Credits

Creative Director: Tim Himsel
Executive Editor: Bryan Trandem
Editorial Director: Jerri Farris
Managing Editor: Michelle Skudlarek
Lead Editor: Thomas G. Lemmer
Senior Editor: Phil Schmidt
Editor: Nancy Baldrica
Lead Art Director: Kari Johnston
Art Director: Dave Schelitzche
Mac Designers: Patti Goar, Andrew Karre, Joe Fahey
Project Manager: Julie Caruso
Copy Editor: Barbara Harold
Technical Illustrator: Jon Simpson
Illustrator: Jan Willem Boer
Technical Photo Editor: Paul Gorton
Photo Editor: Angela Hartwell
Studio Services Manager: Marcia Chambers
Lead Photographer: Tate Carlson
Photographers: Chuck Nields, Andrea Rugg
Scene Shop Carpenters: Scott Ashfield, Dan Widerski
Production Service Manager: Kim Gerber
Production Staff: Laura Hokkanen, Helga Thielen

Copyright ©2002
Creative Publishing international, Inc.
5900 Green Oak Drive
Minnetonka, MN 55343
1-800-328-3895
www.creativepub.com

President/CEO: Michael Eleftheriou
Vice President/Publisher: Linda Ball
Vice President/Retail Sales & Marketing: Kevin Haas

Printed on American paper by: R. R. Donnelley & Sons Co.
10 9 8 7 6 5 4 3 2 1

Created by: The Editors of Creative Publishing international, Inc.,
in cooperation with Black & Decker.®
Black & Decker is a trademark of the Black & Decker
Corporation and is used under license.

Contributing Editors, Art Directors, Set Builders, and Photographers

Cy DeCosse, William B. Jones,
Gary Branson, Bernice Maehren,
John Riha, Paul Currie,
Greg Breining, Tom Carpenter,
Jim Huntley, Gary Sandin,
Mark Johanson, Dick Sternberg,
John Whitman, Anne Price-Gordon,
Barbara Lund, Dianne Talmage,
Diane Dreon, Carol Harvatin,
Ron Bygness, Kristen Olson,
Lori Holmberg, Greg Pluth,
Rob Johnstone, Dan Cary,
Tom Heck, Mark Biscan, Christian Dick
Abby Gnagey, Joel Schmarje,
Jon Simpson, Dave Mahoney,
Andrew Sweet, Bill Nelson,
Barbara Falk, Dave Schelitzche,
Brad Springer, Lori Swanson,
Daniel London, Jennifer Caliandro
John Hermansen, Geoffrey Kinsey,
Phil Juntti, Tom Cooper,
Earl Lindquist, Curtis Lund,
Tom Rosch, Glenn Terry,
Wayne Wendland, Patrick Kartes,
John Nadeau, Mike Shaw,
Mike Peterson, Troy Johnson,
Jon Hegge, Jim Destiche,
Christopher Wilson, Tony Kubat,
Phil Aarrestad, Kim Bailey, Rex Irmen,
John Lauenstein, Bill Lindner,
Mark Macemon, Charles Nields,
Mette Nielsen, Cathleen Shannon,
Hugh Sherwood, Rudy Calin,
Dave Brus, Paul Najlis, Kevin Walton
Mike Parker, Mark Scholtes,
Mike Woodside, Rebecca Hawthorne,
Paul Herda, Brad Parker,
Susan Roth, Ned Scubic,
Stewart Block, Mike Hehner,
Doug Deutscher, Paul Markert,
Steve Smith, Mary Firestone.

Library of Congress Cataloging-in-Publication Data

The complete photo guide to outdoor home
improvement : more than 150 projects
    p. cm.
  ISBN 1-58923-043-4
  I. Dwellings--Remodeling--Amateurs' manuals.
  2. Dwellings--Maintenance and repair--Amateurs' manuals.
  I. Black & Decker Corporation (Towson, MD.)

TH4816.C648 2002
643'.7--dc21   2001052998

BLACK & DECKER®

THE COMPLETE PHOTO GUIDE TO

OUTDOOR
HOME IMPROVEMENT

More than

150

Projects

CREATIVE
PUBLISHING
international

www.creativepub.com

Contents

Projects for Your Outdoor Home

Your yard and landscape are an important and valuable part of your home. This book covers everything you need to plan, design, and build the elements of your outdoor home.

The book opens with the Planning section, which takes you through each step of developing outdoor building projects. This section contains information on choosing materials, working with building codes, and drawing plans.

In the next section, Basic Techniques, you'll learn how to work with some of the most common building materials used in outdoor projects, such as concrete, stone, and copper. There are also projects and tips provided to help you prepare your building site for construction.

The next seven sections of the book are devoted to the building projects. There are a wide range of projects, some of which can be completed in a weekend using tools you probably already own, and others that require more time, rented tools or machinery, or specific skills. Among the projects included are: flagstone pathway, picket fence, arbor, children's play structure, wraparound deck, basic shed, gazebo, and three-season porch. Each project has easy-to-follow instructions, complete tools & materials lists, and full color photos and illustrations to walk you through every step of the building process.

Sections with large-scale projects—such as decks, porches, and sheds—include a subsection containing project planning and design information, detailed anatomy drawings, and step-by-step basic building techniques. Each of the projects also contains full building plans. Make sure to work with your local building department, and when possible, invite family and friends to help you with these projects.

Even if you're a beginner, you'll find many projects in this book that are well within your abilities. And remember: with each project you tackle, you'll acquire new skills and gain the confidence to take on larger ones.

Planning

Homeowners no longer think of their yards as great expanses of lawn, but as outdoor living spaces. Permanent outdoor structures can add to the beauty and function of these outdoor rooms. For example, a deck can provide additional space for entertaining or relaxing, a wall can provide privacy and texture, and a walkway or path can unify areas.

But before you can begin building, you have to organize your ideas and create a plan for materials, tools, inspections, measuring, and construction. Proper planning will help you create an outdoor project that is beautiful now and will last for years to come—an important consideration, since landscaping contributes about 30% to your home's total value.

This opening section will provide you with all the information you need in order to plan and design the projects of your choice. We'll look at new and standard materials for outdoor projects—including wood, metal, plastic, manufactured and natural stone, and concrete—and show you how to estimate and order supplies. You will find information on basic and specialty tools, and a discussion of the common types of hardware and fasteners used for outdoor projects. We'll also review the basics of building codes, including permits and inspections. And to ensure you get the results you want, we'll show you the techniques you'll need to design your own projects.

By following these planning strategies, you will save time and money and enjoy your outdoor home for years to come.

IN THIS CHAPTER:

Bark mulch

Cedar bark wood chips

Cedar lattice

Teak

Redwood

Pine

Building Materials

The building materials you choose should reflect both the function and the appearance of your outdoor project. Materials impact not only the style, but the durability, maintenance requirements, and overall cost of a project. Wood, stone, and brick are traditional favorites, but the versatility and ease of installation you get with PVC vinyl, metal and aluminum, and concrete make them attractive options for certain applications.

Lumber

Wood remains the most common building material in outdoor construction, and it is usually less expensive than stone or brick. Its versatility lends itself to just about any project, from the plain and practical to the elegant and ornate. It is ideal for decks and walkways, fences and retaining walls, pergolas and screens, outdoor furniture, and of course, outbuildings. And it is beautiful, blending with most architectural styles. It looks especially good in settings surrounded by trees.

Most home centers and lumberyards carry a wide selection of dimension lumber, as well as convenient preassembled fence panels, posts, pickets, rails, balusters, floor boards, stringers, and stair railings. Inspect all lumber for flaws, sighting along each board to check for warping, twisting, or loose knots. Boards used for structural parts should have only small knots that are tight and ingrown. Also inspect the end grain. Lumber with a vertical grain will cup less as it ages. Return any boards with serious flaws.

Framing lumber—typically pine or pressure-treated pine—comes in a few different grades: Select Structural (SEL STR), Construction (CONST) or Standard (STAND), and Utility (UTIL). For most applications, Construction Grade No. 2 offers the best balance between quality and price. Utility grade is a lower-cost lumber suitable for blocking and similar uses but should not be used for structural members. Board lumber, or *finish* lumber, is graded by quality and appearance, with the main criteria being the number and size of knots present. "Clear" pine, for example, has no knots.

The most important consideration in choosing lumber is its suitability for outdoor use. Select a wood that is not prone to rot or insect attack. Three types generally are recommended: heart cedar, heart redwood, and pressure-treated lumber. Redwood and cedar are attractive, relatively soft woods with a natural resistance to moisture and insects—ideal qualities for outdoor applications. "Heart" or "heartwood" varieties will be identified on the grade stamp. In both redwood and cedar, heartwood has better resistance to decay than lighter-colored sapwoods.

Western red cedar (WRC) or incense cedar (INC) for decks should be heartwood (HEART) with a maximum moisture content of 15% (MC15).

Pressure-treated pine is stronger and more durable than redwood or cedar, and is more readily available and less expensive in many areas. Although this lumber has a noticeable green color due to its preservative, the wood either can be stained or left to weather to a pleasing gray.

Plywood designated as exterior-grade is made with layers of cedar or treated wood and a special glue that makes it weather-resistant. Always cover exposed plywood edges to prevent water intrusion.

Some homeowners shy away from pressure-treated lumber, due to the chemicals used to treat it. Despite popular fears, the chemicals in pressure-treated pine do not easily leach into the soil, nor are they easily absorbed through the skin. In fact, it can be argued that pressure-treated lumber is actually a good environmental choice, because it lasts longer in projects, thereby reducing the harvest of new trees. When using pressure-treated lumber, however, take some commonsense precautions: Avoid prolonged skin contact by wearing gloves and protective clothing, and avoid breathing the dust by wearing a particle mask.

If you live in an arid climate, such as in the Southwest, you can use untreated pine lumber, because wood will not rot if its moisture content is less than 20%. However, it's always a good idea to use pressure-treated lumber for deck posts or any other framing members that are in contact with the ground.

Teak and white oak are hardwoods usually reserved for top-of-the-line outdoor furniture. These woods have a dense cell structure that makes them resistant to water penetration. However, because these woods are expensive, they generally aren't practical to use for large structures, such as decks or fences. They are better suited for accent pieces, such as benches or large planters.

Remember that although treated woods do resist rot, they will not last indefinitely without regular maintenance. They should have a fresh coat of stain or sealer every two years to maintain durability and appearance. Sealing cut edges of lumber—including pressure-treated wood—will prevent rotting of the end grain.

Apply a coat of sealer-preservative or staining sealer to all sides of outdoor structures. Make sure sealer is applied to all end-grain. Even pressure-treated lumber is vulnerable to moisture and rot.

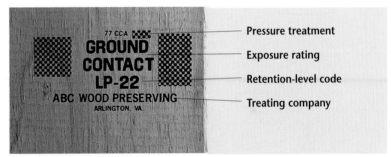

Pressure-treated lumber stamps list the type of preservative and the chemical retention level, as well as the exposure rating and the name and location of the treating company.

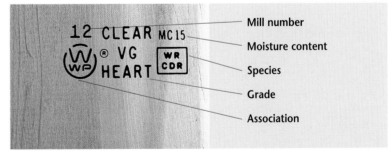

Cedar grade stamps list the mill number, moisture content, species, lumber grade and membership association. Western red cedar (WRC) or incense cedar (INC) for decks should be heartwood (HEART) with a maximum moisture content of 15% (MC15).

Chain link

Landscape edging

Landscape fabric

Pre-fabricated plastic stones, lattice, and decking

Metals & Plastics

Plastic and aluminum products have become popular alternatives to traditional outdoor building materials, because they are low maintenance, versatile, and easy to install. Though these materials are typically more expensive than wood and other alternatives, their durability makes them attractive options.

Plastics are now available in several colors, and they can be used in most applications where wood is appropriate. They can be found in fencing and timbers for use in decks, walkways, fences, and arbors. PVC vinyl and fiberglass reinforced plastic (FRP) are becoming popular choices for fencing and decking materials. Many styles and sizes are available, and they are strong, versatile, and require no maintenance. Materials are often sold as kits, making installation easy. Before choosing PVC, check manufacturers' specifications on expansion and contraction variances to see if it is suitable for your project.

Composite materials blend together wood fibers and recycled plastics to create a rigid product that, unlike wood, will not rot, splinter, warp, or crack. These boards can be cut to size with a circular saw, and do not required painting or staining.

Metal is often used in outdoor applications, such as in fencing and gates. Aluminum offers a sturdy, lightweight, and waterproof material that is available in a variety of designs, ranging from the simple to the elaborate. Availability may be limited, so check with local building centers. Galvanized chain-link steel has long been a popular choice for fencing, because it is relatively maintenance free and can be used to create a secure outdoor wall at a reasonable price. Options, such as vinyl-coated mesh and color inserts, can increase privacy and boost style. Traditional wrought iron, though more expensive and less common today, is used for fencing, railings, and patio furniture to add a touch of elegance.

Copper pipe is a unique and unexpected material that is well suited to temperature swings and water exposure, making it ideal for outdoor use. This metal is inexpensive and available at nearly any home center or hardware store.

Although many of these materials may be more expensive initially, they often carry lifetime warranties, which can make them more economical than wood over time. Before choosing any alternative building material, check on restrictions with your local building department.

Metals and plastics are replacing more traditional materials, as they have minimal maintenance and allow environmentally conscientious consumers to use recycled products.

Manufactured Stone

Manufactured stone is often designed to resemble natural stone, but it offers distinct advantages over the real thing. Greater uniformity makes installation easier, and it is often less expensive than natural alternatives.

Although poured concrete isn't as attractive as natural stone, new masonry techniques help it rival natural stone for visual appeal. Brick, concrete, and glass block are available in a growing variety of sizes and styles, providing the flexibility to build distinctive, reasonably priced outdoor structures. Many of these products are well-suited to do-it-yourselfers, because their weights are manageable and installation is easy.

Decorative concrete block can be used to make screen walls and is available in many colors. A decorative block wall is one of the most economical choices for a stone landscape wall.

Concrete paver slabs, available in several shapes and sizes, can be used for laying simple walkways and patios. They are available in a standard finish, a smooth aggregate finish, or colored and molded to resemble brick. Concrete paver slabs are relatively inexpensive and quite easy to work with. They're usually laid in a bed of sand and require no mortar. Their surface is generally finished so the smooth gravel aggregate is exposed, but they are also available in plain pavers and aggregate.

Paver bricks resemble traditional kiln-dried clay bricks, but are more durable and easier to install. Paver bricks are available in a variety of colors and geometric shapes for paving patios, walkways, and driveways. Many varieties are available in interlocking shapes that can be combined with standard bricks to create decorative patterns, such as herringbone and basket weave. Paver bricks have largely replaced clay bricks for landscape use, and can be set into a bed of sand for patios and driveways, where mortar is not required.

Edging blocks are precast in different sizes for creating boundaries to planting areas, lawns, loose-fill paths, and retaining walls.

Brick and concrete block are available in a growing variety of sizes and styles, allowing you to build distinctive outdoor structures.

Interlocking retaining wall blocks

Molded paver slabs

Paver bricks

Exposed aggregate paver slabs

Concrete paver slabs

Natural Stone

Natural stone is one of the finest building materials you can use. It offers beautiful color and texture, along with unmatched durability and elegance, making it a classic building material for landscape floors, ornamental walls, retaining walls, and walkways. Because of its beauty, it is also a choice material for decorative features, such as rock gardens, ponds, fountains, and waterfalls.

These virtues come at a price, however: Natural stone is one of the more expensive building materials you can select, and using it can be a challenge. It can be heavy and difficult to work with.

Natural stone includes a wide range of materials, from microscopic sands to enormous boulders and carefully cut granite, marble, limestone, slate, and sandstone. It is sold in many forms, so you'll have to choose what type, form, texture, and shade to use for your project.

Fieldstone, sometimes called river rock, is any loose stone gathered from fields, dry river beds, and hillsides. It is often used to build retaining walls, ornamental garden walls, and rock gardens, where it creates an informal, natural look. When split into smaller pieces, fieldstone can be used in projects with mortar. When cut into small pieces, or quarried stone, fieldstone is called cobblestone, a common material in walks and paths.

Ashlar, sometimes called wall stone, is quarried stone—such as granite, marble, or limestone—that has been smooth-cut into large blocks, ideal for creating clean lines with thin mortar joints. Cut stone works well for stone garden walls, but because of its expense, its use is sometimes limited to decorative wall caps.

Flagstone is large slabs of sedimentary rock with naturally flat surfaces. Limestone, sandstone, slate, and shale are the most common types of flagstone. It is usually cut into pieces up to 3" thick, for use in walks, steps, and patios. Smaller pieces—less than 16" square—are often called steppers.

Veneer stone is natural or manufactured stone cut or molded for use in non-load-bearing, cosmetic applications, such as facing exterior walls or freestanding concrete block walls.

Rubble is irregular pieces of quarried stone, usually with one split or finished face. It is widely used in wall construction.

Each type of stone offers a distinctive look, as well as a specific durability and workability. Often the project dictates the form of stone to use. Ask your local stone supplier to suggest a stone that meets your cost, function, and workability needs.

NOTE: You may find different terms used for various types of stone. Ask your supply yard staff to help you.

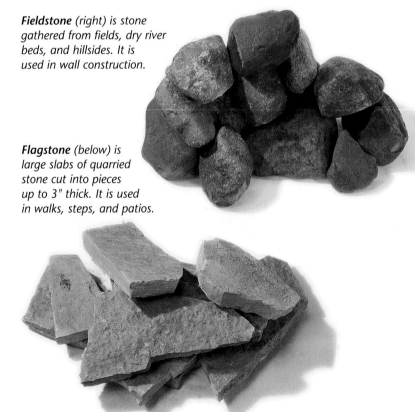

Fieldstone (right) is stone gathered from fields, dry river beds, and hillsides. It is used in wall construction.

Flagstone (below) is large slabs of quarried stone cut into pieces up to 3" thick. It is used in walks, steps, and patios.

A stone yard is a great place to get ideas and see the types of stone that are available. This stone yard includes a display area that identifies different types of stone and suggests ways they can be used.

Concrete

Poured concrete has long been a favorite for driveways, walkways, and patios because of its exceptional strength, but new tinting and surface finishing techniques give concrete a decorative look that makes it attractive for landscaping. It's much less expensive than natural stone, and because it's poured while in a semi-liquid state, it can be formed into curves and other shapes, such as landscape ponds or fountains. Using simple tools, you can even finish concrete to simulate brick pavers or flagstone.

Concrete is made up of a mixture of portland cement, sand, coarse gravel, and water. Premixed bags of dry concrete are available at home centers, and are easy and efficient to use.

Mix concrete in a wheelbarrow for smaller projects, or rent a power mixer to blend larger amounts of cement, gravel, sand, and water quickly. Buy ready-mixed concrete for large jobs.

Timing and preparation are the most important factors in working with concrete. Concrete will harden to its final form, regardless of whether you have finished working with it. Start with smaller-scale projects until you're comfortable working with concrete. A concrete walkway is a good starter project. Recruit helpers when you're ready to take on a large project.

Premixed concrete products contain all the components of concrete. Just add water, mix, and pour.

To mix concrete ingredients in a wheelbarrow, use a ratio of 1 part portland cement (A), 2 parts sand (B), and 3 parts coarse gravel (C).

Prepackaged mortar mixes are available at home centers. Simply select the proper mortar mixture for your project, mix in water, and start to trowel.

Mortar

Masonry mortar is a mixture of portland cement, sand, and water. Ingredients, such as lime and gypsum, are added to improve workability or control "setup" time.

Every mortar mixture balances strength, workability, and other qualities. Make sure to use the mortar type that best suits your needs:

Type N is a medium-strength mortar for above-grade outdoor use in non-load-bearing (freestanding) walls, barbecues, chimneys, soft stone masonry, and tuck pointing.

Type S offers high-strength mortar for exterior use at or below grade. It is generally used in foundations, brick-and-block retaining walls, driveways, walks, and patios.

Type M is a very high strength specialty mortar for load-bearing exterior stone walls, including stone retaining walls and veneer applications.

Glass Block Mortar is a specialty white type S mortar for glass block projects. Standard gray type S mortar is also acceptable for glass block projects.

Refractory Mortar is a calcium aluminate mortar that does not break down with exposure to high temperatures; it is used for mortaring around firebrick in fireplaces and barbecues. Chemical-set mortar will cure even in wet conditions.

To mix mortar, always read and follow the manufacturer's specifications on the mortar mix package.

Estimating & Ordering Materials

Whether pouring a small slab or building an elaborate archway, it is important to estimate the dimensions of your project as accurately as possible. This will allow you to create a complete and concise materials list, and help eliminate extra shopping trips and delivery costs.

Begin compiling a materials list by reviewing your building plans. These plans should include scaled plans that will make estimating easier.

Once you have developed a materials list, add 10% to the estimate for each item. This will help you manage small oversights and allow for waste when cutting.

The cost of your project will depend upon which building materials you choose. But because some materials may not be readily available in your area, plan your projects and place orders accordingly. Lumber, stone, manufactured stone, and alternate materials, such as metals and plastics can vary widely in price. It's unfortunately true that the most attractive building materials are usually the most expensive as well.

In addition to lumber, fasteners, hardware, hand tools, and power tools, many home centers also carry masonry tools and materials, such as concrete, mortar, and stucco mix, typically in premixed bags. Consider the scale of your project before buying concrete or stucco by the bag, however. For large projects, you may want to hire a ready-mix supplier to deliver fresh concrete.

If you plan on working with specialty or alternative materials, such as vinyl fencing or composite decking, many home centers will have a select range of styles and sizes on-hand. Contacting manufacturers directly will lead to greater choices of products, and you will be able to place an order directly with them or be directed to a retailer near you.

Local building suppliers can be a great asset to do-it-yourselfers. The staff can offer professional advice, and yards often carry the tools and other materials necessary to complete your project. Often you can receive help in designing your project, and advice on estimating the materials, applicable local building codes, and regional climate considerations.

Many centers also offer coordinating services for landscapers and contractors to work with you. You may also find class offerings in masonry construction or other techniques to help you develop the skills to complete your project.

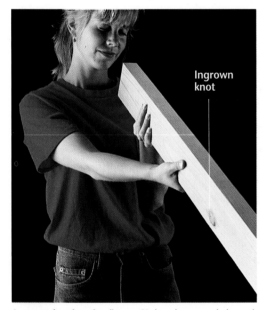

Inspect lumber for flaws. Sight along each board to check for warping and twisting. Return any boards with serious flaws. Check for loose knots. Boards used for structural parts should have only small knots that are tight and ingrown.

HOW TO ESTIMATE MATERIALS

Sand, gravel, topsoil (2" layer)	surface area (sq. ft.) ÷ 100 = tons needed
Standard brick pavers for walks (2" layer)	surface area (sq. ft.) × 5 = number of pavers needed
Standard bricks for walls and pillars (4 × 8")	surface area (sq. ft.) × 7 = number of bricks needed (single brick thickness)
Poured concrete (4" layer)	surface area (sq. ft.) × .012 = cubic yards needed
Flagstone	surface area (sq. ft.) ÷ 100 = tons needed
Interlocking block (2" layer)	area of wall face (sq. ft.) × 1.5 = number of stones needed
Ashlar stone for 1-ft.-thick walls	area of wall face (sq. ft.) ÷ 15 = tons of stone needed
Rubble stone for 1-ft.-thick walls	area of wall face (sq. ft.) ÷ 35 = tons of stone needed
8 × 8 × 16" concrete block for freestanding walls	height of wall (ft.) × length of wall (ft.) × 1.125 = number of blocks needed

Local brick and stone suppliers will often help you design your project and advise you about estimating materials, local building codes, and climate considerations.

AMOUNT OF CONCRETE NEEDED (CUBIC FEET)

Number of 8"-Diameter Footings	Depth of Footings (feet)			
	1	2	3	4
2	¾	1½	2¼	3
3	1	2¼	3½	4½
4	1½	3	4½	6
5	2	3¾	5¾	7½

Dry Ingredients for Self-mix

Amount of Concrete Needed (cubic feet)	94-lb. bags of portland cement	Cubic feet of sand	Cubic feet of gravel	60-lb. bags of premixed dry concrete
1	⅙	⅓	½	2
2	⅓	2/3	1	4
3	½	1½	3	6
4	¾	1¾	3½	8
5	1	2¼	4½	10
10	2	4½	9	20

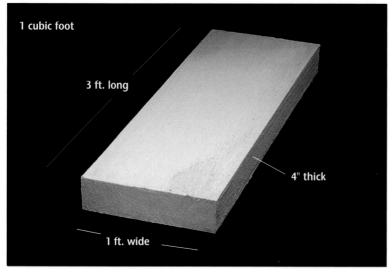

Measure the width and length of the project in feet, then multiply the dimensions to get the square footage. Measure the thickness in feet (4" thick equals ⅓ ft.), then multiply the square footage times the thickness to get the cubic footage. For example, 1 ft. × 3 ft. × ⅓ ft. = 1 cu. ft. Twenty-seven cubic feet equals one cubic yard.

CONCRETE COVERAGE

Volume	Thickness	Surface Coverage
1 cu. yd.	2"	160 sq. ft.
1 cu. yd.	3"	110 sq. ft.
1 cu. yd.	4"	80 sq. ft.
1 cu. yd.	5"	65 sq. ft.
1 cu. yd.	6"	55 sq. ft.
1 cu. yd.	8"	40 sq. ft.

Basic Tools

The right tool always makes the job easier. As a homeowner, you may already own many of the tools needed for the projects in this book. If you don't have the necessary tools, you can borrow them, rent them, or buy them.

If you decide to purchase new tools, invest in the highest-quality products you can afford. High-quality tools perform better and last longer than less-expensive alternatives. Metal tools should be made from high-carbon steel with smoothly finished surfaces. Hand tools should be well balanced and have tight, comfortably molded handles.

Quality tools may actually save you money over time, because you eliminate the expense of replacing worn out or broken tools every few years.

Level

Quick clamp

Cat's paw

Chisel

Mason's string

Tape measure

Trowel

Shovel

Hoe

Rubber mallet

Caulk gun

Mason's hammer

Combination square

Rafter square

Flat pry bar

Line level

Scratch awl

Pipe clamp

Metal snips

Compass

Ratchet wrench & sockets

Plumb bob

22-oz. claw hammer

Chalk line

Putty knife

Framing square

Clamshell posthole digger

Hand tools for outdoor building should be rated for heavy-duty construction. Always purchase the highest quality tool you can afford; there is no substitute for quality.

Power & Rental Tools

Outdoor building projects and landscaping work often require the use of power tools and specialty tools.

Home centers will have in stock the common power tools you will require, but if your project demands a tool that you will only use once or that is expensive, consider renting. Many home centers now have rental equipment on site. Also check your local rental center outlets for tool availability.

When renting, always read the owner's manual and operating instructions to prevent damage to tools and personal injury. Some rental centers also provide training and assistance on specialty tools.

To ensure your safety, always use a ground-fault circuit-interrupter (GFCI) extension cord with power tools, and wear protective gear, such as work glasses, particle masks, and work gloves, when sawing or handling pressure-treated lumber and masonry products.

Power tools include: power miter saw (A), 14.4-volt cordless trim saw with a 5⅜"-blade (B), reciprocating saw with 6" and 8" blades (C), ⅜" drill and bits (D), jig saw (E), ½" hammer drill and bits (F).

Landscaping tools for preparing sites include: power auger (A), power tamper (B), power sod cutter (C), pick (D), weed trimmer (E), come-along (F), garden rake (G).

19

Masonry Tools

Masonry work involves two steps: preparing the site and laying the concrete. To work effectively with masonry products, you will have to buy or rent some special-purpose tools.

You may want to purchase some smaller landscaping tools, including a pick for excavating hard or rocky soil; a weed trimmer, for removing brush and weeds before digging; a posthole digger, for digging just one or two holes; a come-along, for moving large rocks and other heavy objects without lifting; and a garden rake, for moving small amounts of soil and debris.

To lay concrete you will need trowels, floats, edgers, and jointers. These are hand tools used to place, shape, and finish concrete and mortar. Chisels are used to cut and fit brick and block. You can also equip your circular saw with blades and your power drill with bits designed for use with concrete and brick.

Always make sure you have the necessary safety equipment on hand before you start a masonry project, including gloves and protective eye wear.

Mason's tools include: a darby (A) for smoothing screeded concrete; mortar hawk (B) for holding mortar; pointing trowel (C) for tuck pointing stone mortar; wide pointing tool (D) for tuck pointing or placing mortar on brick and block walls; jointer (E) for finishing mortar joints; brick tongs (F) for carrying multiple bricks; narrow tuck-pointer (G) for tuck-pointing or placing mortar on brick and block walls; mason's trowel (H) for applying mortar; masonry chisels (I) for splitting brick, block, and stone; bullfloat (J) for floating large slabs; mason's hammers (K) for chipping brick and stone; maul (L) for driving stakes; square-end trowel (M) for concrete finishing; side edger (N) and step edger (O) for finishing inside and outside corners of concrete; joint chisel (P) for removing dry mortar; control jointer (Q) for creating control joints; tile nippers (R) for trimming tile; sled jointer (S) for smoothing long joints; steel trowel (T) for finishing concrete; magnesium or wood float (U) for floating concrete; screed board (V) for screeding concrete.

Fasteners & Hardware

Because you will be building outdoor structures, the connecting hardware, fasteners, and materials you use must hold up to extreme weather conditions. The better the materials, the longer the life of the structure.

Any metal connecting hardware and fasteners, including nails and screws, should be made from rust-resistant material, such as galvanized steel, aluminum or stainless steel. Although galvanized metals will not stain treated wood, they may react with natural chemicals in cedar and redwood, causing staining. Stainless steel fasteners won't cause staining in any wood, but they are expensive.

Seal screwheads set in counterbored holes with silicone caulk to prevent water damage. Also be aware that when combining dissimilar metals, you will need a plastic spacer to prevent the electrochemical reaction known as galvanic action from occurring, which causes corrosion.

A common type of hardware you'll find throughout this book is the metal anchor, used to reinforce framing connections. Many of the anchors called for in the various projects (and all of the anchors in the sheds and outbuilding projects) are Simpson Strong-Tie® brand, which are commonly available at lumberyards and home centers. If you can't find what you need on the shelves, look through the manufacturer's catalog, or visit their website (see page 493). Always use the fasteners recommended by the manufacturer.

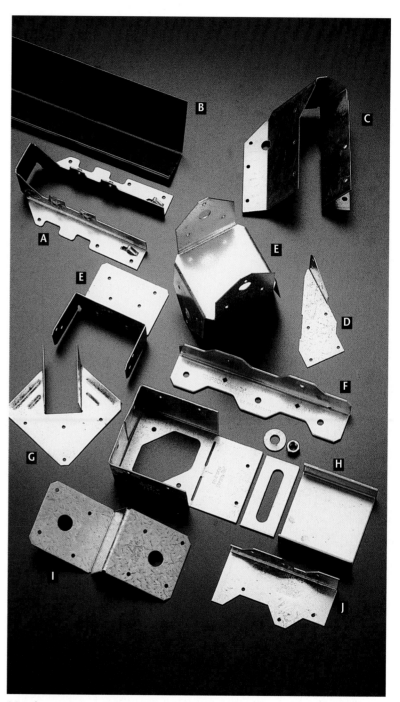

Metal connectors commonly used include: *joist hanger (A), flashing (B), angled joist hanger (C), rafter tie (D), post-beam caps (E), stair cleat (F), hurricane tie (G), post anchor with washer and pedestal (H), joist tie (I), angle bracket (J).*

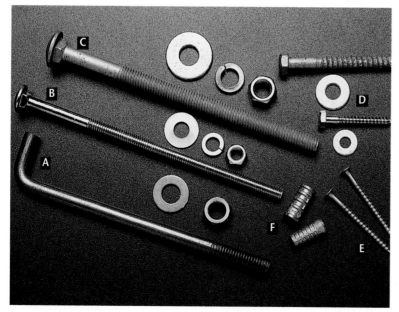

Common types of fasteners include: *J-bolt with nut and washer (A), carriage bolts with washers and nuts (B, C), galvanized lag screws and washers (D), corrosion-resistant deck screw (E), masonry anchors (F).*

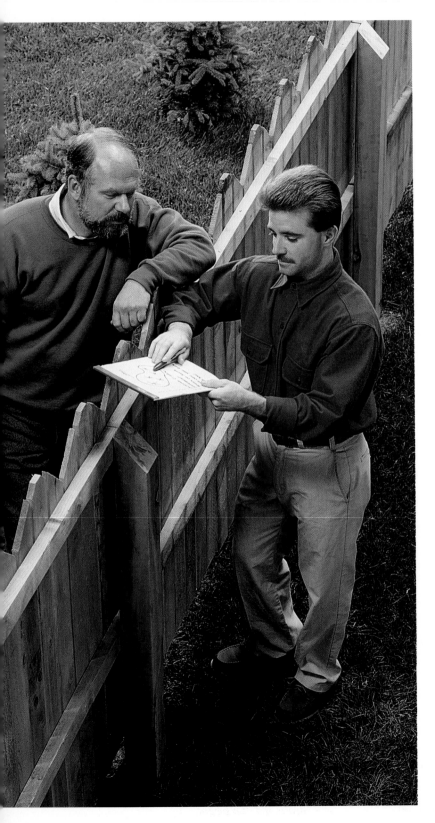

Codes & Courtesies

Almost anytime you build—whether indoors or out—there are local regulations you'll have to consider. Building codes, zoning ordinances, and permits are the legal issues you'll have to contend with, but you should also consider neighborhood standards and the impact your project will have on adjoining and adjacent properties.

Building codes govern the materials and construction methods of your project to ensure safety, and zoning laws govern the size, location, and style of your structure to preserve aesthetic standards. Permits and inspections are required to ensure your plans meet all local building and zoning restrictions.

Requirements and restrictions vary from one municipality to another, so check the codes for your area. If your plans conflict with local codes, authorities will sometimes grant a variance, which allows you to compromise the strict requirements of the code.

Consult with your local building inspection department early in your planning process to determine if your project requires a permit and whether you must submit plans for approval. The permit process can take several weeks or months, so checking early can help you avoid unnecessary delays or changes to your plans. Then fill out the necessary forms, pay any applicable fees, and wait for your approval.

In the meantime, it's a good idea to discuss your plans with neighbors. A fence, wall, or gate on or near a property line is as much a part of your neighbors' landscapes as your own. The tall hedge you have planned for privacy, for example, may cast a dense shadow over your neighbor's sunbathing deck. The simple courtesy of apprising your neighbors of your plans can help you avoid strained relationships or even legal disputes.

You may find that discussing your plans with neighbors reaps unexpected rewards. For instance, you and your neighbor may decide to share labor and expenses by landscaping both properties at once. Or you may combine resources on a key feature that benefits both yards, such as a stone garden wall or shade tree. When several neighbors put their heads together to create an integrated landscape plan for their yards, the results benefit everyone. Individual landscapes look larger when the surrounding yards share a complementary look and style.

In addition, check with your local utility companies to pinpoint the locations of any underground electrical, plumbing, sewer, or telephone lines on your property. The locations of these features can have an obvious impact on your plans, if your project requires digging or changes to your property's grade. There is no charge to have utility companies locate these lines, and it can prevent you from making an expensive or life-threatening mistake. In many areas, the law requires that you have this done before digging any holes.

On the following pages, you'll find some common legal restrictions for typical landscape projects.

FENCES

• **Height:** The maximum height of a fence may be restricted by your local building code. In some communities, backyard fences are limited to 6 ft. in height, while front yard fences are limited to 3 ft. or 4 ft.—or prohibited altogether.

• **Setback:** Even if not specified by your building code, it's a good idea to position your fence 12" or so inside the official property line to avoid any possible boundary disputes. Correspondingly, don't assume that a neighbor's fence marks the exact boundary of your property. For example, before digging an elaborate planting bed up to the edge of your neighbor's fence, it's best to make sure you're not encroaching on someone else's land.

• **Gates:** Gates must be at least 3 ft. wide. If you plan to push a wheelbarrow through it, your gate width should be 4 ft.

DRIVEWAYS

• **Width:** Straight driveways should be at least 10 ft. wide; 12 ft. is better. On sharp curves, the driveway should be 14 ft. wide.

• **Thickness:** Concrete driveways should be at least 6" thick.

• **Base:** Because it must tolerate considerable weight, a concrete or brick paver driveway should have a compactible gravel base that is at least 6" thick.

• **Drainage:** A driveway should slope ¼" per foot away from a house or garage. The center of the driveway should be crowned so it is 1" higher in the center than on the sides.

• **Reinforcement:** Your local building code probably requires that all concrete driveways be reinforced with iron rebar or steel mesh for strength.

SIDEWALKS & PATHS

• **Size of sidewalks:** Traditional concrete sidewalks should be 4 ft. to 5 ft. wide to allow two people to comfortably pass one another, and 3" to 4" thick.

• **Width of garden paths:** Informal pathways may be 2 ft. to 3 ft. wide, although steppingstone pathways can be even narrower.

• **Base:** Most building codes require that a concrete or brick sidewalk be laid on a base of compactible gravel at least 4" thick. Standard concrete sidewalks may also need to be reinforced with iron rebar or steel mesh for strength.

• **Surface & drainage:** Concrete sidewalk surfaces should be textured to provide a non-slip surface, and crowned or slanted ¼" per foot to ensure that water doesn't puddle.

• **Sand-set paver walkways:** Brick pavers should be laid on a 3"-thick base of sand.

STEPS

• **Proportion of riser to tread depth:** In general, steps should be proportioned so that the sum of the depth, plus the riser multiplied by two, is between 25" and 27". A 15" depth and 6" rise, for example, is a comfortable step (15 + 12 = 27); as is an 18" depth and 4" rise (18 + 8 = 26).

• **Railings:** Building codes may require railings for any stairway with more than three steps, especially for stairs that lead to an entrance to your home.

CONCRETE PATIOS

• **Base:** Concrete patios should have a subbase of compactible gravel at least 4" thick. Concrete slabs for patios should be at least 3" thick.

• **Reinforcement:** Concrete slabs should be reinforced with wire mesh or a grid of rebar.

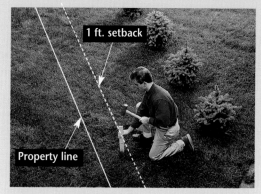

Fences should be set back at least 1 ft. from the formal property lines.

Driveways should be at least 10 ft. wide to accommodate vehicles.

Concrete paving should be laid on a bed of gravel to provide drainage.

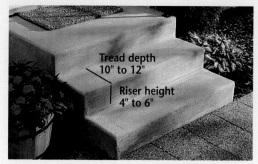

Concrete steps should use a comfortable tread depth and riser height.

Concrete patios require reinforcement with steel mesh or rebar.

Frost line

Mortared garden walls need to be supported by concrete footings.

A pool requires a protective fence to keep neighborhood children and animals from falling in.

GARDEN WALLS

• **Footings:** Mortared brick or stone garden walls more than 4 ft. in height often require concrete footings that extend below the winter frost line. Failure to follow this regulation can result in a hefty fine or a demolition order, as well as a flimsy, dangerous wall.

• **Drainage:** Dry-set stone garden walls installed without concrete footings should have a base of compactible gravel at least 6" thick to ensure the stability of the wall.

SWIMMING POOLS

• **Fences:** Nearly all building codes require a protective fence around swimming pools to keep young children and animals away from the water.

• **Location:** In some areas, building codes require that below-ground swimming pools be at least 10 ft. away from a building foundation.

SHEDS

• **Permits:** Sheds greater than 120 sq. ft. generally require a permit, but temporary buildings generally do not. Additionally, if you live in a city or a suburban association, there may be restrictions on where and how you may build a shed. If you live in a rural community, you may not need a permit if the shed will not house humans or animals.

• **Site:** Choose a location that enhances your property in all seasons. Consider setback requirements, yard grade, drainage, sun exposure, foliage, and the shed's function.

• **Size:** Choose a shed size based on what will be housed in the shed, and how much room is needed to maneuver objects inside. Most sheds are built with a 3 to 4 ratio, 6-ft. wide by 8-ft. long, for example.

• **Style:** Zoning laws may dictate acceptable shed styles for your area. Try to choose a design that blends with existing home and neighborhood architecture.

• **Foundation:** The type of foundation you will need will depend on the shed's size and purpose, as well as the climate and soil conditions in your region. Cost and local building codes may also play a role in foundation type.

PORCHES

• **Permits:** Permits are required for any additions to a home. Have all gas or electrical elements added to the porch inspected before walls or floors are closed up and finished. In some areas, inspections may also be required for the footings, framing, and insulation.

• **Slope:** When building an open porch, slope floors away from the home to permit water runoff, and construct a roof overhang of 16" to enjoy the porch in the rain.

• **Cost:** To reduce costs, build a porch on a wooden deck, rather than on a concrete slab.

• **Foundation:** Always prime and paint wood support members before installation, including the ends, to prevent rot.

FIRE PITS & BARBECUES

• **Clearance:** Requirements vary by municipality, but in general, permanent open fire or barbecue pits are not permitted less than 25 ft. from your home, garage, shed, wood pile, or wooden fences.

• **Diameter:** Most cities limit the size of a fire or barbecue pit to 3 ft. in diameter, but check with your building or fire department for local requirements. The pit must be ringed with a non-combustible material, such as stone, clay, concrete, or driveway pavers. Some cities may even require a ring of sand around the pit to prevent grass fires.

• **Permits:** An inspector from the fire department will visit your site and determine whether the pit meets local safety codes. If your built-in barbecue will incorporate gas lines or electrical outlets or fixtures, additional permits and inspections will be required. If the pit passes inspection, you will be issued a recreational burning permit for a fee.

• **Burning:** Most localities do not permit burning rubbish or waste. The use of flammable or combustible liquid accelerants is generally prohibited in fire pits. Some may even restrict the size of cut wood that may be burned.

• **Safety:** Most cities require an adult present at a pit fire until all flames are extinguished. If conditions are too windy or dry, or produce excess smoke, you may be asked to extinguish all flames. A connected garden hose or other extinguisher must be near the site.

RETAINING WALLS

• **Height:** For do-it-yourself construction, retaining walls should be no more than 4 ft. high. Higher slopes should be terraced with two or more short retaining walls.

• **Batter:** A retaining wall should have a backward slant (batter) of 2" to 3" for dry-set stones; 1" to 2" for mortared stones.

• **Footings:** Retaining walls higher than 4 ft. must have concrete footings that extend down below the frost line. This helps ensure the stability of the wall.

PONDS

• **Safety:** To ensure child safety, some communities restrict landscape ponds to a depth of 12" to 18", unless surrounded by a protective fence or covered with heavy wire mesh.

DECKS

• **Structural members:** Determining the proper spacing and size for structural elements of a deck can be a complicated process, but if you follow these guidelines, you will satisfy code requirements in most areas:

BEAM SIZE & SPAN

Beam size	Maximum spacing between posts
two 2 x 8s	8 ft.
two 2 x 10s	10 ft.
two 2 x 12s	12 ft.

JOIST SIZE & SPAN

Joist size	Maximum distance between beams (Joists 16" apart)
2 x 6	8 ft.
2 x 8	10 ft.
2 x 10	13 ft.

• **Decking boards:** Surface decking boards should be spaced so the gaps between boards are no more than ¼" wide.

• **Railings:** Any deck more than 24" high requires a railing. Gaps between rails or balusters should be no more than 4".

• **Post footings:** Concrete footings should be at least 8" in diameter. If a deck is attached to a permanent structure, the footings must extend below the frost line in your region.

A series of short retaining walls, rather than one tall wall, is the best way to handle a slope.

Railing balusters are required by building code to be spaced no more than 4" apart to keep small children from slipping through or being trapped between them.

Sheds larger than 120 square feet may require a permit, but temporary structures typically do not.

Measuring

You will have to accurately measure and note the features of your yard on a rough sketch, called a yard survey. From this survey, you can draw a detailed scale drawing, called a site plan. The sketch for the yard survey can be rough, but the measurements must be exact.

If possible, enlist someone to help you take these measurements. If you haven't already done so, ask your local utility companies to mark buried utility lines.

You will also have to mark your property lines. If you don't have a plot drawing (available from the architect, developer, contractor, or possibly, the previous owner) or a deed map (available from city hall, county courthouse, title company, or mortgage bank) that specifies property lines, hire a surveyor to locate and mark them. File a copy of the survey with the county as insurance against possible boundary disputes in the future.

THE YARD SURVEY:

Accurate yard measurements are critical for estimating quantities and cost of materials. To sketch your survey, follow these steps:

Step A: Sketch your yard and all its main features on a sheet of paper. Assign a key letter to each point. Measure all straight lines and record the measurements on a notepad.

Step C: Plot irregular boundaries and curves, such as shade patterns or low-lying areas that hold moisture after a rainfall. Plot these features by taking a series of perpendicular measurements from a straight reference line, such as the edge of your house or garage.

Step B: Take triangulated measurements to locate other features, such as trees that don't lie along straight lines. Triangulation involves locating a feature by measuring its distance from any two points whose positions are known.

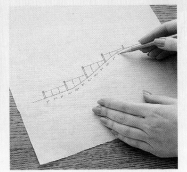

Step D: Sketch elevations to show slopes. Measure the vertical drop of a slope using different-sized stakes and string. Connect the string to the stakes so it is perfectly horizontal. Measure the distance between the string and ground at 2-ft. intervals along the string.

Challenges

Planning an outdoor project often involves dealing with obstacles in your chosen path. You may have to go around a tree or rock outcropping, handle a hill or grade change, cross a depression, or work around buried electric, telephone, gas, cable, and water lines on your property.

You can easily cope with such challenges by removing the interference, when possible, or relocating or rerouting your structure. Contact local utility companies to locate and mark lines before you draw up plans. Law requires that these companies inspect your site on request and mark the location of buried lines.

Another option is to incorporate obstacles into your project layout. For example, on a hillside you can step a fence down in level sections, or follow the contour of the slope. If a tree is in your path, try adapting your structure to incorporate the tree's current size and future growth. For example, plan a deck to flow around a large shade tree.

Rocks can be dealt with in much the same way. Incorporate boulders into wall design, or use them as focal points along a pathway.

Board, louver, basket-weave, and panel fences are good choices for stepped fences. More geometric in shape, they can also be more difficult to design and build.

Inset framing makes it possible to save mature trees when building a deck. Keeping trees and other landscape features intact helps preserve the value and appearance of your property.

Drawing Plans

Not every project needs extensive plans and maps, but the more steps there are to the construction process, the more important it is to carefully consider all the details. Good plans make it possible to efficiently complete a project. Plotting the location of an outdoor structure on paper makes it much easier to determine a realistic budget, make a materials list, and develop a practical work schedule.

From your yard survey, create a site map, or scale drawing, that establishes the position of all elements of the existing site on paper. A site map is an overhead view of your yard, and is the basis for the finished project design.

A scale of ⅛" = 1 ft. is common for site maps and project plans. At this scale, you'll be able to map a yard as big as 60 ft. × 80 ft. on a sheet of 8½" × 11" drafting paper; or an 80-ft. × 130-ft. yard on an 11" × 17" sheet. If your yard is too large to fit on one sheet of paper, simply tape several sheets together.

On a copy of the site map, locate and draw your project's layout. Consider how to handle obstacles like large rocks, trees, and slopes. Be sure to take into account local setback regulations and other pertinent building codes. Also make determinations for posts, footings, and accessibility to your structure.

Depending on the complexity of your project, your final plans may also include several different scale drawings, each showing a different aspect. You may create a bubble plan, a final design, and several working plans. An elevation chart may also be helpful if you have significant slope to contend with.

A bubble plan, or zone plan, is a rough sketch that indicates how the new project or projects will be laid out on your site. Draw several variations of your ideas. Even experienced professional designers go through as many as a dozen bubble plans before settling on a favorite. To save time, sketch ideas on photocopies of a tracing of your site map.

For the final design drawings, illustrate all the features of the new project in color. A final design drawing requires careful, detailed work. Expect some trial and error as you transform your bubble plan into a polished drawing.

Strive to integrate your new projects into your existing or planned landscape, establishing a continuous flow from your project to your landscape. Disguise unavoidable straight lines, such as property lines and walkways, by incorporating flowing planting beds or walls that have curved borders.

Also strive for a feeling of continuity between the various rooms of your outdoor home. Many people use lawn grass as the unifying element. Repeated use of building materials or shrubbery and flowers can also provide unity.

The best plans are the result of playful exploration and fearless

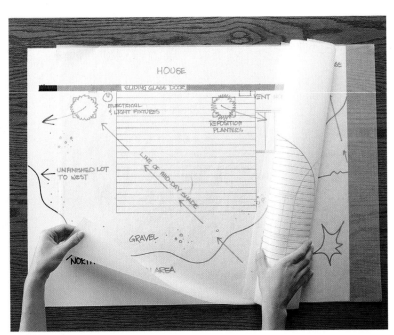

Experiment with project ideas by sketching different designs on separate sheets of tissue paper.

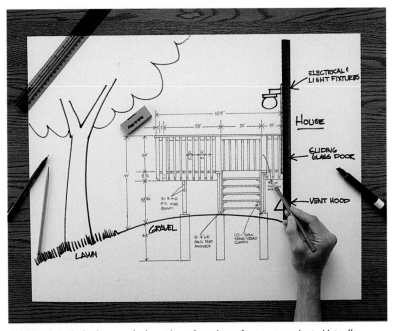

Create detailed plan and elevation drawings for your project. List all dimensions on the drawing, and indicate size, type, and quantities of lumber and hardware needed.

trial and error. Take your time, experiment with many different layouts, and don't be afraid to make mistakes and changes.

Once you've worked out the details and decided on a final layout, convert the scale dimensions from the site map to actual measurements. From this information, draw up a materials estimate, adding 10% to compensate for errors and oversights.

An elevation plan shows a side view of your planned project. It's not always necessary to draw the entire structure when making an elevation drawing. If you're planning a fence or garden wall on a flat yard, for example, you can draw the elevation for a small section that represents the construction pattern for the entire structure.

Before you begin your project, there is one more set of plans to complete: the working plans. Working plans for a project serve the same function as blueprints do for a building. A working plan is a bare-bones version of a plan drawing and elevation that includes only the measurements and specifications needed to actually construct the project.

Working plans help you estimate the amounts of materials you'll need and make it easier to schedule and organize work. Unless your project is very simple, it's a good idea to create several working plans: a demolition plan, a resurfacing plan, a building plan, and a re-landscaping plan. If your projects are quite large, you will want to create separate plans for each part of your overall project plan.

DECIMAL EQUIVALENTS:

Converting actual measurements to scale measurements often produces decimal fractions, which then must be converted to ruler measurements. Use this chart to determine equivalents.

Decimal	Fraction
.0625	1/16
.125	1/8
.1875	3/16
.25	1/4
.3125	5/16
.375	3/8
.4375	7/16
.5	1/2
.5625	9/16
.625	5/8
.6875	11/16
.75	3/4
.8125	13/16
.875	7/8
.9375	15/16

Test different bubble plans in your yard by outlining the walls with rope or a hose, and by positioning cardboard cutouts to represent stepping stones and walkways.

Hang tarps or landscape fabric over a stake-and-string frame to get a sense of the size of the structure and its impact on the landscape.

Basic Techniques

Before undertaking any outdoor project, you will need to understand how to effectively work with the basic materials you've chosen, in order to get the results you are after. This section provides the basic techniques you will need when working with common building materials.

While in the planning phase of your project, an assessment of your yard could reveal that you have a drainage problem, which could pose future complications for your planned outdoor structures. Techniques and tips on regrading and creating adequate drainage are provided to help you rectify these issues.

As you move into the actual construction stages, refer to this section to find thorough information on preparing the surface of your yard for paving projects and working with concrete—including building wood forms and placing concrete for walkways and patios, and pouring footings for garden walls.

Because many outdoor projects incorporate brick, natural stone, or manufactured stone in their design, special material placement techniques illustrate how to cut, fit, and mortar stone pieces for pathways, garden walls, or firepits. In addition, steps for cutting and soldering copper are provided, since more and more homeowners are finding beautiful and unique uses for this inexpensive material in their yards.

Throughout this book, references will be made to this section, specifying the techniques used in each particular project.

Grading

Unless your yard has the proper grade, or slope, rainwater can flow toward the foundation of your house—and possibly into your basement. An improper grade can also cause water to collect in low-lying areas, creating boggy spots where you'll have trouble growing grass and other plants. When graded correctly, your yard should have a gradual slope away from the house of about ¾" per horizontal foot.

Although the initial grading of a yard is usually done by a landscape contractor, you can do the work yourself to save money. The job is a bit time-consuming, but it isn't difficult. Typically, creating a grade at this stage involves spreading a 4" to 6" layer of topsoil over the yard, then distributing and smoothing it to slope away from the house.

Established landscapes often require regrading, especially if the house has settled. If you find signs of basement moisture problems or puddle-prone areas in the yard, you need to correct the slope. The measuring and grading techniques featured here will help you remove and distribute soil as needed.

TOOLS & MATERIALS

- Basic tools (page 18)
- Line level
- Grading rake
- Stakes
- String
- Tape
- Topsoil
- Hand tamp

HOW TO MEASURE & ESTABLISH A GRADE

Step A: Measure the Slope

1. Drive a pair of stakes into the soil, one at the base of the foundation, and another at least 8 ft. out into the yard along a straight line from the first stake.

2. Attach a string fitted with a line level to the stakes and adjust the string until it's level. Measure and flag the string with tape at 1-ft. intervals.

3. Measure down from the string at the tape flags, recording your measurements as you work. Use these

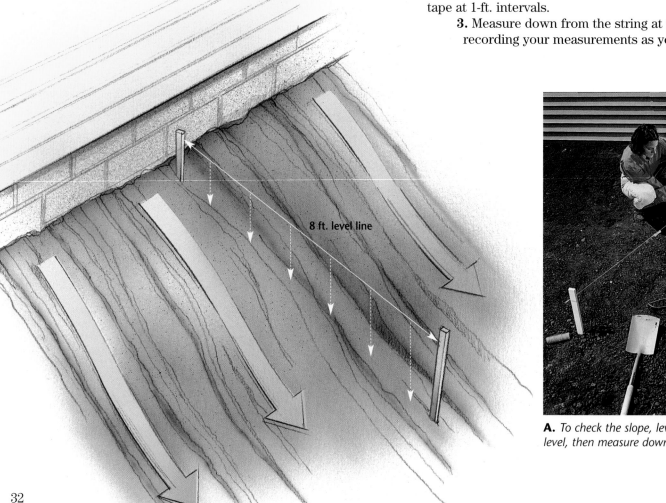

8 ft. level line

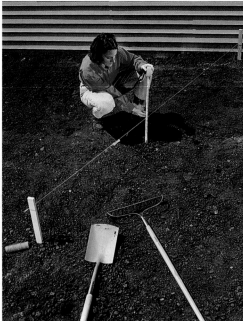

A. *To check the slope, level the string with a line level, then measure down at 1-ft. intervals.*

measurements as guidelines for adding or removing soil to create a correct grade.

Step B: Add & Distribute Soil

1. Starting at the base of the house, add soil to low areas until they reach the desired height.

2. Using a garden rake, evenly distribute the soil over a small area. Measure down from the 1-ft. markings as you work to make sure that you are creating a ¾" per 1 ft. pitch as you work.

3. Add and remove soil as needed, working away from the house until soil is evenly sloped. After you've completed an area, repeat steps A and B to grade the next section of your yard.

Step C: Lightly Tamp the Soil

Use a hand tamp to lightly compact the soil. Don't overtamp the soil or it could become too dense to grow a healthy lawn or plants.

Step D: Remove Debris

After all the soil is tamped, use a grading rake to remove any rocks or clumps. Starting at the foundation, pull the rake in a straight line down the slope. Dispose of any rocks or construction debris. Repeat the process, working on one section at a time until the entire area around the house is graded.

VARIATION: CREATING LEVEL AREAS

You may want to create some perfectly level areas for playing lawn sports such as croquet, badminton, volleyball, and lawn bowling. Level areas also make safe play surfaces for small children and a good base for play structures.

Outline the perimeter of the area with evenly placed stakes. Extend a string fitted with a line level between a pair of stakes and adjust the string until it's level. At 2-ft. intervals, measure down from the marked areas of the string to the ground. Add and remove topsoil as necessary, distributing it with a garden rake until the surface under the string is level. Repeat the process until the entire area is leveled.

B. *Beginning at the foundation, use a garden rake to distribute soil, checking and adjusting the slope as you work.*

C. *Use a hand tamp to lightly compact the soil in the graded area.*

D. *Pull a grading rake in a straight line down the slope to remove rocks, clumps, and debris.*

Drainage Swale

If your yard has areas where rainwater collects and creates boggy spots or has slopes that send runoff water into unwanted places, you need to improve or redirect its drainage. You can fill small low-lying areas by top-dressing them with black soil, but in large areas, the best solution is to create a swale.

A swale is a shallow ditch that carries water away from the yard to a designated collection area, usually a gutter, sewer catch bin, stream or lake. Some communities have restrictions regarding redirecting runoff water, so contact your city or county inspector's office to discuss your plans before you begin. This is especially important if you're planning a swale that empties into a natural water source, such as a stream, pond, or lake.

If you're building a swale between your house and a neighboring yard, talk to your neighbor about the project before you begin. If drainage is a problem in their yard as well, they may be willing to share the expense and the work of the project.

Building a swale is relatively simple, but it involves the labor of digging a trench. We'll show you how to construct the swale using a shovel, but there are rental tools that you might want to use instead. For larger yards or those with very dense soil, renting a trencher is an option worth considering. This machine, which can be adjusted to dig to an approximate depth, makes quick work of loosening the soil. If you decide to use a trencher, you'll still need to use a shovel to create the "V" shape and to smooth the sides of the trench, as pictured below.

Another machine you may want to rent is a sod cutter, which cuts the sod into even strips that can be replaced when the swale is complete. If you plan to reuse the sod, store it in a shady area and keep it slightly moist until you replant it.

TOOLS & MATERIALS

- Basic tools (page 18)
- Stakes
- Trenching spade
- Sod cutter (optional)

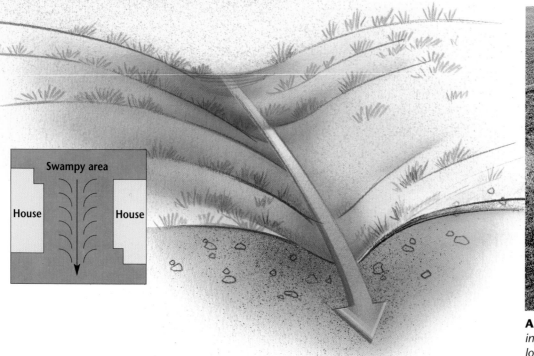

A. *Mark a route for the swale with stakes, making sure that the outlet for the water is at the lowest point.*

VARIATION: SWALE WITH DRAIN

If you have very dense soil with a high clay content or severe drainage problems, you'll need to lay perforated drain pipe in the trench for the swale. Follow these steps to make a swale with drain tile:

Step A:
Dig a 1-ft.-deep trench, angled downward to the outlet point. Line the trench with landscape fabric. Spread a 2" layer of coarse gravel along the bottom of the swale, then lay perforated drain pipe over the gravel, with the perforations facing down. Cover the pipe with a 5" layer of gravel, then wrap landscape fabric over the top of the gravel.

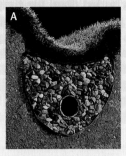

Step B:
Cover the swale with soil and the original or fresh sod. Set a splash block at the outlet under the exposed end of the drain pipe to distribute the runoff water and prevent erosion.

HOW TO MAKE A DRAINAGE SWALE

Step A: Mark the Route

After identifying the problem area, use stakes to mark a swale route that directs water toward an appropriate runoff area. To promote drainage, the outlet of the swale must be lower than any point in the problem area or along the planned route.

Step B: Remove the Sod

Carefully remove the sod from the outlined area. Set it aside and keep it moist, so that it can be replaced when the swale is complete.

Step C: Dig the Trench

Following the marked route, dig a 6"-deep "V"-shaped trench with wide, rounded sides. Shape the trench so it slopes gradually downward toward the outlet, making sure that the bottom and sides of the trench are smooth. Set the topsoil aside for other projects.

Step D: Replace the Sod

Lay the sod back into the trench. Compress it thoroughly, so the roots make contact with the soil and there are no air pockets beneath it. Water the sod and keep it moist for several weeks.

B. *Carefully remove the sod with a spade and set it aside, keeping it moist until you're ready to replace it.*

C. *Dig a 6"-deep trench that slopes to the center, creating a "V" shape. Use the shovel to smooth the sides as you work.*

D. *Replace the sod, compressing it against the soil. Water the sod and keep it moist for several weeks.*

Dry Well

A dry well is a simple method for channeling excess water out of low-lying or water-laden areas, such as the ground beneath a gutter downspout. A dry well system typically consists of a buried drain tile running from a catch basin positioned at the problem spot to a collection container some distance away.

A dry well system is easy to install and surprisingly inexpensive. In the project shown here, a perforated plastic drain tile carries water from a catch basin to a dry well fashioned from a plastic trash can, which has been punctured, then filled with stone rubble. The runoff water percolates into the soil as it makes its way along the drain pipe and through the dry well.

HOW TO INSTALL A DRY WELL

Step A: Dig the Trench

1. Using stakes, mark a path running from the problem area to the location of the dry well. Carefully remove a 12" strip of sod and set it aside, keeping it moist so you can reuse it later. Dig a trench, 10" wide and 14" deep, along the staked path.

2. Slope the trench slightly toward the dry well, about 2" for

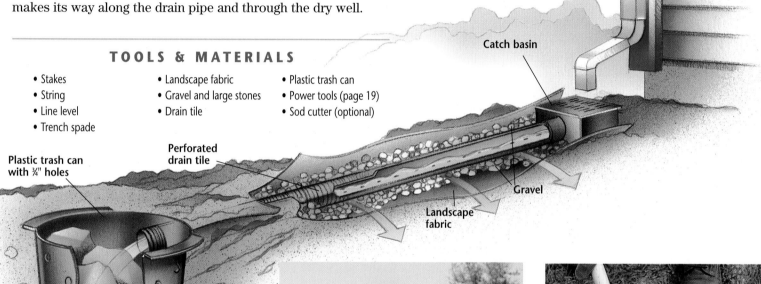

Catch basin

TOOLS & MATERIALS

- Stakes
- String
- Line level
- Trench spade

- Landscape fabric
- Gravel and large stones
- Drain tile

- Plastic trash can
- Power tools (page 19)
- Sod cutter (optional)

Perforated drain tile

Gravel

Landscape fabric

Plastic trash can with ¾" holes

Large stones

A. Dig a 10"-wide, 14"-deep trench along the planned route from the catch basin to the dry well.

B. Line the trench with landscape fabric, then lay a 1" layer of gravel along the bottom of the trench.

every 8 ft., to ensure that water flows easily along the drain tile. To check the slope, place a stake at each end of the trench, then tie a string between the stakes. Use a line level to level the string, then measure down from it at 2-ft. intervals. Add or remove soil as needed to adjust the slope of the trench.

3. Remove the sod in a circle, 4" wider than the dry well container, then dig a hole at least 4" deeper than the container's height.

Step B: Lay the Drain Tile

1. Line the trench and hole with landscape fabric, folding the excess fabric back over each side of the trench and around the edges of the hole.

2. Lay a 1" layer of gravel along the bottom of the trench, then lay the drain tile in place, with the perforations facing down.

Step C: Create the Dry Well

1. About 3" from the top, trace the outline of the drain tile onto the side of the trash can, then use a jig saw to cut a hole. Using a power drill and a ¾" bit, drill drainage holes through the sides and bottom of the trash can, one hole every 4" to 6".

2. Place the trash can in the hole, positioning it so the large hole faces the trench. Insert the drain tile, perforated side down, with at least 2" of the tile extending inside the trash can.

3. Fill the trash can with large stones. Arrange the top layer of stones so they are flat in the container.

4. Fold the landscape fabric over the rocks, then fill the

TIP: GRAVEL

Gravel comes in two forms: rough and smooth. When buying gravel for shaping projects, select rough gravel. Smooth gravel typically is used as a decorative ground cover. When used for shaping projects, it tends to slide toward the middle of the trench. Rough gravel clings to the sides of the trench, creating a more even drainage layer.

---

hole with soil.

Step D: Connect the Catch Basin

At the other end of the trench, opposite the dry well, connect the catch basin to the drain tile. Position the catch basin so excess water will flow directly into it.

Step E: Refill the Trench

1. Fill the trench with gravel until the drain tile is covered by 1" of gravel. Fold the edges of the landscape cloth down over the gravel-covered drain tile.

2. Fill the trench with the soil you removed earlier.

3. Replace the sod, lightly tamp it with the back of a shovel, then water it thoroughly.

C. *Prepare the dry well container, then place it in the excavation, insert the drain tile and fill it with large rocks.*

D. *Attach a catch basin to the drain tile opening, and position the basin to collect the excess water in the problem area.*

E. *Cover the drain tile with 1" of gravel, then backfill the trench with soil and fold the landscape fabric over it.*

Surface Preparation

A well-constructed base is crucial to the success of any paving project. The quality of the base, which protects the paving project from time- and weather-inflicted damage, determines the longevity of the project. Whether you're building a stepping-stone path, a concrete patio, or a brick walkway, surface preparation is vital to the success of your project.

The best material for a paving base is compactible gravel. The gravel is applied and compressed over evenly excavated soil, cre-ating a smooth surface to pave. In addition, gravel drains water easily, preventing erosion and frost heave.

For most paving projects, it's best to cover the base with a layer of landscape fabric. The fabric prevents grass and weeds from growing up through the paving. Cut the landscape fabric into sheets and arrange them so that the edges overlap by 6". For some projects, you'll need to add a layer of sand over the land-scape fabric.

The most important part of surface preparation is excavating and creating a smooth base with the proper slope for drainage. Before you begin excavating, evaluate the grade of the area you're paving, as shown in "Grading" (page 32). If the area is uneven or has a severe slope, you'll probably need to excavate or fill the area, then level it before you begin paving.

HOW TO PREPARE SURFACES FOR PAVING
Step A: Outline the Excavation Area
1. If you're paving a straight design, outline the area with stakes and string. Place the stakes so that they're at least 1 ft. outside the site the intersecting strings will mark—the actual corners of the paved surface. Use a line level to level the strings. (For curves, use a rope or garden hose to lay out the design.)

TOOLS & MATERIALS

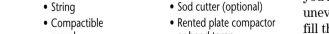

- Basic tools (page 18)
- Line level
- Stakes
- Long 2 x 4
- String
- Compactible gravel
- Landscape fabric
- Measuring tape
- Sod cutter (optional)
- Rented plate compactor or hand tamp
- Shovel

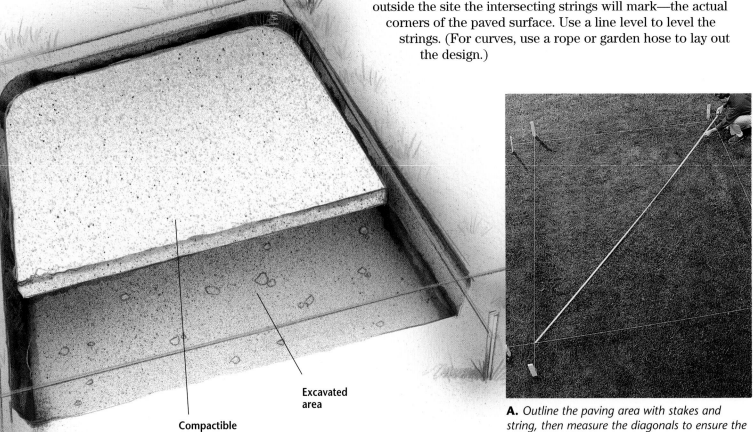

Excavated area

Compactible gravel

A. Outline the paving area with stakes and string, then measure the diagonals to ensure the outline is square.

2. Measure diagonally across the corners to make sure the outline is square. Adjust the stakes until these diagonal measurements are equal. For straight designs with rounded corners, as shown below, use a rope or garden hose to mark the curves.

Step B: Excavate the Area

1. Starting at the outside edge, use a shovel to evenly excavate the outlined area so it's about 5" deeper than the thickness of the planned paving.

2. Use a long 2 × 4 to check the surface for high and low spots, then redistribute soil as necessary to create a smooth, even surface across the entire area.

3. If you're building a paver patio or walkway, excavate 6" beyond the planned width and length of the project, which allows room for the edging.

Step C: Add Compactible Gravel

1. Pour compactible gravel over the excavated area, then rake it into a smooth layer at least 4" deep. The thickness of this base layer can vary to compensate for any unevenness in the excavation.

2. Use the 2 × 4 to check the surface once again for high and low spots, and add or remove gravel as needed to make the surface even.

TIP: RENTING A SOD CUTTER

You may want to rent a sod cutter to strip grass from your pathway or patio site. Sod cutters, available at most rental centers, help you save time on big projects. These machines excavate at a very even depth, allowing you to roll up the removed sod. The cut sod can be replanted in other areas of your yard.

Step D: Compact the Gravel

1. Use a rented plate compactor to pack the gravel into a firm, even surface. For small areas, you can pack down the gravel with a hand tamp.

2. Check the evenness of the gravel base with a 2 × 4. Remove or add gravel as needed, then repack the base with the plate compactor.

B. *Remove soil from the outlined layer with a shovel until the excavation is 5" deeper than the height of the paving.*

C. *Pour compactible gravel into the excavated area, then rake it into a smooth 4" layer.*

D. *Use a rented plate compactor (pictured) or a hand tamp to pack the gravel into a firm, flat surface.*

Working with Concrete

Poured concrete is one of the most versatile and durable building materials available. You can use it in building just about any type of outdoor structure.

Concrete costs less than other building materials, such as pressure-treated lumber or brick pavers. And with a decorative finish, such as exposed aggregate, or a tint added to the wet mixture, you can tailor concrete's appearance to suit your desired project designs and ideas.

While all concrete mixtures are basically the same—containing portland cement, sand, and a combination of aggregates—make sure to use the proper type of concrete for your project. Varying the ratios of the ingredients creates special properties that are better suited for specific situations.

General-purpose concrete is usually the least expensive, and is suitable for most do-it-yourself, poured concrete projects.

Fiber-reinforced concrete contains strands of fiberglass that increase the strength of the concrete. If approved by your local building inspector, you can use fiber-reinforced concrete for some slabs, instead of general-purpose concrete, eliminating the need for metal reinforcement.

High-early-strength concrete contains agents that cause it to set quickly—a desirable property if you are pouring in cold weather.

Sand mix contains no mixed aggregate, and is used only for surface repairs where larger aggregate is not desirable.

If your project requires more than one cubic yard of concrete, have a supplier deliver pre-mixed concrete to your site, and have lots of hands ready to help. If you will mix your own concrete, consider renting a power concrete mixer to get the proper consistency.

Concrete will harden to its final form, whether you have finished working with it or not. The best insurance policy against running out of time is thorough site preparation. Proper site preparation varies from project to project and site to site, but the following steps are basic to any project:

1. Lay out the project, using stakes and strings.

2. Clear the project area and remove sod.

3. Excavate the site to allow for a subbase, footings

When pouring concrete next to structures, *glue a ½"-thick piece of asphalt-impregnated fiber board to the adjoining structure to keep the concrete from bonding with the structure. The board creates an isolation joint, allowing the structures to move independently, minimizing the risk of damage.*

Reinforcement materials: *Metal rebar, available in sizes ranging from #2 (⅛" diameter) to #5 (⅝" diameter), is used to reinforce narrow concrete slabs, like sidewalks, and in masonry walls. For most projects, #3 rebar (⅜" diameter) is suitable. Wire mesh (or "re-mesh") is most common in 6 × 6" grids. It is usually used for broad surfaces, like patios. Bolsters suspend rebar and wire mesh off the subbase. Fiber additive is mixed into concrete to strengthen small projects that receive little traffic.*

(as needed), and concrete.

4. Lay a subbase for drainage and stability, and pour footings, as needed.

5. Build and install reinforced wood forms.

Ask your local building inspector if your project will require frost footings (pages 48 to 51) or metal reinforcement, such as rebar, reinforcing mesh, rebar bolsters, or fiber additives. For large-scale or elaborate concrete projects, a landscape engineer or building inspector can advise you on how to prepare your yard.

Before you even start digging for any concrete project, there are a few preliminary tasks to take care of. Contact your local public utility companies to locate and mark all buried electric and gas lines. Check your yard's grade (page 32) in the project area. Correct any drainage problems (pages 34 to 37) to eliminate boggy areas and to protect your project's new foundation.

With your yard prepared, you can then stake out your project area and prepare the surface (page 38) by excavating, leveling, and readying the area with compactible gravel. In addition to providing a level, stable foundation for the concrete, com-

pactible gravel also improves drainage. This is especially true if you are building on soil that is high in clay content. Make a story pole to ensure you excavate the site to a consistent depth as you dig along your slope line (photo below left).

Build forms (pages 42 to 43) and gather the necessary tools before you begin working. Good preparation means fewer delays at critical moments, and it leaves you free to focus on placing and smoothing the concrete, not on staking down loose forms or locating misplaced tools. For driveways and walkways, construct a curved screed board for crowning the concrete surface to prevent water from pooling (below right).

Whatever type of concrete project you are undertaking, remember that timing and preparation are the most important factors in working with concrete. Poured concrete yields the most durable and attractive final finish when it is poured at an air temperature between 50° and 80°F, and when the finishing steps are completed carefully. Using simple tools you can finish concrete in many different ways, from simulating brick pavers or flagstone (pages 72 and 73), to crafting stepping stones with a personality all their own (page 66).

Install stakes and strings when laying out straight walkways, and measure from the strings to ensure straight sides and uniform excavation depth.

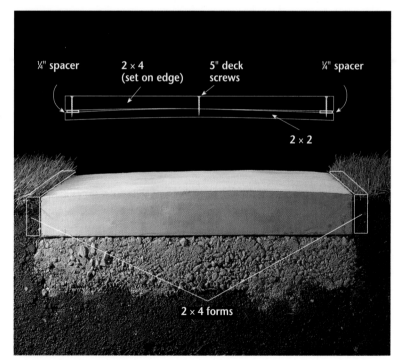

Build a curved screed board to crown the top of concrete surfaces to prevent water from pooling.

Building Wood Forms

Poured concrete requires some type of form to give it shape. Forms are frames, usually made from 2 × 4 lumber, built around a project site to contain poured concrete and establish its thickness.

The mason's strings that outline your project (pages 38 to 39) are a good reference guide for setting form boards in place. Most concrete surfaces should have a slight slope to direct water runoff, especially if they are near your house. To create a standard slope of ⅛" per ft., multiply the distance between the stakes on one side (in feet) by ⅛". For example, if the stakes are 10 ft. apart, the result would be ¹⁰⁄₈ (1¼"), and you will move the strings down 1¼" on the stakes on the low ends.

Forms also can be constructed from other materials, such as plywood for tall-form projects like concrete steps (pages 334 to 337) and cardboard tube forms for footings (pages 218 to 219). For some projects, the earth itself can be used as a form for footings (pages 48 to 51). When building with brick or block where the footing will be visible, use standard wood forms for the tops of footings. Curves can be created with ⅛" hardboard attached at the inside corners of a form frame, with stakes driven behind the curved form for support (see "TIP" on opposite page).

Some projects and building codes require adding metal reinforcement to concrete to boost its durability. For most projects, #3 rebar is suitable. Sidewalks and masonry walls, for example, are often reinforced with rebar. Wire mesh is used to support broad surfaces, like patios (page 40).

If you are installing metal reinforcement, leave at least 1" of clearance between forms and the edges or ends of metal reinforcement. Use bolsters or small chunks of concrete to raise wire mesh reinforcement off the subbase, but make sure it is at least 2" below the tops of the forms.

Cut metal rebar with a reciprocating saw that is equipped with a metal-cutting blade. (Cutting metal rebar with a hacksaw can take 5 to 10 minutes per cut.) Use bolt cutters to cut wire mesh.

Overlap joints in metal rebar by at least 12", then bind the ends together with heavy-gauge wire. Overlap seams in wire mesh reinforcement by 12".

TOOLS & MATERIALS

- Circular saw or handsaw
- Hammer
- Level
- Wood-trimming knife
- 2 × 4s
- 3" deck screws
- Vegetable oil or commercial release agent

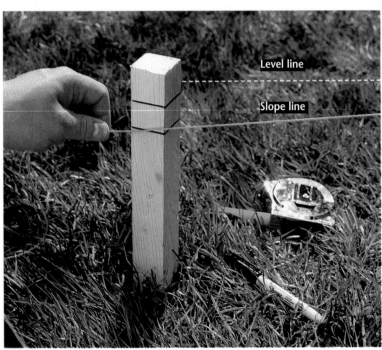

A. *Lay out the project area with stakes and mason's string, then determine a ⅛" per ft. slope and adjust the strings accordingly.*

B. *Starting with the longest form board, position the boards so the inside edges are directly below the mason's string outlines.*

HOW TO BUILD WOOD FRAMES

Step A: Set the Slope

1. Outline and excavate the project area (pages 38 to 39).

2. Establish a slope of ⅛" per foot, (pages 32 to 33), adding and removing soil as needed, and working away from the house until the soil is evenly sloped.

Step B: Prepare the Forms

1. Cut 2 × 4s to create a frame with inside dimensions equal to the total size of the project.

2. Starting with the longest form board, position the boards so the inside edges are directly below the mason's strings that outline the project.

Step C: Prepare the Stakes

1. Cut several pieces of 2 × 4, at least 12" long, to use as stakes. Trim one end of each stake to a sharp point.

2. Drive the stakes at 3-ft. intervals at the outside edges of the form boards, positioned to support any joints in the form boards.

Step D: Assemble the Forms

1. Drive 3" deck screws through the stakes and into the form board on one side, so the form board is about 1" above ground level.

2. Set a level so it spans the staked side of the form and the opposite form board, and use the level as a guide as you stake

the second form board so it is level with the first.

3. Once the forms are staked and leveled, drive 3" deck screws at the corners.

4. Coat the insides of the forms with a vegetable oil or a commercial release agent to prevent the concrete from bonding with them.

5. Tack nails to the outsides of the forms to mark locations for control joints at intervals roughly 1½ times the slab's width (but no more than 30 times its thickness).

6. Install metal reinforcement, if necessary.

TIP: CREATING CURVES

Create curves with ⅛" hardboard attached at the inside corners of a form frame. Drive support stakes behind the curved form.

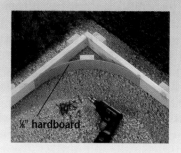

⅛" hardboard

C. *Trim one end of each 2 × 4 stake to a sharp point, then drive the stakes at 3-ft. intervals at the outside edges of the form boards, positioned to support any joints in the form boards.*

D. *Set a level so it spans the staked side of the form and the opposite form board, level the second form board with the first, and attach to the stakes with 3" deck screws.*

Mixing Concrete

Concrete prepared on-site can be blended from separate ingredients or mixed with water and bags of premixed concrete. The basic ingredients of concrete are the same, whether the concrete is mixed from scratch, purchased premixed, or delivered by a ready-mix company. Portland cement is the bonding agent, sand and a combination of aggregates add volume and strength, and water activates the cement.

Premixed concrete is usually sold in 60-lb. bags that yield roughly ½ cu. ft. However, remember that coverage rates for poured concrete are determined by the thickness of the slab. To estimate how much concrete you will need, measure the width and length of your project in feet, then multiply the dimensions to get the square footage. Measure the thickness in feet, then multiply the square footage times the thickness to get the cubic footage. (For more information on estimating and ordering concrete, see the charts on page 17.)

Always prepare a full bag of mix, since key ingredients can settle to the bottom. All mixes come with mixing recommendations printed on the bag. Remember, however, that depending upon conditions on the day you mix, you may either have to add or subtract water.

If you are mixing in a mortar box or wheelbarrow, pour a bag of premixed concrete into the container and form a hollow in the mound of dry mix. Add water to the hollow, starting with one gallon of clean tap water per 60-lb. bag. (Keep track of how much water you use for mixing subsequent batches.)

Mix with a hoe while continuing to add water, until a good consistency is achieved. A batch of properly mixed concrete is damp enough to form in your hand when you squeeze it, and dry enough to hold its shape.

If you are mixing in a power mixer, pour in ½ gallon of water for each 60-lb. bag of concrete you will use in the batch, then add all of the dry ingredients. Mix for one minute, adding water as needed until the proper consistency is formed. Then mix for an additional three minutes. Empty the concrete and rinse out the drum immediately.

Remember that concrete sets quickly. Have help on hand to pour and work concrete before it hardens.

Have ready-mix concrete delivered for large projects. Prepare the site and build the forms, and try to have helpers on hand to help you place and tool the concrete when it arrives.

For smaller projects, mix concrete in a mixing box or wheelbarrow, or use a power mixer (INSET). Mix the concrete, adding water until a good consistency is achieved. Be careful not to overwork the mix.

Placing Concrete

Placing concrete involves pouring it into forms, then leveling and smoothing it with special masonry tools. Attention to detail when placing your concrete will result in a professional finished appearance for your project.

When pouring concrete, never overload your wheelbarrow, and always load from the front—not the side—to avoid tipping. Experiment with sand or dry mix to find a comfortable, controllable load—or "pod." This also helps you get a feel for how many wheelbarrow loads it will take to complete your project.

To avoid disturbing your building site, lay planks over the forms to make a ramp for the wheelbarrow. Make sure you have a flat, stable surface between the concrete source and the forms, and use supports for your plank ramp. Always remember to start pouring concrete at the farthest point from the concrete source, and work your way back.

After you fill the forms, rap the sides with a hammer or the blade of a shovel to help settle the concrete. This draws finer aggregates in the concrete against the forms, creating a smoother surface on the sides. This is especially important when building steps.

Once the surface is smooth and level, cut control joints around the edges. Control joints are designed to control where the slab cracks in the future, as natural heaving and settling occurs. Without control joints, a slab may develop a jagged, disfiguring

crack. You can also create round edges for a more professional appearance.

If you are building a walkway or driveway, crown the surface of the concrete to prevent water from pooling on the surface.

To make a crown, construct a curved screed board (page 41) by cutting a 2 × 2 and a 2 × 4 long enough to rest on the walkway forms. Butt them together edge-to-edge and insert a ¼" spacer between them at each end. Attach the parts with 4" deck screws driven at the center and the edges. The 2 × 2 will be drawn up at the center, creating a curved edge. Screed the concrete with the curved edge of the screed board facing down.

HOW TO PLACE CONCRETE
Step A: Place Concrete in the Forms

1. Make sure you have a clear path from the source to the site. Use 2 × 6 lumber to build a ramp, if necessary. Lay planks over your forms, and use supports for your plank ramp. Then load your wheelbarrow with fresh concrete. Remember to load from

A. *Pour concrete in evenly spaced loads (called a "pod"), starting at the end farthest from the concrete source.*

B. *Use a masonry hoe to distribute concrete evenly in the project area, working the concrete until it is fairly flat, and the surface is slightly above the top of the forms. Remove excess concrete with a shovel.*

the front, not the side, to avoid tipping.

2. Pour concrete in evenly spaced loads, or "pods," starting at the end farthest from the concrete source and working forward. Do not pour too close to the forms: Pour so the top of the pod is a few inches above the top of the forms. If using a ramp, stay clear of the end of the ramp.

3. Continue to place concrete pods next to preceding pods, working away from the first pod. Do not pour too much concrete at one time, or it may harden before you can start tooling.

Step B: Distribute the Concrete

1. Distribute the concrete evenly in the project area, using a masonry hoe. Work the concrete until it is fairly flat, and the surface is slightly above the top of the forms. Remove any excess concrete with a shovel.

2. Immediately work the blade of a spade between the inside edges of the form and the concrete to remove trapped air bubbles that can weaken the concrete.

3. Rap the forms with a hammer or the blade of the shovel to help settle the concrete and draw the finer aggregates in the concrete against the forms.

Step C: Screed the Surface

1. Use a screed board—a straight piece of 2 × 4 long enough to rest on opposite forms—to remove the excess concrete before bleed water appears.

2. Move the screed board in a sawing motion from left to right, and keep the screed flat as you work. If screeding leaves any valleys in the surface, add fresh concrete to the low areas and screed to level.

Step D: Cut the Control Lines

Cut control joints at marked locations with a mason's trowel, using a straight 2 × 4 as a guide. Control joints help prevent jagged, disfiguring cracks that can occur as natural heaving and settling occur.

Step E: Float the Concrete Surface

Wait until bleed water disappears (see "Tip" on opposite page), then float in an arcing motion, with the leading edge of the tool up. Stop floating as soon as the surface is smooth.

Step F: Groove the Control Joints

Once any bleed water has dried, draw a groover across the precut control joints, using a straight 2 × 4 as a guide. You may have to make several passes to create a smooth control joint.

Step G: Shape the Edges

1. Shape the edges of the concrete with an edging tool placed between the forms and the concrete. You may have to make several passes to create a smooth, finished appearance.

2. Use a wood float to smooth out any marks left by the groover or edger.

C. *Use a screed board to remove excess concrete before bleed water appears. Use a sawing motion from left to right, keeping the screed flat.*

D. *Cut control joints at marked locations with a mason's trowel, using a straight 2 × 4 as a guide.*

E. *When bleed water disappears, float in an arcing motion, with the leading edge of the tool up. Stop floating as soon as the surface is smooth.*

F. *Once any bleed water has dried, draw a groover across the precut control joints, using a straight 2 × 4 as a guide. Make several passes, if necessary, to create a smooth control joint.*

G. *Shape concrete with an edging tool between the forms and the concrete, then use a wood float to smooth out marks left by the groover or edger.*

TIP: UNDERSTANDING BLEED WATER

Timing is key to an attractive concrete finish. When concrete is poured, the heavy materials gradually sink, leaving a thin layer of water—known as bleed water—on the surface. To achieve an attractive finish, it's important to let bleed water dry before proceeding with other steps. Follow these rules to avoid problems:

• Settle and screed the concrete and add control joints (steps B through C) immediately after pouring and before bleed water appears. Otherwise, crazing, spalling, and other flaws are likely.

• Let bleed water dry before floating or edging. Concrete should be hard enough that foot pressure leaves no more than a ¼"-deep impression.

• Do not overfloat the concrete; it may cause bleed water to reappear. Stop floating (step E) if a sheen appears, and resume when it is gone.

NOTE: Bleed water does not appear with air-entrained concrete, which is used in regions where temperatures often fall below freezing.

Pouring Footings

Footings provide a stable, level base for brick, block, stone, and poured concrete structures. They distribute the weight of the structure evenly, prevent sinking, and keep structures from moving during seasonal freeze-thaw cycles.

The required depth of a footing is usually determined by the frost line, which varies by region. The frost line is the point nearest ground level where the soil does not freeze. In colder climates, it is likely to be 48" or deeper. Frost footings (footings designed to keep structures from moving during freezing temperatures) should extend 12" below the frost line for the area. Your local building inspector can tell you the frost line depth for your area.

Footings for walls should be twice as wide as the structure. They should also extend at least 12" past the ends of the project area.

TIP: PLANNING FOOTINGS

- Describe the proposed structure to your local building inspector to find out whether it requires a footing, and whether the footing needs reinforcement. In some cases, 8"-thick slab footings can be used, as long as the subbase provides plenty of drainage.

- Keep footings separate from adjoining structures by installing an isolation board (pages 40 and 51).

- For smaller poured concrete projects, consider pouring the footing and the structure as one unit.

- A multi-wall project such as a barbecue may require a floating footing (pages 476 to 479).

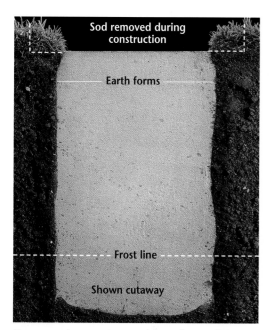

For poured concrete, *use the earth as a form. Strip sod from the project area, then rest the edges of a board on the earth to screed.*

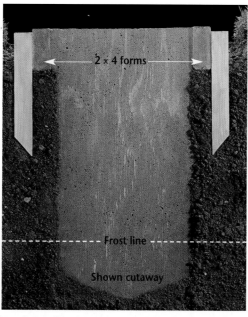

For brick, block, and stone, *build level, recessed wood forms. Rest the board on the frames when you screed the concrete.*

Add tie-rods *if you will be pouring concrete over the footing. After the concrete sets up, press 12" sections of rebar 6" into the concrete.*

TIP: USING A WATER LEVEL

Water levels take advantage of the fact that water in an open tube will level itself, no matter how many bends and turns the tube has. This makes a water level ideal for working with long structures, around corners, or on sites where a conventional level won't work. Typical commercially available water levels consist of clear plastic tubes that screw onto the ends of a garden hose (right, top).

Mark off 1" increments on each tube. Attach the tubes to the ends of a garden hose, then fill the hose until water is visible in both tubes. Working with a helper, hold the tubes at the ends of the site. Adjust the tubes until the water is at the same mark in each tube (right, bottom). Drive stakes or mark off the level points on your structure.

OPTION: Pricier water levels contain an electronic gauge that's useful when you need precise readings.

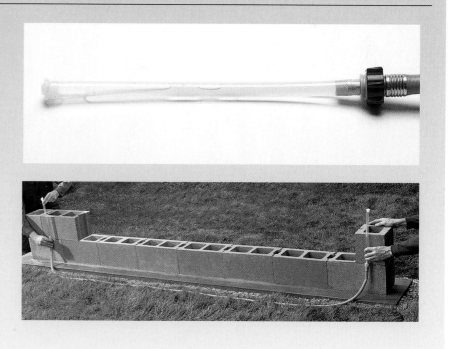

A. *Strip away sod 6" outside the project area on all sides, then excavate the trench for the footing to a depth 12" below the frost line.*

B. *Build and install a 2 × 4 form frame for the footing, aligning it with the mason's strings. Stake the form in place, and adjust to level.*

TOOLS & MATERIALS

- Rope or hose
- Mason's string
- Tape measure
- Shovel
- Framing square
- Level
- Compactible gravel
- Hand tamp
- 2 × 4 lumber
- Circular saw or handsaw

- Wood-trimming knife
- Hammer
- 3" deck screws
- Stakes
- Fiber board
- Construction adhesive
- #3 rebar
- 16-gauge wire
- Concrete
- Mixing container

- Wheelbarrow
- Hoe
- Circular saw
- Long, straight 2 × 4
- Tie-rods, if needed
- Float
- Plastic sheeting
- Vegetable oil or commercial release agent
- Bolt cutters

HOW TO POUR A FOOTING

Step A: Dig Rough Trenches for the Footings

1. Lay out the location of the project using rope or hose, then use stakes and mason's string to outline footings that are twice as wide as the proposed project.

2. Measure the diagonals to make sure the staked outline is square, then use a framing square to make sure the corners are square. Adjust if necessary.

3. Strip away sod 6" outside the project area on all sides, then excavate the trench for the footing to a depth of 12" below the frost line. The bottom of the trench should be roughly level.

4. Lay a 6" layer of compactible gravel subbase into the trench. Tamp the subbase thoroughly.

Step B: Build Forms & Add Reinforcement

1. Build and install 2 × 4 forms to outline the footings, aligning the forms with the mason's string. Drive stakes along the outside of the forms to anchor them in position, then adjust the forms to level.

2. If your project abuts another structure, such as a house foundation, slip a piece of ½"-thick asphalt-impregnated fiber board into the trench between the footing and the structure to create an isolation joint. The board allows the structures to move independently, minimizing the risk of damage. Use a few dabs of construction adhesive to hold the board in place.

3. Make two #3 rebar grids to reinforce each footing. For each grid, use bolt cutters to cut two pieces of #3 rebar 8" shorter than the length of the footing and two pieces 4" shorter than the depth of the footing. For longer footings, make many smaller grids to cover the greater spans.

4. Bind the pieces of rebar together with 16-gauge wire, forming a rectangle. Set the rebar grids upright in the trench, leaving 4" of space between the grids and the walls of the trench.

5. Coat the inside edges of the forms with vegetable oil or commercial release agent.

Step C: Pour the Footings

1. Make sure you have a clear path from your concrete source to your project area. Build a ramp, if necessary, from 2 × 6 lumber. Mix the concrete according to manufacturer's instructions. Work the concrete with a shovel to remove any air pockets. Do not overwork the mix.

2. Pour the concrete in evenly spaced loads, starting at the end farthest from the concrete source. Pour the concrete so it reaches the tops of the forms (pages 45 to 47). Do not pour too close to the forms.

3. Screed the surface of the concrete by dragging a short 2 × 4 along the top of the forms. Add concrete to any low areas that form. Screed the surface again, and add tie-rods, if needed. Float the concrete until it is smooth and level.

4. When the concrete is hard to the touch, cover the footings with plastic and let the concrete cure for 2 to 3 days. Remove the forms and backfill around the edges of the footings. Add compactible gravel to bring the surrounding areas level with the surface of the footings.

5. Let the footings cure for 1 week to maximize strength.

C. *Mix and pour concrete, so it reaches the tops of the forms. Screed the surface, using a 2 × 4. Add tie-rods if needed. Float the concrete until it is smooth and level.*

TIP: MAKING ISOLATION JOINTS

If your project abuts another structure, such as a house foundation, slip a piece of fiber board into the trench to create an isolation joint between the footing and the structure (page 40).

Use a few dabs of construction adhesive to hold it in place.

Building with Brick

Bricks are easy to work with if you have the right tools and use good techniques. Before starting a brick project, plan carefully, evaluate the bricks you're using, and practice handling them. When working with bricks, wear gloves to protect your hands whenever possible. And always wear eye protection when cutting or splitting bricks, or any other masonry units, whether by hand or with a saw.

With bricks, as with any building material, planning minimizes problems during construction. Remember that you need to build a frost footing if the proposed brick structure is more than 3 ft. tall or if it will be tied to another permanent structure. Frost footings should extend about 12" past the frost line in your area.

Don't add mortar joint thickness to the total dimensions when you're planning a brick project. The actual size of a brick is ⅜" smaller than the nominal size, which allows for ⅜"-wide mortar joints. For example, a 9" (nominal) brick actually measures 8⅝", so four 9" bricks set with ⅜" mortar joints will measure 36" in length. To make sure planned dimensions work, test project layouts using ⅜" spacers between bricks. Whenever possible, make plans that use whole bricks, eliminating extensive cutting.

You'll need to learn a few brick-handling skills before you begin building projects. Even after you've learned these skills, be

TOOLS & MATERIALS

- T-square
- Pencil
- Sand
- Mason's chisel
- Hammer
- Masonry cutting blade
- Pipe clamps or bar clamps
- Straightedge
- Eye protection
- Circular saw

sure to buy extra bricks for every project. Bricks vary in density and the type of materials used to make them, which greatly affects how they respond to cutting and the way they absorb moisture. You'll always need to make practice cuts on a sample and test the water absorption rate to determine their density before you begin a project.

To test the absorption rate of a brick, use an eyedropper to drop 20 drops of water onto one spot and check it after 60 seconds. If the surface is completely dry, dampen the bricks with water before you lay them. Otherwise, they'll wick the moisture out of the mortar before it has a chance to set properly.

HOW TO MARK & CUT BRICKS
Step A: Mark Straight Cutting Lines

When you can't avoid cutting bricks, the first thing you have to do is mark the cuts. If you're making many identical cuts, use a T-square and pencil to mark groups of bricks at the same time.

A. Use a T-square and pencil to mark several bricks for cutting. Make sure the ends of the bricks are all aligned.

B. Use a circular saw with a masonry-cutting blade to score a group of bricks. Clamp the bricks, ends aligned.

C. To split a brick, align a mason's chisel on a scored line. Tap the chisel with a hammer until the brick splits.

Align the ends and hold the bricks in place as you mark.

Step B: Score Straight Cuts

1. To avoid cracking them, set the bricks on a bed of sand as you work. If the cutting line falls over the core, score the brick on two sides; if it falls over the web area, score all four sides.

2. For small jobs, use a mason's chisel and hammer both to score and to cut the bricks. To score a brick, use a hammer to tap on the mason's chisel, leaving cut marks ⅛" to ¼" deep. For large jobs, you can ensure uniformity and speed up the process by scoring the bricks with a circular saw and a masonry-cutting blade. Set the saw's blade depth between ⅛" and ¼". Carefully align the ends of the bricks, and clamp them securely at each end, using pipe clamps or bar clamps.

Step C: Make Straight Cuts

Use a mason's chisel and a hammer to split the bricks. Hold the chisel at a slight angle and tap it firmly with the hammer.

Step D: Mark Angled Cuts

Set the bricks in position, allowing ⅜" for mortar joints, where necessary. Mark cutting lines, using a straightedge to make sure the cutting lines are straight and accurate.

Step E: Score Angled Cuts

Making angled cuts is a gradual process—to avoid ruining the brick you have to make a series of cuts that move toward the final cutting line. First, score a straight line in the waste area of the brick, about ⅛" away from the starting point of the marked

---

TIP: USING A BRICK SPLITTER

If your project requires many cuts, it's a good idea to rent a brick splitter, a tool that makes accurate, consistent cuts in bricks and pavers. Always read and follow manufacturer's instructions on a rental tool, and refer questions to the rental center.

In general, though, a brick splitter is easy to use. Just mark a cutting line, and then set the brick on the table of the splitter. Align the cutting line on the brick with the cutting blade on the splitter.

Once the brick is in position on the splitter table, pull down sharply on the handle. The cutting blade will cleave the brick along the cutting line.

NOTE: Always wear eye protection when cutting masonry products, including bricks and pavers.

---

cutting line and perpendicular to the side of the brick.

Step F: Complete Angled Cuts

To make the remaining cuts, keep the chisel stationary at the point of the first cut. Pivot it slightly; score and split again. Keep the pivot point of the chisel at the edge of the brick. Repeat the process until all of the waste area is removed.

D. To mark angled cuts, set the bricks in position and mark the angle of the cut, using a pencil and a straightedge.

E. Mark a line in the waste area of the brick, about ⅛" away from the starting point of the cutting line.

F. Make a series of cuts, gradually removing angled sections until all of the waste area is removed.

HOW TO MIX & THROW MORTAR

Mixing the mortar properly is critical to the success of a brick project. If the mortar's too thick, it falls off the trowel in a heap. If it's too watery, it's impossible to control. Finding the perfect water ratio calls for experimentation. Mix only as much mortar as you can use within about 30 minutes—once mortar begins to set up, it's difficult to work with and yields poor results.

Step A: Mix the Mortar

1. Empty the mortar mix into a mortar box or wheelbarrow and form a depression in the center. Pour about ¾ of the recommended amount of water into the depression, and then mix it in with a masonry hoe. Be careful not to overwork the mix. Continue mixing in small amounts of water until the mortar clings to a trowel just long enough for you to deliver it in a controlled, even line that holds its shape after settling. Take careful notes on how much water you add to each batch, and record the ratios for the best mixture.

2. Set a piece of plywood on blocks at a convenient height, and place a shovelful of mortar on the surface. Slice off a strip of mortar from the pile, using the edge of a mason's trowel. Slip the trowel, point-first, under the section of mortar and lift up. Snap the trowel gently downward to dislodge any excess mortar clinging to the edges. A good load of mortar is enough to set three

bricks. Don't get too far ahead of yourself—if you throw too much at one time, it will set up before you're ready.

Step B: Throw the Mortar

Position the trowel at your starting point. In one motion, begin turning your wrist over, and quickly move the trowel across the surface to spread the mortar consistently along the bricks. Don't worry if you don't get this right the first time. Throwing mortar is a quick, smooth technique that takes time to perfect, but even a beginning bricklayer can successfully use the basic technique in pretty short order. Keep practicing until you can consistently throw a rounded line about 2½" wide and about 2 ft. long.

Step C: Furrow the Mortar Line

Drag the point of the trowel through the center of the mortar line in a slight back-and-forth motion. This action, called "furrowing," helps distribute the mortar evenly.

HOW TO LAY BRICKS

Step A: Mark Reference Lines & Lay the First Course

1. Before you can lay any bricks, you have to create a sturdy, level building surface. So, first pour a footing or slab, as required for your project (see pages 48 to 51), and let that concrete cure.

2. Dry-lay the first course of bricks, centered on the footing or slab, using a ⅜"-diameter dowel for spacing. Mark reference lines

A. *Mix the mortar. Place a shovelful on a plywood work surface, and slice off a strip of mortar.*

B. *Throw the mortar in a rounded line about 2½" wide and about 2 ft. long.*

C. *"Furrow" the mortar line by dragging the trowel point through its center, using a back-and-forth motion.*

around the bricks.

3. Dampen the footing or slab with water, and dampen the bricks if necessary (see page 52).

4. Mix mortar and throw a bed of mortar inside the reference lines. Butter the inside end of the first brick. Press this brick into the mortar, creating a ⅜" mortar bed. Cut away the excess mortar.

5. Plumb the face of the end brick, using a level. Tap lightly with the handle of the trowel to adjust the brick if it's not plumb. Level the brick end to end.

6. Butter the end of a second brick, and then set it into the mortar bed, pushing it toward the first brick to create a joint of ⅜". Continue to butter and place bricks, using the reference lines as a guide and following the plans for the specific project.

Step B: Check Your Work with a Level

Add courses, frequently checking your work with a level to make sure it's both level and plumb. Adjust any bricks that are misaligned by tapping them lightly with the handle of the trowel.

Step C: Tool the Joints & Complete the Project

Every 30 minutes, stop laying bricks and tool all joints that have hardened enough to resist minimal finger pressure. Tooling joints involves drawing a jointing tool across each joint in a fluid

TIP: BUTTER YOUR BRICKS

"Buttering" is a term used to describe the process of applying mortar to a brick before adding it to the structure being built. To butter a brick, apply a heavy layer of mortar to one end, then cut off the excess with a trowel.

motion to smooth away excess mortar. Tool the horizontal joints first, then the vertical ones. Use a trowel to cut away any excess mortar you pressed from the joints. When the mortar is set, but not completely hardened, brush any excess off the faces of the bricks.

A. Dry-lay the first course and mark reference lines. Lay a bed of mortar, butter the bricks, and lay the bricks.

B. Frequently check your work with a level; adjust bricks as necessary.

C. Every 30 minutes, smooth the joints, using a jointing tool.

Working with Stone

Working with stone demands patience and attention to detail. But the rewards are many. Few masonry materials rival stone for spectacular beauty or durability.

Stone work is a labor-intensive craft, however, so consider assembling a team of helpers for your project. With five or more working, you can complete many stone projects in a weekend, whereas completing a big stone project on your own can take many days.

Cutting stones to fit is an important part of most stone projects. Keep a circular saw equipped with a silicon-carbide or diamond-cutting masonry blade on hand, along with a maul and chisel to remove jagged edges and undesirable bumps. To avoid unnaturally straight lines, you may want to take the first pass with a saw (called "scoring"), then complete splitting with a maul and chisel (see "TIP" on page 59). If you will be splitting a lot of stone, build a banker to provide a sturdy, shock-absorbent work surface (page 57).

Organize stones by size and shape before starting your project. Stack long stones in one area. These will serve as tie stones, tying together shorter stones and increasing your wall's strength.

Filler, or wedge, stones should be grouped together in another area. These pieces will be used to fill gaps between the shaping stones. The remaining stones are put in a third pile. Some of these stones may serve as shiners, a stone that is used when no other stone will fit in a space.

Stone weighs 165 lb./cu. ft., on average, so consider wearing a lifting belt to support your back and stomach muscles, and always bend at the knees when lifting, or use a ramp or towing device (see "TIP" on opposite page).

The ultimate look of your wall, pillar, arch, walk, or other stone project can be varied by the stone type, mortar technique, mortar tint, stone dress, and stone pattern you choose. Methods for laying stone vary, but there are a few general principles:

• Thinner joints are stronger. Joints should be ½" to 1" thick. Whether you are using mortar or dry-laying stone, the more contact between stones, the more resistance to stones dislodging.

• Tie stones are essential in vertical structures, such as walls or pillars. These long stones span at least two-thirds the width of the structure, tying together the shorter stones around them. In

Tie stones are long stones that span most of the width of a wall (pages 160 to 163). As a guide, figure that 20 percent of the stones in a structure should be tie stones.

A shiner is the opposite of a tie stone—a flat stone on the side of a wall that contributes little in terms of strength. Use shiners as seldom as possible, and use tie stones nearby to compensate.

horizontal structures, such as walks, long stones act like tie stones, adding strength by bonding with other stones.

• When working with mortar, most stone masons point their joints deep for æsthetic reasons. The less mortar is visible, the more the stone itself is emphasized.

• Long vertical joints, or head joints, are weak spots in a wall. Close the vertical joints by overlapping them with stones in the next course, similar to a running bond pattern in a brick or block wall. This technique is called "ashlar" construction. With irregular stone, such as untrimmed rubble or field stone, building course by course is difficult. Instead, place stones as needed to fill gaps and to overlap the vertical joints.

• The sides of a stone wall should have an inward slope (called "batter") for maximum strength. This is especially important with dry-laid stone. Use a batter gauge and level to slope the sides of a wall 1" for every 2 ft. of height. Ashlar and freestanding walls slope less; round stone and retaining walls slope twice as much. Place uneven stone surfaces in the bottom course of a dry-laid wall, and remove soil under the stone until it lies flat.

TIP: LIFTING STONE

Stone weighs 165 lb./cu. ft., on average. This can make it difficult to place stones precisely. Wear a lifting belt to support your back and stomach muscles, and always bend at the knees as you lift stone. If you can't lift with this method, the stone is too heavy to lift alone. Find a helper, or use an alternative technique to move the stone into position. Ramps and simple lifting or towing devices, such as chains, simplify the task.

Use a batter gauge and level to slope the wall 1" for every 2 ft. of height, in general. Vary slope according to the type of stone used.

"Dress" a stone, using a pointing chisel and maul, to remove jagged edges or undesirable bumps. Position the chisel at a 30° to 45° angle.

Build a banker out of 2 × 2s, and ¾" plywood. Attach pieces with 3½" coarse-threaded wallboard screws through the sides; fill with sand.

Cutting Stone

You can cut most stone by placing it directly on a bed of flat, soft ground, such as grass or sand, that will absorb some of the shock when the maul strikes the chisel. Use a sandbag for additional support. You can also build a simple cutting platform, called a banker (page 57), to support stones.

Protect yourself by wearing safety glasses and heavy gloves and using the proper tools for the job. A standard brickset chisel and hammer are too light, as is a carpenter's framing hammer, which is brittle and may chip when striking a chisel. The best tools are a pitching chisel for long, clean cuts, a pointing chisel for removing small bumps, a basic stone chisel, and a maul for tapping the chisels. A mason's hammer—with its pick at one end—is also useful for breaking off small chips.

Keep the head of your chisel smooth, by grinding it any time curled edges begin to appear. This "mushrooming" results from repeated blows to the chisel with a maul, and can result in small shards of metal breaking free.

Laying stones works best when the sides (including the top and bottom) are roughly square. The stone should sit flat on its

TOOLS & MATERIALS

- Maul
- Stone chisel
- Pitching chisel
- Pointing chisel
- Mason's hammer
- Circular saw with silicone-carbide or diamond-cutting masonry blades
- GFCI extension cord
- Stone
- Trenching spade
- Sod cutter (optional)

bottom or top side without much rocking. It is often helpful to mark a stone for cutting while it sits in place on a wall or other structure, but never cut a stone while it is in place, even to remove a small bump; you risk splitting surrounding stones or breaking the mortar bond. Move the stone to soft ground or a banker.

HOW TO CUT FIELDSTONE
Step A: Mark the Cut Line

Place the stone on a banker, or prop it with sandbags, and mark with chalk or a crayon all the way around the stone, indicating where you want it to split. If possible, use natural fissures in the stone as cutting lines.

A. *Mark the stone with chalk or a crayon to indicate where you want it to split.*

B. *Score along the reference line using a chisel and maul, then strike solidly along the score line with a pitching chisel to split the stone.*

Step B: Make the Cut

1. Score along the line using moderate blows with a chisel and maul, then strike solidly along the score line with a pitching chisel to split the stone.

2. Dress the stone with a pointing chisel (page 57).

HOW TO CUT FLAGSTONE

Step A: Mark the Stone

Mark the stone on both sides with chalk or a crayon, indicating where you want it to split. Mark your line near a fissure, that is probably where the stone will break naturally.

Step B: Score the Stone

Score the line on the side of the stone that won't be exposed. Move a chisel along the line and use a maul to strike it with moderate blows. OPTION: If you have a lot of cutting to do, use a circular saw to score stones, and a maul and chisel to split them. Keep stones wet during cutting to reduce dust.

Step C: Remove the Waste End

1. Turn the stone over, and place a pipe or 2 × 4 under the chalk line.

2. Strike the maul on the end of the portion to be removed.

3. Dress the stone with a pointing chisel (page 57).

TIP: USING A CIRCULAR SAW

If you have a lot of cutting to do, reduce hammering fatigue by using a circular saw with a silicone-carbide or diamond cutting masonry blade to score the stones ⅛" deep with each pass, then use a maul and chisel to split them completely. Keep the stones wet during cutting with a circular saw to reduce dust.

A. *Mark the cutting line on the piece of flagstone to be trimmed.*

B. *Score along the line on the back side of the stone, using a chisel and maul.*

C. *Place a pipe or 2 × 4 directly under the score line, then strike the portion to be removed with a maul.*

Cutting & Soldering Copper

A soldered pipe joint, also called a sweated joint, is made by heating a copper or brass fitting with a propane torch until the fitting is just hot enough to melt solder. The heat then draws the solder into the gap between the fitting and the copper pipe, forming a strong seal.

Using too much heat is the most common mistake made by beginners. To avoid this error, remember that the tip of the torch's inner flame produces the most heat. Direct the flame carefully—solder will flow in the direction the heat has traveled. Heat the pipe just until the flux sizzles; remove the flame and touch the solder to the pipe. The heated pipe will quickly melt the solder.

Soldering copper pipe and fittings isn't difficult, but it requires some patience and skill. It's a good idea to practice soldering pieces of scrap pipe before taking on a large project.

HOW TO SOLDER COPPER PIPE

Step A: Cut the Pipe

1. Measure and mark the pipe. Place a tubing cutter over the pipe with the cutting wheel centered over the marked line. Tighten the handle until the pipe rests on both rollers.

2. Turn the tubing cutter one rotation to score a continuous line around the pipe. Then rotate the cutter in the other direction. After every two rotations, tighten the handle.

3. Remove metal burrs from the inside edge of the cut pipe, using the reaming point on the tubing cutter or a round file.

Step B: Clean the Pipe & Fittings

To form a good seal with solder, the ends of all pipes and the insides of all fittings must be free of dirt and grease. Sand the ends of pipes with emery cloth, and scour the insides of the fittings with a wire brush.

Step C: Flux & Dry-fit the Pipes

1. Apply a thin layer of water-soluble paste flux to the end of each pipe, using a flux brush. The flux should cover about 1" of the end of the pipe.

2. Insert the pipe into the fitting until the pipe is tight against the fitting socket, and twist the fitting slightly to spread the flux. If a series of pipes and fittings (a run) is involved, flux and dry-fit the entire run without soldering any of the joints. When you're sure the run is correctly assembled and everything fits, take it apart and prepare to solder the joints.

A. Position the tubing cutter, and score a line around the pipe. Rotate the cutter until the pipe separates.

B. Clean inside the fittings with a wire brush, and deburr the pipes with the reaming point on the tubing cutter.

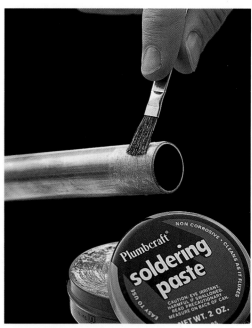

C. Brush a thin layer of flux onto the end of each pipe. Assemble the joint, twisting the fitting to spread the flux.

Step D: Heat the Fittings

1. Shield flammable work surfaces from the heat of the torch. Although heat-absorbent pads are available for this purpose, you can use a double layer of 26-gauge sheet metal. The reflective quality of the sheet metal helps joints heat evenly.

2. Unwind 8" to 10" of solder from the spool. To make it easier to maneuver the solder all the way around a joint, bend the first 2" of the wire solder to a 90° angle.

3. Open the gas valve and light the propane torch. Adjust the valve until the inner portion of the flame is 1" to 2" long.

4. Hold the flame tip against the middle of the fitting for 4 to 5 seconds or until the flux begins to sizzle. Heat the other side of the joint, distributing the heat evenly. Move the flame around the joint in the direction the solder should flow. Touch the solder to the pipe, just below the fitting. If it melts, the joint is hot enough.

Step E: Apply the Solder

Quickly apply solder along both seams of the fitting, allowing capillary action to draw the liquefied solder into the fitting. When the joint is filled, solder begins to form droplets on the bottom. A correctly soldered joint shows a thin bead of silver-colored solder around the lip of the fitting. It typically takes about ½" of solder wire to fill a joint in ½" pipe.

If the solder pools around the fitting rather than filling the joint as it cools, reheat the area until the solder liquifies and is drawn in slightly.

NOTE: Always turn off the torch immediately after you've finished; make sure the gas valve is completely closed.

Step F: Wipe Away Excess Solder & Check the Joint

1. Let the joint sit undisturbed until the solder loses its shiny color. Don't touch it before then—the copper will be quite hot.

2. When the joint is cool enough to touch, wipe away excess flux and solder, using a clean, dry rag. When the joint is completely cool, check for gaps around the edges. If you find gaps, apply more flux to the rim of the joint and resolder it.

3. If, for some reason, you need to take apart a soldered joint, you can reverse the process. First, light the torch and heat the fitting until the solder becomes shiny and begins to melt. Then use channel-type pliers to separate the pipe from the fitting. To remove the old solder, heat the ends of the pipe, and then use a dry rag to carefully wipe away the melted solder. When the pipe is cool, polish the ends down to bare metal, using emery cloth. Discard the old fittings—they can't be reused.

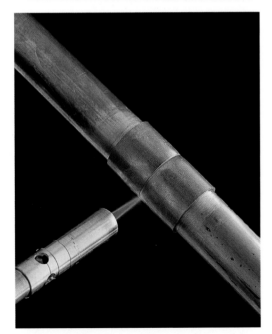

D. *Heat the fitting until the flux begins to sizzle. Concentrate the tip of the torch's flame on the middle of the fitting.*

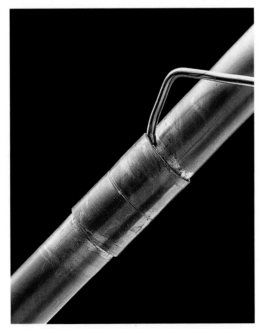

E. *Push ½" to ¾" of solder into each joint, allowing capillary action to draw liquefied solder into the joint.*

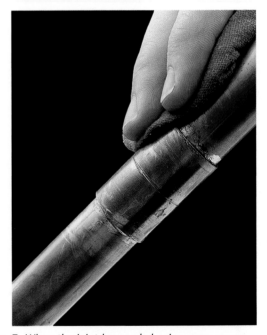

F. *When the joint has cooled, wipe away excess solder with a dry rag. Be careful: pipes will be hot.*

Pathways & Patios

Pathways and patios help transform your yard into a series of living spaces by providing a suitable surface for each room's intended purpose and activities.

By their nature, these outdoor floors must withstand heavy use and the stresses caused by seasonal weather. You will have to carefully select materials, keeping in mind the style and purpose of the area as well as the climate in your region.

There are a variety of materials available. Brick, stone, concrete, wood and gravel can be used alone or in combinations to create attractive, durable outdoor surfaces. Look for ways to repeat materials used elsewhere in your landscape or house. For example, if you have an attractive wood fence, use the same type of wood to create a boardwalk that flows through your flower beds or garden. Or if your home has a distinctive brick facade, repeat the brick element in a matching brick paver patio or walkway.

The projects in this section illustrate the basics of paving with gravel, stone, brick, concrete, and wood. With an understanding of these techniques, you can easily complete projects as demonstrated, or create variations. Many of the projects include suggestions for other materials, applications, or techniques you can apply to the basic principles.

IN THIS CHAPTER:

Loose-fill Pathway

Walkways and paths serve as hallways between heavily used areas of your yard. In addition to directing traffic, paths create visual corridors that direct the eye to attractive features or areas.

A loose-fill pathway is a simple, inexpensive alternative to a concrete or paved path. Lightweight loose materials, such as gravel, crushed rock, bark, or wood chips, are used to "pave" a prepared pathway surface. Because the materials are not fixed within the path, edging is installed around the perimeter of the pathway to hold them in place. In addition to using standard pre-

formed plastic edging, you can fashion edging from common hardscape building materials, such as wood, cut stone, and brick pavers. For professional-looking results, repeat a material used in the exterior of the house or other landscape structures in the pathway edging. Select loose-fill materials that complement the color and texture of your edging.

Our loose-fill project uses brick edging set in soil, which works well for casual, lightly traveled pathways. However, this method should be used only in dense, well-drained soil. Bricks set in loose or swampy soil won't hold their position.

Loose-fill materials are available at most home and garden stores. Many stores sell these materials prebagged, which makes transporting and applying them easier. Aggregate supply companies also sell crushed rock and pea gravel in bulk, which is often a less expensive option. If you buy loose-fill material in bulk, it may be easier to have the supplier deliver it than to transport it yourself.

As you prepare to build a path, consider how it will normally be used, keeping in mind that loose-fill pathways are best suited to light-traffic areas. Also think about how the path will fit into the overall style and shape of your landscape. Curved pathways create a soft, relaxed look that complements traditional landscape designs, while straight or angular paths fit well in contemporary designs. You may want to strategically place the path to lend depth to an area or highlight an interesting element.

TOOLS & MATERIALS

- Rope or garden hose
- Spade
- Rake
- Trowel
- Trenching spade or hoe
- Rubber mallet
- Stakes & string
- Brick pavers
- Landscape fabric
- Loose-fill material

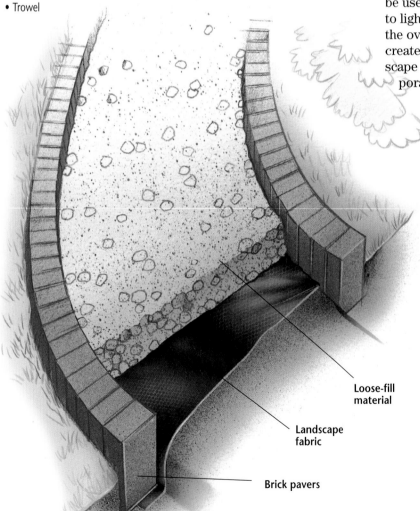

Loose-fill material

Landscape fabric

Brick pavers

A. *Dig narrow trenches for the edging on both sides of the excavated path site. Check the depth with a brick paver.*

HOW TO CREATE A LOOSE-FILL PATHWAY

Step A: Excavate the Path

1. Lay out the shape of the path with a rope or garden hose, then use a spade to excavate the area to a depth of 3". Rake the site smooth.

2. Dig narrow edging trenches along both edges of the path site, using a trenching spade or hoe. Make the trenches about 2" deeper than the path.

3. Test the trench depth with a brick paver placed on end in the trench—the top of the brick should stand several inches above ground. If necessary, adjust the trench to bring the bricks to the correct height.

Step B: Add Landscape Fabric

Line the trench with strips of landscape fabric, overlapping the strips by at least 6". Push the ends of the landscape fabric into the edging trenches.

Step C: Set the Bricks

1. Set the bricks into the edging trenches. Arrange them side by side, with no gaps between bricks.

2. Using a trowel, pack soil behind and beneath each brick. Adjust bricks as necessary to keep rows even.

Step D: Spread the Loose-fill Material

1. Spread the loose-fill material, adding material until it sits slightly above ground level. Level the surface, using a garden rake.

VARIATION: CHILDREN'S PLAY AREA

Using the same techniques shown here for building a path, you can pave the floor of an outdoor room with loose-fill material. Simply excavate and level the area, as shown in "Surface Preparation" (page 38 to 39).

Loose-fill paving, especially pea gravel or sand, works well in a children's play area (pages 458 to 467).

2. Tap the bricks lightly on the inside faces to help set them into the soil. Inspect and adjust the bricks yearly, adding new loose-fill material as necessary.

B. *Place strips of landscape fabric over the path and into the edging trenches, overlapping sections by 6".*

C. *Install bricks end to end and flush against each other in the trenches, then pack soil behind and beneath each brick.*

D. *Fill the pathways with loose-fill material. Tap the inside face of each brick paver with a mallet to help set them permanently in the ground.*

Stepping Stone Path

Whether you are paving a frequently traveled area, or introducing a sense of movement to your landscape, a stepping stone path can be an ideal and inexpensive solution. A thoughtfully arranged stepping stone design almost begs to be walked upon, and its open design complements, rather than overpowers, the landscape.

When designing your path, keep in mind that paths with gentle curves or bends are usually more attractive than straight ones. The distance between the stones is also an important consideration. Set the stones to accommodate a normal stride, so you can effortlessly step from one stone to the next.

There are a variety of materials available for constructing stepping stone paths, from natural stone to prefabricated concrete. To ensure that your path blends with the rest of your landscape, select a material that suits your yard's style and existing materials. Natural stone indigenous to your area is often a good choice. Many stone yards sell 1" to 2½" sedimentary rock "steppers," which are ideal for stepping stone paths. But you can also use cut stone, wood rounds, or precast concrete pavers.

Even if you expect it to be more decorative than functional, your path should be built with methods and materials that keep safety in mind. Select stones that are wide enough to stand on comfortably and have a flat, even, lightly textured surface.

Like other paved surfaces, stepping stones can be adversely affected by the weather. Without a proper base, they can become unstable or settle unevenly. Prepare the base carefully and check the path each spring, adjusting stones as necessary for safety.

TOOLS & MATERIALS

- Spade
- Garden rake
- Stepping stones
- Sand or compactible gravel

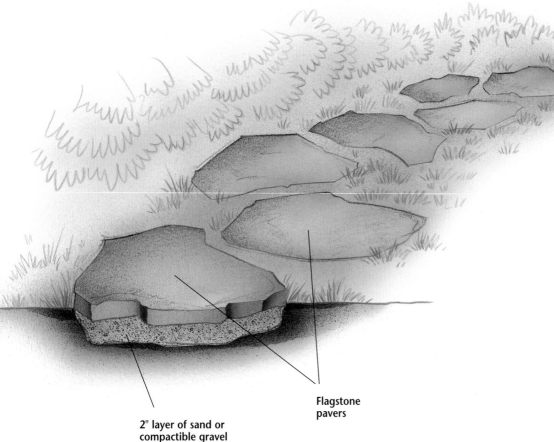

Flagstone pavers

2" layer of sand or compactible gravel

A. Arrange the stepping stones on top of the grass, then test the layout by walking the path. Adjust the stones as necessary.

HOW TO CREATE A STEPPING STONE PATH

Step A: Arrange the Stones

Arrange the stones along the ground in your planned pattern. Walk the full course of the path, then adjust the spacing between the steppers so you can step smoothly from stone to stone.

Step B: Let the Ground Cover Die

If you're installing the path over grass or another living ground cover, leave the stones in place for three to five days. The ground cover beneath the stones will die, leaving a perfect outline of the stones.

Step C: Prepare the Base

1. Using a spade, cut around the outline, creating an excavation 2" deeper than the thickness of the stone.

2. Add a 2" layer of sand or compactible gravel and smooth it out with a garden rake.

Step D: Set & Adjust the Stones

1. Place the stones in the partially filled holes. Rock each stone back and forth several times to help it settle securely into the base.

2. Check to make sure the stones are stable and flush with the ground. Add or remove sand and readjust the stones as necessary.

VARIATION: MAKING STEPPING STONES

You can also design and make your own stepping stones, using quick-setting concrete. Estimate one 40-lb. bag of mix for each 18"-square stone, and then decorate by embedding accent stones or create imprinted patterns with leaves or other materials of your choice.

B. *Leave the stones in place for several days to kill the grass beneath, leaving a visible outline for excavation.*

C. *Dig up the outlined areas, 2" deeper than the height of the stones. Spread a 2" layer of sand in each hole.*

D. *Reposition the stones, adding or removing sand as necessary until they're stable and flush with the ground.*

Flagstone Walkway

Natural flagstone is an ideal material for creating landscape floors. It's attractive and durable, and blends well with both formal and informal landscapes. Although flagstone structures are often mortared, they can also be constructed with the sand-set method. Sand-setting flagstones is much faster and easier than setting them with mortar.

There are a variety of flat, thin sedimentary rocks that can be used for this project. Home and garden stores often carry several types of flagstone, but stone supply yards usually have a greater variety. Some varieties of flagstone cost more than others, but there are many affordable options. When you buy the flagstone for your project, select pieces in a variety of sizes from large to small. Arranging the stones for your walkway is similar to put-

ting together a puzzle, and you'll need to see all the pieces. When you're ready to begin the project, sort the stones by size, and spread them out so that you can see each one.

The following example demonstrates how to build a straight flagstone walkway with wood edging. If you'd like to build a curved walkway, select another edging material, such as brick or cut stone. Instead of filling gaps between stones with sand, you might want to fill them with topsoil and plant grass or some other ground cover between the stones.

HOW TO BUILD A FLAGSTONE WALKWAY
Step A: Prepare the Site & Install the Edging

1. Lay out, excavate and prepare the base for the walkway (page 38). Remove the stakes and string when the base is complete.

2. Form edging by installing 2 × 6 pressure-treated lumber around the perimeter of the pathway.

3. Drive stakes on the outside of the edging, spaced 12" apart. The tops of the stakes should be below ground level. Drive galvanized screws through the edging and into the stakes.

TOOLS & MATERIALS

- Basic tools (page 18)
- Line level
- Hand tamp
- Circular saw with masonry blade
- Power drill
- Masonry chisel
- Maul

- Rubber mallet
- Sod cutter (optional)
- Landscape fabric
- Sand
- 2 × 6 pressure-treated lumber

- Galvanized screws
- Compactible gravel
- Flagstone pavers
- Water

Flagstone pavers

Sand

Landscape fabric

Compactible gravel

2 × 6 wood edging

A. *Drive 12" stakes outside the 2 × 6 pressure-treated edging, then attach them together with galvanized screws.*

B. *Test-fit the flagstones inside the edging, mark them for cutting, then set them aside in the same arrangement.*

Step B: Arrange the Stones

1. Test-fit the stones over the walkway base, finding an attractive arrangement that limits the number of cuts needed. The gaps between the stones should range between ⅜" and 2" wide.

2. Use a pencil to mark the stones for cutting, then remove the stones and place them beside the walkway in the same arrangement. Refer to pages 58 to 59 for techniques on cutting stone.

3. Score along the marked lines with a circular saw and masonry blade set to ⅛" blade depth. Set a piece of wood under the stone, just inside the scored line. Use a masonry chisel and hammer to strike along the scored line until the stone breaks.

Step C: Make a Sand Base

1. Lay strips of landscape fabric over the walkway base, overlapping the strips by 6". (If you plan to grow grass or another ground cover between the stones, skip this step.)

2. Spread a 2" layer of sand over the landscape fabric. Make a "screed board" for smoothing the sand from a short 2 × 6, notched to fit inside the edging (see inset photo). The depth of the notches should equal the thickness of the stones.

3. Pull the screed from one end of the walkway to the other, adding sand as needed to create a level base.

Step D: Lay the Flagstones

1. Beginning at one corner of the walkway, lay the flagstones onto the sand base. Repeat the arrangement you created in Step B, with ⅜"- to 2"-wide gaps between stones.

2. If necessary, add or remove sand to level the stones, then set them by tapping them with a rubber mallet or a length of 2 × 4.

VARIATION: PATIO

Using the same technique for fitting and setting the stones, you can easily create a flagstone patio.

Follow the steps for preparing the patio base, as shown on pages 84 to 85. Then install the wood edging and flagstone as demonstrated below.

Step E: Add Sand Between the Stones

1. Fill the gaps between the stones with sand. (Use topsoil, if you're going to plant grass or ground cover between the stones.)

2. Pack sand into the gaps, then spray the entire walkway with water to help settle the sand.

3. Repeat #2 until the gaps are completely filled and tightly packed with sand.

C. *Spread a 2" layer of sand over the landscape fabric and smooth it out with a screed board made from a notched 2 × 6.*

D. *Lay the flagstones in the sand base leaving a gap between stones. Use a rubber mallet to set them in place.*

E. *Pack the gaps between the stones and the edging with sand, then lightly spray the entire walkway with water.*

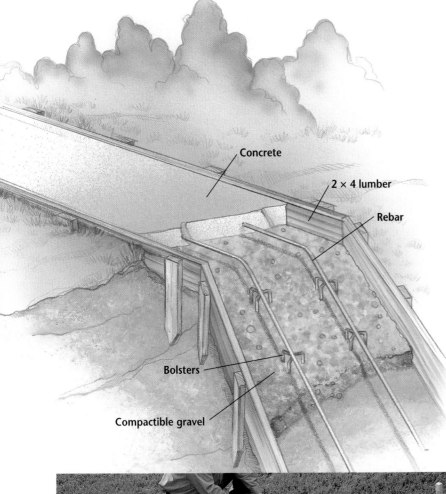

Concrete

2 × 4 lumber

Rebar

Bolsters

Compactible gravel

Concrete Walkway

Pouring a concrete walkway is one of the most practical projects you can master as a homeowner. Once you've excavated and poured a walkway, you can confidently take on larger concrete projects, such as patios and driveways. Refer to pages 40 to 47 for more information on these steps, and the most effective techniques.

HOW TO POUR A CONCRETE WALKWAY
Step A: Lay Out & Prepare the Site
1. Select a rough layout for the walkway, including any turns. Stake out the location and connect the stakes with mason's strings. Set the slope, if needed (pages 32 to 33).

TOOLS & MATERIALS

• Tape measure	• Masonry hoe	• 2½" and 3" deck screws
• Mason's string	• Hammer	• Level
• Line level	• Mason's float	• Isolation board
• Garden stakes	• Straightedge	• Construction adhesive
• Hammer	• Mason's trowel	• Rebar
• Sod cutter (optional)	• Edger	• Bolsters
• Spade	• Groover	• Concrete mix
• Wheelbarrow	• Stiff-bristle broom	• Nails
• Hand tamp	• Compactible gravel	• Plastic sheeting
• Drill	• 2 × 4 lumber	• Concrete sealer

A. *Stake out the location and connect the stakes with mason's string. Set the slope, if needed. Remove the sod, then excavate the site to a depth of 4" greater than the thickness of the concrete walkway.*

B. *Glue an isolation board to any permanent structures that adjoin the walkway.*

2. Remove sod to 4" and 6" beyond the mason's strings, then use a spade to excavate the site to a depth 4" greater than the walkway's thickness, following the slope lines.

3. Pour a 5" layer of compactible gravel as a subbase. Tamp the subbase to an even 4"-thick layer.

Step B: Build & Install the Forms

1. Build and install 2 × 4 forms set on edge (page 41). Miter-cut the ends at angled joints. Position them so the inside edges are lined up with the strings.

2. Connect the forms with 3" deck screws, and drive 2 × 4 stakes on the outside of the forms at 3-ft. intervals. Attach the stakes to the forms with 2½" deck screws.

3. Level the forms or make sure they are set to the desired slope. Drive stakes at each side of angled joints.

4. Use construction adhesive to glue an isolation board to the steps, house foundation, or other permanent structure adjoining the walkway.

5. If necessary, reinforce the walkway with #3 rebar. For a 3-ft.-wide walkway, lay two sections of rebar spaced evenly inside the project area. Use bolsters to support the rebar, but keep it at least 2" below the tops of the forms. Bend rebar to follow any angles or curves, and overlap pieces at angled joints by 12".

6. Mark locations for control joints (to be cut with a groover later) by tacking nails to the outside faces of the forms, spaced roughly at 32-in. intervals.

Step C: Pour the Concrete

1. Mix, then pour concrete into the project area (pages 44 to 47). Use a masonry hoe to spread it evenly within the forms.

2. After all concrete is poured, run a spade along the inside edges of the forms, then use a hammer to tap the outside edges of the forms to help settle the concrete.

3. Build a curved screed board (page 41) and use it to form a crown when smoothing out the concrete.

Step D: Float, Edge & Cut Control Lines

1. Smooth the surface with a float.

2. Cut control joints at marked locations, using a trowel and straightedge.

3. Let the concrete dry until any bleed water disappears.

4. Shape the concrete by running an edger along the forms. Lift the leading edges of the edger and float slightly as you work. Smooth out any marks created by the edger, using a float.

5. Once bleed water has disappeared, draw a groover along the control joints, using a straight 2 × 4 as a guide. Use a float to smooth out any tool marks.

Step E: Finish the Walkway

1. Draw a clean, stiff-bristled broom across the surface of the walkway to create a textured, non-skid surface. Avoid overlapping broom marks.

2. Cover the walkway with plastic and let the concrete cure for one week.

3. Remove the forms, then backfill the space at the sides of the walkway with dirt or sod.

4. Seal the concrete, if desired, according to manufacturer's directions.

C. *Build a curved screed board and use it to form a crown when you smooth out the concrete.*

D. *Smooth the surface with a float. Cut control joints at marked locations. Let the concrete dry until bleed water disappears.*

E. *Remove the forms and backfill at the sides of the walkway with dirt or sod. Seal the concrete, if desired.*

Simulating Flagstone in Concrete

Carving joints in a concrete walk is an easy way to simulate the look of natural flagstones and add interest to an otherwise undistinguished path. By tinting the concrete before pouring it and carving the joints, you can create a walk that resembles a tightly laid flagstone path, hence the name *false flagstone*, often given to this age-old finishing technique.

Start by studying some flagstone paths in your neighborhood and sketching on paper the look you want to recreate. This way, you can also get an idea of the color to aim for when tinting the concrete mix. Keep in mind the color of your house and landscaping, and experiment with tint until you find a complementary hue. For directions on pouring a concrete walk, turn to the walkway project on pages 70 to 71. For further details and techniques for pouring concrete, refer to pages 40 to 47 in the Basic Techniques section.

TOOLS & MATERIALS

- Concrete mix
- Concrete tint
- 2 × 4 lumber
- Circular saw or handsaw
- 3" deck screws
- Level
- Wood-trimming knife
- Vegetable oil or commercial release agent
- Screed board
- Jointing tool or curved ¾" copper pipe
- Magnesium float
- Concrete sealer

HOW TO SIMULATE FLAGSTONE IN A CONCRETE WALKWAY

Step A: Tint & Pour the Concrete

1. Mix concrete and a tinting agent, following the manufacturer's instructions.

2. Pour the concrete into forms (pages 45 to 47), and smooth the surface with a screed board and magnesium float.

Step B: Create Flagstone Pattern

Cut shallow lines in the concrete, using a jointing tool or a curved copper pipe.

Step C: Refloat the Surface

1. Refloat the surface, using a magnesium float. Once the concrete has cured, remove the forms.

2. Protect the surface with a clear concrete sealer, following the manufacturer's instructions.

A. *Pour concrete into forms, and smooth the surface with a screed board and magnesium float.*

B. *Cut shallow lines in the concrete, using a jointing tool or a curved copper pipe.*

C. *Refloat the surface, and remove the forms once the concrete has cured. Protect the surface with a clear concrete sealer.*

Simulating Brick Pavers In Concrete

An alternative to the simulated-flagstone technique (opposite page) is to pour your walk in sections, using a patterned mold to create either a brick paver or stepping stone effect. You won't need to set up forms for this project—the mold shapes the concrete as you place it. Once you've staked out your site and poured a subbase (pages 38 to 39), you can go right to placing the concrete in the mold. But you will need to take extra care each time you place the mold to make sure the walk follows the path you intended. As with the "false flagstone" project (opposite page), you may want to tint the concrete before pouring to recreate the tones of natural stone or pavers. Consider your home and landscaping as you experiment with tint until you find a complementary hue. Turn to the related sections for directions on pouring a concrete walkway on pages 70 to 71, and basic techniques for concrete on pages 40 to 47.

TOOLS & MATERIALS

- Shovel
- Trowel
- Concrete mold
- Isolation board
- Compactible gravel
- Concrete mix
- Concrete tint
- Concrete sealer
- Mason's sand
- Mortar

HOW TO SIMULATE BRICK PAVERS IN A CONCRETE WALKWAY

Step A: Place & Fill the Molds
1. Place the mold at the start of your excavated site.
2. Fill each mold cavity, and smooth the surface flush with the top of the mold, using a trowel.

Step B: Remove the Forms
Let bleed water dry (page 47), then lift the mold and set it aside.

Step C: Finish the Slabs
1. Smooth the edges of the concrete with a trowel, adding concrete to fill voids.
2. To pour subsequent sections, place the mold with the same orientation or rotate it ¼ turn. Continue to place and fill the mold until you reach the end of the walk.
3. In the final placement, fill as many cavities as needed to reach the walk's edge.
4. Wait a week, then apply clear concrete sealer, following the manufacturer's instructions.
5. Finish the walk by filling the joints with sand or dry mortar.

A. Place the mold at the start of your excavated site, and fill each mold cavity. Use a trowel to smooth the surface flush with the top of the mold.

B. Let bleed water dry, then lift the mold and set it aside.

C. Smooth concrete edges with a trowel, adding concrete to fill voids.

Boardwalk

Whether as a garden path or a high-traffic walkway, a boardwalk can add a touch of elegance to any yard. The simplicity of this project's design makes it an easy solution to walkway problems. Frames measuring 29 × 45" are constructed from pressure-treated lumber and recessed in trenches along the project area. Cedar decking boards conceal the frame, creating a lovely walkway surface through your yard.

The boardwalk should be built on a relatively flat stretch. For greater stability, fasten the frames together with 5/16 × 2½" galvanized lag screws driven through both sides of the end boards.

TOOLS & MATERIALS

- Tape measure
- Stakes & string
- Wheelbarrow
- Shovel
- Rake
- Hand tamp
- Framing square
- Circular saw

- Power drill
- Clamps
- Ratchet wrench
- T-bevel
- Landscaping fabric
- Compactible gravel

- 2 × 4 pressure-treated lumber
- 2½" & 3" galvanized deck screws
- 5/16 × 2½" galvanized lag screws with washers
- ¾ × 6 cedar decking boards

HOW TO INSTALL A BOARDWALK

Step A: Excavate the Area

1. Lay out the boardwalk site, using stakes and strings (pages 38 to 39).

2. Dig a trench, 4½" deep and 34" wide, to the length of the site.

3. Line the base of the trench with strips of landscaping fabric, overlapping the strips by 6".

4. Lay a 2" subbase of compactible gravel over the landscaping fabric. Use a hand tamper to pack the gravel into a firm, even surface.

Step B: Build the Frame

1. The boardwalk is constructed as a series of frames attached to one another. For each frame, cut pressure-treated 2 × 4s as follows: three 42" boards (stringers) and two 29" boards (ends).

2. Centered on the face of each end board (14½ from each end), drill a pair of 1/16" pilot holes. Put one hole approximately 3/4" from each edge.

3. Lay out the pieces on a flat surface. Butt the ends of the stringers against the end boards, with the side stringers flush with the ends of the end boards and the middle stringer aligned with the pilot holes at the midpoint. Fasten the pieces together, using 3" galvanized deck screws and checking for square with a framing square.

4. Build as many frames as needed to cover the boardwalk site. For sections

¾ × 6 cedar decking boards

2 × 4 pressure-treated lumber

Compactible gravel

Landscaping fabric

A. *Shovel 2" of compactible gravel into the trench and distribute it with a rake. Compact lightly with a hand tamp.*

Cutting List

Dimensions for one panel:

Part	Type	Size	Qty.
Stringers	2 × 4	42"	3
End boards	2 × 4	29"	2
Decking	¾ × 6	32"	*

*as needed

shorter than 42", cut the stringers for the last frame 3" shorter than the remaining length to allow for the width of the end boards.

Step C: Install the Boardwalk Panels

1. Position the frames in the trench, butting them end-to-end. Clamp the end boards together, making sure the stringers are aligned with one another.

2. Drill four $^3/_{16}$" pilot holes in the end boards, one between each pair of stringers, on both sides of the end boards. Fasten the frames together with $^5/_{16} \times 2\frac{1}{2}$" galvanized lag screws with washers, using a ratchet wrench.

3. Fasten the remaining frame sections together, then backfill the space between the outside edge of the stringers and the trench with compactible gravel for drainage.

Step D: Attach the Decking

1. Cut $^3/_4 \times 6$" decking boards to 32", using a circular saw or handsaw.

2. Starting at one end, center a decking board on the frame so there is a 1½" overhang on each side.

3. Drill pairs of $^1/_{16}$" pilot holes in the decking board at each stringer location, and attach the decking to the frames using 2½" galvanized deck screws.

4. Continue installing the decking, maintaining ¼" spaces between the boards. If necessary, rip the final decking board to size at the end of the boardwalk.

VARIATION: CORNERS

To create a corner, position two frame sections at the angle in the trench with the front corners touching. Tack a string between the back corners, then measure and cut pressure-treated 2 × 4s to size for one corner stringer and two nailers. Use a T-bevel to find the angles created by the turn, and miter-cut the ends of each board to the angle of the turn. Fasten the pieces together with 3" deck screws. For the decking, use the same angle to miter-cut across the face of the boards. Cut them to size as you go.

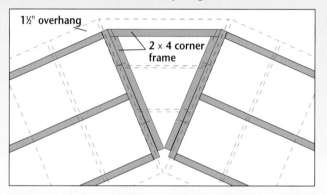

B. *Construct the boardwalk in sections. For each frame, cut three stringers and two end boards. Build as many frames as needed.*

C. *Position the frames in the trench end-to-end, and fasten the ends together with lag screws.*

D. *Install decking boards so they overhang the edges of the stringers by 1½", with ¼" space between boards. Fasten using 2½" deck screws.*

Garden Steps

If you have a steep slope in a high-traffic area of your yard, adding garden steps makes the slope safer and more manageable. Or, if your yard has a long, continuous hill, you can add several sets of steps to get the same results. In addition to making your landscape more accessible, garden steps make your yard more attractive by creating visual interest.

Garden steps are built into an excavated portion of a slope or hill, flush with the surrounding ground. You can build steps from almost any hardscape material: stone, brick, concrete, wood, or even interlocking block. Our version uses two materials: wood

and concrete. The design is simple—the steps are formed by a series of wood frames made from 5 × 6 landscape timbers. The frames are stacked on top of one another, following the run of the slope. After the frames are set in place, they're filled with concrete and given a finished texture.

The exact dimensions of the frames you build will depend on the height of your slope, the size of the timbers you're using and how wide and deep the steps must be. Gradual slopes are best suited to a small number of broad steps. Steeper slopes require a larger number of narrower steps. To keep the stairs easy to use, the risers should be no more than 6" high, and the depth of the frame, also called the tread depth, should be at least 11".

HOW TO PLAN YOUR STEPS

Drive a tall stake into the ground at the bottom of the slope and adjust it until it's plumb. Then drive a shorter stake at the top of the slope. Position a straight 2 × 4 against the stakes, with one end touching the ground next to the top stake. Adjust the 2 × 4 so it's level, then attach it to the stakes with screws (see diagram at left). Measure from the ground to the bottom of the 2 × 4 to find the total vertical rise of the stairway. Divide the total rise by the actual thickness of the timbers to find the number of steps required. Round off fractions to the nearest full number.

Measure along the 2 × 4, between the stakes, to find the total horizontal span. Divide the span by the number of steps to find the tread depth. If the tread depth comes out to less than 11", revise the step layout to extend it.

TOOLS & MATERIALS

- Level
- Reciprocating saw
- Hand tamp
- Power drill
- Spade bit
- Hammer
- Stapler
- Scissors
- Wheelbarrow

- Garden rake
- Edging tool
- Stiff-bristled broom
- Sod cutter (optional)
- 12" spikes
- 2 × 4 lumber
- Timber

- Stakes & string
- Spade
- ¾" pipe
- Plastic sheeting
- Concrete

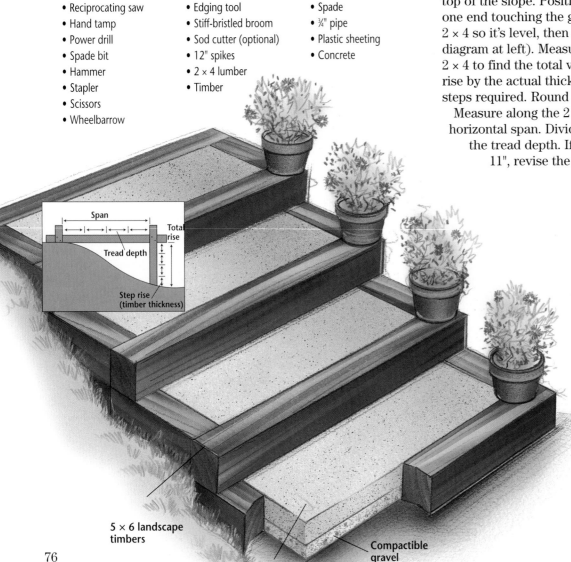

Span
Total rise
Tread depth
Step rise (timber thickness)

5 × 6 landscape timbers

Concrete

Compactible gravel

A. *Arrange the timbers to form the step frame and end nail them together, using 12" spikes.*

HOW TO BUILD GARDEN STEPS
Step A: Build the Frames
Use a reciprocating saw to cut timbers, then assemble the step frames with 12" spikes. In our design, the front timber runs the full width of the step; while the back timber fits between the side timbers.

Step B: Outline the Step Run
1. Mark the sides of the site with stakes and string. Position the stakes at the front edge of the bottom step and the back edge of the top step.

2. Outline the excavation for the first step at the base of the slope, using stakes and string. Remember that the excavation will be larger than the overall tread depth, since the back timber in the frame will be covered by the front timber of the next step.

Step C: Excavate & Install the First Frame
1. Excavate the area for the first frame, creating a flat bed with a very slight forward slope, dropping about ⅛" from back to front. The front of the excavation should be no more than 2" deep. Tamp the soil down firmly, using a hand tamp.

2. Set the timber frame into the excavation. Use a level to make sure that the front and back timbers are level, and that the frame slopes slightly forward.

3. Using a spade bit, drill two 1" guide holes in the front timber and the back timber, 1 ft. from the ends. Anchor the steps to the ground by driving a 2½-ft. length of ¾" pipe through each guide hole until the pipe is flush with the timber.

TIP: PLANNING YOUR STEPS

To simplify the building process, take all necessary measurements, then make a sketch of the site. Indicate the rise, tread depth and width of each step. Remember that actual timber dimensions may vary from the nominal measurements.

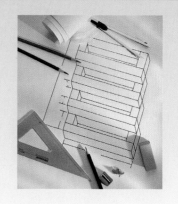

Step D: Add the Second Frame
1. Excavate for the next step, making sure the bottom of the excavation is even with the top edge of the frame you installed for the first step.

2. Position the second step frame in the excavation, lining up the front of the frame directly over the rear timber of the first frame.

3. Nail the first frame to the second with three 12" spikes. Drill guide holes and drive two pipes through the back timber to anchor the second frame in place.

B. *Outline the area for the steps with stakes and string, then measure the height of the slope.*

C. *Excavate the area for the first step, and install the first step frame.*

D. *Excavate the area for the next step, and assemble the frame. Stake the second frame to the first with 12" spikes.*

VARIATION: BRICK-FILLED STEPS

© Crandall & Crandall

If pavers are used elsewhere in your landscape, you may prefer to repeat that element by filling your wood step frames with sand-set pavers. Other variations you can try are shown on the opposite page.

Step E: Place the Remaining Frames

1. Excavate and install the remaining steps in the run. The back of the last step should be flush with the ground at the top of the slope.

2. Staple plastic over the timbers to protect them while the concrete is being poured. Cut away the plastic from the frame openings.

3. Pour a 2" layer of compactible gravel into each frame, and use a scrap 2 × 4 to smooth it out.

Step F: Fill the Steps with Concrete

1. Mix concrete and shovel it into the bottom frame, flush with the top of the timbers. Work the concrete lightly with a garden rake to help remove air bubbles, but don't overwork it.

2. Screed the concrete smooth by dragging a 2 × 4 across the top of the frame. If necessary, add concrete to the low areas and screed the surface again until it is smooth and free of low spots.

3. Use an edging tool to smooth the cracks between the concrete and the timbers.

4. Pour concrete into the remaining steps, screeding and edging each step before moving on to the next.

Step G: Finish the Surface & Cure the Concrete

1. While the concrete is still wet, create a textured, nonskid surface by drawing a clean, stiff-bristled broom across its surface. Brush each surface only one time, and avoid overlapping brush marks.

2. Remove the plastic from around the timbers.

3. When the concrete has hardened, mist it with water, cover it with plastic, and let it cure for one week.

E. *Cover the completed framework with plastic. Pour and smooth a 2" layer of compactible gravel in each frame.*

F. *Shovel concrete into the first frame, then work it with a garden rake to remove air bubbles.*

G. *Texture the surface of the concrete by drawing a stiff-bristled broom across it in one sweeping motion.*

© Michael S. Thompson

These wood-and-paver steps complement the colorful border that surrounds them.

Curving wood steps echo the informal tone of the rest of this landscape.

These attractive steps illustrate how effectively materials such as cement and stone can be combined.

These stone steps suit the rustic site perfectly.

The formality of these brick steps contrasts nicely with the riot of flowers.

Pre-cast Form Steps

Pre-cast concrete step forms are ideal for building attractive steps without building wood forms and pouring concrete yourself. In a few hours, you can excavate, lay pre-cast forms, and fill them with brick pavers.

Many manufacturers sell pavers that are sized to fit inside the forms they make. Determine how many forms you need for your steps and the paver pattern you wish to use, then consult the manufacturer's specifications for the number of pavers required.

To plan the layout for this project, follow "How to Plan Your Steps" on page 76. Adjust the amount of overlap for each step to fit the dimensions of your site or to create a desired appearance.

A. Mark the outline of your steps with stakes and string, then excavate for the first step. Dig a hole 6" deeper than the height of the step and 4" wider and longer than the step on all sides.

TOOLS & MATERIALS

- Tape measure
- Shovel
- Hand tamp
- Rake
- Level
- Rubber mallet
- Broom
- Drill
- Stakes & string
- Compactible gravel
- Step forms
- Sand
- Straight 2 x 4
- Pavers
- Dirt

HOW TO BUILD STEPS WITH PRE-CAST FORMS

Step A: Excavate for the First Step

1. Mark the outline of your steps with stakes and string. Refer to page 38 ("Surface Preparation") for more information on establishing slope and preparing a subbase.

2. Dig a hole 6" deeper than the height of the step and 4" wider and longer than the step on all sides.

Step B: Position the Forms

1. Fill the hole with compactible gravel, and rake the gravel to create a slight downward slope (⅛" per foot) from back to front, for drainage.

2. Tamp the gravel well with a hand tamp, then set the first form in place. Use a level to make sure the form is level from side to side and that it has the proper slope from back to front.

Step C: Install the Brick Pavers

1. Add a layer of gravel inside the form and tamp it well. The distance between the gravel and the top of the form should equal the thickness of a brick paver plus 1".

2. Add a 1"-thick layer of sand over the gravel. Place a 2 x 4 across the form and measure from the bottom of the board to the top of the sand to maintain the correct space for the pavers.

3. Lay the pavers in the form in the desired pattern, keeping them level with the top of the form. Adjust them as needed, by tapping them into place with a rubber mallet or by adding sand underneath them.

Step D: Fill the Joints with Sand and Add Remaining Steps

1. Spread a ½" layer of sand over the step, and use a broom to spread the sand over the pavers to fill the joints.

2. Sweep up the loose sand, then soak the step area thoroughly with water to settle the sand in the joints. Let the surface dry completely. If necessary, add more sand and water until the gaps between the pavers are packed tightly with sand.

3. Excavate for the next step, accounting for the overlap and a 4" space behind and at the sides for gravel. Fill and tamp the gravel so the front is level with the top of the first step, then repeat Step B through Step D.

4. When all the steps are installed, back fill with dirt along the sides.

B. *Fill the hole with compactible gravel. Rake the gravel to create a slight downward slope, then tamp well. Set the first form in place.*

C. *Add a layer of gravel inside the form and tamp it well. Use a 2 x 4 set across the form to measure for the height of the pavers.*

D. *Excavate the next step, providing for overlap and a 4" space behind and at the sides for gravel. Fill and tamp the gravel so the front is even with the top of the first step.*

Brick Paver Landing

The entry area is the first detail that visitors to your home will notice. Create a memorable impression by building a brick paver landing that gives any house a warmer, more formal appearance. You can also add a special touch to the landing by building a permanent planter next to it, using matching brick.

Remember that when adding an adjoining structure, like a planter, you must create a separate building base and be sure to include an isolation joint (pages 40 and 51) so the structure is not connected to the landing area or to the house. An isolation joint will allow the structures to move independently from one another, minimizing the risk of damage to either.

In many cases, a paver landing like the one shown here can be built directly over an existing sidewalk. Make sure the sidewalk is structurally sound and free from major cracks. Pavers often are cast with spacing flanges on the sides, but these are for sand-set projects. Use a spacing guide, like a dowel, when setting pavers in mortar.

HOW TO BUILD A BRICK PAVER LANDING
Step A: Prepare the Site
1. Dry lay the pavers onto the concrete surface and experi-

TOOLS & MATERIALS

- Tape measure
- Drill
- Mason's hoe
- Mason's trowel
- Level
- Straightedge
- Rubber mallet
- Mortar bag

- Jointing tool
- Coarse rag
- Brick pavers
- Isolation board
- Construction adhesive
- Type S mortar
- Plastic sheeting

Isolation board

A. Mix a batch of mortar and dampen the concrete slightly. If the landing will abut an adjoining structure, secure an isolation board in place.

ment with the arrangement to create a layout that uses whole bricks, if possible.

2. Attach an isolation board to the foundation (pages 40 and 51) with construction adhesive to prevent the mortar from bonding with any adjoining structures. Mix a batch of mortar, then dampen the concrete slightly.

Step B: Lay the Border Pavers

1. Lay a bed of mortar for three or four border pavers, starting at one end or corner. Level off the bed to about ½" in depth with a trowel.

2. Lay the border pavers, buttering an end of each paver with mortar as you would a brick. Set the pavers into the mortar bed, pressing them down so the bed is ⅜" thick.

3. Cut off excess mortar from the tops and sides of pavers. Use a level to make sure the pavers are even across the tops. Also, make sure that mortar joints are uniform in thickness.

4. Finish the border section next to the foundation, and check with a level to make sure the row is even in height.

5. Trim off any excess mortar, then fill in the third section, leaving the front edge of the project open to provide easier access for laying the interior field pavers.

Step C: Set the Field Pavers

1. Apply a ½"-thick bed of mortar between the border pavers in the work area closest to the foundation. Because mortar is easier to work with when fresh, mix and apply the mortar in small sections (no more than 4 sq. ft.).

2. Begin setting pavers in the field area, without buttering the edges. Check the alignment with a straightedge, and adjust the pavers' heights as needed, making sure the mortar joints are uniform in width.

3. Fill in the rest of the pavers to complete the pattern in the field area. Apply mortar beds in small sections. Then add the final border sections.

Step D: Mortar the Joints

1. Every 30 minutes add mortar to the joints between the pavers until the joints are level with the tops of the pavers. Use a mortar bag to deliver the mortar into the joints.

2. Smooth and shape the mortar joints with a jointing tool. Tool the full-width "running" joints first, then tool the joints at the ends of the pavers.

3. Let the mortar dry for a few hours, then remove any residue by scrubbing the pavers with a coarse rag and water.

4. Cover the walkway with plastic and let the mortar cure for at least two days. After removing the plastic, do not walk on the pavers for at least one week.

B. *Lay the border pavers, buttering an end of each paver with mortar. Use a level to make sure the pavers are even across the tops.*

C. *Set the pavers in the field area, without buttering the edges. Apply mortar beds in small sections—no more than 4 sq. ft.*

D. *Use a mortar bag to fill mortar joints between pavers. Make sure the joints are even with the tops of the pavers.*

Brick Paver Patio

Brick pavers are versatile and durable, making them an excellent material for paving walkways and patios. They convey an impression of formality, quickly dressing up your landscape. Brick pavers are available in a variety of shapes, patterns and colors to complement your landscape. It's best to use concrete pavers rather than traditional clay bricks. Concrete pavers have self-spacing lugs that make them easy to install. To estimate the number of pavers you'll need, see "Estimating Materials" (page 16).

The easiest way to build a patio or walkway with brick pavers is to set them in sand. With this method, the pavers rest on a 1" layer of sand spread over a prepared base. Pavers are then arranged over the sand, and the joints between them are densely packed with more sand. The sand keeps the pavers in place, but still allows them to shift as the ground contracts and expands with temperature changes.

TOOLS & MATERIALS

- Basic tools (page 18)
- Hand tamp
- Rubber mallet
- Carpenter's level
- Circular saw with masonry blade
- Plate compactor (rented)
- Broom
- Landscape fabric
- Rigid plastic edging
- Galvanized spikes
- 1"-thick pipe or wood strips
- Sand
- 2 × 4 lumber
- Brick pavers

HOW TO BUILD A SAND-SET PAVER PATIO

After you've prepared the foundation for the patio (see "Surface Preparation," page 38), you're ready to begin installing the patio. Leave the stakes and strings in place to use as a reference.

Step A: Prepare the Surface

1. Cut strips of landscape fabric and lay them over the base, overlapping each strip by at least 6".

2. Install rigid plastic edging around the edges of the patio, below the reference strings. Anchor the edging by driving galvanized spikes through the predrilled holes and into the subbase. For curves and

Brick pavers

Sand

Rigid plastic edging

Compactible gravel

Landscape fabric

Staggered   Herringbone   Basket-weave

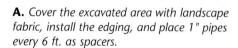

A. Cover the excavated area with landscape fabric, install the edging, and place 1" pipes every 6 ft. as spacers.

B. Remove the spacers from the 1" layer of sand, fill the depressions with sand, and pack the sand with a hand tamp.

rounded patio corners, use rigid plastic edging with notches on the outside flange.

3. Remove the reference strings, then place 1"-thick pipes or wood strips over the landscape fabric, spaced every 6 ft., to serve as depth spacers for laying the sand base.

Step B: Add the Sand Base

1. Spread a 1" layer of sand over the landscape fabric, using a garden rake to smooth it out. The sand should just cover the tops of the depth spacers.

2. Water the layer of sand thoroughly, then lightly pack it down with a hand tamp.

3. Screed the sand to an even layer by resting a long 2 × 4 on the spacers and drawing it across the sand, using a sawing motion. Fill footprints and low areas with sand, then water, tamp, and screed again.

4. Remove the embedded spacers along the sides of the patio base, then fill the grooves with sand and pat them smooth with the hand tamp.

Step C: Set the First Section of Pavers

1. Lay the first border paver in one corner of the patio, making sure it rests firmly against the plastic edging. Lay the next paver snug against the first.

2. Set the pavers by tapping them into the sand with a mallet. Use the depth of the first paver as a guide for setting the

remaining pavers in a 2-ft. section.

3. After each section is set, use a long level to make sure the pavers are flat. Make adjustments by tapping high pavers deeper into the sand, or by removing low pavers and adding a thin layer of additional sand underneath them.

Step D: Complete the Patio

1. Continue installing 2-ft.-wide sections of the border and interior pavers.

2. At rounded corners, install border pavers in a fan pattern with even gaps between the pavers. Gentle curves may accommodate full-sized border pavers, but for sharper bends, you'll need to mark and cut wedge-shaped border pavers to fit. Use a circular saw with a masonry blade to cut the pavers.

3. Lay the remaining interior pavers. Use a 2 × 4 to check that the entire patio is flat. Adjust any uneven pavers by tapping them with the mallet or by adding more sand beneath them.

Step E: Fill Joints & Compact the Surface

1. Spread a ½" layer of sand over the patio, then use the plate compactor to compress the entire patio and pack the sand into the joints.

2. Sweep up the loose sand, then soak the patio area thoroughly to settle the sand in the joints.

3. Let the surface dry completely. If necessary, spread and pack sand over the patio again, until all the joints are tightly packed.

C. *Lay the pavers tight against each other, setting them with the mallet. Check the height with a long level.*

D. *Install border pavers in a fan pattern around the corners, and trim pavers as necessary to make them fit.*

E. *Spread a ½" layer of sand over the patio and pack it into the joints with the plate compactor. Sweep up the loose sand.*

Concrete Patio

Concrete is an inexpensive material for creating durable, low-maintenance outdoor floors. It can be formed into almost any shape or size, making it an ideal choice for walkways, driveways and patios.

The patio in our project is divided into four even quadrants separated by permanent forms. This construction method makes it possible to complete the project in four easy stages—you can pour, tool, and screed each quadrant separately.

An isolation joint separates the patio from the foundation of the house, so footings aren't necessary. When calculating the depth of the base, remember to maintain adequate clearance between the top of the patio and the door threshold. The top of the patio should be at least 2" below the house sill or threshold, so the concrete has room to rise and fall without suffering damage from frost heave.

Concrete may be left as is or finished with a variety of techniques to give the surface an attractive texture or pattern. For this project, we added color and texture with a layer of seeding aggregate.

TOOLS & MATERIALS

- Basic tools (page 18)
- Tape measure
- Circular saw or handsaw
- Wheelbarrow
- Masonry hoe
- Spade
- Hammer
- Wood float

- Concrete edger
- Stiff-bristled brush
- Stakes & string
- Pressure-treated 2 × 4s
- 2½" galvanized deck screws
- Masking tape
- Wire mesh

- Bolsters
- Concrete
- Seeding aggregate
- Plastic sheeting
- Exposed aggregate sealer

HOW TO CONSTRUCT A CONCRETE PATIO

Step A: Prepare the Surface & Build the Forms

1. Lay out the patio, excavate the site and prepare the base (page 38). Leave the stakes and string in place as a reference.

2. Measure and cut pressure-treated 2 × 4s for the permanent form outlining the entire patio.

3. Lay the boards in place, using the strings as guides. Fasten the ends with 2½" deck screws.

4. Temporarily stake the forms at 2-ft. intervals, then use a 2 × 4 and a level to make sure the frame is level.

Step B: Divide the Form into Quadrants

1. Measure, mark, and cut the 2 × 4s that divide the patio into quadrants. Attach these pieces to the frame with toenailed deck screws.

2. Drive deck screws halfway into the inside faces of all the

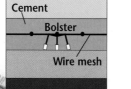

Cement

Bolster

Wire mesh

Seeding aggregate

Concrete

Deck screws

Pressure-treated 2 × 4s

Compactible gravel

Bolster

Wire mesh

A. *Build a permanent form around the patio perimeter and temporarily stake it into place, using a level as you work.*

B. *Install the 2 × 4s that divide the patio into four quadrants, and attach them to the frame with deck screws.*

forms, spacing them every 12". These exposed screws will act as tie rods between the poured concrete and the forms.

3. Cover the tops of the forms with masking tape to protect them when you pour the concrete.

Step C: Pour the Concrete for the First Quadrant

1. Cut reinforcing wire mesh to fit inside each quadrant, leaving 1" clearance on all sides. Use bolsters to raise the mesh off the base, making sure it remains at least 2" below the top of the forms.

2. Mix the concrete in a wheelbarrow, then pour it into the first quadrant. Use a masonry hoe to spread the concrete evenly in the form.

3. Screed the concrete with a straight 2 × 4 that is long enough to reach across a quadrant.

4. Slide a spade along the inside edges of the form, then rap the outer edges with a hammer to settle the concrete into the quadrant.

Step D: Embed the Aggregate and Pour Remaining Quadrants

1. Sprinkle handfuls of seeding aggregate evenly over the wet concrete.

2. Use a float to embed the aggregate, making sure that the aggregate is firmly embedded, but still visible.

3. Tool the edges of the quadrant with a concrete edger, then use a wood float to smooth out any marks left by the tool. Cover the seeded concrete with plastic so it doesn't cure too quickly as you pour and finish the remaining quadrants.

4. Pour concrete into and finish the remaining quadrants, one at a time, using the same technique.

VARIATION: EXPOSED AGGREGATE WALKWAY

Using the same technique as used to finish the patio's surface, you can give a freshly poured concrete walkway an exposed aggregate finish. Apply the finish a section at a time for best results.

Step E: Complete the Finish & Seal the Concrete

1. After the water has evaporated from the concrete surface, mist it with water, then scrub it with a stiff-bristled brush to expose the aggregate.

2. Remove the tape from the forms, then replace the plastic and let the concrete cure for one week. After the concrete has cured, rinse and scrub the aggregate again to remove any remaining residue.

3. Wait three weeks, then seal the patio surface with exposed-aggregate sealer. Apply the sealer according to the manufacturer's directions.

C. *Pour concrete into the first quadrant and screed the concrete smooth with a 2 × 4 that rests on top of the form.*

D. *Sprinkle handfuls of seeding aggregate evenly over the surface of the wet concrete and embed it with a float.*

E. *Mist the surface of the concrete with water and scrub it with a stiff-bristled brush to expose the aggregate.*

New subbase

Old patio

Tiled Patio

It's easy to create a beautiful tiled patio. If you have ever laid ceramic or vinyl tile inside your house, you already have valuable experience that will help you lay patio tile. The project layout and application techniques are quite similar.

The patio tiling project shown here is divided into two separate projects: pouring a new subbase and installing patio tile. If your existing patio is in good condition, you will not need to pour a new subbase. If you do not have a concrete slab in the project area already, you will have to pour one. In that case, skip Step A through Step E and refer to pages 40 to 47.

Make sure you purchase exterior tile for your patio project. Exterior tile is designed to withstand freezing and thawing better than interior tile. There is a wide variety of styles and colors to choose from. Try to select colors and textures that match or complement other parts of your house and yard.

If you have never laid tile before, here are some helpful tips for laying a tiled patio:

• Rent a wet saw from your local rental store for cutting tiles, or use a tile cutter. For curved cuts, use tile nippers.

• Do not mortar more area than you can tile in 15 to 20 minutes.

Start with smaller sections, then increase the size as you get a better idea of your working pace.

• Add a latex-fortified grout additive so excess grout is easier to remove. Also, because patio tile will absorb grout quickly and permanently, remove all excess grout from the surface before it sets. It is a good idea to have helpers when working on large areas.

TOOLS & MATERIALS

- Basic hand tools (page 18)
- Shovel
- Aviation snips
- Masonry hoe
- Mortar box
- Hand tamper
- Magnesium float
- Concrete edger
- Utility knife
- Trowel or putty knife
- Measuring tape
- Tile marker
- Chalkline
- Carpenter's square
- Maul
- Straightedge
- Square-notched trowel
- Rubber mallet

- Tile cutter or wet saw
- Tile nippers
- Needlenose pliers
- Caulk gun
- Sash brush or sponge brush
- Paint roller with extension pole
- 2 × 4 and 2 × 2 lumber
- 2½" & 3" deck screws
- ⅜" stucco lath
- Heavy gloves
- 30# building paper
- Dry floor-mix concrete
- Plastic sheeting
- Dirt
- Roofing cement
- Tile
- Tile spacers

- Dry-set mortar
- Buckets
- Soft cloth for wiping tiles
- ¼"-diameter caulking backer rod
- Grout
- Latex-fortified grout additive
- Grout float
- Grout sponge
- Coarse cloth or abrasive pad
- Latex tile caulk
- Caulk tint
- Grout sealer
- Tile sealer

HOW TO INSTALL A TILED PATIO

Step A: Install Subbase Form Boards

1. Dig a trench 6" wide, and no more than 4" deep, around the patio to create room for 2 × 4 forms. Clean dirt and debris from the exposed sides of the patio.

2. Cut and fit 2 × 4 frames around the patio (pages 86 to 87), joining the ends with 3" deck screws. Cut wood stakes from 2 × 4s and drive them next to the forms, at 2-ft. intervals.

3. Set stucco lath on the surface, and then set a 2 × 2 spacer on top of the lath to establish the subbase thickness. NOTE: Wear heavy gloves when handling metal, such as stucco lath.

4. Adjust the form boards so the tops are level with the 2 × 2. Screw the stakes to the forms with 2½" deck screws.

Step B: Prepare the Site

1. Remove the 2 × 2 spacers and stucco lath, then lay strips of 30# building paper over the patio surface, overlapping seams by 6", to create a bond-breaker for the new surface.

2. Crease the building paper at the edges and corners, making

A. *Adjust the form height by setting stucco lath on the surface, then place a 2 × 2 spacer on top of the lath (their combined thickness should equal the thickness of the subbase).*

B. *Build temporary 2 × 2 forms to divide the project into working sections. The forms also provide rests for the screed board used to level and smooth the fresh concrete.*

C. *Level off the surface of the concrete by dragging a straight 2 × 4 across the top, with the ends riding on the forms.*

D. *Pour and smooth out the next working section. After floating this section, remove the 2 × 2 temporary form between the two sections.*

sure the paper extends past the tops of the forms. Make a small cut in each corner of the paper for easier folding.

3. Lay strips of stucco lath over the building-paper, overlapping seams by 1". Keep the lath 1" away from the forms and the wall. Use aviation snips to cut the lath.

4. Build temporary 2 × 2 forms to divide the project into 3- to 4-ft. sections. Screw the ends of the 2 × 2s to the form boards so the tops are level.

Step C: Place Concrete in the First Section

1. Mix dry floor-mix concrete according to the manufacturer's directions, using either a mortar box or a power mixer (page 43). The mixture should be very dry so it can be pressed down into the voids in the stucco with a tamper.

2. Fill one section with the concrete, up to the tops of the forms. Tamp the concrete thoroughly with a lightweight tamper to force it into the voids in the lath and into the corners.

3. Drag a straight 2 × 4 across the tops of the forms to screed the concrete surface level. Use a sawing motion as you progress to create a level surface and fill any voids in the concrete. If voids or hollows remain, add more concrete and smooth it off.

4. Use a magnesium float to smooth the surface of the concrete. Apply very light pressure and move the float back and forth in an arching motion. Tip the lead edge up slightly to avoid gouging the surface.

Step D: Fill Remaining Sections

1. Pour and smooth out the next section. Float the section then remove the 2 × 2 temporary forms between the two sections.

2. Fill the void left behind with fresh concrete. Float the concrete until it is smooth and level, and blends into the section on each side.

3. Pour and finish the remaining sections one at a time, using the same techniques.

Step E: Finish the Subbase

1. Let the concrete dry until pressing the surface with your finger does not leave a mark, then cut contours around the edges of the subbase with a concrete edger. Tip the lead edge of the edger up slightly to avoid gouging the surface. Using a float, smooth out any marks left by the edger.

2. Cover the concrete with sheets of plastic, and weigh down the edges. Let the concrete cure for at least three days, or according to the manufacturer's directions.

3. After curing is complete, remove the plastic, disassemble and remove the forms, and trim off the building paper around the sides of the patio using a utility knife.

4. Apply roofing cement to two sides of the patio, using a trowel or putty knife to fill and seal the seam between the old and new surfaces. To provide drainage for moisture between the layers, do not seal the lowest side of the patio.

5. After the roofing cement dries, shovel dirt or ground cover

E. *After curing is complete, remove the plastic, disassemble and remove the forms, and trim off the building paper around the sides. Apply roofing cement to two sides of the subbase.*

F. *Adjust the tile to create a layout that minimizes tile cutting. Shift the rows of tiles and spacers until the overhang is equal at each end and any cut portions are less than 2" wide.*

back into the trench around the patio.

Step F: Dry Lay the Tile

1. Dry lay one row of tile vertically and one horizontally on the subbase, so they intersect at the center of the patio. Use tile spacers between tiles to represent joints. Keep the tiles ¼" to ½" away from the house to allow for expansion.

2. Adjust the tile to create a layout that minimizes tile cutting. Shift the rows of tiles and spacers until the overhang is equal at each end and any cut portions are less than 2" wide.

3. With the layout set, mark the subbase at the joint between the third and fourth row out from the house, then measure and mark it at several more points along the subbase. Snap a chalk line to connect the marks.

4. Use a carpenter's square and a long, straight board to mark end points for a second reference line perpendicular to the first. Mark the points next to the dry-laid tile so the line falls on a joint location. Snap a chalk line that connects the points.

Step G: Place First Legs of Tile

1. Mix a batch of dry-set mortar in a bucket, according to the manufacturer's directions.

2. Spread mortar evenly along both legs of the first quadrant near the house, using a square-notched trowel. Apply enough mortar for four tiles along each leg.

3. Use the edge of the trowel to create furrows in the mortar.

G. *Set the first tile in the corner of the quadrant where the lines intersect, adjusting until it is exactly aligned with both reference lines. Position the next tile along one arm of the quadrant, fitting it neatly against the spacer.*

H. *Set tiles into the field area of the first quadrant, saving any cut tiles for last. Cut tile using a wet saw or a tile cutter. For curved cuts, use tile nippers.*

I. *Fill in the remaining quadrants, using a straightedge to check joints occasionally. If any of the joint lines are out of alignment, compensate over several rows of tiles. After all tiles are set, remove spacers.*

Apply enough mortar to completely cover the area under the tiles without covering up the reference lines.

4. Set the first tile in the corner of the quadrant where the lines intersect, pressing down lightly and twisting slightly from side to side. Adjust the tile until it is exactly aligned with both reference lines.

5. Rap the tile gently with a rubber mallet to set it into the mortar. Rap evenly across the entire surface area. Be careful not to break the tile or completely displace the mortar beneath the tile.

6. Set plastic spacers at the corner of the tile that faces the working quadrant.

7. Position the next tile into the mortar bed along one arm of the quadrant. Make sure the tiles fit neatly against the spacers. Rap the tiles with the mallet to set it into the mortar, then position and set the next tile on the other leg of the quadrant. Make certain the tiles align with the reference lines.

8. Fill out the rest of the tiles in the two, mortared legs of the quadrant. Use the spacers to maintain uniform joints between tiles. Wipe off any excess mortar before it dries.

Step H: Fill the First Quadrant

1. Apply a furrowed layer of mortar to the field area of the first quadrant, and then set tiles into it. Save any cut tiles for last. Use a wet saw or a tile cutter for cutting. For curved cuts, use tile nippers.

2. Place several tiles at once, and then set them all with the rubber mallet at one time.

3. As you finish the quadrant, use a needlenose pliers to carefully remove the plastic spacers before the mortar hardens—usually within one hour. Clean all excess mortar from the tiles before it hardens.

Step I: Fill the Remaining Quadrants

1. Apply mortar and fill in tiles in the remaining quadrants, beginning with the next quadrant against the house. Use the same techniques used for the first quadrant.

2. Use a straightedge to check the tile joints occasionally. If any of the joint lines are out of alignment, compensate for the misalignment over several rows of tiles.

3. After all the tiles for the patio are set, make sure all spacers are removed and any excess mortar has been cleaned from the tile surfaces. Cover the project area with plastic for three days to allow the mortar to cure properly.

Step J: Create Expansion Joints

After three days, remove the plastic and insert strips of ¼"-diameter caulking backer rod into the joints between quadrants and over any control joints, to keep grout out of these joints.

Step K: Grout the Joints

1. Mix a batch of tile grout to the recommended consistency. TIP: Add latex-fortified grout additive so excess grout is easier to remove. Use a damp sponge to wipe off grout film.

2. Start in a corner and spread a layer of grout onto a 25-sq.-ft. or less area of the tile surface.

3. Use a rubber grout float to spread the grout and pack it into the tile joints. Scrape diagonally across the joints, holding the float in a near-vertical position. Make sure to scrape off excess grout from the surface of the tile so the tile does not absorb it.

4. Use a damp sponge to wipe the grout film from the surface of the tile. Rinse the sponge out frequently with cool water, and be careful not to press down so hard around joints that you disturb the grout. Wash grout off of the entire surface.

Step L: Finish & Seal the Tile

1. Let the grout dry for four hours, and then poke it with a nail to make sure it has hardened. Use a cloth to buff the surface to remove any remaining grout film. Use a coarser cloth, such as burlap, or an abrasive pad, to remove stubborn grout film.

2. Remove the caulking backer rod from the tile joints, then fill the joints with caulk tinted to match the grout color.

3. Apply grout sealer to the grout lines using a sash brush or small sponge brush. Avoid spilling over onto the tile surface with the grout sealer. Wipe up any spills immediately.

4. After one to three weeks, seal the surface with tile sealer. Follow the manufacturer's application directions, using a paint roller with an extension pole.

J. *After three days, remove plastic sheeting and insert strips of caulking backer rod into the joints between quadrants and control joints.*

K. *Mix a batch of tile grout to the recommended consistency and use a grout float to pack it into tile joints.*

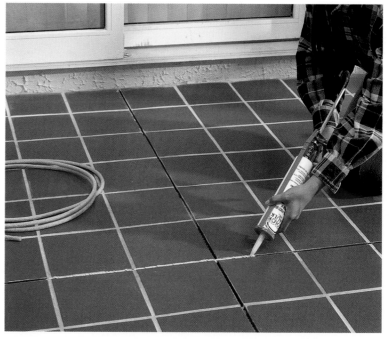

L. *Remove the caulking backer rod, then fill the joints with caulk that is tinted to match the grout color. Apply grout sealer, then seal the entire surface after one to three weeks with tile sealer.*

Concrete Driveway

Pouring a driveway is a lot like pouring a patio or walk, but on a larger scale. It's particularly useful to divide the driveway into sections that you can pour one at a time. A wood divider (pages 89 to 90) is removed after each section is firm and repositioned to pour the next section.

Driveways up to 10 ft. wide are simplest to build because you can pour fiber-reinforced concrete directly over the subbase without additional reinforcement. (Check with your building inspector regarding local requirements.)

For driveways wider than 10 ft., a control joint is added down the center to keep cracks from spreading. Joints cut in the driveway's surface or created with strips of felt placed between sections of the driveway reduce damage to the concrete from cracking and buckling. For a larger slab, add metal reinforcement, using the approach used for a walkway (page 70 to 71).

Pay attention to drainage conditions when planning your driveway. Soil that drains poorly can damage a slab (pages 40 to 41). If drainage is poor, line your site with polyethylene sheeting before pouring. It is critical to establish a gradual slope, and finish the driveway with a crowned surface, so water will run off.

If your driveway must curve or turn, create forms with 1 × 4s by sawing parallel ½"-deep kerfs in one side of each board, and bending the boards to form the proper curves. Attach the curved forms inside the stakes, and backfill beneath all the forms.

NOTE: It's important to handle bleed water carefully as you pour a driveway. Review the section on bleed water (page 47) before beginning your project.

Apron

Isolation joint or Control joint

Control joint (for driveways wider than 10 ft.)

TOOLS & MATERIALS

- Measuring tape
- Shovel
- Hand tamp or power tamp
- Hammer
- Circular saw
- Drill
- Water level
- Power mixer
- Wheelbarrow
- Hoe
- Trowel

- Darby
- Edger
- Concrete groover
- Hand float
- Bucket
- Stakes
- Mason's string
- Crushed stone
- 2 × 4 and 1 × 2 lumber
- 2" deck screws
- ⅜ × 1½" wood spacer
- Felt isolation strip

- Bricks
- Polyethylene vapor barrier
- Vegetable oil or commercial release agent
- Fiber-reinforced concrete
- Screed board
- 6 mil plastic sheeting
- Concrete sealer

A. *Excavate the site to the desired depth, then smooth the bottom of the site with a 2 × 4 and pack the soil with a tamper.*

HOW TO LAY OUT YOUR DRIVEWAY

A proper layout is key to determining how well your driveway functions. Start by calculating the amount of drop per foot on the site. You will need this number to maintain a gradual slope as you excavate.

To find the slope of your driveway, divide the length in feet (the horizontal distance from the apron to the curb) by the vertical drop in inches. This tells you how many inches per foot the new driveway should slope.

To find the vertical drop from the garage to the curb, divide the total drop by the distance in yards to determine the amount of drop per yard. You can use mason's string or a water level to find vertical drop, but it's easiest to use a water level (page 49). Set stakes along the length of the site to mark positions for the forms.

How deep you dig will depend upon the thickness of your slab and subbase, typically 4" each. (Check with your building inspector: building codes in some areas call for a 6" slab—in that case, you will need 2 × 6s instead of 2 × 4s for forms.) Use beveled 12" 1 × 2 stakes and mason's strings to mark the edges of the site, and set the stakes at a consistent height so you can use them to check the depth of the excavated site.

Plan to excavate an area 10" wider than the slab. This will allow room for stakes and forms that will hold the concrete in place (pages 42 to 43).

HOW TO POUR A CONCRETE DRIVEWAY
Step A: Lay Out & Excavate the Site

1. Find the slope and drop (above) of the planned driveway, and determine the thickness of your slab and subbase.

B. *Drive stakes and string at the corners of the site. Position 2 × 4 forms inside the strings, fastening them to stakes with deck screws. INSET: Use a water level to set the slope.*

2. Excavate the site (pages 38 to 39), digging 10" wider than the planned slab to allow room for stakes and forms.

3. Establish the proper slope using stakes and mason's strings. You may have to remove the stakes temporarily to smooth the bottom of the site with a 2 × 4 and pack the soil with a tamp.

4. Pour a 4" layer of crushed stone as a subbase, screed with a long 2 × 4, then tamp the stone. Make small adjustments to the slope of the site, as required, by adjusting the thickness of the subbase.

Step B: Build the Forms

1. Drive stakes at the corners of the site, 3½" in from each side, and connect the stakes on each side with mason's strings.

2. Use a water level (INSET, page 95) to check that the strings are set to the correct slope, and make any adjustments to the stakes as necessary.

3. Position 2 × 4 forms inside the strings, aligning the tops with the strings. Plant stakes every 2 ft. outside the forms, with the tops slightly lower than the tops of the forms.

4. Drive deck screws through the stakes and into the forms. Where forms meet, secure them to a single 1 × 4 stake.

Step C: Build a Divider

1. Construct a divider equal in length to the width of the slab. Set a 1 × 2 on the edge of a 2 × 4, and place a ⅝" × 1½" wood spac-

er midway between them, flush with the edges.

2. Attach the two pieces with 2" deck screws so the screw heads sink below the surface. The curved top of the divider will form the crown of the driveway as you screed.

Step D: Install the Divider

1. Position the divider roughly 6 ft. from the top of the driveway, then drive screws through the forms and into the divider to hold it in place temporarily.

2. Place a felt isolation strip against the divider, propping the strip in place temporarily with bricks.

3. If your site drains poorly (page 32), add a layer of polyethylene over the bottom of the site as a vapor barrier.

4. Coat the dividers and forms with vegetable oil or commercial release agent to prevent the concrete from bonding to the forms' surfaces as it cures.

Step E: Pour Concrete

1. Mix fiber-reinforced concrete for one section of the slab at a time, using a power mixer. Or order concrete from a ready-mix supplier. If you use ready-mix, have helpers on hand so you can pour the concrete as soon as it arrives.

2. Pour pods of concrete (pages 45 to 47) into the first section, and dig into the concrete with a shovel to eliminate any air pockets.

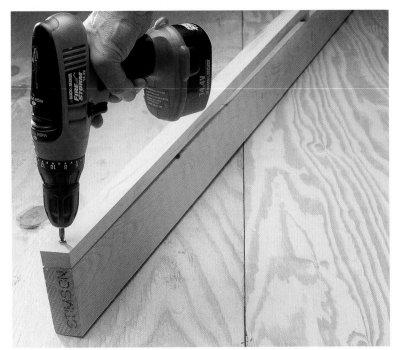

C. *Construct a divider equal in length to the slab's width, using a 1 × 2 set on a 2 × 4, with a ⅝" × 1½" wood spacer midway between them.*

D. *Position the divider roughly 6 ft. from the top of the driveway. Drive screws through the forms and into the divider to secure it temporarily.*

3. Remove the brick props inside the site once there is sufficient concrete in place to prop up the felt strip.

Step F: Screed the Surface

1. Screed the concrete from side to side, using a 2 × 4 resting on the driveway apron and the crowned divider. Raise the leading edge of the board slightly as you move it across the concrete.

2. Add concrete to any low spots, and rescreed if necessary.

Step G: Float, Edge & Finish the Concrete

1. Float the surface with a darby, then let the surface cure for 2 to 4 hours, or until it is solid enough to support your weight.

2. For a slab wider than 10 ft., cut a control joint down the slab's center line (page 46).

3. Use an edger along the inside of the forms to create smooth edges (page 46).

4. Remove the divider and screw it in place to pour the next section. Prop the felt strip in place temporarily with bricks, and remove the bricks when there is sufficient concrete in place to hold the felt.

5. Finish the surface as desired as each section hardens. Cover the sections with polyethylene sheeting, and mist them daily for two weeks.

6. Remove the forms and plastic sheeting, and seal the concrete, following the manufacturer's recommendations.

E. *Pour pods of concrete into the first section, digging into the concrete with a shovel to eliminate air pockets.*

F. *Screed the concrete from side to side, using a 2 × 4 resting on the driveway apron and the crowned divider. Raise the leading edge of the board slightly as you move it across the concrete.*

G. *Float the surface with a darby, then let the surface cure for 2 to 4 hours, or until it is solid enough to support your weight. Finish the surface as desired as each section hardens.*

Pathway & Patio Ideas

© Crandall & Crandall

© Jerry Pavia

(above) **An unexpected pattern** made from smaller concrete slabs makes this driveway easier on the eye than a single, unrelieved slab of concrete.

(left) **A mixture of paving materials** makes this patio unique. The homeowner used broken pieces of tile to create a sunburst pattern within a flagstone and mortar patio.

© Saxon Holt

© Saxon Holt

© R. Todd Davis

(above) **A simple concrete slab patio** balances and anchors this complex landscape design, which features many textures and patterns.

(near right) **Irregular natural stone pavers** blend in well with this informal landscape to create a meandering pathway through the garden.

(far right) **A boardwalk creates unity** in this setting, where the house siding and deck are also made from natural wood.

Fences & Walls

Crawling across a rolling field or guarding a suburban home, a fence or wall defines space and creates a backdrop for the enclosed landscape. Its materials, style, shape, and colors set a tone that may even tell you something about what you'll find on the other side.

Traditional picket fences conjure up images of cottage gardens and children playing. Post and rail fences often surround rustic landscapes or pastures; long expanses of a white board fence can make you believe there might be horses over the next hill. Privacy fences such as board and stringer, or security fences such as chain link, produce images of swimming pools sparkling in the sun.

Landscape walls can serve many purposes: They can define property boundaries, separate living areas within the yard, and screen off unpleasant views or utility spaces. Durable masonry walls, such as glass block, concrete block, stone or stone veneer, can introduce new textures and patterns into your landscape, while living walls, like the framed trellis wall, can provide beautiful backdrops for your favorite vines or lush border gardens.

Using simple building techniques, the projects in this section offer a wide variety of choices for practical, visually appealing fences and walls. Properly constructed, the fences or walls you build should last decades with little maintenance.

Basic Techniques

Once the plans are drawn, the materials delivered, and the tools gathered, it's time to begin the process of building your fence or wall.

Installation begins with plotting the fence or wall line and marking post locations. When installing fences, make a site map and carefully measure each post location. The more exact the posthole positions, the less likely it is that you'll need to cut stringers and siding to special sizes.

For walls, determine the outside edges of the footings along the entire site, as for a fence line. Then plot right angles to find the ends and inside edges of the footings.

Laying out a fence or wall with square corners or curves (page 104) involves a little more work than for a straight fence or wall line. The key in both instances is the same as for plotting a straight fence or wall line: Measure and mark accurately. This will ensure proper spacing between the posts and accurate dimensions for footings, which will provide strength and support.

TOOLS & MATERIALS

- Stakes & mason's string
- Line level
- Tape measure
- Plumb bob
- Reciprocating saw
- Spring clamps
- Masking tape
- Pencil
- Spray paint
- Hand maul

HOW TO PLOT A STRAIGHT FENCE LINE

Step A: Mark the Fence Line

1. Determine the exact property lines. Plan your fence line with a setback of at least 6" from the legal property line. (Local regulations may require a larger setback.)

2. Draw a site map. Make sure it is detailed and takes all aspects of your landscape into consideration, with the location of each post accurately marked.

3. Referring to the site map, mark the fence line with stakes at each end or corner post location, and mason's string between.

4. Adjust the string until it is level, using a line level as a guide.

Step B: Mark the Gate Posts

1. To find the on-center spacing for the gate posts, combine the width of the gate and the clearance necessary for the hinges and latch hardware, then add 4".

2. Mark the string with masking tape to indicate where the gate posts will be installed.

Step C: Mark Remaining Posts

Refer to your site map, and then measure and mark the line post locations on the string, using masking tape. Remember that the tape indicates the center of the post, not the edge.

A. *Mark the fence line with stakes and mason's string. Using a line level as a guide, adjust the string until it is level.*

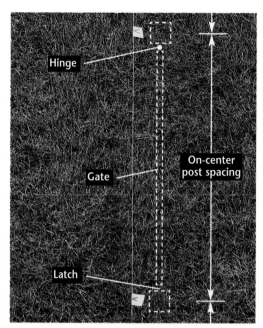

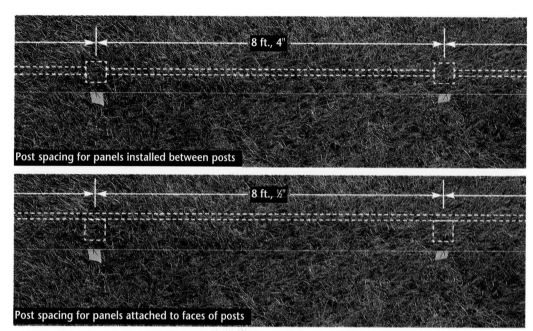

B. *Measure the gate width, including hinge and latch hardware, plus 4" for the on-center spacing between posts. Mark the locations on the string with masking tape.*

C. *Mark the string at remaining post locations. Use masking tape to mark the center of the posts.*

Right Angles

If your fence or wall will enclose a square or rectangular area, you probably want the corners to form 90° angles. The most effective method of plotting right angles for fences, walls, or other construction, such as pillars, is the 3-4-5 triangle method. Have someone help you manage the tape measures, if necessary.

HOW TO PLOT A RIGHT ANGLE
Step A: Mark One Side

1. Begin marking the fence line with stakes and mason's string (page 102).

2. At the location of the outside corner, plant a stake. Connect the corner stake to the previous stake with mason's string.

3. Plant another stake 3 ft. out from the corner stake along the established line.

A. *Stake out the fence line, marking the outside corner of the two adjacent fence sides. Connect the stakes with mason's string, then mark a point 3 ft. along the wall with another stake.*

B. *Position one tape measure at the corner stake and open it past 4 ft. With someone's help, position another tape measure at the 3 ft. stake and open it past the 5 ft. mark. With both tape measures locked, adjust them so they intersect at the 4 ft. and 5 ft. marks.*

Step B: Mark the Adjacent Side

1. Position the end of one tape measure at the outside corner stake, and out along the adjacent, connecting side. Open it past the 4 ft. mark and lock it.

2. Have someone help you position the end of another tape measure at the 3 ft. stake on the first side. Open it past the 5 ft. mark and lock.

3. Angle the second tape measure toward the first, so that the two tapes intersect at the 5 ft. mark for the diagonal measurement, and at the 4 ft. mark for the perpendicular measurement.

4. Run mason's string from this stake to the outside corner stake. The 3 ft. and 4 ft. mason's strings form a right angle. Extend or shorten the mason's string, as needed.

5. Stake out the exact dimensions for the rest of your structure according to your site map.

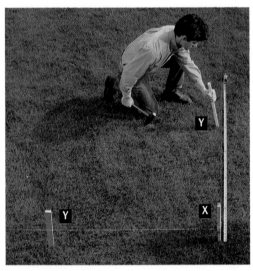

A. *Plot a right angle. Tie mason's string to a pair of stakes equidistant from the corner stake. Plant a stake where the two strings meet, opposite the corner stake, to form a square.*

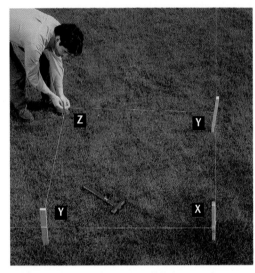

B. *Using mason's string attached to the end stakes, create a square and position a stake at the far corner (Z).*

Curves

A curved wall can add appeal to an otherwise dull landscape. With a few tools, you can make a simple "compass" to plot the curve symmetrically on the ground.

HOW TO PLOT A CURVE
Step A: Form a Square
1. Plot a right angle, using the 3-4-5 triangle method (page 103).

2. Measure and plant stakes equidistant from the outside corner (X) to mark the end points for the curve (Y).

Step B: Create a Compass
1. Tie a mason's string to each end stake, and extend the strings back to the corner stake. Then hold them tight at the point where they meet.

2. Pull this point out, opposite the corner stake, until the strings are taut. Plant a stake (Z) at this point to complete a square.

Step C: Mark the Curve
Tie a mason's string to the stake (Z), just long enough to reach the end points of the curve (Y). Pull the string taut and hold a can of spray paint at the end of it. Moving in an arc between the end points, spray paint the curve on the ground.

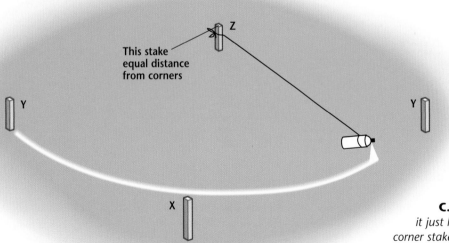

This stake equal distance from corners

C. *Tie a string to the final stake—make it just long enough to reach from the final corner stake to the end stakes. Holding the string taut, spray paint the curve on the ground.*

Handling Slope

It's considerably easier to build a fence when the ground is flat and level along the entire length of the proposed fence line. But few landscapes are entirely flat. Hills, slight valleys, or consistent downward grades are slope issues to resolve while planning your fence. There are two common ways to handle slope: contouring and stepping.

A contoured fence is the easier of the two solutions. The stringers between the posts run roughly parallel with the ground, so the fence line has a consistent height and rolls in unison with the terrain. Contouring works best over large areas of slope, with post-and-rail or picket fences.

A stepped fence, see page 106, takes more time and effort, but creates a more structured look. Each section between posts "steps" down in equal increments, creating a uniform fence line. Stepping works best over gradual slopes. Steep hills or valleys rise too much over short runs, and will cause large gaps between the ground and the bottom of the fence.

Whichever method you use, make sure your posts are plumb and properly set in the ground. If they are not, gravity will work on your fence line and create structural problems over time.

Refer to this information if you need to adapt any of the fence designs in this section for a sloped site.

HOW TO CONTOUR A FENCE
Step A: Determine Post Locations
1. Outline the fence location with stakes and string, as shown on pages 102 to 103. Drive one stake into the ground at the top of the slope and one at the bottom. Make sure the stakes are plumb.

2. Run string between the stakes, 6" above the ground at each stake.

3. Measure and mark equidistant post locations along the string, using pieces of tape.

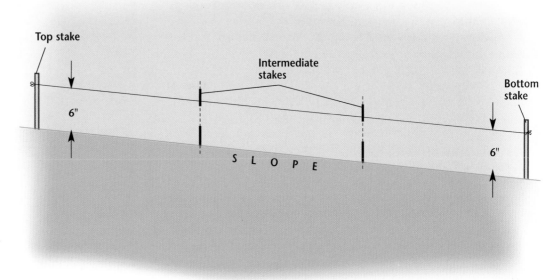

A. *Run a string between stakes at the top and bottom of the slope. Mark the post centers on the string, and drop a plumb bob to determine the posthole locations.*

4. Drop a plumb bob from each piece of tape, and mark the ground with a stake for the posthole location.

Step B: Set the Posts
1. Dig footings and set the posts in concrete (pages 108 to 109). Allow to cure for two days.

2. Measure up from the base of each post and mark cutoff lines for the height, using a framing square.

3. Trim the posts along the cutoff lines using a reciprocating saw or handsaw.

B. *Mark the fence height on each post, and cut to size with a reciprocating saw or handsaw.*

Each post will be the same height, creating a contour fence line that follows any ground variance you may find on your property.

Step C: Build the Framework & Apply the Siding

1. On each post, measure down from the top, and mark a line for both the upper and lower stringer positions.

2. Clamp a board for the upper stringer between two posts, aligning the top edge with the upper stringer reference marks of each. Scribe each post outline on the backside of the stringer. Remove the stringer and cut it to size, using a circular saw.

3. Position the stringer between the two posts and toenail it into place, using galvanized nails or deck screws.

4. Repeat #2 and #3 to install the remaining stringers, both upper and lower, in their proper positions.

5. Apply the siding. Mark each board with a reference line, so each will extend evenly above the upper stringer. If necessary, trim the bottoms to maintain 2" of clearance from the ground. Use spacers between the boards to maintain consistent spacing.

C. Clamp the upper stringer at the reference marks on the posts. Scribe the backside of the stringer where it overlaps the post and cut it to size.

HOW TO STEP A FENCE

Step A: Determine the Slope & Post Locations

1. Drive a short stake into the ground at the top of the slope and a longer stake at the bottom. Make sure the top of the longer stake rises above the bottom of the shorter stake. Check the longer stake for plumb with a level.

2. Run string from the bottom of the short stake to the top of the longer one. Using a line level, adjust the string at the longer stake until it is level. Mark the position on the stake.

3. Measure the length of the string from stake to stake. This number is the run. Divide the run into equal segments that are between 48" and 96". This will give you the number of sections, and posts (number of sections + 1).

Example: 288" (run) ÷ 72" (section size) = 4 (number of sections).

4. Measure the longer stake from the ground to the string mark for the rise. Divide the rise by the number of sections

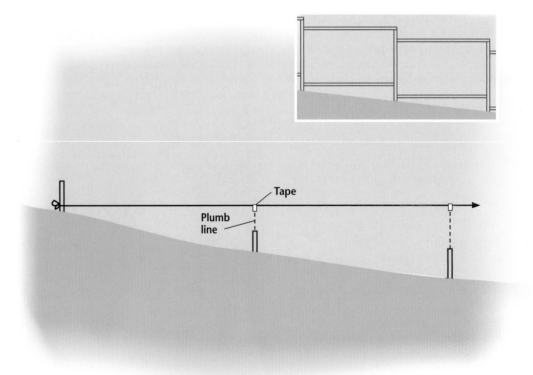

A. Using stakes and string, determine the run and the rise of the slope, then calculate and mark stepped post locations.

you will have on the slope for the stepping measurement.

Example: 24" (rise) ÷ 4 (sections between posts) = 6" (step size).

5. Measure and mark the post locations along the level string with a piece of tape.

6. Drop a plumb bob from each post location mark on the string, and mark the ground with a stake.

Step B: Mark & Cut Posts

1. Dig the postholes and set the posts (pages 108 to 109). Allow the concrete to cure for two days.

2. On the post at the bottom of the slope, measure up from the ground and mark the post height. Cut the post at the mark using a reciprocating saw or handsaw.

3. Use a line level to run a level string from the top of this post to the next post. Mark a reference line on the post.

4. Measure up from this reference line and mark the step size (6" in our example). Cut the post to size with a reciprocating saw or handsaw.

5. Measure down from the reference line and mark the lower stringer position.

6. Repeat #3 through #5 for each post, until you reach the top of the slope.

Step C: Attach the Stringers & Siding

1. Measure across the top of the post to the reference line on the next post. Cut the board for the upper stringer to size.

2. Place the stringer with one end on the post top and the other flush against the next post at the reference mark. Make sure the stringer is level and attach it, using 3" galvanized deck screws.

3. Measure the distance between the posts, and cut the boards for the lower stringers to size. Continue this process until you reach the top of the slope.

4. Apply the siding. Mark each board with a reference line so each will extend evenly above the upper stringer. If necessary, trim the bottoms so they're even below the lower stringer. Use spacers between the boards to maintain consistent spacing.

B. *Run a level string from the top of the previous post. Mark the step size on the post, and cut it to height, using a reciprocating saw or handsaw.*

C. *Cut the upper stringers to size. Attach one end to the post top and the other end flush against the next post at the reference mark.*

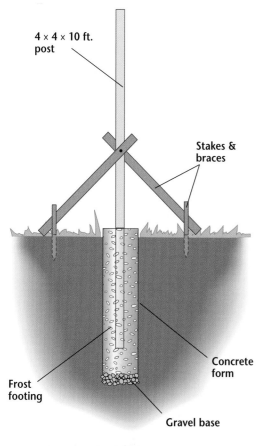

4 × 4 × 10 ft. post

Stakes & braces

Concrete form

Frost footing

Gravel base

Setting Posts

After plotting your fence line with stakes and string, dig the postholes and set the posts. It is critical that the posts be perfectly aligned and plumb. Dig postholes 6" deeper than the post footing depth specified by local building codes, or 12" past the winter frost line in cold climates. Good post-setting techniques let you breeze through this process and on to the most satisfying part: attaching the fencing to the framework.

HOW TO INSTALL POSTS

Step A: Mark Post Locations

1. Transfer the marks from the string to the ground, using a plumb bob to pinpoint the post locations.

2. Mark each post location with a stake, and remove the string.

Step B: Dig Postholes

1. Dig postholes using a power auger (available at rental centers) or posthole digger. Make each hole 6" deeper than the post footing depth specified by local building code or 12" past the frost line in cold climates. Keep the holes as narrow as possible, usually about twice the width of the post. Corner and gate posts usually require wider footings for extra stability. Check local regulations.

TOOLS & MATERIALS

- Plumb bob
- Stakes
- Hand maul
- Power auger or posthole digger
- Shovel
- Coarse gravel

- Carpenter's level
- Concrete
- Mason's trowel
- Pressure-treated, cedar, or redwood 4 × 4 posts
- Scrap lengths of 2 × 4

A. Drop a plumb bob from each post reference mark on the string to pinpoint the post centers on the ground.

B. Dig postholes 6" deeper than specified by local building code. Pour 6" of gravel into each hole to improve drainage.

C. Position each post in its hole. Brace the post with scrap pieces of 2 × 4 on opposite sides, and adjust it until it is plumb.

2. Pour a 6" layer of gravel into each hole for improved drainage.

Step C: Position the Posts

1. Position each post in its hole. Check posts for plumb with a level. Adjust posts to the correct height by adding or removing gravel.

2. Brace each post with scrap 2 × 4s secured to opposite sides.

3. Make sure the fence line is straight, using mason's string. Adjust further if necessary.

Step D: Fill the Postholes

1. Mix concrete and fill each posthole, overfilling them slightly.

2. Check to make sure each post is plumb, then shape the concrete around the bottom of the post to form a rounded crown that will shed water.

3. Let the concrete cure for two days before removing the braces.

D. *Fill the post holes with pre-mixed concrete, overfilling each slightly. Recheck the post for plumb and shape the concrete into a crown to shed water.*

VARIATION: POST SPIKES

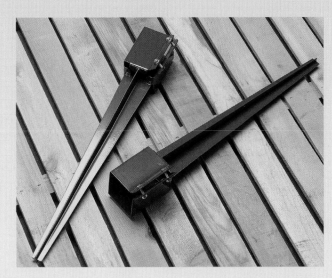

An alternative to setting posts in concrete is to use post spikes. Also called post anchors, supports, or mounting spikes, post spikes are between 24" and 30" in length, and are designed with a socket head to accommodate 4 × 4 or 6 × 6 posts. Post spikes with swivel heads help make adjustments during installation even easier.

With no holes to dig or concrete to mix, it takes little time or effort to install post spikes. To begin, put an 8"-length of post into the socket head, and place the tip of the spike on the post location. Have someone help hold the spike in position as you drive it about 6" into the ground, using a sledgehammer. Check the blades of the spike for plumb with a level to make sure you are driving it in straight. Also, make sure the spike remains properly aligned and doesn't twist. Make any necessary adjustments and continue driving the spike into the ground until the base of the socket head is flush with the ground.

Cut a post to the desired fence height, and insert it into the socket head; check the post for plumb, using a level. Drive 1¼" galvanized deck screws (or the hardware screws that came with the post spike) into the pre-drilled screw holes, one on each side, of the socket head.

It is best to install the post spikes as you install the fencing. This will allow you to easily maintain the proper spacing between posts and save you from having to cut stringers and siding to special sizes.

Board & Stringer Fence

If you want a high-quality, well-built wood fence, a board-and-stringer fence may be the best answer. This fence style is constructed from a basic frame with at least two rails, called stringers, that run parallel to the ground between posts to form the framework. Vertical boards, called siding, are attached to the framework created by the stringers.

A board-and-stringer fence is well-suited for yards of almost any contour. Consult the section on handling slope (pages 105 to 107) for instructions on how to adapt a board-and-stringer fence to a sloped yard.

We used dog-eared siding in this project, but these construction methods can be used with many siding patterns (see page 112). Spend a little time looking at magazines and driving through your favorite neighborhoods—you're certain to find a siding style that appeals to you and suits your property.

HOW TO BUILD A BOARD & STRINGER FENCE
Step A: Trim the Posts & Add the Top Stringers

1. Lay out the fence line (pages 102 to 107) and install the posts (pages 108 to 109). Let the concrete cure at least two days.

2. On each post, measure up from the ground to a point 12" below the planned fence height. Snap a level chalk line across all posts at this height. Trim the posts, using a reciprocating saw.

3. Cut a 2 × 4 to 72" for the top stringer. Coat the ends of the stringers with sealer and let them dry.

4. Place the stringers flat on top of the posts, centering the joints over each post. Attach the stringers to the posts, using 3" galvanized deck screws.

Step B: Install the Remaining Stringers

1. Measuring down from the top of each post, mark lines at 24" intervals to mark the locations for the other stringers in this bay.

2. At each mark, attach a 2 × 4 fence bracket to the inside face of the post, flush with the outside edge, using 4d box nails.

3. Position a 2 × 4 between each pair of brackets. Hold or tack

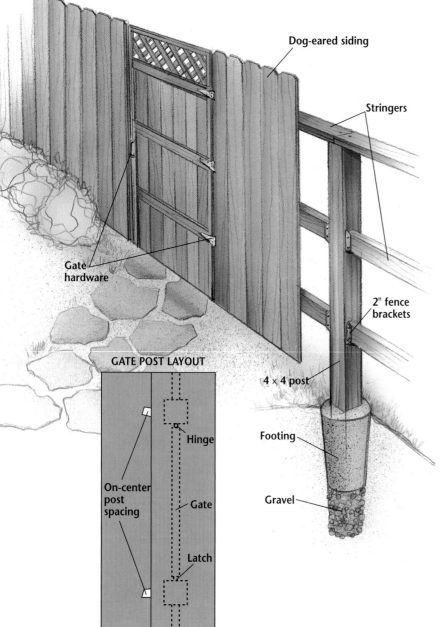

Dog-eared siding

Stringers

Gate hardware

2" fence brackets

4 × 4 post

Footing

Gravel

GATE POST LAYOUT

On-center post spacing

Hinge

Gate

Latch

A. *Trim the posts, and attach the cut stringers on top of the posts with 3" galvanized deck screws.*

TOOLS & MATERIALS

- Tools & materials for setting posts (page 108)
- Tape measure
- Chalk line
- Line level
- Reciprocating saw or handsaw
- Paintbrush
- Circular saw
- Hammer

- Drill
- Level
- Wood sealer/protectant or paint
- Pressure-treated, cedar, or redwood lumber:
  - 4 × 4s, 10 ft.
  - 2 × 4s, 8 ft.
  - 1 × 6s, 8 ft.
- 2" galvanized deck screws

- Galvanized 2 × 4 fence brackets
- 4d galvanized box nails
- 3" galvanized deck screws
- 6d galvanized box nails
- ⅛" piece of scrap wood
- Prefabricated gate & hardware
- Wood scraps for shims

the board against the posts, and scribe the back side along the edges of the posts.

4. Cut the stringers ¼" shorter than marked, so they will slide into the brackets easily. Coat the cut ends of the stringers with sealer and let them dry.

5. Nail the stringers into place, using 6d galvanized box nails. If the stringers are angled to accommodate a slope, bend the bottom flanges of the brackets to match the angles of the stringers.

Step C: Attach the Siding

1. Beginning at an end post, measure from the ground to the top edge of the top stringer and add 8½". Cut a 1 × 6 to this length and seal its edges.

2. Position the 1 × 6 so that its top extends 10½" above the top stringer, leaving a 2" gap at the bottom. Make sure the siding board is plumb, then attach it to the post and rails with pairs of 2" galvanized deck screws.

3. Measure, cut, and attach the remaining siding to the stringers, using the same procedure. Leave a gap of at least ⅛"

between boards, using pieces of scrap wood for spacers. If necessary, rip boards at the ends of the fence to make them fit.

Step D: Hang the Gate

1. Attach three hinges to the gate frame, evenly spaced and parallel to the gate edge.

2. Shim the gate into position between the gate posts. Drill pilot holes and attach the hinges to the gate post, using the screws provided with the hinge hardware.

3. On the opposite side, attach the latch hardware to the fence and to the gate.

4. Open and close the gate to make sure the latch works correctly. Make adjustments if necessary. Paint the fence or coat with sealer.

C. *Measure and cut the siding to size. Attach the siding to the framework, spacing them at least ⅛" apart.*

B. *Attach the fence brackets to the inside faces of the posts. Position the stringers in the brackets, then nail them in place.*

D. *Attach the hinges according to the manufacturer's directions, then hang the gate and install the latch hardware.*

VARIATIONS: BOARD PATTERNS

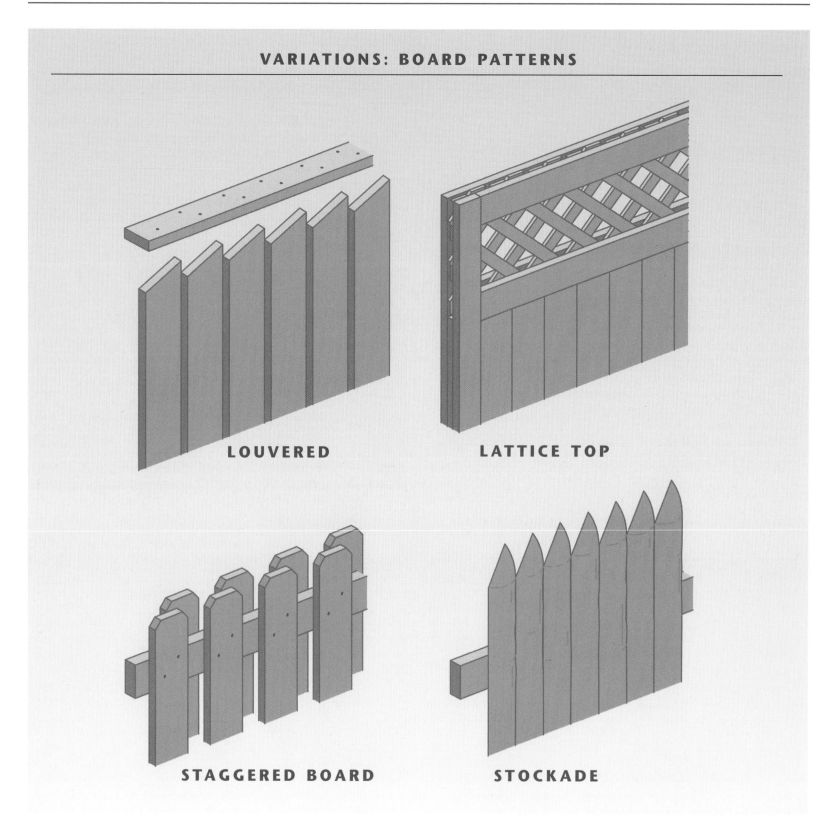

LOUVERED

LATTICE TOP

STAGGERED BOARD

STOCKADE

Panel Fence

Panel fences are one of the easiest, quickest types of fences you can build. They're also reasonably priced and ideal for yards that are flat or have a steady, gradual slope.

Preassembled fence panels come in a wide variety of popular styles. The one disadvantage is that not all panels are as well built as you might like. Shop around to find well-constructed panels made of high-quality materials. Be sure to choose and purchase your panels before setting your posts, so you can space the posts accurately.

Although you can trim panels to fit between the posts if necessary, doing that can be difficult. Try to plan a layout that uses only full-sized panels.

If the fence line includes a slope, decide whether to contour or step the fence (pages 105 to 107) and plan accordingly.

TOOLS & MATERIALS

- Tools & materials for setting posts (page 108)
- Tape measure
- Mason's string
- Carpenter's level
- Line level
- Hammer
- Stepladder
- Reciprocating saw or handsaw

- Paintbrush
- Pressure-treated, cedar, or redwood 4 × 4 posts, 10 ft.
- Prefabricated fence panels
- Galvanized fence brackets
- 4d galvanized box nails

- 1" galvanized deck screws
- Prefabricated gate & hardware
- Post caps
- Galvanized casing nails
- Wood sealer/protectant or paint
- Wood blocks

HOW TO BUILD A PANEL FENCE

Step A: Test-fit the Preassembled Panels

1. Lay out the fence line (pages 102 to 107) and install posts (pages 108 to 109). Space the posts to fit the preassembled panels you've purchased. Let the concrete cure for at least two days.

2. Test-fit the panels, positioning each so the bottom of the panel will be 2" above ground level. Check the panel for plumb, using a level, then outline it on the inside faces of the posts.

3. On level sites, use a line level to ensure that the panels will be level. On a sloped site where panels will be installed step-fashion, try to maintain a uniform vertical drop with each panel.

Step B: Mark Panel Position & Attach Brackets

1. Align and attach a bracket against the bottom of the outline, using 4d box galvanized nails.

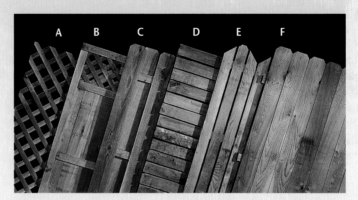

VARIATION: FENCE PANELS

Preassembled fence panels are an attractive, timesaving option when building a fence. The entire panel is attached to the posts, eliminating the need to cut and attach stringers individually.

Some popular styles of prefabricated panels include:

A. Lattice panels
B. Solid panels with lattice tops
C. Staggered board
D. Horizontal board
E. Modified picket
F. Dog-eared board

A. *Lay out the fence line and set the posts. Test-fit a panel and outline its position on the inside faces of the posts.*

B. *Align the bottom of the first bracket 2" above ground level. Evenly space two more brackets inside the outline, attaching each bracket with 4d galvanized nails (INSET).*

2. Attach two more, evenly spaced, brackets inside the outline. Bend the bottom flange of both these brackets flat against the post.

Step C: Attach Fence Panels

1. Working from above, slide the panel into the brackets until it rests on the bottom flange of the lowest bracket.

2. Attach the panels from each side by driving 1" galvanized deck screws through the holes in the brackets.

Step D: Attach the Gate Hardware & the Gate

1. Align three evenly spaced hinges on the gate frame so that the pins are straight and flush with the edge of the gate. Attach the hinges to the gate frame with the screws provided with the hardware.

2. Shim the gate into position between the gate posts, with the hinge pins resting against one post. Attach the hinges to the post, using the screws provided by the manufacturer.

3. Attach the latch hardware to the other gate post and then to the gate, using the screws provided by the manufacturer.

4. Open and close the gate to make sure the latch works correctly, and adjust if necessary.

Step E: Trim & Decorate Post Tops

1. Use a reciprocating saw or handsaw to trim the tops uniformly.

2. Cover flat post tops with decorative wood or metal caps, attaching the caps with galvanized casing nails. If you're not going to use post caps, trim the posts to a point to help them shed water.

3. Paint the fence or coat with wood sealer/protectant.

D. *Attach three evenly spaced hinges to the gate frame. Shim the gate in place and attach the hinges on the gate post. Attach the latch hardware to the gate and then to the opposite post.*

C. *Slide the fence panels into the brackets from above, until they rest on the bottom flanges of the lowest brackets.*

E. *Trim the post tops to size, using a reciprocating saw. Cover each post top with a decorative post cap, or trim it to a point to help shed water. Paint or coat the fence with sealer.*

115

Picket Fence

For generations, the stereotypical dream home has been a vine-covered cottage surrounded by a white picket fence. But these days, the diversity in designs and styles of this classic American fence make it adaptable to any home, from a three-story Victorian to a modest rambler.

The charm of a picket fence lies in its open and inviting appearance. The repetitive structure and spacing create a pleasing rhythm that welcomes family and friends while maintaining a fixed property division.

Traditionally, picket fences are 36" to 48" tall. Our version is 48" tall, the posts are spaced 96" on-center, and the pickets are spaced 1¾" apart. It's important that the spacing appear to be consistent. Using a jig simplifies that process, and, if necessary, you can spread any extra space across many pickets to mask the discrepancy.

Picket fences are traditionally white; however, matching your house's trim color or stain can be an eye-catching alternative. You'll need to apply two coats of paint or stain. If you prime and paint all the materials before construction, apply the second coat after the fence is completed to cover any marks, smudges, and nail or screw heads.

There are a number of picket styles to choose from. Most building centers carry a variety, or you can design your own by simply creating a template. If you need a large quantity of pickets or want to use an intricate design, contact a cabinet shop in your area—the time saved may be worth the added expense.

TOOLS & MATERIALS

- Tools & materials for setting posts (page 108)
- Circular saw
- Jigsaw
- Paintbrush and roller
- Tape measure
- Reciprocating saw or handsaw

- Spring clamps
- Framing square
- Drill
- Pressure-treated, cedar, or redwood lumber:
  - 1 × 4s, 8 ft. (9 per bay)
  - 2 × 4s, 8 ft. (2 per bay)
  - 4 × 4s, 8 ft. (2 per bay)

- Paint, stain, or sealer
- 16d galvanized nails
- 1½" galvanized deck screws
- Fence post finials

HOW TO BUILD A PICKET FENCE

Step A: Prepare the Materials

1. Lay out the fence line with stakes and mason's string (pages 102 to 107). Space the post locations every 96" on-center.

2. Count the 4 × 4 posts and estimate the number of pickets you'll need to complete the project. Since it's likely you'll make a cutting error or two, estimate enough lumber to compensate.

3. If you're creating your own pickets, cut 1 × 4s to length. (Our design calls for 46" pickets.) Cut simple, pointed pickets with a circular saw. For more elaborate designs like the one shown here, make a template, then use a jigsaw to cut the pickets.

4. Apply the first coat of paint, stain, or sealer.

Step B: Set the Posts

1. Set the posts (pages 108 to 109). Allow the concrete footings to cure for two days.

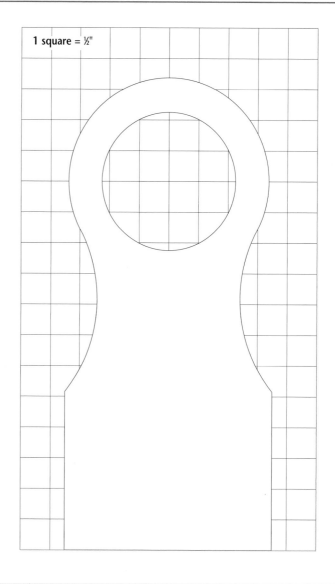

1 square = ½"

A. *Mark the fence line and calculate the number of posts and pickets required. Cut pickets, using a template and a jig saw.*

Cutting List

Each 96" bay requires:

Part	Type	Size	Qty.
Posts	4 × 4	78"	2
Pickets	1 × 4	46"	18
Stringers	2 × 4	92½"	2
Jig	1 × 4	1¾" × 46"	1

2. Measure up 48" from the base of each post and mark cutting lines.

3. Trim the posts along the cutting lines, using a reciprocating saw or handsaw.

Step C: Build the Framework

1. On each post, measure and mark a line 6" down from the top of the post to indicate the upper stringer position, and 36½" from the top to indicate the lower stringer.

B. *Set the posts, then mark cutoff lines and trim them to 48" above ground level.*

C. *Mark the stringer position on the posts, then scribe and cut the stringer to size. Toenail the stringer in place (inset).*

2. At the upper stringer marks on the first two posts, clamp an 8-ft. 2 × 4 with the top edge of the 2 × 4 flush with the mark. Scribe the post outline on the back of the stringer at each end. Remove and cut the upper stringer to size, using a circular saw.

3. Position the upper stringer between the two posts, set back ¾" from the face of the posts. Toenail the stringer into place with 16d galvanized nails.

4. Repeat #2 and #3 to install the remaining stringers, both upper and lower.

Step D: Space & Hang the Pickets

1. To compensate for slope or shorter sections, calculate the picket spacing: Decide on the number of pickets you want between posts. Multiply that number by the width of a single

---

PICKET SPACING EXAMPLE

18 (pickets) × 3½" (picket width) = 63" (total picket width).

92½" (space between posts) – 63" = 29½" (unoccupied space).

29½" ÷ 17 (18 pickets – 1) = 1¾" (space between pickets).

NOTE: Not all calculations will work out evenly. If your figures come out uneven, make slight adjustments across the entire fence section.

D. *Calculate the picket spacing and make a spacing jig. Position the first picket and secure it with 1½" galvanized deck screws. Using the spacing jig, position and install the remaining pickets.*

picket. This is the total width of pickets between the posts. Subtract that number from the total distance between the posts. The remainder equals the unoccupied space. Divide that number by the number of pickets minus 1 (the number of spaces that will exist between the posts). The resulting number equals the picket spacing.

2. To make a spacing jig, rip a 1 × 4 to the spacing size—1¾" in this project. Attach a scrap of wood to one end of the board as a cleat.

3. Draw a reference mark on each picket, 6" down from the peak.

4. Place a picket flat against the stringers and slide it flush against the post. Adjust the picket until the reference line is flush with the top edge of the upper stringer. Drill pilot holes and attach the picket, using 1½" deck screws.

5. Hang the jig on the upper stringer and hold it flush against the attached picket. Position a new picket flush against the jig and attach it. Reposition the jig and continue along the fence line.

Step E: Apply Finishing Details

1. Attach fence post finials for detail. Use a straightedge to draw lines from corner to corner on the top of the post to determine the center. Drill a pilot hole where the lines intersect and screw a finial into the center of each post.

2. For painted fences, apply the second coat.

E. *Determine the center of the post tops, drill pilot holes, and screw in fence post finials.*

VARIATION: PICKET PATTERNS

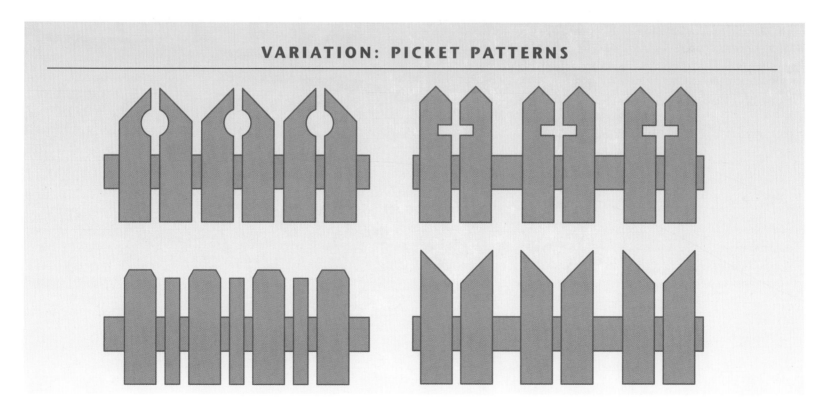

Post & Rail Fence

Post & rail construction can be used to build fences in a surprising range of styles, from a rustic split rail fence to the more genteel post-and-rail fence, with or without a capped top.

Because they use so little lumber, split rail fences are an inexpensive way to cover a large area of land. We show you how to build this fence by setting the posts in gravel-and-dirt footings. This method is common in some regions, but isn't appropriate everywhere. You can set the posts in concrete (pages 108 to 109) if required by the building codes in your area.

One other note: if you don't want to cut mortises, most lumberyards offer pre-mortised posts and tapered stringers that can be used to build split rail fences.

Post-and-rail fences, which typically are painted but sometimes stained and sealed, require more lumber and more upkeep than split rail fences, but in certain settings nothing else will do. There are endless variations on rail placement, but the directions shown on pages 122 and 123 will give you a good understanding of the basics involved. You should be able to adapt the plans and build just about any design that appeals to you.

HOW TO BUILD A SPLIT RAIL FENCE
Step A: Prepare the Posts

1. Plot the fence line (pages 102 to 107), spacing posts every 72" on center. Dig the postholes (pages 108 to 109).

2. From the top of each post, measure and mark points 6" and 26½" down the center. Outline 2"-wide by 4"-tall mortises

at each mark, using a cardboard template.
Step B: Cut the Mortises

1. Drill a series of 1" holes inside each mortise outline, drilling through the backside if necessary. Drill only halfway through for end posts, and halfway through on adjacent sides for corner posts.

TOOLS & MATERIALS

- Tools & materials for plotting a fence line (page 102)
- Cardboard
- Chalk line
- Shovel
- Combination square
- Drill, with 1"-bit

- 2" wood chisel
- Chisel & hammer
- Reciprocating saw with a 6" wood blade
- Rubber mallet
- Lumber (see Cutting List)
- Coarse gravel

Cutting List

Each 72" bay requires:

Part	Type	Size	Qty.
Posts	4 × 4	66"	2
Stringers	4 × 4	72"	2

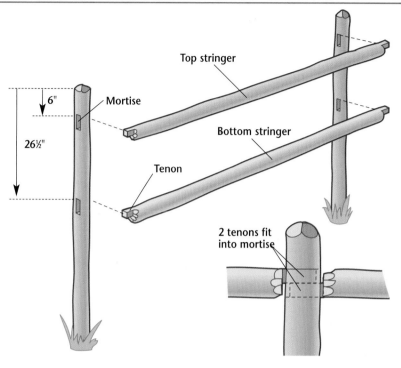

Top stringer
Mortise
6"
26½"
Bottom stringer
Tenon
2 tenons fit into mortise

2. Remove the remaining wood from the mortises with a hammer and chisel.

Step C: Shape the Tenons

1. Snap a straight chalk line down the sides of the stringers.

2. On one end, draw a straight line from

the chalk line mark at the edge, to the center of the timber, using a combination square.

3. At the center, draw a 1½"-long line perpendicular to the first, extending ¾" from each side. From each end of this line, draw perpendicular lines up to the edge of the timber. You will have outlined a rough, 1½ × 1½"-square tenon end.

4. Measure and mark 3½" down from the end stringer for the tenon length.

5. Rough-cut the tenons, using a reciprocating saw with a 6" wood blade. If necessary, shape the tenons with a hammer and chisel to fit the mortises.

Step D: Set the Posts & Attach the Stringers

1. Fill the postholes with 6" of gravel, and insert the first post. Because each post is cut to size, make sure the post top measures 36" from the ground. If it sits too high, lay a board over the post top and tap down with a rubber mallet. If it's too low, add more gravel. Leave 6" of clearance between the position of the bottom stringer and the ground.

2. Begin to fill the posthole with gravel and dirt. Every few inches, tamp the dirt

around the post with the end of your shovel, and check the post for plumb.

3. Place the next post in the posthole without setting it. Insert the tenons of the stringers into the mortises of the first set post. Insert the other ends of the stringers to the unset post. Adjust the post to fit the stringers if necessary.

4. Plumb the post and set with a dirt and gravel footing. Repeat this procedure of setting a post, then attaching the stringers. Alternate the stringers so the tenons of one stringer face up and the tenons of the next stringer face down, creating a tight fit in the mortise. Plumb each post as you go.

TOOLS & MATERIALS

- Tools & materials for setting posts (page 108)
- Tape measure
- Bar clamps
- Circular saw
- Framing square
- Chisel & hammer
- Paintbrush & roller

- Stakes
- Line level
- Drill
- Lumber (see Cutting List)
- Paint, stain, or sealer
- 2" galvanized deck screws

Cutting List

Each 72" bay requires:

Part	Type	Size	Qty.
Posts	4 × 4	66"	2
Stringers	1 × 4	72"*	3

*add 1¼" for end stringers

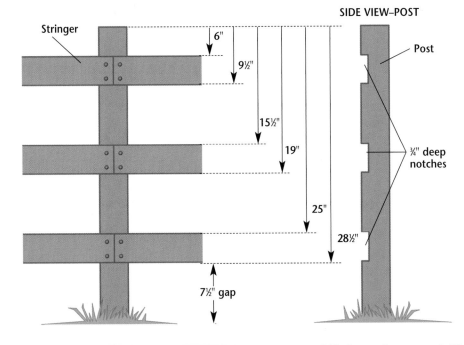

SIDE VIEW–POST

HOW TO BUILD A POST & RAIL FENCE

Step A: Prepare the Posts

1. Mark the fence line (pages 102 to 107). Mark and dig postholes 72" on-center (pages 108 to 109).

2. Cut 4 × 4 posts to 66". Measure and mark at 6", 9½", 15½", 19", 25", and 28½" down from the top of two posts.

3. Gang several posts between the marked posts and clamp them together, using bar clamps. Use a framing square to extend the marks across all the posts. Mark the notches with an "X" between each pair of marks.

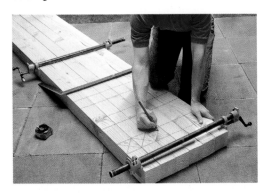

Step B: Notch the Posts

1. Make a series of cuts inside each set

of reference lines, using a circular saw with the blade depth set at ¾".

2. Remove the remaining wood in each notch, using a hammer and chisel. Remove wood only to the depth of the original cuts so the stringers will sit flush with the face of the post.

Step C: Set the Posts & Attach the Stringers

1. Cut the stringers (see Cutting List above). Paint, stain, or seal all the lumber and allow it to dry.

2. Brace the posts into position (pages 108 to 109) with the notches facing out. Run a mason's string and set a level line; keep the notches aligned and the tops of

the posts 36" above the ground. If a post is too high, lay a board over it and tap down, using a rubber mallet. If it's too low, add gravel beneath it. Be sure there is 7½" between the bottom of the lowest notch and the ground. Set the posts in concrete and let it cure for 2 days.

3. Fit a 73½" stringer into the notches in the first pair of posts. Position it to cover the entire notch in the first post and half of the notch in the second. Attach the stringer, using 2" galvanized deck screws. Install the other two stringers to this pair of posts.

4. Butt a stringer against the first one and attach it securely. Repeat with remaining stringers.

TOOLS & MATERIALS

- Tools & materials for setting posts (page 108)
- Tape measure
- Reciprocating saw or handsaw
- Combination square
- Circular saw

- Drill
- Lumber (see Cutting List)
- 2" galvanized deck screws
- 3" galvanized deck screws
- Paint, stain, or sealer

HOW TO BUILD A CAPPED POST & RAIL FENCE

Step A: Set the Posts

1. Mark the fence line (pages 102 to 107), spacing posts 72" on-center.

2. Cut the lumber as indicated on the Cutting List at right. Paint, stain, or seal the posts and let them dry.

3. Dig postholes and set the posts (pages 108 to 109). Let footings cure two days.

4. Measure and mark each post at 36" from the ground. Trim with a reciprocating saw or handsaw. Touch up the finish on top of the posts.

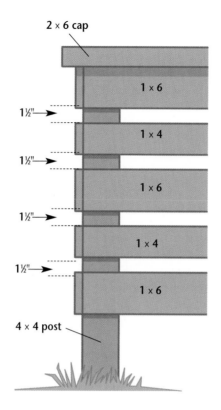

5. Mark a line down the center of the outside face of each post (except the end or gate posts).

Step B: Attach the Stringers

1. Measure from the reference line on one post to the line on the next. For each bay, cut two 1 × 4s and three 1 × 6s to this length. For the last bay, measure from the last reference line to the outside edge of the end post. Paint, stain, or seal the stringers.

2. Position a 1 × 6 against the faces of two posts with its top edge flush with the top of the posts and its ends flush with the reference lines. Clamp the stringer in place, then attach it on both ends, using pairs of 2" galvanized deck screws.

3. On each post, mark a line 1½" from the bottom of the 1 × 6. Position and attach a 1 × 4 as described above.

4. Alternate 1 × 6s and 1 × 4s, spacing them 1½" apart.

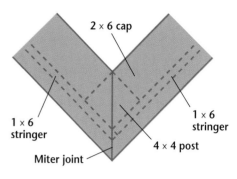

TOP VIEW–DETAIL

Cutting List

Each 72" bay requires:

Part	Type	Size	Qty.
Posts	4 × 4	66"	2
Stringers	1 × 4	72"*	2
	1 × 6	72"*	3
Top cap	2 × 6	72"*	1

*add 1¾" to end post stringers and top cap

Step C: Attach the Cap Stringer

1. Measure and cut 2 × 6s to fit between post tops. Add 1¾" on the end posts so the cap stringers extend beyond the posts. For corners, cut the ends at 45° angles, using a circular saw.

2. Position a cap stringer on the post tops, flush with the back of the posts and extending 1¼" beyond the front. Make sure the ends are centered on the posts, and attach the caps, using 3" galvanized deck screws.

Vinyl Fence

Made of polyvinyl chloride (PVC), the same durable material as vinyl house siding, vinyl fencing is virtually maintenance-free. It will never rust, rot, peel, splinter, or crack. The material itself never needs painting and is UV resistant, so it's unlikely to fade.

Most vinyl fence products are installed in the same general way, but there are some differences between details. It's important to read and follow the manufacturer's instructions precisely. Many manufacturers also provide toll-free numbers where you can get additional advice and help, if necessary.

Vinyl fence materials are pre-cut to length and shipped in unassembled kits. The pre-routed holes in the posts make it easy to insert and lock the pieces together.

It's essential to reinforce each corner, end, and gate post with concrete and rebar. If the fence is 60" or higher, it's a good idea to reinforce each of the posts. If concrete were allowed to seep into the stringers, it would cause them to sag over time. To prevent that problem, tape or plug the ends of each stringer before installing it.

Since most vinyl fencing is ordered directly from the manufacturer or through a distributor, you'll have an opportunity to ask and answer questions before you place an order. Lay out your fence line and consider any special challenges, such as slope issues. With that information in hand, a sales representative may be able to help you customize the materials and simplify the installation process.

TOOLS & MATERIALS

- Tools & materials for setting posts (page 108)
- Cordless drill or screwdriver

- Level
- PVC vinyl fencing materials
- Duct tape

- #3 rebar
- Rebar separator clips
- Construction adhesive

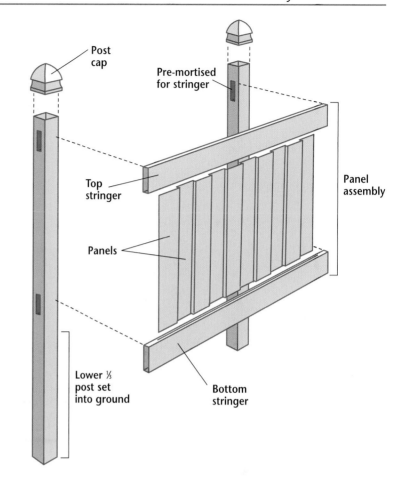

HOW TO INSTALL VINYL FENCING

NOTE: These are general installation tips. Refer to the manufacturer's instructions for your specific fence style.

Step A: Prepare the Materials

1. Mark the fence line (pages 102 to 107), spacing the posthole locations according to the manufacturer's recommendations. Dig the postholes (pages 108 to 109).

2. Sort and check the materials to be sure you have received all the proper fence pieces and hardware.

3. Cover both ends of each stringer with duct tape. Make sure there are no gaps or holes that would allow concrete to seep into the stringer later when you fill the posts.

Step B: Assemble the Panels

1. Insert the panel pieces into the pre-routed holes of the bottom stringer. Make sure each piece fits securely. If not, add duct tape to the bottom of the pieces so the fit is tighter.

2. Attach the top stringer to the panels. Work from one end and adjust the panel pieces to fit into the pre-routed holes. Make sure the stringer fits tightly around the panel pieces.

3. Secure the stringer to the panels with the self-tapping screws provided by the manufacturer.

Step C: Set the First Post

1. Position the first post. Because the posts are manufactured to size, the posts must sit precisely at the height of the fence. If a post is too high, lay a board over the top and gently tap it down, using a rubber mallet. If it's too low, add gravel beneath it. Be sure to leave enough room for a 2" gap between the bottom of the fence and the ground.

2. Mix concrete in a wheelbarrow or mixing trough, and set the post (108 to 109). Use a level on adjacent sides to make sure the post is plumb. Brace the plumbed post into position with stakes and scrap pieces of 2 × 4 tied or taped to the post. Let the concrete cure.

Step D: Attach the Panels

1. Set the next post and pour the concrete footing, but do not brace the post just yet.

2. With the assistance of another person, fit the panel between the posts. Insert the top and bottom stringers to the pre-routed holes of the first (previously set) post.

3. Insert the stringers on the other end of the panel into the

A. *Place tape over the ends of the lower stringers so concrete cannot seep into them from the posts.*

next post. If necessary, adjust the post to accommodate the stringers.

4. Inside of the post, drive a screw (provided with the kit) through the top stringer to secure it.

5. Plumb the post and brace it with 2 × 4s. Repeat this procedure of setting a post, then attaching a panel. Plumb each post

and brace it securely in place before you begin work on the next panel.

Step E: Reinforce the End and Corner Posts

1. If you're installing a gate, mount the hinge and latch hardware to the gate posts.

2. Connect two 72"-lengths of #3 rebar with rebar-separator clips for every end and corner post. Place one clip 6" down from the top of each piece and another 12" up from the bottom.

3. Position the rebar assembly inside the post, with the pieces of rebar sitting in opposing corners.

4. Fill the post with concrete, leaving at least 6" of exposed rebar at the top. Wipe off any excess or seepage.

Step F: Attach the Finishing Details

1. Attach post caps with glue or screws, if provided by the manufacturer. If you use glue, apply it to the inside edge of the cap, and then attach the cap to the post top. Wipe off any excess glue as soon as possible.

2. Cover exposed screw heads with screw caps, if provided.

3. Wash the fence with a mild detergent and water.

NOTE: PVC vinyl can be permanently discolored by some wasp or insect sprays. Use these products with caution around vinyl fences, as well as vinyl siding.

B. *Assemble the panels by working from one end and adjusting them to fit the pre-routed holes of the bottom stringer.*

C. *Keep the posts plumb with 2 × 4 braces attached to stakes driven into the ground. Duct tape is strong enough to hold the braces to the vinyl posts without causing any damage.*

Shown cut away for clarity

D. *Drive a screw through the top stringer inside of the post. The screw should be tight against the inside wall of the post.*

Shown cut away for clarity

E. *Attach the rebar separator clips and set the rebar into position in the posts. Fill the post with concrete to within 6" of the top of the post (INSET).*

F. *Attach each post cap, using glue or screws, if these are provided by the manufacturer.*

VARIATION: LOUVERED FENCES

Louvered fences filter sightlines, providing privacy without completely obscuring the view. They are perfect for extremely windy climates—their variated structure diffuses wind very effectively.

Photo courtesy of CertainTeed EverNew

127

Ornamental Metal Fence

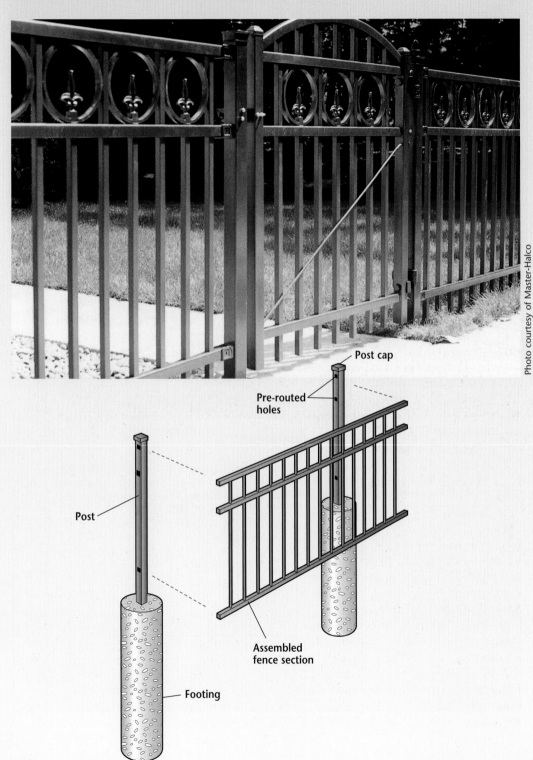

Post cap

Pre-routed holes

Post

Assembled fence section

Footing

Today's ornamental metal fences are designed to replicate the elegant wrought-iron designs of the past. They are made of aluminum and galvanized steel, with a powder-coat finish to help prevent rust. Styles range from the simple to the ornate, and are available in a variety of colors and sizes. These fences have become recent favorites for swimming pool enclosures.

Few home centers stock these materials, but some may be able to order them for you. Many manufacturers and distributors maintain web sites where you can get more information or place orders. A quick search of the internet should yield plenty of options.

As with any prefabricated fence, always read the manufacturer's instructions thoroughly before beginning installation. Installing these fences is generally simple, but does require two people.

The fence sections are manufactured or welded together in 48"- to 96"-long sections, and the posts are pre-cut. In our design, the posts have pre-routed holes for the stringer ends. Other designs use systems of brackets or fasteners.

If a fence section is too long, cut it to fit, using a hacksaw. Make sure to cut off only as much as necessary—it's vital to maintain a tight fit and proper spacing.

When slope is an issue, metal fencing can be contoured with the ground (pages 105 to 106) if the grade's rise is less than 12" over a 72" run. Anything greater will require stepping the fence (pages 106 to 107). If you're using brackets, simply determine the step measurement and set the brackets accordingly. Any routed holes in the posts will have to be cut on site.

TOOLS & MATERIALS

- Tools & materials for setting posts (page 108)
- Tape measure
- Rubber mallet
- Hacksaw
- Drill

- Ornamental metal fencing materials
- 1" self-tapping screws
- 2 × 4 scraps
- Mason's string
- Stakes
- Duct tape

HOW TO INSTALL AN ORNAMENTAL METAL FENCE

NOTE: These are general installation tips. Refer to the manufacturer's instructions for your specific fence.

Step A: Set the First Post

1. Lay out and check the materials to be sure you have all the parts and hardware.

2. Mark the fence line with stakes and

A. Dig postholes and set the first post in concrete. Brace it with 2 × 4s on adjacent sides.

mason's string (pages 102 to 107). Space and dig the postholes according to local codes and the manufacturer's recommendations.

3. Starting with a gate or end post, set the first post in place. Use a level on adjacent sides to make sure the post is plumb. Brace it with stakes and scrap pieces of 2 × 4 tied or taped to the post.

Because the posts are manufactured to size, the top of the post must be at fence height when it's set. Measure the height; if the post is too high, lay a board over it and gently tap it down, using a rubber mallet. If it's too low, add gravel beneath it.

4. Set the post in concrete (pages 108 to 109). Let the concrete cure for two days—you'll use this post as a starting point for the remaining sections of the fence.

Step B: Attach the Panels

1. Set the next post in concrete, but don't brace it yet.

2. With the assistance of another person, insert the top and bottom stringers of a fence section to the pre-routed holes of the fixed end or gate post.

3. At the other end of the section, insert the stringer ends into the line post. If necessary, adjust the line post to accommodate the stringers.

4. For the corners, attach the first section, then trim the stringer ends of the adjacent section approximately 1", using a hacksaw, so the sections remain properly spaced.

Step C: Finish the Installation

1. Drive 1" self-tapping screws through the posts and into each stringer end to secure the fence sections to the posts.

2. Plumb the line post and brace it firmly, using 2 × 4s on adjacent sides.

3. Continue setting posts and attaching sections of fence, plumbing each post as

B. Insert the stringer ends of the fence section into the routed holes of the posts.

you go. Let the concrete cure for at least 24 hours.

4. Attach finials to the posts, using a rubber mallet or set screws, if provided.

C. Secure the stringers to the posts with 1" self-tapping screws.

Chain Link Fence

If you're looking for a strong, durable, and economical way to keep pets and children in—or out—of your yard, a chain link fence may be the perfect solution. Chain link fences require minimal maintenance and provide excellent security. And for yards that include slopes, it's a natural choice—the mesh flexes enough that it can be adjusted to follow the contours of most yards.

A 48"-tall fence—the most common choice for residential use—is what we've demonstrated here. The posts, fittings, and chain link mesh, which are made from galvanized metal, can be purchased at home centers and fencing retailers. The end, cor-

ner, and gate posts, called terminal posts, bear the stress of the entire fence line. They're larger in diameter than line posts and require larger concrete footings. A footing three times the post diameter is sufficient for terminal posts.

The fittings are designed to accommodate slight alignment and height differences between terminal posts and line posts. Tension bands, which hold the mesh to the terminal posts, have one flat side to keep the mesh flush along the outside of the fence line. The stringer ends hold the top stringer in place and keep it aligned. Loop caps on the line posts position the top stringer to brace the mesh.

When the framework is in place, the mesh must be tightened against it. This is done a section at a time with a winch tool called a come-along. As you tighten the come-along, the tension is distributed evenly across the entire length of the mesh, stretching it taut against the framework. One note of caution: It's surprisingly easy to topple the posts if you over-tighten the come-along. To avoid this problem, tighten just until the links of the mesh are difficult to squeeze together by hand.

For added stability, you can weave a heavy-gauge wire through the mesh, approximately 4" above the ground. Pull the wire taut, and secure it to brace bands placed on the terminal posts.

TOOLS & MATERIALS

- Tools & materials for setting posts (page 108)
- Tape measure
- Mason's string
- Stakes
- Chalk
- Wrench & pliers

- Hacksaw or pipe cutter
- Come-along (fence stretcher)
- Duct tape
- Galvanized terminal and line posts

- Galvanized fittings (see diagram)
- Bolts & nuts for chain link fence assembly
- Galvanized chain link mesh

TOP VIEW

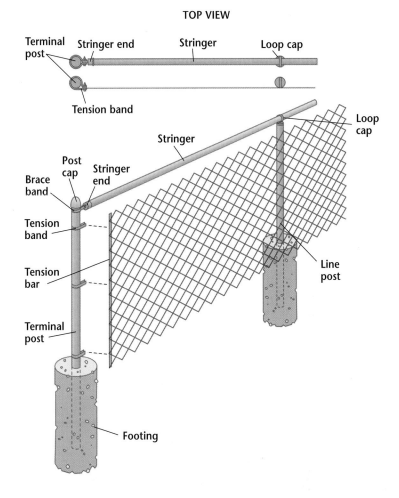

HOW TO INSTALL A CHAIN LINK FENCE

Step A: Set the Posts

1. Mark the fence location with stakes and mason's string (pages 102 to 107). Measure and mark the post locations with stakes, every 96" on-center.

2. Dig the postholes. For terminal posts (end, corner, and gate posts), dig the postholes 8" wide; for line posts, 6" wide.

3. Set the terminal posts in concrete (pages 108 to 109). Each terminal post should be 50" above the ground, or 2" above the fence height. Plumb each post, and brace it on adjacent sides with stakes and scrap pieces of 2 × 4 taped securely to the post.

4. From the top of each terminal post, measure down 4" and mark with chalk. Run a mason's string between the posts at the reference marks.

5. Fill the line postholes with concrete. Keep the post tops level with the mason's string, or 46" above the ground. Plumb each post and brace it on adjacent sides. Let the concrete cure for a day or two.

Step B: Attach the Fittings

1. Place three tension bands on every gate and end post. Place the first band 8" from the top, the second 24" from the top, and the third 8" off the ground. Make sure the flat side of each tension band faces the outside of the fence and points into the fence bay.

2. For corner posts, use six tension bands—two bands at each location. Point the flat sides of the bands in opposite directions.

3. Place a brace band approximately 3" below the top of each terminal post. Connect a stringer end to the brace band with a bolt and nut. The angled connection side of the stringer end should angle downward. Make sure the head of the bolt faces the outside of the proposed fence line.

4. For corners, place two brace bands on top of one another. Connect a stringer end to the upper brace band so the angled connection side points upward, and one to the lower brace band so the angled connection side points downward.

5. Top each terminal post with a post cap and each line post with a loop cap. Make sure the loop cap openings are

A. *Set the posts and brace them into position so they are plumb.*

B. *For a corner, place two brace bands 3" from the top of the post. Attach stringer ends with the angle side up to the upper brace band, and the angle side down to the lower band.*

C. *Cut the last piece of top stringer in a section to size. Adjust the brace band and stringer end to fit it in place.*

perpendicular to the proposed fence line, with the offset side facing the outside of the fence line.

Step C: Attach the Top Stringer

1. Start at one section, between two terminal posts, and feed the non-tapered end of a top stringer piece through the loop caps, toward a terminal post. Insert the non-tapered end into the cup of the stringer end. Make sure the stringer is snug. If necessary, loosen the brace band bolt and adjust it.

2. Continue to feed pieces of top stringer through the loop caps, fitting the non-tapered ends over the tapered ends. Use a sleeve to join two non-tapered ends, if necessary.

3. To fit the last piece of top stringer in the section, measure from where the taper begins on the previous piece to the inside back wall of the stringer end cup. Cut a piece of top stringer to size, using a hacksaw or pipe cutter. Connect the non-tapered end to the tapered end of the previous stringer. Loosen the brace band bolt and insert the cut end to the stringer end assembly. Make sure the fittings remain snug.

4. Repeat for each section of the fence.

Step D: Apply the Chain Link Mesh

1. Unroll chain link mesh on the ground and stretch it along the fence line, from terminal post to terminal post.

2. Weave a tension bar through the end row of the mesh. Secure the tension bar to the tension bands on the terminal post with bolts and nuts. Make sure the bolt heads face the outside of the fence.

3. Pull the mesh taut along the fence line by hand, moving toward the terminal post at the other end. Set the mesh on end and lean it against the posts as you go.

Step E: Stretch the Chain Link Mesh

1. Weave the spread bar of a come-along through the mesh, approximately 48" from the final terminal post. Hook the spread bar of the come-along to the tension bar. Attach the other end of the come-along to the terminal post, roughly in the middle.

2. Tighten the come-along slowly, until the mesh is taut. Make sure to keep the top of the mesh lined up, so that the peaks of the links rise about 1" above the top stringer.

3. Pull the remaining chain link mesh tight to the terminal post by hand, and insert a tension bar where the mesh meets the tension braces.

4. Remove any excess mesh by bending back both knuckle ends of one zig-zag strand in the mesh. Spin the strand counterclockwise so it winds out of the links, separating the mesh into two.

5. Secure the tension bar to the tension bands with bolts and nuts, with the bolt heads facing the outside of the fence.

6. Use tie wire spaced every 12" to attach the mesh to the top stringer and line posts.

7. Repeat #1 through #6 for each section.

D. *Weave a tension bar through the chain link mesh and attach it to the tension braces with bolts.*

E. *Use a come-along to stretch the mesh taut against the fence. The mesh is tight enough when the links are difficult to squeeze together by hand.*

TIP: WEAVING CHAIN LINK MESH TOGETHER

If a section of chain link mesh comes up short between the terminal posts, you can add another piece by weaving two sections together.

With the first section laid out along the fence line, estimate how much more mesh is needed to reach the next terminal post. Over-estimate 6" or so, so you don't come up short again.

Detach the amount of mesh needed from the new roll by bending back the knuckle ends of one zig-zag strand in the mesh. Make sure the knuckles of the same strand are undone at the top and bottom of the fence. Spin the strand counter-clockwise to wind it out of the links, separating the mesh into two.

Place this new section of chain link at the short end of the mesh so the zig-zag patterns of the links line up with one another.

Weave the new section of chain link into the other section by reversing the unwinding process. Hook the end of the strand into the first link of the first section. Spin the strand clockwise until it winds into the first link of the second section, and so on. When the strand has connected the two sections, bend both ends back into a knuckle. Now you can attach the chain link mesh to the fence framework.

Brick & Cedar Fence

This elegant fence is not nearly as difficult to construct as it looks. It does, however, require some time and effort, and will make use of both your carpentry and masonry skills. There are also quite a few necessary materials, which does increase the expense. But when the project is complete, you'll have an attractive, durable structure that will be the envy of the neighborhood.

The 72" brick pillars replace the posts of most fences. The footings need to be 4" longer and wider than the pillar on each side, 16 × 20" for this project.

To maintain an even ⅜" mortar joint spacing between bricks, create a story pole using a 2 × 2 marked with the spacing. After every few courses, hold the pole against the pillar to check the joints for a consistent thickness. Also make sure the pillars remain as plumb, level, and square as possible. Poor pillar construction greatly reduces strength and longevity of the pillars.

Attaching the stringers to the pillars is much easier than you may imagine. Fence brackets and concrete screws are available that have as much

holding power as lag bolts and anchors. Although other brands are available, we used ¼"-diameter concrete screws. The screws come with a special drill bit to make sure the embedment holes are the right diameter and depth, which simplifies the process for you.

The part of this project that looks the trickiest is creating the arched top of the cedar-slat fence sections. It can be achieved relatively easily by using a piece of PVC pipe. With the ends anchored, the pipe is flexible enough to bend into position and rigid enough to hold the form of the arch so it can be traced.

HOW TO BUILD A BRICK & CEDAR FENCE
Step A: Install the Footings

1. Measure and mark the fence line with stakes and mason's string (pages 102 to 107).

2. Determine the center of each pillar location along the fence line. To space the pillars at 96" edge to edge, drop a plumb bob 12" in from the end of the fence line, and then every 116". Place a stake at each pillar location.

3. Outline 16 × 20" pillar footings at each location, then dig the

TOOLS & MATERIALS

- Tools & materials for pouring footings (page 48)
- Tape measure
- Level
- Plumb bob
- Wheelbarrow or mortar box
- Mason's trowel
- Jointing tool
- Aviation snips
- Drill
- Circular saw
- Hammer

- Jig saw
- Standard modular bricks (4 × 2⅔ × 8", 130 per pillar)
- 2 × 2 lumber, 10 ft.
- Chalk
- Type N mortar mix
- ¼" wooden dowel & vegetable oil
- ¼" wire mesh
- Capstone or concrete cap
- ⅜"-thick wood scraps
- 2 × 6 fence brackets (6 per bay)

- 1¼" countersink concrete screws
- Concrete drill bit
- Pressure-treated, cedar, or redwood lumber:
  1 × 6, 8 ft. (16 per bay)
  2 × 6, 8 ft. (3 per bay)
- 1½" stainless steel deck screws
- 1½" finish nails (3)
- 96"-length of flexible ¼" PVC pipe

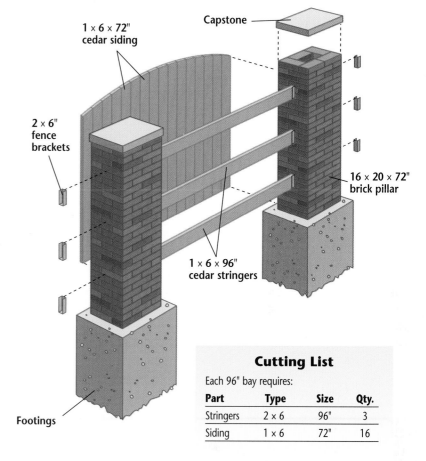

trenches and pour the footings (pages 48 to 51). Let the footings cure for two days.

Step B: Lay the First Course

1. On a flat work surface, lay out a row of bricks, spaced ⅜" apart. Mark the identical spacing on a 2 × 2 to create a story pole.

2. Dry-lay the first course of five bricks—center them on the footing, leaving ⅜" spaces between them. Mark reference lines around the bricks with chalk.

3. Set the bricks aside and trowel a ⅜"-layer of mortar inside the reference lines. Set a brick into the mortar, with the end

Cutting List

Each 96" bay requires:

Part	Type	Size	Qty.
Stringers	2 × 6	96"	3
Siding	1 × 6	72"	16

A. *Pour footings that are 4" longer and wider than the pillars on each side. This project calls for 16 × 20" footings.*

B. *Trowel a bed of mortar inside the reference lines and lay the first course. Create a weep hole in the mortar with a dowel to ensure the drainage of any moisture that seeps into the pillar.*

aligned with the reference lines. Set a level on top of the brick, then tap the brick with the trowel handle until it's level.

4. Set the rest of the bricks in the mortar, buttering the mating ends with mortar. Use the reference lines to keep the bricks aligned, and make sure they are plumb and level.

5. Use a pencil or dowel coated with vegetable oil to create a weep hole in the mortar of the first course of bricks, so that any moisture that seeps into the pillar will drain away.

Step C: Lay the Subsequent Courses

1. Lay the second course, rotating the pattern 180°, so the joints of the first course are overlapped by the bricks of the second course.

2. Lay the subsequent courses, rotating the pattern 180° with each course. Use the story pole and a level to check the faces of the pillar after every other course. Use the story pole after every few courses to make sure the mortar joints are consistent.

3. After every fourth course, cut a strip of ¼" wire mesh and place it over a thin bed of mortar. Add another thin bed of mortar on top of the mesh, then add the next course of brick.

4. After every five courses, use a jointing tool to smooth the joints when they have hardened enough to resist minimal finger pressure.

Step D: Lay the Final Course

1. For the final course, lay the bricks over a bed of mortar and wire mesh. After placing the first two bricks, add an extra brick in the center of the course. Lay the remainder of the bricks to fit around it.

2. Fill the remaining joints, and work them with the jointing tool as soon as they become firm.

3. Build the other pillars in the same way as the first. Use the story pole to maintain identical dimensions and a 96" length of 2 × 2 to keep the spacing between pillars consistent.

Step E: Install the Top Cap

1. Select a capstone 3" longer and wider than the top of the pillar. Mark reference lines on the bottom of the capstone to help you center it.

2. Spread a ½"-thick bed of mortar on top of the pillar. Center the capstone on the pillar, using the reference lines. Strike the mortar joint under the cap so it's flush with the pillar. If mortar

C. *Lay each new course so the bricks overlap the joints of the previous course. Use a jointing tool after every five courses to smooth the firm mortar joints.*

D. *Lay the final course over a bed of mortar and wire mesh, with an additional block added to the center. Fill the joints with mortar, and work them with a jointing tool as soon as they become firm.*

E. *Spread a ½"-thick bed of mortar on top of the pillar, and center the cap, using the reference lines.*

squeezes out of the joints, press ⅜"-thick wood scraps into the mortar at each corner to support the cap. Remove the scraps after 24 hours and fill the gaps with mortar.

Step F: Attach the Stringers

1. On the inner face of each pillar (the face perpendicular to the fence line), measure down from the top and use chalk to mark at 18", 36", and 60".

2. At each mark, measure in 6¾" from the outside face of the pillar and mark with the chalk. Position a 2 × 6 fence bracket at the point where the reference marks intersect. Mark the screw holes on the pillar face, two or three per bracket.

3. Drill 1¾"-deep embedment holes at each mark, using the bit provided with the concrete screws. The hole must be ¼" deeper than the length of the screw.

4. Align the fence bracket screw holes with the embedment holes, and drive the 1¼" concrete screws into the pillar. Repeat for each pillar, attaching three fence brackets on each side of each line pillar.

5. Measure the distance from a fence bracket of the first pillar to the corresponding fence bracket of the next to determine the exact length of the stringers. If necessary, mark and then cut a cedar 2 × 6 to length, using a circular saw.

6. Insert a 2 × 6 stringer into a pair of fence brackets and attach it with 1½" stainless steel screws. Repeat for each stringer.

Step G: Cut the Section Arch

1. Cut 1" off the ends of the cedar 1 × 6s to create a square edge.

2. On a large, flat surface, such as a driveway, lay out sixteen 1 × 6s, with approximately ½" of space between them and the cut ends flush.

3. On the two end boards, measure up from the bottom and mark 64". Tack a 1½" finish nail into each mark, 2" from the edge of the board.

4. Draw a line connecting the nails. Measure and mark the center (48" from the edge in our project). At the center, mark a point 6" above the original line. This mark indicates the height of the arch.

5. Place a 96"-long piece of flexible PVC piping against the two nails. At the mid-point, bend the PVC pipe until it meets the height mark. Tack a 1½" finish nail behind the PVC pipe to hold it in place, then trace along the PVC pipe to form the arch. Cut the arch, using a jig saw, along the marked line.

Step H: Attach the Siding

1. Run a mason's string 2" above the bottom of the fence line as a guide.

2. Attach the siding to the stringers, using 1½" stainless steel deck screws. Maintain a 2" gap at the bottom of the fence, and make sure the boards are plumb. Use ½" scraps of wood as spacing guides between boards.

3. Repeat for each section of fence.

F. *Attach 2 × 6 fence brackets to the pillars, using 1¼" concrete screws.*

G. *Align cedar slats for a 96" section, and tack two nails on opposite sides, 64" from the bottom. Deflect a piece of PVC pipe against the nails, 6" up from the middle, and trace the arch.*

H. *Attach the cedar slats to the stringers with 1½" stainless steel deck screws. Maintain their order to properly form the arch top.*

Brick Archway

Building an arch over a pair of pillars is a challenging task made easier with a simple, semi-circular plywood form. With the form in place, you can create a symmetrical arch by laying bricks along the form's curved edge. Select bricks equal in length to those used in the pillars.

When building new pillars (pages 134 to 137, Step A through Step E), use the colors and textures of your home exterior and landscape to guide your choice of brick. Brickyards sells mortar tint to complement the color of your bricks. Once you settle on the amount of tint to add to the mortar, record the recipe, so you can maintain a consistent color in every batch.

TOOLS & MATERIALS

- Joint chisel
- Mason's hammer
- Pry bar
- Jig saw
- Circular saw
- Drill
- Compass
- Level
- Mason's string
- Trowel

- Jointing tool
- Tuck-pointer
- ¾" plywood
- ¼" plywood
- 1" & 2" wallboard screws
- Bricks
- Type N mortar mix
- 2 × 4 & 2 × 8 lumber
- Shims

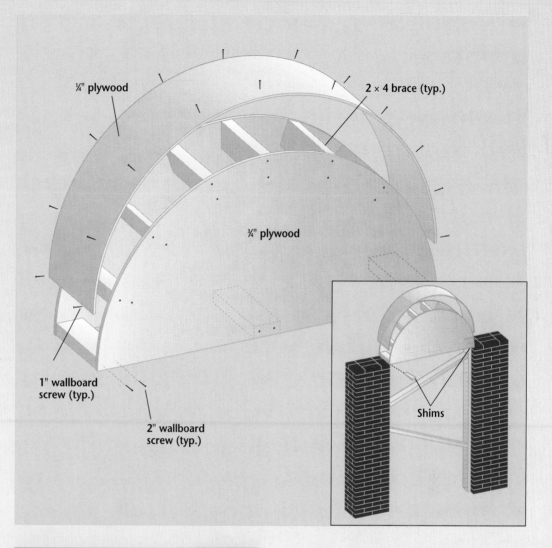

¼" plywood

2 × 4 brace (typ.)

¾" plywood

1" wallboard screw (typ.)

2" wallboard screw (typ.)

Shims

HOW TO BUILD THE ARCH FORM

Refer to the illustrations at the right.

Determine the distance between the inside edges of the tops of your pillars. Divide the distance in half, and then subtract ¼". Use this as the radius.

Mark a point at the center of a sheet of ¾" plywood. Use a pencil and a piece of string to scribe the circle on the plywood, using the radius calculated above. Cut out the circle with a jig saw. Then mark a line through the center point of the circle and cut the circle in half with a jig saw or a circular saw.

Construct the form by bracing the two semicircles, using 2" wallboard screws and 2 × 4s. To calculate the length of the 2 × 4 braces, subtract the combined thickness of the plywood sheets—1½"—from the width of the pillars, and cut the braces to length. Cover the top of the form with ¼" plywood, attached with 1" wallboard screws.

If your pillars are capped, remove the caps before building an arch. Chip out the old mortar from underneath, using a hammer and joint chisel. With a helper nearby to support the cap, use a pry bar and shims to remove each cap from the pillar.

HOW TO BUILD A BRICK ARCH
Step A: Mark Brick Spacing on Form

1. Center a brick at the peak of the form. Set a compass to the width of one brick plus ¼". Place the compass point at

A. Mark reference lines along the form, using a compass.

B. *Cut two 2 × 8 braces, ½" shorter than pillar height, and prop one against each pillar with 2 × 4 cross braces.*

one edge of the brick and mark the form with the pencil.

2. Place the compass point on the new mark and make another mark along the curve. Continue to make marks along the curve until less than a brick's width remains.

3. Divide the remaining width by the number of compass marks, and increase the compass setting by the amount. Use a different color to make the final reference marks to each side of the peak.

4. Extend the pencil lines across the curved surface of the form and onto the far edge.

Step B: Mount the Form to the Pillars

1. Cut two 2 × 8 braces, ½" shorter than pillar height. Prop one brace against each pillar with 2 × 4 cross braces.

2. Place shims on top of each 2 × 8 to raise the form so its bottom is even with the tops of the pillars. Rest the plywood form on the braces.

Step C: Lay the First Course

1. Mix mortar and trowel a narrow ⅜" layer on top of one pillar. Place one brick, and then rap the top with a trowel handle to settle it.

2. Butter the bottom of each subsequent brick, and place it in

C. *Place five bricks, then tack a string to the center point of the form on each side, and use the strings to check each brick's alignment.*

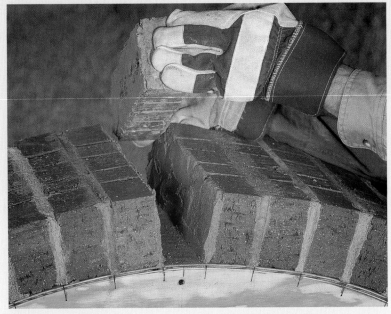

D. *Butter the center, or keystone, brick as accurately as possible and ease it into place. Smooth the remaining joints with a jointing tool.*

position.

3. Place five bricks, then tack a string to the center point of the form on each side, and use the strings to check each brick's alignment. Switch to the other side of the form and place five more bricks, to balance the weight on the form.

4. Continue to place bricks on alternate sides of the form, until the space for one brick remains. Take care not to dislodge other bricks as you tap a brick into position.

5. Smooth previous joints with a jointing tool as they become firm.

Step D: Place the Keystone in the First Course

Butter the final brick in the first course, the center brick or keystone, as accurately as possible and ease it into place. Smooth the remaining joints with a jointing tool.

Step E: Lay the Second Course

1. Lay a bed of mortar over the first course, and then lay the second course halfway up each side. Maintain the same mortar joint thickness as in the first layer. Some of the joints will be staggered, adding strength to the arch.

2. Dry-lay several more bricks on one side—using shims as substitutes for mortar joints—to check the amount of space remaining.

3. Remove the shims and lay the final bricks with mortar. Smooth the joints with a jointing tool.

Step F: Tuck-point the Underside of the Arch

Leave the form in place for one week, misting occasionally. Carefully remove the braces and form. Tuck-point and smooth the joints on the underside of the arch.

E. *Lay the second course halfway up each side of the area. Dry-lay several more bricks on one side—using shims as substitutes for mortar joints—to check the amount of space remaining. Remove the shims and lay the final bricks.*

F. *Leave the form in place for a week, misting occasionally. Remove the braces and form, then tuck-point the joints on the underside of the arch.*

Cedar & Copper Fence

This cedar-and-copper fence can wear many faces: By staining the lumber and sealing the copper, you can give it a tailored, contemporary look; by leaving the lumber and copper unfinished, you can create a weathered, rustic look. Or, by painting the lumber and sealing the copper to keep it bright, you can create a fresh, crisp look.

Regardless of the finish you choose, this clever combination of cedar and copper pipe produces a durable fence with an interesting appearance. It provides security without completely compromising your view—in fact, we first saw a fence similar to this one, separating a swimming pool from a wildlife area.

The design was perfect for that situation: The height and the vertical nature of the fence made it difficult to breach, but the openness preserved the natural view beyond the fence line. Of course, regulations regarding fences around swimming pools vary by municipality, so it's especially important to check local building codes before planning such a fence.

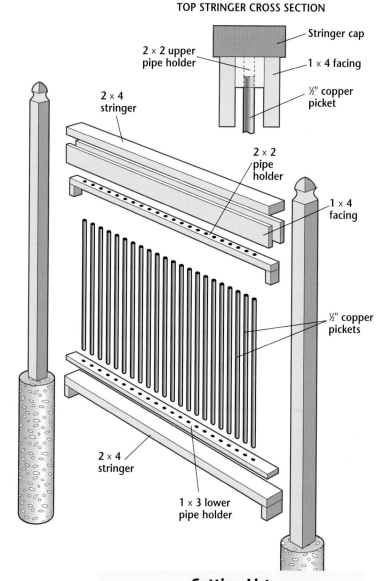

TOP STRINGER CROSS SECTION

Stringer cap
2 × 2 upper pipe holder
1 × 4 facing
½" copper picket
2 × 4 stringer
2 × 2 pipe holder
1 × 4 facing
½" copper pickets
2 × 4 stringer
1 × 3 lower pipe holder

TOOLS & MATERIALS

- Tools & materials for setting posts (page 108)
- Paintbrush & roller
- Combination square
- Drill & spade bit
- Tubing cutter or hacksaw
- Chalk line
- Line level
- Framing square

- 4 × 4 shaped cedar fence posts (2 per bay)
- Paint, stain, or sealer
- Pressure treated, cedar, or redwood lumber:
  - 1 × 2, 8 ft. (1 per bay)
  - 1 × 3, 8 ft. (1 per bay)
  - 2 × 2, 8 ft. (1 per bay)
  - 2 × 4, 8 ft. (2 per bay)
  - 1 × 4, 8 ft. (2 per bay)

- ½" copper pipe, 10 ft. (11 per bay)
- 2½" galvanized deck screws
- 2" galvanized deck screws
- Stakes & mason's string

HOW TO BUILD A CEDAR & COPPER FENCE

Step A: Set the Posts & Prepare the Materials

1. Mark the fence line with stakes and mason's string (page 102).

2. Calculate the post spacing based on the contour of the land along the fence line (pages 105 to 107) and mark the post locations. Set the posts (pages 108 to 109), and adjust each post so that it is 66" above ground level.

3. Cut the lumber as described in the Cutting List at right. Paint, stain, or seal all the pieces.

A. *Cut the lumber, then paint, stain, or seal the pieces. Mark the fence line and set the posts.*

Cutting List

Each 96" bay requires:

Part	Type	Size	Qty.
Posts	4 × 4	10 ft.	2
Upper pipe holder	2 × 2	92"	1
Lower pipe holder	1 × 3	92"	1
Upper stringer supports	2 × 2	2"	2
Lower stringer supports	2 × 4	3"	2
Stringers	2 × 4	92"	2
Facings	1 × 4	92"	2
Copper pipe	½"	55"	22

B. Mark 4" on-center spacing on the edge of a 1 × 2. Mark a center line on the pipe holder lumber, then transfer the spacing marks. Drill ½" holes, using a drill and spade bit.

Step B: Make the Pipe Holders

1. Make a story board for the pipe spacing: On the edge of a 1 × 2, make a mark every 4"—you'll have a total of 22 marks.

2. For each bay, you'll need one 1 × 3 holder for the bottom of the fence and one 2 × 2 holder for the top. Use a combination square to draw a center line along the length of each pipe holder. Line up the story board along the center line and transfer the marks.

3. Drill a ½" hole at each mark, using a drill and spade bit. To keep the boards from splitting, place the 2 × 2 over a piece of scrap lumber as you drill.

4. Calculate the number of pipes necessary for your fence line, and cut the appropriate number of 55" pieces of ½" copper pipe, using a tubing cutter or hacksaw.

Step C: Attach the Stringer Supports

1. At the first post, mark a level line across the inside face of the post, 2" from the ground. Align a 2 × 4 stringer support above that line and fasten it to the post with 2½" galvanized deck screws.

C. Mark a level line and then attach a stringer support on the inside face of each post.

D. Fasten the stringers to the posts, then center the lower pipe holder on top of the stringer. Drive screws down through the 1 × 3 and into the stringer.

2. Using a chalk line and line level, mark a level position on the opposite post. Use a framing square to transfer that mark to the inside face of the post, then fasten a stringer support to that post.

Step D: Install the Lower Stringer & Pipe Support

1. Set a 2 × 4 on top of the stringer supports and drive 2½" galvanized deck screws at an angle, through the stringer and support, and into the post.

2. Set a 1 × 3 pipe holder in place, centered on top of the stringer. Drive 2" galvanized deck screws through the pipe holder and down into the stringer. Add screws between every other pair of holes in the 1 × 3.

Step E: Install the Upper Pipe Holder

1. Mark a level line on the inside face of the post, 3" down from the flare of the post. Measure the distance between the top of the lower stringer and the bottom of the upper stringer support. Transfer that measurement to the inside face of the opposite post and draw a level line.

2. On each post, align a stringer support below the mark and fasten it to the post with 2½" galvanized deck screws.

3. Set a 2 × 2 pipe holder on top of the stringer supports and drive 2½" galvanized deck screws at an angle through the support and into the post.

Step F: Place the Pipes & Add the Facings

1. Working from above the upper pipe holder, insert a pipe into each hole and settle it into the corresponding hole in the bottom pipe holder.

2. Position a 1 × 4 facing on the one side of the pipe holder, flush with the top of the 2 × 2. Fasten the 1 × 4 in place, using 2" galvanized deck screws. Add a second facing on the other side of the fence.

3. Center a 2 × 4 stringer on top of the structure; secure it with 2½" galvanized deck screws.

NOTE: Built one bay at a time as described, this design can accommodate a slight slope. If you have a more radical slope to deal with, refer to pages 105 to 107 for further information.

E. *Mark positions for the upper stringer supports and attach them to the inside faces of the posts. Add the upper pipe supports and secure them, using 2½" galvanized deck screws.*

F. *Insert the pipes into the holes in the upper pipe holder and settle them into the corresponding holes in the lower pipe holder. Add 1 × 4 facings, then top the structure with a 2 × 4 stringer.*

Framed Trellis Wall

This simple design creates a sophisticated trellis wall that would work in many settings. Part of its appeal is that the materials are inexpensive and the construction remarkably simple.

It can be used as an accent wall, a backdrop to a shallow garden bed, or a screen to block a particular view. As a vertical showcase for foliage or flowers, it can support a wide display of colorful choices. Try perennial vines such as Golden Clematis (*Clematis tangutica*) or Trumpet Creeper (*Campsis radicans*). Or, for spectacular autumn color, plant Boston Ivy (*tricuspidata*). If you prefer annual vines, you might choose Morning Glories (*Ipomoea tricolor*) or a Black-eyed Susan Vine (*Thunbergia alata*). The possibilities go on and on—just make sure that the plants you select are well-suited to the amount of sunlight they'll receive.

Depending on the overall look you want to achieve, you can paint, stain, or seal the wall to contrast with or complement your house or other established structures. Well-chosen deck post finials can also help tie the wall into the look of your landscape.

This project creates three panels. If you adapt it to use a different number of panels, you'll need to revise the list of materials.

TOOLS & MATERIALS

- Tools & materials for setting posts (page 108)
- Tape measure
- Framing square
- Hammer
- Chalk line
- Line level
- Reciprocating saw or handsaw

- Paintbrush & roller
- Circular saw
- Drill
- Caulk gun
- Nail set
- Paint, stain, or sealer
- 10d galvanized casing nails
- 4d galvanized finish nails

- 6d galvanized finish nails
- Construction adhesive
- Pressure-treated, cedar, or redwood lumber:
  - 4 × 4 posts, 10 ft. (4)
  - 2 × 4s, 10 ft. (3)
  - 1 × 4s, 10 ft. (12)
  - 1 × 1s, 10 ft. (12)
  - 4 × 8-ft. lattice panels (3)
- Deck post finials (4)

A. *Set posts and let the concrete dry thoroughly. Snap level chalk lines to indicate the positions for the stringers. At the line for the top stringer, measure up 10" and draw a cutting line on each post.*

HOW TO BUILD A FRAMED TRELLIS WALL

Step A: Set the Posts

1. Mark the post positions 4 ft. apart, as indicated in the diagram at right. Dig holes and set the posts (pages 108 to 109). It's important to maintain the 4-ft. spacing between posts as accurately as possible.

2. On the first post, measure and mark a point 77" from the ground. Using a framing square, draw a level line across the post at the mark. Tack a nail in place along the line, and tie a chalk line to it. Stretch the chalk line to the opposite post, then use a line level to level it. Remove the line level and snap a line across all four posts.

3. On each post, measure down 75" from the chalk line and draw a line across the post, using a framing square.

4. Mark a line 10" above the chalk line. Trim off the posts

Cutting List

Part	Type	Size	Qty.
Posts	4 × 4	10 ft.	4
Stringers	2 × 4	48"	6
Back frame			
Top & bottom	1 × 4	41"	6
Sides	1 × 4	72"	6
Front frame			
Top & bottom	1 × 4	48"	6
Sides	1 × 4	65"	6
Stops			
Top & bottom	1 × 1	48"	12
Sides	1 × 1	70½"	12
Lattice panels	4 × 8	48 × 72"	3
Post caps	1 × 6	4½ × 4½"	4

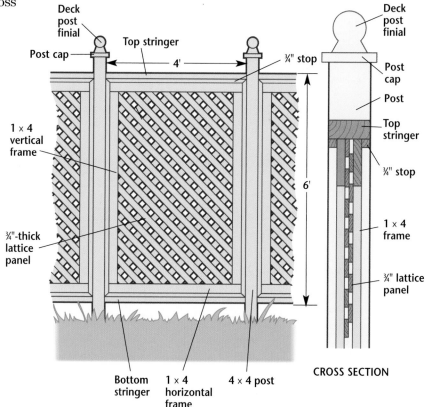

Deck post finial
Post cap
Top stringer
4'
¾" stop
Deck post finial
Post cap
Post
Top stringer
1 × 4 vertical frame
¾"-thick lattice panel
¾" stop
6'
1 × 4 frame
¾" lattice panel
Bottom stringer
1 × 4 horizontal frame
4 × 4 post

CROSS SECTION

along these lines, using a reciprocating saw or handsaw. Paint, stain, or seal the posts, including the cut ends.

Step B: Prepare Pieces & Position Stringers

1. Cut the stringers, back and front frame pieces, stops, lattice panels and post caps as indicated on the Cutting List on page 149. Paint, stain, or seal these pieces.

2. Transfer the level lines to the inside face of the posts, using a framing square.

3. Working between the two center posts, position the top stringer; make sure the top of the stringer is even with the marked line. Attach the stringer, toenailing it with 10d galvanized casing nails. Align the bottom stringer with the marked line and secure it in the same way.

Step C: Add Stops to the Back of the Fence Frame

Position a 1 × 1 stop flush with the back edge of the stringer and post, as indicated on the Cross Section on page 149. Drill pilot holes approximately every 8", then drive 6d galvanized finish nails through the stop and into the fence frame.

Step D: Set up the Back Frame

1. On a level work surface, position the pieces of the back frame to form a 4 × 6-ft. rectangle with butted joints. Measure the opposite diagonals. Adjust the frame until these measurements are equal, ensuring that the frame is square.

2. Run a bead of construction adhesive around the center of the back frame. Set the lattice panel in place, making sure it's square within the frame.

Step E: Attach the Front Frame

Set the front frame in place, with the joints butted in the opposite direction of those on the back frame. Square the frame as described in Step D, then secure the frame with 4d galvanized finish nails driven every 6". Sink the nails, using a nail set. Let the adhesive cure, according to manufacturer's directions.

Step F: Install the Framed Lattice Panel

1. Set the panel in place between the center posts, positioned

B. *Transfer the level lines to the inside of the posts, using a framing square. Install the first set of stringers between the center posts, even with the marked lines.*

C. *Add the stops to the back side of the fence frame. Drill pilot holes and nail the stops in place with 6d galvanized finish nails.*

firmly against the stops.

2. Position 1 × 1 stops around the front edges of the frame. Push the stops in until they hold the panel snugly in place. Drill pilot holes approximately every 6" and drive 6d galvanized finish nails through the stops and into the fence frame.

Step G: Complete the Wall

1. Repeat Steps B through F to install the left and right panels.

2. Set a post cap over each post, positioned so that the overhang is equal on all sides. Nail the trim in place, using 6d galvanized finish nails.

3. On top of each post cap, draw diagonal lines from corner to corner, forming an "X". Drill a pilot hole through the center of each "X", then install a deck post finial in each hole.

D. Set up the pieces of the back frame, butting the joints. Square the frame, then apply a bead of construction adhesive along the center of the frame. Carefully set the lattice panel in place.

E. Set the front frame in place, butting the pieces in the opposite direction of the back frame. Drive 4d galvanized finish nails every 6" to secure the front frame to the lattice panel and back frame.

F. Set the panel in place between the center pair of posts. Add stops on the front side, then drill pilot holes and nail the stops in place, using 6d galvanized nails.

G. Install the remaining panels and add post caps to the posts. Add a deck finial to each post.

Mortarless Block Wall

Far from an ordinary concrete block wall, this tile-topped, mortarless block wall offers the advantages of block—affordability and durability—as well as a flair for the dramatic. Color is the magic ingredient that changes everything. We added tint to the surface-bonding cement to produce a buttery yellow that contrasts beautifully with the cobalt blue tile. You can use any combination that matches or complements your wall's surroundings.

Mortarless block walls are simple to build. You set the first course in mortar on a footing that's twice as wide as the planned wall, and extends 12" beyond each end. Then you stack the subsequent courses in a running bond pattern.

The wall gets its strength from a coating of surface-bonding cement that's applied to every exposed surface. Tests have shown that the bond created between the blocks is just as strong as traditional block-and-mortar walls.

The wall we have built is 24" tall, using three courses of standard 8 × 8 × 16" concrete blocks and decorative 8 × 12" ceramic tiles for the top cap.

Choose a durable, exterior ceramic tile and use a thinset exterior tile mortar. Be sure to select an exterior grout as well.

TOOLS & MATERIALS

- Stakes & mason's string
- Hammer
- Line level
- Tape measure
- Shovel
- Wheelbarrow or mortar box
- Hand maul
- Hand tamp
- 4-ft. level
- Hacksaw
- Chalk line
- Circular saw with masonry-cutting blade
- Masonry chisel
- Line blocks
- Mason's trowel

- Notched trowel
- Square-end trowel
- Groover
- Tile cutter
- Caulk gun
- Rubber grout float
- Sponge
- Small paintbrush
- Compactible gravel
- 2 × 4s for footings
- #3 rebar
- 16-gauge wire
- Vegetable oil or release agent
- Cement mix
- Sheet plastic
- Concrete blocks (end, half, & stretcher)

- Type N mortar
- Corrugated metal ties
- Wire mesh
- Surface-bonding cement
- Fortified thinset exterior mortar
- 8 × 12" ceramic tile rated for exterior use
- Matching bullnose tile
- Tile spacers
- Sand-mix exterior grout
- Silicone caulk
- Grout sealer

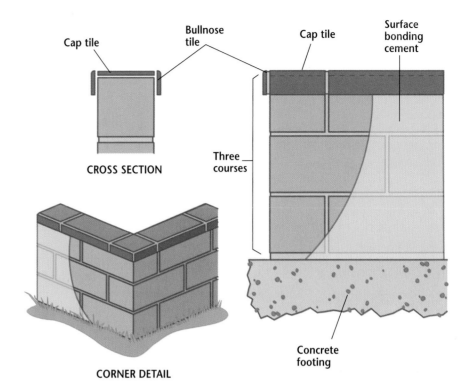

CROSS SECTION

CORNER DETAIL

HOW TO BUILD A MORTARLESS BLOCK WALL

Step A: Install the Footings & Lay Out the First Course

1. Lay out the location of the wall (pages 102 to 103), then use stakes and mason's string to outline footings that are twice as wide as the proposed wall. Measure the diagonals to make sure the staked outline is square, then use a framing square to make sure the corners are square. Adjust if necessary.

2. Dig the trenches and set the footings, as described on pages 48 to 51. When the concrete is hard to the touch, cover the footings with plastic and let the concrete cure for two to three days. Remove the wood forms and backfill around the edges, then let the footings cure for a week.

3. Lay out the blocks for the entire first course. If you need to use less than half a block, trim two blocks instead. For example, if you need 3½ blocks, use four and cut two of them to ¾ their length—this produces a stronger, more durable wall.

4. Use a level to make sure the course is plumb and a framing square to make sure the corners are square. Set a mason's string flush with the height of the course, along the outside of the wall.

5. Mark the position of the end and corner blocks on the footing, using a pencil.

6. Remove the blocks. Snap chalk lines to connect the end and corner marks for reference lines.

Step B: Set the First Course

1. Mix a batch of mortar, then mist the footing with water, roughly three or four block lengths from the end of the wall. Lay

A. *Lay out the first course of block, cutting blocks as necessary. Mark the ends and corners, then remove the blocks and snap reference lines.*

153

a ⅜"-thick bed of mortar on the misted area, covering only the area inside the reference lines.

2. Set an end block into the mortar bed at the corner. Place a stretcher block into the mortar bed directly against the end block with no spacing between the blocks. Place the next stretcher block in exactly the same manner. Use the mason's string as a guide to keep the blocks level and properly aligned.

3. Repeat this process, working on 3 to 4 ft. at a time, until the first course is complete. Periodically check to make sure the wall is plumb and level and that the corners are square.

Step C: Build Up the Corners & Ends

1. At a corner, begin the second course with a full-sized end block stacked so that it spans the vertical joint where the two runs meet. Make sure the block is level and plumb. If a block requires leveling, cut a piece of corrugated metal tie and slip it underneath. If a block is off by more than ⅛", remove the block, trowel a dab of mortar underneath, and reposition the block.

2. Butt a full-sized stretcher block against the end block to form the corner. Use a framing square to make sure the corner is square.

3. Build the corner up three courses high. Keep blocks level and plumb as you go, and check the position with a level laid diagonally across the corners of the blocks.

4. Build up the ends of the wall three courses high; use half-sized end blocks to offset the joints on the ends of the wall.

Step D: Fill in the Subsequent Courses

1. Set your mason's string level with the corner and end blocks of the second course.

2. Fill the second course with stretcher blocks, alternating from the end to the corner until the blocks meet in the middle. Maintain a standard running bond with each block overlapping half of the one beneath it. Trim the last block if necessary, using a circular saw and masonry-cutting blade, or a hammer and chisel.

3. Use a level to check for plumb, and line blocks and a line level to check for level. Lay wire mesh on top of the blocks.

4. Install the top course, then fill block hollows with mortar and trowel the surface smooth.

Step E: Apply Surface-bonding Cement

1. Starting near the top of the wall, mist a 2 × 5-ft. section on one side of the wall with water. (The water keeps the blocks from absorbing all the moisture from the cement once the coating is applied.)

2. Mix the cement in small batches, according to the manufacturer's instructions, and apply a ¹⁄₁₆"- to ⅛"-thick layer to the damp

B. *Mist the footing with water, then lay a ⅜"-thick bed of mortar inside the reference lines.*

C. *Starting at the first corner, stack a full-sized end block so it overlaps the vertical joint at the corner. Build the corners and then the ends three courses high.*

D. *Fill in the subsequent courses. On the next to the last course, lay wire mesh over the block, then install the final course. Fill the block hollows with mortar.*

blocks, using a square-end trowel. Spread the cement evenly by angling the trowel slightly and making broad upward strokes.

3. Use a wet trowel to smooth the surface and to create the texture of your choice. Rinse the trowel frequently to keep it clean and wet.

4. To prevent random cracking, use a groover to cut control joints from top to bottom, every 48". Seal the hardened joints with silicone caulk.

Step F: Set the Tiles

1. Lay out the 8 × 12" ceramic tiles along the top of the wall, starting at a corner. If any tiles need to be cut, adjust the layout so that the tiles on the ends of the wall will be the same size.

2. Apply latex-fortified exterior thinset mortar to the top of the wall, using a notched trowel. Spread the mortar with the straight edge, then create clean ridges with the notched edge. Work on small sections at a time.

3. Place the corner tile, twist it slightly, and press down firmly to embed it in the mortar. Place each tile in this same manner, using tile spacers to keep the tiles separated.

4. Lay out the bullnose tile on each side of the wall. Again, start in a corner and make sure that the tiles at the ends of the wall will be the same size. Cut tile as necessary.

5. Apply mortar to the sides of the wall. Set the bullnose tile in the same way that you set the top tile. Tape the tile in place until the mortar dries.

6. Remove the spacers and let the mortar cure for at least 24 hours.

Step G: Grout the Tile

1. Mix a batch of sanded grout. NOTE: Adding latex-fortified grout additive makes it easier to remove excess grout.

2. Spread a layer of grout onto a 4- to 5-ft. area of tile. Use a rubber grout float to spread the grout and pack it into the joints between tiles. Use the grout float to scrape off excess grout from the surface of the tile. Scrape diagonally across the joints, holding the float in a near-vertical position.

3. Use a damp sponge to wipe the grout film from the surface of the tile. Rinse the sponge frequently with cool water, and be careful not to press down so hard that you disturb the grout.

4. Continue working along the wall until you've grouted and wiped down all the tile. Let the grout dry several hours, then use a cloth to buff the surface until any remaining grout film is gone.

5. Apply grout sealer to the grout lines.

E. *Apply the surface-bonding cement to damp blocks, using a square-end trowel. Smooth the cement and cut grooves as necessary.*

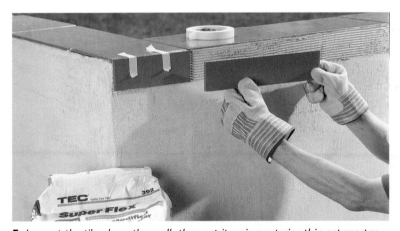

F. *Lay out the tile along the wall, then set it, using exterior thin-set mortar.*

G. *Grout the joints, using a rubber grout float. Wipe the film from the tile and let it dry. Polish the tile with a soft, dry rag.*

Mortared Block Wall

In some regions, mortared concrete block walls stand sentry at the borders of many yards. They're a durable, economical way to provide privacy and security. In some situations their utilitarian look is just what's called for, but in others a little decorative flair is in order. Adding decorative blocks as shown below or covering the blocks with stone veneer as shown on page 159 adds some style to these perennial favorites.

The wall we demonstrate here is 36" tall. If you're planning a wall taller than 36", you'll have to reinforce it by adding rebar and filling the block hollows with mortar. And, of course, a concrete block wall requires a footing that is twice as wide as the wall and reaches at least 12" below the frost line. Check your local building codes for installation requirements for both the wall and the footings

before you begin this or any block project.

There are three basic block types: Stretcher blocks have flanges on both ends and are used to build the body of the wall. End blocks are smooth on one end with flanges on the other. They are used for the wall ends and corners, with the smooth-face out. Half-blocks are also used to achieve the proper staggered block pattern. When using any type of block, make sure the side with the wider flanges is facing upward. These wider flanges provide more surface for the mortar.

Laying block is a matter of applying mortar to the footing and blocks and positioning them properly—proper positioning is the key to the strength and durability of a block wall. Keep in mind that although laying block isn't difficult, it is heavy work. If possible, recruit a friend or two to help you.

TOOLS & MATERIALS

- Tools & materials for pouring footings (page 48)
- Stakes & mason's string
- Tape measure
- Hammer
- Pencil
- Circular saw with a masonry-cutting blade

- Chalk line
- Line level
- Wheelbarrow or mortar box
- Mason's trowel
- 4-ft. carpenter's level
- V-shaped jointing tool
- Mortar bag
- Concrete blocks (end, stretcher, & cap)

- Type N mortar
- ⅜" wood strips or dowels

FOR VARIATION:
- Wire lath
- Self-tapping masonry anchors
- Stone veneer

HOW TO BUILD A MORTARED BLOCK WALL

Step A: Install the Footings

1. Plot the wall line with stakes and mason's string (pages 102 to 103). Outline the footings and measure the diagonals to make sure the outline is square. Adjust if necessary.

2. Dig the trenches and pour the footings, as described on pages 48 to 51.

Step B: Lay Out the First Course

1. Test-fit a course of blocks on the footing, using end and stretcher blocks. Use ⅜"-thick wood strips or dowels as spacers to maintain even gaps for the mortar. Cut blocks as necessary, using a circular saw and masonry-cutting blade.

2. Mark the ends of the course on the footing with a pencil, extending the lines well past the edges of the block. Snap chalk lines for reference marks on each side of the footing, 3" from the blocks.

3. Remove the blocks and set them nearby.

Step C: Set the Ends & Corners of the First Course

1. Mix mortar in a wheelbarrow or mortar box, following the manufacturer's directions. (The mortar should hold its shape when squeezed with your hand.)

2. Dampen the center of the footing, then trowel thick lines of mortar, slightly wider and longer than the base of the end block.

3. Set an end block into the mortar, with the end aligned with the pencil mark on the footing. Set a level on top of the block, then tap the block with a trowel handle until it's level. Use the chalk line as a reference point for keeping the block in line.

4. At the opposite end of the footing, apply mortar, then set and level another end block.

5. Stake a mason's string flush with the top outside corners of the end blocks. Check the string with a line level, and then adjust the blocks to align with the string. Remove any excess mortar, and fill the gaps beneath the blocks.

Step D: Fill the First Course

1. Apply mortar to the vertical flanges on one side of a standard block and to the footing. Set the block next to the end

block, leaving a ⅜" layer of mortar between blocks. Tap the block into position with a trowel handle, using the mason's string as a guide.

2. Install the remaining blocks, working back and forth from each end. Maintain ⅜" joints, and keep the course level, plumb, and aligned with the string.

3. When you reach the middle of the course, apply mortar to the flanges on both ends of the last block. Slide the block into

A. *Dig trenches and pour footings twice as wide as the proposed wall.*

B. *Test-fit a course of blocks, placing end blocks and half blocks as necessary. Use ⅜" wood strips or dowels as spacers.*

place and line it up with the string.

Step E: Build Up the Ends of the Wall

1. Trowel a 1" layer of mortar along the top flanges of one end block of the first course. Scrape off any mortar that falls onto the footing. Start the second course with a half-sized end block,

C. *Lay a mortar bed, then set the end blocks. Stake a mason's string flush with the top outside corners of the blocks.*

D. *Apply mortar to the flanges on one end of each block (INSET) and set the first course, alternating ends. At the center, apply mortar to both flanges of the last block and set it in place.*

which will offset the vertical joints.

2. Build the ends up three courses high. Keep the blocks plumb and aligned with the mason's string.

NOTE: If the wall includes a corner, begin the second course with a full-sized end block placed to span the vertical joint formed at the junction of the two runs. Build up three courses of the corners as you build the ends. For further information on corners, see page 154.

Step F: Fill in the Subsequent Courses

1. Install the second course of stretcher blocks, using the same method as with the first course. When the second course is completed, use line blocks to set your mason's string for the new course line.

2. Scrape off excess mortar, and tool the joints with a V-shaped mortar tool.

3. Install each additional course of blocks by repeating this process. Finish the joints as each course is completed. Use a level to make sure the wall remains plumb.

Step G: Lay the Top Cap

1. Apply mortar to the top of the finished wall. Ease the end (and corner, if necessary) cap blocks into position. Place them gently so their weight doesn't squeeze the mortar out of the joints.

2. Make sure the cap blocks are level and plumb, using a 4-ft. level.

E. *Start the second course with a half-size end block, which will result in staggered vertical joints. Make sure the wall remains plumb as you work.*

F. Fill in the field blocks of the second course, alternating from one end to the other. Tool the joints with a V-shaped jointing tool, then install remaining courses.

G. Lay a bed of mortar along the top of the finished wall. Apply mortar to one end of each cap block and set it in place.

VARIATION: APPLYING STONE VENEER

If a mortared block wall fits into your plans, but you don't like the appearance, you can set stone veneer over the finished wall.

Start by attaching wire lath to the entire surface of the wall, using self-tapping masonry anchors.

Next, apply a ½"-thick layer of mortar over the lath. Scratch grooves into the damp mortar, using the trowel tip. Let the mortar dry overnight.

Apply mortar to the back of each veneer piece, then press it onto the wall with a twisting motion. Start at the bottom of the wall and maintain a ½" gap between pieces. Let the mortar dry for 24 hours.

Fill the joints with fresh mortar, using a mortar bag. Use a V-shaped jointing tool to finish the joints.

Stone veneer can dress up the surface of a block wall. Veneer, which is lightweight and easy to handle, is available in many styles and colors. Shaped end and corner pieces greatly simplify the process of setting it.

Dry Stone Wall

Many homeowners—especially dedicated gardeners—dream of using low stone walls to form the boundaries of their yards or gardens. Sadly, many of them think those stone walls are destined to remain merely dreams. If you're one of those people, you'll be happy to know that you don't have to hire a professional mason or learn to throw mortar in order to build a durable stone wall.

You can construct a low stone wall without mortar, using a centuries-old method known as "dry laying." With this technique, the wall is actually formed by two separate stacks that lean together slightly. The position and weight of the two stacks support each other, forming a single, sturdy wall.

While dry walls are simple to construct, they do require a fair amount of patience. The stones must be carefully selected and sorted by size and shape. They must also be correctly positioned in the wall so that weight is distributed evenly. Long, flat stones work best. A quarry or aggregate supply center will have a variety of sizes, shapes, and colors to choose from. For this project you'll need to purchase a number of stones in these four sizes:

- Shaping: half the width of the wall
- Tie: the same width as the wall
- Filler: small shims that fit into cracks
- Cap: large, flat stones, wider than the wall

Because the wall relies on itself for support, a concrete footing is unnecessary, but the wall must be at least half as wide as it is tall. This means some stones may need to be shaped or split to maintain the spacing and structure of the wall.

To shape a stone, score its surface using a circular saw outfitted with a masonry blade. Place a mason's chisel on the cut and strike it with a hand sledge until the stone breaks. Always wear safety glasses when cutting or shaping stone.

TOOLS & MATERIALS

- Tools & materials for plotting a fence line (page 102)
- Shovel
- Circular saw with masonry blade

- Hand sledge
- Mason's chisel
- 4-ft. level
- Mason's trowel
- Safety glasses

- Stones of various shapes and sizes
- Capstone
- Type M mortar
- Rough-textured rag

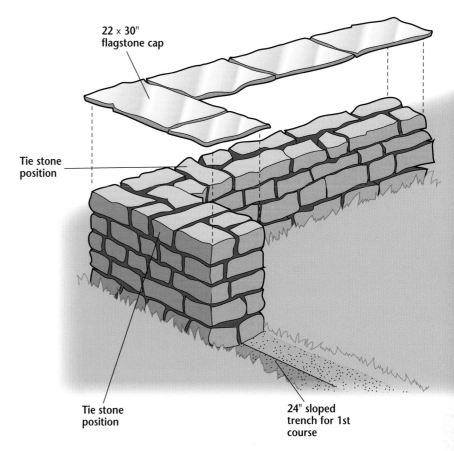

22 × 30" flagstone cap

Tie stone position

Tie stone position

24" sloped trench for 1st course

HOW TO BUILD A DRY STONE WALL

Step A: Dig the Trench

1. Sort the stones by size and purpose, placing them in piles near the building site.

2. Lay out the wall site with stakes and mason's string (pages 102 to 103). Measure the diagonals to make sure the outline is square, and use a framing square to make sure the corners are square. Adjust if necessary.

3. Dig a 24"-wide trench, 4" to 6" deep, along the site. Create a slight "V" shape by sloping the sides toward the center. The center of the trench should be about 2" deeper than the sides.

Step B: Build the First Course

1. Lay pairs of shaping stones in two rows along the bottom of the trench. Position them flush with the edges of the trench and sloping toward the center. Use stones similar in height. If stones have uneven surfaces, position them with the uneven sides facing down.

A. *Sort the stones by size and purpose. After planning the wall location, dig a V-shaped trench for the wall.*

B. *Lay the first course of shaping stones in the trench, adjusting them so that they slope toward each other. At corners, stagger the stones so the seams between stones are not aligned.*

161

C. *Build up the corner two courses high, with tie stones across the width of each just before they meet. Lay the rest of the course, working from the corner to the end of the wall.*

D. *Add the third course of stone over the second, using tie stones every 36", checking periodically with a level.*

E. *Once all the courses are in place, mortar the capstones to the top course of stone, then seal all the gaps between them.*

2. Form a corner by laying the last stone of the outer row so it covers the end of the stone in the outer row of the adjacent wall course. Lay the inner row in the same manner.

3. Fill any significant gaps between the shaping stones with filler stones.

Step C: Build Up the Corners

1. Lay the stones for the second course corner so they cover the joints of the first course corner. Use the same steps as forming the first course corner. Use stones that have long, square sides.

2. Build up the corner two courses high. Place tie stones across the width of each wall just before the corner.

3. Build the wall ends in this same way. Use stones of varying lengths so that each joint is covered by the stone above it.

4. Wedge filler stones into any large gaps.

Step D: Fill the Subsequent Courses

1. Lay the second course using shaping stones. Work from the corner to the end of the wall. Make sure to stagger the joints; stones of varying lengths will help offset them.

2. If necessary, shape or split the final stones of the course to size with a masonry saw or hand sledge and chisel. Carefully place the stones without disrupting the others.

3. For the third course, place tie stones every 36". Lay shaping stones between the tie stones and continue to place filler stones into any cracks on the surface or sides of the wall.

4. Continue laying courses, maintaining a consistent height along the wall and adding tie stones to every third course. Build up the corners first, and then build the courses with shaping stones, working from the corner to the end. Check for level as you go.

Step E: Set the Capstones

1. When the wall is approximately 36" high, check it for level.

2. Apply mortar to the center of the wall using a trowel. Keep the mortar at least 6" from the edges.

3. Center the capstones over the wall and set them as close together as possible.

4. Carefully fill the cracks between the capstones with mortar. Let any excess mortar dry until crumbly, then brush it off. After two or three days, scrub off any residue using water and a rough-textured rag.

162

VARIATION: SLOPES AND CURVES

If slope is an issue along your wall site, you can easily step a dry stone wall to accommodate it. The key is to keep the stones level so they won't shift or slide with the grade, and to keep the first course below ground level. This means digging a stepped trench.

Lay out the wall site with stakes and mason's string. Dig a trench 4" to 6" deep along the entire site, including the slope. Mark the slope with stakes at the bottom where it starts, and at the top where it ends.

Begin the first course along the straight-line section of the trench, leading up to the start of the slope. At the reference stake, dig into the slope so a pair of shaping stones will sit level with the rest of the wall.

To create the first step, excavate a new trench into the slope, so that the bottom is level with the top of the previous course. Dig into the slope the length of one-and-a-half stones. This will allow one pair of stones to be completely below the ground level, and one pair to span the joint where the new trench and the stones in the course below meet.

Continue creating steps, to the top of the slope. Make sure each step of the trench section remains level with the course beneath. Then fill the courses, laying stones in the same manner as for a straight-line wall. Build to a maximum height of 36", and finish by stepping the top to match the grade change, or create a level top with the wall running into the slope.

If you'd like a curved wall or wall segment, lay out each curve, as demonstrated on page 104. Then dig the trench as for a straight wall, sloping the sides into a slight "V" toward the center.

Lay the stones as for a straight wall, but use shorter stones; long, horizontal stones do not work as well for a tight curve. Lay the stones so they are tight together, off-setting the joints along the entire stretch. Be careful to keep the stone faces vertical to sustain the curve all the way up the height of the wall.

If the wall goes up- or downhill, step the trench, the courses, and the top of the wall to keep the stones level.

To build a curved wall, lay out the curve using a string staked to a center point, and dig the trench and set stones as for a straight wall.

© Crandall & Crandall this page

Mortared Stone Wall

The classic look of a mortared stone wall adds a sense of solidity and permanence to a landscape that nothing else can match. Although building a mortared wall takes more work than building a dry-laid one, in some cases, the tailored look of mortared stone is just what's needed.

Plan and position your wall carefully—making changes requires a sledgehammer and a fair amount of sweat. Before you begin work, check local building codes for regulations regarding the size and depth of the footings as well as construction details. And remember, in most communities any building project that requires a footing requires a building permit.

Plan to make your wall no more than 18" wide. Purchase a generous supply of stone so that you have plenty to choose from as you fit the wall together. Laying stone is much like putting a jigsaw puzzle together, and the pieces must fit well enough that gravity and their weight—rather than the strength of the mortar—will hold the wall together. Your stone supplier can help you calculate the tonnage necessary for your project, but you can make rough estimates with the formulas on page 165.

© Crandall & Crandall

TOOLS & MATERIALS

- Tools & materials for pouring footings (page 48)
- Stakes & string
- Line level
- Tape measure
- Wheelbarrow or mortar box
- Hand maul
- Masonry chisel
- Chalk
- Mason's trowel
- Batter gauge
- 4-ft. level
- Jointing tool
- Stiff-bristle brush
- Stones of various shapes and sizes
- Type N mortar
- ⅜" wood shims

A. Pour footings and let them cure. Dry-fit stones to follow the mason's string guides, staggering the joints.

HOW TO BUILD A MORTARED STONE WALL

Step A: Pour the Footings & Dry-fit the First Course

1. Plot the wall line with stakes and mason's string (pages 102 to 107), then follow the instructions on pages 48 to 51, Steps A through C, to pour the footings. Let the concrete cure for 48 hours, then remove the forms and backfill around the footings. Let the footings cure for a week.

2. Sort the stones by size and shape. Set aside long, thin stones for tie stones. Using stakes, string, and a line level, set up a guide for the height of the first course of the wall.

3. Using larger stones, dry-fit the first course. Center a tie stone on the cement slab, extending from the front to the back. Lay out 3 to 4 ft. of the wall at a time, leaving ½ to ¾" between stones. Chisel or cut the stones as necessary.

4. Trace the outline on the footing with chalk. Remove the stones and set them aside, following the layout you have established.

Step B: Lay the First Course

1. Mix a batch of mortar, following manufacturer's directions. Mist the first 3 to 4 ft. of the footing with water, and then lay a 2"-thick mortar bed on the area.

2. Working along one side of the first course, set stones into the mortar bed. Wiggle each stone after you set it in place, then use the handle of a trowel to tap it down, just firmly enough to remove any air bubbles from the mortar bed.

3. Set the other side of the first course in the mortar bed. Fill the center with smaller stones and mortar; leave the center slightly lower than the outer edges. If you need to reposition a stone, wash off the mortar before resetting it.

4. Pack mortar between the stones, keeping the mortar about 1" from the face of the wall.

5. Continue setting 3 to 4 ft. of the wall at a time until you've completed the entire first course.

Step C: Add Successive Courses

1. Adjust the string and line level to indicate the height of the next course.

2. Dry-fit the second course, 3 to 4 ft. at a time; add a tie stone at the beginning of each section. Stagger the vertical joints by setting one stone over two and two over one.

3. Set the stones aside in the layout you have established. Lay a 2" bed of mortar over the first course, then replace the stones. Check the slope with a batter gauge, and use wood shims to support large stones so their weight doesn't displace the mortar. Keep the side relatively plumb, checking with a 4-ft. level.

4. When the mortar is set enough to resist light finger pressure (about 30 minutes), smooth the joints, using a jointing tool. Keep the mortar 1" back from the faces of the stones. Remove the shims and fill the holes. Remove dry spattered mortar with a dry, stiff-bristle brush.

Step D: Add the Capstones

1. Create a level, 1"-thick mortar bed on top of the wall. Center flat stones over the wall and tap them into the mortar.

2. Fill the spaces between stones with mortar. Tool the joints when the mortar is dry enough to resist light finger pressure.

ROUGH TONNAGE CALCULATIONS:

Ashlar: the area of the wall face (sq. ft.) divided by 15 equals the number of tons needed.

Rubble: the area of the wall face (sq. ft.) divided by 35 equals the number of tons necessary.

B. *Apply mortar to the footing and set the stones in position, according to the layout. If necessary, use wood shims to keep the stones in position.*

C. *Add courses, staggering the vertical joint. Fill between the two sides of the courses with smaller stones and mortar.*

D. *Center flat cap stones on top of the wall, setting them in a level bed of mortar.*

Stone Moon Window

You can build circular openings into brick or stone walls, using a single semicircular wood form (page 139). Moon windows can be built to any dimension, although lifting and placing stones is more difficult as the project grows larger, while tapering stones to fit is a greater challenge as the circle gets smaller. To minimize the need for cutting and lifting stone, we built this window 2 ft. in diameter atop an existing stone wall. Before doing this, you'll need to check with your local building inspector regarding restrictions on wall height, footings, and other design considerations. You may need to modify the dimensions to conform with the local building code.

Make sure to have at least one helper on hand. Building with stone is always physically demanding, and steps such as installing the brace and form require a helper.

TOOLS & MATERIALS

- Jig saw
- Circular saw
- Drill
- Tape measure
- Level
- Mortar box
- Mason's hoe
- Trowels
- Jointing tool or tuck-pointer
- Mortar bag
- Stone chisel

- Maul
- ¾" plywood
- ¼" plywood
- 1" & 2" wallboard screws
- Tapered shims
- 2 x 4 lumber
- 2 x 8 lumber
- 4 x 4 posts
- Type M mortar (stiff mix)
- Ashlar stone

HOW TO BUILD A STONE MOON WINDOW

Step A: Dry-lay the Stones

1. Build a plywood form, following the instructions on page 139.

2. For the top of the circle select stones with sides that are squared off or slightly tapered.

3. Dry-lay the stones around the outside of the form, spacing them with shims that are roughly ¼" thick at their narrow end.

4. Number each stone and a corresponding point on the form, using chalk, then set the stones aside.

5. Turn the form around and label a second set of stones for the bottom of the circle. Use letters to label the bottom set of stones instead of numbers to avoid confusion.

Step B: Set the First Stone

1. Prepare a stiff mix of type M mortar (page 54).

2. Lay a ½"-thick mortar bed on top of the wall for the base of the circle. Center the stone that will be at the base of the circle in the mortar.

Step C: Build the Form Support

1. Construct a sturdy scaffold to hold the plywood arch form in place. Use pairs of 2 × 4s nailed together to create the legs and horizontal supports of the bracing structure (see diagram above).

2. Set the form on top of the stone at the base of the circle and check it for level in both directions. Adjust the braces as required.

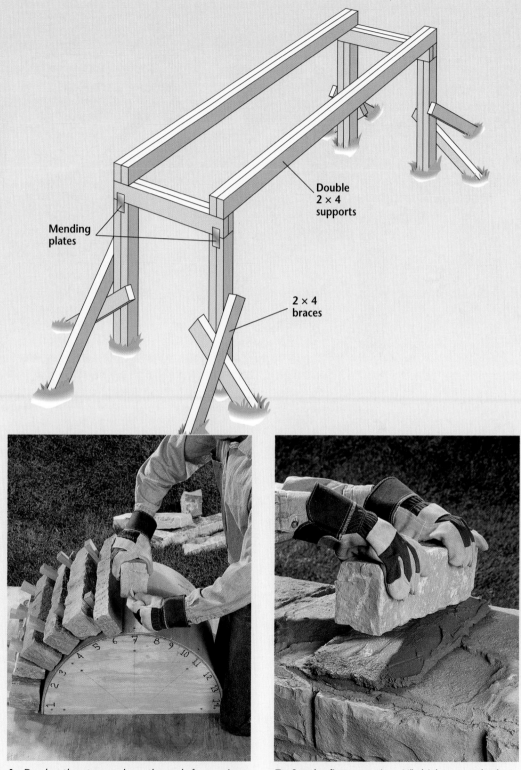

Double
2 × 4
supports

Mending
plates

2 × 4
braces

A. Dry-lay the stones along the arch form using ¼" shims as spacers. Number the stones and the form at corresponding points.

B. Set the first stone in a ½" thick mortar bed at the base of the window circle.

3. Screw the braces to the form, so the edges are at least ¼" in from the edges of the form.

Step D: Lay the Lower Course

1. Extend the mortar bed along the wall and add stones. Butter one end of each stone, and tap them into place with a trowel. Keep the joint width consistent with the existing wall, but set the depth of new joints at about 1", to allow for tuck-pointing.

2. Attach mason's string at the center of the front and back of the form. Use the strings to check the alignment of each stone.

3. Stagger the joints as you build upward and outward. Alternate large and

C. Build a 2 × 4 scaffold for the arch form. Position the form on the first stone, level the scaffold, and brace the legs with 2 × 4s.

D. Install the lower course of stones in a bed of mortar, building up the rest of the wall as you work. Check the alignment using a mason's line.

E. Invert the arch form, reattaching it so it will complete the top half of the window. Check to make sure it is level before fastening to the scaffold.

small stones for maximum strength and a natural look. Smooth joints that have hardened enough to resist minimal finger pressure.

4. Dress stones (pages 56 to 59) with large bumps or curves if necessary, so the sides are roughly squared off.

Step E: Position the Form for the Upper Course

1. Invert the form on the top of the wall in preparation for laying the top half of the circle. The bottom edge of the form should be set roughly ½" higher than the top of the lower half of the circle.

2. Check the braces for level (both lengthwise and widthwise). Adjust them as necessary, and reattach them to the posts.

Step F: Lay the Upper Course

1. Lay stones around the circle as for the lower course. Work from the bottom up and alternate from one side of the form to the other to balance the weight on the form. The top stone, or keystone, will be laid last.

2. If mortar oozes from the joints, insert temporary shims between joints. Remove the shims after two hours, and pack the voids with mortar.

3. Once the keystone is in place, smooth the remaining joints. Let the wall set up overnight, and then mist it several times a day for a week.

Step G: Tuck-point Inside of Circle

1. After a week, remove the form.

Remove any excess mortar from the joints inside the circle.

2. Mist lightly, and then tuck-point all joints with stiff mortar so they are of equal depth.

3. Once the joints reach a putty-like consistency, tool them with a jointing tool. Let the mortar harden overnight. Mist the wall for five more days.

F. Lay the stones around the circle, working from the bottom up, so the keystone is laid last. If necessary, use wood shims to prevent mortar from seeping out of the joints.

G. Mist the stones lightly and tuck-point each joint with stiff mortar, then tool them, using a jointing tool.

Glass Block Wall

A translucent wall can be an elegant addition to a contemporary landscape. Glass block provides the feeling of privacy while allowing light to pass through. Glass may not immediately come to mind as a material for landscaping projects, but it's versatile, durable, and easy to work with if you keep a couple caveats in mind.

First, a glass block wall cannot function as a load-bearing wall. It has to be supported by another structure, such as a concrete block support column or an existing wall. Second, glass block can't be cut, so you have to plan your project carefully.

You work with glass block in much the same way you work with brick. Mix the special glass block mortar a little drier than standard mortar for brick, because glass doesn't wick water out of the mortar the way brick does. You can find glass block and installation products at a specialty distributor or home center. There are a variety of sizes, with different textures and patterns that offer varying degrees of privacy. Bullnose end blocks and corner blocks work well for finishing exposed edges; radial blocks are good for right angles or curves.

There are several items particular to this installation. T-spacers are plastic molds placed between blocks to ensure consistent mortar joints and help support the weight of the block to prevent mortar from squeezing out before it sets. Reinforcement wire adds strength and helps keep the courses properly aligned. And panel anchors are used to secure courses to the support structures.

Because installation techniques may vary from project to project, ask a glass block retailer or manufacturer for advice about the best products and methods for your project. If you'd like to build your wall on an existing foundation, such as a concrete patio, check with your local building department for structural requirements.

HOW TO BUILD A GLASS BLOCK WALL
Step A: Dry-Lay the First Course

1. Plot the wall line (pages 102 to 103). Outline and pour the footings, following the directions on pages 48 to 51, Steps A through C. Let the footings cure for two days.

2. Dry-lay the first course of the glass block over the center of the footing. Lay ¼" wood spacers between blocks to set gaps for the mortar joints.

3. Set a concrete block at each end of the course for the support columns, then center the glass block against the concrete blocks.

4. Mark reference lines on the footings, then remove the blocks.

TOOLS & MATERIALS

- Tools & materials for pouring footings (page 48)
- Tape measure
- Chalk
- Wheelbarrow or mortar box
- Mason's trowel with rubber-tipped handle
- Level
- Wire cutters
- Jointing tool
- Sponge & pail
- Nylon- or natural-bristle brush
- Cloth
- 8 × 8" glass block
- ¼" wood spacers
- 6 × 8 × 8" concrete block
- Glass block mortar
- Glass block T-spacers
- Glass block panel anchors
- 6"-wide capstone
- Brick sealer
- Reinforcement wire
- 16-gauge wire

Step B: Lay the First Course

1. Mist the footings, then lay a ¼"-thick bed of mortar inside the reference lines.

2. Set the concrete support block first. Make sure it is properly aligned so the glass block can be centered against it.

3. Begin at the concrete block, and set the glass block for the first course. Butter the leading edge of each glass block liberally to fill the recesses on the sides of both blocks. Use T-spacers beneath the blocks at the joints to maintain the proper joint spacing.

4. At the end of the course, set the concrete block for the second support column. Make sure it's properly aligned and level with the rest of the course.

5. Check each block with a level to make sure it's level and plumb. Make adjustments by tapping lightly with a rubber-tipped trowel handle (not a metal hammer).

6. Fill the gaps between the tops of the blocks with mortar. Set in the appropriate T-spacers.

Step C: Lay the Subsequent Courses

1. Apply another ¼"-thick mortar bed for the next course.

2. Lay the blocks for the subsequent course in the same way, beginning with the concrete block for the support column. Make sure the blocks of the new course are aligned directly on top of the one beneath. Use T-spacers in the joints to maintain the

A. *Dry-lay the entire first course, with ¼" spacers between the blocks to set gaps for the mortar joints, then mark reference lines.*

B. *Set the first course in mortar, using T-spacers to keep the glass blocks evenly spaced. Gently tap with a rubber-tipped trowel handle to adjust.*

C. *Fill the gaps between the tops of the blocks with mortar, then position T-spacers. Apply a mortar bed, and lay the subsequent courses.*

proper spacing. Repeat for each course, building the concrete block support columns as you lay each course, until reaching the desired wall height.

Step D: Add Reinforcement Wire

1. Add reinforcement wire across the entire wall, every other course.

D. *Add reinforcement wire after every other course. Where more than one piece is needed, overlap the wire by 6".*

2. Lay half (⅛") of the mortar bed, then set two parallel rails of the wire in the mortar, centered on the blocks. Overlap the wire by 6" where more than one piece is needed.

3. For corners, cut the inner rail of the reinforcement wire, then bend the outer rail to fit the corner. Tie the cut ends of the inner rail together with 16-gauge wire to secure it.

4. Cover the wire with the remaining half (another ⅛") of the mortar and build the next course.

Step E: Add Panel Anchors

1. Tie the glass block to the support columns using glass block panel anchors on every other course.

2. Use the same method as for the reinforcement wire to embed the anchors in the mortar, spanning the concrete block.

Step F: Tool the Mortar Joints

1. Smooth out the joints with a mortar jointing tool when the fresh mortar hardens enough to resist light finger pressure (within 30 minutes).

2. Remove excess mortar from the glass surface before it sets, using a damp sponge. You can also use a nylon- or natural-bristle brush, but take care not to damage the joints. Don't use steel wool or other abrasive materials that can scratch the glass surface.

Step G: Install the Capstone

1. Lay a ¼" bed of mortar on the final course.

2. Butter the leading edge of each capstone, and position it on the mortar bed. (Use a capstone that is as wide as the cement

E. *Embed anchors in the mortar of every other course to tie the glass block to the concrete block support columns.*

F. *Tool the joints and remove excess mortar from the glass blocks for an even look, within 30 minutes of laying fresh mortar. Use a mortar jointing tool and a damp sponge.*

G. *Lay a ¼" bed or mortar, then add a single course of capstone to complete the wall.*

H. *Clean the glass block with a wet sponge to remove grit. After the surface dries, remove any cloudy residue with a clean, dry cloth.*

block you've used in the support columns.)

3. Tool the joints and remove any excess mortar with a damp sponge or nylon- or natural-bristle brush.

Step H: Clean, Cure & Seal the Wall

1. Clean the glass block thoroughly, using a wet sponge.

Rinse the sponge frequently.

2. Allow the surface to dry, then remove any cloudy residue by rubbing the surface of the blocks with a clean, dry cloth.

3. Let the mortar cure for two weeks, then apply a brick sealer to protect the wall from water damage.

VARIATION: A MATTER OF STYLE

The wide variety of glass block styles and textures offers some options. You can use all one style of blocks or get creative by mixing styles. Consider making a checkerboard pattern with two complementary styles or even creating smooth "windows" within a textured wall.

The variety of available styles also offers options for topping your wall with something other than the traditional capstone. For the final course of a glass block wall, consider laying a style of glass block different from the previous courses. Bullnose end blocks and corner blocks are both good options.

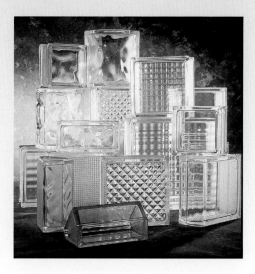

Retaining Wall

Retaining walls are often used to manage steep slopes in a landscape. They not only prevent erosion, but also create flat space for a garden bed, patio, or hedge. Retaining walls are not limited to sloped yards, however. They can also be used to add the illusion of slope to a flat yard. After these decorative retaining walls are constructed, the area behind the wall is backfilled with soil for a planting area.

Interlocking block is the easiest material to work with when constructing retaining walls. The biggest advantage of interlock-ing block is that no mortar is required. Blocks are available in many styles and colors that will blend with or provide an accent to your landscape. Some of these products have a natural rock finish that resembles the texture of cut stone, which adds a distinctive touch to a wall.

Although the wall itself does not require any type of fixative, the coordinating capstones are held securely in place by con-struction-grade adhesive. We've used coordinating capstones for this project, but you could also use mortared natural stone, which creates a pleasing contrast.

Limit the height of retaining walls to 4 ft. Taller walls are sub-ject to thousands of pounds of pressure from the weight of the soil and water. They require special building techniques and per-mits, and are best constructed by professionals. If your slope is greater than 4 ft., build a series of terraced walls over the course of the slope, instead of a single, tall wall.

HOW TO BUILD A RETAINING WALL

Step A: Excavate the Site

1. Excavate the slope to create a level area for the retaining wall. Allow at least 12" of space for the gravel backfill between the back of the wall and the hillside.

2. Use stakes to mark the front edge of the wall at the ends, and at any corners or curves. Connect the stakes with string, and use a line level to check the string, adjusting until it's level.

3. Dig a trench for the first row of block. Make the trench 8"

TOOLS & MATERIALS

- Basic tools (page 18)
- Rented plate compactor
- Stakes
- String
- Line level
- Landscape fabric
- Compactible gravel
- Interlocking block
- Perforated drain tile
- Gravel
- Hand tamp
- Construction-grade adhesive
- Capstones
- Caulk gun

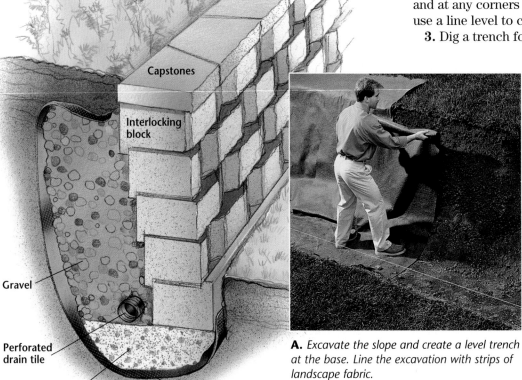

Capstones

Interlocking block

Gravel

Perforated drain tile

Compactible gravel

Landscape fabric

A. *Excavate the slope and create a level trench at the base. Line the excavation with strips of landscape fabric.*

B. *Lay the first row of interlocking block over the compacted gravel base in the trench, checking with a level as you work.*

deeper than the thickness of the block. Measure down from the string as you work to make sure the trench remains level.

4. Line the excavated area with strips of landscape fabric cut 3 ft. longer that the planned height of the wall. Overlap the strips by at least 6".

Step B: Build a Base & Lay the First Row

1. Spread a 6" layer of compactible gravel into the trench. Compact the gravel, using a plate compactor.

2. Lay the first row of blocks into the trench, aligning the front edges with the string. If you're using flanged blocks, install the first row of blocks upside down and backward in the trench.

3. Check the blocks frequently with a level, and adjust them by adding or removing gravel.

Step C: Install Drain Tile & Add Rows

1. Lay the second row of blocks according to the manufacturer's instructions, making sure the joints are staggered with the course below. As you work, check to make sure the blocks are level.

2. Add 1" to 2" of gravel, as needed, to create a slight downward pitch as the drain tile runs toward the outlet.

3. Place perforated drain tile on top of the gravel, about 6" behind the blocks, with the perforations facing down. Make sure that at least one end of the pipe is unobstructed so runoff water can escape.

4. Lay the additional rows until the wall is about 18" high, offsetting vertical joints in successive rows.

5. Fill behind the wall with coarse gravel, and pack it down with a hand tamp.

> ## TIP: CREATING HALF-BLOCKS
>
> Half-blocks are often needed for making corners, and to ensure that vertical joints between blocks are staggered between rows. To make a half-block, score a full block with a circular saw outfitted with a masonry blade, then break the blocks along the scored line with a maul and chisel.

Step D: Lay the Remaining Rows & Backfill

1. Lay the remaining rows of block, except the cap row, backfilling with gravel and packing it down with a hand tamp as you work.

2. Fold the landscape fabric down over the gravel backfill. Add a thin layer of topsoil over the landscape fabric, then lightly pack down the soil, using the hand tamp.

3. Fold any excess landscape fabric back over the tamped soil.

Step E: Add the Capstones

1. Apply construction adhesive to the top blocks. Lay the capstones in place.

2. Use topsoil to fill in behind the wall and to fill in the trench at the base of the wall.

3. Add sod or other plants, as desired, both above and below the wall.

C. *Lay a section of perforated drain tile behind the wall over the gravel, then lay the remaining rows of blocks.*

D. *Fold the excess landscape fabric over the gravel, then cover it with a layer of soil. Compress the soil with a hand tamp.*

E. *Apply adhesive along the top blocks, then lay the capstones so the joints are staggered with those below.*

Fence & Wall Ideas

© Jerry Pavia

© Saxon Holt

(above) **Posts made from unstripped logs** *create a fenceline that blends in wonderfully with this rustic landscape. "Stringers" of weathered metal chain establish a visual boundary.*

(left) **A bamboo variation of a post-and-panel fence** *makes perfect sense in this oriental-theme garden, with its exotic rhododendrons.*

© Charles Mann (all photos this page)

(above) **A masonry wall adds texture** *to an area, and sometimes color, as in this landscape with its stucco-surfaced concrete block wall.*

(right, top) **A brightly colored fence adds interest,** *and also creates harmony, when painted to match the trim color of the home.*

(right, bottom) **A garden wall can be a work of art,** *especially here, where a masonry wall is embellished with a painted-tile picture and a spectacular flowering shrub.*

© Saxon Holt

Gates

Although gates are uncomplicated, we ask a lot of them. These simple structures need to welcome family and invited guests at the same time that they turn away intruders. Successful gates need to operate smoothly and keep their attractive appearance for many years with little maintenance.

A gate's allure and interest depend on its materials, color, and pattern, but its strength and durability depend on its structural design and how well it's built. No book can describe gates for every situation, but once you understand the fundamental elements of building a gate, a world of possibilities opens up. The style of your fence and existing landscape will strongly influence your decisions, but after reading through this section, you should be able to build a range of gates—from a dramatic trellis gate combination to a security-conscious arch gate.

Building a gate offers you the opportunity to stretch your imagination and make use of unexpected materials. For example, copper pipe and plumbing fittings, salvaged metal, and stained glass make quite a splash when recycled into gates.

As these projects show, gates give you a chance to make a statement. We hope they also show you that gates are about connection—not just to a fence or wall, but to the lives of the people on the other side.

Basic Gates

If you understand the basic elements of gate construction, you can build a sturdy gate to suit almost any situation. The gates shown here illustrate the fundamental elements of a well-built gate.

To begin with, adequate distribution of the gate's weight is critical to its operation. Because the posts bear most of a gate's weight, they're set at least 12" deeper than fence posts. Or, depending on building codes in your area, they may need to be set below the frost line in substantial concrete footings.

However they're set, the posts must be plumb. A sagging post can be reinforced by attaching a sag rod at the top of the post and running it diagonally to the lower end of the next post. Tighten the knuckle in the middle until the post is properly aligned. A caster can be used with heavy gates over smooth surfaces to assist with the weight load.

The frame also plays an important part in properly distributing the gate's weight. The two basic gate frames featured here are the foundation for many gate designs. A Z-frame gate is ideal for a light, simple gate. This frame consists of a pair of horizontal braces with a diagonal brace running between them. A perimeter-frame gate is necessary for a heavier or more elaborate gate. It employs a solid, four-cornered frame with a diagonal brace.

In both styles, the diagonal brace must run from the bottom of the hinge side to the top of the latch side, to provide support and keep the gate square.

There are a multitude of hinge, latch, and handle styles available. Whichever you choose, purchase the largest hinges available that are in proportion with your gate, and a latch or handle appropriate for the gate's purpose.

Z frame

Perimeter frame

© Jerry Pavia

TOOLS & MATERIALS

- Tape measure
- Level
- Framing square
- Circular saw
- Paintbrush
- Drill
- Spring clamps

- Jig saw
- Combination square
- Pressure-treated, cedar, or redwood lumber as needed:
  1 × 2s
  2 × 4s

- Paint, stain, or sealer
- Hinge hardware
- Gate handle or latch
- 2" galvanized deck screws
- 2½" galvanized deck screws

HOW TO BUILD A Z-FRAME GATE

Step A: Calculate the Width & Cut the Braces

1. Check both gate posts on adjacent sides for plumb, using a level. If a post is not plumb, reinforce it with a sag rod. When both posts are plumb, measure the opening between them.

2. Consult the packaging on your hinge and latch hardware for the clearance necessary between the frame and gate posts. Subtract this figure from the measurement of the opening. The result will be the finished width of the gate. Cut 2 × 4s to this length for the frame's horizontal braces.

3. Paint, stain, or seal the lumber for the frame as well as the siding for the gate, and let it dry completely.

Step B: Attach the Diagonal Brace

1. On the fence, measure the distance from the bottom of the upper stringer to the top of the lower stringer. Cut two pieces of scrap 2 × 4 to this length to use as temporary supports.

2. On a flat work surface, lay out the frame, placing the temporary supports between the braces. Square the corners of the frame, using a framing square.

3. Place a 2 × 4 diagonally from one end of the lower brace across to the opposite end of the upper brace. Mark and cut the brace, using a circular saw.

4. Remove the temporary supports, and toenail the brace into position, using 2½" galvanized deck screws.

Step C: Apply the Siding

1. Position the frame so the diagonal brace runs from the bottom of the hinge side to the top of the latch side, then plan the lay out of the siding to match the position and spacing of the fence siding. If the final board needs to be trimmed, divide the difference and trim two boards instead. Use these equally trimmed boards as the first and last pieces of siding.

A. *Make sure the gate posts are plumb, then measure the distance between them and calculate the dimensions of the gate.*

B. *Place a 2 × 4 diagonally across the temporary frame, from the lower corner of the hinge side to the upper corner of the latch side, and mark the cutting lines.*

Copper Gate

This copper gate is an example of how ordinary materials can be used in extraordinary ways. Despite its elegant appearance, the gate actually is nothing more than simple combinations of copper pipe and fittings and a few pieces of inexpensive hardware.

The best setting for this gate is one in which it is largely ornamental. Although it's sturdy and fully operational, it isn't meant to provide security or handle a constant flow of traffic in and out of your yard. However, set into a living wall or a section of fence where it receives light use, it can provide decades of service.

Copper pipe and fittings are intended to be exposed to water,

heat, and cold, so they're entirely suited to outdoor use. The finish can be protected to maintain the bright color or allowed to develop a patina. To maintain the original color, spray the new copper with an acrylic sealer. On the other hand, if you don't want to wait for the patina to develop on its own, rub the finished piece with the cut face of a lemon or a tomato—the acid will speed the chemical process that creates the patina.

We used a copper watering can for an accent piece, but there's really no limit to what you could choose. If an object appeals to you and can be wired or soldered securely into place, you can make it work. You may have to adjust the dimensions of the display frame, but that's a simple matter of making a few calculations before you begin cutting the copper.

C. A attac to th

2. plac end: brac **3.** Ste **1.** free **2.** hol ed **3.** the bac mal pro pos **4** pos Fas har **5** cat

TOOLS & MATERIALS

- Tape measure
- Tubing cutter
- Paintbrush
- 4-ft. level
- Reciprocating saw or hand saw
- Locking pliers or pipe wrench
- Drill
- Emery cloth
- Wire brush
- Flux
- Solder
- Propane torch
- 4 × 4 posts, 8 ft. (2)
- Paint, stain, or sealer
- Tools & materials for setting posts (page 108)
- Deck post cap & finial
- ¾" copper pipe, 20 ft.
- ½" copper pipe, 10 ft.
- ⅝ × ¾ × 1 brass flange bearings (3)
- ¾" 90° elbows (10)
- ¾ to ½" reducing tees (12)
- ¾" tees (3)
- Lag screwhinges for chain link fence (2)
- ⅜" flexible copper tubing
- 8-gauge copper wire (about 8")
- Copper watering can
- 16-gauge copper wire (about 24")
- Galvanized finish nails

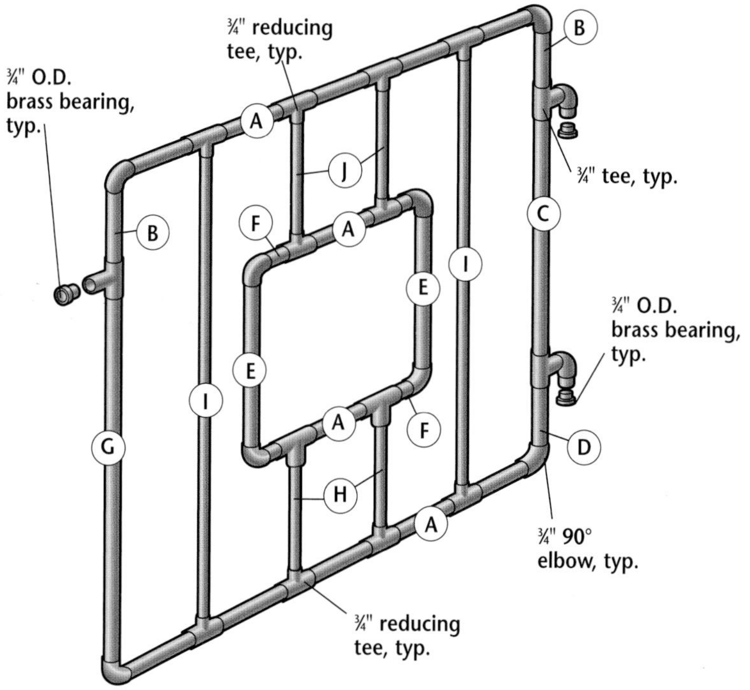

¾" reducing tee, typ.
¾" O.D. brass bearing, typ.
¾" tee, typ.
¾" O.D. brass bearing, typ.
¾" 90° elbow, typ.
¾" reducing tee, typ.
A
B
C
D
E
F
G
H
I
J

HOW TO BUILD A COPPER GATE

Step A: Cut the Copper Parts

1. Measure and mark the pipe, according to the Cutting List and diagram at right.

2. Cut the copper pipe to length, using a tubing cutter. Place the tubing cutter over the pipe, with the cutting wheel centered over the marked line. Tighten the handle until the pipe rests on both rollers. Turn the tubing cutter one rotation to score a continuous line around the pipe. Then rotate the cutter in the other direction. After every two rotations, tighten the handle of the cutter. Remove metal burrs from the inside edge of the cut pipe, using the reaming point on the tubing cutter or a round file.

3. Sand the ends of all the pipes with emery cloth, and scour the insides of the fittings with a wire brush. Apply flux to all the mating surfaces.

Step B: Assemble the Gate Pieces

1. Dry-fit the pieces of the top of the gate and the display frame, referring to the diagram above.

2. Assemble the bottom run of the gate, again referring to the diagram as necessary.

3. Join the top and bottom sections of the gate. Measure from

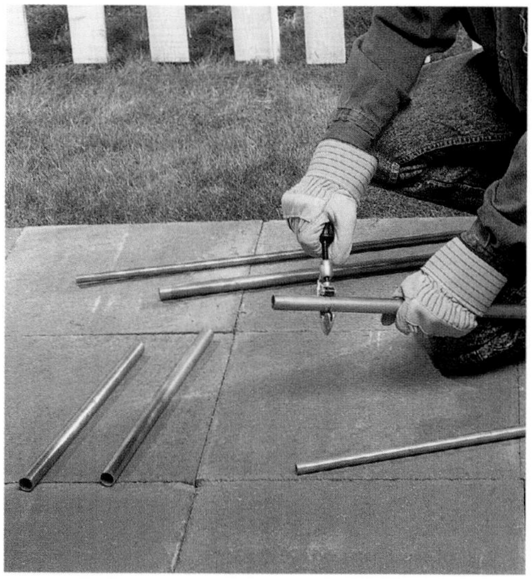

A. *Measure, mark, and cut the copper pipe, using a tubing cutter. Clean and flux the pipe and fittings.*

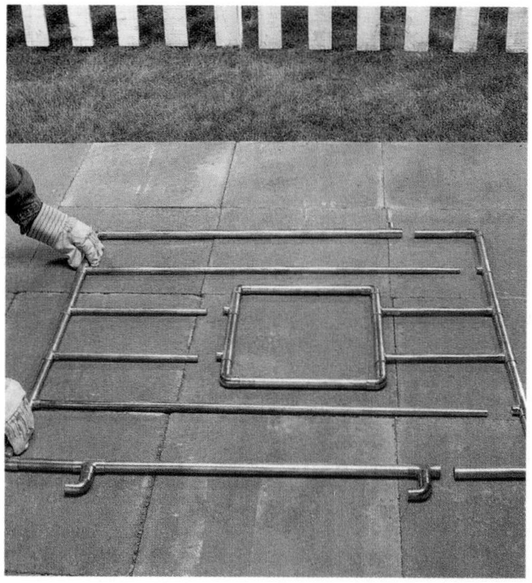

B. *Dry-fit the bottom assembly of the gate, and then the top assembly. Connect the two assemblies.*

Cutting List

Key	Part	Length	Qty.
A¾"	pipe	6½"	12
B¾"	pipe	6"	2
C	¾" pipe	23¾"	1
D	¾" pipe	5"	1
E	¾" pipe	12½"	2
F	¾" pipe	2½"	4
G	¾" pipe	29½"	1
H	½" pipe	10"	2
I	½" pipe	36¾"	2
J	½" pipe	12¼"	2

one corner of the gate to the diagonally opposite corner. Repeat at the opposite corners. Adjust the pieces until these measurements are equal, which indicates that the gate is square.

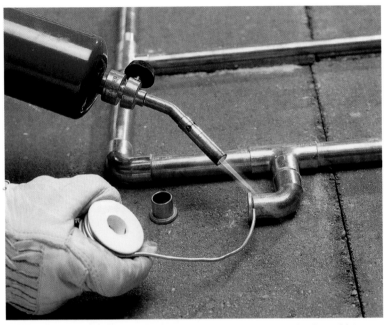

C. Solder the joints of the gate. Add brass bushings to the latch and hinge extensions and solder them in place.

Step C: Solder the Joints & Add the Bushings

1. Solder each joint, beginning at the bottom of the gate and working toward the top.

2. At each of the hinge extensions and at the latch extension, add a brass flange bearing. As you solder these bearings in place, direct the torch's flame more toward the bearing than toward the elbow—brass heats more slowly than copper.

Step D: Install & Mark the Gate Posts

1. Paint, stain, or seal the posts.

2. Mark the post positions 49½" apart on-center. Dig the holes and set the posts (pages 108 to 109). As you plumb the posts, maintain the spacing between them as accurately as possible.

3. On the first post, measure and mark a point 47½" from the ground. Using a 4-ft. level, draw a line across the post at the mark, then across the opposite post. Trim off the posts along these lines, using a reciprocating saw or handsaw. Paint, stain, or seal the cut ends of the posts.

4. Set a deck post cap and finial on top of each post and nail it in place, using galvanized finish nails.

5. Cut two 4¼" spacers. Center the gate between the posts, resting it on the spacers. Mark the hinge-side post to indicate the locations of the hinge extensions. Mark the latch-side post to indicate the location of the latch extension.

Step E: Install the Lag Screws for the Hinges

1. At each of the marked locations on the hinge-side post, drill

D. Install the gate posts, then position the gate and mark the locations for the latch and for the hinge extensions.

E. Drill pilot holes at the marked locations on the hinge-side post. Drive a lag screw hinge into each pilot hole. Make sure the hinge pin is facing up when the screw hinge is in position.

a ½" pilot hole approximately 2¾" into the post. Drill these holes carefully—they must be as straight as possible.

2. Drive a lag screwhinge into each pilot hole, using a locking pliers or pipe wrench to twist it into place. The hinge pin needs to be facing up when the lag screw is in its final position.

Step F: Add the Latch

1. At the marked location on the latch-side post, drill a ½" hole through the post. Again, take care to drill the hole straight through the post.

2. Cut 15 to 18" of ⅜" flexible copper. Drill a hole through the tubing, 2½" from one end. At the opposite end, form a decorative coil. Cut a 2" piece of #8 copper wire and form a decorative coil at one end.

3. Insert the latch through the hole in the latch-side post. Thread the wire through the hole in the tubing, then create a small loop below the tubing. This wire loop keeps the latch from falling out of the post.

Step G: Hang the Watering Can

1. Position the watering can within the display frame on the gate. Mark the spots where the handle and spout will meet the copper pipe; clean and flux those areas. Wrap 16-gauge copper wire around the handle of the watering can, using 6 or 8 wraps of wire to connect it to the display frame in the marked spot. Add a little more flux, then solder the handle to the frame. The flux will draw the solder into the crevices between the wire

---

TIP: SOLDERING COPPER JOINTS

To solder, hold the flame tip of a propane torch against the middle of a fitting for 4 to 5 seconds, or until the flux begins to sizzle. Heat the other side of the joint, distributing the heat evenly. Move the flame around the joint in the direction you want the solder to flow.

Quickly apply solder along both seams of the fitting, allowing the capillary action to draw the liquefied solder into the fitting. When the joint is filled, solder will begin to form droplets on the bottom of the joint. It typically takes ½" of solder wire to fill a joint in a ½" pipe.

Let the joint sit undisturbed until the solder loses its shiny color. When the joint is cool enough to touch, wipe away excess flux and solder, using a clean, dry cloth.

---

wraps to create a strong, solid joint.

2. Thread a piece of 16-gauge copper wire through a hole in the spout of the watering can. Wrap the other end of the wire around the display frame in the marked location. Flux and solder the wire wrap as described above.

F. *Drill a hole on one end of a piece of flexible copper. At the opposite end, bend a coil. Insert the tubing through the hole in the latch-side post, and thread a loop of wire through the hole in the tubing.*

G. *Set the watering can into position and secure it, using 16-gauge wire. Solder the wrapped wire to the gate frame.*

Arched Gate

With its height and strategically placed opening, this gate is a great choice for maintaining privacy and enhancing security with style.

No ordinary "peephole," the decorative wrought iron provides a stunning accent and gives you the opportunity to see who's heading your way or passing by. The arch of the gate also adds contrast to the fence line and draws attention to the entryway.

This gate is best suited to a situation where you can position it over a hard surface, such as a sidewalk or driveway. The combined weight of the lumber and the wrought iron makes for a heavy gate. To avoid sagging and to ease the gate's swing, you'll need to include a wheel on the latch side of the gate. Over a solid surface such as concrete or asphalt, the wheel will help you open and close the gate easily.

Shaping the top of the arch is a simple matter: Just enlarge the pattern provided on page 193 and trace it onto the siding. Then cut the shape, using a jig saw.

This piece of wrought iron came from a banister we found at a salvage yard. We used a reciprocating saw with a metal-cutting blade to cut it to a usable size.

HOW TO BUILD AN ARCHED GATE

Step A: Prepare the Lumber

1. Measure the opening between the gate posts and determine the finished size of your gate. (Check the packaging of your hinge and latch hardware for clearance allowances.) Compare your actual dimensions to those in the diagram at right, then check the Cutting List and make any necessary adjustments. Cut the lumber for the gate.

2. Paint, stain, or seal the pieces on all sides and edges. Let them dry thoroughly.

Step B: Build the Frame

1. Lay out the parts of the frame and mark the cutting lines for the half-lap joints (see diagram, opposite page). To make a half-lap joint, set the depth of a

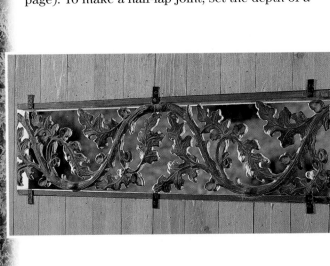

TOOLS & MATERIALS

- Tape measure
- Circular saw with wood- & metal-cutting blades
- Paintbrushes & roller
- Hammer
- Chisel
- Drill
- Jig saw
- Level
- Framing square
- Spring clamps

- Caulk gun
- Salvaged piece of ornamental metal
- Paint, stain, or sealer
- Pressure-treated, cedar, or redwood lumber:
  2 × 4s, 10 ft. (3)
  1 × 4s, 8 ft. (13)
- Posterboard or cardboard
- Construction adhesive

- 1¼" galvanized deck screws
- 16d nails
- 2" galvanized deck screws
- 1½" mending plates (8)
- 2½" bolts and nuts (8)
- Gate wheel
- Hinge & latch hardware
- Gate handle
- Finish nails

Cutting List

Key	Part	Type	Length	Qty.
A	Siding brace	1 × 4	42¾"	1
B	Horizontal braces	2 × 4	42¾"	3
C	Vertical braces	2 × 4	63"	2
D	Diagonal brace	2 × 4	6 ft.	1
E	Siding	1 × 4	8 ft.	12

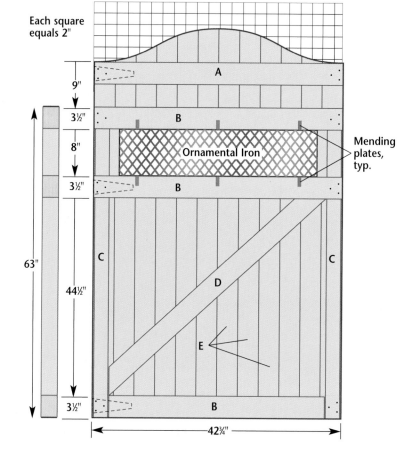

A. *Measure the gate opening and finalize the dimensions of the gate. Cut the pieces, and then paint, stain, or seal the lumber.*

B. *Set the blade depth on a circular saw to ¾". Mark the half-lap joint, then make a cut every ⅛" to ¼" in the joint area. Remove the waste material, using a hammer and chisel.*

Gate Ideas

© Saxon Holt

© Angela Hartwell

(above) **This gate welcomes visitors,** *aided by blooming vines weaving through its latticework. The entire design hints at the friendly atmosphere within.*

(left) **A gate can be purely ornamental,** *as with this bamboo gate that blends curved and angled components.*

© The Image Finders/Jim Barron

© Charles Mann

© Saxon Holt

(top) **Formal gates** *are best suited to large land-scapes, and should match the fencing materials used, as in this estate-sized property.*

(above) **A truly unique gate**, *made from tree branches, creates surprise and whimsy in a land-scape, especially when paired with traditional building materials used in a wall or fence.*

(right) **This heavy panel door** *painted a bright color creates a sturdy security gate that doesn't scare off invited guests. Such a door defines the outdoor landscape as part of the owner's home.*

Decks

A deck is the perfect way to create a comfortable and practical outdoor living space, whether for cookouts with family and friends, or time alone with a cup of coffee and the Sunday paper.

A great deck design makes the best possible use of available outdoor space while meshing gracefully with the beauty and functionality of your home. Decks provide options for almost every space configuration—from wraparound decks that take advantage of small yards by using the space surrounding the house, to detached decks located anywhere in the yard.

This section begins with important information on working with your local building officials and codes, to prepare you for obtaining a building permit before you begin construction.

Next, you will find basic deck building techniques showing you how to lay out and install the deck you have designed on paper. Step-by-step instructions explain how to build each component of a basic deck: ledgers, footings, posts, beams, joists, decking, stairs, and railings. The specific tools and materials required for each of these techniques are listed. Also, information regarding the recent trends in alternative decking materials, such as plastic/wood composites and PVC vinyl are discussed, complete with full how-to steps.

Everything is here to help you design, plan, and build a cost-effective deck that will provide years of enjoyment. All you have left to do now is choose from one of the six popular designs included here, and begin planning your new deck.

Anatomy of a Deck

Before you begin your project, it's important to know the structural parts of a deck. They include posts, beams, ledgers, and joists. They support and distribute the weight of the deck. For economy and durability, use pressure-treated lumber for these parts (and most building codes require it). The other parts of a deck include the decking, facing, railings, and stairway. You may want to use redwood or cedar for these visible parts.

Each part has a specific function, and one part often works in conjunction with another. For example, a ledger anchors an attached deck to a house, and supports one end of all joists.

Concrete footings with post anchors support the weight of the deck and hold the deck posts in place. They are made by pouring concrete into tube forms. Local climates and building codes determine the depth of footings. Post anchors should be made of galvanized steel to resist corrosion.

Posts transfer the weight of the deck to the footings. They are attached to the post anchors with galvanized nails.

Beams provide the main structural support for the deck. A beam is usually made from a pair of 2 × 8s or 2 × 10s fastened to deck posts.

Joists support the decking. For an attached deck, the joists are fastened at one end to the ledger, and at the other end to the header joist. The outside joists can be covered with redwood or cedar facing boards for enhanced appearance.

Decking is the main feature of any deck. The decking boards are attached to the joists with galvanized screws or nails.

Railing parts include railing posts and balusters attached to the header and outside joists, a horizontal rail, and a cap. Building codes may require railings on decks 24" or more above ground level.

A stairway is made from a pair of stringers fastened to the side of the deck, and a series of treads are attached to the stringers with metal cleats.

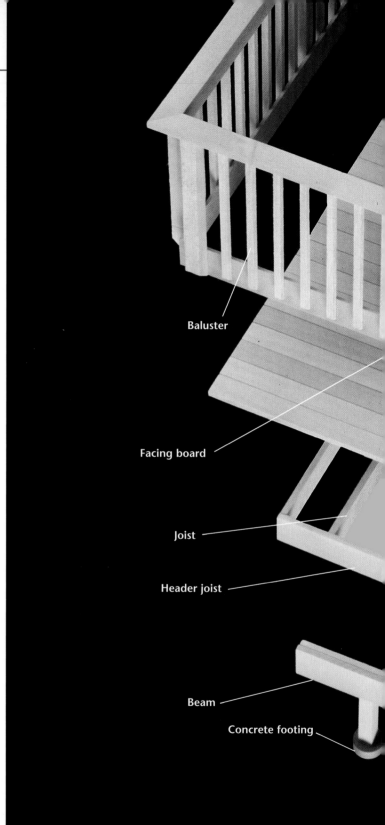

Baluster

Facing board

Joist

Header joist

Beam

Concrete footing

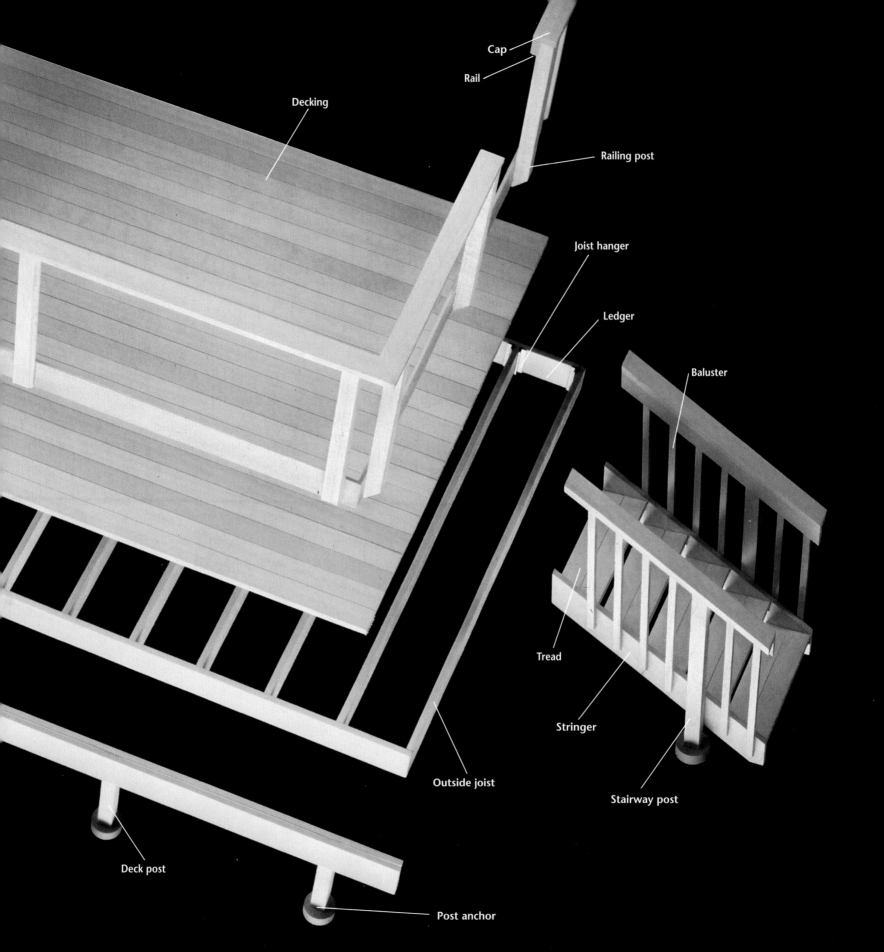

Cap

Rail

Decking

Railing post

Joist hanger

Ledger

Baluster

Tread

Outside joist

Stringer

Stairway post

Deck post

Post anchor

Working with Building Officials

In most regions, you must have your plans reviewed and approved by a building official if your deck is attached to a permanent structure or if it is more than 30" high. The building official makes sure that your planned deck meets building code requirements for safe construction.

These pages show some of the most common code requirements for decks. But before you design your project, check with the building inspection division of your city office, since code regulations can vary from area to area. A valuable source of planning information, the building official may provide you with a free information sheet outlining the relevant requirements.

When you have a rough idea of what you want your deck to look like, you'll need to develop the concept into a workable plan. Especially for complicated, elaborate decks, it is crucial that you have detailed plan drawings to help organize and direct your work. Good plans also make it possible to create an accurate materials list. You can hire a landscape designer, or use computer printouts generated by deck-design software programs. You can also adapt an existing deck plan borrowed from a book or magazine, or purchased in blueprint form. And, you can always rely on good-old-fashioned graph paper and ruler.

Whatever your method, remember to create both overhead plan drawings and side elevation drawings of the project. Also, be sure to consider sun patterns and the locations of existing

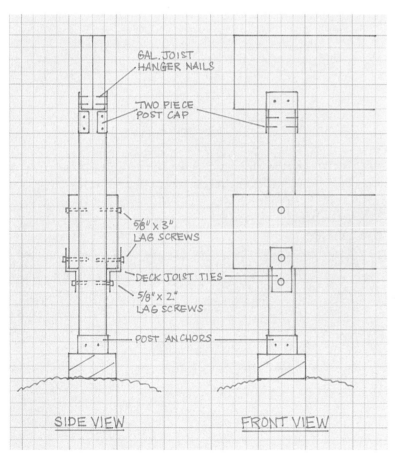

Draw detailed illustrations of the joinery methods you plan to use on all structural members of your deck. Your building official will want to see details on post-footing connections, post-beam joints, beam-joist joints, and ledger connections.

PLAN-APPROVAL CHECKLIST:

When the building official reviews your deck plans, he or she will look for the following details. Make sure your plan drawings include this information when you visit the building inspection office to apply for a building permit.

• Overall size of the deck.

• Position of the deck relative to buildings and property lines. The deck must be set back at least 5 ft. from neighboring property.

• Location of all beams and posts.

• Size and on-center (OC) spacing of joists.

• Thickness of decking boards.

• Height of deck above the ground.

• Detailed drawings of joinery methods for all structural members of the deck.

• Type of soil that will support the concrete post footings: sand, gravel, or clay.

• Species of wood you will be using.

• Types of metal connectors and other hardware you plan to use when constructing your deck.

landscape features of the site.

As you refine your ideas about the deck, there are several factors to take into consideration. For instance, the deck must be sturdy enough to easily support the heaviest anticipated load. This not only includes the substantial weight of the surface decking and railings, but also the weight of people, deck furnishings, and, in some climates, snow. Because different species of wood have different strengths, you must choose accordingly.

The design of the deck as well as the size and spacing of its structural members—posts, beams, joists—also help determine what lumber to choose.

Here are a few other things to consider as you prepare the design for your deck:

- The span limit of a board is the safe distance it can cross without support from underneath. The maximum safe span depends on the size and wood species of the board.

- Footing diameter and depth is determined by your building official, based on the estimated load of the deck and on the composition of your soil. In regions with cold winters, footings must extend below the frost line. Minimum diameter for concrete footings is 8".

- Beams may overhang posts by no more than 1 ft. Some local building regulations require that, wherever possible, beams should rest on top of posts, secured with metal post-beam caps.

- Engineered beams, such as a laminated wood product or steel girder, should be used on decks with very long joist spans, where standard-dimension lumber is not adequate for the load.

- Railings are required for any deck more than 24" above the ground; railings must be at least 36" in height, and the bottom rail must be positioned so there is no more than 6" of open space below it. Vertical balusters can have no more than 4" between them.

Once you have completed the plans for your deck, return to the building inspections office and have the official review them. If your plans meet code, you will be issued a building permit, usually for a small fee. Regulations may require that a field inspector review the deck at specified stages in the building process. If so, make sure to comply with the review schedule.

Metal flashings must be used to prevent moisture from penetrating between the ledger and the wall.

36" minimum

4" maximum

34" to 38"

4" to 8"

At least 9"

Stairs must be at least 36" wide. Vertical step risers must be between 4" and 8" apart, and treads must have a horizontal run of at least 9". A single staircase can have no more than 12 steps; for longer runs, two staircases are required, separated by a landing. Stair railings should be 34" to 38" above the noses of the step treads, and there should be no more than 6" of space between the bottom rail and the steps. The space between the rails or balusters should be no more than 4".

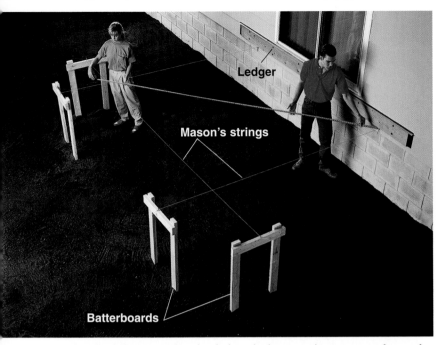

A. *Install a ledger to anchor the deck to the house and to serve as reference for laying out footings (pages 212 to 214). Use batterboards and mason's strings to locate footings, and check for square by measuring diagonals (pages 215 to 217).*

Basic Deck Building Techniques:

Step-by-Step Overview

You will find it helpful to review the directions on pages 212 to 241 before beginning deck construction. It is a good idea to build the deck in several stages, and gather tools and materials for each stage before beginning. Also, arrange to have at least one helper for the more difficult stages.

Next, check with local utilities for the location of underground electrical, telephone, or water lines. Then, apply for a building permit, where required, and make sure a building inspector has approved the deck design before beginning work.

The time it takes to build a deck depends on the size and complexity of the design. A rectangular deck, about 10 ft. × 14 ft., for instance, can be completed in two or three weekends.

B. *Pour concrete post footings (pages 218 to 219), and install metal post anchors (page 220). Set and brace the posts, attach them to the post anchors, and mark posts to show where beam will be attached (page 221).*

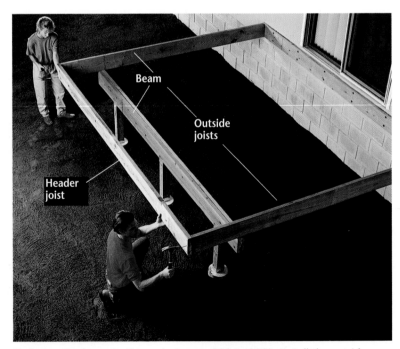

C. *Fasten the beam to the posts (pages 222 to 225). Install the outside joists and header joist, using galvanized nails (pages 226 to 227).*

D. Install metal joist hangers on the ledger and header joist, then hang the remaining joists (*pages 226 to 227*). Most decking patterns require joists that are spaced 16" on center.

E. Lay decking boards, and trim them with a circular saw. If desired for appearance, cover pressure-treated header and outside joists with redwood or cedar facing boards (*pages 228 to 229*).

F. Build deck stairs (*pages 234 to 237*). Stairs provide access to the deck and establish traffic patterns.

G. Install a railing around the deck and stairway (*pages 238 to 241*). A railing adds a decorative touch and may be required on any deck that is more than 24" above the ground.

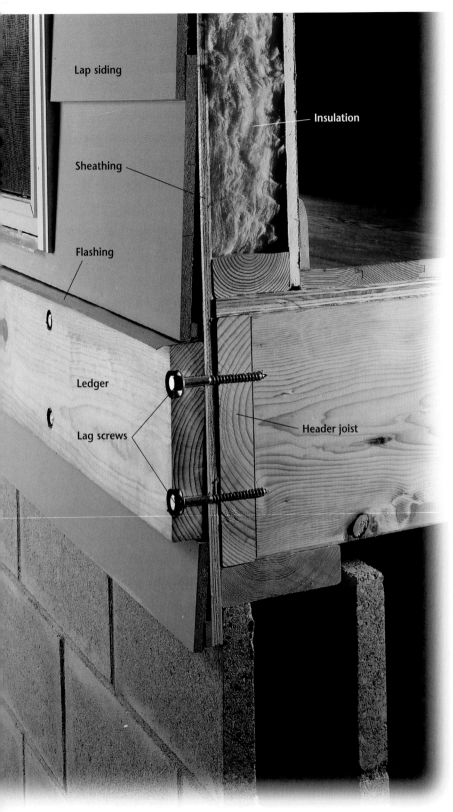

Lap siding

Insulation

Sheathing

Flashing

Ledger

Lag screws

Header joist

Attaching a Ledger

The first step in building an attached deck is to fasten the ledger to the house. The ledger anchors the deck and establishes a reference point for building the deck square and level. The ledger also supports one end of all the deck joists, so it must be attached securely to the framing members of the house.

Install the ledger so that the surface of the decking boards is 1" below the indoor floor level. This height difference prevents rainwater or melted snow from seeping into the house.

If your deck sits very close to the ground, it may be necessary to anchor the ledger to the foundation.

TOOLS & MATERIALS

- Pencil
- Level
- Circular saw with carbide blade
- Chisel
- Hammer
- Metal snips
- Caulk gun

- Drill and bits (¼" twist, 1" spade, ⅜" and ⅝" masonry)
- Ratchet wrench
- Awl
- Rubber mallet
- Pressure-treated lumber
- Galvanized flashing

- 8d galvanized common nails
- Silicone caulk
- ⅜ x 4" lag screws and 1" washers
- Lead masonry anchors for ⅜" lag screws (for brick walls)
- 2 x 4s for braces

A. *Set the circular saw blade depth to the same thickness as the siding, and cut out the siding along the outline.*

HOW TO ATTACH A LEDGER TO LAP SIDING

Step A: Outline the Ledger & Cut the Siding

1. Draw an outline showing where the deck will fit against the house, using a level as a guide. Include the thickness of the outside joists and any decorative facing boards that will be installed.

2. Cut out the siding along the outline, using a circular saw. Set the blade depth to the same thickness as the siding, so that the blade does not cut into the sheathing.

3. Use a chisel to finish the cutout where the circular saw blade does not reach. Hold the chisel with the bevel-side in.

Step B: Tack the Ledger in Position

1. Measure and cut the ledger from pressure-treated lumber. Remember that the ledger will be shorter than the overall length of the cutout.

2. Cut galvanized flashing to the length of the cutout, using metal snips. Slide the flashing up under the siding.

3. Center the ledger in the cutout, underneath the flashing.

4. Brace it in position, and then tack the ledger into place with 8d galvanized nails.

5. Apply a thick bead of silicone caulk to the crack between the siding and the flashing.

TIP: VINYL & ALUMINUM

You can treat vinyl and aluminum siding the same when it comes to cutting into it for installing a ledger. Mark the layout as you would for lap siding, using a permanent marker. Then, make the initial cut with a utility knife and straightedge. Follow the pattern you've drawn and finish the cutting with aviation snips for vinyl or tin snips for aluminum.

Step C: Secure the Ledger to the House Header Joist

1. Drill pairs of ¼" pilot holes spaced every 2 ft., through the ledger and sheathing and into the header joist. Counterbore each pilot hole to ½" depth, using a 1" spade bit.

2. Attach the ledger to the wall with ⅜ × 4" lag screws and washers, using a ratchet wrench.

3. Seal the lag screw heads with silicone caulk. Seal the crack between the wall and the sides and bottom of the ledger.

B. *Center the ledger in the cutout, brace in position, and tack into place with 8d galvanized nails.*

C. *Attach the ledger to the wall with ⅜ × 4" lag screws and washers, using a ratchet wrench.*

A. *Drive lead masonry anchors for lag screws into drilled holes, using a rubber mallet.*

B. *Seal the cracks between the wall and ledger with silicone caulk. Also seal the lag screw heads.*

HOW TO ATTACH A LEDGER TO MASONRY
Step A: Mark the Ledger Position & Install Masonry Anchors

1. Measure and cut the ledger. The ledger will be shorter than the overall length of the outline.

2. Drill pairs of ¼" pilot holes every 2 ft. in the ledger. Counterbore each pilot hole to ½" depth, using 1" spade bit.

3. Draw an outline of the deck on the wall, using a level as a guide. Center the ledger in the outline on the wall, and brace it in position.

4. Mark the pilot hole locations on the wall, using an awl or nail. Remove the ledger.

5. Drill anchor holes 3" deep into the masonry, using a ⅝" masonry bit. Drive lead masonry anchors for ⅜" lag screws into the drilled holes, using a rubber mallet.

Step B: Attach the Ledger

1. Attach the ledger to the wall with ⅜ × 4" lag screws and washers, using a ratchet wrench. Tighten the screws firmly, but do not overtighten.

2. Seal the cracks between the wall and the ledger with silicone caulk. Also seal the lag screw heads.

HOW TO ATTACH A LEDGER TO STUCCO
Step A: Mark the Ledger Position

1. Draw the outline of the deck on the wall, using a level as a guide.

2. Measure and cut the ledger, and drill pilot holes (as with masonry, above).

3. Brace the ledger against the wall, and mark the hole locations, using a nail or awl.

Step B: Drill Pilot Holes & Attach the Ledger

1. Remove the ledger. Drill pilot holes through the stucco layer of the wall, using a ⅜" masonry bit.

2. Extend each pilot hole through the sheathing and into the header joist, using a ¼" bit. Reposition the ledger and brace it in place.

3. Attach the ledger to wall with ⅜ × 4" lag screws and washers, using a ratchet wrench.

4. Seal the lag screw heads and the cracks between the wall and the ledger with silicone caulk.

A. *With the ledger braced against the wall inside the outline, mark the lag screw hole locations, using a nail or an awl.*

B. *Attach the ledger to the wall with lag screws and washers, using a ratchet wrench.*

Locating Post Footings

You will need to establish the exact locations of all concrete footings by stretching mason's strings across the site. Use the ledger board as a starting point. These perpendicular layout strings will be used to locate holes for concrete footings, and to position metal post anchors on the finished footings. You can anchor the layout strings with temporary 2 × 4 supports, often called batterboards.

HOW TO LOCATE POST FOOTINGS

Step A: Build Batterboards

1. Cut 2 × 4 stakes for batterboards, each about 8" longer than the post height. Trim one end of each stake to a point, using a circular saw.

2. Cut 2 × 4 cross pieces, each about 2 ft. long.

3. Assemble the batterboards by attaching the crosspieces to the stakes with 2½" deck screws. The crosspieces should be about 2" below tops of the stakes.

TOOLS & MATERIALS

- Tape measure
- Felt-tipped pen
- Circular saw
- Screwgun
- Framing square
- Masonry hammer
- Hammer

- Line level
- Plumb bob
- 2 × 4s
- 10d nails
- 2½" deck screws
- Mason's strings
- Masking tape

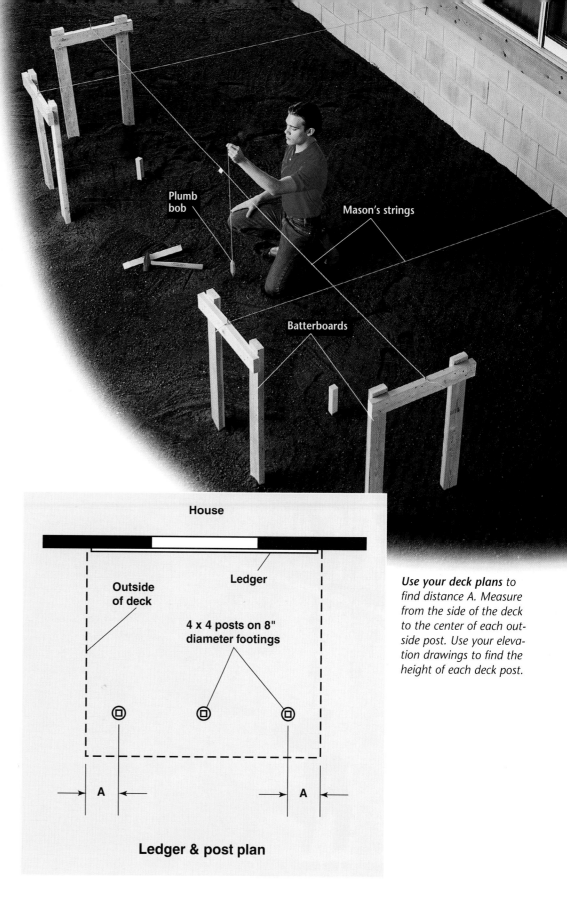

Plumb bob

Mason's strings

Batterboards

House

Outside of deck

Ledger

4 x 4 posts on 8" diameter footings

A   A

Ledger & post plan

Use your deck plans to find distance A. Measure from the side of the deck to the center of each outside post. Use your elevation drawings to find the height of each deck post.

A. *Assemble batterboards by attaching crosspieces to stakes with deck screws.*

Step B: Find Rough Post Location

1. Use your deck plans to find the distance from the outermost edge of the deck to the center point of the post footing.

2. On the ledger, measure in from each end and mark reference points. When measuring, remember to allow for the outside joists and facing that will butt to the ends of the ledger.

3. Drive a batterboard 6" into the ground, about 2 ft. past the post location. The crosspiece of the batterboard should be parallel to the ledger.

4. Drive a 10d nail into the bottom of the ledger at the reference point, and attach mason's string to the nail.

5. Extend the mason's string so that it is taut and perpendicular to the ledger, and secure it temporarily by wrapping it several times around the batterboard. Use a framing square as a guide.

Step C: Square the Mason's String to the Ledger

1. Check the mason's string for square using the "3-4-5 carpenter's triangle." Here's how it works. First, measure along the ledger 3 ft. from the mason's string and mark a point, using a felt-tipped pen.

2. Measure the mason's string 4 ft. from the edge of the ledger. Mark it with masking tape.

3. Measure the distance between the marks. If the string is perpendicular to the ledger, the distance will be exactly 5 ft. If

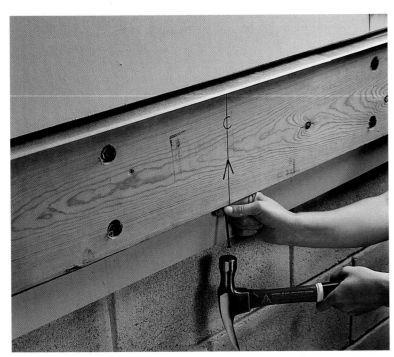

B. *Drive a 10d nail into the bottom of the ledger at the reference point and attach a mason's string to it.*

C. *Check the mason's string for square using the "3-4-5 carpenter's triangle": measure the distance between the marks. If the string is perpendicular to the ledger, the distance will be exactly 5 ft. Adjust if necessary.*

necessary, move the string left or right on the batterboard until distance between the marks is 5 ft. When it is, your "triangle" should be perfect.

4. Drive a 10d nail into the top of the batterboard at the string location. Leave about 2" of nail exposed. Tie the string to the nail.

5. Hang a line level on the mason's string. Raise or lower the string until it's level.

6. Locate the other outside post footing, repeating steps A to C.

Step D: Find Post Locations on Mason's Strings

1. Measure along the mason's strings from the ledger to find the centerpoints of the posts. Mark the centerpoints on the strings using masking tape.

2. Drive additional batterboards into the ground, about 2 ft. outside the mason's strings, and lined up with the post centerpoint marks.

3. Align a third cross string with the centerpoint marks on the first strings. Drive 10d nails in the new batterboards, and tie off the cross string on the nails. The cross string should be close to, but not touching, the first strings.

4. Check the strings for square by measuring distances A-B and C-D. Measure diagonals A-D and B-C from the edge of the ledger to the opposite corners. If the strings are square, the measurement A-B will be the same as C-D, and the diagonal A-D will be the same as B-C. If necessary, adjust the strings on the batterboards until they are square.

Step E: Transfer Footing Locations to the Ground

1. Measure along the cross string and mark the centerpoints of any posts that will be installed between the outside posts.

2. Use a plumb bob to mark the post centerpoints on the ground, directly under the marks on the mason's strings. Drive a stake into the ground at each point. Remove the mason's strings before digging the footings.

D. *Check strings for square. The outline is square when measurements A-B and C-D are the same, and diagonal A-D is the same as B-C. If necessary, adjust strings on batterboards until square.*

E. *Drop a plumb bob from each piece of tape on the mason's string, and mark the ground with a stake at that point to mark the exact centerpoint of the footings.*

Digging & Pouring Footings

Concrete footings hold deck posts in place and support the weight of the deck. Check local codes to determine the size and depth of footings required for your area. In cold climates, for example, footings must be deeper than the soil frost line.

To help protect posts from water damage, each footing should be poured so that it is 2" above ground level. Tube-shaped forms let you extend the footings above ground level.

It is easy and inexpensive to mix your own concrete by combining portland cement, sand, gravel, and water. See pages 16 to 17 for more information on buying concrete, and page 44 for mixing concrete.

Before digging, consult local utilities for the location of any underground electrical, telephone, or water lines that might interfere with footings.

HOW TO DIG & POUR POST FOOTINGS

Step A: Dig the Footings

1. Dig holes for post footings with a clamshell digger or power

TOOLS & MATERIALS

- Power auger or clamshell posthole digger
- Tape measure
- Pruning saw
- Shovel
- Reciprocating saw or handsaw
- Torpedo level
- Hoe
- Trowel
- Shovel
- Old toothbrush
- Plumb bob
- Utility knife
- 8" concrete tube forms
- Portland cement
- Sand
- Gravel
- J-bolts
- Wheelbarrow
- Scrap 2 × 4

auger. Center the holes on the layout stakes. For holes deeper than 35", use a power auger.

2. Measure the hole depth. Local building codes specify the depth of footings. Cut away tree roots, if necessary, using a pruning saw.

3. Pour 2" to 3" of loose gravel in the bottom of each footing hole to provide drainage under the concrete footings.

4. Add 2" to the hole depth (so footings will be above ground level) and cut concrete tube forms to length, using a reciprocating saw or handsaw. Make sure the cut is straight.

5. Insert the tubes into the footing holes, leaving

A. Insert the tube forms into footing holes, leaving about 2" of tube above ground level.

about 2" of tube above ground level. Use a level to make sure the tops of the tubes are level.

6. Pack soil around the tubes to hold them in place.

Step B: Mix & Pour the Concrete

1. Mix dry ingredients for concrete in a wheelbarrow, using a hoe.

2. Form a hollow in the center of the dry concrete mixture. Slowly pour a small amount of water into the hollow. Blend in the dry mixture with a hoe. Add more water gradually, mixing thoroughly until concrete is firm enough to hold its shape when sliced with a trowel.

3. Pour concrete slowly into the tube form. Guide it from the wheelbarrow with a shovel. Use a long stick to tamp the concrete, filling any air gaps in the footing.

4. Level the concrete by pulling a 2 × 4 across the top of the tube form, using a sawing motion. Add concrete to any low spots.

5. Retie the mason's strings on the batterboards, and recheck the measurements.

Step C: Insert the J-bolt into the Concrete

Insert a J-bolt at an angle into the wet concrete at the center of the footing. Lower the J-bolt slowly, wiggling it slightly to eliminate any air gaps.

TIP: PREMIXED CONCRETE

Buy premixed bags of dry concrete for small jobs. A 60-lb. bag creates about ½ cubic foot of concrete, and a 90-lb. bag creates about ⅔ cubic foot.

Step D: Position the J-bolt

1. Set the J-bolt so ¾" to 1" is exposed above the concrete. Brush away any wet concrete on the bolt threads with an old toothbrush.

2. Use a plumb bob to make sure the J-bolt is positioned exactly at the center of the post location.

3. Use a torpedo level to make sure the J-bolt is plumb. If necessary, adjust the bolt and repack the concrete. Let the concrete cure, and then cut away the exposed portion of the tube with a utility knife.

B. *Fill the tube forms with concrete. Use a long stick to tamp the concrete, filling any air gaps.*

C. *Insert a J-bolt at an angle into the wet concrete at the center of the footing.*

D. *Use a torpedo level to make sure the J-bolt is plumb. If necessary, adjust the bolt and repack the concrete.*

Setting Posts

Posts support the deck beams and transfer the weight of the deck to the concrete footings. For maximum strength, the posts must be plumb.

To prevent rot or insect damage, use pressure-treated lumber for posts, and make sure the factory-treated end faces down.

Metal post anchors are used to attach the posts to the concrete footings. They have drainage holes and pedestals that raise the ends of the wood posts above the concrete footings. Follow the manufacturer's specifications to determine specific nail size.

TOOLS & MATERIALS

- Pencil
- Framing square
- Ratchet wrench
- Tape measure
- Miter saw or circular saw
- Hammer
- Screwgun
- Level
- Combination square
- Metal post anchors
- Nuts for J-bolts
- Lumber for posts
- 10d or 16d joist hanger nails
- 2" deck screws
- Long, straight 2 × 4; 1 × 4s; pointed 2 × 2 stakes.

HOW TO SET POSTS

Step A: Install Post Anchors

1. Lay a long, straight 2 × 4 flat across two or three concrete footings, parallel to the ledger, with one edge tight against the J-bolts. Draw a reference line across each concrete footing, using the edge of the 2 × 4 as a guide. Remove the 2 × 4.

2. Place a metal post anchor on each concrete footing, and center it over the J-bolt. Use a framing square to make sure the post anchor is positioned square to the reference line drawn on the footing.

3. Thread a nut over each J-bolt, and tighten it securely with a ratchet wrench.

Step B: Set the Posts

1. Use the elevation drawing from your deck plans to find the height of each post. Add 6" for a cutting margin, then cut the posts with a miter saw or circular saw. Make sure factory-treated ends of posts are square. If necessary, trim with a miter saw or

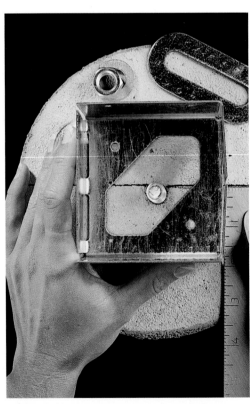

A. Use a framing square to make sure the post anchor is positioned square to the reference line drawn on the footing.

B. Place each post in an anchor, and tack into place with a single 10d joist hanger nail.

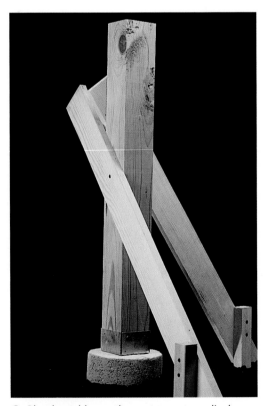

C. Plumb and brace the post on perpendicular sides.

circular saw to square the ends.

2. Place the metal pedestal into the anchor. Set the post in the anchor, on top of the pedestal. Tack into place with a single 10d or 16d joist hanger nail.

Step C: Brace the Posts

1. To brace the posts, place a 1 × 4 flat across the post, so that it crosses the post at a 45° angle about halfway up. Attach the brace to the post temporarily with a single 2" deck screw.

2. Drive a pointed 2 × 2 stake into the ground next to the end of the brace. Use a level to make sure the post is plumb, adjusting the post, as necessary. Attach the brace to the stake with two 2" deck screws, then plumb and brace the post on the side perpendicular to the first brace using the same methods.

4. Attach the post to the post anchor with the manufacturer's specified nail size, typically 10d or 16d joist hanger nails.

Step D: Mark the Joist Positions

1. Position a straight 2 × 4 with one end on the ledger and the other end across the face of the post. Level it, then lower the end at the post ¼" for every 3 ft. between the ledger and the post (for water runoff).

2. Draw a line on the post along the bottom of the 2 × 4 to indicate the top of the joists.

Step E: Mark the Beam Locations

1. From the line indicating the tops of the joists, measure down and mark on the posts a distance equal to the width of the joists. This line is the top of the beam.

2. If you are installing a sandwich-type beam (pages 224 to 225), use a combination square to draw a line completely around the post. This line will indicate the top of the beam.

If installing a saddle-type beam (pages 222 to 223) or notched-post-type beam (pages 223 to 224), repeat #1 and #2 to determine the bottom of the beam, and mark around the entire post using a combination square.

D. *Position a straight 2 × 4 with one end on the ledger and the other end across the face of the post. Create a slope for water runoff, then draw a reference line on the post to indicate the top of the joists.*

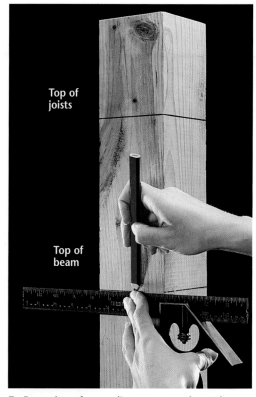

Top of joists

Top of beam

E. *From the reference line, measure down the post and mark the top of the beam.*

Installing Beams

Deck beams attach to the posts to help support the weight of the joists and decking. There are three different ways to attach them. The installation method you choose depends on the deck design and local codes, so check with a building inspector to determine what is acceptable in your area.

In a saddle-type beam construction, the beam is attached directly on top of the posts. Metal fasteners, called post-beam caps, are used to align and strengthen the beam-to-post connection.

A notched-post deck requires 6 × 6 posts notched at the post top to accommodate the full size of the beam. The deck's weight bears directly on the posts, as in the saddle type.

A sandwich-type beam has two beam members that "sandwich" the posts. Because this method has less strength than a saddle beam design, some local codes may restrict its use, or may require that the beam members be reinforced with joist ties (see Step B, page 224).

TOOLS & MATERIALS

- Tape measure
- Pencil
- Circular saw
- Paint brush
- Combination square
- Screwgun
- Drill
- ⅜" auger bit
- 1" spade bit
- Ratchet wrench
- Caulk gun
- Reciprocating saw or handsaw
- Pressure-treated lumber
- Clear sealer-preservative
- 2½" galvanized deck screws
- 10d joist hanger nails
- ⅜ × 8" carriage bolts with washers and nuts
- ⅜ × 2" lag screws
- Silicone caulk

HOW TO INSTALL A SADDLE BEAM
Step A: Prepare Beam Members
1. Measure and mark two straight, pressure-treated boards to length. Cut the boards with a circular saw, and seal the cut ends with a clear sealer-preservative.

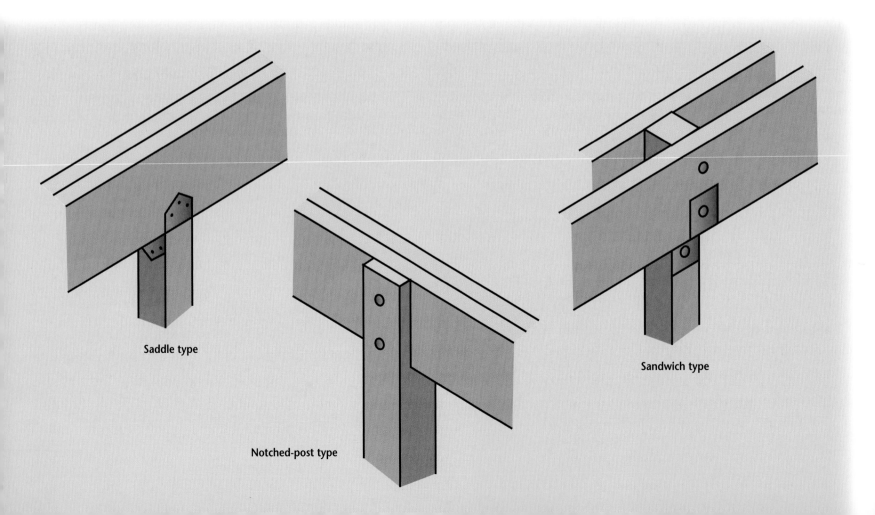

Saddle type

Notched-post type

Sandwich type

2. Fasten the boards together with 2½" galvanized deck screws, to form the beam.

3. Measure and mark the post locations on the tops and sides of the beam, using a combination square as a guide.

Step B: Prepare the Post

1. Cut each post at the line indicating the bottom of the beam (page 221), using a reciprocating saw.

2. Attach post-beam caps to the top of the posts, using 10d joist hanger nails.

Step C: Attach the Beam

1. With someone's help, lift the beam into the post-beam caps. Make sure the crown side is up.

2. Align the post location marks with the post-beam caps. Fasten the post-beam cap to the beam on both sides, using 10d joist hanger nails.

HOW TO INSTALL A NOTCHED-POST BEAM
Step A: Prepare the Beams & Posts

1. Measure and mark two straight, pressure-treated boards to length. Cut the boards with a circular saw, and seal the cut ends with a clear sealer-preservative.

2. Fasten the boards together with 2½" galvanized deck screws, to form the beam.

A. *Mark the post locations on the tops and sides of the beam boards, using a combination square.*

B. *Attach post-beam caps to the top of posts, using joist hanger nails.*

C. *With someone's help, lift the beam into the post-beam caps, and align the post location marks with the edges of the caps.*

A. *Use a circular saw to rough-cut the notches, then a reciprocating saw or handsaw to finish.*

B. *Drill counterbored pilot holes through the beam and the post, then secure with carriage bolts.*

3. Measure and mark the post locations on the tops and sides of the beam, using a combination square as a guide.

4. Remove the 6 × 6 posts from the post anchors and cut them at the finished height.

5. Measure and mark a 3 × 7½" notch at the top of each post. Trace the lines on all sides, using a framing square.

6. Use a circular saw to rough-cut the notches, then a reciprocating saw or handsaw to finish.

Step B: Install the Beam

1. Reattach the posts to the post anchors (pages 220 to 221), with the notch-side facing away from the deck.

2. With someone's help, lift the beam (crown side up) into the notches. Align the beam and clamp to the posts.

3. Counterbore two ½"-deep holes, using a 1" spade bit, then drill ⅜" pilot holes through the beam and post, using a ⅜" auger bit.

4. Insert carriage bolts into each pilot hole. Add a washer and nut to the counterbore-side of each, and tighten using a ratchet. Seal both ends with silicone caulk.

HOW TO INSTALL A SANDWICH BEAM

Step A: Prepare & Attach the Beam Members

1. Measure and mark two straight, pressure-treated boards to length. Cut the boards with a circular saw. Seal the cut ends with a clear sealer-preservative.

2. Hold the beam members together. Measure and mark the post locations on the tops and sides of the boards, using a combination square as a guide.

3. With the crown side up, place one beam member against the inner side of the posts. Align the post location marks on the beam member with the beam height marks on the posts. Tack in position with 2½" deck screws.

4. Repeat for the second beam member on the outer side of the posts.

Step B: Fasten the Beam Members to the Post

1. On the inner beam member, counterbore two holes ½" deep, using a 1" spade bit.

2. At the center of the counterbore holes, drill ⅜" pilot holes through the entire beam-post-beam assembly, using a ⅜" auger bit.

3. Thread a ⅜ × 8" carriage bolt through each pilot hole, with a washer and nut on the inner side with the counterbore. Tighten with a ratchet wrench until the nut is snug and recessed in the counterbore hole. NOTE: Beam members can be reinforced with joist ties (inset).

4. Seal around the nuts in the counterbore holes with silicone caulk.

Step C: Finish the Beam Construction

1. Cut the tops of posts flush with the top edge of the beam, using a reciprocating saw or handsaw.

2. Seal the cut ends of the posts with clear sealer-preservative.

A. *Place the beam members against the side of the posts, aligned with the beam height marks, and tack in position with deck screws.*

B. *Thread a carriage bolt through each pilot hole, with a washer and nut on the counterbored side. INSET: Beam members can be reinforced with joist ties.*

C. *Cut the tops of the posts flush with the top edge of the beam, and seal the cut ends with clear sealer-preservative.*

VARIATION: ANGLE BRACES

Reinforce elevated decks with beveled 4 × 4 angle braces. For a solid beam (left), attach with lag screws to the sides of the post and the bottom of the beam. For a sandwich beam (right), use carriage bolts to mount the braces in between the two beam members.

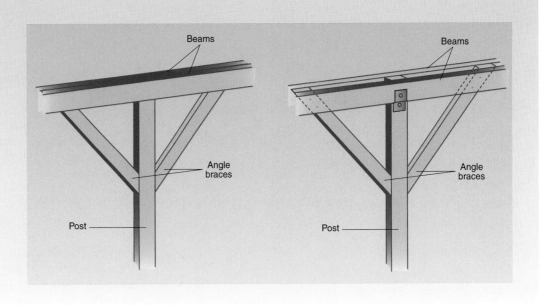

Hanging Joists

Joists provide support for the decking boards. They are attached to the ledger and header joist with galvanized metal joist hangers, and are nailed to the top of the beam.

For strength and durability, it is best to use pressure-treated lumber for all joists. The exposed outside joists and header joist can be faced with redwood or cedar boards for a more attractive appearance (page 229).

The decking pattern determines the spacing and layout of the joists. For example, a normal, straight decking pattern requires joists that are spaced 16" on-center. A diagonal decking pattern requires that the joist spacing be 12" on-center. Parquet patterns and some other designs may require extra support, like double joists or extra blocking.

HOW TO HANG JOISTS

Step A: Build the Joist Frame

1. Use your deck plans to find the length of the outside joists and the header joist.

2. Measure and mark lumber for the outside joists, using a combination square as a guide, then cut them with a circular saw. Seal the cut ends with a clear sealer-preservative.

3. Drill three ⅟₁₆" pilot holes, spaced about 3" apart, through one end of each outside joist.

4. Fasten the outside joists in position at the ends of the ledger, using 16d galvanized common nails.

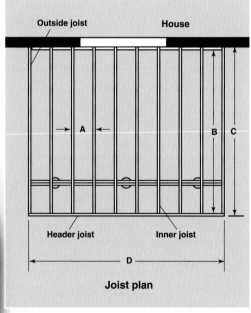

Use your design plan to find the spacing (A) between joists, and the length of inner joists (B), outside joists (C), and header joist (D). Measure and mark lumber for outside joists, using a combination square as a guide. Cut joists with a circular saw. Seal cut ends with clear sealer-preservative.

5. Attach the outside joists to the top of the beam by toenailing them with 16d galvanized common nails.

6. Measure and cut the header joist. Seal the cut ends with a clear sealer-preservative.

7. Drill 1/16" pilot holes at each end of the header joist. Attach the header joist to the ends of the outside joists with 16d galvanized common nails.

8. Strengthen each inside corner of the deck frame with an angle bracket. Attach the brackets with 10d joist hanger nails nails.

Step B: Mark the Joist Locations

1. Measure along the ledger from the edge of the outside joist, and mark where the joists will be attached to the ledger.

2. Draw the outline of each joist on the ledger, using a combination square as a guide.

3. Measure along the beam from the outside joist, and mark where joists will cross the beam. Draw the outlines across the top of both beam members.

4. Measure along the header joist from the outside joist, and mark where joists will be attached to the header joist. Draw the outlines on the inside of the header, using a combination square as a guide.

Step C: Attach the Joist Hangers

1. Position each hanger so that one of the flanges is against the joist outline, and then nail the flanges to the framing member with 10d or 16d galvanized common nails.

2. Cut a scrap board to use as a spacer. Hold the spacer inside each joist hanger, then close the hanger around the spacer.

3. Nail the remaining side flange to the framing member with 10d or 16d galvanized common nails. Remove the spacer.

Step D: Install the Joists

1. Measure and mark the lumber for the joists, using a combination square as a guide. Cut the joists with a circular saw, then seal the cut ends with a clear sealer-preservative.

2. Place the joists in the joist hangers with the crown side up. At the ledger, attach the joists to the joist hangers with 10d joist hanger nails. Drive nails into both sides of each joist.

3. Align the joists with the outlines drawn on the top of the beam. Anchor the joists to the beam by toenailing from both sides with 10d galvanized common nails.

4. Attach the joists to the header joist hangers with 10d joist hanger nails. Drive nails into both sides of each joist.

A. *Install the outside joists, then measure and cut the header joist. Attach the header to the ends of the outside joists with 16d common nails.*

B. *Draw the outline of each joist on the ledger, using a combination square as a guide.*

C. *Use a scrap piece as a spacer and hold it inside each joist hanger, then close the hanger around the spacer and attach it to the ledger.*

D. *Seal the cut ends with clear sealer-preservative, and place the joists in hangers with the crown side up.*

Laying Decking

Buy decking boards that are long enough to span the width of the deck, if possible. If boards must be butted end-to-end, make sure to stagger the joints so they do not overlap from row to row. The best way to prevent screws or nails from splitting the wood is to predrill the ends of boards.

Install decking so that there is a ⅛" gap between boards to provide drainage. Because boards naturally "cup" as they age, lay the boards with the bark side facing down, so that the cupped surface cannot hold standing water.

If you don't begin building right away, store the lumber so that it says dry and warp-free. Use supports to keep the wood stack

a few inches off the ground. Use spacer blocks to support each row, and to allow air circulation between boards. Cover the lumber stack with heavy plastic or a waterproof tarp.

HOW TO LAY DECKING
Step A: Position the First Decking Board
   1. Using the dimensions from your deck plans, choose a deck-

TOOLS & MATERIALS

- Tape measure
- Circular saw
- Screwgun
- Hammer

- Drill
- ⅛" twist bit
- Pry bar
- Chalk line
- Jig saw or handsaw
- Decking boards

- 2½" corrosion-resistant deck screws
- 8d & 10d galvanized common nails
- Redwood or cedar facing boards

A. Position the first row of decking flush against the house. Attach with pairs of deck screws into each joist.

ing board for the first row that is perfectly straight and cut it to length, using a circular saw.

2. Position the first row of decking flush against the house. Attach it by driving a pair of 2½" corrosion-resistant deck screws into each joist.

Step B: Position & Install the Remaining Decking

1. Position the remaining decking boards so that their ends overhang the outside joists. Space boards about ⅛" apart. Attach boards to each joist with a pair of 2½" deck screws driven into each joist.

2. Drill ⅛" pilot holes in the ends of boards before attaching them to the outside joists. Pilot holes prevent screws from splitting decking boards at the end.

3. After every few rows of decking are installed, measure from the edge of the decking board to the edge of the header joist. If measurements show that the last board will not fit flush against

the edge of the deck, adjust the board spacing.

4. Adjust the board spacing by changing the gaps between the boards by a small amount over three or four rows of boards. Very small spacing changes will not be obvious to the eye.

Step C: Trim the Ends

1. Use a chalk line to mark the edge of the decking flush with the outside of the deck.

2. Cut off the decking, using a circular saw. Set the saw blade ⅛" deeper than the thickness of the decking so that the saw will not cut the side of the deck.

3. At areas where the circular saw cannot reach, finish the cut-off with a jig saw or handsaw.

Step D: Attach the Facing

For a more attractive appearance, face the deck with redwood or cedar facing boards. Miter-cut corners, and attach boards with deck screws or 8d galvanized nails.

B. *Position the remaining decking boards so that the ends overhang the outside joists. Space boards about ⅛" apart and fasten in place.*

C. *Cut off the long ends of the decking flush with the side of the deck, using a circular saw.*

D. *Face the deck with redwood or cedar facing boards. Miter-cut corners, and attach boards with deck screws or galvanized nails.*

Alternative Decking Materials

Composite materials

Composite materials

PVC vinyl

Fiberglass reinforced plastic (FRP)

The variety of decking materials on the market today offers some good lower-maintenance alternatives to wood. Although these materials may initially be somewhat more expensive than wood, they often carry lifetime warranties and can be much cheaper over the long run.

- Composite materials blend together wood fibers and recycled plastics to create a rigid product that, unlike wood, will not rot, splinter, warp, or crack. Painting or staining is unnecessary. Like wood, these deck boards can be cut to size, using a circular saw with a large-tooth blade.

  Plastic/wood composites are available in colors that complement any wood tone. The decking is installed with screws driven through the top of the deck boards into the joists, in the same way as with standard lumber. Other composites use a tongue-and-groove system for fastening deck boards to the joists. This blind-screw method leaves no visible holes in the deck floor.

- PVC vinyl and plastic decking materials are typically shipped in kits that contain everything necessary, except deck screws, to install the decking. The kits are pre-ordered to size, usually in multiples of the combined width of a deck board and the fasteners. The drawback of PVC vinyl decking is that it expands and contracts with freeze/thaw cycles.

  PVC vinyl and plastic deck materials also use a blind-screw method. A T-clip system simplifies installation and creates a uniform decking pattern.

- Fiberglass-reinforced plastic (FRP) decking will last a lifetime. Many of the manufacturers claim that the material is three times as strong as wood and not affected by heat, sunlight, or severe weather. The decking is pre-ordered to size but, if necessary, it can be cut using a circular saw with diamond-tip blade or masonry cut-off disc.

Fiberglass decking is installed with retaining clips, so each deck board snaps easily into place. The result is a sturdy structure that will last a lifetime.

• Aluminum decking systems are considerably more expensive than the other wood alternatives and are not widely available, but they offer sturdy, lightweight, and waterproof outdoor flooring. Simple designs using aluminum decking are very easy to install, although more elaborate designs and floor patterns can be quite difficult.

Most of these products are specifically designed with the do-it-yourselfer in mind. Though the installation methods and fastening systems vary from manufacturer to manufacturer, most of them are designed to accommodate the standard building dimensions, such as 16" joist spacing.

Prior to placing an order for any material, check with your local building department. Some areas may require a permit or have restrictions against certain materials. Also remember that these are general installation instructions. You should always follow the installation methods recommended by the manufacturer of the product you select.

HOW TO LAY COMPOSITE DECKING

Step A: Install First Rows

1. Lay composite decking as you would wood decking (pages 228 to 229). Position it with the factory crown up so water will run off, and space rows ⅛" to ¼" apart for drainage.

2. Predrill pilot holes at ¾ the diameter of the fasteners, but do not countersink them. Composite materials allow fasteners to set themselves. Use spiral shank nails, hot-dipped galvanized ceramic coated screws, or stainless nails or deck screws.

Step B: Install the Remaining Rows

Lay the remaining decking. If your deck plan calls for boards 16 ft. or shorter, leave a gap at deck ends and any butt joints, 1/16" for every 20°F difference between the temperature at the time of installation and the expected high temperature for the year.

A. *Lay composite decking as you would wood decking.*

B. *For boards 16 ft. or shorter, leave a gap at deck ends and any butt joints.*

HOW TO LAY TONGUE-AND-GROOVE DECKING

Step A: Install the Starter Strip

1. Position the starter strip at the far end of the deck. Make sure it is straight and properly aligned.

2. Attach the starter strip with 2½" galvanized deck screws driven into the lower runner found under the lip of the starter strip.

Step B: Lay the Decking

1. Fit the tongue of a deck board into the groove of the starter strip. There will be approximately a ¼" gap between the deck boards and the starter strip.

2. Fasten the deck boards to the joists with 2½" galvanized deck screws, working from the middle out to the sides of the deck.

3. Continue to add rows of decking. When you lay deck boards end-to-end, leave a ⅛" gap between them, and make sure any butt joints are centered over a joist.

Step C: Install Final Row of Decking

1. Place the final deck board in its position and attach it with 2½" galvanized deck screws driven through the top of the deck board into the joist. If necessary, rip the final board to size, and then support the board with a length of 1 × 1 and attach both to the joist.

2. For a neater appearance, attach facing boards to conceal the exposed ends of the deck boards.

A. *Position the starter strip at the far end of the deck, make sure it is straight, then fasten with deck screws.*

B. *Fit the tongue of a deck board into the groove of starter strip, and fasten. Work from the middle out to the sides of the deck.*

C. *Drive deck screws through the top of the final deck board into the joist, or into a length of 1 × 1 attached to the joist.*

HOW TO LAY DECKING WITH A T-CLIP SYSTEM

Step A: Attach T-clips to the Ledger

Insert 2" galvanized deck screws into the T-clips. Loosely attach one T-clip to the ledger at each joist location.

Step B: Install First Decking Board

1. Position a deck board tight against the T-clips.

2. Loosely attach T-clips against the bottom lip on the front side of the deck board, just tight enough to keep the board in place.

3. Be sure to fully tighten the T-clips at the back of the board, which is against the house.

Step C: Install Remaining Boards

1. Push another deck board tightly against the front T-clips, attach more T-clips at the front of the new board, and then fully tighten the previous set of T-clips.

2. Continue adding deck boards one by one, repeating the process to the end of the deck.

3. Cover the exposed deck board ends with facing boards. Miter cut the corners of the facing and drill pilot holes ¾ the diameter of the screws. Attach with 3" galvanized deck screws.

A. *Loosely attach one T-clip to the ledger at each joist location, using deck screws.*

B. *Loosely attach T-clips against the bottom lip on the front side of the deck board, then tighten at the back.*

C. *Install cedar facing to cover the exposed deck board ends, using deck screws.*

HOW TO LAY FIBERGLASS DECKING
Step A: Install the Retaining Clips

1. Place a length of retaining clips on top of the first joist. Center it on the joist and fasten with 2" galvanized deck screws.

2. Attach lengths of retaining clips to the subsequent joists. It's very important that the clips are perfectly aligned with the first length of clips, creating straight rows.

Step B: Install the Deck Boards

1. Place the open face of a decking board perpendicular to the joists, resting on top of the row of clips. Work along the row, applying firm pressure to the top of the deck board until the decking snaps into place over the retaining clips.

2. Attach the remaining deck boards in place, snapping each onto a row of retaining clips. The best method is to gently step on the deck board with one foot.

Step C: Finish the Deck

1. Cut the over-hanging ends of the decking boards flush with the outside joists, using a circular saw with a carbide-tipped blade or a masonry cut-off disc.

2. Use the self-drilling screws provided in the kit to attach the prefabricated facing, covering the exposed hollow ends and creating a decorative trim.

3. As a finishing touch, you will want to cover the screw heads with screw caps.

A. *Attach retaining clips so they are perfectly aligned across the joists, creating straight rows.*

B. *Place the decking boards across the top of a row of clips, then apply firm pressure until the decking snaps into place over the retaining clips.*

C. *Use the self-drilling screws provided in the kit to attach the facing. Cover screw heads with screw caps.*

Building Stairs

The goal of any stairway is to allow people to move easily and safely from one level to another.

Building deck stairs requires four calculations. The number of steps depends on the vertical drop of the deck. The vertical drop is the distance from the surface of the deck to the ground.

Rise is the vertical space between treads. Building codes require that the rise measurement be about 7".

Run is the depth of the treads. A convenient way to build deck stairs is to use a pair of 2 × 6s for each tread.

Span is figured by multiplying the run by the number of treads. The span lets you locate the end of the stairway, and position support posts.

If the deck is high off the ground, you may want to incorporate a landing, which is really just an oversized step. It provides a convenient spot from which to change the direction of the stairway, and a great spot to catch your breath momentarily while climbing.

Landings should be at least 36" square, or as wide as the staircase itself. And they very often require reinforcement with diagonal cross braces between the support posts. Designing and building a stairway with a landing can be one of the most challenging elements of a deck project. Precision is crucial, since building codes have very exact standards.

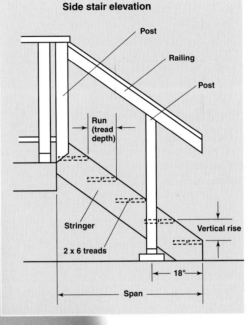

A common deck stairway is made from two 2 × 12 stringers, and a series of 2 × 6 treads attached with metal cleats. Posts set 18" back from the end of the stairway help to anchor the stringers and the railings. Calculations needed to build stairs include the number of steps, the rise of each step, the run of each step, and the stairway span.

TOOLS & MATERIALS

- Tape measure
- Pencil
- Framing square
- Level
- Plumb bob
- Clamshell posthole digger
- Wheelbarrow
- Hoe
- Circular saw
- Hammer
- Drill
- ⅛" twist bit
- 1" spade bit
- Ratchet wrench
- Caulk gun
- Sand
- Portland cement

- Gravel
- J-bolts
- Metal post anchors
- 4 × 4 posts
- 2 × 12 lumber
- Metal cleats
- ¼ × 1¼" lag screws
- Joist angle brackets
- 10d joist hanger nails
- ⅜" × 4" lag screws and 1" washers
- 2 × 6 lumber
- 16d galvanized common nails
- Silicone caulk
- Long, straight 2 × 4
- Pointed stakes
- Masking tape

HOW TO BUILD DECK STAIRS

Step A: Locate & Install the Posts

1. Use the stairway elevation drawings (page 234) to find measurements for your stair stringers and posts. Use a pencil and framing square to outline where the stair stringers will be attached to the side of the deck.

2. Locate the post footings so they are 18" back from the end of the stairway span. Lay a straight 2 × 4 on the deck so that it is level and square to the side of the deck.

3. Use a plumb bob to mark the ground at the centerpoints of the footings.

4. Dig holes and pour footings for posts (page 218 to 219). Attach metal post anchors to footings and install 4 × 4 posts (pages 220 to 221).

Step B: Lay Out the Stair Stringers

1. Use tape to mark the rise measurement on one leg of a framing square, and the run measurement on the other leg. Beginning at one end of the stringer,

A. *Locate the post footings 18" back from the end of the stairway span, using a straight 2 × 4 as a guide and a plumb bob to mark the ground at the centerpoints of the footings.*

HOW TO FIND MEASUREMENTS FOR A STAIRWAY LAYOUT		Sample Measurements (39" High Deck)
1. Find number of steps: Measure vertical drop from deck surface to ground. Divide by 7. Round off to nearest whole number.	Vertical drop:	39"
	÷ 7 =	5.57"
	Number of steps: =	= 6
2. Find step rise: Divide the vertical drop by the number of steps.	Vertical drop:	39"
	Number of steps: ÷	÷ 6
	Rise: =	= 6.5"
3. Find step run: Typical treads made from two 2 × 6s have a run of 11¼". If your design is different, find run by measuring depth of tread, including any space between boards.		
	Run:	11¼"
4. Find stairway span: Multiply the run by the number of treads. (Number of treads is always one less than number of steps.)	Run:	11¼"
	Number of treads: ×	× 5
	Span: =	= 56¼"

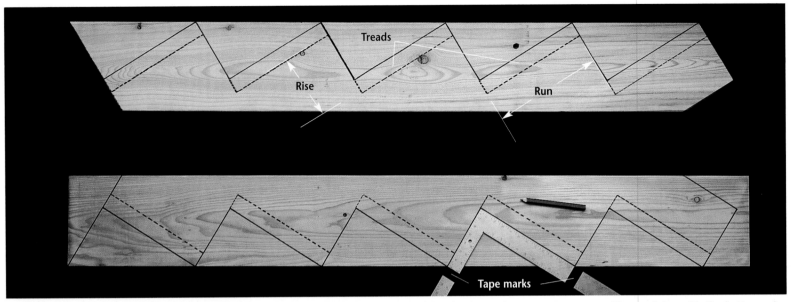

B. *To lay out the stair stringers, use a framing square with each leg marked with tape for the rise and run measurements. Align each leg with the bottom edge of the stringers, then draw in the tread outline against the bottom of each run line.*

C. *Attach angle brackets to the upper ends of stringers, using joist hanger nails. Brackets should be flush with the cut ends of the stringers.*

D. *Drill two counterbored pilot holes through each stringer and into each adjacent post, then fasten with lag screws and washers.*

position the square with the tape marks flush with the edge of the board, and outline the rise and run for each step.

2. Draw in the tread outline against the bottom of each run line. Use a circular saw to trim the ends of the stringers as shown.

Step C: Attach Tread Cleats & Angle Brackets

1. Attach metal tread cleats flush with the bottom of each tread outline, using ¼ × 1¼" lag screws. Drill ⅛" pilot holes to prevent the screws from splitting the wood.

2. Attach angle brackets to the upper ends of the stringers, using 10d joist hanger nails. Brackets should be flush with the cut ends of the stringers.

Step D: Attach the Stair Stringers to the Deck

1. Position the stair stringers against the side of the deck, over the stringer outlines. Align the top point of the stringer flush with the surface of the deck.

2. Attach the stringers by nailing the angle brackets to the deck with 10d joist hanger nails.

3. Drill two ¼" pilot holes through each stringer and into each adjacent post. Counterbore each hole to a depth of ½", using a 1" spade bit.

4. Attach stringers to posts with ⅜ × 4" lag screws and washers, using a ratchet wrench. Seal screw heads with silicone caulk.

Step E: Install the Step Treads

1. Measure the width of the stair treads. Cut two 2 × 6s for each tread, using a circular saw.

2. For each step, position the front 2 × 6 on the tread cleat, so that the front edge is flush with the tread outline on the stringers.

3. Drill ⅛" pilot holes, then attach the front 2 × 6s to the cleats with ¼ × 1¼" lag screws.

4. Position the rear 2 × 6s on the cleats, allowing a small space between boards. Use a 16d nail as a spacing guide. Drill ⅛" pilot holes, and attach 2 × 6s to cleats with ¼ × 1¼" lag screws.

E. *Drill pilot holes, then attach the front 2 × 6s to the cleats with lag screws.*

VARIATION: NOTCHED STRINGERS

Notched stringers precut from pressure-treated wood are available at building centers. Edges of cutout areas should be coated with sealer-preservative to prevent rot.

Notched stringers can also be custom cut from 2 × 10 or 2 × 12 lumber. Refer to pages 334 to 337 in the Porches section, and pages 438 to 439 in the Sheds & Outbuildings section for detailed techniques.

Installing Railings

Railings must be sturdy, and firmly attached to the framing members of the deck. Railing posts should never be attached to the surface decking. Most building codes require that railings be at least 36" above decking. Vertical balusters should be spaced no more than 4" apart. In some areas, a grippable handrail for any stairway over four treads may be required. Check with your local building inspector for the codes in your area.

To give your deck railing a customized look, you can install pre-fabricated railing inserts, which come in a variety of designs. Or, you can paint the railing to match or complement your house trim. Painted railings create an elegant contrast to the natural wood colors found in the decking boards and stair treads.

TOOLS & MATERIALS

- Tape measure
- Pencil
- Miter saw
- Drill
- Twist bits (¼", ⅛", ¹⁄₁₆")
- 1" spade bit
- Combination square
- Awl

- Ratchet wrench
- Caulk gun
- Level
- Reciprocating saw or circular saw
- Jig saw with wood-cutting blade
- Railing lumber (4 × 4s, 2 × 6s, 2 × 4s, 2 × 2s)

- Paint brush
- Clear sealer-preservative
- ⅜ × 4" lag screws and 1" washers
- Silicone caulk
- 2½" corrosion-resistant deck screws
- 10d galvanized common nails

HOW TO INSTALL A DECK RAILING

Step A: Prepare the Posts

1. Refer to your deck plans for the length of railing posts and balusters.

2. Measure and cut 4 × 4 posts, using a miter saw or circular saw. Cut off the tops of the posts square,

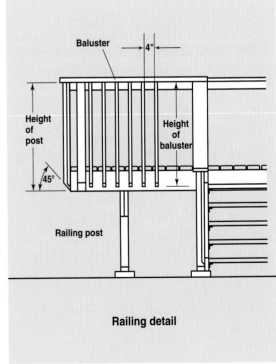

Baluster 4"

Height of post

Height of baluster

45°

Railing post

Railing detail

and cut the bottoms at a 45° angle. Seal the cut ends with a clear sealer-preservative.

3. Drill two ¼" pilot holes through the bottom end of each post, spaced 4" apart. Counterbore each pilot hole to ½" depth, using a 1" spade bit.

Step B: Prepare the Balusters

1. Measure and cut 2 × 2 balusters for the main deck, using a power miter saw or circular saw. Cut off the tops of the balusters square, and cut bottoms at a 45° angle. Seal the cut ends with a clear sealer-preservative.

2. Drill two ⅛" pilot holes near bottom end of each baluster, spaced 4" apart. Drill two ⅛" pilot holes at top of each baluster, spaced 1½" apart.

Step C: Attach the Posts

1. Measure and mark the position of the posts around the outside of the deck, using a combination square as a guide. Posts should be spaced no more than 6 ft. apart. Plan to install a post on the outside edge of each stair stringer.

2. Position each post with the beveled end flush with the bottom of the deck. Plumb the post with a level, then insert a screwdriver or nail into the pilot holes and mark the side of the deck. Remove the post and drill ¼" pilot holes into the side of the deck.

3. Attach the railing posts to the side of the deck with ⅜ × 4" lag screws and washers, using a ratchet wrench. Seal screw heads with silicone caulk.

Step D: Install Side Railings

1. Measure and cut 2 × 4 side rails. Position the rails with the edges flush to the tops of the posts. Attach the rails to the posts with 2½" corrosion-resistant deck screws.

2. For long rails, join 2 × 4s by cutting the ends at a 45° angle. Drill 1/16" pilot holes to prevent nails from splitting the end grain, and attach the rails with 10d galvanized nails. (Screws may split mitered ends.)

3. Attach the ends of the rails to the stairway posts, flush with the edges of the posts. Drill ⅛" pilot holes, and attach rails with 2½" deck screws.

A. *Use a miter saw or circular saw to cut the railing post tops square and the bottoms at a 45° angle.*

B. *Drill two pilot holes near the bottom end of each baluster, spaced 4" apart, and two pilot holes at the top, spaced 1½" apart.*

C. *Mark their positions and then drill pilot holes into the side of the deck at the reference marks.*

Step E: Mark the Stairway Rail Position

1. At the stairway, measure from the surface of the decking to the top of the upper stairway post.

2. Transfer the measurement to the lower stairway post, measuring from the edge of the stair stringer.

3. Position the 2 × 4 rail against the inside of the stairway posts. Align the rail with the top rear corner of the top post, and with the pencil mark on the lower post. Have a helper attach the rail temporarily with 2½" deck screws.

Step F: Install the Stair Railing

1. Mark the outline of the post and the deck rail on the backside of the stairway rail, and the outline of the stairway rail on the lower stairway post.

2. Use a level to mark a plumb cutoff line at the bottom end of the stairway rail. Remove the rail.

3. Extend the pencil lines across both sides of the stairway post, using a combination square as a guide.

4. Cut off the lower stairway post along the diagonal cutoff line, using a reciprocating saw or circular saw. Use a jig saw to cut the stairway rail along the marked outlines.

5. Position the stairway rail flush against the top edge of the posts. Drill ⅛" pilot holes, and then attach the rail to the posts

with 2½" deck screws.

Step G: Install the Balusters

1. Refer to your deck plans to find the spacing distance between the balusters. Cut a scrap piece of 2 × 6 to the spacing distance to use as a spacer block to ensure equal spacing between balusters.

2. Beginning next to a plumb railing post, position each baluster tight against the spacer block, with the top of the baluster flush with the top of the rail. Attach each baluster with 2½" deck screws.

3. For the stairway, position a baluster against the stringer and rail, and adjust it for plumb. Draw a diagonal cutoff line on the top of the baluster, using the top of the stair rail as a guide. Cut the baluster on the marked line, using a miter saw. Seal the ends with a clear sealer-preservative.

4. Beginning next to the upper stairway post, position each baluster tight against the spacer block, with the top flush to the top of the stair rail. Attach balusters with 2½" deck screws.

Step H: Install the Railing Top Cap

1. Position the 2 × 6 top cap so the edge is flush with the inside edge of the rail.

2. Drill ⅛" pilot holes, and attach the cap to the rail with 2½"

D. *Cut the ends of long rails at a 45° angle, drill pilot holes to prevent the nails from splitting the end grain, and attach with box nails.*

Rail parallel to stringer

E. *Position and mark a 2 × 4 rail against inside of the stairway posts, and attach the rail temporarily with deck screws.*

F. *Position the stairway rail flush against top edge of the posts. Drill pilot holes, then attach with deck screws.*

deck screws driven every 12". Also drive screws into each post and into every third baluster.

3. For long caps, bevel the ends at 45°. Drill ¹⁄₁₆" pilot holes, and attach at posts using 10d nails.

4. At the corners, miter-cut the ends of the railing cap at 45°. Drill ⅛" pilot holes, and attach the cap to the post with 2½" deck screws.

5. At the top of the stairs, cut the top cap so that it is flush with the stairway rail. Drill ⅛" pilot holes and attach the cap with 2½" deck screws. NOTE: Some areas may require a grippable hand rail. Check your local building codes.

Step I: Install the Railing Top Cap to the Stairway

1. Measure and cut the top cap for the stairway rail. Mark the outline of the post on the side of the cap, and bevel-cut the ends of the cap.

2. Position the top cap over the stairway rail and balusters so that the edge of the cap is flush with the inside edge of the rail. Drill ⅛" pilot holes, and attach the cap to the rail with 2½" deck screws driven every 12". Also drive screws through the cap into the stair posts and into every third baluster.

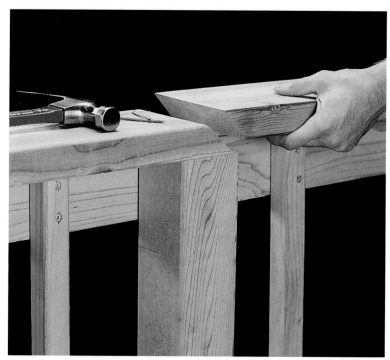

H. Position the top cap flush with the inside edge of the rail, drill pilot holes, and attach with deck screws. For long caps, bevel the ends at a 45° angle.

G. Position each baluster tight against a spacer block with the top flush to the top of the stair rail. Attach each baluster with deck screws.

I. Position a cap over the stairway rail and balusters so the edge is flush with the inside edge of the rail, drill pilot holes, and attach with deck screws.

High Rectangular Deck

This simple rectangular deck provides a secure, convenient outdoor living space. The absence of a stairway prevents children from wandering away or unexpected visitors from wandering in. It also makes the deck easier to build.

Imagine how handy it will be to have this additional living area only a step away from your dining room or living room, with no more need to walk downstairs for outdoor entertaining, dining, or relaxing.

MATERIALS

- 12" diameter concrete footing forms (3)
- J-bolts (3)
- 6 × 6" metal post anchors (3)
- 2 × 10" joist hangers (26)
- 2½" & 3" galvanized deck screws
- 10d joist hanger nails
- ⅜ × 4" lag screws and washers (28)
- ¼ × 5" lag screws and washers (16)
- 5⁄16 × 7" carriage bolts, washers, and nuts (6)
- 16d galvanized common nails
- Metal flashing (18 ft.)
- Silicone caulk (3 tubes)
- Concrete as required

Cutaway View

OVERALL SIZE:
18'-0" LONG
14'-0" WIDE
9'-2" HIGH

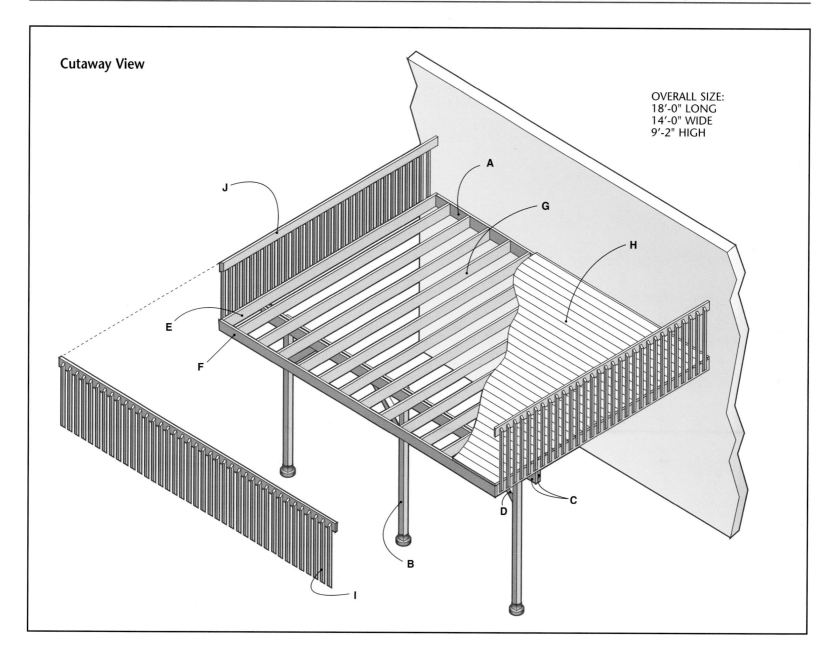

Lumber List

Qty.	Size	Material	Part
2	2 × 12" × 20'	Trtd. lumber	Beam boards (C)
2	2 × 10" × 18'	Trtd. lumber	Ledger (A), Rim joist (F)
15	2 × 10" × 14'	Trtd. lumber	Joists (G), End joists (E)
3	6 × 6" × 10'	Trtd. lumber	Deck posts (B)

Lumber List

Qty.	Size	Material	Part
2	4 × 4" × 8'	Trtd. lumber	Braces (D)
32	2 × 6" × 18'	Cedar	Decking (H), Top rail (J)
2	2 × 6" × 16'	Cedar	Top rail (J)
50	2 × 2" × 8'	Cedar	Balusters (I)

Framing Plan

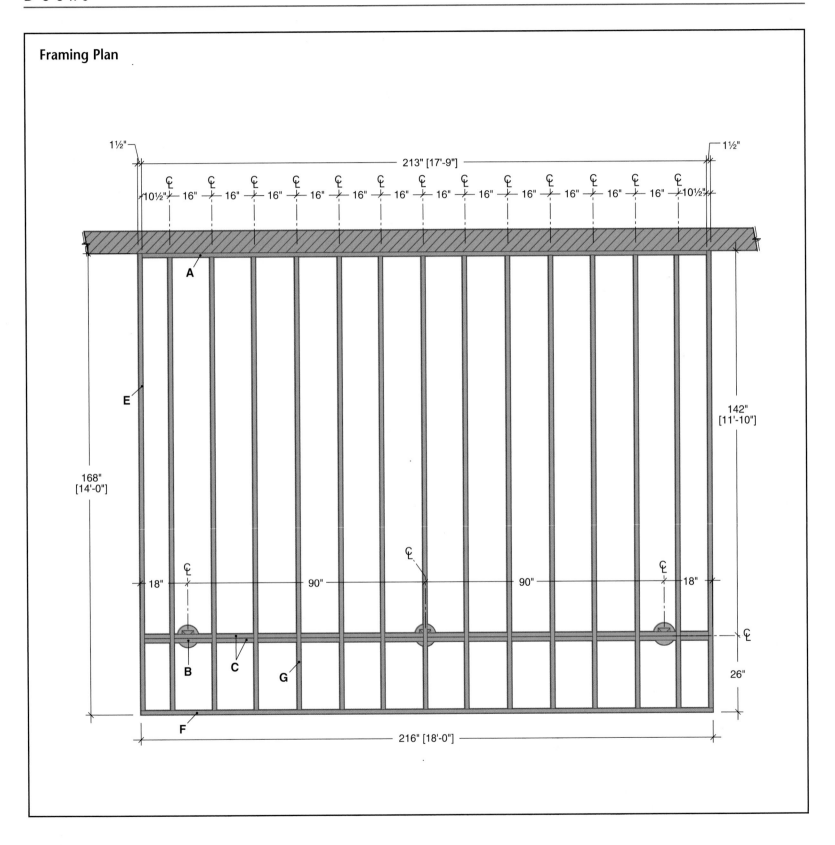

Elevation

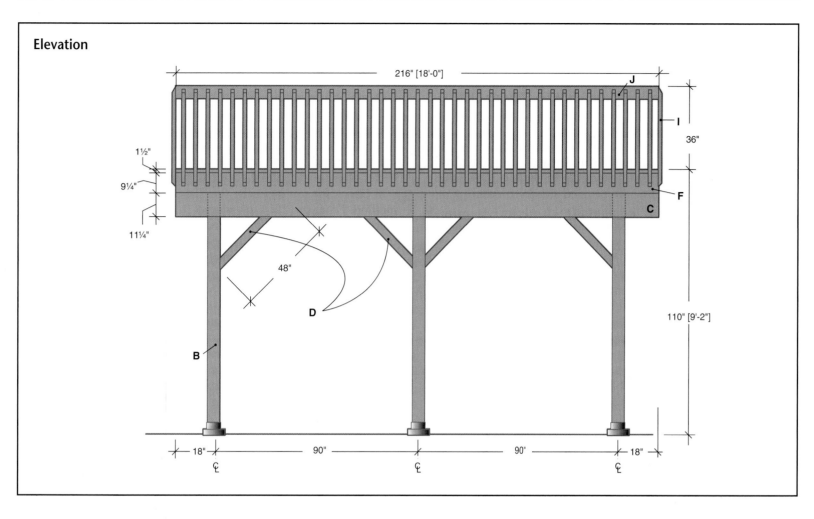

Railing Detail

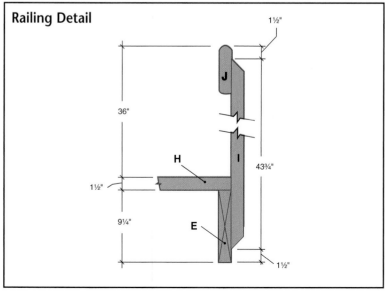

Face Board Detail

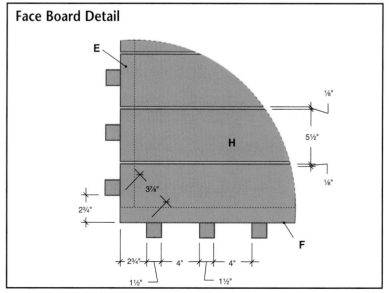

clamp the beam to the posts. NOTE: Installing boards of this size and length, at this height, requires care. You should have at least two helpers.

4. Counterbore two ½"-deep holes using a 1" spade bit, then drill ⁵⁄₁₆" pilot holes through the beam and post.

5. Thread a carriage bolt into each pilot hole. Add a washer and nut to the counterbore-side of each bolt and tighten with a ratchet wrench. Seal both ends of the bolts with silicone caulk.

6. Cut the tops of the posts flush with the top edge of the beam, using a reciprocating saw or handsaw.

Step G: Install the Frame

1. Measure and cut the end joists (E), using a circular saw.

2. Attach end joists to ends of ledger with 16d galvanized common nails.

3. Measure and cut the rim joist (F) to length with a circular saw. Fasten to the ends of the end joists with 16d galvanized common nails.

4. Square up the frame by measuring corner-to-corner and adjusting until the measurements are equal. When the frame is square, toenail the end joists in place on top of the beam.

5. Trim the ends of the beam flush with the faces of the end joists, using a reciprocating saw or a handsaw.

Step H: Install the Braces

1. Cut the braces (D) to length (see Elevation, page 245) with a circular saw or miter saw. Miter both ends at 45°.

2. Install the braces by positioning them against the beam boards and against the posts. Make sure the outside faces of the braces are flush with the outside faces of the beam and the posts. Temporarily fasten with deck screws.

3. Secure the braces to the posts with ¼" × 5" lag screws. Drill two ¼" pilot holes through the upper end of each brace into the beam. Counterbore to a ½"-depth using a 1" spade bit, and drive lag screws with a ratchet wrench. Repeat for the lower end of the braces into the posts.

Step I: Install the Joists

1. Measure and mark joist locations (see Framing Plan, page 244) on the ledger, rim joist, and beam. Draw the outline of each joist on the ledger and rim joist, using a combination square.

2. Install a joist hanger at each joist location. Attach one flange of the hanger to one side of the outline, using 10d common nails. Use a spacer cut from scrap 2 × 8 lumber to achieve the correct spread for each hanger, then fasten the remaining side flange with 10d common nails. Remove the spacer and repeat the same procedure for the remaining joist hangers.

E. *Measure and mark a 3 × 7½" notch at the top of each post. Trace the lines on all sides, using a framing square.*

F. *Fasten the beam to the posts with carriage bolts fitted with a washer and nut. Tighten with a ratchet wrench.*

3. Measure, mark, and cut lumber for joists (G), using a circular saw. Place joists in hangers with crown side up and attach with 10d joist hanger nails. Align joists with the outlines on the top of the beam, and toenail in place.

Step J: Lay the Decking

1. Measure, mark, and cut the decking boards (H) to length.

2. Position the first row of decking flush against the house. Attach by driving a pair of 3" galvanized deck screws onto each joist.

3. Position remaining boards, leaving ⅛" gaps between boards to provide for drainage. Attach to each joist with deck screws.

4. Every few rows of decking, measure from the edge of the decking to the outside edge of the deck. If the measurement can be divided evenly by 5⅝, the last board will fit flush with the outside edge of the deck as intended. If the measurement shows that the last board will not fit flush, adjust the spacing as you install the remaining rows of boards.

5. If the decking overhangs the end joists, snap a chalk line to mark the outside edge of the deck and cut flush with a circular saw set to a 1½" depth. If needed, finish the cut with a jig saw or handsaw where a circular saw can't reach.

G. Secure the end joists to the ledger, using angle brackets and 10d joist hanger nails.

H. Cut 4 × 4 beam braces with ends cut at a 45° angle. Drill pilot holes in ends of braces, and attach them to the beams and posts with 5" lag screws.

I. Fasten the joists in the joist hangers with 10d joist hanger nails. Drive nails into both sides of each joist.

Rectangular Deck

Here's a deck that's classic in its simplicity. Moderately sized and easy to build, this rectangular deck won't cost you an arm and a leg—in either time or money. The framing and decking plans are quite straightforward, and you can likely build the entire deck in just two or three weekends, even with limited carpentry and building experience. Within just a few weeks' time, you can transform your yard into a congenial gathering place for cooking, entertaining, and just plain relaxing—a place where you, your family, and your friends can enjoy the fresh air in convenience and comfort.

MATERIALS

- 8"-diameter concrete footing forms (5)
- Gravel
- J-bolts (5)
- 4 × 4" metal post anchors (5)
- 4 × 4" metal post-beam caps (3)
- 2 × 8" joist hangers (16)
- 1½ × 6" angle brackets (6)
- 1½ × 10" angle brackets (10)
- 2½" & 3" galvanized deck screws
- 16d galvanized common nails
- ⅜ × 4" lag screws and washers (20)
- 10d joist hanger nails
- ⅜ × 5" lag screws and washers (22)
- ¼ × 1¼" lag screws and washers (80)
- Flashing (12 ft.)
- Exterior silicone caulk (3 tubes)
- Concrete as needed

Cutaway View

OVERALL SIZE:
12"-0" LONG
10"-0" WIDE
3'-5" HIGH

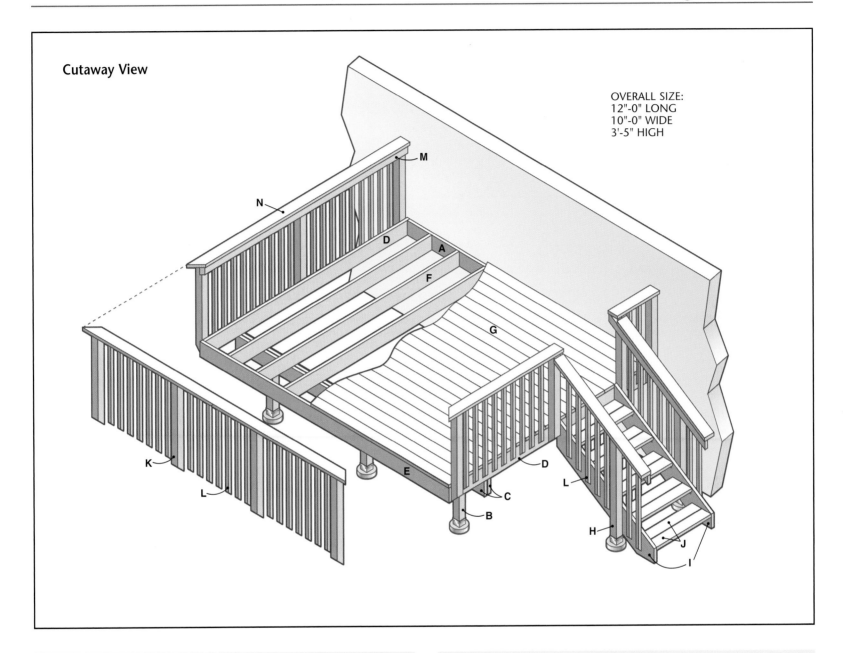

Lumber List			
Qty.	Size	Material	Part
4	2 x 8" x 12'	Trtd. lumber	Ledger (A), Beam bds (C), Rim joist (E)
1	4 x 4" x 8'	Trtd. lumber	Deck posts (B)
10	2 x 8" x 10'	Trtd. lumber	End joists (D), Joists (F)
25	2 x 6" x 12'	Cedar	Decking (G), Rail cap (N)
7	4 x 4" x 8'	Cedar	Stair posts (H), Rail post (K)

Lumber List			
Qty.	Size	Material	Part
2	2 x 12" x 8'	Cedar	Stringers (I)
5	2 x 6" x 6'	Cedar	Treads (J)
32	2 x 2" x 8'	Cedar	Balusters (L)
2	2 x 4" x 12'	Cedar	Top rail (M)
2	2 x 4" x 10'	Cedar	Top rail (M)

Framing Plan

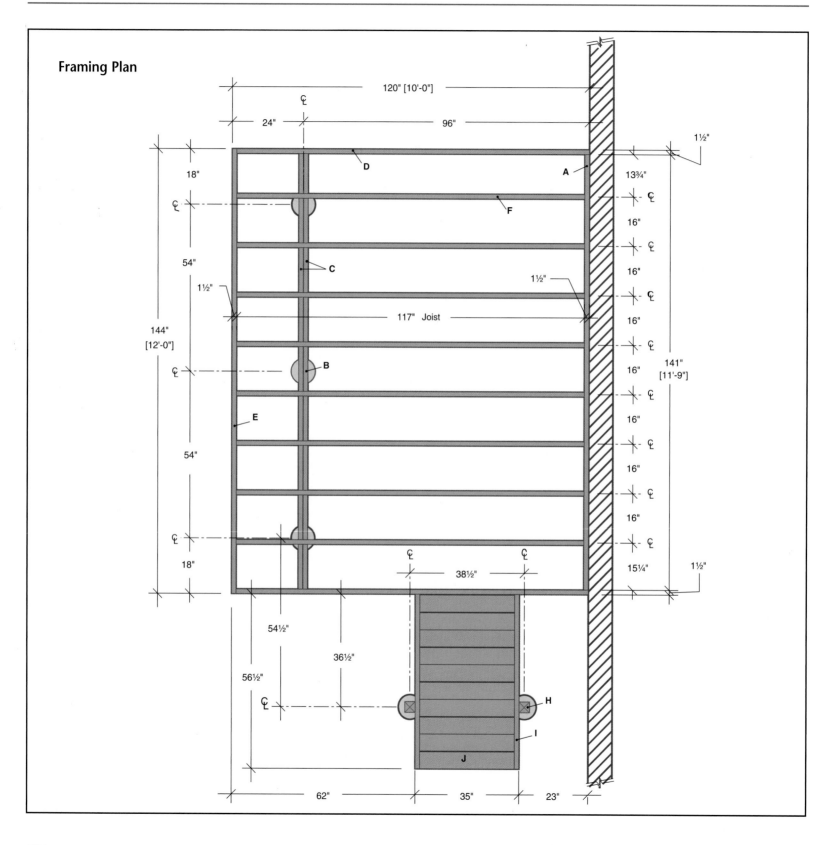

120" [10'-0"]

24" 96"

1½"

18"

13¾"

A

D

C̶L

C̶L 16"

F

C̶L 16"

C

144"
[12'-0"]

1½"

117" Joist

1½"

C̶L 16"

C̶L 16"

B

C̶L 16"

E

C̶L 16"

54"

C̶L 16"

C̶L 16"

141"
[11'-9"]

C̶L

18"

15¼"

1½"

38½"

54½"

36½"

56½"

H

I

J

62" 35" 23"

Elevation

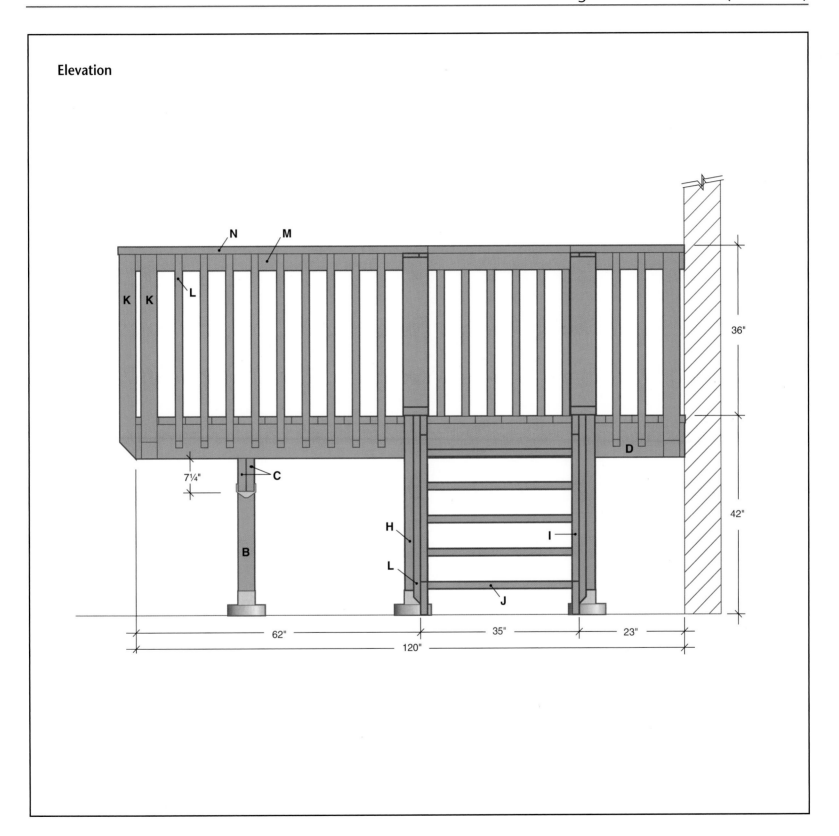

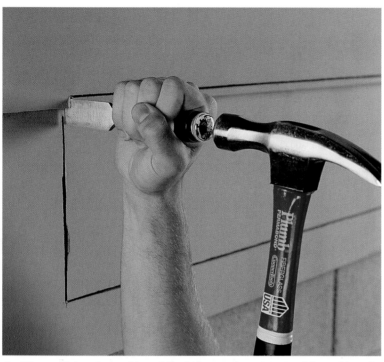

A. *After outlining the position of the ledger and cutting the siding with a circular saw, use a chisel to finish the corners of the cutout.*

B. *Check the strings for square, by measuring from corner to corner. If the measurements are not equal, adjust the strings on the batterboards. When the diagonal measurements are equal, the outline is square.*

HOW TO BUILD A RECTANGULAR DECK

Step A: Attach the Ledger

1. Draw a level outline on the siding to show where the ledger and the end joists will fit against the house. Install the ledger so that the surface of the decking boards will be 1" below the indoor floor level. This height difference prevents rainwater or melted snow from seeping into the house.

2. Cut out the siding along the outline with a circular saw. To prevent the blade from cutting the sheathing that lies underneath the siding, set the blade depth to the same thickness as the siding. Finish the cutout with a chisel, holding the beveled side in to ensure a straight cut.

3. Cut galvanized flashing to the length of the cutout, using metal snips. Slide the flashing up under the siding at the top of the cutout.

4. Measure and cut the ledger (A) from pressure-treated lumber. Center the ledger end-to-end in the cutout, with space at each end for the end joists.

5. Brace the ledger in position under the flashing. Tack the ledger into place with galvanized deck screws.

6. Drill pairs of ¼" pilot holes at 16" intervals through the ledger and into the house header joist. Counterbore each pilot hole ½", using a 1" spade bit. Attach the ledger to the wall with ⅜ × 4" lag screws and washers, using a ratchet wrench.

7. Apply a thick bead of silicone caulk between the siding and flashing. Also seal the lag screw heads and the cracks at the ends of the ledger.

Step B: Locate the Footings

1. Referring to the measurements shown in the Framing Plan on page 254, mark the centerlines of the two outer footings on the ledger and drive nails at these locations.

2. Set up temporary batterboards and stretch a mason's string out from the ledger at each location. Make sure the strings are perpendicular to the ledger, and measure along the strings to find the centerpoints of the posts.

3. Set up additional batterboards and stretch another string parallel to the ledger across the post centerpoints.

4. Check the mason's strings for square, by measuring diagonally from corner to corner and adjusting the strings so that the measurements are equal.

5. Measure along the cross string and mark the center post location with a piece of tape.

6. Use a plumb bob to transfer the footing centerpoints to the ground, and drive a stake to mark each point.

Step C: Pour the Footings

1. Remove the mason's strings and dig the post footings, using a clamshell digger or power auger. Pour 2" to 3" of loose gravel into each hole for drainage. NOTE: When measuring the footing size and depth, make sure you comply with your local building code, which may require flaring the base.

2. Cut the footing forms to length, using a reciprocating saw or handsaw, and insert them into the footing holes, leaving 2" above ground level. Pack soil around the forms for support, and fill the forms with concrete, tamping with a long stick or rod to eliminate any air pockets.

3. Screed the tops flush with a straight 2 × 4. Insert a 3" J-bolt into each footing, set so ¾" to 1" of thread is exposed. Retie the mason's strings and position the J-bolts at the exact center of the posts, using a plumb bob as a guide. Clean the bolt threads before the concrete sets.

Step D: Set the Posts

1. Lay a long, straight 2 × 4 flat across the footings, parallel to the ledger. With one edge tight against the J-bolts, draw a reference line across each footing.

2. Place a metal post anchor on each footing, centering it over the J-bolt and squaring it with the reference line. Attach the post anchors by threading a nut over each bolt and tightening with a ratchet wrench.

3. Cut the posts to length, adding approximately 6" for final trimming. Place the posts in the anchors and tack into place with one nail.

4. With a level as a guide, use braces and stakes to plumb the posts. Finish nailing the posts to the anchors.

5. Determine the height of the beam by extending a straight 2 × 4 from the bottom edge of the ledger across the face of a post. Level the 2 × 4, and draw a line on the post.

6. From that line, measure 7¼" down the post and mark the bottom of the beam. Using a level, transfer this line to the remaining posts.

7. Use a combination square to extend the level line completely around each post. Cut the posts to this finished height, using a reciprocating saw or handsaw.

Step E: Install the Beam

1. Cut the beam boards (C) several inches longer than necessary, to allow for final trimming.

C. *Pour concrete into the tube form, guiding it from a wheelbarrow with a shovel. Use a long stick to tamp the concrete, filling air gaps in the footing.*

D. *After the posts have been set in place and braced plumb, use a straight 2 × 4 and a level to mark the top of the beam on each post.*

E. *With the beam in place, align the reference marks with the post-beam caps and fasten using 10d joist hanger nails.*

2. Join the beam boards together with 2½" galvanized deck screws. Mark the post locations on the top edges and sides, using a combination square as a guide.

3. Attach the post-beam caps to the tops of the posts. Position the caps on the post tops and attach using 10d joist hanger nails.

4. Lift the beam into the post-beam caps, with the crown up. Align the post reference lines on the beam with the post-beam caps. NOTE: You should have at least two helpers when installing boards of this size and length.

5. Fasten the post-beam caps to the beam using 10d joist hanger nails.

Step F: Install the Frame

1. Measure and cut the end joists to length using a circular saw.

2. Attach end joists to the ends of the ledger with 16d galvanized common nails.

3. Measure and cut the rim joist (E) to length with a circular saw. Fasten it to end joists with 16d galvanized common nails.

4. Square up the frame by measuring corner-to-corner and

F. *Cut the rim joist to length, and attach to the ends of end joists with 16d galvanized common nails.*

adjusting until measurements are equal. Toenail the end joists in place on top of the beam, and trim the beam to length.

5. Reinforce each inside corner of the frame with an angle bracket fastened with 10d joist hanger nails.

Step G: Install the Joists

1. Mark the outlines of the inner joists (F) on the ledger, beam, and rim joist (see Framing Plan, page 254) using a tape measure and a combination square.

2. Attach joist hangers to the ledger with 10d common nails and to the rim joist with 10d joist hanger nails, using a scrap 2 × 8 as a spacer to achieve the correct spread for each hanger.

3. Measure, mark, and cut lumber for inner joists, using a circular saw. Place the joists in the hangers with crown side up, and attach at both ends with 10d joist hanger nails. Be sure to use all the holes in the hangers.

4. Align the joists with the marks on top of the beam, and toenail in place.

Step H: Lay the Decking

1. Cut the first decking board (G) to length, position it against the house, and attach by driving a pair of 2½" galvanized deck screws into each joist.

2. Position the remaining decking boards with the ends overhanging the end joists. Leave a ⅛" gap between boards to provide for drainage, and attach the boards to each joist with a pair of deck screws.

3. Every few rows of decking, measure from the edge of the decking to the outside edge of the deck. If the measurement can be divided evenly by 5⅞, the last board will fit flush with the outside edge of the deck as intended. If the measurement shows that the last board will not fit flush, adjust the spacing as you install the remaining rows of boards.

4. If your decking overhangs the end joists, snap a chalk line to mark the outside edge of the deck and cut flush with a circular saw. If needed, finish the cut with a jig saw or handsaw where a circular saw can't reach.

Step I: Build the Stairway

1. Refer to the Framing Plan (page 254) for the position of stairway footings.

2. Locate the footings by extending a 2 × 4 from the deck, dropping a plumb bob, and marking the centerpoints with stakes.

3. Dig postholes with a clamshell digger or an auger, and pour the stairway footings using the same method as for the deck footings.

4. Attach metal post anchors to the footings, and install posts (H), leaving them long for final trimming.

5. Cut the stair stringers (I) to length and use a framing square

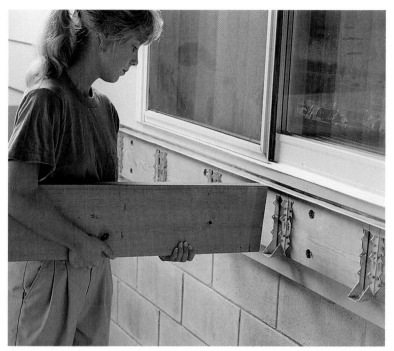

G. *Install joists in hangers with the crown side up, and fasten with 10d joist hanger nails.*

H. *Adjust the board spacing by changing the gaps between the boards by a small amount over three or four rows of boards.*

to mark the rise and run for each step (see Stairway Detail, below). Draw the tread outline on each run. Cut the angles at the end of the stringers with a circular saw. (For more information on building stairways, see pages 234 to 237.)

6. Position a 1½ × 10" angle bracket flush with the bottom of each tread line. Attach the brackets with 1¼" lag screws.

7. Fasten angle brackets to the upper ends of the stringers, using 1¼" lag screws; keep the brackets flush with the cut ends on the stringers. Position the top ends of the stringers on the side of the deck, making sure the top point of the stringer and the surface of the deck are flush.

8. Attach the stringers by driving 10d joist hanger nails through the angle brackets into the end joist, and by drilling ¼" pilot holes from inside the rim joist into the stringers and fastening with ⅜ × 4" lag screws.

9. To connect the stringers to the stair posts, drill two ¼" pilot holes and counterbore the pilot holes ½" deep with a 1" spade bit. Use a ratchet wrench to fasten the stringers to the posts with 4" lag screws and washers.

10. Measure the length of the stair treads (J) and cut two 2 × 6 boards for each tread. For each tread, position the front board on the angle bracket so the front edge is flush with the tread outline on the stringers. Attach the tread to the brackets with ¼ × 1¼" lag screws.

11. Place the rear 2 × 6 on each tread bracket, keeping ⅛" spaces between the boards. Attach with 1¼" lag screws.

12. Attach the treads for the lowest step by driving deck screws through the stringers.

Step J: Install the Railing

1. Cut posts (K) and balusters (L) to length (see Railing Detail, page 261) with a miter saw or circular saw. Cut the top ends square, and the bottom ends at a 45° angle.

2. Mark and drill two ¼" pilot holes at the bottom end of each post. Holes should be spaced 4" apart and counterbored ½", with a 1" spade bit.

Stairway Detail

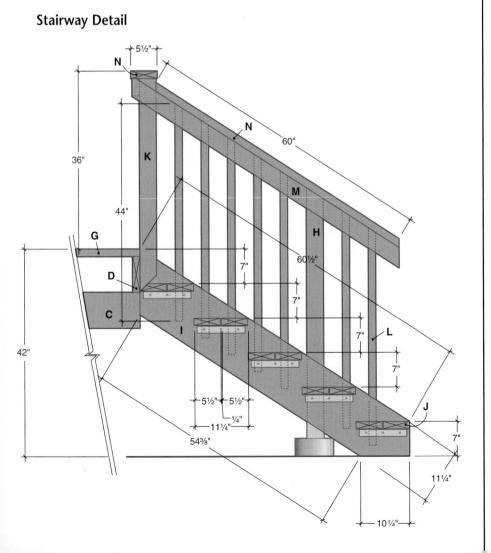

I. *After attaching the stringers to the deck, fasten them to the posts. Drill and counterbore two pilot holes through the stringers into the posts, and attach with lag screws.*

3. Drill two ⅛" pilot holes, 4" apart, near the bottom of each baluster. At the top of each baluster, drill a pair of ⅛" pilot holes spaced 1½" apart.

4. Using a combination square, mark the locations of the posts on the outside of the deck. NOTE: Position corner posts so there is no more than 4" clearance between them.

5. Clamp each post in place. Keep the beveled end flush with the bottom of the deck, and make sure the post is plumb. Use an awl to mark pilot hole locations on the side of the deck. Remove posts and drill ¼" pilot holes at marks. Attach the railing posts to the side of the deck with ⅜ × 5" lag screws and washers.

6. Cut top rails (M) to length, with 45° miters on the ends that meet at the corners. Attach to posts with 2½" deck screws, keeping the top edge of the rail flush with the top of the posts. Join rails by cutting 45° bevels at ends.

7. Temporarily attach stairway top rails with 3" galvanized screws. Mark the outline of the deck railing post and top rail on the back side of the stairway top rail. Mark the position of the top rail on the stairway post. Use a level to mark a plumb cutoff line at the lower end of the rail. Remove the rail.

Step K: Install the Balusters & Top Caps

1. Cut the stairway post to finished height along the diagonal mark, and cut the stairway rail along outlines. Reposition the stairway rail and attach with deck screws.

2. Attach the balusters between the railing posts at equal intervals of 4" or less. Use deck screws, and keep the top ends of balusters flush with the top rail. On the stairway, position the balusters against the stringer and top rail, and check for plumb. Draw a diagonal cut line at top of baluster and trim to final height with a miter saw.

3. Confirm measurements, and cut rail cap sections (N) to length. Position sections so that the inside edge overhangs the inside edge of the rail by ¼". Attach cap to rail with deck screws. At corners, miter the ends at 45° and attach caps to posts.

4. Cut the cap for the stairway rail to length. Mark the angle of the deck railing post on the side of the cap, and bevel-cut the ends of the cap. Attach the cap to top rail and post with deck screws. NOTE: Local building codes may require a grippable handrail for any stairway over four treads. Check with your building inspector.

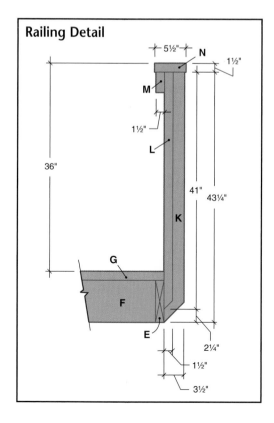

Railing Detail

J. *Position the stairway top rail in place against the posts. Attach temporarily and mark for cutting to size.*

K. *Position the rail cap over the posts and balusters. Make sure mitered corners are tight, and attach with deck screws.*

Inside Corner Deck

With the help of a diamond decking pattern, this inside corner deck provides a focal point for recreational activities and social gatherings. At the same time, the corner location can offer intimacy, privacy, shade, and a shield from the wind.

The design calls for double joists and blocking for extra strength and stability where decking boards butt together. Joists are spaced 12" on center to support diagonal decking.

It takes a little more time to cut the decking boards and match the miter cuts, but the results are spectacular and well worth the effort.

MATERIALS

- 8"-diameter concrete footing forms (8)
- J-bolts (8)
- 4 × 4" metal post anchors (8)
- 2 × 8" single joist hangers (50)
- 2 × 8" double joist hangers (30)

- 1½ × 10" angle brackets (12)
- 2½" & 3" galvanized deck screws
- 16d galvanized common nails
- 10d joist hanger nails
- ⅜ × 4" lag screws and washers (78)

- ¼ × 1¼" lag screws (96)
- ½ × 7" carriage bolts, washers, and nuts (12)
- Exterior silicone caulk (6 tubes)
- Concrete as needed

Cutaway View

OVERALL SIZE:
14'-5" LONG
13' WIDE
4'-1" HIGH

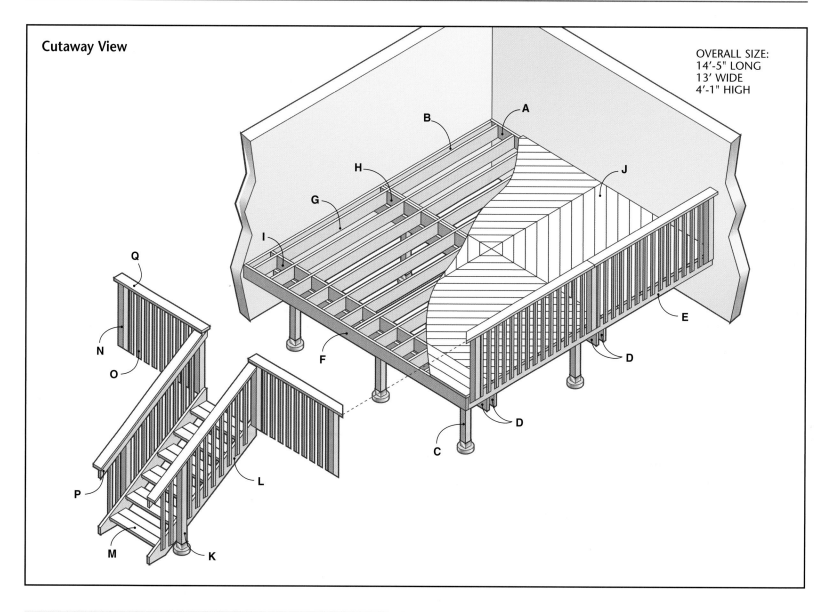

Lumber List

Qty.	Size	Material	Part
6	2 × 8" × 14'	Trtd. lumber	Short ledger (A), Long ledger (B), Beam boards (D)
14	2 × 8" × 16'	Trtd. lumber	Joists (G), Single blocking (I)
3	2 × 8" × 8'	Trtd. lumber	Double blocking (H)
3	4 × 4" × 8'	Trtd. lumber	Deck posts (C)
1	2 × 8" × 16'	Cedar	End joist (E)
1	2 × 8" × 14'	Cedar	Rim joist (F)

Lumber List

Qty.	Size	Material	Part
42	2 × 6" × 8'	Cedar	Decking (J), Railing caps (Q)
16	2 × 6" × 14'	Cedar	Decking (J)
1	4 × 4" × 10'	Cedar	Stair posts (K)
6	2 × 6" × 8'	Cedar	Treads (M)
4	4 × 4" × 8'	Cedar	Railing posts (N)
2	2 × 10" × 8'	Cedar	Stringers (L)
33	2 × 2" × 8'	Cedar	Balusters (O)
6	2 × 4" × 8'	Cedar	Top rails (P)

Framing Plan

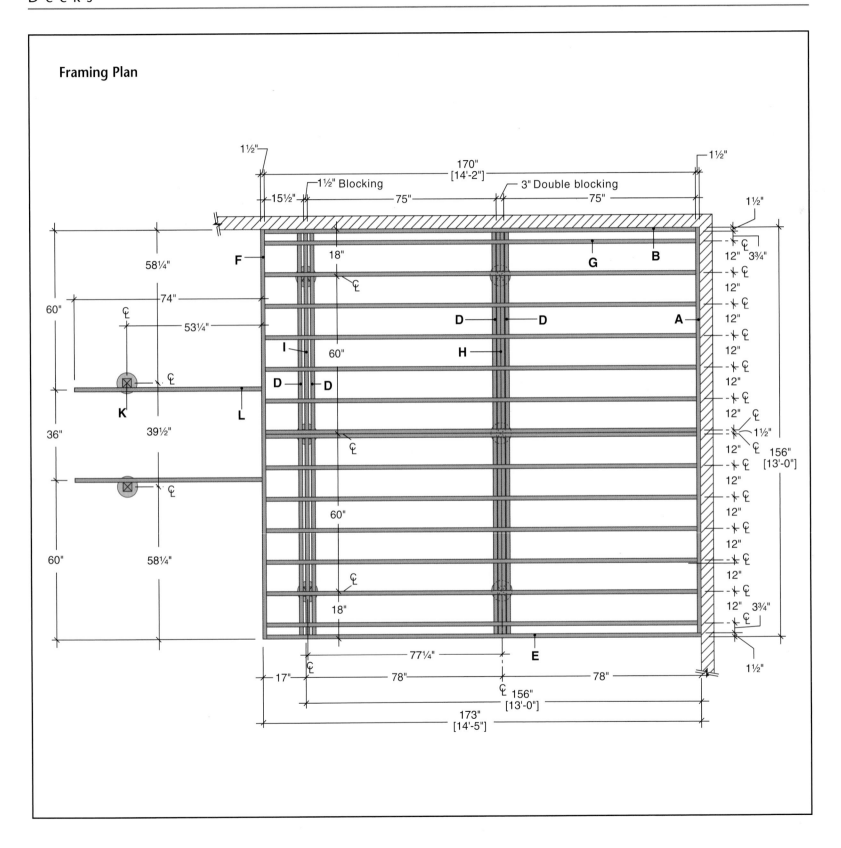

Railing Detail

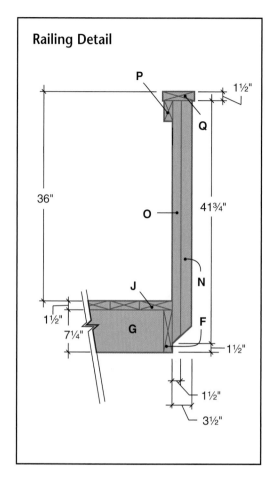

Stairway Detail

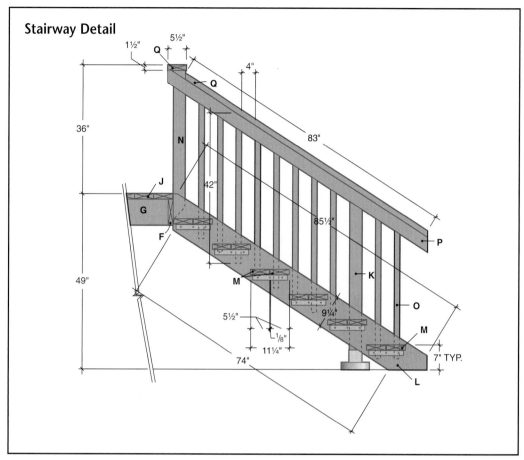

Elevation

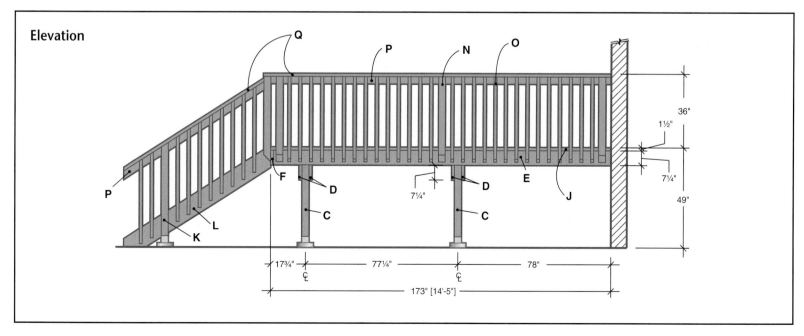

HOW TO BUILD AN INSIDE CORNER DECK

Step A: Attach the Ledgers

1. To show where the ledgers will be attached to the house, draw outlines on the wall, using a level as a guide. To locate the top of the ledger outline, measure down from the indoor floor surface 1" plus the thickness of the decking boards. This height difference prevents rain and melting snow from seeping into the house.

2. Measure and cut the ledgers to length. They will be shorter than the outline on the wall to allow for the width of the rim joist and end joist.

3. Drill pairs of ¼" pilot holes through the ledgers at 16" intervals. Counterbore the pilot holes ½" with a 1" spade bit.

4. Brace the short ledger (A) in place, and insert a nail or an awl through the pilot holes to mark the hole locations on the wall.

5. Repeat the process to mark the hole locations for the long ledger (B).

6. Remove the ledgers and drill pilot holes into the stucco with a ⅜" masonry bit. Then, use a ¼" bit to extend each pilot hole through the sheathing and into the header joist.

7. Position and brace the ledgers against the walls. Use a ratchet wrench to attach the ledgers to the walls with ⅜ × 4" lag screws and washers. Seal the screw heads and all cracks between the wall and ledger with silicone caulk.

Step B: Pour the Deck Footings

1. Referring to the measurements shown in the Framing Plan (page 264) mark the centerlines of the footings on the ledgers and drive a nail into the ledger at each location.

2. Set up temporary batterboards and stretch a mason's string out from the ledger at each location. Make sure the strings are perpendicular to the ledger.

3. Check the mason's strings for square, using the "3-4-5 carpenter's triangle" method. From the point where each string meets the ledger, measure 3 ft. along the ledger and make a mark. Next, measure 4 ft. out along the string and mark with tape. The distance between the points on the ledger and the string should be 5 ft. If it's not, adjust the string position on the batterboard accordingly.

4. Drop a plumb bob to transfer the footing centerpoints to the

A. *Once pilot holes have been drilled and the ledger has been positioned and braced against the wall, use a ratchet wrench to attach the ledger with lag screws and washers.*

B. *To locate the centerpoints of the footings on the ground, drop a plumb bob from the intersections of the mason's strings. Then, drive a stake into the ground to mark each centerpoint.*

ground, and drive a stake to mark each point. Remove the strings.

5. Dig the post footings, using a clamshell digger or power auger. Pour 2" to 3" of loose gravel into each hole for drainage. NOTE: Make sure the footing size and depth comply with your local building code, which may require flaring the base to 12".

6. Cut the footing forms to length, using a reciprocating saw or handsaw, and insert them into the footing holes so that they extend 2" above grade. Pack soil around the forms for support, and fill the forms with concrete, tamping with a long stick or rod to eliminate any air pockets.

7. Screed the tops of the footings flush, using a 2 × 4. Insert a J-bolt into the wet concrete of each footing, and set it, with ¾" to 1" of thread exposed. Retie the mason's strings and position each J-bolt at the exact center of the post location, using the plumb bob as a guide. Clean the bolt threads before the concrete sets.

Step C: Set the Posts

1. Lay a long, straight 2 × 4 flat across each row of footings, parallel to the short ledger. With one edge tight against the J-bolts, draw a reference line across the top of each footing.

2. Center a metal post anchor over the J-bolt on each footing, and square it with the reference line. Attach the post anchors by threading a nut over each bolt and tightening with a ratchet wrench.

3. Cut the posts, leaving an extra 6" for final trimming. Place each post in an anchor and tack it in place with one nail.

4. With a level as a guide, use braces and stakes to ensure that each post is plumb. Finish nailing the posts to the anchors.

5. Determine the height of the inside beam by extending a straight 2 × 4 from the bottom edge of the long ledger across the row of posts. Level the 2 × 4, and draw a line on the posts. Use the same method to determine the height of the outer beam.

Step D: Install the Beams

1. Cut the beam boards (D), leaving an extra few inches for final trimming.

2. Position one beam board, crown up, against the row of posts. Tack the board in place with deck screws.

3. Attach the remaining beam boards to the posts in the same way.

4. Drill two ½" holes through the boards and posts at each joint

C. *Install the post anchors and then tack the anchors to the posts. Plumb the posts and nail them to the anchors.*

D. *Position the beam against the posts, and attach it temporarily with deck screws.*

and counterbore the pilot holes ½" with a 1" spade bit. Secure the beam boards to the posts with carriage bolts, using a ratchet wrench.

5. Cut the tops of the posts flush with the tops of the beams, using a reciprocating saw or handsaw.

Step E: Install the Joists

1. Measure, mark, and cut the end joist (E) and the rim joist (F), using a circular saw.

2. Attach the end joist to the short ledger and the rim joist to the long ledger, using 16d galvanized common nails.

3. Nail the rim joist to the end joist.

4. Toenail the end joist to the tops of the beams, and cut the ends of the beams flush with the end joist.

5. Measure, mark, and install the double center joist at the precise center of the deck, with double joist hangers.

6. Measure both ways from the double joist, and mark the centerpoints of the remaining joists at 12" intervals. Using a combination square, mark the outlines of the joists on the ledger, beams, and rim joist.

7. Nail the joist hangers to the short ledger and rim joist, using a scrap 2 × 8 as a spacer to achieve the correct spread for each hanger.

8. Cut the joists (G) to length. Insert the joists into the hangers with the crown up, and attach them with joist hanger nails. Align the joists with the marks on the beams and toenail them in place.

Step F: Install the Blocking

1. To locate the rows of blocking, measure from the inside corner of the house along the long ledger (see Framing Plan, page 264). Drive one screw or nail at 78", and another at 156". Make corresponding marks across from the ledger on the end joist.

2. Snap chalk lines across the joists, between the ledger and the end joist. The line at 78" is the centerline of the double blocking. The line at 156" is the outer edge of the single blocking. Don't be concerned if the blocking is not directly over the beams.

3. Cut double blocking pieces from 2 × 8s nailed together with 16d galvanized common nails.

4. Install the blocking by alternating end nailing and using

E. *Drive 16d galvanized nails through the rim joist and into the end joist.*

F. *Working from a plywood platform, install double blocking to support the ends of the deck boards. Attach the blocking by alternating endnailing and using double joist hangers.*

galvanized joist hangers.

Step G: Lay the Decking

1. Begin at the center of the diamond pattern, where the double joist and the double blocking intersect. Cut four identical triangles, as large as possible, from 2 × 6" cedar stock.

2. Drill ⅛" pilot holes in the ends, position the pieces as shown, and attach with 3" deck screws.

3. To install the remaining courses, measure, cut, drill, and attach the first three boards in each course. Then, measure the actual length of the last board to achieve the best fit. For best results, install the decking course by course. Maintain a ⅛" gap between courses.

4. Once the diamond decking pattern is complete, cut and install the three remaining deck boards.

Step H: Install the Stairway Posts & Build the Stairs

1. For the position of the stairway footings, refer to the Framing Plan (page 264). Locate the footings by extending a 2 × 4 from the deck, perpendicular to the rim joist, dropping a plumb bob, and marking the centerpoints on the ground with stakes.

2. Dig postholes with a clamshell digger or an auger, and pour footings using the same method as for the deck footings. Insert J-bolts, leaving ¾" to 1" of thread exposed. Allow the concrete to set. Attach metal post anchors.

3. Cut the stairway posts (K) to length, adding approximately 6" for final trimming. Place the posts in the anchors.

4. Use a level to ensure that the posts are plumb, and attach the posts to the anchors with 16d galvanized common nails.

5. Cut the stringers (L) to length and use a framing square to mark the rise and run for each step (see Stairway Detail, page 265). Draw the tread outline on each run. Cut the angles at the ends of the stringers with a circular saw.

6. Position an angle bracket flush with the bottom of each tread outline. Drill ⅛"

pilot holes in the stringers, and attach the angle brackets with 1¼" lag screws.

7. The treads (M) fit between the stringers, and the stringers fit between the stairway posts. Measure and cut the treads (M) to length, 3" shorter than the distance between the stairway posts.

8. Assemble the stairway upside down on sawhorses. Mark and drill ⅛" pilot holes at the ends of the treads. Position each front tread with its front edge flush to the tread outline, and attach to the angle brackets with ¼ × 1¼" lag screws.

9. Attach the rear treads in similar fashion, leaving a ⅛" gap between treads.

TIP: DECKING BOARDS

When laying decking, install boards that have a flat grain with the bark side down. Flat-grain boards tend to cup to the bark side and, if installed bark-side-up, often trap water on the deck.

G. *Measure the actual length of the last deck board in each course before cutting to achieve the best fit.*

H. *Drill pilot holes and then attach the treads to the stringers, using 1¼" lag screws and angle brackets.*

I. *Fasten the stair to the deck with a ratchet wrench, using 4" lag screws.*

Step I: Install the Stairs

1. Position the stairway in place against the edge of the deck, making sure the top of the stringer is flush with the surface of the deck. From underneath the deck, drill ¼" pilot holes through the rim joist into the stringers. Attach the stringers to the rim joist with 4" lag screws, using a ratchet wrench.

2. To fasten the stairway to the stair posts, drill two ¼" pilot holes through each stringer into a post. Counterbore the pilot holes ½" deep with a 1" spade bit, and use a ratchet wrench to drive 4" lag screws with washers. Seal the screw heads with silicone caulk.

Step J: Install the Deck Railing

1. Cut the railing posts (N) and balusters (O) to length (see Railing Detail, page 265) with a miter saw or circular saw. Cut the tops square and the bottoms at 45° angles.

2. Drill two ¼" pilot holes at the bottom end of each railing post, positioned so the lag screws will attach to the rim joist. Counterbore the holes ½" deep with a 1" spade bit.

3. Drill two ⅛" pilot holes near the bottom of each baluster, spaced 4" apart. At the top of each baluster, drill a pair of ⅛" pilot holes spaced 1½" apart.

4. With the help of a combination square, draw the outlines of the railing posts around the perimeter of the deck. The posts at the corner must be spaced so there is less than 4" between them.

5. Hold each railing post in its position, with the end 1½" above the bottom edge of the deck platform (see Railing Detail, page 265). Make sure the post is plumb, and insert an awl through the counterbored holes to mark pilot hole locations on the deck.

6. Set the post aside and drill ¼" pilot holes at the marks. Attach the railing posts to the deck with ⅜ × 4" lag screws and washers. Seal the screw heads with silicone caulk.

7. Cut the top rails (P) to length with the ends mitered at 45° where they meet in the corner. Attach them to the railing posts with 3" deck screws, keeping the edges of the rails flush with the tops of the posts.

8. To position the balusters, measure the total distance between two railing posts, and mark the centerpoint on the top rail. The two railing sections on the long side of this deck will have a baluster at the centerpoint; the two railing sections on the stairway side will have a space at the centerpoint. NOTE: If the dimensions of your deck vary from the plan, calculate whether you will have a baluster or a space at the center of each section.

9. Cut a spacer slightly less than 4" wide. Start at the center of each railing section, and position either a baluster or a space over the line. Measure out from the center both ways, marking the outlines of the balusters on the top rail. The end spaces may be narrow, but they will be symmetrical.

10. To install the balusters, begin next to a railing post and make sure the first baluster is plumb. Install the remaining balusters, holding each one tight against the spacer and flush with the top rail. Attach the balusters with 2½" deck screws.

11. Cut the deck railing cap (Q) to length, with the ends mitered at 45° where they meet in the corner. Position the railing cap sections so the inside edge overhangs the inside edge of the top rail by ¼". Attach the cap with 3" deck screws.

Step K: Install the Stairway Railing

1. Determine the exact size and shape of the stairway top rail. Tack a cedar 2 × 4 across the faces of the stairway post and deck post with 10d galvanized nails. Make sure the angle of the 2 × 4 is parallel with the angle of the stringer below.

2. On the back side of the 2 × 4, mark the outline of the deck railing post and the end of the deck top rail. On the stairway post, mark a diagonal cutoff line at the top edge of the 2 × 4. At the lower end of the 2 × 4, use a level to mark a plumb cutoff line directly above the end of the stringer.

3. Remove the 2 × 4 and make the cuts.

4. Drill ⅛" pilot holes through the stairway top rail. Place in position and attach with 2½" deck screws.

5. To trim the top ends of the stairway balusters, hold a baluster against the stairway post and draw a diagonal cut line along the top edge of the rail. Trim the baluster. Using this baluster as a template, mark and cut the remaining stairway balusters.

6. Install the stairway balusters with 2½" deck screws, using the same procedure as for the deck balusters.

7. Measure the railing caps for the stairway. Cut the caps to size, with the upper ends beveled to fit against the deck posts, and the lower ends beveled to align with the end of the top rail. Install the caps by drilling ⅛" pilot holes and attaching them with 2½" deck screws.

J. *After the top rail and balusters have been installed, install the railing cap with its inside edge overhanging the inside face of the top rail by ¼".*

K. *With the stairway top rail cut to size and installed, attach the railing cap with deck screws.*

Footing Location Diagram

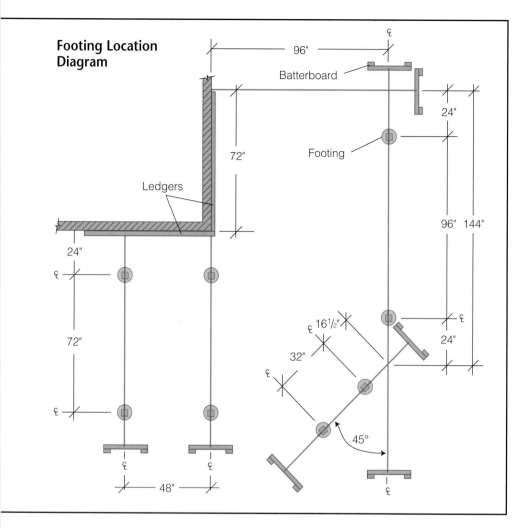

HOW TO BUILD A WRAPAROUND DECK

Step A: Attach the Ledgers

1. Draw a level outline on the siding to show where the ledgers and the adjacent end joist and rim joist will fit against the house.

2. Position the top edge of the ledgers so that the surface of the decking boards will be 1" below the indoor floor level. This height difference prevents rainwater or melted snow from seeping into the house. Draw the outline long enough to accommodate the thickness of rim joist F-1 and end joist E-2.

3. Cut out the siding along the outline with a circular saw. To keep the blade from cutting the sheathing underneath the siding, set the blade depth to the same thickness as the siding. Finish the corners of the cutout with a chisel, holding the beveled side in to ensure a straight cut.

4. Cut galvanized flashing to the length of the cutout, using metal snips, and slide the flashing up under the siding.

5. Measure and cut the ledgers (A) to length from pressure-treated lumber, using a circular saw. Remember, the ledger boards should be shorter than the overall length of the cutouts.

6. Position the ledgers in the cutout, underneath the flashing, and brace them in place. Fasten them temporarily with deck screws.

7. Drill pairs of ¼" pilot holes through the ledger and sheathing and into the house header joist at 2-ft. intervals. Counterbore each pilot hole ½" deep, using a 1" spade bit. Attach the ledgers to the wall with ⅜ × 4" lag screws and washers, using a ratchet wrench.

8. Apply a thick bead of silicone caulk between the siding and the flashing. Also seal the lag screw heads and any gaps between the wall and the ledger.

Step B: Pour the Footings

1. Referring to the Footing Location Diagram (above), stretch mason's strings across the site, using 2 × 4 batterboards. Check the mason's strings for square, using the "3-4-5 carpenter's triangle" method. From the point where each string meets the ledger, measure 3 ft. along the ledger and make a mark. Next, measure 4 ft. out along the mason's string and mark with tape. The distance between the points on the ledger and the string should be

A. Attach the ledgers to the walls with ⅜ × 4" lag screws and washers, using a ratchet wrench.

5 ft. If not, adjust the mason's strings accordingly. Measure along the strings to locate the centerpoints of the footings. Mark the locations with tape.

2. Drop a plumb bob at the tape locations and drive stakes into the ground to mark the centerpoints of the footings.

3. Remove the mason's strings and dig holes for the footings, using a clamshell digger or power auger.

4. Pour 2" to 3" of loose gravel into each hole for drainage. Make certain the hole dimensions comply with your local building code, which may require flaring the footings to 12" at the base.

5. Cut the footing forms to length, using a reciprocating saw or handsaw. Insert the forms into the holes, leaving 2" of each form above grade. Pack soil around the forms.

6. Fill the forms with concrete and tamp the concrete with a long stick to eliminate any air pockets. Screed the tops flush with a flat 2 × 4. Insert a J-bolt into each footing, leaving ¾" to 1" of thread exposed.

7. Retie the mason's strings and drop a plumb bob to position each J-bolt at the exact center of the footing. Clean the bolt threads before the concrete sets.

Step C: Set the Deck Posts

1. Start by laying a long, straight 2 × 4 flat across each pair of footings. With one edge tight against the J-bolts, draw a reference line across each footing.

2. Place a metal post anchor on each footing, center it over the J-bolt, and square it with the reference line. Thread a nut over each J-bolt and tighten each of the post anchors in place.

3. Cut the posts (C) to their approximate length, adding several inches for final trimming. Place the posts in the anchors and tack them into place with one nail each.

4. With a level as a guide, use braces and stakes to plumb the posts. Once the posts are plumb, finish nailing them to the anchors.

5. To determine the height of the posts, make a mark on the house, 7¼" down from the bottom edge of the ledger. Use a straight 2 × 4 and a level to extend this line across a post. Transfer this line to the remaining posts.

6. Cut the posts off with a reciprocating saw or a handsaw and attach post-beam caps to the tops, using 10d joist hanger nails.

Step D: Install the Beams

1. Cut the beams from 2 × 10" lumber, adding several inches to each beam for final trimming. Position the beam boards (C) so the crowns face the same direction, and fasten them together

B. *Add 2" to the hole depth and cut the concrete tube forms to length, using a reciprocating saw or handsaw. Make sure the cut is straight.*

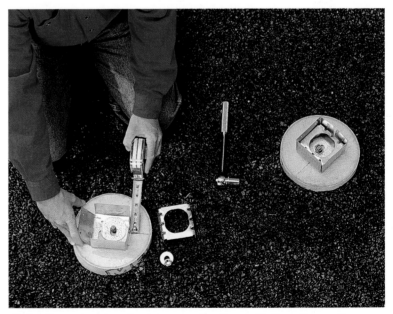

C. *Set the post anchors in place, squaring them with the reference line scribed on the footings.*

with 10d galvanized common nails spaced every 16".

2. Position beams C-1 and C-2 in their post-beam caps and attach them with nails.

3. Mark and cut the angled end of beam C-3 by mitering it at 22½°. Position the beam in the post caps.

4. Make a 22½° miter cut at one end of beam C-4 to form a 45° corner with beam C-3. Leave the other end long for final trimming. Place beam C-4 in the post-beam caps.

5. Fit the beams tightly together, fasten them with 3" deck screws, and attach them to the post caps with 10d joist hanger nails.

Step E: Install the Joists

1. Referring to the Framing Plan on page 274, cut rim joist F-1 to final length, and cut end joist E-1 generously long, to allow for final trimming.

2. Fasten one end of rim joist F-1 to the ledger with 16d galvanized common nails. Rest end joist E-1 in place on beams C-1 and C-2. Fasten F-1 and E-1 together with 16d galvanized common nails.

3. Use a framing square to finalize the location of E-1 on the beams. Mark the beams and trim them to length. Toenail E-1 in

place on the beams.

4. Cut end joist E-2 to length. Install it by nailing it to the end of the ledger, checking for square, and toenailing it to the top of beam C-3. Trim the beam to length.

5. Mark the outlines of the inner joists (D) on the ledger, beams and rim joist F-1 (see Framing Plan, page 274), using a tape measure and a combination square.

6. Attach joist hangers to the ledger and rim joist F-1 with 10d joist hanger nails, using a scrap 2 × 8 as a spacer to achieve the correct spread for each hanger. NOTE: Spacing between the joists is irregular to accommodate the installation of railing posts.

7. Place the inside joists in the hangers on the ledger and on rim joist F-1, crown up, and attach them with 10d joist hanger nails. Be sure to use all the nail holes in the hangers. Toenail the joists to the beams and leave the joists long for final trimming.

8. Mark the final length of the inside joists by making a line across the tops of the joists from the end of end joist E-2. Check for square. Brace the inside joists by tacking a board across their edges for stability. Cut them to length with a circular saw.

9. Cut rim joist F-2 long to allow for final trimming, and nail into position with 16d galvanized common nails.

D. *Fit beam C-4 tightly against beam C-3 and attach the two beams to each other with 10d common nails.*

E. *Mark the three remaining inside joists for cutting by snapping a chalk line. Brace and miter-cut the three inside joists.*

10. To mark the remaining joists for trimming at a 45° angle, make a mark 139" from the 90° corner on end joist E-1. Make a second mark 139" from the other 90° corner along rim joist F-2. The distance between these two points should be at least 70". If necessary, move the line back until it measures 70". Regardless of the overall dimensions of your deck, this length will ensure adequate space for mounting the railing posts at the top of the stairway.

11. Mark the last three joists for cutting by snapping a chalk line between the marked points on end joist E-1 and rim joist F-2. Transfer the cut marks to the faces of the joists with a combination square, and cut the miters with a circular saw.

12. Measure, cut, and attach rim joist F-3 across the angle with 16d galvanized common nails.

Step F: Install the Railing Posts

1. Cut the railing posts (G) to size and notch the lower ends to fit around the rim joists (see Railing Detail, page 275).

2. Clamp all but two of the posts together to lay out and cut ¾ × 3½" notches, or dadoes, for the horizontal rails. NOTE: The posts at the stairway are not notched for rails.

3. Cut the dadoes by making a series of parallel ¾"-deep cuts

within each 3½" space, about ¼" apart, with a circular saw. Knock out the waste wood between the cuts, using a hammer. Then, chisel smooth the bottom of each dado.

4. To locate the railing posts on the diagonal corner, find the centerline of rim joist F-3 and measure 18" in both directions. These points are the inner faces of the railing posts and the outer faces of the stringers. Drill ¼" pilot holes through the railing posts into the rim joist, and secure the posts with lag screws.

5. To position the corner railing posts, measure 3" both ways from the outside corners of rim joist F-3. Predrill the posts, and use a ratchet wrench to attach them to the rim joists with lag screws.

6. Use the Framing Plan (page 274) and the Corner Post Detail (below) to locate the remaining railing posts.

Step G: Install the Decking, Nailer & Face Boards

1. Measure, mark, and cut the decking (H) to size, making notches to fit around the railing posts. Position the first board above the stairway, and attach it by driving a pair of deck screws into each joist.

2. Position the remaining decking boards so that the ends overhang the deck, leaving ⅛" gaps between the boards to allow

F. Drill pilot holes through the posts and into the rim joists, and attach the posts with lag screws. Note the unnotched stairway post.

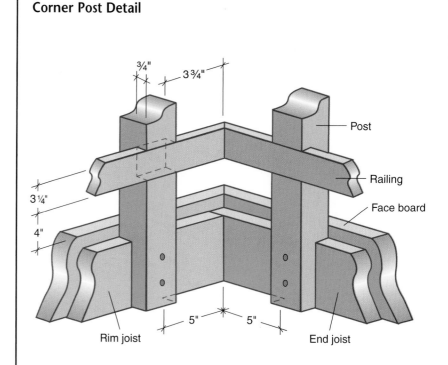

Corner Post Detail

Post

Railing

Face board

Rim joist

End joist

¾"

3¾"

3¼"

4"

5"

5"

G. Cut the notches for the first decking board and position it above the stairway.

H. Drill pilot holes through the treads to prevent splitting. Then, attach the treads to the stringers with deck screws, using a power driver.

for drainage.

3. Where more than one board is required to span the deck, cut the ends at 45° angles and make the joint at the center of a joist.

4. Snap a chalk line flush with the edge of the deck, and cut off the overhanging ends of the deck boards with a circular saw set for a 1½"-deep cut.

5. Measure, mark, and cut the stairway nailer (I) to size and attach it to the rim joist with a mending plate and deck screws (see Stairway Detail, page 275).

6. Measure, mark, and cut the face boards (J) to length, making 45° miter cuts at the right angle corners, and 22½° miter cuts at the stairway corners. Attach the face boards to the rim and end joists with pairs of deck screws at 2-ft. intervals.

Step H: Pour the Concrete Pad & Build the Stairway

1. Determine the location for the pad. Add 6" in each direction, and excavate the area approximately 8" deep.

2. Lay and tamp a 4" base of compactible gravel.

3. Build a form from 2 × 6" lumber (see Framing Plan, page 274). Level the form at 42" below the finished surface of the deck, to accommodate six 7" stairway rises. Stake the form into place.

4. Fill the form with concrete, screed it flush with a 2 × 4, and let the concrete set overnight.

5. Lay out and cut the stringers (K) to size, according to the Stairway Detail (page 275). The center stringer is notched at the top and bottom to fit around the gussets. Mark the rises and runs with a framing square. Cut the notches with a circular saw, using a reciprocating saw or handsaw to finish the corners.

6. Measure, mark, and cut the gussets (L) to length. Assemble the stairway framework by nailing the gussets in place between the outer stringers with 16d galvanized common nails. Turn the framework upside down and attach the center stringer by nailing through the gussets.

7. Position the framework against the deck, and attach with deck screws driven through the upper gusset into the face board and nailer. Drill pilot holes through the lower gusset into the concrete pad, and attach with masonry screws.

8. Cut the stairway railing posts (N) to length. To install the railing posts, clamp them in place against the stringers, drill pilot holes through the stringers into the posts, and attach the posts with ⅜ × 4" lag screws.

9. Measure, mark, and cut the treads (O) to length. For the bottom treads, use a piece of railing post scrap to trace a line for the notch. Then, cut the notch with a circular saw. Attach the treads to the stringers with deck screws.

Step I: Build the Railing

1. Measure and cut to length the 10-ft. rails, each with one end mitered at 45°. Install the rails, using 1½" deck screws.

2. Miter one end of the long rails at 45°. Leave the other end long for final trimming.

3. Clamp each long rail in place and use a straightedge to mark cut lines at the angled corner. Transfer this line to the face of each rail, using a combination square. Remove the rails and miter-cut the ends for the angled corners at 22½°.

4. Reposition the rails and attach them to the railing posts with 1½" deck screws.

5. Measure, mark, and cut the short rails to length with one end mitered at 22½° and the other end cut square.

6. Fasten the ends of the short rails to the railing posts above the stairway with angle brackets. Use ⅝" galvanized screws to attach the brackets to the rails and 1½" deck screws to attach them to the posts. Attach them to the notched post as well, using 1½" deck screws.

7. Measure, mark, and cut the deck railing cap (Q), and install

it with 3" deck screws.

Step J: Build the Stairway Railing

1. To mark the stairway posts for trimming, hold the edge of a straight 2 × 4 across the deck post at the top of the stairs and the stairway post below. With the upper end of the 2 × 4 against the underside of the deck railing cap, and the 2 × 4 parallel to the stairway stringer, mark a cut line on the stairway post along the underside of the 2 × 4. Cut the post to length.

2. Repeat the process to mark and cut the other stairway post to length.

3. Measure, mark, and cut the stairway railing caps (see Stairway Detail, page 275). Place a cedar 2 × 6 on top of the stairway posts, mark the angles for the ends, and cut to length, allowing for a 1" overhang at the end of the stairway.

4. Install the stairway railing caps with 3" deck screws.

5. To cut the stairway rails, hold each one tight against the bottom of the cap and mark the ends. Cut the rails to length so that they fit tight between the posts.

6. To install the rails, mark the positions of the rails on the posts and attach them with angle brackets, using ⅝" screws and 1½" deck screws.

I. *Clamp the long rails, mark the ends, and transfer the lines across the face of the board with a combination square to ensure a tight-fitting 22½° miter with the short rail.*

J. *Use angle brackets to attach the stairway railing pieces and angled rails. To attach the brackets to the rails, use ⅝" galvanized screws.*

Low-profile Deck

This low-profile deck creates a distinctive focal point for homes with ground-level entries. The composite decking complements the rich tones of the cedar, and the V-pattern directs your view to the centerpoint of the deck. This deck is ideal for flat, level lots or for covering up an old cement patio, and requires no posts, so construction is easier than building a higher deck. Since this deck is less than 24" high, there's also no requirement for a railing. This deck can hold a BBQ, table, chairs, and lots of other accessories. Our plan also calls for a suspended step that's perfect for areas with snow and frost.

MATERIALS

- 8"-diameter concrete footing forms (6)
- 3" direct-bearing hardware (6)
- 2 × 8" double joist hangers (4)
- 2½" composite decking screws
- 2 × 8" joist hangers (72)
- 10d joist hanger nails
- 16d galvanized box nails
- 12d galvanized casing nails
- ⅜ × 4" carriage bolts, washers, and nuts (12)
- ⅜ × 4" lag screws (22)
- Lead masonry anchors (22)
- Ledger flashing (20 ft.)
- Exterior silicone caulk (3 tubes)
- Concrete as required

Cutaway View

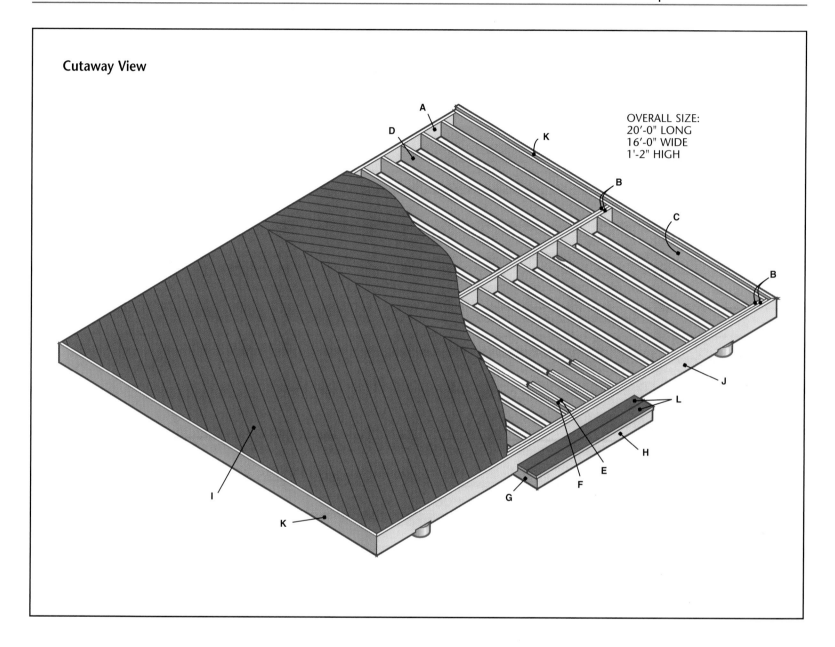

OVERALL SIZE:
20'-0" LONG
16'-0" WIDE
1'-2" HIGH

Lumber List			
Qty.	Size	Material	Part
5	2 × 8" × 20'	Trtd. lumber	Ledger (A) & Beam bds (B)
2	2 × 8" × 16'	Trtd. lumber	End joists (C)
40	2 × 8" × 8'	Trtd. lumber	Joists (D)
3	2 × 4" × 8'	Trtd. lumber	Step support spacers (E)
2	2 × 6" × 8'	Trtd. lumber	Interior step supports (F)
1	2 × 6" × 6'	Cedar	End step supports (G)

Lumber List			
Qty.	Size	Material	Part
2	2 × 6" × 6'	Cedar	Step riser (H)
74	2 × 6" × 10'	Composite	Decking (I)
2	2 × 6" × 6'	Composite	Tread (L)
1	2 × 10" × 20'	Cedar	Front face bd (J)
2	2 × 10" × 16'	Cedar	Side face bds (K)

HOW TO BUILD A LOW-PROFILE DECK

Step A: Attach the Ledger

1. Measure and cut the ledger (A) to length. Drill pairs of ¼" pilot holes at 2-ft. intervals. Counterbore each hole ½", using a 1" spade bit.

2. Determine ledger location and draw its outline on the wall. Make sure you include a 3" space at each end of the ledger for the end joists and side face boards. Temporarily brace the ledger in position, using 2 × 4s. Make sure the ledger is level and mark the hole locations on the wall with an awl or nail.

3. Remove the ledger and drill anchor holes 3" deep, using a ⅜" masonry bit. Drive lead anchors into the drilled holes, using a rubber mallet, and attach the ledger to the wall with lag screws and washers, using a ratchet wrench.

4. Seal the screw heads, and the joint between the wall and ledger, with silicone caulk.

Step B: Pour the Footings

1. To locate the footings, refer to the measurements in the Framing Plan (page 284) and mark the centerline for each pair of footings on the ledger.

2. Construct three temporary 2 × 4 batterboards. Position the batterboards out from the footing marks, approximately 19 ft. from the ledger. Stretch mason's string from the bottom of the ledger at each mark to the corresponding batterboard, making sure that the strings are level and perpendicular to the ledger.

3. Check for square, using the "3-4-5 carpenter's triangle" method. From the point where each string meets the ledger, measure 3 ft. along the ledger and make a mark. Next, measure 4 ft. out along the string and mark with tape. The distance between the points on the ledger and the string should be 5 ft. If it's not, adjust the string position on the batterboard accordingly.

4. To locate the centers of the six footings, build four more batterboards and stretch two additional mason's strings parallel to the house (refer to the Framing Plan, page 284 for measurements). Use a plumb bob to transfer the footing centerpoints to the ground, and drive a stake to mark each point.

A. *Attach the ledger to the masonry wall with lag screws and washers, using a ratchet wrench.*

B. *Level the footing forms against the mason's strings, pour the concrete, and set the direct-bearing hardware into the wet concrete, using the layout strings to ensure accurate alignment (inset).*

5. Remove the mason's strings and dig the footings, using a clamshell digger or power auger. Pour 2" to 3" of loose gravel into each footing hole for drainage. NOTE: When measuring the footing size and depth, make sure you comply with your local building code, which may require flaring the base to 12".

6. Cut the footing forms to length, using a reciprocating saw or handsaw, and insert them into the footing holes.

7. Retie the mason's strings, making sure they are level.

8. Level the tops of the forms by setting them flush with the mason's strings and packing soil around them to hold them securely in place.

9. Remove the mason's strings and fill the footing forms with concrete, tamping with a long stick or rod to eliminate any air gaps.

10. Screed the concrete flush, using a straight 2 × 4, then insert direct-bearing hardware into each footing while the concrete is still wet. Reattach the layout strings to ensure that the hardware is aligned correctly.

Step C: Install the Beams

1. Measure, mark, and cut the beam boards (B) to length, using a circular saw. NOTE: Three of the beam boards are the same length as the ledger. The fourth board is 3" longer to accommodate the 1½" end joist on each end.

2. Make each beam by fastening two beam boards together with pairs of box nails driven at 16" intervals. At both ends of the outer beam, the long beam board overhangs 1½", creating a notch for attaching the end joist.

3. Position the beams crown-side-up on the direct-bearing hardware. Double-check that both beams are correctly aligned with the ledger, and attach to the hardware with carriage bolts.

Step D: Install the Joists

1. Measure, mark, and cut the end joists (C) to length. The end joists extend from the house to the notch in the end of the outer beam. In our plan the end joists are 189" long, but verify this measurement before cutting. Attach the end joists to the ledger and beams with box nails.

2. Measure, mark, and cut double center joists (D). Mark the centerline of the deck on

C. *Set the beams in the direct-bearing hardware on the footings. Note the "notch" for the end joist at the end of the outer beam.*

D. *Measure, cut, and install the joists with joist hangers, verifying the length of each one as you go.*

E. *Cut notches for the step supports in the outer beam with a reciprocating saw or handsaw. Finish the notches with a hammer and chisel.*

F. *Lay composite decking boards with a ⅛" to ¼" gap to allow for drainage, expansion, and contraction.*

the ledger and beams, install double joist hangers at each mark, and nail the joists in place. Seal the seam between the beam boards in the double joists with silicone caulk to protect against moisture.

3. Locate the remaining joists by measuring along the ledger and beams from the center joists, and marking centerlines at 12" intervals (see Framing Plan, page 284). Install a joist hanger at each centerline.

4. Measure, mark, and cut the inner joists (D), verifying the actual lengths, and install in joist hangers with joist hanger nails.

Step E: Build the Step

1. Measure, mark, and cut the step support spacers (E). Set the spacers back approximately 1" from the front beam, and attach to the deck joists with deck screws (see Step Detail, page 289).

2. Cut 1½ × 1½" notches in the bottom edge of the front beam, adjacent to the step support spacers. Use a reciprocating saw or handsaw to make the vertical cuts, and finish each notch with a chisel and hammer.

3. Measure, mark, and cut the step supports (F) and end step

supports (G) to length. Make a 45° miter cut at the front of the end step supports where they meet the step riser. Attach the step supports to the spacers with deck screws. The interior step supports extend 11¼" beyond the beam, while the end step supports extend 12¾" to allow for the miter joints at the riser.

4. Measure, mark, and cut the step riser (H) to length, with 45° mitered ends. Attach the riser to the step supports with 12d galvanized casing nails.

Step F: Lay the Decking

1. To create reference lines, mark a point in the center of the front of the deck. Measure equal distances along the double center joist, and along the outer beam, then snap a chalk line between these points. As you progress with rows of decking, periodically measure between the ends of the decking boards and the reference line to help you maintain a consistent angle.

2. Begin laying the composite decking at the front center of the deck. Cut one end of the first decking board at a 45° angle and leave the other end slightly long. Position it above the step, aligning the 45° cut with the centerline of the double joist, and fasten with 2½" composite screws.

3. Cut and attach the next deck board in similar fashion, leaving ⅛" to ¼" spaces between the boards.

4. Cut and attach the remaining deck boards, periodically checking the angle of the decking against the reference lines and making any necessary adjustments.

5. After installing the decking, trim the excess that overhangs the deck ends. For boards 16 ft. or smaller, leave a gap at the deck ends and at any butt joints—¹⁄₁₆" for every 20°F difference between the temperature at the time of installation and the expected high for the year—as composite decking will expand and contract. Set the blade depth on your circular saw at slightly more than 1½", and trim the decking to size.

Step G: Install the Face Boards

1. Measure, mark, and cut the front face board (J) to size (see Detail, page 285), and notch it to fit around the step supports. Cut 45° miters on both ends.

2. Temporarily clamp the face board in place and mark for notching around the footings. Also mark the points where the carriage bolts in the direct-bearing hardware contact the back of the board.

3. Remove the board, cut the footing notches, and chisel out the back of the board to accommodate the carriage bolts. Attach the face board with 12d galvanized casing nails.

4. Measure, mark, and cut the side face boards (K) to length, making 45° miter cuts at the front ends. Attach the face boards to the end joists with deck screws.

5. Complete the suspended step by cutting the composite treads (L) to length and attaching them to the step supports, using 2½"composite screws. Leave a ½" gap at the front face board, and a ¼" gap between the treads.

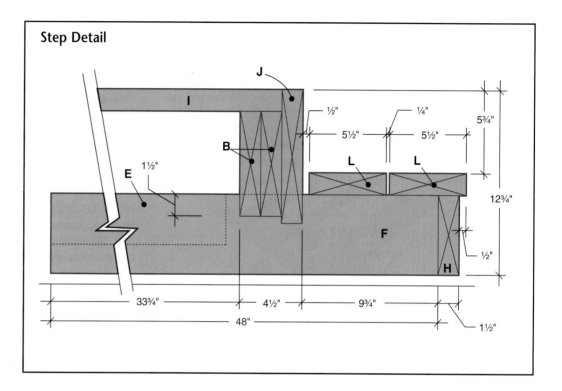

Step Detail

G. Cut the composite step treads to length and attach with composite screws, leaving a ½" gap between the first tread and the face board.

Deck Ideas

Photo courtesy of Archadeck

(above left) **A space too small for a practical yard** can be ideal for an expansive deck. This large deck occupies virtually the entire back yard of this home.

Photo courtesy of California Redwood Association

(right) **This well-integrated deck** features a low-profile design that takes advantage of a natural alcove in the home's design. Its decking, arbor, and trim are painted and stained to match the house.

Photo courtesy of Lindal Cedar Homes, Inc.; Seattle, WA

(left) **This elevated, panoramic deck** is designed to take advantage of a magnificent view of the surrounding countryside. The shaded space underneath the deck is ideal on sunny days.

(above) **This elaborate, custom-designed deck** adds great value to this home. Its rustic flavor helps it blend into the surrounding natural landscape.

(left) **A multi-level rooftop deck** makes good use of a limited yard space that has almost no level areas. Several separate activity areas have been established here, each of which can be accessed from many different points of the home or yard.

Porches

Few elements of your home will conjure up sweeter memories than a breezy front porch on a perfect summer evening. Linking your home to your landscape, a porch creates a traditional threshold to your home.

Porch designs and styles are endless, limited only by your imagination. For instance, a porch can wrap around your home to allow you to take advantage of a spectacular view. If insects are a problem where you live, a screened-in porch can be beneficial. Or if you simply want to dress up a bare entry, a portico not only can provide decoration, but also keep rain and snow from falling directly over the entrance.

This section will help you plan, design, and build your porch from the ground up. Tips are offered on evaluating your property, working with building codes and authorities, and drawing working plans. And because every porch project is unique, step-by-step instructions are provided to assist you in understanding the parts and techniques needed in building a standard porch, from attaching ledgers to installing railings. In addition, detailed projects are included for building concrete steps and constructing a three-season porch.

Whether you're looking to create a comfortable spot to contemplate your flower garden, or simply make your home's entrance more inviting, a porch will not only increase your home's value, but it will create a new outdoor living space you'll enjoy for years to come.

Planning & Designing Porches

As with any addition you make to your home, a porch requires some fore-thought. There will be the fun of dreaming up ideas and designs, but you will also have to do research and planning. An evaluation of your property will help you determine if, in fact, you have the space available to build the porch you envision. Your local zoning ordinances and building codes will specify where and how you can build. Finally, you will have to create detailed plans that comply with those building codes in order to obtain a building permit.

Because porches and entries come in many shapes and forms, choosing the best design for your home is an important decision, worthy of careful consideration. The choices you make will affect your property's value, so make sure your porch design not only meets your needs, but makes sense when viewed with the rest of your home. Browse through magazines, walk through neighborhoods, and visit libraries to gather as much information as you can, then jot down ideas that can be incorporated into your design. A professional designer or architect can also help you plan a project to meet your specific needs and budget, while satisfying local building codes.

Review your list of porch ideas and uses, and compare it to your site. Take stock of your property. Determine whether there is room to build in the proposed location, or if it is possible to build around existing landscape elements without running afoul of your local building and zoning restrictions. Also:

• Note the location of windows, electrical service lines, and any other obstructions that might affect the position or design of your porch.

Anatomy of a Porch

This illustration shows each part of a typical porch. Though the structural components are standard, the decorative details may differ, based on your specific porch details and design.

Ledgers anchor the porch deck to the house, supporting one side of the joists.

Concrete footings with post anchors support the weight of the porch and hold it in place.

Posts transfer the weight of the porch roof and porch deck to the footings.

Joists are horizontal members that support the porch floor.

Porch flooring commonly consists of tongue-and-groove porch boards installed over a plywood subfloor. The subfloor is attached to the joists. Trim, called the **apron**, is added to conceal the joist frame.

Beams distribute bearing loads of the roof to the posts.

Trusses and **rafters** bear on the beams, and give shape and stability to the roof. The angle of the rafter chords creates the roof pitch, allowing water to shed.

Sheathing ties the framing members together, creating rigidity and strength in the structure.

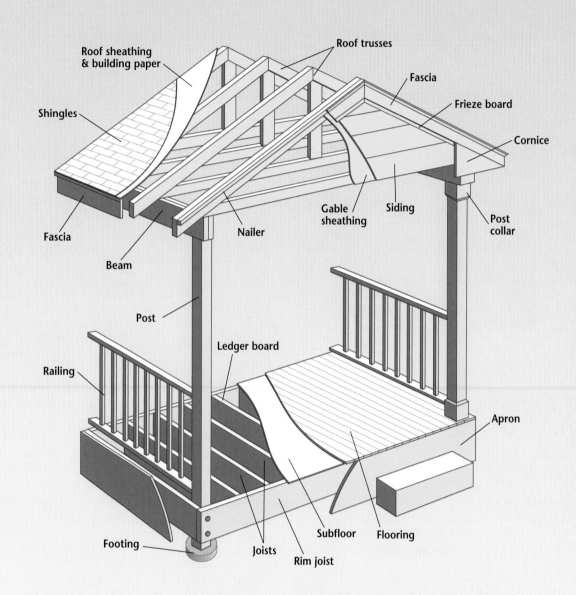

Fascia boards are the trim at the gable ends and eaves of a roof. **Frieze boards** are blocking between the sheathing and fascia boards.

Roofing materials (such as building paper, drip-edge, and asphalt shingles) shed water to protect the structural members of the roof from rot.

Post collars, cornices, soffits, and ceilings all help to conceal the framing members and decorate the structure.

Railings create a security barrier between the edge of the porch and the ground, while steps allow access to and from the porch and yard.

A floor plan shows overall project dimensions, the size and spacing of floor joists, the size and location of posts, and the types of hardware to be used for connecting and anchoring structural members.

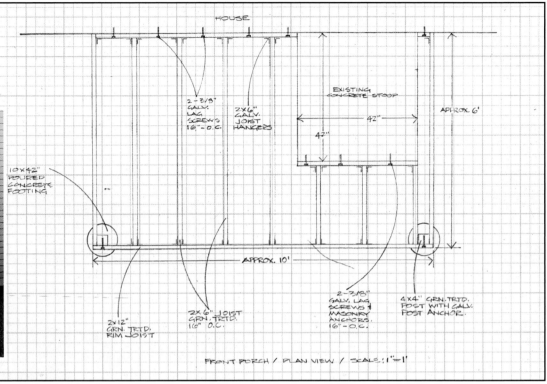

- Note whether the proposed porch area is exposed to direct sun or wind, which can be determining factors in the porch design.
- Consider the style and construction of your house and what porch roof style would blend best with your home.
- Mark your property lines and measure distances from the planned project area to municipal sidewalks or streets. (To avoid future disputes, mark property lines 1 ft. in from your actual property boundaries.)
- Measure the slope of the proposed building site to determine whether you must regrade. If the slope is greater than 1" per foot, you may have to consult a landscape architect.

It is also important to assess the building materials used in and around the planned project area. If you have stucco siding, for example, allow extra time for siding removal.

Contact your local building departments early in the planning process. The types of projects that require building permits vary among localities, but it is safe to say that a major project—such as a porch—will require a permit. Inspections may be required before, during, and even after porch construction.

The building department can also be a helpful resource. The staff inspectors can grant building permits, answer questions, and provide information. For example, if your porch will occupy space near property borders or municipal streets or sidewalks,

an inspector can tell you whether you will need a variance from the local zoning commission.

Building codes often prescribe minimum sizes for structural members of your project, like deck joists, beams, posts, and ledgers. The height, width, and estimated weight of the project must be suitable for the support methods used, and comply with any neighborhood covenants. Screw sizes and spacing are usually indicated for most parts of the project, from structural elements to roof covering. Depending upon where you live, there may be special requirements for your project. For example, in cold climates, concrete frost footings of 48" or deeper sometimes are required. You also will be required to pay a permit fee, which likely will be based on your project's estimated cost.

Before issuing a building permit for your porch project, the building department will require a detailed plan that includes both an elevation drawing and a floor plan. There are some very specific conventions you must follow to create these drawings, so get assistance if you have not done this kind of work before. Refer to pages 28 to 29 for more information and techniques on drawing plans.

Begin by drawing a site map on which you can sketch your final ideas and plans. Your site map should include relevant features, such as shade patterns, trees, and other landscaping details. Also measure the height of door thresholds and the length and height of any walls or buildings adjacent to the proposed project area. Use tracing paper to try out a few different design ideas before drawing up your final plans. Remember, your local building department may require changes to your plans based on codes and zoning restriction.

If you have a larger-scale or elaborate porch project in mind, you may need to enlist the aid of an architect or designer to help you develop your ideas into detailed drawings.

Once you have your permit, you can begin construction, but take some commonsense precautions to work safely outdoors:

- Always follow basic safety rules for working with ladders and scaffolding, and provide level, stable footing for extension ladders.
- Set up your work site for quick disposal of waste materials, and create a storage surface to keep tools safely off the ground.
- Wear sensible clothing and use protective equipment, including a cap, eye protection, a particle mask, work gloves, full-length pants, and a long-sleeved shirt.
- Plan your work days to avoid extreme heat, take frequent breaks, and drink plenty of fluids.

Because of the size of the structure and the amount of work involved, make sure to enlist some help during the building of your porch.

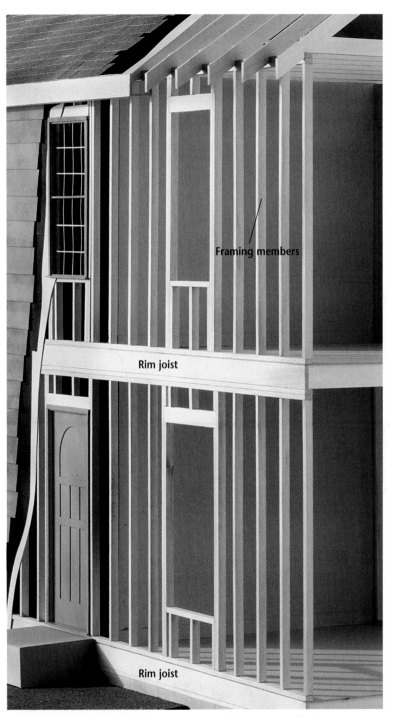

Try to use the same roof slope as your house. *To measure, hold a carpenter's square against the roofline with the long arm perfectly horizontal. Position the square so the long arm intersects the roof at the 12" mark. On the short arm, measure down to the point of intersection: the number of inches gives you the roof slope in a 12" span. For example, if the top of the square is 4" from the roofline, then your roof slope is 4-in-12.*

Learn about house construction. *The model above shows the basic construction of a platform-framed house—by far the most common type of framing today. Pay special attention to locations of rim joists and framing members, since you likely will need to anchor any large porch or patio project to one or both of these elements.*

Building a Basic Porch:

Step-by-Step Overview

Every porch project is different, because each home offers special challenges and every owner has specific design considerations in mind. However, there are some elements of a porch that are constant. From the ground up, the bare bones of porches are the same.

The following directions on pages 306 to 333 are the basic techniques you will need in order to build a porch. As with a deck, it is a good idea to build a porch in several stages, gathering tools and materials for each stage before beginning. And because of the size and complexity of most porch designs, have at least one helper for the more difficult stages.

Have the local utilities lines for electrical, telephone, and water lines marked, and refer to your building plans often. Use the techniques illustrated in this project as a guide to help you convert your own porch plan into a reality.

A. *Install a ledger to anchor the porch deck to the house, then use it as reference to lay out the footings and posts (pages 306 to 309). If building over old steps, attach a step ledger to the riser of the top step (pages 311).*

B. *Build the porch deck frame, then install metal joist hangers on the ledger and rim joist, and install the remaining joists (pages 310 to 311).*

C. *Install a plywood subfloor over the joists, then tongue-and-groove porch boards (pages 312 to 313). The porch boards, usually made of fir, are nailed to the subfloor with a floor nailer tool (shown).*

D. *Install a roof ledger and beams, then hoist the trusses up onto the beams, and fasten into place (pages 314 to 317).*

E. *Lay plywood sheathing across the trusses, then install the gable sheathing, frieze boards, and fascia boards (pages 318 to 319). Finish the roof with asphalt shingles (pages 393 to 395), using step flashing when tying into the house (page 320 to 321).*

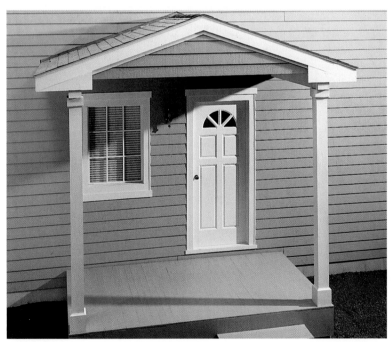

F. *Wrap the posts and beams with finish-grade lumber to give them a more solid, proportional look (pages 322 to 323). Install cornices and finish the gable siding (pages 324 to 325). Install soffits and ceilings to hide the remaining construction details (pages 326 to 327).*

G. *With the porch completed, you will need to add railings (pages 328 to 329) if your porch deck is higher than 20". Build wooden steps to provide access to the porch (pages 330 to 333).*

Attaching Ledgers & Installing Posts

You want your porch to be permanent, and permanence requires a sturdy foundation and a strong roof. After all, you don't want to discover that your porch has drifted away from your home or that your roof sags as time goes by.

Ledger boards and posts will support the roof and the deck of a porch for its entire life. A ledger board is a sturdy piece of lumber, anywhere from a 2 × 6 to a 2 × 12, that is secured to a house wall to support joists or rafters for the porch. The techniques for installing a porch ledger are the same as for a deck. Refer to pages 212 to 214 for more information on installing ledgers to different types of siding materials.

Ledgers must be attached to the wall at framing member loca-tions, or attached directly to the house rim joist, if the rim joist is at the correct height. Before starting ledger installation, you must locate and mark framing members.

Posts used in most porch projects are 4 × 4 or 6 × 6 lumber that is attached to concrete footings with post-anchor hardware.

In most cases, porches are built with posts at the front only. A ledger is installed at deck level to support the floor, and another is usually installed at ceiling level to anchor the roof beams and the rafters or trusses.

The project shown here incorporates a set of old concrete steps for the foundation (also refer to page 311), by making a cutout in the deck-level ledger board that is the same width and position as the steps, and attaching the cut section to the face of the top riser with masonry anchors. If this is not the case for your project, install a standard ledger board.

A. *(left) Mark the center and endpoint of the ledger location, then mark the ledger height. Use a straight, scrap 2 × 4 and a level to ensure the ledger is at the same height as the steps.*

Drip-edge flashing

B. *Apply exterior panel adhesive to the flashing, and slip the flashing behind the siding at the top of the cutout.*

TOOLS & MATERIALS

- Tape measure
- Hammer
- Circular saw or handsaw
- Chisel
- Metal snips or aviator's snips
- Drill and bits (¼" twist & 1" spade, or ⅜" & ⅝" masonry)
- Caulk gun
- Carpenter's level
- Framing square

- Ratchet wrench
- Awl & rubber mallet
- Mason's string
- Straightedge
- Plumb bob
- Line level
- Shovel
- Wheelbarrow
- Combination square
- Construction plans
- Framing lumber

- Metal or vinyl drip-edge flashing
- Exterior panel adhesive or caulk
- Concrete
- Concrete footing tube forms
- Post anchors
- 10d joist hanger nails
- 8d galvanized nails
- ⅜ × 4" lag screws
- 2½" deck screws

HOW TO INSTALL THE LEDGER & POSTS

Step A: Mark the Ledger Outline

1. Mark the center of the project area onto the wall of your house to use as a reference point for establishing the layout.

2. Measure out from the center and mark the endpoints of the ledger location, then mark the ledger height at the centerline. The top of the ledger should be even with the back edge of the steps. Use a straightedge and a level to extend the height mark to the endpoints of the ledger location.

3. Mark cutting lines for the ledger board cutout on the siding, ½" around the ledger layout. Extend the marks across the project area with the level and straightedge.

Step B: Remove the Siding & Install the Flashing

1. Remove the siding at the cutting lines (pages 212 to 214). For wood siding, set the blade of your circular saw so it cuts through the thickness of the siding. Cut along the cutting lines, and finish the cuts at the corners with a wood chisel.

2. Cut a piece of metal or vinyl drip-edge flashing to fit the length of the cutout area. Apply caulk or exterior panel adhesive to the back face of the flashing, and slip the flashing between the siding at the top of the cutout.

Step C: Mark Joist Locations on the Ledger & Rim Joist

1. Cut a 2 × 8 ledger board to size, which should be 4" shorter than the full length of the porch. Also cut the rim joist from 2 × 12 lumber, according to your project plans.

2. Lay the ledger board next to the rim joist to gang-mark deck joist locations onto the ledger and the rim joist. Set a 2 × 6 spacer at each end of the ledger to make up for the difference in length between the two, then mark the joist locations onto the ledger and the rim joist. Start 15¼" from one end of the rim joist, and mark deck joist locations 16" apart on-center.

C. *Align the ledger and the rim joist. Mark on-center joist locations on both boards every 16", using a straightedge.*

D. *Cut the ledger to size, using a circular saw or handsaw.*

Step D: Mark, Cut & Install the Ledger

1. Position the ledger on the back steps, and mark cutting lines onto the full-length ledger board at the edges of the steps. Cut the ledger into sections.

2. Position the ledger board sections in the cutout areas, up against the drip-edge flashing. Tack in place with 8d galvanized common nails.

3. Drill two counterbored pilot holes into the ledger at framing member locations, or at 16" intervals if attaching at the rim joist. Drive ⅜ × 4" galvanized lag screws, with washers, into the pilot holes to secure the ledger.

Step E: Locate the Footings

1. Build two batterboards (page 215 to 216) and drive one into the ground at each side of the porch, 12" past the front of the project area, aligned with the project edge.

2. Drive a nail at each end of the ledger, and tie a mason's string to each nail. Tie the other end of each string to a batterboard.

3. Square the string with the ledger, using the 3-4-5 method

(pages 215 to 217, or page 103): Mark the ledger board 3 ft. from the end, then mark the mason's string 4 ft. out from the same point. Adjust the mason's string until the endpoints from the 3-ft. and 4-ft. marks are exactly 5 ft. apart, then retie. Make sure the mason's string is taut.

4. Measure out from the ledger board and mark the post centers on the mason's string with a piece of tape.

5. Hang a plumb bob from each piece of tape, then drive a stake into the ground at the post-center location.

Step F: Pour the Footings

1. Set an 8"-diameter concrete tube form onto the ground, centered around the stake. Mark the edges of the form onto the ground. Remove the form and the stake, and dig a hole past the frost-line depth (page 108). Avoid moving the mason's string.

2. Set the concrete tube form into the hole so the top is about 2" above the ground. Use a level to make sure the top of the form is level. Repeat for the other post footing.

3. Mix concrete and fill the forms. Screed the surface of the concrete with a scrap of 2 × 4.

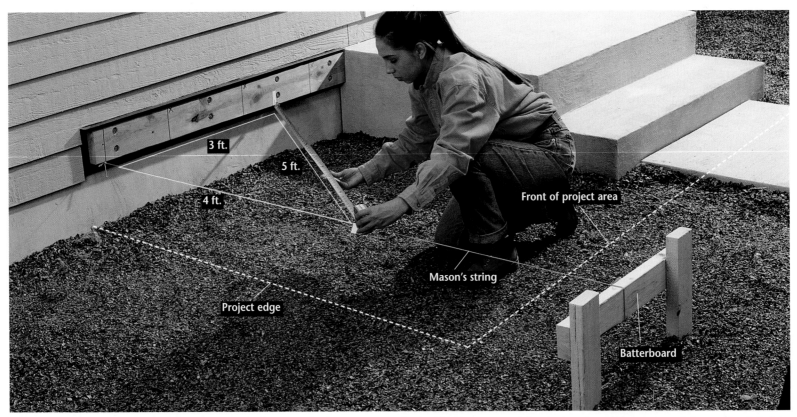

3 ft.

5 ft.

4 ft.

Front of project area

Mason's string

Project edge

Batterboard

E. *Establish square lines for the sides of the porch, by using the 3-4-5 carpenter's triangle, then measure for the location of the posts and drop a plumb bob to transfer the center point of the post to the ground.*

4. Drop a plumb bob from the tape marks on the mason's string to find the post centers on the surface of the concrete. Insert a J-bolt into the concrete at that point. The threaded end of the J-bolt should extend up at least 2". Let the concrete cure for three days.

Step G: Install the Posts

1. Set a metal post anchor over the J-bolt, and secure with a washer and nut.

2. Cut a post that is at least 6" longer than the planned post height.

3. With a helper, set the post into the post anchor and secure with 8d galvanized nails driven through the pilot holes in the post anchor. Install both posts.

4. Brace each post with a pair of 2 × 4s attached to stakes driven in line with the edges of the posts, but outside of the project area. Secure the braces to the stakes with 2½" deck screws, then use a level to make sure the posts are plumb. Attach the braces to the posts with 2½" deck screws.

F. *Drop a plumb bob to determine the exact center of the footing, and then install a J-bolt at the point to attach the post anchor.*

G. *Having someone help you, install the post in the post anchor and brace on adjacent sides with 2 × 4s staked to the ground.*

Installing Porch Floors

Like most of the floors inside your home, the floor of your porch is built in layers to increase its strength and durability. The joists provide the bottom layer, giving the floor form and size. The subfloor—usually plywood—provides a stable base. And the porch boards, the layer you see, provides the finished outer layer. "Trim" is achieved with side skirt boards and a front apron that can be cut from exterior-grade plywood to conceal the outer joists and the rim joist, creating a cleaner appearance.

For maximum strength, the joists are usually installed parallel to the house, then the subfloor is laid perpendicular to the joists. Before laying the porch boards, it is helpful to make a cleat and

spacer from two pieces of scrap lumber that are similar in thickness to the skirt board—usually ¾" (see Step E). The cleat provides a secure, straight edge for aligning the first porch board, and the spacer creates an overhang for the skirt board.

To save time and simplify installation, use a floor nailer to attach porch boards directly to the subfloor. Check your local rental center for availability of this specialty tool.

TOOLS & MATERIALS

- Tape measure
- Circular saw & handsaw
- Caulk gun
- Speed square
- Jig saw
- Drill
- Hammer

- Floor nailer
- Mallet
- Nail set
- ¾" Exterior-grade plywood
- Exterior-grade construction adhesive

- Tongue-and-groove flooring
- Finish flooring
- Floor nailer nails
- 1¼", 1½" & 2" galvanized deck screws
- 8d siding nails

HOW TO INSTALL PORCH FLOORS

Step A: Install the Subfloor

1. Measure and cut ¾" exterior-grade plywood to length, so that any seams fall over joists. Keep a slight (⅛") expansion gap between the pieces. Notch any pieces to fit around posts.

2. Nail a 2 × 4 cleat to any posts that are not fitted against joists. Make sure the cleat is flush with the tops of the joists.

3. Fasten the plywood pieces with 1½" deck screws. If you are installing the floor over old steps, apply exterior-grade construction adhesive to the steps to bond with the plywood.

Step B: Cut the Starter Board

1. To create a starter board, ripcut the grooved edge off a tongue-and-groove porch board with a circular saw.

2. Measure, mark, and cut the starter board 1" longer than the

A. Cut pieces of plywood subfloor to size and install with deck screws. INSET: Notch plywood pieces to fit around posts, and fasten to nailing cleats attached to posts.

B. Mark the location of the post on the starter board, then notch-out with a jig saw.

finished length, including a ¾" overhang for the porch apron.

3. Position the starter board so the tongue edge is pressed against the post. Mark the location of the post onto the board.

4. Measure and mark the cutting depth to fit around the post. Notch the board with a jig saw.

Step C: Install the Cleat & Spacer

1. Sandwich together two pieces of scrap lumber that are the same thickness as the skirt board—usually ¾" (see Step E). Align the top edge of the outer piece (the cleat) at least 2" above the top edge of the inner piece (the spacer). Fasten the cleat to the spacer with 1¼" deck screws.

2. Attach the cleat and spacer to the outer joist, with the top of the spacer just below the top of the outer joist. Tack in place with 2" deck screws.

Step D: Install the Porch Boards

1. Draw reference lines on the subfloor, perpendicular to the house, to be used to check the alignment of the porch boards.

2. Butt the notched porch board against the cleat so it fits around the post. Nail it in place, spacing the nails every 6" to 8". If you are using a tongue-and-groove floor nailer, load a nail strip, then position the nailer over the exposed tongue and rap the striking head with a mallet to discharge and set the nails.

3. Cut and position the next porch board (notch for the post, if needed) so the groove fits around the tongue of the first board,

and nail it in place.

4. Continue installing porch boards. Occasionally check the alignment by measuring from a porch board to the nearest reference line, making sure the distance is equal at all points. Adjust the position of the boards, as needed.

5. Notch and install porch boards to fit around the other post.

6. Ripcut the last board to size, leaving an overhang equal to the starter board overhang (typically ¾"). Position the board, and drive galvanized finish nails through the face of the board and into the subfloor. Set the nail heads with a nail set, then remove the cleat and spacer.

Step E: Install the Skirt Boards & Apron

1. Mark several porch boards ¾" out from the front edge of the rim joist to create an overhang to cover the top of the apron. Snap a chalk line to connect the marks, creating a cutting line.

2. Use a straightedge as a guide and trim off the boards at the cutting line, using a circular saw. Use a handsaw to finish the cuts around the posts.

3. Cut skirt boards for the sides of the porch from exterior-grade plywood so they are flush with the front edge of the rim joist. Install them beneath the porch board overhangs and nail them in place with 8d siding nails.

4. Cut the front apron long enough to cover the edge grain of the skirt boards. Fasten it to the rim joist with 8d siding nails.

C. *Sandwich a cleat and spacer together that are the same thickness as the apron, and fasten so the cleat is 2" above the top of the outer joist.*

D. *Cut porch flooring to size, notching pieces to fit around posts where necessary. Install using a tongue-and-groove floor nailer and mallet.*

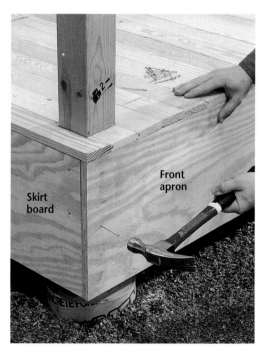

E. *Cut exterior-grade plywood to size for side skirt boards and the front apron. Secure with 8d siding nails.*

Step C: Mark the Beam Locations

1. Lay out the locations for the beams onto the ledger, according to your construction plan.

2. Insert a pair of lumber scraps with the same dimensions as the beam members (2 × 8s used here) into the double-joist hanger. Position the hanger against the ledger, using a torpedo level to make sure it is plumb. Fasten the double-joist hangers to the ledger with 10d common nails.

3. Set a straight board in each joist hanger, and hold the free end against the post. Use a carpenter's level to adjust the height of the board until it is level. Mark the post where it meets the bottom of the straight board. Draw cutting lines on all sides of the post at the height mark, using a combination square.

4. Steady the post, having a helper brace the post from below, and trim off the top at the cutting line.

Step D: Create the Beams

1. Refer to your construction plan to determine the dimensions of the beam members (2 × 8s are used here). Measure the distance from the ledger at the double-joist hangers to 1½" past the fronts of the posts. Cut the beam members to size.

2. Nail pairs of beam members together, using 10d common nails, to create the beams. Drive the nails at slight angles, in rows of three, and spaced every 12" to 16".

3. Lay out truss locations onto the tops of the beams, starting at the beam-ends that will fit into the double-joist hangers. Mark both edges of each truss, drawing an "X" between the lines for reference. Generally, trusses should be spaced at 24" intervals. Check your construction plan for exact placement.

Step E: Attach the Beams

1. Set a metal post cap onto the top of each post, and nail it in place with 10d joist hanger nails.

2. With a helper, raise the beams, and set them into the post caps and double-joist hangers. Secure the beams with 10d joist hanger nails.

3. For beams that are thinner than the posts, cut plywood spacers and install them between the inside edges of the beams and the inner flange of the post cap. The spacers should fit snugly, and be trimmed to roughly the size of the post cap flanges. Drive 10d joist hanger nails through the post cap flanges, into the spacers and beams.

Step F: Attach the First Truss

1. With help, turn the first truss upside down (to make it easier

C. *Hold a straight 2 × 4 in the double-joist hanger and against the post, level, and mark a cutting line on the post.*

D. *Nail the beam members together in pairs, then lay out the truss locations 24" on-center across the tops, using a framing square.*

E. *Set the beam in the double-joist hanger at the ledger and in the saddle fastener at the post. Fasten with 10d joist hanger nails.*

F. *Install the first truss flush against the house, with the peak aligned with the project centerline and the rafter tails overhanging the beams equally on both sides. Make sure it is plumb and fasten to the framing members with 20d common nails.*

to handle), and hoist it into position. Rest one end of the truss on a beam, then slide the other end up and onto the opposite beam.

2. Invert the truss so the peak points upward, and position it against the house, with the peak aligned on the project centerline.

3. Make sure that the first truss is flush against the siding, with the peak aligned on the project centerline and that the rafter tails overhang the beams evenly on each side. Nail the rafter chords and bottom chord of the truss to the house at framing member locations, using 20d common nails.

Step G: Attach the Subsequent Trusses

1. Lift the remaining trusses onto the beams.

2. Install the trusses at the locations marked on the beams, working away from the house, by toenailing through the bottom chords and into the beams with 8d common nails. Install the remaining trusses so the rafter tails overhang the beams equally.

3. Nail the last truss flush with the ends of the beams.

4. Use a level to plumb each truss, then attach 1 × 4 braces to the underside of each row of rafter chords, using 2" deck screws.

G. *With all the truss in place, Check each for plumb, then fasten 1 × 4 bracing to the undersides of the rafter chords.*

317

Installing Sheathing & Fascia

Plywood sheathing ties the structural elements of the roof together and provides a work and nailing surface for installing roofing.

When installing sheathing, make sure seams between sheets of plywood fall on framing members, such as rafter chords or studs. Leave a ⅛" gap between sheets of plywood, and a ¼" gap at the peak. Fasten sheathing with 8d galvanized box nails driven every 6" around the edges, and every 12" in the field. If necessary, install nailers to create a nailing surface for the roof sheathing overhang at the gable end.

Fascia adds a finished look to your roof, and helps prevent moisture and pests from damaging the structural elements of the roof. Fascia is usually fashioned from 1× lumber and fastened to the rafter chord tails, lookouts, or face, using finish nails.

Often, frieze boards are installed in conjunction with the fascia to create a nailer for the fascia, and to bridge the seam from the siding. A ⅜" to ¼" plowed groove can be routed into the side fascia to accommodate soffit panels (pages 326 to 327).

TOOLS & MATERIALS

- Tape measure
- Hammer
- Drill
- Circular saw and handsaw
- Rafter square
- Framing square
- T-square
- Router with ⅜" to ½" straight bit
- 4d box nails
- 8d galvanized box nails
- 8d galvanized finish nails
- 2 × 2 lumber
- 1× lumber
- ¾" exterior-grade plywood sheathing
- 1½" & 2½" deck screws

HOW TO INSTALL ROOF SHEATHING & FASCIA BOARDS
Step A: Attach the Roof Sheathing

1. Cut 2 × 4 nailing strips to match the dimensions of the front-truss rafter chords. Attach the nailing strips to the rafter chords using 2½" deck screws.

2. Cut ¾" exterior-grade plywood sheathing to cover the trusses and nailing strips. The sheathing should be flush with the ends of the rafter tails, and seams should fall over rafter locations. Leave ⅛" gaps between pieces, and fasten sheathing with 8d galvanized box nails, nailing every 6" at the edges, and every 12" in the field.

3. Fill in the rest of the sheathing, saving the pieces that butt together at the peak for last. Leave a ¼" gap at the peak.

Step B: Attach the Gable Sheathing

1. Measure the triangular shape of the gable end, from the bottom of the truss to the bottoms of the nailing strips. Divide the area into two equal-sized triangular areas, and cut ¾" exterior-

A. *Install plywood roof sheathing, working from the rafter tails to the peak. Leave a ⅛" gap between sheets, and a ¼" at the peak.*

grade plywood to fit.

2. Butt the pieces together directly under the peak, and attach them to the front truss with 1½" deck screws.

Step C: Attach the Frieze Boards & Fascia

1. Cut 1 × 4 frieze boards to fit against the plywood gable sheathing, beneath the nailing strips. Use a rafter square to cut the ends at the angle of the roof pitch (page 314). Attach the frieze boards to the gable sheathing with 4d box nails.

2. Cut 1 × 6 fascia boards long enough to extend several inches past the ends of the rafter tails. Use a speed square to cut the ends at the angle of the roof pitch (page 314). Nail the fascia boards to the nailing strips, aligning the tops flush with the tops of the roof sheathing.

Step D: Attach the Side Fascia Boards

1. Calculate the length of the side fascia boards by measuring from the house to the back faces of the gable-end fascia boards.

2. Cut the side fascia boards to fit, and rout a plowed groove for the soffit panels, if necessary. Attach fascia boards with 8d galvanized finish nails driven into the ends of the rafter tails. Make sure the tops of the side fascia boards do not protrude above the plane of the roof sheathing.

3. Trim off the ends of the gable-end fascia boards, so they are flush with the side fascia boards, using a handsaw.

4. Drive two or three 8d galvanized finish nails through the gable-end fascia boards and into the ends of the side fascia boards.

B. *Measure the triangular shape of the gable, divide into two pieces, and cut ¾" exterior-grade plywood to size.*

C. *Cut fascia boards long enough to extend several inches past the ends of the rafter tails and attach using 8d galvanized finish nails.*

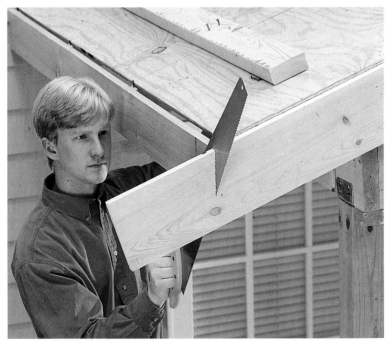

D. *Cut side fascia boards to fit between the house and the back faces of the gable-end fascia, then trim off the gable-end fascia boards with a handsaw.*

319

Installing Step Flashing

Make a flashing-bending jig with screws lined up along a piece of scrap wood.

Step flashing is used to tie a gable roofline into an existing wall. The galvanized metal or rubber barrier protects seams and makes water flow over shingled surfaces, away from gaps around roofing elements or at the tie-in points in the siding.

Step flashing is typically available in 5 × 7" and 5 × 10" aluminum or metal blanks. These blanks are then bent into "ells" (and trimmed to size with aviation snips, if necessary), and installed with one leg of the ell behind the siding and the other underneath the shingles. To ensure water won't seep between pieces, each subsequent blank of flashing overlaps the next; one blank for each row of shingles.

To bend your own flashing, make a bending jig by driving screws into a piece of scrap wood, creating a line one-half the width of the flashing when measured from the edge of the board. Clamp the bending jig to a worksurface, then press a step flashing blank flat on the board, then bend it over the edge.

Step flashing is installed at the same time as the roofing material. Roofing material comes in many different styles and materials—from asphalt shingles to cedar shakes. It protects your roof and home from water seepage and the elements. For techniques on installing building paper, drip-edge, and asphalt shingles, refer to pages 393 to 395 in the Sheds & Outbuildings section of this book.

A. Cut away 2" of siding above the roof sheathing.

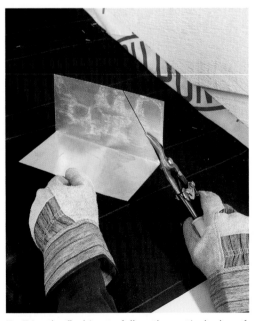

B. Trim the flashing to follow the vertical edge of the roof with aviation snips.

C. Apply roofing cement to the base of the flashing, then tuck the flashing under the siding and secure it to the roof.

TOOLS & MATERIALS

- Tape measure
- Circular saw
- Reciprocating saw
- Aviation snips
- Caulk gun
- Hammer

- Trowel
- Pry bar
- Galvanized metal step flashing blanks
- Roofing cement
- Roofing nails

- Rubber gasket nails
- Scrap wood
- Screws
- #30 building paper
- Asphalt shingles
- Drip-edge flashing

HOW TO INSTALL STEP FLASHING

Step A: Remove the Siding

1. Remove siding about 2" above the roof sheathing, using a circular saw with the cutting depth set to the siding thickness.

2. Use a reciprocating saw held at a very low angle to cut the siding flush with the top of the roof.

3. Connect the cuts at the ends with a wood chisel, and remove the siding.

Step B: Begin Roofing & Cut the Flashing

1. Install building paper, drip-edge flashing, and shingles (pages 393 to 395). Carefully pry up the siding and tuck at least 2" of paper under the siding. Leave the siding unfastened until after you install the step flashing.

2. Shingle up to the siding, trimming the last shingle if necessary. Bend a piece of step flashing in half and set it next to the lowest corner of the roofline. Mark a trim line on the flashing, following the vertical edge of the roof.

3. Cut and remove the waste portion of the flashing, using aviation snips.

Step C: Install the Flashing

1. Pry out the lower courses of siding and any trim that's in the way. Insert spacers to prop the siding or trim away from the work area.

2. Apply roofing cement to the base of the flashing in the area where the overlap with the step flashing will be formed. Tuck the trimmed piece of step flashing under the siding and secure the flashing. Fasten the flashing with one rubber-gasket nail driven near the top, and into the roof deck.

Step D: Add the Shingles

1. Apply roofing cement to the top side of the first piece of step flashing, where it will be covered by the next shingle course.

2. Install the shingle by pressing it firmly into the roofing cement. Don't nail through the flashing underneath.

Step E: Continue Shingling

1. Tuck another piece of flashing under the trim or siding, overlapping the first piece of flashing by at least 2". Set the flashing into roofing cement applied on the top of the shingle.

2. Nail the shingle in place, taking care not to drive nails through the flashing.

3. Continue shingling and flashing the roof. Make sure shingle tabs are staggered in regular patterns, with a consistent exposed area on shingle tabs.

4. Cut off shingle tabs and use them to create the roof ridge.

D. *Apply roofing cement to the flashing, then press the shingle into it. Do not nail through the flashing when attaching the shingle.*

E. *Continue to shingle and flash the roof, maintaining a regular shingle pattern with a consistent exposed area on the shingle tabs.*

Finishing the Cornice & Gable

The cornice and gable are prominent features on the front of any porch. The cornice, sometimes called the "cornice return" or the "fascia return," is usually fitted with trim that squares off the corner where it meets the soffit. The gable is the area just below the peak, which is usually covered with trim and siding material.

The cornice and gable are finished to match the siding and the trim on your house. Make sure to caulk all seams at the peak of the gable and between the fascia boards and the cornice (photo at left). Use ¾" sanded plywood or 1× finish-grade lumber to make the cornice, and use siding that matches your house for the gable trim. To make installation easier, paint the siding materials before installation.

Caulk all seams between the fascia boards and cornice, and at the peak of the gable (INSET).

TOOLS & MATERIALS

- Tape measure
- Caulk gun
- Framing square
- Hammer
- Circular saw

- Nail set
- Chalkline
- Rafter square
- Caulk
- Finish-grade lumber

- 8d galvanized finish nails
- 4d galvanized finish nails
- Siding
- 4d siding nails

A. Lay out the dimensions of the cornice pieces on 1× finish-grade lumber, using a framing square.

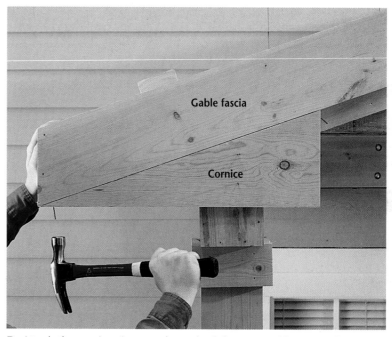

B. Attach the cornice pieces to the ends of the wrapped beams with 8d finish nails, and to the bottom edge of the fascia with 4d finish nails.

A framing square or speed square can be used to find the slope for the ends of the siding pieces, but an optional technique also exists. First, position a scrap board on the horizontal chalk line on the gable sheathing and mark the points where the edges of the board intersect with the frieze board. Connect the points to establish the slope line, the cut the scrap board on the line. Use the board as a template to mark your siding for cutting.

HOW TO INSTALL A CORNICE
Step A: Cut the Cornice Pieces
1. At each end of the front porch, measure the area from the end of the gable fascia to a spot about 6" inside the porch beam.

2. Lay out a triangular piece of plywood or finish-grade lumber to fit the area, using a framing square to create right angles.

3. Cut out the cornice pieces, using a circular saw and straight-edge guide.

Step B: Attach the Cornice Pieces
1. Test-fit the cornice pieces over the ends of the porch gable, then install with 8d finish nails driven into the ends of the beams, and 4d nails driven up through the ends of the cornice pieces and into the underside of the gable fascia.

2. Use a nail set to embed the heads of the nails below the surface of the wood, being careful not to split the cornice pieces.

3. Caulk the seams between the fascia boards and the cornice.

HOW TO INSTALL GABLE SIDING
Step A: Cut the Siding to Size
1. Caulk the seam at the peak of the gable.

2. Measure the dimensions of the area covered by the gable sheathing on the house. If you have installed fascia and frieze boards, measure from the bottom of the frieze boards. Add 2" of depth to the area to make sure that the siding will cover the edges of the ceiling once the ceiling and soffits are installed.

3. Snap a horizontal chalk line near the bottom of the gable sheathing as a reference line for installing the siding.

4. Mark a cutting line that matches the slope of the roof onto the end of one piece of siding. Use a framing square or a rafter square (page 314) to mark the slope line.

5. Cut the bottom siding board to length, cutting the ends along the slope reference line.

Step B: Install the Siding
1. Use 4d siding nails to install the bottom siding board so it is flush with the bottom edge of the frieze boards. The bottom edge of the siding board should be 2" lower than the bottom of the gable sheathing.

2. Cut the next siding board so it overlaps the first board from above, creating the same amount of exposed siding as on the rest of the house. Be careful to keep the siding level.

3. Continue cutting and installing siding pieces until you reach the peak of the gable.

A. *Mark cutting lines on the pieces of siding to match the slope of the roof, using a framing square or a rafter square and a straightedge.*

B. *Measure from the bottom edge of the frieze boards to find the size of the subsequent pieces of siding. Overlap the siding so the reveal matches the siding on your house.*

2. Make sure the stringers are square to the rim joist, then position the gussets between the bases of the stringers. Drill holes through the gussets and into the concrete, ¼" deeper than the embedment length of the screw. NOTE: Use a masonry bit recommended by the manufacturer of the masonry screws you choose. Oversized holes will make it difficult to set the masonry screws.

3. Clean out the holes, then fasten the gussets to the concrete with 3" masonry screws.

Step D: Attach the Railing Posts

1. Cut the 4 × 4 posts for the step railing to height. Position the posts at the outside face of an outside stringer. Make sure the posts are plumb, using a level, then clamp them in position. Drill ⅜" guide holes through the posts and the stringer.

2. Drive ⅜ × 6" carriage bolts through the guide holes and secure each with a washer and nut on the inside face of the stringer.

Step E: Install the Step Risers & Treads

1. Measure the stringers for the dimensions of the risers. Cut to size, then attach the risers to the vertical edges of the stringers, using 2½" deck screws.

2. Measure the depth of the step treads, adding 1" to 2" to both the depth and the length to create an overhang. Cut to size, using a circular saw. Notch the treads for the top and bottom steps to fit around the posts, using a jig saw.

3. Position the treads, then attach to the horizontal edges of the stringers, using 2½" deck screws.

Step F: Install the Bottom & Top Rails

1. Lay a 2 × 4 on the steps flush against the posts, then mark a cutting line on the 2 × 4 where it meets at each inside post edge. Use the 2 × 4 as a template for marking cutting lines on the top and cap rails.

2. Set the blade of a circular saw to match the angle of the cutting marks on the 2 × 4, then gang the 2 × 4 with a 2 × 2 for the top railing and a piece of cap railing for cutting. Gang-cut the rails at the cutting lines.

3. Toenail the bottom rail to the posts, using 3" deck screws driven through pilot holes and into the inside faces of the posts. The bottom of the rail should be level with the noses of the steps.

4. Attach the 2 × 2 top rail so it is parallel to the bottom rail, 2" down from the finished post height.

Step G: Install the Balusters & Top Cap

1. Hold a 2 × 2 flush against a post, so the ends extend past the top and bottom rails. Mark cutting lines on the 2 × 2 at the bottom edge of the top rail, and the top edge of the bottom rail. Use

D. *Clamp railing posts into position, making sure they are plumb. Drill ⅜" holes through the posts and stringer, then secure with ⅜ × 6" carriage bolts with washers.*

E. *Measure the dimensions for the risers and treads (adding 1" to 2" to treads for an overhang), and cut to size. Notch the treads to fit around posts as necessary. Attach with 2½" deck screws.*

the 2 × 2 as a template for making cutting lines on all railing balusters.

2. Mark layout lines for the balusters on the top and bottom rails, spacing the balusters no more than 4" apart.

3. Drill ⅛" holes in the center of the top rail at baluster locations, then drive 2½" deck screws into the baluster ends. Toenail balusters to the bottom rail with 8d finish nails.

4. Cut the cap rail to size, then position over the top rail. Fasten with 2½" deck screws.

5. Install a bottom rail, top rail, and cap rail in a horizontal position between the railing post at the top step and the end post for the porch railing. If the distance between posts is more than 4", install balusters between the rails.

Step H: Close off Gaps & Finish the Steps

1. Attach nailing strips to the undersides of the outer stringer, set back far enough to create a recess for the wood or lattice.

2. Cut a piece of wood or lattice to fit, and install it with 8d casing nails.

3. Check the post tops with a straightedge to make sure they follow the slope of the railing. Trim to height, if necessary, then attach decorative post caps, if desired.

4. Apply sealer/protectant or paint the steps and railing to match the porch and house.

F. *Cut a 2 × 4 bottom rail to size, position between the posts, and toenail in place with 3" deck screws. Install the 2 × 2 top rail similarly, but centered on the posts.*

G. *Measure along the top rail and mark the baluster location so they are no more than 4" apart. Drill pilot holes through the top rail for fastening the balusters.*

H. *Install nailing strips behind the stringers. Measure and cut finished lumber to size to close off the gap, and fasten in place with 8d casing nails.*

Landing depth
Door width plus 12" minimum

Riser height

6" - 8"

Tread depth

Overall rise

10" - 12"

Overall run

Concrete Steps

New concrete steps give a fresh, clean appearance to your house. And if your old steps are unstable, replacing them with concrete steps that have a non-skid surface will create a safer living environment.

Like wooden steps, concrete step design requires some calculations and some trial and error. As long as the design meets safety guidelines, you can adjust elements, such as the landing depth and the dimensions of the steps. However, there are some code requirements that must be met. For example, steps with more than two rises will require a handrail. Ask your local building inspector about other requirements in your area.

Before demolishing your old steps, measure them to see if they meet safety guidelines. If so, you can use them as a reference for

your new steps. If not, start from scratch so your new steps do not repeat any design errors. Sketching your plan on paper will make the job easier.

If you will need to remove or demolish existing concrete steps, set aside the rubble to use as fill material for the new steps. Make sure to wear protective gear, including eye protection and gloves, when demolishing concrete.

When installing railings with mounting plates, install J-bolts before the concrete sets (page 219), or choose railings with surface-mounted hardware (page 337) that can be attached after the steps are completed.

Refer to pages 40 to 51 in the Basic Techniques section for additional tips and techniques for working with concrete.

TOOLS & MATERIALS

- Tape measure
- Sledge hammer
- Shovel
- Drill
- Reciprocating saw
- Level
- Mason's string
- Hand tamper
- Mallet
- Concrete mixing tools
- Jig saw

- Clamps
- Ruler or framing square
- Float
- Step edger
- Broom
- 2 × 4 lumber
- Steel rebar grid
- Wire
- Bolsters
- Construction adhesive
- Compactible gravel

- Fill material
- ¾" exterior-grade plywood
- 2" deck screws
- Isolation board
- #3 rebar
- Stakes
- Latex caulk
- Vegetable oil or commercial release agent

The rise of each step should be between 6" and 8". For example, if the overall rise is 21" and you plan to build three steps, the rise of each step would be 7" (21 divided by 3"), which falls within the recommended safety range for riser height.

5. Measure the width of your door and add at least 12"—this number is the minimum depth you should plan for the landing area of the steps. The landing depth plus the depth of each step should fit within the overall run of the steps. If necessary, you can increase the overall run by moving the stake at the planned base of the steps away from the house, or by increasing the depth of the landing.

6. Sketch a detailed plan for the steps, keeping these guidelines in mind: Each step should be 10" to 12" deep, with a riser height between 6" and 8", and the landing should be at least 12" deeper than the swing radius (width) of your door. Adjust the parts of the steps as needed, staying within the given ranges. Take time to create the final sketch; it is worth doing carefully.

HOW TO INSTALL CONCRETE STEPS

Step A: Design the Steps

1. Attach a mason's string to the house foundation, 1" below the bottom of the door threshold.

2. Drive a stake where you want the base of the bottom step to fall. Attach the other end of the string to the stake and use a line level to level it. Measure the length of the string—this distance is the overall depth, or run, of the steps.

3. Measure down from the string to the bottom of the stake to determine the overall height, or rise, of the steps.

4. Divide the overall rise by the estimated number of steps.

Step B: Install the Footings

1. Remove or demolish the existing steps; if the old steps are concrete, set aside the rubble to use as fill material.

2. Dig 12"-wide footing trenches that extend past the frost line (page 48 to 51). Locate the trenches perpendicular to the foundation, spaced so the footings will extend 3" wider than the outside edges of the steps.

3. Install steel rebar grids for reinforcement, then affix

A. *Determine the rise and run dimensions for your steps, then use them to draw scale plans.*

B. *Install footings that extend past the frost lines. Once bleed water disappears, insert 12"-long pieces of rebar, spaced at 12" intervals.*

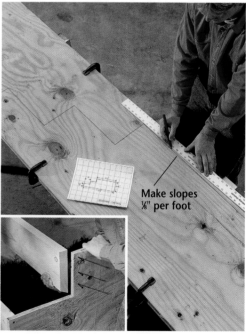

Make slopes ⅛" per foot

C. *Transfer your plan dimensions onto plywood to create the side forms. Cut the risers to size, beveling the bottom edge (INSET). Build the form.*

isolation boards to the foundation wall inside each trench, using construction adhesive (page 51).

4. Mix the concrete. Work it with a shovel to remove any air pockets, but do not overwork the mix. Pour the concrete in evenly spaced loads, starting at the end farthest from the concrete source.

5. Level and smooth the concrete with a screed board. NOTE: You do not need to float the surface afterward. When bleed water disappears (page 47), insert 12" sections of rebar 6" into the concrete, spaced at 12" intervals and centered side-to-side. Leave 1 ft. of clear space at each end. Let the footings cure for two days.

Step C: Build the Step Form

1. Excavate the area between the footings 4" deep. Fill the area in with compactible gravel to create a subbase. Tamp until it is level with the footings, adding gravel as needed.

2. Following your drawing plans, transfer the measurements for the side forms onto ¾" exterior-grade plywood. Add a ⅛"-per-foot back-to-front slope to the landing part of the form.

3. Clamp a second piece of plywood to the first, marked piece to cut both side forms at the same time. Cut along the cutting lines, using a jig saw.

4. Cut form boards for the risers to fit between the side forms. Bevel the bottom edges of the boards when cutting to create clearance for the float at the back edges of the steps.

5. Attach the riser forms to the side forms with 2" deck screws.

Step D: Place & Support the Step Form

1. Cut a 2 × 4 to make a center support for the riser forms. Attach 2 × 4 cleats to the riser forms with 2" deck screws, then attach the support to the cleats. Check to make sure all corners are square.

2. Cut an isolation board and affix it to the house foundation at the back of the project area, using construction adhesive.

3. Set the form onto the footings, flush against the isolation board. Add 2 × 4 bracing arms to the sides of the form, attaching them to cleats on the sides and to stakes driven into the ground.

Step E: Add the Clean Fill

1. Fill the form with clean fill (broken concrete or rubble). Stack the fill carefully, keeping it 6" away from the sides, back, and top edges of the form.

2. Shovel smaller fragments onto the pile to fill the void areas.

3. Lay pieces of #3 rebar on top of the fill at 12" intervals, and attach them to bolsters with wire to keep them from moving when the concrete is poured. Keep rebar at least 2" below the top of the forms. Mist the pile of rubble.

Step F: Pour Concrete in the First Step

1. Coat the forms with vegetable oil or a commercial release agent, then mist with water so concrete won't stick to the forms.

D. *Secure isolation boards to the foundation of the house. Position the form against the house and brace with 2 × 4s.*

E. *Carefully add clean fill and rebar inside the form, keeping it at least 6" away from the sides, back, and top edges of the form.*

2. Mix concrete and shovel into the bottom step of the form first. Settle and smooth it with a screed board.

3. Press a piece of #3 rebar 1" down into the "nose" of each tread for reinforcement.

4. Float the steps (pages 45 to 47), working the front edge of the float underneath the beveled edge at the bottom of each rise form.

Step G: Fill the Remainder of the Form

1. Shovel concrete into the forms for the remaining steps and the landing. Keep an eye on the poured concrete as you work, and stop to float any concrete as soon as the bleed water disappears. Press rebar into the nose of each step.

2. Once the concrete sets, shape the steps and landing with a step edger, and float the surface.

3. Sweep with a stiff-bristled broom for maximum traction.

Step H: Finish the Steps

1. Remove the forms as soon as the surface is firm to the touch, usually within several hours.

2. Smooth rough edges with a float. Add concrete to fill any holes. NOTE: If forms are removed later, more patching may be required. Backfill the area around the base of the steps, and seal the concrete.

3. If installing a railing, follow the manufacturer's directions.

F. *Pour concrete in the first step, smooth with a screed board, and add lengths of rebar 1"-deep into the nose of each tread.*

G. *Fill the remainder of the form with concrete, smooth with a screed board, and press rebar into the nose of each step. Once bleed water disappears, float and edge the surface of the concrete (INSET).*

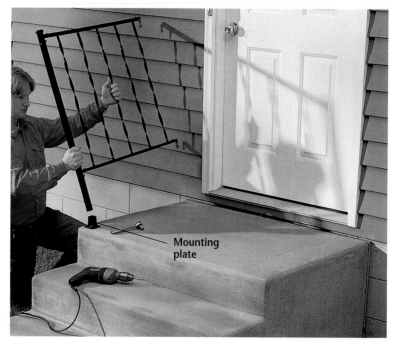

Mounting plate

H. *Remove the forms once the concrete is firm to the touch, and smooth the rough edges with a float. Backfill around the area and install a railing, if necessary.*

Screening-in a Porch

If you have ever built a stud wall and repaired a window screen, you already have most of the skills needed for a screen-in project. A screen-in can be accomplished on many areas of a house or yard, including decks, patios, and gazebos. But by far the most popular is the front porch. The quick and simple front porch screen-in demonstrated here is a good example of how to make outdoor living spaces more livable.

There are many strategies you can take to accomplish a front porch screen-in. Porches and entryways covered by the main roof of the house often can be screened-in simply by attaching the screen materials directly to the existing structure of the porch, using retaining strips to fasten the screens. Or, check with your local building center to learn more about manufactured screen-in systems. Generally, these systems use rubber spline cords and tracks to secure the screens, allowing the installer to create greater screen tension and reduce the need for screen frames.

Another easy way, demonstrated here, is to build a self-contained frame inside the railings, posts, and beams to support the screening. The self-contained frame is a versatile option that can be used in almost any outdoor structure.

If your floor is constructed of deck boards, cover the gaps between the boards from below, using retaining strips and brads to tack fiberglass insect mesh to the bottom edges of the floor joists. If you cannot reach from below, the best solution is to remove the deck boards, attach a layer of insect mesh to the tops of the joists, and then reinstall the boards.

If you plan to paint the frames a different color than the surrounding porch surfaces, paint all of the wood parts for the screen-in before you install them.

TOOLS & MATERIALS

- Tape measure
- Chalkline
- Framing square
- Circular saw or handsaw
- Carpenter's level
- Hammer
- Drill
- Wood chisel
- Screwdrivers
- Staple gun
- Utility knife
- Framing lumber
- 3" deck screws
- 16d casing nails
- Screen door
- 2½" door hinges (3)
- ¾" wood screws
- 1" wood screws
- Fiberglass insect mesh screening
- Screen retaining strips
- 1¼" brass brads

HOW TO SCREEN-IN A PORCH

Step A: Outline the Screen Walls

1. Outline the project area on the porch floor, using a chalkline. Create the largest possible space not obstructed by beams, posts, railings, trim, or the ceiling.

2. Check the corners of the outline with a framing square to make sure the chalk lines are square.

3. Mark the door rough opening—the door width plus 3" for the door frame and ½" for clearance.

Step B: Install the Sole Plates

1. Measure and cut 2 × 4s to length for sole plates, using a circular saw. Attach to the porch floor inside the chalk line, using 3" deck screws driven at 12" intervals. Do not install sole plates in the door rough opening.

2. Mark 2 × 4 door frames at the sides of the door rough opening, using a straightedge. The door frames should rest on the floor, butted against the sole plates.

3. Mark doubled 2 × 4 posts at the front corners of the project outline, and mark 2 × 4 end posts on the sole plate next to the wall of the house.

4. Mark 2 × 4 studs for screen supports, spaced at even intervals of 24" to 36", depending on the total distance spanned.

Step C: Install the Top Plates

1. Cut 2 × 4 top plates to match the sole plates, using a circular saw. Lay the top plates next to the sole plates, and copy the post and stud marks onto the top plates. The top plate over the door opening is not cut out.

2. Using a straight 2 × 4 and a level, mark the locations for the top plates on the ceilings directly above the sole plates.

3. Attach the top plates to the ceiling with 3" deck screws driven into joists or beams, if possible. Make sure the top plates are aligned directly above the sole plates, with the framing member marks also in alignment.

Step D: Install the Studs

1. Measure the distance between the bottom plate and top plate at each stud location, then cut studs and posts to length, using a circular saw.

2. Position and install the studs and posts at the marks on the top plates and

A. *Outline the project area on the floor, using a chalk line. Check the corners with a framing square to make sure the outline is square.*

Door rough opening
Door frame locations

B. *Cut 2 × 4s for sole plates to length, align with the reference lines, and fasten to the porch floor with 3" deck screws.*

C. *Mark the locations for the top plates on the ceiling directly above the sole plates using a straight 2 × 4 and a level.*

D. *Install studs and posts at reference marks on the top and sole plates. Toenail in place with 16d casing nails.*

E. *Measure and cut 2 × 4 spreaders to size, and fasten between studs at the height of the railings.*

the sole plates. Toenail them in place with 16d casing nails.

3. Install the 2 × 4 door frames by nailing through the frames and into the ends of the sole plates.

NOTE: If the ledger board sticks out past the siding, work around it when installing the 2 × 4 end posts. Butt two 2 × 4s together so one fits between the floor and the ledger, with the edge against the wall. Toenail the other 2 × 4 into the top plate and sole plate, and nail it to the edge of the first 2 × 4.

Step E: Install the Spreaders

Cut 2 × 4 spreaders to fit between the studs and posts, using a circular saw. Position the spreaders at the same height as the porch railing, then toenail them with 16d casing nails. NOTE: The spreaders prevent framing members from warping and provide a nailing surface for screen retaining strips.

Step F: Install the Door Header & Stop Molding

1. Install a 2 × 4 door header to create a rough opening that is ¾" higher than the height of the screen door.

2. Nail door-stop molding to the inside faces of the door frames and header. Recess the molding back from the outside edges of the door frame to match the thickness of the door, so when the door closes, it is flush with the outside edges of the door frame.

Step G: Install the Door

1. Measure and mark the locations for the door hinges on the edge of the door. Mark at 12" from the top of the door and 12" from the bottom, then space the third hinge evenly between the two.

2. Cut a mortise to the depth matching the thickness of the hinges into the edge

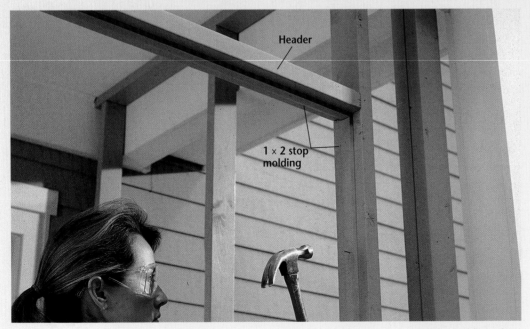

Header

1 × 2 stop molding

F. *Install the door header ¾" higher than the actual height of the door. Attach 1 × 2 stop molding along the inside face of the door frame so it creates a recess the same thickness as the door.*

of the door at each location, using a wood chisel. Attach the hinges with ¾" wood screws.

3. Set the door in the opening, using ½"-thick spacers to hold it up off the floor. Outline the hinge plates onto the front edge of the door frame.

4. Remove the door and cut mortises into the door frame at the hinge locations, using a wood chisel. The mortises should be deep enough so the hinge plate will be flush with the surface of the wood.

5. Set the door in the opening, and screw the hinges to the frame with 1" wood screws.

6. Install desired door hardware, including a door pull, a closer or spring, a wind chain, a latch or lock, and a rubber door

sweep for the bottom of the door, if desired. Follow the manufacturer's directions for each piece of hardware.

Step H: Attach the Screen

1. Measure and mark centerlines along the inside faces of all studs and posts for reference lines when installing the screens.

2. Use a scissors to cut strips of screening so they are at least 4" wider and 4" longer than the opening in the framework where each screen will be installed.

3. Cut wooden retaining strips—for fastening the screens—to the width of the framework openings.

4. Begin attaching screens at the tops of the framework openings by securing them with the retaining strips. Attach the

retaining strips with 1¼" brass brads at 6" to 12" intervals.

Step I: Finish Securing the Screen

1. With a helper, pull the screen down until taut. Use a retaining strip (cut to the width of the opening) to press the screen against the reference line, then attach near the ends of the strip with 1¼" brass brads.

2. Staple the screen at the sides, flush against the reference lines, then attach retaining strips over the staples at the reference lines with 1¼" brass brads.

3. Install screens in all remaining openings, then use a utility knife to trim the excess screening at the edges of the retaining strips.

G. *Mark the hinge locations onto the door frame, then chisel mortises deep enough so the hinge plate will be flush with the surface of the frame.*

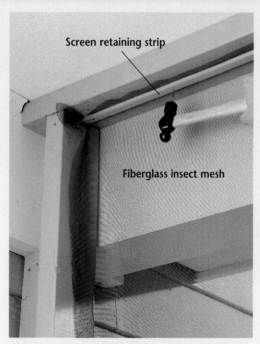

Screen retaining strip

Fiberglass insect mesh

H. *Mark center reference lines on the inside faces of all studs and posts. Align mesh and retaining strips with the lines, then fasten with brass brads.*

I. *Secure the screen at the stretcher with retaining strips and brads. At the sides, pull the screen taut and staple in place, then cover with retaining strips and fasten with brads.*

Portico

A portico is essentially the same as a very small porch, but without the deck floor. It creates an awning that dresses up an ordinary entryway, and shields the entrance from falling rain and snow.

Most of the same techniques used to build a porch can be used to build a portico, with a few exceptions. Because a porch deck will not be built, the posts are fastened directly to the concrete steps using masonry fasteners and metal post anchors. The edges of the post anchors should be a minimum of 2" from the edges of the steps. Also, your concrete stoop will need footings that extend below the frost line (refer to pages 334 to 337). Check with your local building inspector for specific codes and regulations in your area.

You will also need to order prefabricated trusses built to the specific dimensions of your project. When ordering, make sure you know the roof pitch, truss span (the distance from the outside edge of one beam to the other), and the rafter tail overhang (typically 12"). Also let the truss manufacturer know of any special design details you'd like, such as scissor trusses to create a slightly vaulted ceiling.

The measurements used in this project are based on a 48 × 72 × 18" concrete stoop. Though these dimensions are specific to this particular size stoop, this project can easily be adapted to not only various stoop sizes, but differing roof pitches. Make sure to draw up detailed and specific plans, and work with your local building inspector. Refer to pages 304 to 333 in this section for basic porch building techniques.

TOOLS & MATERIALS

- Tape measure
- Hammer drill with ⅜" masonry bit
- Hammer
- Level
- Circular saw
- Chalkline
- Chisel (or aviator's snips)
- Electronic stud finder (optional)
- Drill
- 1" spade bit
- Ratchet wrench
- Torpedo level
- Rafter square
- Handsaw
- Reciprocating saw
- Straightedge
- Nail set
- Caulk gun
- Jig saw
- Paintbrush
- ⅜ × 3" masonry fasteners
- 4 × 4 metal post anchors
- 10d joist hanger nails
- 1¼", 2" & 2½" deck screws
- 10d, 16d & 20d common nails

- ⅜ × 4" lag screws
- 2 × 8 double joist hangers
- Metal post caps
- 8d siding nails
- 8d galvanized casing nails
- 4d & 8d finish nails
- Roofing materials (see pages 393 to 395)
- Exterior-grade caulk
- Quarter-round molding
- 4d ringshank siding nails
- ¾" cove molding
- Wood putty
- Cedar scallops

Lumber (as needed):
- 2 × 4s (braces & stakes)
- 2 × 8s (ledger, beam members)
- ¼", ½" & ¾" exterior-grade plywood
- 1 × 6s (beam brace, frieze boards, fascia, post collar wrap)
- Trusses (order to size)
- 1 × 4 (truss braces, post wrap)
- 2 × 2 (nailing strips)
- 1 × 10 finish lumber (beam wrap)

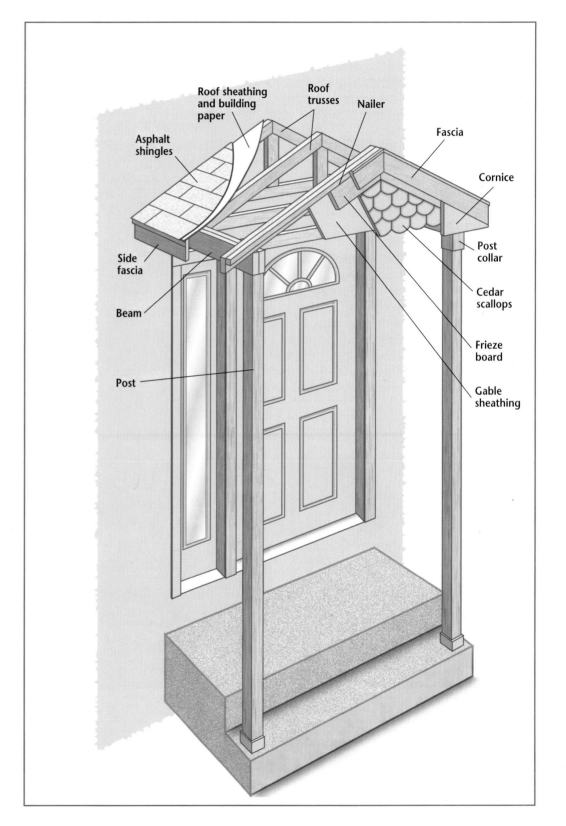

HOW TO BUILD A PORTICO

Step A: Install Post Anchors

1. On the first step of the concrete stoop, measure in from each side and mark at 3¾", then at 3¾" from the front of the step to mark the position of the concrete fasteners.

2. At the two locations, drill 2" into the stoop, using a hammer drill with a ⅜" masonry bit.

3. Clean out the holes so they are free of dirt and debris. Tap ⅜ × 3" masonry fasteners into the holes, using a hammer. Leave ¾" to 1" of thread exposed.

4. Position and align 4 × 4 metal post anchors over the threads. Secure the anchors to the stoop with the masonry fastener's fitted washer and nut, using a ratchet wrench.

Step B: Install the Posts

1. Cut two 4 × 4 posts 6" longer than the planned post height.

2. Place metal pedestals into each post anchor, then set a post in each anchor, on top of the pedestal. Tack each post in place with a single 10d joist hanger nail.

3. Brace each post with a pair of 2 × 4s attached to stakes driven into the ground. Secure the braces to the stakes with deck screws, then use a level to make sure the posts are plumb. Attach the braces to the posts with deck screws.

4. Finish attaching the posts to the post anchors with 10d joist hanger nails.

Step C: Install the Ledger

1. Measure to find the midpoint of the stoop, then transfer a centerline to the peak area of the planned roof, using a long, straight 2 × 4 and a level.

2. At the centerline, measure and mark the bottom edge of the ledger at 12" above the brickmold of the entrance. From that mark, measure up and mark at 8¼"—the width of the 2 × 8 ledger board plus 1".

3. Set a 2 × 8 for the ledger board on the first step so it extends past the edges of both posts. Mark the outside edges of the posts onto the ledger for the beam locations. Also, mark at each edge of the step for the ends of the ledger. Cut the ledger at the step-edge marks (a length of 60" in this project), using a circular saw.

4. Make a reference mark at the midpoint on the ledger board, then measure from the midpoint to one end (30" in our project).

5. At the centerline on the house, measure out level from each ledger reference mark, in each direction, a distance equal to the measurement in #4 plus ½" (30½" for our project), and mark. Snap chalk lines from mark to mark, creating a ledger board outline that is enlarged ½" on all sides.

6. Remove the siding in the outlined area, using a circular saw and chisel for lap siding, or aviator's snips for aluminum and vinyl siding.

7. Locate the framing members by finding the visible nail

A. *Position post anchors over the exposed threads of the masonry fasteners (INSET), and secure with the fastener's washer and nut.*

B. *Fasten the posts to the post anchors with joist hanger nails. Check posts for plumb, then brace with 2 × 4s fastened to stakes in the ground.*

C. *With the circular saw blade set to the siding depth, cut away the siding, following the ledger board outline.*

heads, and mark. Use an electronic stud finder, if necessary.

8. Position the ledger in the outline and tack in place with 10d common nails. Drill pairs of pilot holes through the ledger and into the framing members. Counterbore each pilot hole ½" deep using a 1" spade bit, then fasten the ledger to the framing members with pairs of ⅜ × 4" lag screws, using a ratchet wrench.

Step D: Install the Beam

1. Insert a pair of 2 × 8 scraps (the same dimension as the beam members) into a double joist hanger, and position it against the ledger at the beam location mark. Use a torpedo level to make sure it is plumb. Fasten the hangers to the ledger with 10d common nails at both beam locations.

2. Set a straight 2 × 4 in each double joist hanger and hold the free end against the post. Level the 2 × 4, then mark the post where it meets the bottom of the 2 × 4.

3. Draw cutting lines on all sides of the post at the height mark using a combination square. Steady the post, having a helper brace it from below, and trim off the top at the cutting line.

4. Measure the distance from the ledger at the double joist hangers to the front edge of the posts. Cut four 2 × 8s to length.

5. To create the beams, nail the 2 × 8s together in pairs, using 16d common nails. Drive the nails at slight angles, in rows of three, spaced every 12" to 16".

6. Lay out truss locations on the tops of the beams, starting at the end that will fit into the double joist hangers. Space trusses at 16" to 24" intervals. Mark both edges of each truss, drawing an "X" between the lines for reference.

7. Nail a metal post cap onto the top of each post, using 10d joist hanger nails. With a helper, raise the beams and set them into the double joist hangers and post caps. Secure the beams with 10d joist hanger nails. NOTE: For beams that are thinner than the posts, cut ½" plywood spacers roughly the size of the post cap flanges, and install them between the inside face of the beams and the post cap flange. The spacers should fit snugly.

8. Make sure the posts are plumb, then attach a 1 × 6 across the ends of the beams for a brace support.

Step E: Install the Trusses

1. With help, turn the first truss upside down (to make it easier to handle) and hoist it into position. Rest one end of the truss on a beam, then slide the other end up and onto the opposite beam.

2. Invert the truss so the peak points upward, and position it against the house, with the peak aligned on the project centerline. Make sure it is flush against the siding, then nail the rafter and bottom chords of the truss to the framing members, using 20d common nails.

3. Lift the remaining trusses onto the beams and install them at the locations marked on the beams, working away from the house, by toenailing through the bottom chords and into the

D. *Place one end of the beams in the double joist hanger at the ledger and the other in the post cap. Fasten in place with joist hanger nails.*

E. *With help, align the truss with the reference marks on the beams and toenail in place. Make sure each truss is plumb, then secure with braces.*

F. *Sheath the roof and the gable, using exterior-grade plywood sheathing and siding nails.*

beams with 10d common nails.

4. Nail the last truss flush with the ends of the beams. If the bottom chord of the first truss overhangs the beams, install the rest of the trusses with equal overhangs.

5. Use a level to plumb each truss, then attach 1 × 4 braces to the underside of each row of rafter chords, using 2" deck screws.

Step F: Install the Roof & Gable Sheathing

1. Cut 2 × 2 nailing strips to the same length as the rafters of the front truss. Attach the nailing strips flush with the top edge of the rafters, using 2½" deck screws.

2. Cut ¾" exterior-grade plywood roof sheathing to cover the trusses and nailing strips. The sheathing should be flush with the ends of the rafter tails.

3. Install sheathing from the bottom to the peak, using 8d siding nails driven every 6" around the edges and every 12" in the field. Be sure to leave a ¼" gap at the peak.

4. Measure the triangular shape of the gable end, from the bottom of the truss to the bottoms of the nailing strips. Cut ¾" exterior-grade plywood to fit. Attach the gable sheathing to the front truss with 8d siding nails driven every 6" around the edges and every 12" in the field.

Step G: Install the Fascia

1. Remove the 1 × 6 brace at the beam ends. Cut 1 × 6 frieze boards to fit against the plywood gable sheathing, beneath the nailing strips. Use a rafter square to cut the ends at angles to match the roof pitch—6-in-12 here. Attach the frieze boards to the gable sheathing with 1¼" deck screws.

2. Cut 1 × 6s for fascia boards long enough to extend several inches past the ends of the rafter tails. Cut the peak ends to match the roof pitch, using a rafter square. Nail the fascia boards to the nailing strips, with the top edge flush with the surface of the roof sheathing, using 8d galvanized casing nails.

3. Measure from the house to the back face of the gable fascia boards for the length of the side fascia boards. Cut 1 × 8 fascia boards to size, then rout a ⅜" plowed groove 1" from the bottom edge of the board.

4. Attach the fascia board to the ends of the rafter tails with 8d galvanized casing nails. Make sure the top of the fascia boards do not protrude above the plane of the sheathing.

5. Trim the ends of the gable fascia boards so they are flush with the side fascia boards, using a handsaw, then drive two or three 8d finish nails through the gable fascia boards and into the ends of the side fascia boards.

Step H: Install the Roofing Materials

1. Cut the siding about 2" above the roof sheathing using a circular saw with the cutting depth set to the siding thickness. Use a reciprocating saw held at a very low angle to cut the siding flush with the top of the roof. Connect the cuts at the ends with

G. *With the frieze boards and gable fascia in place, measure from the house to the end of the gable fascia. Cut the side fascia board to length and attach with casing nails.*

H. *Install the roofing, using step flashing where the new roof line meets the siding of the house.*

a wood chisel, and remove the siding.

2. Refer to pages 393 to 395 in the Sheds & Outbuildings section for information on installing building paper, drip-edge flashing, and asphalt shingles. Refer to pages 320 to 321 in the Porches section for installing step flashing. Make sure shingle tabs are staggered in regular patterns, with a consistent exposed area on shingle tabs.

Step I: Wrap the Beams & Attach the Post Collars

1. Use finish lumber to cover the beams and any metal hardware. Cut 1 × 10 boards for the sides of the beams to the same length as the beams, and attach with 8d finish nails. If necessary, add ½" plywood strips at the top and bottom of the beam to compensate for the ½" spacers in the post caps. Also, cut 1 × 4s to length to cover the bottoms of the beams.

2. Create a 3" top collar where the posts meet the beam. Cut pieces of 1× finish lumber for three sides of each post to size, making sure the side pieces cover the ends of the back piece. Fasten the pieces together and in place with 4d finish nails.

3. Measure the ends of the beams and cut 1 × 10 finish lumber to create an end cap for each beam, covering the ends of the beam, beam wrap, and the top collar pieces. Nail the end caps over the end of each beam, using 4d finish nails.

4. Create 3" bottom collars for each post, cutting 1× finish lumber to the same dimensions as the pieces of the top collar. Cut the front collar pieces to cover the ends of the side pieces.

Nail the pieces together and in place with 4d finish nails.

Step J: Wrap the Ledger Board

Measure the exposed ledger and cut a piece of finish lumber to size. If the ledger protrudes past the siding, cut a furring strip to cover the gap between the inside face of the ledger cover and the siding. Install the ledger cover with 8d finish nails.

Step K: Finish the Cornice

1. At each end of the portico roof, measure the area from the end of the gable fascia to a spot about 6" past the beam. Lay out a triangular piece of finish-grade lumber to fit the area, using a framing square to create right angles. Cut the cornice pieces, using a straightedge and circular saw.

2. Test-fit the cornice pieces over the ends of the gable, then install with 8d finish nails driven into the ends of the beams, and 4d finish nails driven up through the ends of the cornice pieces and into the underside of the gable fascia.

3. Set the nail heads, being careful not to split the cornice pieces, then caulk the seams between the fascia boards and the cornice.

Step L: Install the Soffits

1. Use a torpedo level to transfer the top height of the plowed groove of the side fascia board to one end of the beam, then mark the groove height at the other end of the beam. Connect the marks with a chalk line.

2. Measure and cut 2 × 2 nailers to length, then install just

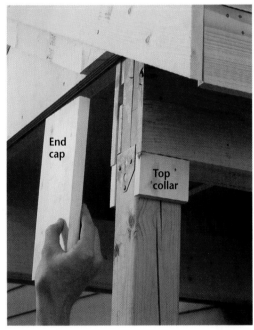

I. *Wrap the beams with 1 × 10 finish lumber. For posts, add 1 × 4 top collars and 1 × 6 bottom collars.*

J. *If the ledger protrudes past the siding, cut a furring strip to cover the gap between the inside face of the ledger cover and the siding.*

K. *Measure, mark and cut each cornice out of finish lumber, then attach at each cornice location with finish nails.*

above the chalk line, using 8d casing nails.

3. Measure from the back of the plowed groove to the beam, just below the nailer, to find the required width of the soffit panel. Measure and cut a piece of ¼"-thick plywood to fit.

4. Insert one edge of the soffit panel into the plow, then nail the other edge to the nailer with 4d finish nails.

5. Add quarter-round molding at the joint between the soffit and the beam, or fill the gaps with tinted exterior-grade caulk.

Step M: Install the Ceiling

1. If installing an exterior light fixture in the ceiling, mount the cast-aluminum or PVC plastic fixture box, run the cables, and wire the circuit, or hire a professional electrician to install it.

2. Measure the ceiling space and cut ½" plywood or your chosen ceiling material to size. Cut ceiling pieces so that any seams fall on the centers of the rafters. Use 4d ringshank siding nails to attach the plywood, spacing nails at 8" to 12" intervals. Do not drive nails next to one another on opposite sides of joints.

3. Install ¾" cove molding around the edges of the ceiling to cover the gaps and create a more decorative look. Miter the corners and attach with 4d finish nails. Set the nail heads slightly, and cover with wood putty.

Step N: Install the Gable Siding

1. Caulk the seams at the peak of the gable, and between the fascia boards and the cornice.

2. Measure along the bottom edge of the gable sheathing—

from the edge of one frieze board to the other—and mark the center of the gable area. Snap a chalk line or use a straightedge to draw a reference line from the mark to the peak. Also draw a horizontal reference line a few inches above the bottom edge of the gable sheathing—so the cedar scallops will conceal the rough edge.

3. Starting at the centerline, align a cedar scallop with the intersecting reference lines, and fasten in place with a pair of 4d finish nails. Continue installing scallops, working from the center to the edges of the frieze boards.

4. At the frieze boards, position the scallops and mark the points where they intersect the frieze boards, transfer cutting lines across the face of each scallop, and cut to size with a jig saw. Reposition the scallops, making sure they fit snug, then fasten in place with 4d finish nails.

5. Install subsequent rows similarly, but stagger the scallops so the joints between two scallops in the preceding row are covered by a single scallop in the following row. Continue cutting and installing scallops until reaching the peak of the gable.

Step O: Finish the Trim & Paint

1. Add decorative trim, stock moldings, and gable ornamentation to soften hard lines and and personalize the project, in keeping with the existing elements and details of your house.

2. Paint or stain any exposed wood to match the house trim.

Side facia

Plowed groove

L. *Install the soffit panels by inserting one edge into the plowed groove* (INSET) *and fastening the panel to the nailers with finish nails.*

M. *Cut the finish material for the ceiling to size and fasten to the bottom chords of the trusses with ringshank siding nails.*

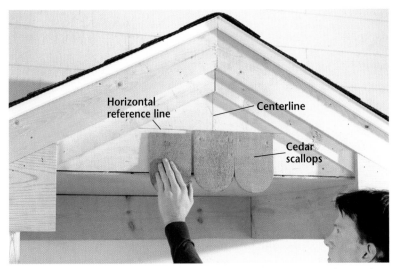

N. *Mark a centerline and reference line on the gable sheathing. Align cedar scallops with the reference lines and fasten with finish nails.*

O. *Add decorative moldings and embellishments to match house details, then finish with paint or stain to match the color of your house and trim.*

VARIATION: BUILDING YOUR OWN TRUSSES

Because of the small scale of a portico roof, you may be able to build your own trusses. Your local building inspector will need to approve detailed truss construction plans that include the roof pitch, the span of the bottom chord, the size of lumber used, and most importantly, the materials used to fasten the joints.

In some instances metal nailing plates may be used, but most often homemade trusses are built using ½" plywood gussets with construction adhesive and 6d common nails. Your truss plans should also include how many nails per gusset are used.

To build trusses, begin by cutting and laying out all the pieces for one truss—the bottom chord, two rafter chords, and the struts—using a rafter square (refer to page 314). Make sure each piece is cut to its exact size and shape specified in your plan. Recheck all measurements and test-fit the pieces. Recut pieces as necessary.

Use these pattern pieces to cut all the remaining pieces for the trusses, then lay out and fasten together a pattern truss. Make sure the joints are tight, then fasten together on both sides of the truss with ½" plywood gussets. Nail wood guides to the chords to create the truss pattern, then build all remaining trusses on top of the pattern truss. NOTE: gable-end trusses only require gussets on one side, as the sheathing will secure the outside face.

If you'd like to build larger trusses that will bear substantial loads, you will need to follow an engineered design approved by an architect or structural engineer.

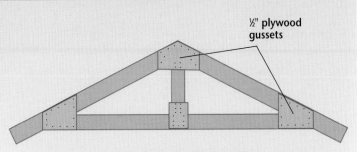

½" plywood gussets

Truss pattern guides

Three-season Porch

A three-season porch blends indoor comforts with an outdoor atmosphere—it is a transition space between your home and yard. Windows line each wall to provide plenty of fresh air and an enjoyable view of your landscape, while keeping insects and inclement weather at bay.

Building a three-season porch is an ambitious project, but like any large-scale project, it can be divided into simple, manageable steps, making the construction process less daunting. This project is split into three building phases: the Deck Frame, the Rough Frame, and the Exterior Finish. Each phase begins with a brief overview of the construction process it covers, with page references to the building techniques you will need.

Building plans are also provided (pages 352 to 355), detailing the parts and dimensions we used in our project. But because each building situation is different, you'll need to tailor these plans to the specific details and dimensions of your home and yard. For example, the distance from the ground to your home's entrance will vary, affecting the height of the deck frame posts and the steps and landing. Make sure any changes or alterations comply with your local building codes and zoning laws. If you are unfamiliar with building plans, refer to page 373 in the Sheds & Outbuildings section for more information.

For ideas on finishing the interior of your three-season porch, see page 367.

TOOLS & MATERIALS

- Basic Tools (page 18)
- Circular saw
- Drill
- 1" spade bit
- Caulk gun
- Power auger or clamshell digger
- Reciprocating saw
- Handsaw
- Wheelbarrow & shovel
- Hand tamp
- T-bevel
- Miter saw

- Nail set
- Stapler
- Jig saw
- Hammer drill
- Galvanized flashing
- 8d, 10d, 16d & 20d galvanized common nails
- 2 x 4 lumber (for batterboards & braces)
- ⅜ x 4" galvanized lag screws & washers
- Silicone caulk
- Masking tape

- 2 x 2 lumber (for stakes)
- Compactible gravel
- 12"-dia. concrete footing forms (3)
- Concrete
- ⅝"-dia. x 6" J-bolts (3)
- 6 x 6 metal post anchors (3)
- 2 x 10 double joist hanger (2)
- 2 x 10 joist hangers (16)
- Metal angle brackets (4)
- 8d & 10d joist hanger nails
- Construction adhesive
- 4d, 6d, 8d & 10d box nails

- 2" & 2½" deck screws
- Hurricane truss ties (16)
- Metal H-clips for sheathing
- 15# building paper
- Galvanized drip edge & step flashing
- Asphalt shingles (to cover 209 sq. ft.)
- 2d roofing nails
- Roofing cement
- 4d, 6d, 8d & 16d galvanized finish nails
- 4d, 8d & 10d galvanized casing nails

- 28 x 55" storm windows (4)
- 32 x 55" storm windows (5)
- 32 x 80" storm door
- 32" aluminum door threshold
- 12 x 12" aluminum louvered vent
- 6d siding nails
- 3" masonry screws
- 2 x 4 trusses, 8-in-12 pitch, 12 ft. span (8)
- Siding to match house

Lumber List

Qty.	Size	Material	Part
Phase One: The Deck Frame			
1	2 x 10 x 12'	Pressure-treated	Ledger
1	6 x 6 x 8'	Pressure-treated	Posts*
2	2 x 10 x 12'	Pressure-treated	Double rim joist
16	2 x 10 x 10'	Pressure-treated	End joists, sister end joists, double mid-joist, joists
2	2 x 10 x 8'	Pressure-treated	Joist blocking
Phase Two: The Rough Frame			
4	⅝" x 4' x 8'	Exterior-grade tongue & groove plywood	Subfloor
5	2 x 4 x 8'	SPF	Blocking for interior walls
2	2 x 4 x 12'	SPF	Endwall plates
4	2 x 4 x 10'	SPF	Sidewall & doorwall plates
2	2 x 8 x 12'	SPF	Endwall header
4	2 x 8 x 10'	SPF	Sidewall & doorwall header
1	½" x 4' x 8'	Plywood	Header spacers
22	2 x 4 x 8'	SPF	Common studs
6	2 x 4 x 8'	SPF	King studs
10	2 x 4 x 8'	SPF	Cripple studs, rough sills, wall blocking
1	2 x 6 x 6'	SPF	Door header
3	2 x 4 x 12'	SPF	Double top plates
2	2 x 4 x 8'	SPF	Gable plates
6	2 x 4 x 10'	SPF	Gable studs, lookouts, barge rafters
2	1 x 4 x 6'	SPF	Truss braces
7	½" x 4' x 8'	Exterior-grade plywood	Roof sheathing
2	1 x 6 x 10'	Cedar	Gable fascia
3	1 x 8 x 8'	Cedar	Side fascia
9	½" x 4' x 8'	Exterior-grade plywood	Wall sheathing
Phase Three: The Exterior Finish			
5	1 x 2 x 6'	SPF	Sill nailers
3	2 x 8 x 10'	Cedar	Window sills
10	2 x 2 x 8'	SPF	Window nailers
3	1 x 6 x 8'	SPF	Door jambs
3	¼" x 4' x 8'	Exterior-grade plywood	Soffits
10	1 x 2 x 8'	Cedar	Inner window trim
4	1 x 10 x 10'	Cedar	Corner trim
2	1 x 6 x 8'	Cedar	End trim
2	1 x 12 x 6'	Cedar	Endwall header trim
2	1 x 12 x 10'	Cedar	Sidewall & doorwall header trim
2	1 x 6 x 6'	Cedar	Endwall sill trim
2	1 x 6 x 10'	Cedar	Sidewall & doorwall sill trim
2	1 x 8 x 6'	Cedar	Endwall skirt trim
2	1 x 8 x 10'	Cedar	Sidewall & doorwall skirt trim
1	1 x 10 x 6'	Cedar	Door header trim
4	1 x 6 x 10'	Cedar	Window trim
4	2 x 6 x 8'	Pressure-treated	Landing ledger, rim joist & landing joists
3	2 x 4 x 8'	Pressure-treated	Landing wall plates, landing wall studs*, gussets
1	2 x 12 x 8'	Pressure-treated	Step stringers*
2	2 x 10 x 8'	Cedar	Facing boards
1	2 x 4 x 6'	Cedar	Step nailer
7	¾" x 6" x 8'	Cedar	Decking boards

*Number and length of boards needed will vary based on the height from your home's entrance to the ground.

DECK FRAMING PLAN

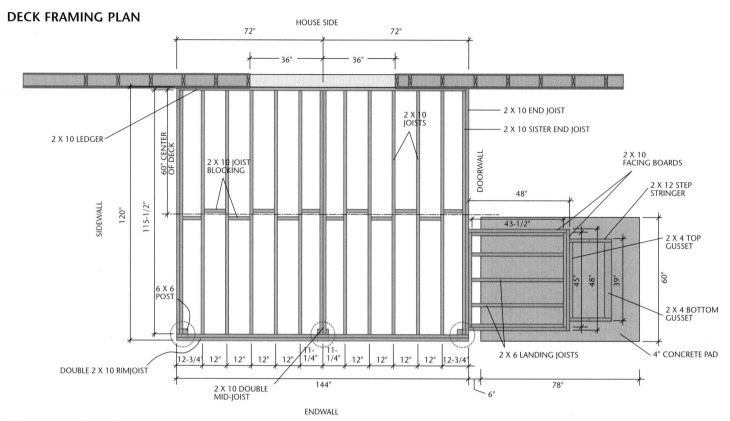

HOUSE SIDE

72" 72"

36" 36"

2 X 10 LEDGER

2 X 10 END JOIST

2 X 10 SISTER END JOIST

2 X 10 JOISTS

2 X 10 JOIST BLOCKING

60" CENTER OF DECK

115-1/2"

120"

SIDEWALL

DOORWALL

2 X 10 FACING BOARDS

2 X 12 STEP STRINGER

48"

43-1/2"

2 X 4 TOP GUSSET

45"

48"

39"

60"

2 X 4 BOTTOM GUSSET

6 X 6 POST

DOUBLE 2 X 10 RIMJOIST

12-3/4" 12" 12" 12" 12" 11-1/4" 11-1/4" 12" 12" 12" 12" 12-3/4"

2 X 6 LANDING JOISTS

4" CONCRETE PAD

2 X 10 DOUBLE MID-JOIST

144"

78"

6"

ENDWALL

ROOF FRAMING PLAN

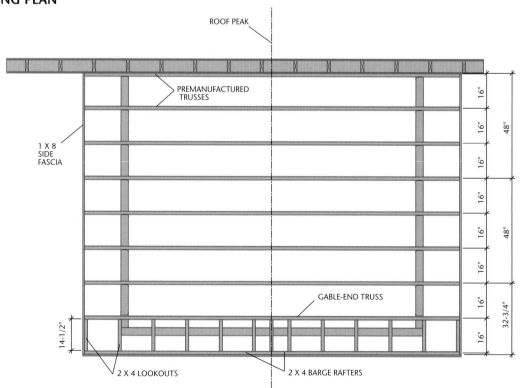

ROOF PEAK

PREMANUFACTURED TRUSSES

1 X 8 SIDE FASCIA

16"

16"

16"

16"

48"

16"

16"

48"

16"

GABLE-END TRUSS

16"

32-3/4"

16"

14-1/2"

2 X 4 LOOKOUTS

2 X 4 BARGE RAFTERS

TYING TO EXISTING WALL

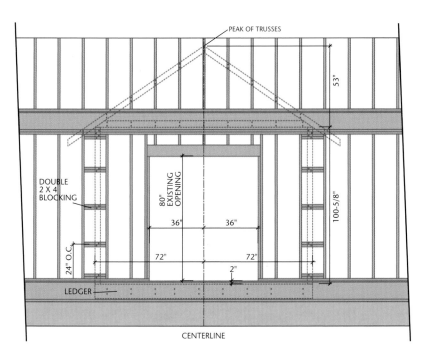

PEAK OF TRUSSES

53"

100-5/8"

DOUBLE 2 X 4 BLOCKING

80" EXISTING OPENING

36" 36"

72" 72"

24" O.C.

2"

LEDGER

CENTERLINE

DOORWALL FRAMING PLAN

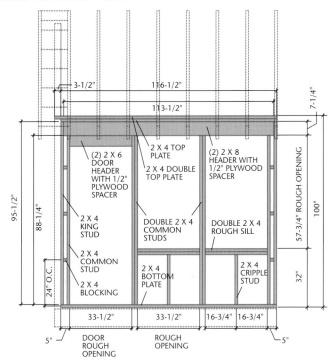

3-1/2" 116-1/2" 7-1/4"

113-1/2"

2 X 4 TOP PLATE

(2) 2 X 6 DOOR HEADER WITH 1/2" PLYWOOD SPACER

2 X 4 DOUBLE TOP PLATE

(2) 2 X 8 HEADER WITH 1/2" PLYWOOD SPACER

95-1/2"

88-1/4"

57-3/4" ROUGH OPENING

100"

2 X 4 KING STUD

DOUBLE 2 X 4 COMMON STUDS

DOUBLE 2 X 4 ROUGH SILL

2 X 4 COMMON STUD

24" O.C.

2 X 4 BLOCKING

2 X 4 BOTTOM PLATE

2 X 4 CRIPPLE STUD

32"

33-1/2" 33-1/2" 16-3/4" 16-3/4"

5" DOOR ROUGH OPENING ROUGH OPENING 5"

SIDEWALL FRAMING PLAN

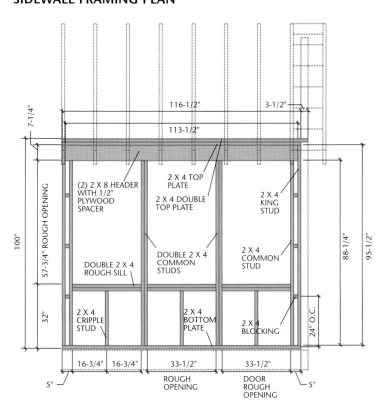

7-1/4" 116-1/2" 3-1/2"

113-1/2"

(2) 2 X 8 HEADER WITH 1/2" PLYWOOD SPACER

2 X 4 TOP PLATE

2 X 4 DOUBLE TOP PLATE

2 X 4 KING STUD

100"

57-3/4" ROUGH OPENING

88-1/4"

95-1/2"

DOUBLE 2 X 4 ROUGH SILL

DOUBLE 2 X 4 COMMON STUDS

2 X 4 COMMON STUD

32"

2 X 4 CRIPPLE STUD

2 X 4 BOTTOM PLATE

2 X 4 BLOCKING

24" O.C.

16-3/4" 16-3/4" 33-1/2" 33-1/2"

5" ROUGH OPENING DOOR ROUGH OPENING 5"

ENDWALL FRAMING PLAN

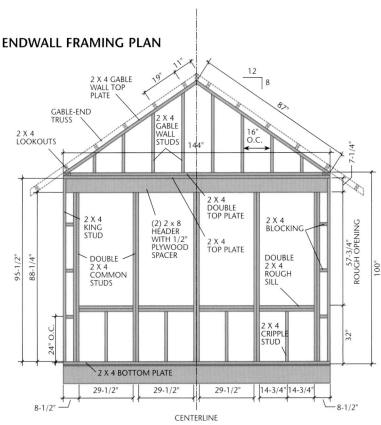

19" 11" 12 8

2 X 4 GABLE WALL TOP PLATE

GABLE-END TRUSS

2 X 4 GABLE WALL STUDS

87"

2 X 4 LOOKOUTS

144"

16" O.C.

7-1/4"

2 X 4 KING STUD

2 X 4 DOUBLE TOP PLATE

2 X 4 BLOCKING

95-1/2"

88-1/4"

(2) 2 x 8 HEADER WITH 1/2" PLYWOOD SPACER

2 X 4 TOP PLATE

DOUBLE 2 X 4 COMMON STUDS

DOUBLE 2 X 4 ROUGH SILL

57-3/4" ROUGH OPENING

100"

24" O.C.

2 X 4 CRIPPLE STUD

32"

2 X 4 BOTTOM PLATE

8-1/2" 29-1/2" 29-1/2" 29-1/2" 14-3/4" 14-3/4" 8-1/2"

CENTERLINE

353

FLOOR PLAN

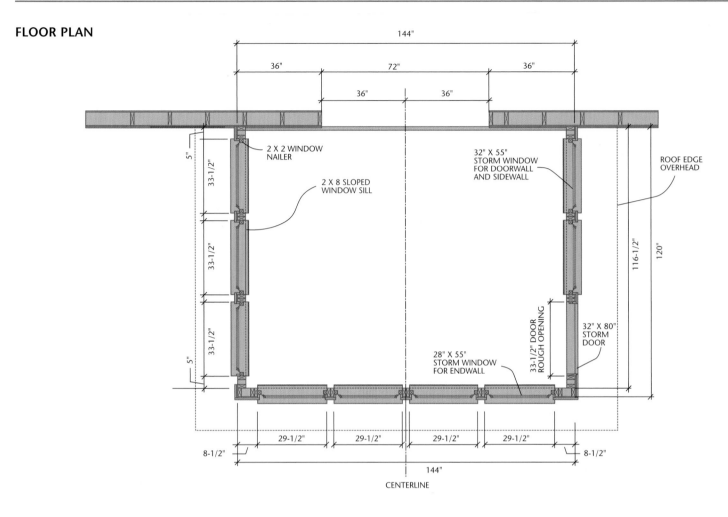

144"

36" 72" 36"

36" 36"

5"

33-1/2"

2 X 2 WINDOW NAILER

2 X 8 SLOPED WINDOW SILL

32" X 55" STORM WINDOW FOR DOORWALL AND SIDEWALL

ROOF EDGE OVERHEAD

33-1/2"

116-1/2"

120"

33-1/2"

5"

28" X 55" STORM WINDOW FOR ENDWALL

33-1/2" DOOR ROUGH OPENING

32" X 80" STORM DOOR

8-1/2" 29-1/2" 29-1/2" 29-1/2" 29-1/2" 8-1/2"

144"

CENTERLINE

CORNER TRIM DETAIL

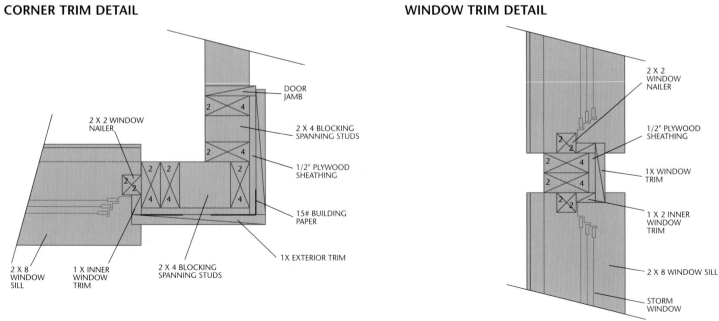

DOOR JAMB

2 X 2 WINDOW NAILER

2 X 4 BLOCKING SPANNING STUDS

1/2" PLYWOOD SHEATHING

15# BUILDING PAPER

1X EXTERIOR TRIM

2 X 8 WINDOW SILL

1 X INNER WINDOW TRIM

2 X 4 BLOCKING SPANNING STUDS

WINDOW TRIM DETAIL

2 X 2 WINDOW NAILER

1/2" PLYWOOD SHEATHING

1X WINDOW TRIM

1 X 2 INNER WINDOW TRIM

2 X 8 WINDOW SILL

STORM WINDOW

SECTION ELEVATION

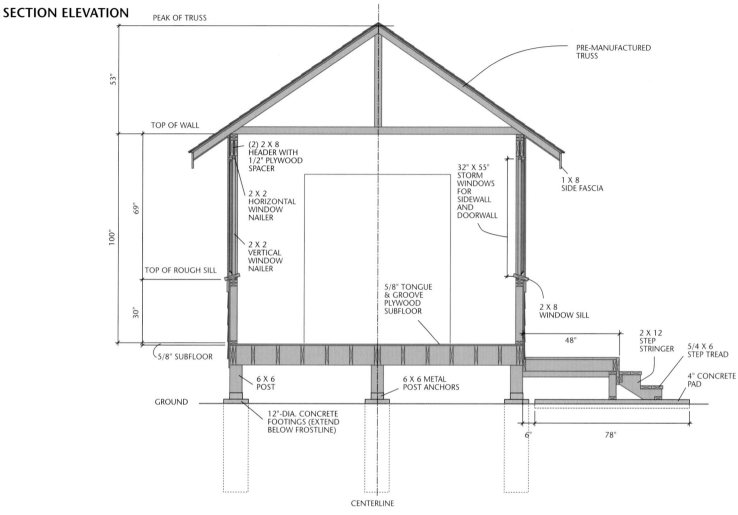

PEAK OF TRUSS

53"

TOP OF WALL

100"

69"

TOP OF ROUGH SILL

30"

PRE-MANUFACTURED TRUSS

(2) 2 X 8 HEADER WITH 1/2" PLYWOOD SPACER

2 X 2 HORIZONTAL WINDOW NAILER

2 X 2 VERTICAL WINDOW NAILER

32" X 55" STORM WINDOWS FOR SIDEWALL AND DOORWALL

5/8" TONGUE & GROOVE PLYWOOD SUBFLOOR

1 X 8 SIDE FASCIA

2 X 8 WINDOW SILL

48"

2 X 12 STEP STRINGER

5/4 X 6 STEP TREAD

5/8" SUBFLOOR

6 X 6 POST

6 X 6 METAL POST ANCHORS

4" CONCRETE PAD

GROUND

12"-DIA. CONCRETE FOOTINGS (EXTEND BELOW FROSTLINE)

6"

78"

CENTERLINE

SECTION DETAIL AT HEADER

SECTION DETAIL AT SILL

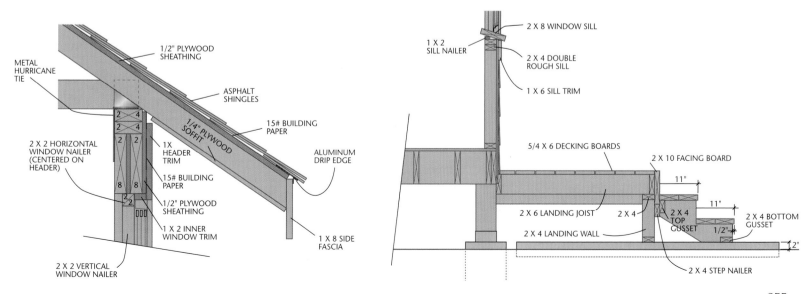

METAL HURRICANE TIE

1/2" PLYWOOD SHEATHING

ASPHALT SHINGLES

1/4" PLYWOOD SOFFIT

15# BUILDING PAPER

2 X 2 HORIZONTAL WINDOW NAILER (CENTERED ON HEADER)

1X HEADER TRIM

15# BUILDING PAPER

1/2" PLYWOOD SHEATHING

1 X 2 INNER WINDOW TRIM

ALUMINUM DRIP EDGE

2 X 2 VERTICAL WINDOW NAILER

1 X 8 SIDE FASCIA

2 X 8 WINDOW SILL

1 X 2 SILL NAILER

2 X 4 DOUBLE ROUGH SILL

1 X 6 SILL TRIM

5/4 X 6 DECKING BOARDS

2 X 10 FACING BOARD

11"

2 X 6 LANDING JOIST

2 X 4

2 X 4 TOP GUSSET

11"

1/2"

2 X 4 BOTTOM GUSSET

2 X 4 LANDING WALL

2"

2 X 4 STEP NAILER

355

Phase One: The Deck Frame

The first phase in building a three-season porch is essentially to build a deck. This requires that you are familiar with basic deck building techniques (pages 204 to 241). Refer to the DECK FRAMING PLAN on page 352, and make sure to follow your approved building plans.

Step A: Attach the Ledger

1. Measure and mark the center of your entrance, then measure out from that centerpoint 72" in both directions and mark for the ends of the ledger outline.

2. Draw an outline 2" below the threshold to mark where the ledger will fit against the house. Use a level as a guide and make the outline 9¼" wide (the width of the ledger) and 144" long.

3. Set your circular saw blade to the depth of the siding, then cut along the outline. Use a wood chisel to finish the cuts at the corners. Remove the siding. NOTE: If your house has fiberboard sheathing rather than plywood sheathing, you may also have to trim it away. Consult your local building inspector.

4. Cut a 2 × 10 ledger at 141" and mark its centerpoint. Position the ledger in the cutout, aligning the centerpoint with the centerpoint of the entrance. Make sure the ledger is level, then brace with 2 × 4s and tack in place with 10d common nails.

5. Drill pairs of ½"-deep counterbore holes spaced every 16", using a 1" spade bit, then drill ¼" pilot holes through the center of each

and into the rim joist of the house. Fasten the ledger to the rim joist with ⅜ × 4" lag screws and washers, using a ratchet wrench. Cover the heads of the lag screws with silicone caulk.

Step B: Locate the Footings

1. Measure in 1¼" from each end of the ledger and tack a nail to mark the centerpoints of the outer footings. Do not nail through the flashing.

2. Build and set up batterboards (pages 215 to 216). Run a mason's string out from each nail at the ledger. Stretch the strings taut and level them using a line level. Make sure the strings are perpendicular to the ledger, using the 3-4-5 carpenter's triangle method (pages 216 to 217).

3. From the ledger, measure along each string and mark the centerpoints of the footings at 115¾". Set up additional batterboards and stretch a mason's string across the centerpoints. Check the strings for square by measuring diagonally from corner to corner, adjusting the strings until the measurements are equal.

4. From one outer footing centerpoint, measure along the cross string and mark at 69¼" for the centerpoint of the middle footing.

5. Transfer the centerpoints of the footings to the ground, using a plumb bob. Mark each point with a stake.

Step C: Pour the Footings

1. Remove the mason's strings and dig three holes for 12"-dia. footings, using a power auger or clamshell digger. Pour 2" to 3" of compactible gravel into each hole for drainage. Check your

A. *Brace the ledger in place, then drill counterbored pilot holes into the rim joist of the house. Secure the ledger with ⅜ × 4" lag screws.*

B. *Transfer each footing centerpoint to the ground, using a plumb bob. Mark each location with a stake.*

C. *Pour concrete footings, then insert 6" J-bolts at the center of each concrete footing, leaving ¾" to 1" of thread exposed.*

local building codes—they may require footings that extend past the frostline and have flared bases.

2. Cut three 12"-dia. concrete footing forms to length and set them into the footing holes so the tops are 2" above ground. Make sure the tops of the forms are level, then pack soil around them for support.

3. Mix concrete and fill each form. Work the concrete with a long stick or rod to eliminate any air pockets, then screed the tops with a straight 2 × 4.

4. Retie the mason's strings and use a plumb bob to set 6" J-bolts in the centers of the footings. Leave ¾" to 1" of bolt thread exposed. Let the concrete cure for two to three days.

Step D: Set the Posts

1. Lay a long, straight 2 × 4 flat across the footings with one edge tight against the J-bolts. Trace a reference line across the top of each footing to help orient the 6 × 6 metal post anchors.

2. Place a post anchor on each footing, centered over the J-bolt and square with the reference line. Thread a nut over each bolt and tighten it with a ratchet wrench.

3. Cut each 6 × 6 post at least 6" longer than specified in your plans to allow for final trimming. Place the posts in the anchors and temporarily tack each in place with a 16d common nail. Check the posts for plumb, then brace them with 2 × 4s and stakes.

4. Run a level mason's line from the bottom edge of the ledger to one end post, and mark the post height. Transfer the mark to each side of the post, using a combination square. Run a level mason's string across all the posts at the post height and mark

the remaining posts.

5. Remove the posts from the anchors and cut them to the finished height, using a reciprocating saw. Return the posts to the anchors, make sure they are plumb, and fasten them with 16d galvanized common nails.

Step E: Build the Floor Frame

1. Measure from one end of the ledger and mark the joist locations, following the DECK FRAMING PLAN on page 352. Mark the outline for a joist hanger at each location, using a combination square. Mark a double joist hanger outline at the centerpoint of the ledger.

2. Attach joist hangers at each outline. Fasten one flange of the joist hanger to one side of the outline with a 10d galvanized common nail. Place a scrap 2 × 10 in the hanger for a spacer, align it with the outline and the top of the ledger, then fasten the hanger in place with 10d galvanized common nails. Attach a double joist hanger at the centerpoint of the ledger.

3. Cut two 2 × 10s at 144" for the double rim joist. Check each board for crowning (page 380, Step A), then nail them together with the crowned edge facing up, using 10d galvanized common nails in rows of three, spaced every 16".

4. Mark the centerpoint of the rim joist, then measure from one end and lay out the joist hanger locations as done for the ledger. Fasten the hangers in position with 10d joist hanger nails. Attach a double joist hanger at the centerpoint of the rim joist.

5. Cut two 2 × 10 end joists at 117", and two sister end joists

D. *Run a level mason's string across the faces of the posts, mark the height, then cut each post to its finished height.*

E. *Fasten each joist to the rim joist and ledger, using metal joist hangers and 10d joist hanger nails. Use metal angle brackets (INSET) to fasten the floor frame to the tops of the posts.*

and two mid-joist members at 115½". Construct the deck frame using 16d galvanized common nails, following the DECK FRAMING PLAN on page 352. Endnail the end joists into the ends of the ledger, using 16d galvanized common nails. Nail the mid-joist members together and place them in the double joist hangers at the center of the deck, fastening them with 10d joist hanger nails.

6. Check the deck frame for square by measuring diagonally from corner to corner, making adjustments until the measurements are equal. Make sure the deck frame members are on top of the posts, then toenail them in place with 10d galvanized common nails. Secure the end joists and mid-joist to the post tops, using metal angle brackets fastened with 10d joist hanger nails.

7. Cut ten 2 × 10 joists at 115½". Place the joists in the joist hangers—with the crowned edges facing up—and fasten them in place with 10d joist hanger nails.

Step F: Install the Joist Blocking
1. From the ledger, measure along the top of both end joists and mark at 60". Snap a chalk line between the marks.
2. Measure and cut 2 × 10 blocking to fit in each bay between the joists. Endnail the blocks to the joists with 16d galvanized common nails, staggering the pattern along the chalk line.

Phase Two: The Rough Frame

The second phase of this project involves creating the skeletal frame of your porch. Though a non-standard wall layout is used here, an understanding of basic wall framing techniques is help-

ful. Refer to pages 382 to 385 for more information.

You will need to strip down the siding to the sheathing in order to tie the porch walls to the framing members of the house. If your house has fiberboard sheathing rather than plywood sheathing, you may also have to trim it away. Consult your local building inspector. When removing the siding, make an outline that is 1½" larger on each side than the dimensions of the porch frame to allow for the porch's sheathing, building paper, and trim. You will also need to remove sections of the interior wall surfaces so 2 × 4 blocking can be installed in the stud bays at the tie-in points for the porch walls.

Step A: Remove the Siding
1. To find the peak of the planned roof, measure 154" up the wall from the centerpoint of the deck frame. Drop a plumb bob from that point and align it with the deck centerpoint, then mark the exact location of the peak on the wall (page 419, photo G). Also mark the top of the wall cutout at 102" at the deck centerpoint. Use a level to trace a plumb reference line between the two marks.
2. From both the 102" mark and the deck frame centerpoint, measure out horizontally in both directions and mark at 73½". Snap chalk lines to connect the marks and create a 102" × 147" outline on the exterior wall.
3. Set your circular saw blade to the depth of the house siding, and cut along the outline. Remove the siding, using a pry bar.

Step B: Install Blocking in the Existing Walls
NOTE: Refer to TYING TO EXISTING WALL, page 353.
1. Transfer the centerpoint of the deck frame to the interior of

F. *Install 2 × 10 blocking between the joists, staggering the pattern. Endnail through the joists using 16d galvanized common nails.*

A. *Snap chalk lines to mark the porch outline, then cut along the lines, using a circular saw with the blade set to the depth of the siding. Remove the siding within the outline, using a pry bar.*

the house. From that point, measure out in each direction 72" and mark the interior walls at the stud bay in which the 2 × 4 blocking will be installed. Remove as much of the finish material from the interior walls as necessary so that there is an open stud bay on both sides of the bays that will contain the blocking.

2. In each stud bay that will contain blocking, mark for blocking against the bottom plate, then measure up and mark the studs every 24" up to the top plate. Also mark for blocking at the top plate.

3. Cut 2 × 4s to size and install them in pairs centered over each reference mark, using 16d common nails. If necessary, also install 2 × 4 vertical blocking in each stud bay to provide a nailer for the loose ends of the house siding created by the cutout.

4. On the exterior of the house, measure from the centerpoint of the deck frame and mark the location of blocking on the wall.

Step C: Install the Subflooring

1. Snap a control line across the joists at 48" from the house for the first row of subflooring, and at 96" for the second row.

2. In the section nearest the house, apply construction adhesive to the tops of the joists and install a full sheet of ⅝" exterior-grade tongue-and-groove subflooring with 8d box nails, spaced every 6" along the edges and 12" in the field (if necessary, trim the sheet so the end breaks on the center of a joist). Measure and cut the next piece to size for the remainder of the row. Leave a ⅛" gap between the two pieces, and fasten the second piece in place.

3. Install the next row, beginning with a half sheet of subflooring to stagger the joints. Cut the final two pieces for the third row to size. Apply construction adhesive to the joists and fasten

the sheets in place.

Step D: Frame the Walls

NOTE: Refer to pages 382 to 385 for wall framing techniques.

1. Cut a 4" to 6" piece of plate material to use as a spacer. Position the spacer at one corner of the floor, with its outside edge flush with the outside of the floor frame. Mark a pencil line along the inside edge of the spacer. Use the spacer to mark the wall ends at each corner of the floor (six marks total). Snap chalk lines through the marks. These lines represent the inside edges of the bottom plates of the three walls.

2. Build the wall headers from pairs of 2 × 8s cut to length with a ½" plywood spacer sandwiched between; cut the endwall header at 141", and both the sidewall and doorwall headers at 113½".

3. Cut two 2 × 4 plates at 144" for the endwall, and four plates at 116½" for the sidewall and doorwall. Then cut six 2 × 4 king studs at 95½", and twenty-two common studs at 88¼".

4. Refer to the WALL FRAMING plans on page 353 to lay out and mark the stud locations onto the bottom plates and headers of each of the three walls. Assemble the walls one at a time, using 16d common nails for endnailing and 10d common nails for toenailing. Measure and cut the double rough sills and cripple studs to size, and make a door header using a pair of 2 × 6s with a ½" plywood spacer. Use 8d box nails to fasten 2 × 4 blocking between king studs and common studs at the ends of the walls.

5. Raise the walls one at a time and brace them with 2 × 4s staked to the ground. Begin with the sidewall, followed by the doorwall, and finally the endwall. Make sure each wall is plumb,

B. In the interior, install double 2 × 4 blocking every 24" between the studs where the porch walls will be tied to the house.

C. Install tongue-and-groove plywood subflooring, using construction adhesive and 8d box nails. Stagger the seams, making sure they fall on joists.

D. Frame the walls according to your plans. With help, raise the walls one at a time, bracing them with 2 × 4s staked to the ground.

then fasten to the floor frame with 16d common nails spaced every 16", but do not nail through the bottom plate in the door rough opening. Tie the walls together and to the house with 16d common nails. NOTE: You may need to drive nails at a slight angle at the ends of the walls in order to fasten them together.

6. Measure the sidewall and doorwall—from the house to the front edge of the endwall—and cut the 2 × 4 double top plates to length. Install them, using 10d common nails. Measure and cut the double top plate for the endwall and install it.

Step E: Install the First Truss

NOTE: Refer to pages 314 to 317 for installing trusses.

1. At the top of the wall cutout, find the visible nail heads on the siding to locate the framing members of the house. Draw reference lines on the outside wall, up to the planned roof peak.

2. With help, hoist the first truss into position against the house. Align the peak of the truss with the centerline marked on the siding.

3. With the truss flush against the siding, make sure the rafter tails overhang the double top plates evenly on both sides. Nail the chords of the truss to the framing members of the house, using 20d common nails.

Step F: Install the Remaining Trusses

NOTE: Refer to the ROOF FRAMING PLAN on page 352.

1. Lay out the truss locations every 16" on-center on the double top plates of both the sidewall and doorwall. From the first truss, measure from the side against the house and mark at 15¼". Then measure from the 15¼" line and mark every 16" until you

reach the ends of the walls. Draw an "X" at the endwall-side of each line to indicate the truss location.

2. Lift the remaining trusses into place and install them at the marks, working away from the house. Make sure the rafter tails overhang the top plates evenly on both sides, then toenail through the bottom chords with 10d common nails to fasten.

3. Use a level to plumb each truss, then attach 1 × 4s to the undersides of the rafter chords at the peak with 2" deck screws—the boards will act as a temporary brace to keep the trusses plumb. Secure the trusses with hurricane ties—drive 8d common nails into the top plate and 8d joist hanger nails into the rafter chords.

Step G: Build the Gable Wall

NOTE: Refer to the ENDWALL FRAMING PLAN on page 353 for the gable wall layout.

1. On the double top plate of the endwall, mark the gable wall stud locations every 16" on center.

2. Set the two 2 × 4 gable plates on edge and use a rafter square (page 314) to mark one end at an 8-in-12 pitch for the peak. Cut the peak ends using a miter saw, then mark each plate at 87".

3. Use a T-bevel to find the angle formed where the bottom edge of the rafter chord meets the top edge of the bottom chord on the gable-end truss. Mark the angle onto the edge of each gable plate at the 87" mark, and cut the ends, using a miter saw.

4. Position the gable plates on the endwall—make sure the top of the plates line up with the bottom of the rafter chords of the gable-end truss. Fasten the plates in place, using 10d common nails.

E. *Position the first truss flush against the siding of the house, then fasten it to the framing members of the house with 20d common nails.*

F. *Install the trusses following the layout marks on the top plates. Toenail the trusses in place, then secure them with hurricanes ties (INSET).*

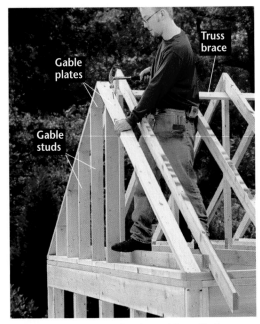

G. *Cut 2 × 4s to size for the gable wall plates and studs. Install them following the layout marks, using 10d common nails.*

5. Use a plumb bob to transfer the stud layout marks from the endwall to the gable plates (see page 419, photo G). Cut one end of each gable wall stud at an 8-in-12 pitch, using a miter saw, then measure and cut the studs to length.

6. Install the studs, following the layout. Fasten them in place—toenail to the endwall and endnail through the gable plates, using 10d common nails.

Step H: Build the Gable Overhang

NOTE: See the ENDWALL FRAMING PLAN on page 353 and the ROOF FRAMING PLAN on page 352 for the gable overhang layout.

1. Mark the lookout layout. From the peak of the gable-end truss, measure down along each rafter chord and mark at 11". Then from the 11" line, mark every 19" until you reach the ends of the chords.

2. Use a rafter square to transfer the marks to the faces of the rafter chords. Draw an "X" at the peak side of each line to indicate the lookout locations. Then, use a framing square to transfer the lookout locations to the top of the gable plates.

3. Cut thirteen 2 × 4 lookouts at 14½". Align the lookouts with the location lines, then fasten them to the rafter chords and gable plates with 10d common nails. At the peak, fasten a lookout so it's plumb and the corners are flush with the top edges of the rafter chords.

4. Use a rafter square to mark one end of the two 2 × 4 barge rafters at an 8-in-12 pitch for the peak. Cut the peak ends, then measure and cut each board long enough to extend several inches past the ends of the truss rafter tails.

5. With help, lift the barge rafters into position one at a time. Align the rafters so the top edges are flush with the top edges of the lookouts, then fasten the rafters in place, using 16d galvanized common nails.

6. To trim the tails of the barge rafter, align a straight 2 × 4 across the bottom edge of the rafter tails and the end of the barge rafters. Mark the barge rafters, then use a rafter square to transfer the line to the face of the rafters. Trim the ends to size with a handsaw.

Step I: Install the Roof Sheathing

Cut ½" exterior-grade plywood sheathing to cover the trusses and gable overhang. Install sheathing from the rafter tails to the peak, using 8d box nails driven every 6" along the edges and 12" in the field of the sheets—the sheathing should not protrude beyond the rafter tail ends, and any seams should fall on rafter chords. Use metal H-clips between sheets to ensure a ⅛" gap at horizontal seams, and leave a ¼" gap at the peak.

Step J: Attach the Fascia

1. Use a rafter square to mark one end of the two 1 × 6 gable fascia boards at an 8-in-12 pitch for the peak. Cut the peak ends, then measure and cut each board long enough to extend several inches past the ends of the rafter tails.

2. Position the fascia boards so the top edges are flush with the top of the sheathing. Fasten the fascia in place, using 8d galvanized finish nails.

3. Measure from the house to the back face of the gable fascia, and cut 1 × 8 side fascia boards to length. Install the fascia so the

H. *Transfer the lookout locations from the rafter chords to the gable wall. Fasten the lookouts in place with 16d common nails.*

I. *Install ½" plywood roof sheathing, using 8d box nails. Use metal H-clips (INSET) to create ⅛" gaps between sheathing pieces.*

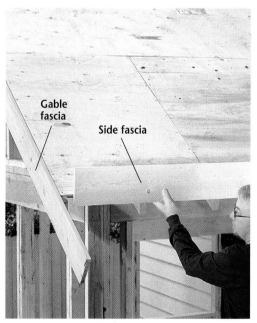

J. *Cut the side fascia to length and fasten it to the rafter tails with 8d finish nails.*

tops of the boards do not project above the sheathing. Fasten the fascia to the rafter tails with 8d galvanized finish nails.

4. Trim off the ends of the gable fascia boards so they are flush with the side fascia boards, using a handsaw. Then drive two or three 8d galvanized finish nails through the gable fascia boards and into the ends of the side fascia.

K. *Install the shingles so the tabs are staggered in regular patterns, with a consistent exposed area on the shingle tabs.*

Step K: Install the Roofing

1. Remove the house siding about 2" above the roof sheathing, using a circular saw with the blade depth set to the siding thickness, then use a reciprocating saw held at a very low angle to cut along the top of the roof. Use a wood chisel to connect the cuts at the ends, and remove the siding.

2. Install drip edge and building paper (pages 392 and 393), step flashing (pages 320 to 321), and asphalt shingles (pages 393 to 394).

Step L: Attach the Wall Sheathing & Building Paper

1. Cut away the bottom plate in the door rough opening, using a reciprocating saw or handsaw. Do not cut into the subfloor.

2. Install ½" exterior-grade plywood sheathing to the framing, using 6d box nails driven every 6" along the edges and 12" in the field of the sheets. Make sure all seams fall on studs. For the gable wall, measure the triangular area, from the header to the lookouts. Divide the area into three sections and cut sheathing to size. For the remaining wall areas, measure and cut sheathing to size.

3. Apply 15# building paper in horizontal strips over all of the wall surfaces, using staples spaced roughly 12" apart. Also wrap the door and window openings with paper.

Phase Three: The Exterior Finish

In this last phase of construction, all of the finish elements—windows, siding, and steps—are installed. To ensure tight joints, measure and cut each piece of trim and siding to size as you work. If installing wooden lap siding (as shown here), you may need to rip-

L. *Cut ½" plywood sheathing to size, and install with 6d box nails every 6" along the edges and every 12" in the field.*

A. *Attach a 1 × 2 sill nailer along the back edge of the rough sill, then install the finished sill so the back edge extends 1" out from the edge of the rough framing members.*

cut some trim and siding boards to width (see page 396 for trim installation techniques). After the siding and trim is installed, prime and paint, or stain and seal, your porch to match your house.

Step A: Attach the Window Sills

1. Cut four 1 × 2 sill nailers at 29½" for the endwall, and five at 33½" for the sidewall and doorwall. Align each nailer flush with the interior edge of the rough sills and fasten it with 4d box nails. (see SECTION ELEVATION, page 355.)

2. Cut four 2 × 8 window sills at 29½" for the endwall, and five at 33½" for the sidewall and doorwall.

3. Install the sills in the rough openings so they slope downward and their back edges extend 1" from the interior edges of the rough openings. Fasten them in place with 16d galvanized finish nails.

Step B: Install the Windows

NOTE: Refer to the SECTION ELEVATION on page 355.

1. At each rough window opening, measure in 1" from the interior edges of the framing members and mark the nailer locations.

2. Cut the 2 × 2 horizontal nailers to the size of the rough openings. Align the nailers with the reference lines and attach them with 10d galvanized casing nails. For the vertical nailers, use a T-bevel to determine the angle at the sill, then mark and cut one end of the vertical nailers using a miter saw before cutting them to length. Align the nailers at the reference lines and install.

3. Place the storm windows against the nailers so the flanges are roughly ¾" from the framing members of the walls. Make sure each window is plumb, then fasten them it to the nailers using

the screws specified by the window manufacturer. Run a thick caulk bead between the windows and the sills.

Step C: Install the Door Frame

1. Beginning at the door header, measure, mark, and cut finish-grade 1 × 6 lumber to size for the door jambs. Rip the pieces to width, if necessary.

2. Install the jambs for the door header and the latch side so they are flush with the outside face of the sheathing. Fasten them to the framing members with 8d casing nails.

3. For the hinge-side jamb, measure the exact width of your storm door including the frame—if the width of the door is ⅜" or greater than the width of the finished door opening (the rough opening plus the thickness of both side jambs), install wood spacers between the hinge-side jamb and the framing member—the finished opening should be ⅛" wider than the door. Make sure the jamb is plumb, then fasten it in place, using 8d casing nails.

Step D: Install the Door

NOTE: The following are only general storm door installation instructions. Read and follow the manufacturer's instructions for your specific storm door.

1. Remove all windows and screens from the 32 × 80" storm door. Position the door in the opening so the hinge side of the door is tight against the door jamb, then draw a reference line onto building paper, following the edge of the door frame. Drill pilot holes spaced every 12" through the hinge-side frame and into the sheathing, then attach the frame with mounting screws.

2. With the door closed, drill pilot holes and attach the latch-

B. *Attach 2 × 2 nailers 1" in from the inside edge of the rough window openings. Install the storm windows, then run a caulk bead where the window meets the finished sill.*

C. *Cut the door jambs to size, beginning with the top jamb at the header. Install the jambs, using 8d casing nails.*

side frame to the sheathing. Keep an even gap between the door and the frame. Then, center the door frame top piece on top of the frame sides. Drill pilot holes and fasten it to the door header.

3. Attach lock and latch hardware as directed by the manufacturer, then reinstall all windows and screens.

Step E: Install the Soffits

D. *Push the door frame tightly against the hinge-side jamb, then drill pilot holes and attach the door frame to the sheathing.*

Measure and cut soffit panels to size from ¼" exterior-grade plywood. Install the panels at the gable-end overhang first, then along the sidewall and doorwall eaves. Hold each panel flush against the lookouts or rafter tails, with the front edge tight against the fascia boards, and fasten, using 4d galvanized casing nails.

Step F: Install the Trim

NOTE: Refer to the plans on pages 354 to 355 for trim placement and details.

1. Measure and cut the inner window trim for each window from 1 × 2 cedar, beginning with the horizontal pieces at the header. Install them flush with the exterior face of the wall sheathing, with the back edges against the window flanges. Attach the trim with 4d galvanized finish nails.

2. Measure the dimensions for each corner trim piece (see CORNER TRIM DETAIL, page 354). The trim should extend from 1" below the bottom edge of the wall sheathing up to the soffits. Cut the pieces to size from 1 × cedar—rip the boards to width and notch them to fit around the window sills, as necessary. Fasten them in place with pairs of 8d galvanized finish nails.

3. Measure and cut the end trim—where the sidewall and doorwall tie into the house. Measure from 1" below the bottom edge of the deck frame up to the soffits, ripping 1 × cedar to width, as necessary. Fasten the boards in place with 8d galvanized finish nails.

4. Measure and cut to length all of the horizontal trim pieces—the header trim (1 × 12s ripped to size), sill trim (1 × 6s), and skirt trim (1 × 8s). Fasten all boards in place, using 8d galvanized finish nails. The skirt trim should extend 1" below the wall

E. *Cut ¼" plywood to size for soffits. Fasten the panels flat against the lookouts on the gable overhang, and against the rafter tails of the trusses.*

F. *Cut all trim pieces to size—rip trim boards to width, as necessary. Fasten the trim pieces in place with 8d galvanized finish nails.*

sheathing. Finally, measure and cut the vertical window trim to size, ripping 1 × 6s to the proper width, and install them.

5. On the floor of the finished door opening, measure the space between the jambs and cut the aluminum threshold to size. Make sure it fits snugly against the jamb and floor frame pieces. Center the threshold under the door, so it covers the edges of the sheathing and trim, and attach it to the subflooring using the fasteners specified by the manufacturer.

Step G: Install the Gable Vent

NOTE: The gable vent used here is an aluminum louvered wall vent that is surface-mounted to the sheathing. For installation of a recessed or framed vent, follow the manufacturer's directions.

1. At the gable wall, mark the location for the vent, then drill ⅛" holes at each corner. Draw reference lines between the holes and cut at the lines, using a jig saw.

2. Position the vent over the opening, make sure it is level, then fasten to the sheathing with 4d galvanized box nails.

Step H: Install the Siding

NOTE: If the trim is thicker than the finished siding you are installing, install galvanized flashing between the skirt trim and the first piece of siding.

1. To install wood lap siding, first mark the centers of the wall studs onto the building paper to facilitate nailing, then cut 1"-wide strips from the top edge of siding pieces to use as starter strips. Check to make sure the skirt trim is level, then install the starter strips flush along the top edge of the trim, using 6d siding nails.

2. Cut the first course of siding to fit snugly between the corner trim boards, but not so tightly that you have to force it into place. Fasten it with a 6d siding nail driven at each stud location, about 1¼" from the bottom edge, or just above the top edge of the siding below. If you need two boards to span the wall, center the inside ends over a stud, leaving a ⅛" gap between them; drive two nails at each end. Make sure to stagger end joints between courses.

3. From the top edge of the first course of siding, measure up and mark the reveal dimension of your house siding, and snap a level chalk line—this is the reference lines for the top edge of the next course. Measure from that mark—using the reveal dimension—to mark for the remaining courses. Use a level to transfer the line onto the adjacent wall, so the courses are aligned horizontally.

4. Cut the remaining pieces of siding to size, aligning the top edges with the chalk lines, then fasten at the stud locations with 6d siding nails. At the gable wall, install siding as for the lower walls, marking angled cuts with a pattern made from scrap siding (pages 324 to 325).

5. Rip-cut the final pieces to size, if necessary, and fasten at the stud locations with 6d nails along the bottom and top edges. Caulk all the joints between the siding and trim, including where the end trim meets the house and around the gable vent.

Step I: Dig & Pour the Concrete Pad for the Steps

1. Determine and lay out the location of the 60" × 78" concrete pad, referring to the DECK FRAMING PLAN on page 352. Excavate the area to approximately 8" deep.

2. Lay and tamp a 4" base of compactible gravel, then build forms from 2 × 6 lumber, so the top of the form is 2" above

G. *Cut the hole for the gable vent. Position the vent and fasten it to the sheathing, using 4d galvanized box nails.*

H. *Cut the gable siding to length, trimming the ends to match the pitch of the roof. Fasten the siding, using 6d siding nails.*

ground level. Make sure the form is level, then stake it in place.

3. Mix concrete and fill the form. Screed the surface with a straight 2 × 4, then let the concrete cure overnight.

Step J: Build the Landing Frame

I. *Mark the layout for the concrete pad with stakes and string. Transfer the corners to the ground with a plumb bob, and mark them with stakes.*

NOTE: Refer to the DECK FRAMING PLAN on page 352 and the SECTION DETAIL AT SILL on page 355.

1. Build the 2 × 6 landing frame: cut a ledger and rim joist at 45", and five joists at 43½". On both the ledger and rim joist, mark the joist locations at 11¼", 23¼", and 37¼" then transfer the marks to the inside faces of both boards, using a combination square. Following the layout, assemble the landing frame, using 16d galvanized common nails. Make sure to install each board with the crowned edge facing up (page 380, Step A).

2. To determine the position of the landing, measure the distance from the top of the porch subflooring to the concrete pad. Divide the dimension by 4 for the rise of the steps.

3. Mark the centerpoint of the finished door opening, then measure down and mark the rise dimension plus the thickness of the decking material (1¼" for this project) on the skirt trim below the door. Mark the centerpoint of the landing ledger, then temporarily prop up the landing frame so the ledger is flush against the skirt trim, with its centerpoint aligned with the door centerpoint. Make sure the landing frame is level, then trace the outline of the ledger onto the skirt trim. Measure the distance from the bottom of the rim joist to the concrete pad to determine the height of the landing wall.

4. Build the 2 × 4 landing wall. Cut two plates at 45" and five studs to size. To determine the length of the studs, add the thickness of the plates and the width of the rim joist (8½" total, in this project), then subtract that number from the height dimension. Lay out the stud locations on the plates using the same measurements as for the landing joists, then assemble the wall using 16d

J. *With the landing frame in position, drill counterbored pilot holes through the ledger and into the end joist of the porch, then fasten it with lag screws.*

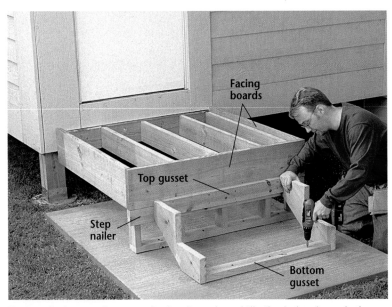

K. *Attach the step frame to the landing, then drill pilot holes through the bottom gusset and fasten it to the concrete pad with 3" masonry screws.*

galvanized common nails. Attach the landing wall to the bottom of the landing frame at the rim joist, using 10d galvanized common nails. Make sure the wall is flush with the ends and front face of the rim joist.

5. Set your circular saw blade depth to the thickness of the skirt trim, and cut out the trim at the outline. Install galvanized flashing under the trim, then reposition and level the landing frame against the porch. Make sure it is level, then drill four ½"-deep counterbore holes into the ledger, using a 1" spade bit, one between each pair of joists. Also drill ¼" pilot holes through the ledger and into the porch end joist, and fasten the landing using ⅜ × 4" lag screws with washers.

6. Drill pilot holes through the bottom plate of the landing wall into the concrete pad, and secure it with 3" masonry screws. Seal the heads of the lag screws and masonry screws with silicone caulk.

Step K: Install the Steps & Decking

NOTE: Refer to the DECK FRAMING PLAN on page 352 and the SECTION DETAIL AT SILL on page 355.

1. Cut three 2 × 10 face boards to size. Position the top edges 1¼" above the top of the landing frame, so they will be flush with the decking surface. Attach them to the frame, using 2½" deck screws. Also cut a 2 × 4 step nailer at 48", and attach it to the landing wall, flush with the ends of the face board, using 2½" deck screws.

2. Lay out the step stringers on 2 × 12 stock, using a framing square (pages 330 to 333). The riser dimension should equal the dimension found in Step J #2, and the run should be 10½". Cut out the stringer steps, using a circular saw and handsaw.

3. Cut two 2 × 4 gussets at 36", then endnail the step stringers to the gussets (see SECTION DETAIL AT SILL, page 355).

4. Center the step frame flush against the landing. Drive 10d galvanized common nails through the top gusset, into the landing. Drill pilot holes through the bottom gusset into the concrete pad, and fasten it with 3" masonry screws.

5. Cut four ⅝ × 6" decking boards at 43", and attach two for each step tread with 2½" deck screws. Overhang the front of the notches by ½", and the ends by 2".

6. Cut the decking boards for the landing to size, and attach them with 2½" deck screws. If necessary, rip the final deck board to the proper width.

INTERIOR FINISH IDEAS

Because a three-season porch is treated as an outdoor space, finish the interior using materials suited for indoor/outdoor applications. They will hold up best over time and against exposure to the elements.

Wood paneling or tongue-and-groove wainscoting (Photo A) are the most practical choices for finishing the porch walls. Both are easy to install, and are much more durable than wallboard.

Ceilings can also be finished with paneling or with a suspended ceiling system. Use finish-grade lumber or decorative moldings to trim out corners and windows (photo B).

The flooring of your porch should be resilient enough to handle heavy traffic, dirt, and water. Vinyl flooring is durable and comes in sheets (photo C) or tiles that are simple to install. Indoor/outdoor carpet is inexpensive and resistant to stains and mildew. Both are low-maintenance materials, and available in a wide variety of colors and styles.

Before you finish the walls and ceiling, install all electrical receptacle and fixture boxes and run the cables (photo D) (the porch should be wired on a separate circuit). You may also want to run a second circuit for electric baseboard heaters, which would help make the space usable during cold seasons.

367

Porch Ideas

© Crandall & Crandall

© Crandall & Crandall

© Andrea Rugg

(above) **This large back yard porch with screen walls** *provides all the benefits of outdoor living, while protecting from inclement weather and pests.*

(left) **This wraparound, plantation-style porch** *creates a feeling of genteel relaxation and easy living.*

(below left) **A small, inviting porch,** *like this example, can be a perfect fit in a suburban or urban neighborhood. This classic porch also makes a cozy perch during balmy evenings.*

© Angela Hartwell

© Andrea Rugg

© Angela Hartwell

(above and right) **This portico includes interesting design features,** *such as lengthy shutters and decorative latticework. A brick stoop helps define the home's entrance.*

(left) **Sun screens help create interesting light and shadow patterns,** *as in this steel-post and I-beam construction. The structure helps filter out sunlight without completely concealing the entrance.*

Sheds & Outbuildings

Constructing your own outbuilding is a satisfying process—from hand-picking the lumber to nailing off the final piece of trim. In the end, you'll have a well-built, custom structure that will far outlast any typical wood or sheet metal kit building. And if you're a beginner, you'll enjoy the added reward of learning the fundamentals of carpentry and building design.

Each of the five building projects in this section includes a complete set of architectural plans and step-by-step instructions for completing the construction. If you need more detail on any of the procedures, look for it in the Basic Construction Techniques section, starting on page 374.

The Techniques section gives you general information on the most popular types of finishes, as well as how-to projects for installing the finishes used in the projects. You'll also learn the basic construction methods for building foundations, framing floors, walls, and roofs, and completing the finish carpentry. For general information on lumber and hardware, see pages 10 and 21.

When you're ready to start planning, read Choosing the Site, on page 372. This includes tips for selecting the best area for your outbuilding and a discussion of the building codes and zoning regulations that may apply to your project.

Choosing the Site

The first step in choosing a site for your building doesn't take place in your backyard but at the local building and zoning departments. By visiting the departments, or making calls, you must determine a few things about your project before you can make any definite plans. Most importantly, find out whether your proposed building will be allowed by zoning regulations and what specific restrictions apply to your situation. Zoning laws govern such matters as the size and height of the building and the percentage of your property it occupies, the building's location, and its position relative to the house, neighboring properties, the street, etc.

From the building side of things, ask if you need a permit to build your structure. If so, you'll have to submit plan drawings (the drawings in this book should suffice), as well as specifications for the foundation and materials. Once your project is approved, you must buy a permit to display on the building site, and you may be required to show your work at scheduled inspections.

Because outbuildings are by nature detached and freestanding, building codes typically govern them much more loosely than they do houses. Many impose restrictions or require permits only on structures larger than 100, or even 120, square feet. Others draw the line with the type of foundation used. In some areas, buildings with concrete slab or pier foundations are classified as "permanent" and thus are subject to a specific set of restrictions (and taxation, in some cases), while buildings that are set on skids and can—in theory at least—be moved are considered temporary or accessory and may be exempt from the general building codes. Again, municipal laws vary greatly, so you'll have to find out which ones apply to you.

Once you get the green light from the local authorities, you can tromp around your yard with a tape measure and stake your claim for the new building. Of course, you'll have plenty of personal and practical reasons for placing the building in a particular area, but here are a few general considerations to keep in mind:

Sunlight: How much light you want will depend on the building's purpose. South-facing windows and doors bring in the most sunlight; a playhouse or gazebo may benefit from some shade. Also consider what the building itself will shade, lest you block essential light to your garden.

Soil & drainage: To ensure that your foundation will last (whatever type it is), plant your building on solid soil, in an area that won't collect water.

Access: For trucks, wheelbarrows, kids, etc. Do you want access in all seasons?

Utility lines: Contact the local utilities to find out where the water, gas, and electrical lines run through your property. This is essential not only for digging in the ground, but also because you don't want your building sitting over lines that may need repair.

Setback requirements: Most zoning laws dictate that all buildings, fences, etc., in a yard must be set back a specific distance from the property line. This *setback* may range from 6" to 3 ft. or more.

Neighbors: To prevent civil unrest, or even a few weeks of ignored greetings, talk to your neighbors about your project.

View from the house: Do you want to admire your handiwork from the dinner table, or would you prefer that your outbuilding blend in with the outdoors? A playhouse in plain view makes it easy to check on the kids.

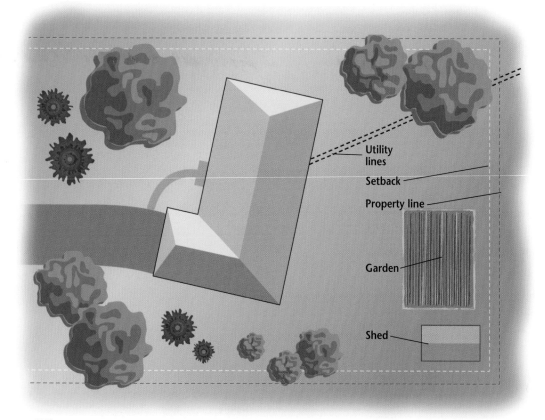

Utility lines

Setback

Property line

Garden

Shed

Working with Plans

Architectural plan drawings are two-dimensional representations of what a building looks like from five different perspectives, or *views*: front, rear, right side, left side, and plan view. The first four are called ELEVATIONS, and they show you what you would see with a direct, exterior view of the building. There are elevation drawings for the framing and for the exterior finishes. PLAN views have an overhead perspective, looking straight down from above the building. FLOOR PLANS show the wall layout, with the top half of the building sliced off. There are also roof framing plans and other drawings with plan views.

To show close-up views of specific constructions or relationships between materials, there are various DETAILS. And all plans include a comprehensive building SECTION—a side view of the building sliced in half down the middle, showing both the framing and finish elements.

Because plan drawings are two-dimensional, it's up to you to visualize the building in its actual, three-dimensional form. This can be done by cross-referencing the different drawings and confirming the quantities and sizes of materials using the materials list. It helps to spend some time just looking over the drawings. Chances are, you'll find yourself absorbed in solving the puzzle of how it all fits together.

NOTE: the plan drawings in this section are not sized to a specific scale, but all of the elements within each drawing are sized proportionately. And although the plan dimensions are given in feet and inches (6'-8", for example), the instructions provide dimensions in inches, so you don't have to make the conversion.

Here are some of the common terms and conventions used in the drawings in this section:

• **Wall height** is measured from the top of the finished floor to the top of the wall framing.

• **Rough openings** for doors and windows are measured between the framing members inside the opening. An opening's width and height often are given on separate drawings.

• **Grade** represents the solid, level ground directly beneath the building.

• **Door & window details** typically show a gap between the 1 × frame and the framing of the rough opening—this represents the shim space needed for installing the frames using shims.

• **Framing layout** is noted with a dimension (usually 16" or 24"), followed by "on center" or "O. C." This describes the spacing between the center of one framing member to the center of the next member. Use the spacing for the general layout, adding extra members, such as for corners and door or window frames, where noted. The last space in a layout is often smaller than the given on-center dimension.

BUILDING SECTION

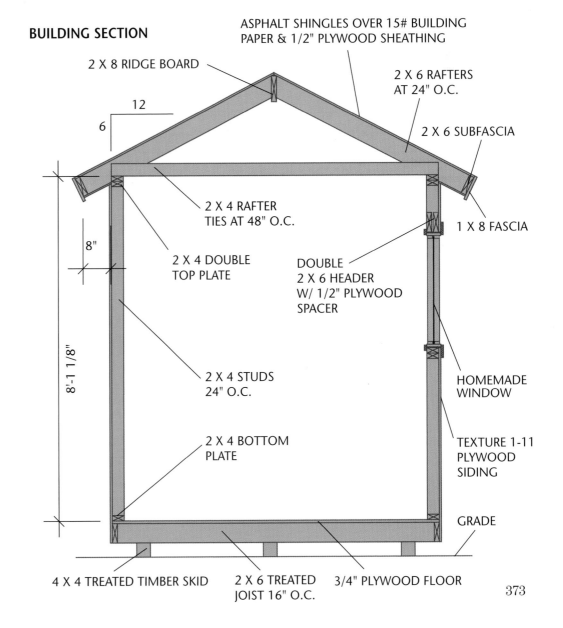

ASPHALT SHINGLES OVER 15# BUILDING PAPER & 1/2" PLYWOOD SHEATHING

2 X 8 RIDGE BOARD

2 X 6 RAFTERS AT 24" O.C.

2 X 6 SUBFASCIA

2 X 4 RAFTER TIES AT 48" O.C.

1 X 8 FASCIA

2 X 4 DOUBLE TOP PLATE

DOUBLE 2 X 6 HEADER W/ 1/2" PLYWOOD SPACER

HOMEMADE WINDOW

2 X 4 STUDS 24" O.C.

TEXTURE 1-11 PLYWOOD SIDING

2 X 4 BOTTOM PLATE

GRADE

4 X 4 TREATED TIMBER SKID

2 X 6 TREATED JOIST 16" O.C.

3/4" PLYWOOD FLOOR

373

Basic Construction Techniques:

Anatomy of a Shed

Shown as a cutaway, this shed illustrates many of the standard building components and how they fit together. It can also help you understand the major construction stages—each project in this section includes a specific construction sequence, but most follow the standard stages in some form:

1. Foundation—including preparing the site and adding a drainage bed;

2. Framing—the floor is first, followed by the walls, then the roof;

3. Roofing—adding sheathing, building paper, and roofing material;

4. Exterior finishes—including siding, trim, and doors and windows.

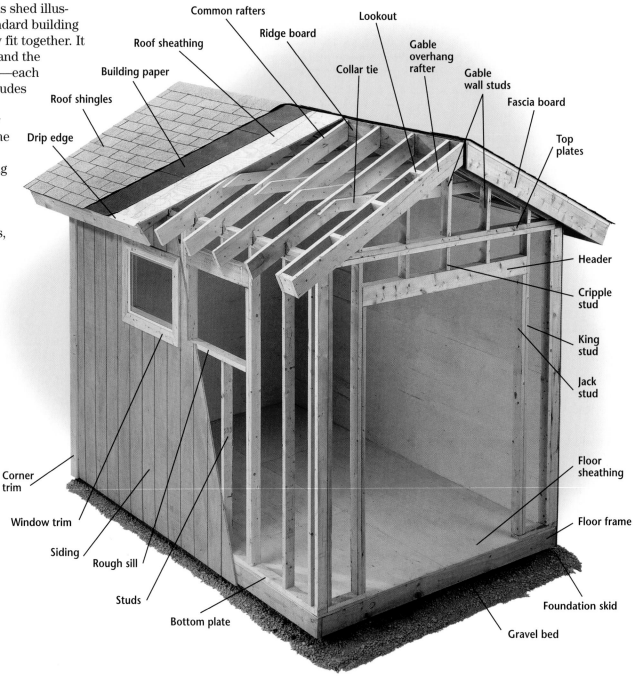

Common rafters

Lookout

Ridge board

Roof sheathing

Gable overhang rafter

Collar tie

Building paper

Gable wall studs

Roof shingles

Fascia board

Drip edge

Top plates

Header

Cripple stud

King stud

Jack stud

Floor sheathing

Floor frame

Corner trim

Window trim

Siding

Rough sill

Studs

Bottom plate

Foundation skid

Gravel bed

Foundations

Like a house, a shed or outbuilding needs a foundation to provide a sturdy base to build upon and to protect the structure from the damaging effects of moisture and soil. In some cases the foundation ties the building to the earth (an important requirement for umbrella-like gazebos) or keeps the building from shifting during seasonal freeze-thaw cycles.

You can build a shed with a variety of foundations; the most commonly used types are the wooden skid and the concrete slab. In addition to being far easier and cheaper to construct, a skid foundation allows you to move the shed if you need to. It also ensures—in most areas—that the building is classified as a temporary structure (see page 372). A concrete slab, by contrast, gives you a nice, hard-wearing floor as well as an extremely durable foundation. But a concrete foundation means the building is considered "permanent," which could affect the tax assessment of your property; you'll also most likely need a permit for the project.

Gazebos must be securely anchored to the ground, as mentioned, and are typically built on concrete pier—also called *footings*—or slab foundations. The gazebo project in this section has nine concrete piers, which you can pour using cardboard tube forms. See pages 215 to 219 for help with laying out and pouring concrete piers.

Wooden Skid Foundation

A skid foundation couldn't be simpler: two or more treated wood beams or landscape timbers (typically 4 × 4, 4 × 6 or 6 × 6) set on a bed of gravel. The gravel provides a flat, stable surface that drains well to help keep the timbers dry. Once the skids are set, the floor frame is built on top of them and is nailed to the skids to keep everything in place.

Building a skid foundation is merely a matter of preparing the gravel base, then cutting, setting, and leveling the timbers. The timbers you use must be rated for ground contact. It is customary, but purely optional, to make angled cuts on the ends of the skids—these add a minor decorative touch and make it easier to *skid* the shed to a new location, if necessary.

Because a skid foundation sits on the ground, it is subject to slight shifting due to frost in cold-weather climates. Often a shed that has risen out of level will correct itself with the spring thaw, but if it doesn't, you can lift the shed with jacks on the low side and add gravel beneath the skids to level it.

TOOLS & MATERIALS

- Basic tools (page 18)
- Shovel
- Rake
- 4-ft. level
- Straight, 8-ft. 2 x 4
- Hand tamper
- Circular saw
- Square
- Treated wood timbers
- Compactible gravel
- Wood sealer-preservative

A. *Excavate the building site and add a 4" layer of compactible gravel. Level, then tamp the gravel with a hand tamper or rented plate compactor (INSET).*

HOW TO BUILD A WOOD SKID FOUNDATION

Step A: Prepare the Gravel Base

1. Remove 4" of soil in an area about 12" wider and longer than the dimensions of the building.

2. Fill the excavated area with a 4" layer of compactible gravel. Rake the gravel smooth, then check it for level using a 4-ft. level and a straight, 8-ft.-long 2 × 4. Rake the gravel until it is fairly level.

3. Tamp the gravel thoroughly using a hand tamper or a rented plate compactor. As you work, check the surface with the board and level, and add or remove gravel until the surface is level.

Step B: Cut & Set the Skids

1. Cut the skids to length, using a circular saw or reciprocating saw. (Skids typically run parallel to the length of the building and are cut to the same dimension as the floor frame.)

2. To angle-cut the ends, measure down 1½" to 2" from the top edge of each skid. Use a square to mark a 45° cutting line down to the bottom edge, then make the cuts.

3. Coat the cut ends of the skids with a wood sealer-preservative and let them dry.

4. Set the skids on the gravel so they are parallel and their ends are even. Make sure the outer skids are spaced according to the width of the building.

Step C: Level the Skids

1. Level one of the outside skids, adding or removing gravel from underneath. Set the level parallel and level the skid along its length, then set the level perpendicular and level the skid along its width.

2. Place the straight 2 × 4 and level across the first and second skids, then adjust the second skid until it's level with the first. Make sure the second skid is level along its width.

3. Level the remaining skids in the same fashion, then set the board and level across all of the skids to make sure they are level with one another.

B. *If desired, mark and clip the bottom corners of the skid ends. Use a square to mark a 45° angle cut.*

C. *Using a board and a level, make sure each skid is level along its length and width and is level with the other skids.*

Concrete Slab Foundation

The slab foundation commonly used for sheds is called a slab-on-grade foundation. This combines a 3½"- to 4"-thick floor slab with an 8"- to 12"-thick perimeter footing that provides extra support for the walls of the building. The whole foundation can be poured at one time using a simple wood form.

Because they sit above ground, slab-on-grade foundations are susceptible to frost heave and in cold-weather climates are suitable only for detached buildings. Specific design requirements also vary by locality, so check with the local building department regarding the depth of the slab, the metal reinforcement required, the type and amount of gravel required for the subbase, and whether a plastic or other type of moisture barrier is needed under the slab.

The slab shown in this project has a 3½"-thick interior with an 8"-wide × 8"-deep footing along the perimeter. The top of the slab sits 4" above ground level, or *grade*. There is a 4"-thick layer of compacted gravel underneath the slab and the concrete is reinforced internally with a layer of 6 × 6" 10/10 welded wire mesh (WWM). (In some areas, you may be required to add rebar in the foundation perimeter—check the local code.) After the concrete is poured and finished,

8"-long J-bolts are set into the slab along the edges. These are used later to anchor the wall framing to the slab.

A slab for a shed requires a lot of concrete (see TIP, right). Considering the amount involved, you'll probably want to order ready-mix concrete delivered by truck to the site (most companies have a one-yard minimum). Order *air-entrained* concrete, which will hold up best; and tell the mixing company that you're using it for an exterior slab. An alternative for smaller slabs is to rent a concrete trailer from a rental center or landscaping company. They fill the trailer with one yard of mixed concrete and you tow it home.

If you've never worked with concrete, finishing a large slab can be a challenging introduction, and you might want some experienced help with the pour.

(see TIP, right)

TIP: ESTIMATING CONCRETE

Calculate the amount of concrete needed for a slab of this design using this formula:

Width × Length × Depth, in ft. (of main slab)

Multiply by 1.5 (for footing edge and spillage)

Divide by 27 (to convert to cubic yards).

Example—for a 12 × 12-ft. slab:
12 × 12 × .29 (3½") = 41.76
41.76 × 1.5 = 62.64
62.64 ÷ 27 = 2.32 cubic yards

TOOLS & MATERIALS

- Basic tools (page 18)
- Circular saw
- Drill
- Mason's line
- Sledgehammer
- Line level
- Framing square
- Shovel
- Wheelbarrow
- Rented plate compactor
- Bolt cutters
- Bull float
- Hand-held concrete float
- Concrete edger
- Compactible gravel
- 2 x 3 & 2 x 4 lumber
- 1¼" & 2½" deck screws
- ¾" A-C plywood
- 8d nails
- 6 x 6" 10/10 welded wire mesh
- 1½" brick pavers
- 8" J-bolts
- 2"-thick rigid foam insulation

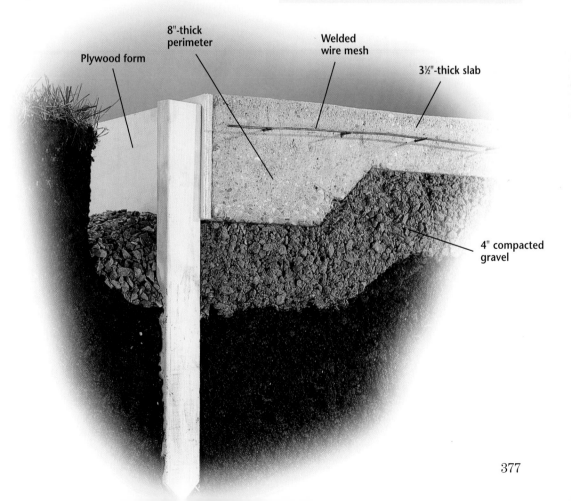

Plywood form

8"-thick perimeter

Welded wire mesh

3½"-thick slab

4" compacted gravel

HOW TO BUILD A CONCRETE SLAB FOUNDATION

Step A: Excavate the Site

1. Set up batter boards (see pages 215 to 216) and run level mason's lines to represent the outer dimensions of the slab. Use the 3-4-5 method (see "Right Angles" on page 103) to make sure your lines are perpendicular, and check your final layout for squareness by measuring the diagonals.

2. Excavate the area 4" wider and longer than the string layout—this provides some room to work. For the footing portion along the perimeter, dig a trench that is 8" wide × 8" deep.

3. Remove 3½" of soil over the interior portion of the slab, then slope the inner sides of the trench at 45° (see page 377). Set up temporary cross strings to check the depth as you work.

4. Add a 4" layer of compactible gravel over the entire excavation and rake it level. Compact the gravel thoroughly, using a rented plate compactor.

Step B: Build the Form

1. Cut sheets of ¾" A-C plywood into six strips of equal width—about 7⅞", allowing for the saw cuts. To make sure the cuts are straight, use a table saw or a circular saw with a straightedge.

2. Cut the plywood strips to length to create the sides of the form. Cut two sides 1½" long so they can overlap the remaining two sides. For sides that are longer than 8 ft., join two strips with a mending plate made of scrap plywood; fasten the plate to the back sides of the strips with 1¼" screws.

3. Assemble the form by fastening the corners together with screws. The form's inner dimensions must equal the outer dimensions of the slab.

Step C: Set the Form

1. Cut 18"-long stakes from 2 × 3 lumber—you'll need one stake for every linear foot of form, plus one extra stake for each corner. Taper one end of each stake to a point.

2. Place the form in the trench and align it with the mason's lines. Drive a stake near the end of each side of the form, setting the stake edge against the form and driving down to 3" above grade.

3. Measuring down from the mason's lines, position the form 4" above grade. Tack the form to the stakes with partially driven 8d nails (drive through the form into the stakes). Measure the diagonals to make sure the form is square and check that the top of the form is level. Drive the nails completely.

4. Add a stake every 12" and drive them down below the top edge of the form. Secure the form with two 8d nails driven into each stake. As you work, check with a string line to make sure the form sides are straight and measure the diagonals to check for square.

Step D: Add the Metal Reinforcement

1. Lay out rows of 6 × 6" 10/10 welded wire mesh so their ends are 1" to 2" from the insides of the forms. Cut the mesh with bolt cutters or heavy pliers, and stand on the unrolled mesh as you cut, to prevent it from springing back. Overlap the rows of mesh by 6" and tie them together with tie wire.

A. *Measure down from the temporary cross strings to check the depth of the excavation.*

B. *Assemble the form pieces with 2½" deck screws, then check the inner dimensions of the form. For long runs, join pieces with plywood mending plates.*

C. *Drive stakes every 12" to support the form, using the mason's lines to make sure the form remains straight.*

2. Prop up the mesh with pieces of 1½"-thick brick pavers or metal bolsters.

3. Mark the layout of the J-bolts onto the top edges of the form, following your plan. (J-bolts typically are placed 4" to 6" from each corner and every 4 ft. in between.)

Step E: Pour the Slab

1. Starting at one end, fill in the form with concrete, using a shovel to distribute it. Use the shovel blade or a 2 × 4 to stab into the concrete to eliminate air pockets and settle it around the wire mesh and along the forms. Fill with concrete to the top of the form.

2. As the form fills, have two helpers screed the concrete, using a straight 2 × 4 or 2 × 6 that spans the form: drag the screed board along the top of the form, working it back and forth in a sawing motion. Throw shovelfuls of concrete ahead of the screed board to fill low spots. The goal of screeding is to make the surface of the concrete perfectly flat and level, if not smooth.

3. Rap the outsides of the form with a hammer to settle the concrete along the inside faces of the form. This helps smooth the sides of the slab.

Step F: Finish the Concrete & Set the J-bolts

1. Immediately after screeding the concrete, make one pass with a bull float to smooth the surface. Add small amounts of concrete to fill low spots created by the floating, then smooth those areas with the float. Floating forces the aggregate down

and draws the water and sand to the surface.

2. Set the J-bolts into the concrete 1¾" from the outside edges of the slab. Work the bolts into the concrete by wiggling them slightly to eliminate air pockets. The bolts should be plumb and protrude 2½" from the slab surface. After setting each bolt, smooth the concrete around the bolt, using a magnesium or wood concrete float.

3. Watch the concrete carefully as it dries. The bull-floating will cause water (called *bleed water*) to rise, casting a sheen on the surface. Wait for the bleed water to disappear and the surface to become dull. Pressure-test the concrete for firmness by stepping on it with one foot: if your foot sinks ¼" or less, the concrete is ready to be finished. NOTE: Air-entrained concrete may have very little bleed water, so it's best to rely on the pressure test.

4. Float the concrete with a hand-held magnesium or wood float, working the float back and forth until the surface is smooth. If you can't reach the entire slab from the sides, lay pieces of 2"-thick rigid foam insulation over the concrete and kneel on the insulation. Work backward to cover up any impressions.

5. Use a concrete edging tool to round over the slab edge, running the edger between the slab and the form. If you want a very smooth finish, work the concrete with a trowel.

6. Let the concrete cure for 24 hours, then strip the forms. Wait an additional 24 hours before building on the slab.

D. *Lay out rows of wire mesh, tie the rows together, then prop up the mesh with brick pavers or metal bolsters.*

E. *Screed the concrete after filling the form, using two people to screed, while a third fills low spots with a shovel.*

F. *Float the slab with a bull float, then set the J-bolts at the marked locations (INSET).*

Framing

Framing is one of the most satisfying phases of a building project. Using basic tools and materials, you'll assemble the skeleton of the structure, piece-by-piece, and in the process learn the fundamentals of carpentry. The style of framing shown here is standard 2 × 4 framing, also called *stick framing*.

The tools you'll use for most framing are the circular saw (and power miter saw, if you have one), framing square, level, chalk line, and, of course, a framing hammer. Nails used for most framing are called common nails. These have a larger diameter than box nails, making them stronger, but also more likely to split thinner stock. Box nails are better for siding, trim, and other nonstructural materials. The three most commonly used nailing techniques are shown in the TIP to the right. Some framing connections, such as where rafters meet wall plates, require metal anchors for increased strength.

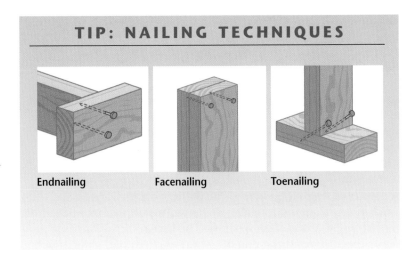

TIP: NAILING TECHNIQUES

Endnailing   Facenailing   Toenailing

Floor Framing

Floor frames for sheds are simple versions of house floor frames. They have outside, or *rim*, joists that are set on edge and nailed to the ends of the common joists. Gazebos have floor frames similar to decks, with angled joists that are connected to support beams with joist hangers (see TIP, page 381). On top of floor frames, a layer of tongue-and-groove plywood (or decking boards, for a gazebo) provides the floor surface and adds strength to the frame. To prevent rot, always use pressure-treated lumber and galvanized nails and hardware for floor frames.

HOW TO BUILD A SHED FLOOR FRAME
**Step A: Cut the Joists &
Mark the Layout**

1. Cut the two rim joists and the common joists to length, making sure all ends

are square. Note that rim joists run the full length of the floor, while common joists are 3" shorter than the floor width.

2. Check the rim joists for crowning—arching along the narrow edges. Pick up one end of the board and hold it flat. With one eye closed, sight down the narrow edges. If the board arches, even slightly, mark the edge on the top (convex) side of the arch. This is the crowned edge and should always be installed facing up. If the board is crowned in both directions, mark the edge with the most significant crowning.

3. Lay one rim joist flat on top of the other so the edges and ends are flush and the crowned edges are on the same side. Tack the joists together with a few 8d nails. Turn the joists on-edge and mark the common joist layout on the top edges: mark 1½" and 15¼" from the end of one joist. Then, measuring from the 15¼" mark, make a mark every 16"—at 32", 48", 64" and so on, to the end of the board (if the plan calls for 24" spacing, make a mark at 1½" and 23¼", then every 24" from there). Don't worry if the last space before the opposite end joist isn't as wide as the others. Make a mark 1½" in from the remaining end. After each mark, draw

a small X designating to which side of the line the joist goes—this is a handy framers' trick to prevent confusion. This layout ensures that the edges of a 4-ft. or 8-ft. board or sheet will fall, or *break*, on the center of a joist.

4. Using a square, draw lines through each of the layout marks, carrying them

A. *Tack together the rim joists, then mark the joist layout. Use a square to transfer the marks to the second rim joist.*

TOOLS & MATERIALS

- Basic tools (page 18)
- Circular saw
- Square
- Pressure-treated
  2 × lumber

- 8d and 16d galvanized
  common nails
- ¾" tongue-and-groove
  exterior-grade plywood

over to the other rim joist. Draw Xs on the other joist, as well. Separate the joists and remove the nails.

Step B: Assemble & Square the Frame

1. Check the two end joists for crowning, then nail them between the rim joists so their outside faces are flush with the rim joist ends and the top edges are flush. Drive two 16d galvanized common nails through the rim joists and into the ends of the end joists, positioning the nails about ¾" from the top and bottom edges.

2. Install the remaining joists, making sure the crowned edges are facing up.

3. Check the frame for squareness by measuring diagonally from corner to corner: when the measurements are equal, the frame is square. To adjust the frame, apply inward pressure to the corners with the longer measurement.

4. If you're building the floor over skids, secure each joist to the outside skids with a metal anchor and toenail the joists to the internal skid(s) with 16d galvanized nails.

Step C: Install the Plywood Floor

1. Lay a full sheet of ¾" tongue-and-groove exterior-grade plywood over the

frame so the groove side is flush with a rim joist and one end is flush with an end joist. Fasten the plywood to the joists with 8d galvanized nails driven every 6" along the edges and every 8" in the field of the sheet. Do not nail along the tongue edge until the next row of plywood is in place.

2. Cut the second piece to fit next to the first, allowing for a ⅛" gap between the sheets. Install the second sheet with

its outside edges flush with the frame.

3. Start the next row with a full sheet (ripped to width, if necessary). Install the sheet starting from the corner opposite the first sheet, so the joints between rows are offset. Make sure the tongue-and-groove joint is tight; if necessary, use a wood block and a sledgehammer to close the joint.

4. Cut and install the remaining piece of plywood.

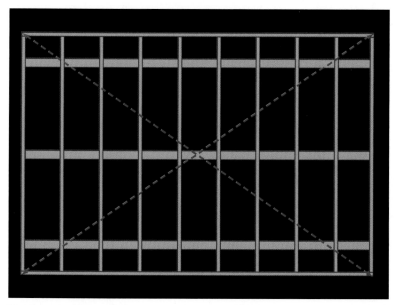

B. *Measure diagonally from corner to corner: if the measurements are equal, the frame is square.*

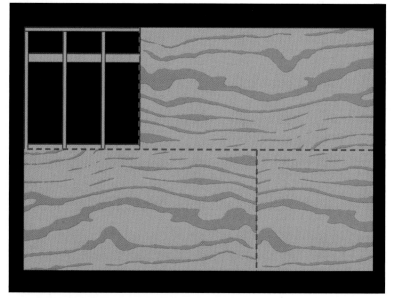

C. *Install the plywood perpendicular to the joists. Start each row with a full sheet and stagger the end-joints between rows.*

Wall Framing

Standard framed walls have vertical 2 × 4 *studs* nailed between horizontal top and bottom *plates*. The top plates are doubled to provide additional support for the roof frame and to strengthen the wall connections. Door and window frames are made up of *king* studs; a *header*, which supports *cripple* studs above the opening; and *jack* studs, which support the header. A window frame also has a *rough sill* and cripple studs below the opening. The opening defined by the frame is called the *rough opening*. Wall frames gain rigidity from plywood sheathing or siding.

Building walls involves three major phases: 1. laying out and framing the wall, 2. raising the wall, and 3. tying the walls together and adding the double top plates. NOTE: If your building has a concrete slab floor, use pressure-treated lumber for the bottom plates and anchor the plates to the J-bolts set in the slab (see page 383).

TOOLS & MATERIALS

- Basic tools (page 18)
- Broom
- Circular saw or power miter saw
- Square
- 4-ft. level
- Handsaw
- 2 × lumber
- 8d, 10d, and 16d common nails
- ½" plywood
- Construction adhesive

HOW TO FRAME WALLS
Step A: Mark the Bottom-plate Layout Lines

1. Sweep off the floor and make sure it's dry. Cut a short (about 4" to 6") piece of plate material to use as a spacer. Position the spacer at one corner of the floor, with its outside edge flush with the outside of the floor frame. Mark a pencil line along the inside edge of the spacer.

2. Use the spacer to mark the wall ends at each corner of the floor (eight marks

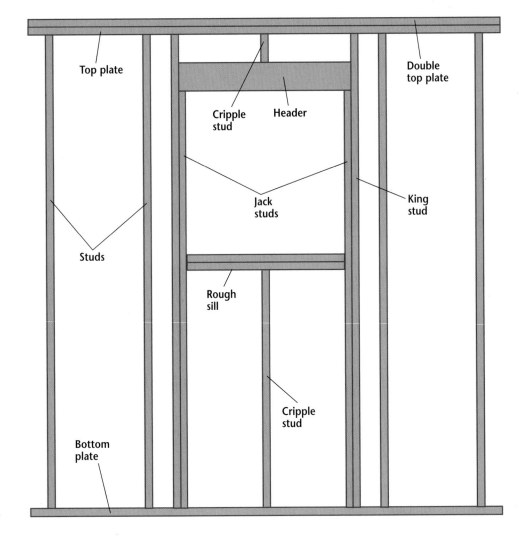

Top plate

Double top plate

Cripple stud

Header

Jack studs

King stud

Studs

Rough sill

Cripple stud

Bottom plate

A. *Use a block cut from plate material to lay out the bottom plates. Mark at the ends of each wall then snap a chalk line.*

total). Snap chalk lines through the marks. These lines represent the inside edges of the bottom plates.

Step B: Lay Out the Plates

1. Measure along the plate layout lines to find the lengths of the plates. NOTE: Follow your project plans to determine which walls run to the edges of the building (called *through* walls) and which butt into the other walls (called *butt* walls).

2. Select straight lumber for the plates. Cut a top and bottom plate for the first wall, making sure their dimensions are the same. Use a circular saw or a power miter saw, but make sure both ends are square. Lay the bottom plate flat on the floor and set the top plate on top of it. Make sure their edges and ends are flush, then tack the plates together with a few 8d nails.

3. Turn the plates on-edge and mark the stud layout onto the front edges. If the wall is a through wall, make a mark at 1½" and 2¾" to mark the end stud and extra corner stud. Then, mark at 15¼" (for 16" on-center spacing) or 23¼" (for 24" on-

SECURING PLATES TO CONCRETE SLABS

When building walls over a concrete slab, drill holes in the bottom plates for the anchor bolts before marking the stud layouts. Position each plate on its layout line with the ends flush with the edges of the slab. Use a square to mark the edges of the bolt onto the plate (top photo). Measure from the layout line to the bolt center and transfer that dimension to the plate. Drill holes through the plates slightly larger in diameter than the bolts. After raising the walls, anchor the plates to the bolts with washers and nuts (bottom photo).

center spacing)—measuring from this mark, make a mark every 16" (or 24") to the end of the plates. Make a mark 1½" in from the opposite end. Following your plan, draw an X next to each mark, designating to which side of the line the stud goes.

Mark the king and jack studs with a K and J respectively, and mark the cripple studs with a C.

If the wall is a butt wall, mark the plate at 1½", then move the tape so the 3½" tape mark is aligned with the end of the plate. Keeping the tape at that position, mark at

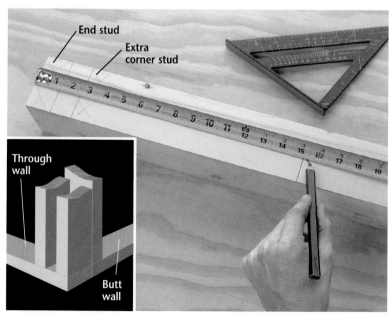

B. Mark the stud layout onto the wall plates, designating the stud locations with Xs. On the plates of the through wall, also mark the location of the extra corner stud (INSET).

C. Construct the headers from 2 × lumber and a ½" plywood spacer. Assemble the pieces with adhesive and nails.

15¼" (for 16" spacing) or 23¼" (for 24" spacing) then mark every 16" (or 24") from there. The 3½" that are "buried" account for the width of the through wall.

4. Using a square, draw lines through each of the layout marks, carrying them over to the other plate. Draw Xs on the other plate, as well.

Step C: Cut the Studs & Build the Headers

1. Cut the studs to length, following the framing plan; make sure both ends are square. (Before cutting, give each stud a quick inspection to check for excessive bowing or crowning; reserve any bad studs for scrap or blocking.)

2. Select straight lumber for the door-frame studs. Cut the jack studs to equal the height of the rough opening minus 1½" (this accounts for the thickness of the bottom plate); cut the jack studs for the window frame to equal the height of the top of the rough opening minus 1½". Cut the king studs the same length as the common studs.

3. To build the headers, cut two pieces of 2 × lumber (using the size prescribed by the plans) to equal the width of the rough opening plus 3". Check the boards for crowning, and mark the top edges (see Step A, page 380). Cut a piece of ½" plywood to the same dimensions as the lumber pieces.

4. Apply two wavy beads of construction adhesive to each side of the plywood and sandwich the lumber pieces around the plywood, keeping all edges flush. Nail the header together with pairs of 16d common nails spaced about 12" apart. Drive the nails at a slight angle so they won't protrude from the other side. Nail from both sides of the header.

Step D: Assemble the Wall

1. Separate the marked plates and remove the nails. Position the plates on-edge, about 8 ft. apart, with the marked edges facing up.

2. Set the studs on-edge between the plates, following the layout marks. Before setting the door- or window-frame studs,

facenail the jack studs to the inside faces of the king studs with 10d common nails staggered and spaced every 12"; make sure the bottom ends and side edges are flush.

3. Nail all of the studs to the bottom plate, then to the top plate. Position each stud on its layout mark so its front edge is flush with the plate edge, and nail through the plate and into the stud end with two 16d common nails (use galvanized nails on the bottom plate if your floor is concrete). Drive the nails about ¾" in from the plate edges.

4. Set the header in place above the jack studs and nail through the king studs and into the header ends with 16d nails— use four nails on each end for a 2 × 6 header, and six for a 2 × 8 header.

For a window frame, measure up from the bottom of the bottom plate and mark the top of the sill on the inside faces of the jack studs—this defines the bottom of the rough opening. Cut two sill pieces to fit between the jack studs and nail them

D. *Frame the walls with 16d nails endnailed through the plates into the studs. Toenail cripples to headers with 8d nails.*

E. *Install a diagonal brace to keep the wall square. Make sure the brace ends won't interfere with the construction.*

together with 10d nails. Toenail the sill to the jack studs with 16d nails.

5. Cut the cripple studs to fit between the header and the top plate (and the sill and bottom plate, for window frames). Toenail the cripple studs to the plates and headers (and sill) with two 8d nails on one side and one more through the center on the other side.

Step E: Square the Wall Frame

1. Check the wall frame for squareness by measuring diagonally from corner to corner: when the measurements are equal, the frame is square. To adjust the frame, apply inward pressure to the corners with the longer measurement.

2. When the frame is perfectly square, install a temporary 1 × 4 or 2 × 4 brace diagonally across the studs and plates. Nail the brace to the frame with 8d nails. Use two nails on the plates and on every other stud. To stabilize the structure, leave the wall braces in place until the walls are sheathed or sided.

3. At each end of the wall, attach a board to brace the wall upright after it is raised; nail it to the end stud with one 16d nail. NOTE: Install only one end brace for the second and third walls; no end brace is needed for the final wall.

Step F: Raise the Wall

1. With a helper, lift the top end of the wall and set the bottom plate on the layout lines you snapped in Step A. Swing out the free ends of the end braces and tack them to the floor frame to keep the wall upright. If you have a slab floor, nail the braces to stakes in the ground.

2. Fine-tune the wall position so the bottom plate is flush with the chalk line, then nail the plate to the floor with 16d nails. Drive a nail every 16" and stagger them so that half go into the rim joist and half go into the common joists. Do not nail the plate inside the door opening.

3. Pull the nails at the bottom ends of the end braces, and adjust the wall until it is perfectly plumb, using a 4-ft. level; set the level against a few different studs to get an accurate reading. Reattach the end braces with 16d nails.

Step G: Complete the Wall Frames & Install the Double Top Plates

1. Build and raise the remaining walls, following the same procedure used for the first wall. After each wall is plumbed and braced in position, nail together the end studs of the adjacent walls with 16d nails, driven every 12". Make sure the wall ends are flush.

2. Cut the double top plates from 2 × 4 lumber. The double top plates must overlap the top plate joints, so that on through walls, the double plate is 3½" shorter on each end than the top plate; on butt walls, the double plate is 3½" longer on each end. Nail the double top plates to the top plates with 10d nails. Drive two nails at the ends of the plates that overlap intersecting walls, and one nail every 16" in between.

3. Use a handsaw or reciprocating saw to cut out the bottom plate in the door opening.

F. Nail the bottom plate to the floor frame, then plumb the wall and secure it with end braces.

G. Nail together the corner studs of intersecting walls (INSET). Add the double top plates, overlapping the wall corners.

Roof Framing

A roof frame is an important structure not only because it supports the roofing and helps keep the building dry, but because its style and shape have a great impact on the character of the building, the feel of the interior space, and the amount of storage space available.

There are four common roof types shown in this book. A *gable* roof is the classic, triangular design, with two sloped sides meeting at the peak, and flat ends (called *gable ends*). *Gambrel* roofs are like gable roofs with an extra joint on each side, resulting in two different slopes. A *hip* roof is structurally similar to a gable, but has no gable ends. *Shed* roofs are the simplest style, with only one sloped plane. They can be built with frames or, for small structures, a sheet of plywood.

All of these roof styles have a designated slope, which is the degree of angle of each side. The slope is expressed in a ratio that states the number of inches of vertical rise per 12" of horizontal run. For example, a roof that rises 6" for every 12" of run is said to have a slope of 6-in-12. Roof slope is indicated in plan drawings by a triangular symbol known as the *roof-slope indicator* (see page 387). You'll use the roof slope to lay out rafters and fascia.

In standard roof framing, rafters are the principal structural members, rising from the walls to the ridge board (or *hub*, in gazebos) at the peak of the roof. Rafters in outbuildings typically are made from 2 × 4s or 2 × 6s, are spaced 16" or 24" on center, and are installed perpendicular to the length of the building. To keep the roof planes from spreading apart, *rafter ties*, or *collar ties*, are nailed between opposing rafters to form a structural triangle. With shed-style roofs, the rafters span from wall-to-wall and no ridge board or ties are needed.

The key to successful roof framing is making accurate cuts on the rafters. Take your time to cut the first two rafters, making any necessary adjustments, then use one as a pattern for marking the rest. The project on pages 387 through 389 shows you how to cut and install rafters in a gable roof frame, but the basic procedures are the same for gambrel and hip roofs.

As an alternative to rafter framing, you can take your plans to a truss manufacturer and have custom trusses built for your project. However, this will cost you more and probably will limit your storage space: the internal supports in truss frames leave little room for storage.

Ridge board · Roof sheathing · Collar tie · Rafters

TOOLS & MATERIALS

- Basic tools (page 18)
- Circular saw
- Framing square
- 4-ft. level
- 2 × lumber
- 8d, 10d, and 16d common nails

TIP: MARKING ANGLES WITH A RAFTER SQUARE

A rafter square is a handy tool for marking angled cuts—using the degree of the cut or the roof slope. Set the square flange against the board edge and align the PIVOT point with the top of the cut. Pivot the square until the board edge is aligned with the desired DEGREE marking or the rise of the roof slope, indicated in the row of COMMON numbers. Mark along the right-angle edge of the square.

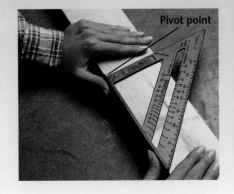
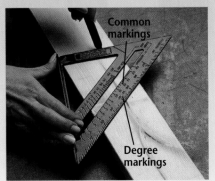

HOW TO BUILD A ROOF FRAME

NOTE: The following instructions are based on the sample rafter template shown here, which is designed for a 6-in-12 roof slope.

Step A: Mark the Plumb Cuts

1. Select a straight board to use for the pattern rafter. Mark the top plumb cut near one end of the board: position a framing square with the 6" mark of the tongue (short part) and the 12" mark of the blade (wide part) on the top edge of the board. Draw a pencil line along the outside edge of the tongue.

2. Starting from the top of the plumb-cut mark, measure along the top edge of the board and mark the overall length of the rafter, then use the square to transfer this mark to the bottom edge of the board. Position the square so the tongue points down, and align the 6" mark of the tongue and the 12" mark of the blade with the bottom board edge, while aligning the tongue with the overall length mark. Draw a line along the tongue. If the bottom end cut of the rafter is square (perpendicular to the edges) rather than parallel to the top end, mark a square cut at the overall length mark.

Step B: Mark the Bird's Mouth Cuts

1. Measure from the bottom of the lower plumb cut and mark the plumb cut of the bird's mouth. Position the square as you did for the lower plumb cut and draw a line across the board face at the new mark.

2. Measure along the bird's mouth plumb cut and mark the

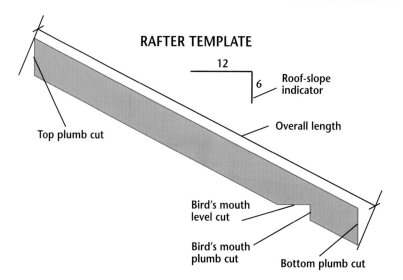

RAFTER TEMPLATE

Top plumb cut

12

6 — Roof-slope indicator

Overall length

Bird's mouth level cut

Bird's mouth plumb cut

Bottom plumb cut

bird's mouth level cut. Use the square to draw the level cut—it must be perpendicular to the bird's mouth plumb cut.

Step C: Make the Cuts

1. Cut the rafter ends at the plumb-cut lines, using a circular saw or power miter saw.

2. Set the base of a circular saw to cut at the maximum depth. Make the bird's mouth cuts, overcutting slightly to complete the cut through the board. As an alternative to overcutting (for aesthetic reasons), you can stop the circular saw at the line intersections, then finish the cuts with a handsaw.

A. Position the framing square at the 6" and 12" marks to draw the top and bottom plumb-cut lines.

B. Mark the bird's mouth level cut by squaring off of the bird's mouth plumb cut.

C. Cut the bird's mouth by overcutting the lines just until the blade cuts entirely through the thickness of the board.

D. *Test-fit the pattern and duplicate rafters, using a 2 × spacer to represent the ridge board.*

E. *Mark the rafter layout onto the wall plates and the ridge board, starting from the same end of the building for each.*

F. *Endnail the first rafter to the ridge, then toenail the second. Reinforce the bottom connection with a metal anchor (INSET).*

3. Select another straight board to use as the duplicate rafter. Use the pattern rafter to trace the cutting lines onto the duplicate, then make the cuts on the duplicate rafter.

Step D: Test-fit the Rafters

1. Cut a 12"-long spacer block from 2 × 6 or 2 × 8 material.

2. With a helper or two, set the two rafters in place on top of the walls, holding the spacer block between the top rafter ends. Make sure the rafters are in line with each other (perpendicular to the walls) and are plumb.

3. Check the cuts for fit: the top-end plumb cuts should meet flush with the spacer block, and the bird's mouths should sit flush against the wall plates. Make sure the top ends are at the same elevation. Recut any angles that don't fit and test-fit the rafters again.

4. Write "PAT" on the pattern rafter, then use it to trace the cutting lines onto the remaining rafters. Before marking, check each rafter for crowning and mark the crowned edge (see Step A on page 380); always install the crowned edge up. If your building has overhangs at the gable ends, mark the end cuts for the overhang rafters but not the bird's mouth cuts—overhang rafters don't have them. Also, if you have the fascia material on-hand, use the pattern rafter to mark the angle for the top ends of the fascia boards (see page 391).

5. Cut the remaining rafters.

Step E: Lay Out the Wall Plates & Ridge Board

NOTE: Start the rafter layouts at the same ends of the walls from where you started the wall stud layouts. This ensures the rafters will fall above the studs. Install rafters aligned with the end studs but not the extra corner studs.

1. Make a mark on the top wall plate, 1½" in from the end. Then, mark at 15¼" (for 16" on-center spacing) or 23¼" (for 24" on-center spacing)—measuring from this mark, make a mark every 16" (or 24") to the end of the wall. Make a mark 1½" in from the remaining end. Following your plan, draw an X next to each mark, designating to which side of the line the rafter goes.

2. Mark the wall on the other side of the building, starting from the same end.

3. Cut the ridge board to length, using the plan dimensions. Check the board for crowning, then lay it on top of the walls next to one of the marked plates, making sure it overhangs the end walls equally at both ends. Use a square to transfer the rafter layout onto both faces of the ridge board.

Step F: Install the Rafters

1. You'll need a couple of helpers and a long, straight 2 × 4 to get the rafters started. Lay the first two rafters on top of the wall, then nail the 2 × 4 to the far end of the ridge board to serve as a temporary support. Set up the rafters at the end of the walls and hold the free end of the ridge board in place between them. Have a helper tack the rafters to the wall plates. Hold a level on the ridge board and make sure it's level, then have a helper tack the support to the far wall to keep the ridge level.

2. Slide one rafter a few inches to the side and endnail the other rafter through the ridge board with three 16d common nails (use two nails for 2 × 4 rafters). Slide the other rafter onto its layout mark and toenail it to the ridge with four 16d nails (three for 2 × 4s). Toenail the lower end of each rafter to the wall plate with two 16d nails, then reinforce the joint with a metal anchor, using the nails specified by the manufacturer.

3. Make sure the rafters are plumb and the ridge is level. Install the remaining rafters, checking for plumb and level periodically as you work.

Step G: Install the Collar Ties

1. Cut the collar ties (or rafter ties) to span between opposing rafters at the prescribed elevation, angle-cutting the ends to match the roof slope.

2. Position the collar tie ends against the rafter faces so the ends are about ½" from the top rafter edges. Make sure the ties are level, then facenail them to the rafters with three 10d common nails at each end.

Step H: Frame the Gable Wall

NOTE: Gable walls consist of top plates that attach to the undersides of the end rafters, and short studs set on top of the wall plates (see page 374). They appear only on gable and gambrel roofs.

1. Cut the top plates to extend from the side of the ridge board to the wall plates. Angle-cut the ends so they meet flush with the ridge and wall plate. The top-end angle matches the rafter plumb cut; the bottom angle matches the level cut of the bird's mouth.

2. Fasten the plates to the rafters so the front plate edges are flush with the outside faces of the rafters; use 16d nails.

3. Mark the gable stud layout onto the wall plate, then use a level to transfer the layout to the gable plates. Cut the gable studs to fit, angle-cutting the ends to match the roof slope. Install the gable studs with 8d toenails. Also install a square-cut stud directly under the ridge board.

Step I: Build the Gable Overhang (Gable & Gambrel Roofs)

NOTE: Gable overhangs are built with additional rafters installed at the gable ends (see page 374). They are supported by the ridge board and blocks—called *lookouts*—attached to the end rafters.

1. Mark the layouts for the lookouts onto the end rafters, following the project plan. Cut the lookouts and toenail them to the rafters with 8d nails (or endnail them with 16d nails) so that the top edges of the blocks are flush with, and parallel to, the tops of the rafters.

2. Install the overhang rafters over the ends of the lookouts with 16d endnails.

G. *Angle-cut the ends of the collar ties to match the roof slope and facenail the ties to the rafters.*

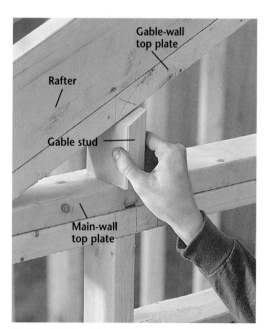

H. *Mark the gable stud layout onto the main-wall top plate and gable-wall top plate, then install the gable studs.*

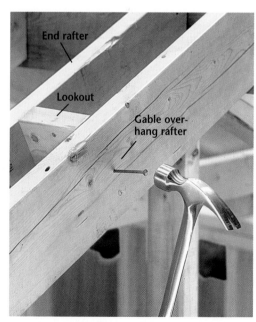

I. *Nail the outer gable overhang rafters to the lookouts, making sure the top edges of the rafters are flush.*

Roofing

The roofing phase typically follows the framing, for most building projects. As it's presented here, roofing includes installing the fascia board, the roof sheathing, and of course, the shingles. You'll also see how to install roof vents.

Fascia board is 1 × trim material, typically made of cedar, that covers the ends of the rafters. On gable and gambrel roofs, fascia also covers the end (or gable overhang) rafters. Sheathing is the structural deck of the roof. Depending on the type of roofing used, the sheathing may be plywood, tongue-&-groove decking boards (see page 442), or spaced 1 × or 2 × lumber.

As for the roofing, deciding on a material is a matter of personal taste and practicality. The most common type used for outbuildings is asphalt shingles, while cedar shingles and metal roofing are also popular options.

Asphalt shingles are the standard roofing material for outbuildings, just as they are for houses. For the money, asphalt shingles are the most durable and low-maintenance material available, and they come in a wide range of colors and styles.

Cedar shingles are a big step up in price from asphalt, but their visual appeal is undeniable. The easiest type to install is the factory-sawn shingle with flat, tapered sides. Contact a roofing professional if you decide to go with cedar shingles.

Metal roofing (used in the Carport project, on pages 444 to 453) has gained popularity in recent years for residential construction. Modern forms of metal roofing are extremely durable and easy to install.

INSTALLING ROOF VENTS

Roof vents, used in conjunction with soffit vents (page 396), can help keep the air in your shed cooler and cleaner. Vents are rated by square inches of ventilation area; most sheds need only two 68" roof vents and two to four 50" soffit vents.

Install roof vents centered between two rafters, about 16" to 24" from the ridge board. Cut a hole through the roof sheathing, following the manufacturer's instructions (below, left). Apply building paper (page 392), then center the vent over the hole and trace around its base flange.

Install shingles to a point at least 2" inside the bottom of the outline—don't cover the hole. Apply roofing cement to the underside of the base flange, then install the vent over the shingles, using rubber-gasket roofing nails driven into all of the flange sides.

Shingle over the side and top vent flanges, leaving the bottom flange exposed; do not nail through the flanges with the shingle nails (below, right).

Fascia & Sheathing

Fascia board and roof sheathing are always installed before the roofing, but which one you install first is up to you. Some buildings also have a 1 × or 2 × board installed behind the fascia, called subfascia or frieze board. Made of rough lumber, the subfascia helps compensate for inconsistency in rafter length, ensuring the fascia will be straight. It also provides a continuous nailing surface for the fascia.

The type of sheathing you use depends on the roof covering. Use CDX plywood (it's exterior-grade) for asphalt and cedar shingles. Depending on the building design, the fascia may be installed flush with the top of the sheathing, or the plywood may overlap the fascia. If you install the fascia first, cut spacers from the sheathing stock and use them when measuring and installing the fascia. Both shingle types must be installed over a layer of 15# building paper (also called tar paper or roofing felt), which goes on after the sheathing and fascia. The paper protects the sheathing from moisture and prevents the shingles from bonding to it.

As an alternative to plywood sheathing, you can use decking boards as a shingle underlayment. Typically sold in ¾ dimension (1¹⁄₁₆" thick), board sheathing creates an attractive "ceiling" for the inside of a building, and nails won't show through as they do with plywood sheathing.

For metal roofing, install purlins—evenly spaced, parallel rows of 1 × or 2 × boards nailed perpendicularly to the rafters. Install the fascia over the ends of the purlins, flush with the tops.

TOOLS & MATERIALS

- Basic tools (page 18)
- Framing square
- Circular saw
- Stapler
- Fascia & trim material

- 6d and 8d galvanized finish nails
- CDX plywood roof sheathing
- 8d box nails
- 15# building paper

HOW TO INSTALL FASCIA BOARD

NOTE: This procedure includes the steps for installing fascia on a gable roof. The basic steps are the same for a gambrel roof. For a hip roof, which has no gable ends, skip Step A and start your installation by tacking the first fascia board to the rafter ends, then working from there.

To install subfascia, follow the same procedure used for fascia, but don't worry about mitering the ends—just overlap the boards at the corners.

Step A: Cut & Fit the Gable-end Fascia

1. Mark a plumb cut on the top end of the first fascia board: If you didn't mark the fascia boards with the pattern rafter (page 388), use a framing square to mark the plumb cut, following the same method used for marking rafters (see page 387). Make the cut with a circular saw or power miter saw.

2. Hold the cut end of the fascia against the end rafter. If the fascia will be flush with the top of the sheathing, use spacers set on the rafter and position the top edge of the fascia flush with the spacers.

3. Have a helper mark the lower end for length by tracing along the rafter end onto the back side of the fascia. Make the cut with a 45° bevel. If you're using a circular saw, tilt the blade to 45° and follow the traced line; if you have a compound miter saw, rotate the blade to match the cutting line and tilt the blade to 45°.

4. Temporarily tack the fascia in place against the rafter with a couple of 8d galvanized finish nails. Repeat this process to mark, cut, and tack-up the opposing fascia piece, then do the same at the other gable end.

Step B: Install the Fascia Along the Eaves

1. Cut a 45° bevel on the end of another fascia piece and fit it against one of the pieces on the gable end. If the board is long enough to span the building, mark the opposite end to length. If you'll need two pieces to complete the eave, mark the board about ¼" from the far edge of a rafter; cut that end with a 45° bevel angled so the longer side of the board will be against the rafter. Cut the remaining piece with a 45° bevel angled in the other direction. This is known as a *scarf* joint—drill pilot holes to prevent splitting and nail these with 8d galvanized finish nails.

2. Make sure the corner joints fit well, then tack the fascia to the rafters.

3. Cut and tack-up the fascia along the other eave. Make sure all of the joints fit well, then fasten the fascia permanently with 8d galvanized finish nails: drive three nails into each rafter end and a pair of nails every 16" along the gable ends.

4. Lock-nail each corner joint with three 6d galvanized finish nails. If necessary, drill pilot holes to prevent splitting.

5. Install any additional trim, such as 1 × 2, called for by the plan. Miter the ends for best appearance.

A. *Mark the bottom end of the gable fascia by tracing along the end of the rafter (or the subfascia). If the fascia will be installed flush with the sheathing, use a spacer for positioning.*

B. *Fasten the fascia to the rafters (or subfascia) with 8d finish nails, then lock-nail the corner joints with 6d nails. Use scarf joints to join boards in long runs (INSET).*

HOW TO INSTALL PLYWOOD SHEATHING & BUILDING PAPER

Step A: Install the Sheathing

1. Lay a full sheet of CDX plywood on top of the rafters at one of the lower corners of the roof. Position the edges of the sheet ⅛" from the fascia (or the outside edges of the rafters) and make sure the inside end of the sheet falls over the center of a rafter; trim the sheet, if necessary.

2. Fasten the sheet to the rafters with 8d box nails spaced every 6" along the edges and every 12" in the field of the sheet.

3. Cut and install the next sheet to complete the first row, leaving a ⅛" gap between the sheet ends.

4. Start the second row with a half-length sheet so the vertical joints will be staggered between rows. Measure from the top of the first row to the center of the ridge board, and rip the sheet to that dimension.

5. Install the first sheet of the second row, then cut and install the remaining sheet to complete the row.

6. Sheath the opposite side of the roof following the same process.

Step B: Install the Building Paper

NOTE: If you are installing asphalt shingles, add the metal drip edge along the eaves before laying the building paper (see page 393).

1. Roll out 15# building paper across the roof along the eave edge. If you've installed drip edge, hold the paper flush with the drip edge; if there's no drip edge, overhang the fascia on the eave by ⅜". Overhang the gable ends by 1" to 2". (On hip roofs, overhang the hip ridges by 6".)

2. Secure the paper with staples driven about every 12".

3. Apply the remaining rows, overlapping the preceding row by at least 2". Overhang the ridge by 6". Overlap any vertical joints by at least 4".

4. Install the paper on the other roof side(s), again overlapping the ridge by 6".

5. Trim the paper flush with the fascia on the gable ends.

A. *Install the plywood sheathing so the vertical joints are staggered between rows. Leave an ⅛" gap between sheets.*

B. *Apply building paper from the bottom up, so the lower paper is overlapped by the paper above it.*

Asphalt Shingles

Asphalt shingles come in a variety of styles, but most are based on the standard three-tab system, in which each shingle strip has notches creating three equally sized tabs on the lower half of the strip. When installed, the tabs cover the solid portion of the shingle below it, giving the appearance of individual shingles.

For durability, use fiberglass-based shingles rather than organic-based. Also check the packaging to make sure the shingles comply with the ASTM D 3462 standard for durability. If you choose a specialty style, such as a decorative shingle or a type that is made to appear natural (like wood or slate), check with the manufacturer for specific installation instructions.

Prepare the roof for shingles by installing building paper and metal drip edge along the roof perimeter. Drip edge covers the edges of the fascia and supports the shingle edges.

TOOLS & MATERIALS

- Basic tools (page 18)
- Metal snips
- Chalk line
- Utility knife
- Straightedge
- Metal drip edge
- Asphalt shingles
- 2d roofing nails
- Roofing cement

HOW TO INSTALL ASPHALT SHINGLES

Step A: Install the Drip Edge

NOTE: Install drip edge along the eaves before applying building paper; install drip edge along the gable ends on top of the paper.

1. Cut a 45° miter on the end of a piece of drip edge, using metal snips. Hold the end flush with the corner of the fascia, and fasten the flange of the drip edge to the sheathing with roofing nails driven every 12". To prevent corrosion, use galvanized nails with galvanized drip edge and aluminum nails with aluminum drip edge. Overlap vertical joints by 2".

2. Apply building paper over the entire roof (see page 392). Install drip edge along the gable ends, over the paper, cutting 45° miters to meet the ends of the eave drip edge. Overlap horizontal joints by 2", overlapping the higher piece on top of the lower. At the roof peak, trim the front flanges so the opposing edge pieces meet at a vertical joint.

Step B: Install the Starter Course of Shingles

1. Snap a chalk line 11½" up from the front edge of the drip edge (this will result in a ½" overlap for standard 12" shingles).

2. Trim off one-half (6") of the end tab of a shingle, using a utility knife and straightedge.

3. Position the shingle upside-down, so the tabs are on the chalk line and the half-tab overhangs the gable drip edge by ⅜".

A. *Install drip edge along the eaves over the sheathing. Add the building paper, then install drip edge along the gable ends.*

B. *Trim 6" from the end tab to begin the starter row. Position the starter row shingles upside-down so the tabs point up.*

Fasten the shingle with four 2d roofing nails, about 3½" up from the bottom edge: drive one underneath each tab, one 2" in from the gable edge, and one 1" from the inside edge. Drive the nails straight and set the heads just flush to avoid tearing the shingle.

4. Use full shingles for the remainder of the row, butting their edges together. Trim the last shingle so it overhangs the gable edge by ⅜".

Step C: Install the Remaining Courses

1. Install the first course of shingles, starting with a full shingle. Position the tabs down and align the shingle edges with those in the starter course. Drive four nails into each shingle: one ⅝" above each tab, and one 1" in from each end, at the same level. Trim the last shingle to match the starter course.

2. Snap a chalk line on the building paper, 17" up from the bottom edge of the first course; this will result in a 5" exposure for each course.

3. Begin the second course with a full shingle, but overhang the end of the first course by ½ of a tab. Begin the third course by overhanging a full tab, then 1½ tabs for the fourth course. Start the fifth course with a full shingle aligned with the first course, to repeat the staggered pattern. Snap a chalk line for each course, maintaining a 5" exposure. After every few courses, measure from the ridge to the shingle edges to make sure the shingles are running parallel to the ridge. If necessary, make slight adjustments with each course until the shingles are parallel to the ridge.

4. Trim the top course of shingles at the ridge. If you are working on a hip roof (gazebo), trim the shingles at each hip ridge.

5. Repeat the procedure to shingle the remaining side(s) of the roof. Overlap the ridge with the top course of shingles and nail them to the other roof side; do not overlap more than 5". On a hip roof, trim the shingles along the hip ridge.

Step D: Install the Ridge Caps

1. Cut ridge caps from standard shingle tabs: taper each tab along the side edges, starting from the top of the slots and cutting up to the top edge. Cut three caps from each shingle—you'll need one cap for every 5" of ridge.

2. Snap a chalk line across the shingles, 6" from the ridge. Starting at the gable ends (for a gable roof) or the bottom edge (for a hip roof), install the caps by bending them over the ridge and aligning one side edge with the chalk line. Fasten each cap with one nail on each roof side, 5½" from the finished (exposed) edge and 1" from the side edge. Maintain a 5" exposure for each shingle. Fasten the last shingle with a nail at each corner, then cover the nail heads with roofing cement.

3. Trim the overhanging shingles along the gable ends: Snap chalk lines along the gable ends, ⅜" from the drip edges (these should line up with the first, fifth, etc., courses). Trim the shingles at the lines. Cover any exposed nails with roofing cement.

C. *Stagger each course of shingles by ½ tab, repeating the pattern after overhanging the edge by 1½ tabs.*

D. *Divide the shingles into thirds, then trim the corners to create the shingle caps (INSET). Install the caps at the ridge.*

Siding & Trim

The siding and exterior trim not only provide an attractive skin for your building, they protect the structure from the weather. It's important to keep this function in mind as you install them: watch for areas where water can pool or trickle in, and make sure all unfinished edges and seams are covered or sealed with caulk.

Apply a protective finish—stain, paint, or varnish—to your siding and trim as soon as possible after installing them. Since conditions vary by region, ask your supplier about the best treatment for your siding, or contact the manufacturer.

Plywood Siding

Plywood siding is the least expensive and easiest to install of all the standard exterior finishes. It's available in 4 × 8-ft., 9-ft., and 10-ft. sheets; ⅜", ½", or ⅝" thicknesses; and in several styles, including striated, rough sawn, channel groove, and board-&-batten. The most common style, Texture 1-11 (shown here), is made to resemble vertical board siding and typically has ship-lap edges that form weather-proof vertical seams.

Plywood siding is exterior-grade, but the layered edges must be protected from moisture. For types with unmilled (square) edges, caulk the gap at vertical seams or install a 1 × 2 batten strip over the joint. All horizontal joints must have metal Z-flashing for moisture protection.

at a corner so one side edge is flush with the corner framing and the other breaks on the center of a stud; hold the top edge on the chalk line. Check with a level to make sure the sheet is plumb, then fasten it with 8d galvanized finish nails, driven every 6" along the perimeter and every 12" in the field of the sheet.

3. Install the remaining sheets, checking each one for plumb and leaving a ⅛" gap between sheets. (For ship-lap edges, first fit the sheets tight, then draw a pencil line along the upper sheet's edge. Slide over the upper sheet ⅛", using the mark as a gauge.) At the joints, do not nail through both sheets with one nail. Overlap the sheets at the corners, if

desired (they will be covered by trim, in any case). Apply siding over door and window openings, but do not nail into the headers if you will install flashing (see page 399). If you start with a trimmed sheet, place the cut edge at the corner.

Step B: Install the Flashing & Second Row

1. Install Z-flashing along the top edge of siding, using 6d galvanized box nails.

2. Install the upper row of siding, leaving a ⅛" gap above the flashing.

3. Cut out the door and window openings with a circular saw, jig saw, or reciprocating saw.

4. Install trim over the flashed joints and at the building corners (see page 396).

TOOLS & MATERIALS

- Basic tools (page 18)
- Chalk line
- Level
- Circular saw
- Jig saw
- Plywood siding
- 8d galvanized finish nails
- 6d galvanized box nails
- Galvanized Z-flashing

HOW TO INSTALL PLYWOOD SIDING
Step A: Install the First Row of Siding

1. Snap a chalk line for the top edges of the siding, accounting for the overhang at the bottom edge: for wood floors, overhang the bottom of the floor frame by ¾" to 1"; for slabs, overhang the top of the slab by 1".

2. Position the first sheet—vertically—

A. *Install the plywood siding vertically. Plumb each sheet and fasten it to the framing with 6d nails.*

B. *Add galvanized metal flashing between rows of siding to prevent water from entering the seam.*

Trim

Trim includes the boards that conceal building seams, cover gaps around window and door frames, finish corners, and perform other decorative and weatherproofing functions. For sheds and outbuildings, simple trim details with 1 × 3, 1 × 4, or 1 × 6 cedar boards work well.

If your building has plywood siding, install the trim after the siding. When installing trim around doors and windows, the simplest method is to use butt joints (photo A). A slightly fancier alternative is to miter them (photo B).

To install window and door trim with butt joints, add the head trim first, then cut the two side pieces to fit. Install mitered trim pieces on opposing sides, (that is, top-bottom, then sides, or vice versa). Leave a ¼" reveal for all window and door trim. This adds interest and makes bowed jambs less noticeable. Exposed doors and windows must have flashing above the trim (see page 399).

To install corner trim (photo C), cut two pieces to length, then nail them together at a right angle, using 6d or 8d galvanized box nails or finish nails. Set the trim on the corner, plumb it with a level, and nail it to the framing with 8d galvanized box nails or finish nails.

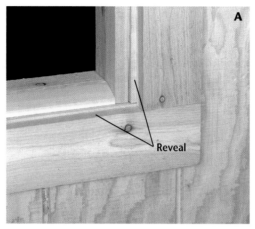

Window trim with butt joints. *Leave a ¼" reveal between the trim and the inside edge of the frame.*

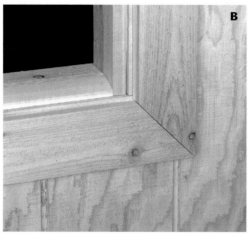

Window trim with miter joints. *Cut all miters at 45° and test-fit the joints before nailing the pieces.*

Install corner trim *by nailing the two pieces together then attaching the assembly to the building.*

FINISHING ROOF OVERHANGS

A common method for finishing the underside of a roof overhang is to install soffit panels that enclose the rafter ends. Soffits can be attached directly to the rafters or to horizontal blocking that extends back to the wall. An alternative to soffitting is leaving the rafter ends exposed. With this application, the wall siding is notched to fit around the rafters.

A roof overhang should also include means for ventilating the building. With soffits, this can be achieved with soffit vents—metal grates (available in rectangular, plug, and strip styles) which cover holes cut into the soffit panels. Exposed overhangs are by nature ventilated but should have bug screen to seal the gaps between the walls and the roof sheathing. To increase ventilation, you can also install roof vents (see page 390).

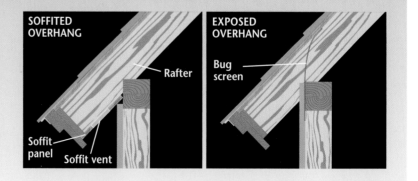

Doors & Windows

Shed doors and windows can be either prehung (factory-built) or homemade. The three shed projects in this section include plans for making your own doors and windows. They're simple designs using basic materials and can be built in an hour or two.

To keep water out, install flashing above the trim of any doors or windows that are exposed—that is, without a roof overhang above. If security is a concern, install a deadbolt for a pre-hung door or a hasp latch and padlock for a homemade door.

Prehung Doors & Windows

Prehung door and window units come in standard sizes, or they can be ordered in custom sizes, though at a higher price. Before framing the walls of your shed, select a door or window and confirm its exact dimensions before sizing the rough openings; be sure to use the outer dimensions of the unit's frame, not of the door or window itself.

Most exterior doors have preattached trim, called *brick molding*, on the outsides of the jambs. You can remove this if you want to add your own trim.

HOW TO INSTALL A PREHUNG WINDOW

NOTE: Window installations vary by product and manufacturer; follow the

TOOLS & MATERIALS

- Basic tools (page 18)
- Level
- Handsaw
- Nail set
- Door or window unit
- Tapered cedar shims
- 10d galvanized casing nails (door) or 1¾" roofing nails (window)

specific instructions provided for your window, including the steps for preparing the rough opening, shimming, flashing, etc. Shown here are the basic steps for installing a utility window with a nailing flange.

Step A: Set & Shim the Window

1. Set the window into the rough opening and center it between the sides. Place

pairs of tapered shims directly beneath the side jambs and at the center of the sill; position the shims so the tapered ends are opposed to form a flat surface.

2. From outside, drive one 1¾" roofing nail through the nailing flange at one of the lower corners of the window, but do not drive the nail completely.

Step B: Level & Fasten the Window

1. Place a level across the sill or top of the jamb, and adjust the shims until the window is perfectly level.

2. Drive one nail through the nailing flange at each corner of the window. Check the window operation to make sure it's smooth, then complete the nailing, following the manufacturer's

A. *Add pairs of tapered shims under the side window jambs and under the center of the sill.*

B. *Level the window, then fasten the unit in place with roofing nails driven through the nailing flange.*

instructions for spacing.

3. If the manufacturer recommends leaving the shims in place, trim the shims with a utility knife, then glue them in place with construction adhesive.

HOW TO INSTALL A PREHUNG DOOR
Step A: Plumb & Fasten the Hinge Jamb

1. Cut out the bottom plate inside the rough opening, using a handsaw. Remove any bracing or nails installed to protect the door during shipping.

2. Set the door into the opening and center it between the sides. Push the brick molding flat against the sheathing or siding; if there's no molding, position the outside edge of the jamb flush with the siding or sheathing. Insert pairs of tapered shims (with the tapered ends opposed to form a flat surface) between the hinge jamb and the framing. Add shims at the top and bottom and at each hinge location.

3. Starting with the top shims, check the hinge jamb with a level to make sure it's plumb, and adjust the shims as needed. Nail through the jamb and shims and into the framing with one 16d casing nail. Repeat at the remaining shim locations.

Step B: Secure the Latch & Head Jambs

1. Standing inside the shed, close the door, and examine the gap between the door and latch jamb. Starting at the top of the latch jamb, install shims between the jamb and the framing. Check the gap to make sure you're not bowing the jamb.

Fasten the jamb and shims with one 16d casing nail.

2. Shim and fasten the latch jamb at four more locations, level with the hinge-side shims, making sure the gap along the door remains consistent.

3. Shim and fasten the head jamb at two locations. For added support, you can replace one screw on each hinge with a 3½" screw, but be careful not to over-tighten them and pull the frame out of square.

4. Nail through the brick molding and into the sheathing (or siding) and framing with 16d casing nails driven every 16".

5. Cut off the shims flush with the framing, using a utility knife. Set all nails with a nail set.

A. Plumb the door jamb, working from the top down. Fasten through the jamb and each shim pair with a casing nail.

B. Shim the latch jamb, using the gap between the door and the jamb as a gauge. Make sure the gap is consistent.

Homemade Doors & Windows

To make your own door or window, build and install the frame, measure the opening, then build and install the door to fit (or add the glass). Use 1 × lumber for the frame, ripping it to width so it spans the wall section of the rough opening.

You can make a homemade door with almost any rigid board: siding, plywood, lumber, etc. Use the door plans provided in the shed project or create your own design.

For windows, you can use standard plate glass, safety glass (tempered), or plexiglass. Plexiglass has more shock-resistance than glass, but it's no less expensive, and it becomes scratched and cloudy over time.

Installing a homemade door or window frame is similar to installing a prehung door: center the frame in the rough opening, shim between the jambs and framing, plumb and level the frame, and fasten it through the jamb and shims (see pages 397 to 398). Because a homemade door frame has no threshold to secure the bottom ends of the side jambs, install a temporary 1 × spreader across the jambs to keep the frame square during installation (illustration at right).

To install a homemade door, mount the hinges to the door, then set the door in the frame and hold it against the stops. Insert shims underneath the door and between the door and latch jamb to set even gaps around the door. Mount the hinges to the wall with screws.

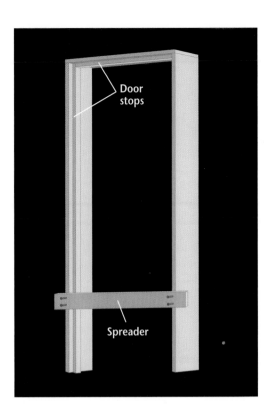

Door stops

Spreader

FLASHING ABOVE DOORS & WINDOWS:

Install metal flashing where siding meets trim to help divert water away from doors, windows, and their frames.

*When the siding is installed **after** the trim:*

Nail the flashing to the sheathing so it laps over the trim, then install the siding over the vertical flange of the flashing.

*When the siding is installed **before** the trim:*

1. Set the trim in place above the door or window, then trace along the top edge and ends of the trim (photo A).

2. Remove the trim and cut out the siding along the traced lines.

3. Slip the flashing underneath the siding and fasten it with nails driven through the siding (complete the siding nailing).

4. Reinstall the cut-out siding below the flashing—to serve as backing—then install the trim (photo B).

A. *Trace along the trim to mark the cutting lines for removing the siding.*

Flashing

B. *Add the flashing, then install the siding cutout and the trim.*

Basic Shed

This 8 × 12-ft. shed features a simple gable roof, double doors, and side and rear windows for natural lighting. With full-height walls and doors, there's ample room for storing large items or creating a comfortable work space. An optional wood ramp helps in moving lawn mowers and other heavy equipment.

The shed's simple construction makes it especially adaptable for different uses. For example, you can easily frame in additional windows—to use the shed as a workshop or potting shed—or omit all of the windows and devote the space entirely to secure storage.

The finish materials for the basic shed also are true to its name: asphalt roof shingles, plywood siding, and simple trim details are appropriately practical for this classic outbuilding design. You can purchase prehung doors and windows, like those shown in the illustration below, or build your own using the project plans.

Materials

Description	Quantity/Size	Material		Description	Quantity/Size	Material
Foundation				**Door**		
Drainage material	1.4 cu. yd.	Compactible gravel		Frame	2 @ 8'-0", 1 @ 6'-0"	¾ × 4¼" (actual) S4S cedar
Skids	3 @ 12'-0"	4 × 4 treated timbers		Stops	2 @ 8'-0", 1 @ 6'-0"	1 × 2 S4S cedar
Floor Framing				Panel material	12 @ 8'-0"	1 × 6 T&G V-joint S4S cedar
Rim joists	2 @ 12'-0"	2 × 6 pressure-treated		Z-brace	4 @ 6'-0"	1 × 6 S4S cedar
Joists	10 @ 8'-0"	2 × 6 pressure-treated		Construction adhesive	1 tube	
Floor sheathing	3 sheets, 4 × 8' ext.-grade plywood	¾" tongue-&-groove		Exterior trim	2 @ 8'-0", 1 @ 6'-0"	1 × 4 S4S cedar
Joist clip angles	20	3" × 3" × 3" × 16 gauge galvanized		Interior trim (optional)	2 @ 8'-0", 1 @ 6'-0"	1 × 2 S4S cedar
Wall Framing				Strap hinges	6, with screws	Exterior hinges
Bottom plates	2 @ 12'-0" 2 @ 8'-0"	2 × 4		**Windows**		
Top plates	4 @ 12'-0" 4 @ 8'-0"	2 × 4		Frames	5 @ 6'-0"	¾ × 4¼" (actual) S4S cedar
Studs	40 @ 92⅝"	2 × 4		Mullion	1 @ 3'-0"	2 × 4 S4S cedar
Headers	2 @ 10'-0", 2 @ 6'0"	2 × 6		Stops	10 @ 6'-0"	1 × 2 S4S cedar
Header spacers	1 @ 9'-0", 1 @ 6'-0"	½" plywood—5" wide		Glazing tape	30 linear ft.	Glazing tape
Gable Wall Framing				Glass	3 pieces—field measure	¼" clear, tempered
Top plates	2 @ 8'-0"	2 × 4		Window muntins (optional)	3 @ 8'-0"	1 × 1 S4S cedar
Studs	2 @ 8'-0"	2 × 4		Exterior trim	5 @ 8'-0"	1 × 4 S4S cedar
Roof Framing				Interior trim (optional)	5 @ 8'-0"	1 × 2 S4S cedar
Rafters	22 @ 6'-0"	2 × 6		**Ramp (Optional)**		
Metal anchors—rafters	10, with nails	Simpson H1		Pads	2 @ 6'-0"	2 × 8 pressure-treated
Rafter ties	3 @ 8'-0"	2 × 4		Stringers	1 @ 8'-0"	2 × 8 pressure-treated
Ridge board	1 @ 14'-0"	2 × 8		Decking	7 @ 6'-0"	2 × 4 pressure-treated
Lookouts	1 @ 8'-0"	2 × 6		**Fasteners**		
Subfascia	1 @ 8'-0", 2 @ 10'-0"	2 × 6		16d common nails	16 lbs.	
Soffit nailers	3 @ 8'-0"	2 × 2		10d common nails	1 lb.	
Exterior Finishes				10d galvanized casing nails	1 lb.	
Plywood siding	10 sheets @ 4 × 9'	⅝" texture 1-11 plywood siding, grooves 8" o.c.		8d common nails	½ lb.	
Z-flashing	2 pieces @ 8 ft.	Galvanized—18- gauge		8d box nails	3 lbs.	
Wall & corner trim	10 @ 10'-0"	1 × 4 S4S cedar		8d galvanized box nails	1½ lbs.	
Fascia	8 @ 8'-0"	1 × 8 S4S cedar		8d galvanized finish nails	7 lbs.	
Plywood soffits	2 sheets @ 4 × 8'	⅜" cedar or fir plywood		⅞" galvanized roofing nails	2 lbs.	
Soffit vents	4 @ 4 × 12"	Louver with bug screen		3d galvanized box nails	¼ lb.	
Flashing (door/window trim)	8 linear ft.	Galvanized—18-gauge		1½" joist hanger nails	80 nails	
Roofing				1¼" wood screws	70 screws	
Roof sheathing	6 sheets @ 4 × 8'	½" ext.-grade plywood		3½" deck screws	12 screws	
Asphalt shingles	150 sq. ft.	250# per square (min.)		3" deck screws	50 screws	
15# building paper	150 sq. ft.			2½" deck screws	40 screws	
Metal drip edge	2 @ 14'-0", 4 @ 6'-0"	Galvanized metal		1¼" deck screws	30 screws	
Roof vents (optional)	2 units			Silicone-latex caulk	1 tube	

FRONT ELEVATION

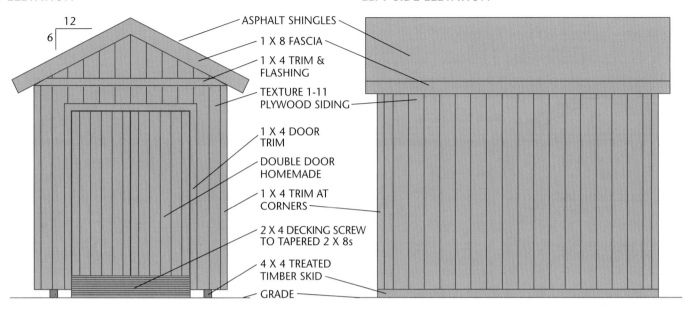

- ASPHALT SHINGLES
- 1 X 8 FASCIA
- 1 X 4 TRIM & FLASHING
- TEXTURE 1-11 PLYWOOD SIDING
- 1 X 4 DOOR TRIM
- DOUBLE DOOR HOMEMADE
- 1 X 4 TRIM AT CORNERS
- 2 X 4 DECKING SCREW TO TAPERED 2 X 8s
- 4 X 4 TREATED TIMBER SKID
- GRADE

12
6

LEFT SIDE ELEVATION

REAR ELEVATION

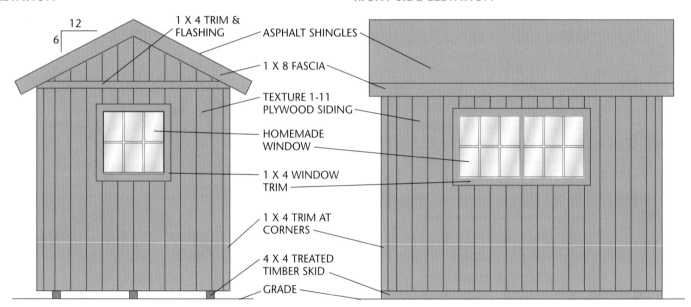

12
6

- 1 X 4 TRIM & FLASHING
- ASPHALT SHINGLES
- 1 X 8 FASCIA
- TEXTURE 1-11 PLYWOOD SIDING
- HOMEMADE WINDOW
- 1 X 4 WINDOW TRIM
- 1 X 4 TRIM AT CORNERS
- 4 X 4 TREATED TIMBER SKID
- GRADE

RIGHT SIDE ELEVATION

HORIZONTAL TRIM DETAIL

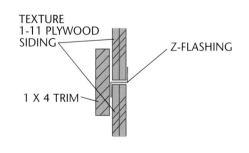

- TEXTURE 1-11 PLYWOOD SIDING
- Z-FLASHING
- 1 X 4 TRIM

DOOR JAMB DETAIL

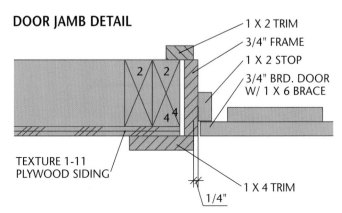

- 1 X 2 TRIM
- 3/4" FRAME
- 1 X 2 STOP
- 3/4" BRD. DOOR W/ 1 X 6 BRACE
- TEXTURE 1-11 PLYWOOD SIDING
- 1 X 4 TRIM
- 1/4"

2 2
4 4

GABLE OVERHANG DETAIL

2 X 6 LOOKOUTS
16" O.C.

ASPHALT SHINGLES OVER
15# BUILDING PAPER

1/2" PLYWOOD

METAL DRIP
EDGE

2 X 6 RAFTER

1 X 8 FASCIA

3/8" PLYWOOD
SOFFIT

6"

2 X 6 RAFTER

2 X 4 STUD
24" O.C.

TEXTURE 1-11
PLYWOOD SIDING

EAVE DETAIL

ASPHALT SHINGLES OVER
15# BUILDING PAPER

1/2" PLYWOOD

2 X 6 RAFTER

METAL DRIP EDGE

2   4
2   4
2 2

2

2 X 2 NAILER

1 X 8 FASCIA

6

2 X 6 SUBFASCIA

2 X 4 STUD
24" O.C.

SOFFIT
VENT

3/8" PLYWOOD
SOFFIT

TEXTURE 1-11
PLYWOOD SIDING

WINDOW JAMB DETAIL

1 X 4 TRIM

1 X 2 TRIM

1 X 2 STOP

GLAZING TAPE
BOTH SIDES

PLYWOOD SIDING

SLOPED STOP
@ SILL

1/4" CLEAR GLASS
TEMPERED

1 X 2 STOP

3/4"

CUT SLOPE FOR
DRAINAGE

1/4"

1/4"

1 X 2 CEDAR STOP @
WINDOW SILL

RAMP DETAIL (OPTIONAL)

2'-0" (OR DESIRED LENGTH)

FLOOR
FRAME

DOOR

2 X 4 DECKING —
SCREW TO
TAPERED 2 X 8s

TAPERED
2 X 8s
(PRESSURE-
TREATED)

2

6

2   8   2   8

COMPACTIBLE
GRAVEL

2 X 8 PADS (PRESSURE-
TREATED) — SET INTO
GRANULAR BASE MATERIAL

DOOR ELEVATIONS

STRAP
HINGE

1 X 6 T&G
V-JOINT
CEDAR
BOARDS

OUTSIDE ELEVATION

5'-0"

(2) 2'-6" DOORS

1 X 6 CEDAR Z-BRACE
GLUED & SCREWED
TO PANEL BOARDS

6'-9 3/4"

INSIDE ELEVATION

BUILDING THE BASIC SHED

Step A: Build the Foundation & Floor Frame

1. Excavate the building site and add a 4" layer of compactible gravel. If desired, add an extension to the base for the optional wood ramp. Tamp the gravel thoroughly, making sure it is flat and level.

2. Cut three 4 × 4 treated timber skids at 144". Arrange and level the skids on the gravel bed, following the FLOOR FRAMING PLAN, on page 403.

3. Cut two 2 × 6 rim joists at 144" and ten joists at 93". Mark the joist layout onto the rim joists, following the plan. Assemble the frame with 16d galvanized common nails; be sure to check each joist for crowning and install it with the crowned edge up.

4. Set the floor frame on top of the skids and measure the diagonals to make sure it's square. Install metal clip angles at each joist along the two outer skids, using 1½" joist hanger nails and 16d galvanized common nails, and toenail each joist to the center skid with 16d galvanized nails.

5. Install the tongue-and-groove floor sheathing, starting with a full sheet at one corner of the frame. Use 8d galvanized nails driven every 6" along the edges and every 12" in the field.

Step B: Frame the Walls

1. Snap chalk lines on the floor for the wall plates.

2. Cut the 2 × 4 wall plates: four at 144" for the side walls and four at 89" for the front and back walls.

3. Mark the stud layouts onto the plates following the FLOOR PLAN, on page 403.

4. Cut thirty-three studs at 92⅝", and cut six at 80½" to serve as jack studs.

5. Build three headers with 2 × 6s and ½" plywood: one at 65" for the door opening, one at 67" for the right side window, and one at 35" for the rear window.

6. Assemble, raise, and brace the walls one at a time, then add the double top plates.

Step C: Frame the Roof

1. Cut a pattern and duplicate rafter, following the RAFTER TEMPLATE, on page 403. Test-fit the rafters using a 2 × 8 spacer block, then cut the remaining twelve common rafters. Cut eight rafters for the gable end overhangs—these do not have bird's mouth cuts.

2. Cut the 2 × 8 ridge board at 156". Draw the rafter layout onto the top plates and ridge board, using 16" on-center spacing. The outsides of the outer common rafters should be 6" from the ends of the ridge board.

3. Install the rafters. Reinforce the rafter-wall connection with metal anchors—install them on all but the outer common rafters.

4. Cut three 2 × 4 rafter ties at 96", and clip the top outer corners so they won't project above the rafters. Position each tie

A. *Secure the joists to the outer skids with metal clip angles. Drive hanger nails into the joists and 16d nails into the skids.*

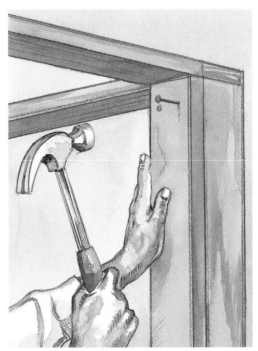

B. *Frame and raise the walls, then fasten adjacent walls together at the corner studs.*

C. *Fasten the bottom ends of the common rafters to the wall plates with metal anchors.*

next to a pair of rafters as shown in the FRAMING ELEVATIONS on page 402. Facenail each tie end to the rafter with three 10d nails, then toenail each tie end to the top wall plate with two 8d nails.

5. Cut the gable-wall plates to reach from the ridge to the wall plates. Install the plates with their outside edges flush with the outer common rafters. Cut and install the gable studs, following the FRAMING ELEVATIONS, on page 402.

Step D: Build the Gable Overhangs

2. Cut sixteen 2 × 6 lookouts at 3". Endnail the lookouts to each of the inner overhang rafters, using 16" on-center spacing (see the GABLE OVERHANG DETAIL, on page 405).

3. Facenail the inner overhang rafters to the outer common rafters with 10d nails.

4. Fasten the outer overhang rafters to the ridge and lookouts, using 16d nails.

Step E: Install the Fascia, Sheathing & Roofing

1. Cut and install the 2 × 6 subfascia along the eaves (see the EAVE DETAIL, on page 405). Keep the ends flush with the outsides of the overhang rafters, and the bottom edges flush with the bottom rafter edges; use 16d nails.

2. Install the 1 × 8 fascia along the gable overhangs, then along the eaves, holding it ½" above the rafters so it will be flush with the sheathing; use 6d galvanized finish nails.

3. Install the ½" plywood sheathing, starting at a lower corner of the roof; use 8d box nails driven every 6" along the edges and every 12" in the field of the sheets.

4. Attach metal drip edge along the eaves, then apply 15# building paper over the sheathing. Add drip edge along the gable ends, over the paper.

5. Install the asphalt shingles, starting at the eave edge. If desired, install roof vents (see page 390).

Step F: Install the Soffits & Siding

1. Cut twelve 2 × 2 nailers to fit between the rafters, as shown in the EAVE DETAIL, on page 405. Fasten the nailers between the rafters with 10d facenails or 8d toenails.

2. Rip the ⅜" plywood soffit panels to fit between the wall framing and the fascia. Fasten the soffits to the rafters with 3d galvanized box nails.

3. Cut holes for four soffit vents: locate one vent in each of the two outer rafter bays, along the eave, on both sides of the building. Install the soffit vents.

4. Install the plywood siding, using 8d galvanized finish nails. Butt the top edges of the siding against the soffits. Don't nail the siding to the rear-window and door headers in this step. At the gable ends, install Z-flashing along the top edge of siding, then continue the siding up to the soffits.

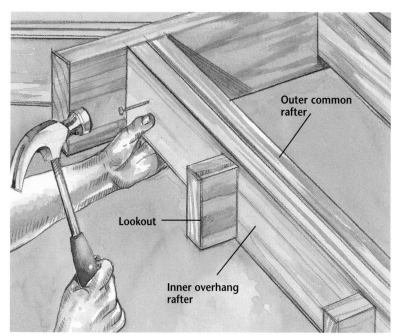

D. *Attach lookouts to four of the overhang rafters, then nail the overhang rafters to the end common rafters.*

E. *Install the plywood roof sheathing after installing the fascia. Nail every 6" at the edges and every 12" in the field.*

F. *Rip the soffit panels to fit between the wall plates and fascia. Fasten the panels to the nailers, rafters and subfascia.*

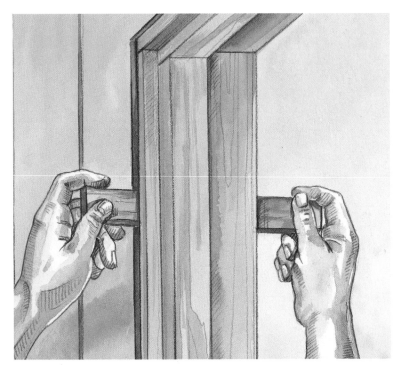

G. *Use pairs of tapered shims to plumb and level the door frame in the rough opening.*

NOTE: Along the side walls, 8-ft. siding will cover the floor plywood by about ½" (this is necessary); if you want the siding to cover the floor framing, use 4 × 9-ft. sheets.

Step G: Build & Install the Doors

1. Cut out the bottom plate from the door opening.

2. Cut the door frame pieces from ¾ × 4½" (actual dimension) cedar: cut the head jamb at 61¼" and the side jambs at 81⅞". Assemble the frame by screwing through the head jamb and into the side jambs with 2½" deck screws.

3. Cut 1 × 2 stops and install them inside the jambs with 1¼" deck screws or 3d galvanized finish nails. If the doors will swing out, install the stops 2¼" from the outside edges of the frame; if they'll swing in, install the stops 2¼" from the inside edges.

4. Install the door frame in the rough opening, using shims and 10d galvanized casing nails (see page 399). Make sure the frame is square and plumb.

5. Cut twelve pieces of 1 × 6 tongue-&-groove boards at 81¾". For each door, fit together six boards with their ends flush, then mark the two end boards for trimming so that the total width is 30". Trim the end boards.

6. Cut the Z-brace boards following the DOOR ELEVATIONS, on page 405. Lay the doors on a flat surface and attach the brace boards using construction adhesive and 1¼" wood screws.

7. Install the hinges and hang the door, using shims to set the gaps at the bottom and top of each door.

8. Install flashing above the door (see page 399), nail-off the siding, then install the 1 × 4 door trim, using 8d galvanized finish nails.

Step H: Build & Install the Windows & Trim

NOTE: If you've bought prehung windows for the shed, install them following the manufacturer's directions (see pages 397 to 399). To build homemade windows, use the following directions.

1. For each window, cut the ¾" × 4¼" frame stock to form a rectangular frame with outer dimensions that are ½" shorter and narrower than the rough opening. Assemble the frame with 2½" deck screws. Cut and install a 2 × 4 mullion in the center of the frame for the side-wall window.

2. Install each window frame in its rough opening, using shims and a level to make sure the frame is plumb and level and the jambs are straight. Fasten the frame with 10d galvanized casing nails.

3. Cut the 1 × 2 stops. Bevel the outer sill stops as shown in the WINDOW JAMB DETAIL, on page 405. Attach the inner stops with 6d galvanized finish nails. Order the glass to fit.

4. Install the glass and outer stops, applying glazing tape to the stops on both sides of the glass. Install the 1 × 4 window trim.

5. Install the horizontal 1 × 4 trim as shown in the ELEVATIONS, on page 404. Fasten the trim with 8d galvanized finish nails.

6. Install the 1 × 4 corner trim so that it butts against the horizontal trim and extends to the bottom edges of the siding.

7. Caulk along all trim joints, where trim meets siding, and around the door and window trim.

Step I: Build the Ramp (Optional)

Determining the width and length (and thus the slope) of the ramp is up to you, but here is the basic construction procedure:

1. Determine the best slope for the ramp using boards or plywood set on the ground and the shed floor. Mark the ground to represent the end of the ramp.

2. Cut two 2 × 8 pads to the full width of the ramp.

3. Measure the distance from the ground to the shed floor; subtract 2" from that dimension to get the height of the tapered stringers.

4. Use the ground marking to determine the length of the stringers—be sure to account for the 1½" thickness of the decking. Cut the tapered stringers from 2 × 8 lumber: cut one for each end and one for every 16" to 24" in between.

5. Attach the pads to the stringers with 16d galvanized nails driven through the bottom faces of the pads and into the stringers.

6. Cut 2 × 4s for the ramp decking—the number needed depends on the length of the sloping sides of the stringers. Allow for a ⅛" gap between decking boards when calculating the number needed.

7. Attach the decking boards to the supports with 16d galvanized nails or 3" deck screws, maintaining a ⅛" gap between boards.

8. Set the ramp in place against the shed and fasten it by toenailing through the end stringers and top decking board with 3½" deck screws.

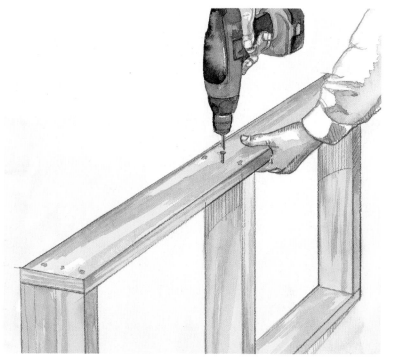

H. *Assemble the window frames with screws. Add a 2 × 4 mullion in the center of the side window frame.*

I. *Build the ramp with pressure-treated 2 × 8s and 2 × 4s, following the plan's size or building it to a custom size.*

Lawn-tractor Garage

Following classic barn designs, this 12 × 12-ft. garage has several features that make it a versatile storage shed. The garage's floor is a poured concrete slab with a thickened edge that allows it to serve also as the building's foundation. Designed for economy and durability, the floor can support a lawn tractor, large stationary tools, or other heavy equipment. See pages 377 to 379 for detailed information on the foundation and how to build it.

For easy access with large items, there's a full-width sectional garage door. The door opening is sized for an 8-ft.-wide × 7-ft.-tall door, but you can buy any size or style—just make sure to get the door before you start framing.

Another functional (and equally aesthetic) feature of this shed is its gambrel roof, a style commonly used for barns because it maximizes the usable interior space.

Beneath the roof is a sizable storage attic—a 315 cubic-ft. space with its own double-doors above the garage door.

Materials

Description	Quantity/Size	Material
Foundation		
Drainage material	1.75 cu. yds.	Compactible gravel
Concrete slab	2.5 cu. yds.	3,000 psi concrete
Mesh	144 sq. ft. welded wire mesh	6 × 6", W1.4 × W1.4
Wall Framing		
Bottom plates	4 @ 12'-0"	2 × 4 pressure-treated
Top plates	8 @ 12'-0"	2 × 4
Studs	47 @ 92⅝"	2 × 4
Headers	2 @ 10'-0", 2 @ 6'-0"	2 × 8
Header spacers	1 @ 9'-0", 1 @ 6'-0"	½" plywood—7" wide
Angle braces	1 @ 4'-0"	2 × 4
Gable Wall Framing		
Plates	2 @ 10'-0"	2 × 4
Studs	7 @ 10'-0"	2 × 4
Header	2 @ 6'-0"	2 × 6
Header spacer	1 @ 5'-0"	½" plywood—5" wide
Attic Floor		
Joists	10 @ 12'-0"	2 × 6
Floor sheathing	3 sheets @ 4 × 8'	¾" tongue-&-groove ext.-grade plywood
Kneewall Framing		
Bottom plates	2 @ 12'-0"	2 × 4
Top plates	4 @ 12'-0"	2 × 4
Studs	8 @ 10'-0"	2 × 4
Nailers	2 @ 14'-0"	2 × 8
Roof Framing		
Rafters	28 @ 10'-0"	2 × 4
Metal anchors—rafters	20, with nails	Simpson H2.5
Collar ties	2 @ 6'-0"	2 × 4
Ridge board	1 @ 14'-0"	2 × 6
Lookouts	1 @ 10'-0"	2 × 4
Soffit ledgers	2 @ 14'-0"	2 × 4
Soffit blocking	6 @ 8'-0"	2 × 4
Exterior Finishes		
Plywood siding	14 sheets @ 4 × 8'	⅝" texture 1-11 plywood siding, grooves 8" o. c.
Z-flashing—siding	2 pieces @ 12'-0"	Galvanized 18-gauge
Horizontal wall trim	2 @ 12'-0"	1 × 4 S4S cedar
Corner trim	8 @ 8'-0"	1 × 4 S4S cedar
Fascia	6 @ 10'-0", 2 @ 8'-0"	1 × 6 S4S cedar
Subfascia	4 @ 8'-0"	1 × 4 pine
Plywood soffits	1 sheet @ 10'-0"	⅜" cedar or fir plywood
Soffit vents	4 @ 4 × 12"	Louver w/bug screen
Flashing—garage door	1 @ 10'-0"	Galvanized 18-gauge
Roofing		
Roof sheathing	12 sheets @ 4 × 8'	½" plywood
Shingles	3 squares	250# per square (min.)
15# building paper	300 sq. ft.	
Metal drip edge	2 @ 14'-0", 2 @ 12'-0"	Galvanized metal
Roof vents (optional)	2 units	

Description	Quantity/Size	Material
Window		
Frame	3 @ 6'-0"	¾ × 4" (actual) S4S cedar
Stops	4 @ 8'-0"	1 × 2 S4S cedar
Glazing tape	30 linear ft.	
Glass	1 piece—field measure	¼"clear, tempered
Exterior trim	3 @ 6'-0"	1 × 4 S4S cedar
Interior trim (optional)	3 @ 6'-0"	1 × 2 S4S cedar
Door		
Frame	2 @ 8'-0"	1 × 6 S4S cedar
Door sill	1 @ 6'-0"	1 × 6 S4S cedar
Stops	1 @ 8'-0", 1 @ 6'-0"	1 × 2 S4S cedar
Panel material	4 @ 8'-0"	1 × 8 T&G V-joint S4S cedar
Door X-brace/panel trim	4 @ 6'-0", 2 @ 8'-0"	1 × 4 S4S cedar
Exterior trim	1 @ 8'-0", 1 @ 6'-0"	1 × 4 S4S cedar
Interior trim (optional)	1 @ 8'-0", 1 @ 6'-0"	1 × 2 S4S cedar
Strap hinges	4	
Garage Door		
Frame	3 @ 8'-0"	1 × 8 S4S cedar
Door	1 @ 8'-0" × 6'-8" w/2" track	Sectional flush door
Rails	2 @ 8'-0"	2 × 6
Trim	3 @ 8'-0"	1 × 4 S4S cedar
Fasteners		
Anchor bolts	16	⅜" × 8", with washers & nuts
16d galvanized common nails	2 lbs.	
16d common nails	17 lbs.	
10d common nails	2 lbs.	
10d galvanized casing nails	1 lb.	
8d common nails	3 lbs.	
8d galvanized finish nails	6 lbs.	
8d box nails	6 lbs.	
6d galvanized finish nails	20 nails	
3d galvanized box nails	½ lb.	
⅞" galvanized roofing nails	2½ lbs.	
2½" deck screws	24 screws	
1¼" wood screws	48 screws	
Construction adhesive	2 tubes	
Silicone-latex caulk	2 tubes	

FRONT FRAMING ELEVATION

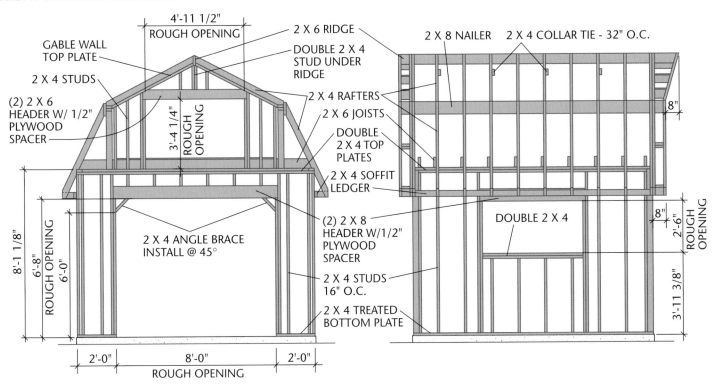

4'-11 1/2"
ROUGH OPENING

2 X 6 RIDGE

DOUBLE 2 X 4 STUD UNDER RIDGE

GABLE WALL TOP PLATE

2 X 4 STUDS

(2) 2 X 6 HEADER W/ 1/2" PLYWOOD SPACER

2 X 4 RAFTERS

2 X 6 JOISTS

3'-4 1/4" ROUGH OPENING

DOUBLE 2 X 4 TOP PLATES

2 X 4 SOFFIT LEDGER

(2) 2 X 8 HEADER W/1/2" PLYWOOD SPACER

2 X 4 ANGLE BRACE INSTALL @ 45°

2 X 4 STUDS 16" O.C.

2 X 4 TREATED BOTTOM PLATE

8'-1 1/8"

6'-8" ROUGH OPENING

6'-0"

2'-0"   8'-0"   2'-0"
ROUGH OPENING

LEFT SIDE FRAMING ELEVATION

2 X 8 NAILER   2 X 4 COLLAR TIE - 32" O.C.

8"

DOUBLE 2 X 4

8"

2'-6" ROUGH OPENING

3'-11 3/8"

REAR FRAMING ELEVATION

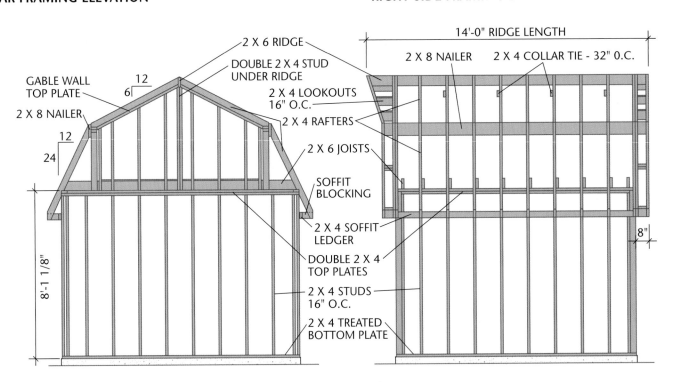

2 X 6 RIDGE

DOUBLE 2 X 4 STUD UNDER RIDGE

2 X 4 LOOKOUTS 16" O.C.

GABLE WALL TOP PLATE

12
6

2 X 8 NAILER

12
24

2 X 4 RAFTERS

2 X 6 JOISTS

SOFFIT BLOCKING

2 X 4 SOFFIT LEDGER

DOUBLE 2 X 4 TOP PLATES

2 X 4 STUDS 16" O.C.

2 X 4 TREATED BOTTOM PLATE

8'-1 1/8"

RIGHT SIDE FRAMING ELEVATION

14'-0" RIDGE LENGTH

2 X 8 NAILER   2 X 4 COLLAR TIE - 32" O.C.

8"

BUILDING SECTION

RAFTER TEMPLATE-LOWER RAFTER

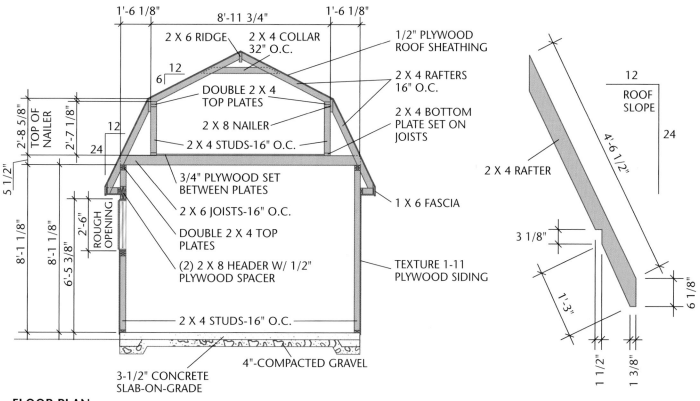

1'-6 1/8"
8'-11 3/4"
1'-6 1/8"

2 X 6 RIDGE
2 X 4 COLLAR 32" O.C.
1/2" PLYWOOD ROOF SHEATHING

12
6

DOUBLE 2 X 4 TOP PLATES

2 X 4 RAFTERS 16" O.C.

2 X 8 NAILER

2 X 4 BOTTOM PLATE SET ON JOISTS

2'-8 5/8"
TOP OF NAILER
2'-7 1/8"

12
24

2 X 4 STUDS-16" O.C.

3/4" PLYWOOD SET BETWEEN PLATES

1 X 6 FASCIA

5 1/2"

2 X 6 JOISTS-16" O.C.

8'-1 1/8"
8'-1 1/8"
ROUGH OPENING
2'-6"
6'-5 3/8"

DOUBLE 2 X 4 TOP PLATES

(2) 2 X 8 HEADER W/ 1/2" PLYWOOD SPACER

TEXTURE 1-11 PLYWOOD SIDING

2 X 4 STUDS-16" O.C.

3-1/2" CONCRETE SLAB-ON-GRADE

4"-COMPACTED GRAVEL

12
ROOF SLOPE
24

2 X 4 RAFTER

4'-6 1/2"

3 1/8"

1'-3"

6 1/8"

1 1/2"
1 3/8"

FLOOR PLAN

RAFTER TEMPLATE-UPPER RAFTER

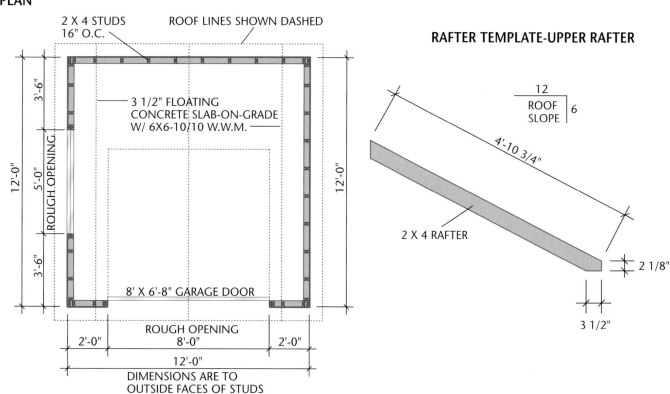

2 X 4 STUDS 16" O.C.
ROOF LINES SHOWN DASHED

3'-6"

3 1/2" FLOATING CONCRETE SLAB-ON-GRADE W/ 6X6-10/10 W.W.M.

12'-0"
5'-0"
ROUGH OPENING
12'-0"

3'-6"

8' X 6'-8" GARAGE DOOR

2'-0"
ROUGH OPENING 8'-0"
2'-0"

12'-0"

DIMENSIONS ARE TO OUTSIDE FACES OF STUDS

12
ROOF SLOPE
6

4'-10 3/4"

2 X 4 RAFTER

2 1/8"

3 1/2"

FRONT ELEVATION

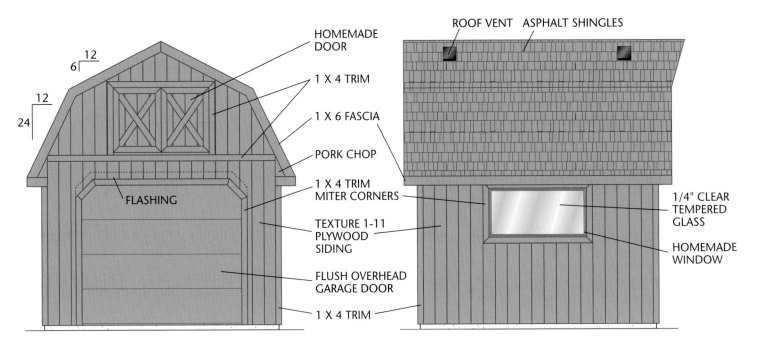

HOMEMADE DOOR

1 X 4 TRIM

1 X 6 FASCIA

PORK CHOP

1 X 4 TRIM MITER CORNERS

TEXTURE 1-11 PLYWOOD SIDING

FLUSH OVERHEAD GARAGE DOOR

1 X 4 TRIM

FLASHING

12
6

12
24

LEFT SIDE ELEVATION

ROOF VENT   ASPHALT SHINGLES

1/4" CLEAR TEMPERED GLASS

HOMEMADE WINDOW

REAR ELEVATION

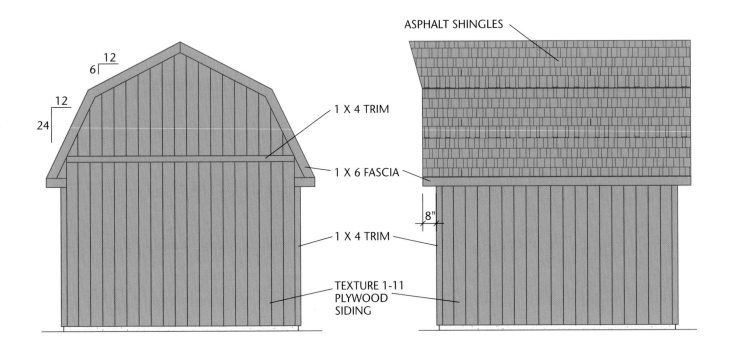

12
6

12
24

1 X 4 TRIM

1 X 6 FASCIA

1 X 4 TRIM

TEXTURE 1-11 PLYWOOD SIDING

RIGHT SIDE ELEVATION

ASPHALT SHINGLES

8"

GABLE OVERHANG DETAIL

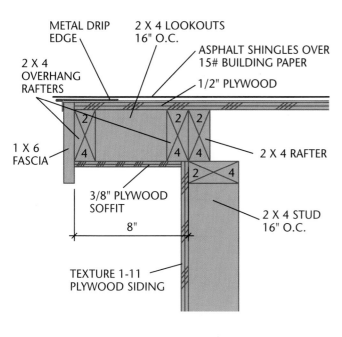

METAL DRIP EDGE

2 X 4 LOOKOUTS 16" O.C.

ASPHALT SHINGLES OVER 15# BUILDING PAPER

2 X 4 OVERHANG RAFTERS

1/2" PLYWOOD

1 X 6 FASCIA

2 X 4 RAFTER

3/8" PLYWOOD SOFFIT

8"

2 X 4 STUD 16" O.C.

TEXTURE 1-11 PLYWOOD SIDING

GABLE OVERHANG RAFTER DETAIL

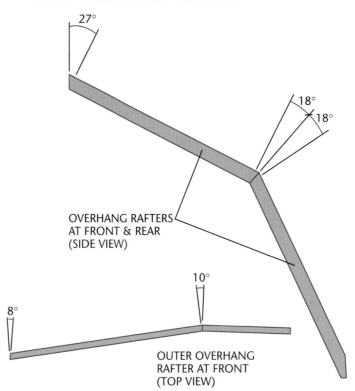

27°

18°

18°

OVERHANG RAFTERS AT FRONT & REAR (SIDE VIEW)

8°

10°

OUTER OVERHANG RAFTER AT FRONT (TOP VIEW)

EAVE DETAIL

SILL DETAIL

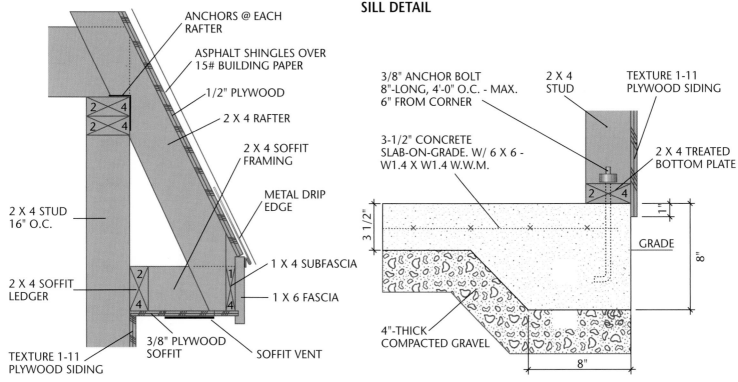

ANCHORS @ EACH RAFTER

ASPHALT SHINGLES OVER 15# BUILDING PAPER

1/2" PLYWOOD

2 X 4 RAFTER

2 X 4 SOFFIT FRAMING

METAL DRIP EDGE

2 X 4 STUD 16" O.C.

2 X 4 SOFFIT LEDGER

1 X 4 SUBFASCIA

1 X 6 FASCIA

TEXTURE 1-11 PLYWOOD SIDING

3/8" PLYWOOD SOFFIT

SOFFIT VENT

3/8" ANCHOR BOLT 8"-LONG, 4'-0" O.C. - MAX. 6" FROM CORNER

2 X 4 STUD

TEXTURE 1-11 PLYWOOD SIDING

3-1/2" CONCRETE SLAB-ON-GRADE. W/ 6 X 6 - W1.4 X W1.4 W.W.M.

2 X 4 TREATED BOTTOM PLATE

3 1/2"

1"

GRADE

8"

4"-THICK COMPACTED GRAVEL

8"

ATTIC DOOR ELEVATION

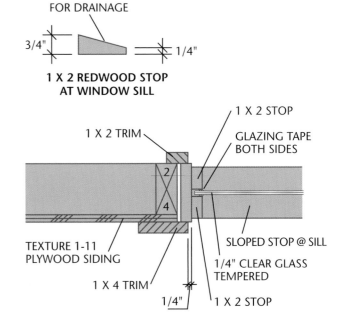

4'-9 1/4"

3'-2"

1 X 4 BOARDS GLUED
AND SCREWED TO
1 X 8 BOARDS

1 X 8 T&G V-JT
BOARDS-VERTICAL

STRAP HINGE

ATTIC DOOR JAMB DETAIL

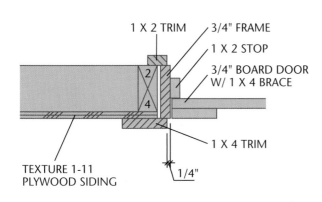

1 X 2 TRIM   3/4" FRAME

1 X 2 STOP

3/4" BOARD DOOR
W/ 1 X 4 BRACE

2

4

1 X 4 TRIM

TEXTURE 1-11
PLYWOOD SIDING

1/4"

GARAGE DOOR TRIM DETAIL

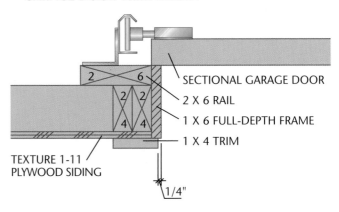

2   6

2   2

4   4

SECTIONAL GARAGE DOOR

2 X 6 RAIL

1 X 6 FULL-DEPTH FRAME

1 X 4 TRIM

TEXTURE 1-11
PLYWOOD SIDING

1/4"

ATTIC DOOR SILL DETAIL

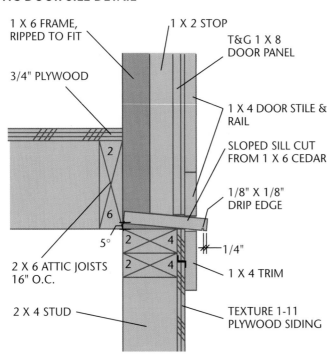

1 X 6 FRAME,
RIPPED TO FIT

1 X 2 STOP

T&G 1 X 8
DOOR PANEL

3/4" PLYWOOD

1 X 4 DOOR STILE &
RAIL

SLOPED SILL CUT
FROM 1 X 6 CEDAR

1/8" X 1/8"
DRIP EDGE

2

6

5°   2   4

2   4

1/4"

1 X 4 TRIM

2 X 6 ATTIC JOISTS
16" O.C.

2 X 4 STUD

TEXTURE 1-11
PLYWOOD SIDING

WINDOW JAMB DETAIL

CUT SLOPE
FOR DRAINAGE

3/4"   1/4"

**1 X 2 REDWOOD STOP
AT WINDOW SILL**

1 X 2 TRIM

1 X 2 STOP

GLAZING TAPE
BOTH SIDES

2

4

TEXTURE 1-11
PLYWOOD SIDING

1 X 4 TRIM

1/4"

SLOPED STOP @ SILL

1/4" CLEAR GLASS
TEMPERED

1 X 2 STOP

BUILDING THE LAWN-TRACTOR GARAGE

Step A: Pour the Slab Foundation

1. Follow the steps on pages 377 to 379 to prepare the building site, build the concrete form, and pour the slab. The top of the slab should sit 4" above grade and measure exactly 144" × 144". Reinforce the slab with 6 × 6"-W1.4 × W1.4 welded wire mesh.

2. After floating the concrete, set ⅜" × 8" J-bolts into the slab, 1¾" from the outer edges; install a bolt 6" from each corner and every 4 ft. in between (do not add bolts inside the garage door rough opening). The bolts should extend 2½" above the surface of the slab. Let the concrete cure for at least two days.

Step B: Frame the Walls

1. Snap chalk lines on the slab for the wall plates.

2. Cut the 2 × 4 wall plates—use pressure-treated lumber for all bottom wall plates. Cut two bottom and two top plates at 137" for the side walls, and cut two bottom and two top plates at 144" for the front and rear walls.

3. Mark the stud layouts onto the plates following the FLOOR PLAN, on page 413.

4. Cut thirty-eight studs at 92⅝". Cut two jack studs at 78½" for the garage door opening and two at 75⅞" for the window opening.

5. Build two headers with 2 × 8s and ½" plywood: one at 99" for the garage door opening and one at 63" for the window.

6. Assemble, raise, and brace the walls one at a time. Use 16d galvanized common nails for attaching the studs to the bottom plates. When framing the front wall, assemble the studs, plates and header, then square the frame before cutting and installing the two 2 × 4 angle braces, as shown in the FRONT FRAMING ELEVATION, on page 412. Add the double top plates after raising the walls.

Step C: Install the Attic Floor Joists

1. Cut ten 2 × 6 attic joists at 144". Check each joist for crowning, then cut off the top corner at each end with a 1½" long 45° cut (this prevents the corners from projecting beyond the rafters).

2. Draw the rafter layout and attic joist layout onto the side walls, following the FRAMING ELEVATIONS, on page 412. The outside face of each end joist should fall 3½" from the outer faces of the front and rear wall, respectively (this leaves room for the 2 × 4 gable wall framing).

3. Install the joists with their ends flush with the side walls, fastening each end to the wall plate with three 8d toenails (two nails on one side, one on the opposite side).

Step D: Frame the Attic Kneewalls

1. Cut four 2 × 4 top plates at 144" and two bottom plates at 137". Cut twenty 2 × 4 studs at 26⅝" and four end studs at 33⅝".

2. Lay out the plates so the studs fall over the floor joists. The bottom plates should be flush with the outer faces of the end floor joists; the top plates should be even with the outsides of the front and rear walls. Position the end studs at the ends of the top plates, their bottom ends on top of the wall plates below.

A. *Set the J-bolts into the wet concrete slab so they are plumb and extend 2½" above the surface.*

B. *Frame, square, and brace the front wall, then install the angle braces at the corners of the garage door opening.*

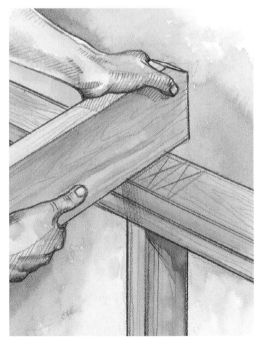

C. *Install the joists perpendicular to the side walls. All but the two outer joists sit next to a rafter.*

D. *Install the kneewalls perpendicular to the attic joists. The kneewall top plates extend past the bottom plates by 3½".*

E. *Fasten the soffit ledgers to the studs, then cut and install blocks that run horizontally from the rafters to the ledgers.*

3. Snap chalk lines for the bottom plates, 18⅛" in from the ends of the floor joists.

4. Frame and raise the kneewalls, fastening their bottom plates to the attic joists with 16d nails. Plumb the walls and install temporary braces.

5. Install ¾" plywood over the joists between the kneewalls. Run the sheets perpendicular to the joists, and keep the outside edges flush with the end joists. Drive 8d nails every 6" along the edges and every 12" in the field of the sheets.

Step E: Frame the Roof

1. Cut two 2 × 8 nailers at 160". Fasten the nailers to the outsides of the kneewalls so their top edges are 32⅝" above the tops of the attic joists and their ends overhang the walls an equal amount at both ends of the building—use 16d nails (see ELEVATIONS, page 412). Mark the rafter layout onto the top edges and outside faces of the nailers.

2. Cut the 2 × 6 ridge board at 168", angle-cutting the front end at 16°.

3. Draw the rafter layout onto the ridge. The outer common rafters should be 16" from the front and 8" from the rear end of the ridge, respectively.

4. Cut two UPPER pattern rafters following the RAFTER TEMPLATE, on page 413, and cut one LOWER pattern rafter. Test-fit the rafters, then cut the remaining common rafters of each type. Cut six additional upper rafters and eight lower rafters for the gable overhangs (do not make bird's mouth cuts on the lower overhang rafters).

5. Install the common rafters. Nail the upper rafters to the ridge and kneewalls with 16d nails. Toenail the lower rafters to the nailer with 16d nails. Nail the rafters to the wall plate, then reinforce the connection with metal anchors, using the recommended nails. Facenail the attic joists to the rafters with two 10d nails at each end.

6. Cut the four 2 × 4 collar ties at 34" and fasten them between pairs of upper rafters, as shown in the BUILDING SECTION, on page 413 and the FRAMING ELEVATIONS, on page 412.

7. At each end of the building, level over from the bottom ends of the outer rafters and mark the wall studs. Snap a chalk line through the marks. This line represents the bottom edge of the soffit ledger (see the EAVE DETAIL, on page 415).

8. Cut two 2 × 4 soffit ledgers at 160", and nail them to the wall studs with their bottom edges on the chalk lines and their ends overhanging the walls by 8"—use 16d nails.

9. Cut twenty-four 2 × 4 blocks to fit between the soffit ledger and the outside ends of the rafters, as shown in the EAVE DETAIL, on page 415. Toenail the blocks to the ledgers and facenail them to the rafters with 10d nails.

Step F: Build the Gable Overhangs

1. Cut 2 × 4 lookouts at 5" and nail them to the inner overhang rafters, using 16" on-center spacing. Don't install lookouts for the angled section of the front gable in this step.

2. Facenail the inner overhang rafters to the outer common rafters with 10d nails.

3. Cut the two angled overhang rafters for the front gable, measuring from the ridge to the 2 × 8 nailers to find the overall lengths. The end cuts on the upper rafters are compound: see the GABLE OVERHANG RAFTER DETAIL, on page 415 for the angles. Cut and test-fit the rafters and adjust the angles as needed. Fasten the rafters to the ridge and nailers with 16d nails. Cut and install lookouts to fit between the common rafters and overhang rafters.

4. Nail the remaining overhang rafters to the lookouts to complete the gable overhangs.

Step G: Frame the Gable Walls

1. Cut the gable wall top plates to reach from the ridge to the attic kneewalls. Install the plates with their outside edges flush with the outer common rafters.

2. Mark the layouts for the gable studs onto the top plates of the main walls, following the FRONT and REAR FRAMING ELE-VATIONS, on page 412. Use a plumb bob or a level to transfer the layout marks to the top plates. Install the gable studs with 8d nails.

3. Build the door header for the front wall, and cut off the top corners to follow the slope of the top plates. Install the header.

Step H: Install the Front Siding, Fascia & Soffits

NOTE: The fascia along the eaves is plowed—it has grooves cut into the inside faces to receive the soffit panels. The fascia along the gable ends is not plowed.

1. Install the plywood siding on the front and rear walls, starting at the corners. Hold the siding 1" below the top of the concrete slab, and fasten it to the wall framing with 8d galvanized finish nails. At the gable ends, install Z-flashing along the top edge of siding, then continue the siding up to the rafters. Below the attic door opening, stop the siding about ¼" below the top wall plate, as shown in the ATTIC DOOR SILL DETAIL, on page 416. Don't nail the siding along the garage door header until the flashing is installed.

2. Mill a ⅜"-wide × ¼"-deep groove into the fascia for the eave sides and gable ends—about 36 linear ft. (see the EAVE DETAIL, on page 415). Use a router or a table saw with a dado-head blade. Locate the groove so its bottom edge is ⅞" above the bottom edge of the fascia.

3. Install the 1 × 4 subfascia along the eaves, using 8d box nails (see the EAVE DETAIL, on page 415). Hold the bottom edge flush with ends of the rafters and the ends flush with the outer faces of the outer-most rafters.

4. Install the plowed fascia along the eaves so the top of the groove is flush with the bottom edge of the subfascia—use 8d

F. Install the angled overhang rafters at the front gable, then cut and install lookouts to support the overhang rafters.

G. Use a plumb bob to transfer the gable stud layout to the top plate (overhang framing shown cutaway for clarity).

galvanized finish nails.

5. Cut perpendicular fascia pieces at the eave ends (where they meet the gable overhangs). The inside ends of these pieces should line up with the 1 × 4 corner trim, when it is installed (see the FRONT and REAR ELEVATIONS, on page 414). Cut short return pieces to run from the perpendicular fascia back to the wall. Make miter joints at all of the corners. Do not install the end and return pieces until the soffit panels are in place.

6. Install the fascia along the gable ends, holding it ½" above the rafters so it will be flush with the top of the roof sheathing. Angle-cut the bottom ends to meet flush with the end pieces.

7. Cut the soffit panels to fit between the fascia and the wall framing, allowing for the grooves and gable-end returns. Install the soffit panels, fastening them to the rafters (and soffit ledgers) with 3d galvanized box nails.

8. Install the end and return fascia pieces.

9. Using plowed fascia, cut a triangular piece (called a *pork chop*) to finish the intersection between the gable and eave soffits. Cut a piece of soffit to enclose the space between the pork chop and the walls. Install these pieces.

10. Cut holes in the soffits and install four 4 × 12" soffit vents, as shown in the EAVE DETAIL, on page 415. Locate the vents within the second rafter bay from each end, on both sides of the building.

Step I: Install the Sheathing & Roofing

1. Install the ½" plywood roof sheathing, starting at a lower corner—use 8d box nails.

2. Attach metal drip edge along the eaves, then apply 15# building paper over the sheathing. Add drip edge along the gable ends, over the paper.

3. Install the asphalt shingles, starting at the eave edges. If desired, install roof vents (see page 390).

Step J: Install the Side Siding, Trim & Garage Door

1. Install the plywood siding along the side walls, butting the top edges against the soffit panels.

2. Install the 1 × 4 horizontal trim to cover the Z-flashing on the rear wall, but do not attach the piece at the front wall in this step. Install the corner trim so the bottom ends are flush with the bottom edges of the siding.

3. Cut the two 2 × 6 rails that will support the garage door tracks (consult the manufacturer's instructions to determine the length). Fasten them at the sides of the rough opening with 16d nails (see the GARAGE DOOR TRIM DETAIL, on page 416).

4. Rip cedar 1 × 8s for the door frame to match the depth of the garage door rough opening. Install the pieces around the opening, mitering the ends at about 22½° at the corner joints.

5. Cut the 1 × 4 trim to fit around the door frame, mitering the ends at the corner joints. Install flashing along the top of the

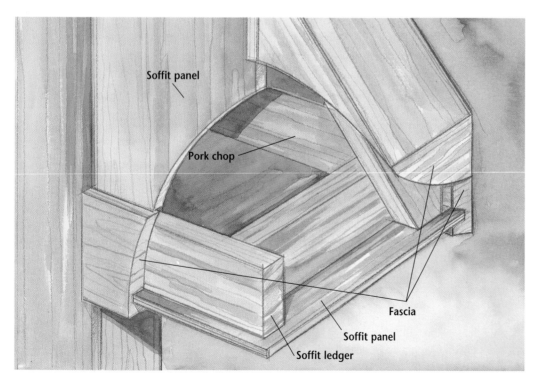

Soffit panel

Pork chop

Fascia

Soffit panel

Soffit ledger

H. *Install the fascia and soffits at the eaves and gable overhangs. Add the return fascia pieces and a vertical soffit panel capped with a pork chop. (Drawing shown cutaway for clarity).*

I. *Nail the sheathing every 6" along the edges and every 12" in the field.*

door before installing the trim (see page 399). Install the trim.

6. Install the garage door, following the manufacturer's instructions.

Step K: Build the Window

1. Using ¾" × 4" stock, cut the window frame pieces to form a rectangular frame that is ½" shorter and narrower than the rough opening. Assemble the frame with 2½" deck screws.

2. Install the window frame in the rough opening, using shims. Make sure the frame is plumb and level and the jambs are straight, and fasten the frame with 10d galvanized casing nails.

3. Cut eight 1 × 2 stops. Bevel the outer sill stop as shown in the WINDOW JAMB DETAIL, on page 416. Attach the inner stops with 6d galvanized finish nails. Order the glass to fit.

4. Install the glass and outer stops, applying glazing tape to the stops on both sides of the glass.

5. Install the 1 × 4 window trim.

Step L: Build & Install the Attic Door

1. Rip cedar 1 × 6s to match the depth of the door rough opening. Cut the head jamb for the door frame at 59" and the side jambs at 39".

2. From full-width 1 × 6 stock, cut the sill at 57½". Cut a drip edge into the bottom face of the sill by making a ⅛"-deep saw cut about ¼" from front edge.

3. Fasten the head jamb to the ends of the side jambs with 2½"

deck screws. Fasten the sill between the side jambs so it slopes down from back to front at 5° (see the ATTIC DOOR SILL DETAIL, on page 416.) Install 1 × 2 stops at the sides and top of the frame, ¾" in from the front edges.

4. Install the frame in the rough opening, using shims or cedar shingles set on the bottom of the rough opening to support the sill along its length (this will prevent it from warping or splitting underfoot). Install the frame with shims and 10d galvanized casing nails. The front edges of the side and top frame pieces should be flush with the face of the siding.

5. Build the storage doors following the ATTIC DOOR ELEVATION, on page 416. The outer dimensions of each door should be 28⅝" × 38½". Cut the 1 × 8 panel boards about ⅛" short along the bottom to compensate for the slope of the sill (see the ATTIC DOOR SILL DETAIL, on page 416). Fit the panel boards together, and trim the side pieces, if necessary. Fasten the boards to the 1 × 4 frame pieces with wood glue and 1¼" screws. Install the doors.

6. Install the horizontal 1 × 4 trim piece across the front wall, butting its top edge against the sill. Add trim around the top and sides of the door frame, butting the bottom ends of the sides on top of the horizontal trim.

J. *Frame the garage door rough opening with 1 × 8s ripped to fit.*

K. *Apply glazing tape to the inside window stops, then add the glass.*

L. *Set the attic door frame on shims to support the frame's sloped sill.*

Step C: Frame the Roof

1. Cut six 2 × 6 rafters, following the RAFTER TEMPLATE, on page 426.

2. Cut the 2 × 6 ledger at 70¾" and rip it down to 4⁵⁄₁₆" in overall width, cutting a 26½° bevel along the top edge. Mark the rafter layout onto the front face of the ledger and the top plate of the front wall, following the ROOF FRAMING PLAN, on page 423.

3. Position the ledger on the rear wall, so its outside face is flush with the outside of the wall and its ends are flush with the outsides of the side walls. Toenail the ledger to the wall plates with 10d nails.

4. Install the rafters, toenailing to the wall plates and endnailing to the ledger with 16d nails.

Step D: Complete the Side Wall Framing

1. Cut a 2 × 4 top plate to fit between the front and rear wall plates, at each side of the bin, angle-cutting the ends at 26½°. Position the plates against the undersides of the rafters so their edges are flush with the outside rafter faces. Fasten the plates to the rafters with 16d nails.

2. Use a plumb bob to transfer the stud layout marks from the bottom plates to the top plates.

3. Cut the remaining four studs to fit between the plates, angling the top ends at 26½°. Toenail the studs to the plates with 8d nails.

Step E: Install the Siding & Fascia

1. Install the plywood siding on the side and rear walls, using 8d galvanized finish nails. Hold the bottom edges ½" below the floor frame, and cut the top edges flush with the tops of the rafters. Stop the siding flush with the outside face of the front wall framing, and overlap the siding at the rear corners.

2. Cut and install the 1 × 4 fascia along the front rafter ends and the 1 × 8 fascia along the rear ends, holding the boards ½" above the top edges of the rafters to account for the thickness of the roof sheathing. You can join the corner of the fascia with mitered or butted joints (for butt joints, consider from which sides of the building the butt ends of the boards will be visible). Fasten the fascia to the framing with 8d galvanized finish nails.

3. Custom-cut the side 1 × 8 fascia boards. Angle the bottom ends so they are parallel to the horizontal cut of the rafters and so they taper to 3½" at the end—to meet the 1 × 4 fascia at the front. Mark and cut the rear ends to meet the rear 1 × 8 fascia.

Step F: Install the Sheathing & Roofing

1. Install the ½" plywood sheathing perpendicular to the rafters. Rip the first piece to width at about 41" and install it at the lower roof edge, then rip the upper piece to fit, and install it. Fasten the sheathing with 8d box nails driven every 6" along the edges and every 12" in the field of the sheets.

2. Attach metal drip edge along the front edge of the roof, then

C. *Toenail the ledger to the rear wall plates, then install the rafters. Endnail through the ledger and into the rafters.*

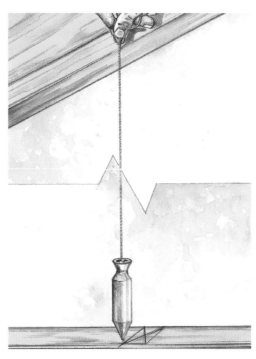

D. *Transfer the stud layout by holding a plumb bob on the stud markings and marking where the string hits the plate.*

E. *Mark the side fascia so it tapers with a horizontal line that meets the bottom edge of the 1 × 4 front fascia.*

apply 15# building paper over the sheathing. Add drip edge along the side and rear edges, on top of the paper.

3. Install the asphalt shingles, starting at the front edge of the roof. Finish the roof along the top edge with custom-cut shingles, or install a continuous roofing strip (starter strip). Cover all exposed nail heads with roofing cement.

Step G: Build & Install the Doors

1. Cut out the bottom plate from the door opening.

2. From ¾ × 3½" (actual dimension) cedar, cut the head jamb of the door frame at 57" and the side jambs at 63⅞". Set the head jamb over the side jamb ends and fasten the pieces with 2½" deck screws.

3. Cut the 1 × 2 stops and install them ¾" from the outside edges of the frame (see the DOOR JAMB DETAIL, on page 426).

4. Install the frame in the rough opening, using shims and 10d galvanized casing nails. Make sure the frame is square and plumb and the front edges of the frame are flush with the outside of the wall framing.

5. For each door, cut six pieces of 1 × 6 tongue-and-groove siding at 63¾". Fit the boards together with their ends flush, then mark the two end boards for trimming so that the total width is 27⅞". Trim the end boards.

6. Cut the 1 × 6 Z-brace boards following the DOOR ELEVA-TIONS, on page 426. (Keep the braces 1" away from the side edges.) Lay the door on a flat surface and attach the brace boards using construction adhesive and 1¼" wood screws.

7. Install the hinges and hang the door.

Step H: Add the Trim

1. Staple fiberglass bug screen to the front wall plate and the roof sheathing, to block each rafter bay (see the OVERHANG DETAIL, on page 426).

2. Cut and install the 1 × 8 trim above the door (see the OVERHANG DETAIL), overlapping the side door jambs about ¼" on each side. Notch the top edge of the board to fit around the rafters. Fasten the trim with 8d galvanized finish nails.

3. Rip two 1 × 10 vertical door trim boards to width so they will cover the 1 × 4 corner trim and about ½" of the door jamb, as shown in the DOOR JAMB DETAIL, on page 426. Cut them to length so they reach from the bottom edge of the siding to the top edge of the 1 × 8 above the door. Notch the top ends to fit around the rafters, and install the trim.

4. Cut and install a horizontal 1 × 8 bottom door trim board between the vertical boards, with its top edge flush with the floor. Install the 1 × 4 corner trim, overlapping the pieces at the rear corners.

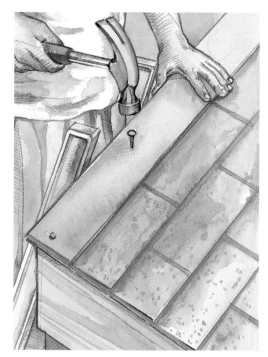

F. *Install shingle courses up to the rear edge, then finish the edge with cut shingles or a solid starter strip.*

G. *Fasten the horizontal Z-brace boards, then lay the angled board over them and mark it for cutting.*

H. *Rip the vertical door trim boards to width then notch them to fit around the rafters.*

Victorian Gazebo

A backyard gazebo provides open-air shelter from hot sun or summer showers and is by itself a decorative landscape centerpiece. The classic octagonal gazebo in this project measures 9 feet across and has a cedar-decked floor perched about two feet above the ground. Its eight posts and floor deck are supported by poured concrete piers—your local building department will tell you how deep to make them.

To improve the

look of the gazebo on the inside, the roof is framed with cedar lumber instead of pine or fir. The roof sheathing is made up of 1 × 6 tongue-and-groove cedar boards and creates an attractive paneled ceiling.

By the nature of its shape, constructing a gazebo involves many angled cuts—for these, it will help you enormously to buy or rent a compound miter saw, or better yet, a sliding compound miter saw, which will cut angles on larger pieces of lumber.

Materials

Description	Quantity/Size	Material
Foundation		
Concrete	field measure	3,000 PSI concrete
Concrete tube forms	1 @ 16"-dia., 8 @ 12"-dia.	
Framing		
Posts	8 @ 10'-0"	6 × 6 cedar
Perimeter beams	8 @ 8'-0"	2 × 6 pressure-treated
Double joists	8 @ 10'-0"	2 × 6 pressure-treated
Angled joists	8 @ 8'-0"	2 × 6 pressure-treated
Roof beams	4 @ 10'-0"	6 × 8 cedar
Hip rafters	8 @ 8'-0"	2 × 6 cedar
Intermediate rafters	4 @ 10'-0"	2 × 6 cedar
Purlins	2 @ 8'-0"	2 × 6 cedar
Collar ties	4 @ 10'-0"	2 × 6 cedar
Rafter hub	1 @ 2'-0"	8 × 8 cedar
Wood sphere	1 @ 10"-dia., with dowel screw	
Pad (center pier)	Cut from stringers	2 × 12 pressure-treated
Framing anchors		
Perimeter beams to posts	8, with nails	Simpson U26-2
Angled joists to perim. beams	16, with nails	Simpson U26
Angled joists to double joists	16, with nails	Simpson LSU26
Anchor bolts	9 @ ⅝" × 12"	Galvanized J-bolt
Posts to piers	8, with fasteners	Simpson ABU66
Perimeter beams to posts	32	½" × 6" lag screws & washers
Metal anchors—rafters to beams	24	Simpson H1
Metal anchors—rafters to hub	8, with nails	Simpson FB26
Posts to beams	8, with fasteners	Simpson 1212T
Beams to beams	8, with nails	3" × 12" × 14-gauge galv. plate
Stringers to perimeter beam	8, with nails	Simpson L50
Stairs		
Compactible gravel	4.5 cu. ft.	
Concrete form	2 @ 8'-0"	2 × 4
Stair pad	7 @ 60-lb. bags	Concrete mix
Stringers	3 @ 8'-0"	2 × 12 pressure-treated

Description	Quantity/Size	Material
Stairs (cont.)		
Stair treads	2 @ 10'-0"	2 × 6 cedar
Stair risers	1 @ 10'-0"	1 × 8 cedar
Finishing Lumber		
Decking	15 @ 8'-0", 6 @ 10'-0"	2 × 6 cedar
Deck starter	1 @ 1'-0"	2 × 8 cedar
Fascia	4 @ 10'-0"	2 × 4 cedar
Lattice	4 panels @ 4 × 8'	Cedar lattice
Stops	15 @ 8'-0" (horizontal)	5/4 × 5/4 cedar
	10 @ 10'-0" (vertical)	
Rails	11 @ 8'-0"	2 × 4 cedar
Roofing		
Roof sheathing	26 @ 8'-0", 14 @ 10'-0"	1 × 6 T&G
	V-joint cedar	
Asphalt shingles	256 sq. ft.	
15# building paper	300 sq. ft.	
Metal drip edge	36 linear ft.	
Galvanized flashing	3 linear ft.	
Roofing cement	1 tube	
Fasteners		
16d common nails	2½ lbs.	
16d galvanized common nails	1 lb.	
16d galvanized box nails	3 lbs.	
16d galvanized casing nails	1 lb.	
10d galvanized common nails	4½ lbs.	
8d galvanized box nails	3½ lbs.	
8d galvanized finish nails	2 lbs.	
3d galvanized finish nails	⅛ lb.	
1½" galvanized joist hanger nails	24 nails	
Masonry screws or nails	6 screws/nails	
3" deck screws	650 screws	
Construction adhesive	1 tube	

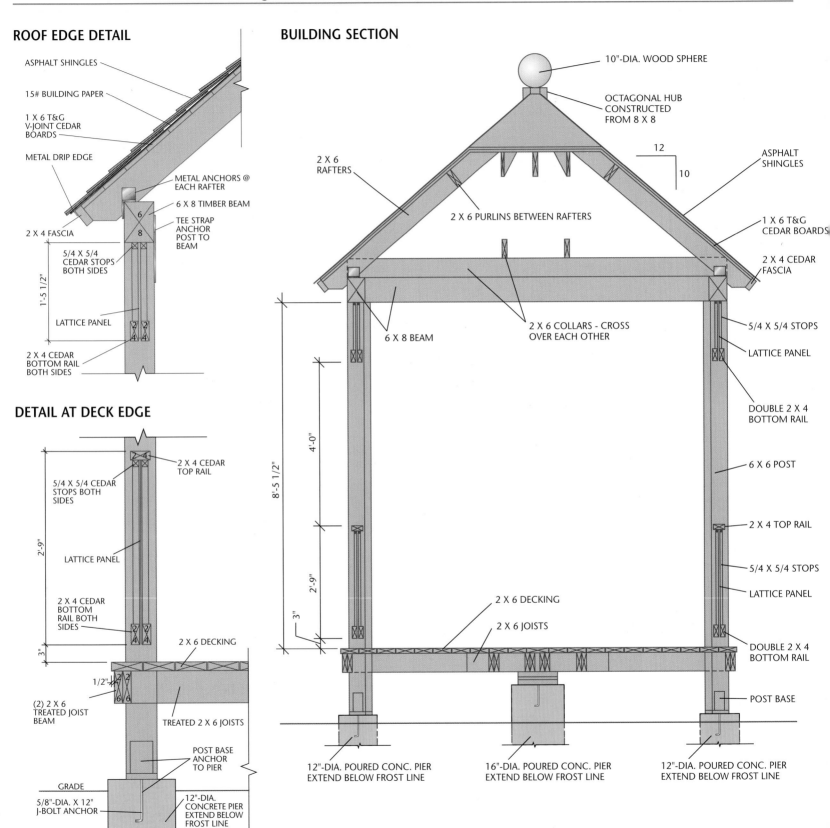

ROOF EDGE DETAIL

ASPHALT SHINGLES

15# BUILDING PAPER

1 X 6 T&G
V-JOINT CEDAR
BOARDS

METAL DRIP EDGE

METAL ANCHORS @
EACH RAFTER

6 X 8 TIMBER BEAM

TEE STRAP
ANCHOR
POST TO
BEAM

2 X 4 FASCIA

5/4 X 5/4
CEDAR STOPS
BOTH SIDES

1'-5 1/2"

LATTICE PANEL

2 X 4 CEDAR
BOTTOM RAIL
BOTH SIDES

6
8

DETAIL AT DECK EDGE

2 X 4 CEDAR
TOP RAIL

5/4 X 5/4 CEDAR
STOPS BOTH
SIDES

2-9"

LATTICE PANEL

2 X 4 CEDAR
BOTTOM
RAIL BOTH
SIDES

3"

1/2"

2 X 6 DECKING

(2) 2 X 6
TREATED JOIST
BEAM

TREATED 2 X 6 JOISTS

POST BASE
ANCHOR
TO PIER

GRADE

5/8"-DIA. X 12"
J-BOLT ANCHOR

12"-DIA.
CONCRETE PIER
EXTEND BELOW
FROST LINE

BUILDING SECTION

10"-DIA. WOOD SPHERE

OCTAGONAL HUB
CONSTRUCTED
FROM 8 X 8

12

10

ASPHALT
SHINGLES

2 X 6
RAFTERS

2 X 6 PURLINS BETWEEN RAFTERS

1 X 6 T&G
CEDAR BOARDS

2 X 4 CEDAR
FASCIA

2 X 6 COLLARS - CROSS
OVER EACH OTHER

6 X 8 BEAM

5/4 X 5/4 STOPS

LATTICE PANEL

DOUBLE 2 X 4
BOTTOM RAIL

8'-5 1/2"

4'-0"

2'-9"

3"

6 X 6 POST

2 X 4 TOP RAIL

5/4 X 5/4 STOPS

LATTICE PANEL

2 X 6 DECKING

2 X 6 JOISTS

DOUBLE 2 X 4
BOTTOM RAIL

POST BASE

12"-DIA. POURED CONC. PIER
EXTEND BELOW FROST LINE

16"-DIA. POURED CONC. PIER
EXTEND BELOW FROST LINE

12"-DIA. POURED CONC. PIER
EXTEND BELOW FROST LINE

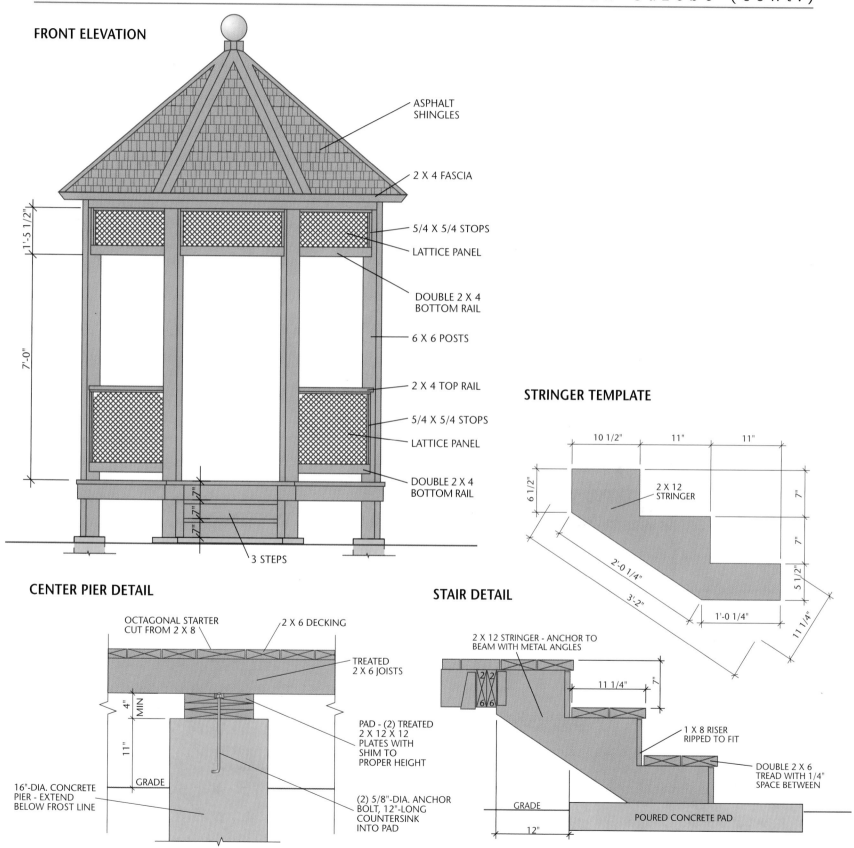

FRONT ELEVATION

ASPHALT SHINGLES

2 X 4 FASCIA

5/4 X 5/4 STOPS

LATTICE PANEL

DOUBLE 2 X 4 BOTTOM RAIL

6 X 6 POSTS

2 X 4 TOP RAIL

5/4 X 5/4 STOPS

LATTICE PANEL

DOUBLE 2 X 4 BOTTOM RAIL

1'-5 1/2"

7'-0"

7"

7"

7"

3 STEPS

STRINGER TEMPLATE

10 1/2"   11"   11"

6 1/2"

2 X 12 STRINGER

7"

7"

5 1/2"

2'-0 1/4"

3'-2"

1'-0 1/4"

11 1/4"

CENTER PIER DETAIL

OCTAGONAL STARTER CUT FROM 2 X 8

2 X 6 DECKING

TREATED 2 X 6 JOISTS

PAD - (2) TREATED 2 X 12 X 12 PLATES WITH SHIM TO PROPER HEIGHT

4" MIN

11"

GRADE

16"-DIA. CONCRETE PIER - EXTEND BELOW FROST LINE

(2) 5/8"-DIA. ANCHOR BOLT, 12"-LONG COUNTERSINK INTO PAD

STAIR DETAIL

2 X 12 STRINGER - ANCHOR TO BEAM WITH METAL ANGLES

2 X 2

6 X 6

11 1/4"   7"

1 X 8 RISER RIPPED TO FIT

DOUBLE 2 X 6 TREAD WITH 1/4" SPACE BETWEEN

GRADE

12"

POURED CONCRETE PAD

BUILDING THE VICTORIAN GAZEBO
Step A: Pour the Concrete Pier Footings

NOTE: See pages 215 to 219 for instructions on laying out and pouring concrete pier footings. Use 12"-dia. cardboard tube forms for the eight outer piers and a 16"-dia. form for the center pier.

1. Set up batter boards in a square pattern, and attach tight mason's lines to form a 9 × 9-ft. square. Take diagonal measurements to make sure the lines are square to one another. Attach two more lines that run diagonally from the corners and cross in the center of the square—this intersection represents the center of the center footing.

2. Measure 31⅝" in both directions from each corner and make a mark on a piece of tape attached to the line. These points represent the centers of the eight outer footings.

3. At each of the nine points, use a plumb bob to transfer the point to the ground, and mark the point with a stake. Remove the mason's lines.

4. Dig holes for the forms and add a 4" layer of gravel to each hole. Set the forms so the tops of the outer forms are 2" above grade and the center form is 12" above grade. Level the forms

and secure them with packed soil. Restring the mason's lines and confirm that the forms are centered under the nine points.

5. Fill each form with concrete, then screed the tops. Insert a ⅝" × 12" J-bolt in the center of the form, using a plumb bob to align the J-bolt with the point on the line layout. On the outer footings, set the bolts so they protrude ¾" to 1" from the concrete; on the center footing, set the bolt at 5". Let the concrete cure completely.

Step B: Set the Posts

1. Use a straight board to mark reference lines for squaring the post anchors. Set the board on top of one of the outer footings and on the center footing. Holding the board against the same side of the J-bolts, draw a pencil line along the board across the tops of the footings. Do the same for the remaining footings.

2. Place a metal post anchor on each footing and center it over the J-bolt. Use a framing square to position the anchor so it's square to the reference line (see photo A, on page 220). Secure the anchor with washers and a nut.

3. Set each post in an anchor, tack it in place with a nail, then brace it with temporary cross braces so that it's perfectly plumb. Secure the post to the anchor, using the fasteners recommended

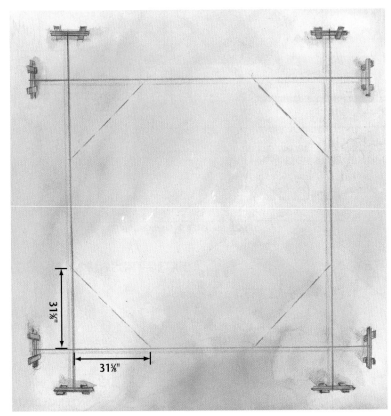

A. *Measure in 31⅝" from the corners of the string layout to mark the centers of the outside piers.*

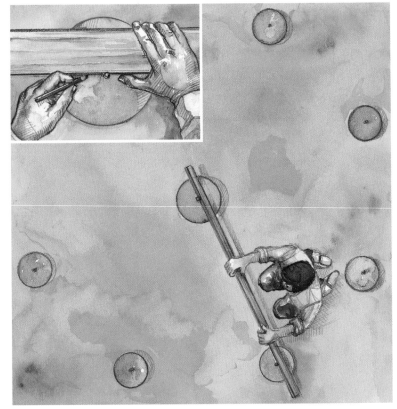

B. *Set a board across the center and each outer footing, and mark a line across the top of the outer footing (INSET).*

by the manufacturer. NOTE: You will cut the posts to length during the construction of the roof frame.

Step C: Install the Perimeter Floor Beams

1. Starting at one of the posts that will be nearest to the stairs, measure from the ground and mark the post at 19". Draw a level line at this mark around all four sides of the post. Transfer this height mark to the other posts, using a mason's line and a line level. These marks represent the tops of the 2 × 6 perimeter beams and the double joists of the floor frame.

2. Measure down 5½" from the post marks and make a second mark on all sides of each post. Notch the outer posts to accept the inner member of the perimeter floor beams, as shown in the FLOOR BEAM SUPPORT DETAIL, on page 434, using a handsaw or circular saw and a chisel.

3. Cut the inner members of the perimeter floor beams to extend between the centers of the notches of adjacent posts, angling the ends at 22½°. Set the members into the notches and tack them to the posts with two 16d galvanized common nails.

4. Cut the outer members of the perimeter beams to fit around the inner members, angling the ends at 22½° so they fit together at tight miter joints (you may have to adjust the angles a little). Anchor the perimeter beams to the posts with two ½" × 6" lag screws at each end, as shown in the FLOOR BEAM SUPPORT DETAIL. Fasten the inner and outer beams together with pairs of 10d galvanized common nails driven every 12".

Step D: Install the Double Joists

1. Fasten metal anchors to the centers of the posts so the tops of the joists will be flush with the upper line drawn in Step C (also, see the FLOOR FRAMING PLAN, on page 434).

2. Cut two 2 × 6 joists to span between two opposing posts, as shown in the FLOOR FRAMING PLAN (check the boards for crowning, and make sure to install them crown-up). Nail the joists together with pairs of 10d galvanized common nails spaced every 12".

3. Set the double joist into the hangers and leave it in place while you build and fit the wood pad that supports the joists at the center pier (see the CENTER PIER DETAIL, on page 433).

4. Cut two 2 × 12 plates—one from two of the boards you'll use for the stair stringers—and cut a shim at 11¼". Use treated plywood or treated lumber for the shim (if necessary, sand a lumber shim to the correct thickness with a belt sander.) Test-fit the pad, then remove the joist.

5. Fasten together the plates and shim with 16d galvanized nails. Drill a counterbore hole for the anchor nut and washer into the top plate, then drill a ⅝" hole through the center of the plates and shim. Secure the pad to the pier with construction adhesive and an anchor nut and washer.

6. Install the double joist, fastening it to the anchors with the recommended nails and toenailing it to the center pad with 10d

C. Cut the post notches by making horizontal cuts with a handsaw then removing the material with a chisel.

D. Miter the ends of four of the double joists so they meet flush with the full-length joist and those perpendicular to it.

galvanized nails.

7. Cut and assemble two double joists that run perpendicular to the full-length double joist. Install the joists at the midpoint of the full-length joist, toenailing them to the joist and pad.

8. Cut the remaining four double joists so their inside ends taper together at 45°. Install the joists following the FLOOR FRAMING PLAN, on page 434.

Step E: Install the Angled Floor Joists

1. Mark the perimeter beam 11" from the post sides to represent the outside faces of the sixteen floor joists (see the FLOOR FRAMING PLAN, on page 434). Then, measure from the inside face of each post toward the center and mark both sides of the double joists at 25"—this mark represents the outside face of the angled joist.

2. Install metal joist anchors on the perimeter beams and skewable anchors on the double joists, using the recommended fasteners.

3. Cut and install the 2 × 6 angled floor joists, following the anchor manufacturer's instructions.

Step F: Pour the Stair Pad

NOTE: The concrete pad sits square to one side of the floor frame, 12" from the outside face of the perimeter beam (see the STAIR DETAIL, on page 433).

1. Using stakes or mason's line, mark a rectangular area that is 39 × 49", positioning its long side 10½" from the perimeter beam. Center the rectangle between the two nearest posts.

2. Excavate within the area to a depth of 7". Add 4" of compactible gravel and tamp it thoroughly.

3. Build a form from 2 × 4 lumber that is 36" × 42" (inner dimensions). Set the form with stakes so that the inside face of its long side is 12" from the perimeter beam and the form is centered between the nearest posts. Make sure the top of the form is level and is 19½" from the top of the perimeter beam.

4. Fill the form with concrete, screed the top flat, and float the concrete, if desired (see pages 45 to 47). Round over the edges of the pad with a concrete edger. Let the concrete cure for 24 hours, then remove the form and backfill around the pad with soil or gravel.

Step G: Build the Stairs

NOTE: The STRINGER TEMPLATE, on page 433, is designed for a gazebo that measures 21" from the stair pad to the top of the floor deck. If your gazebo is at a different height, adjust the riser dimension of the steps to match your project: divide the floor height (including the decking) by three to find the riser height for each step.

1. Use a framing square to lay out the first 2 × 12 stair stringer,

E. *Fasten the angled floor joists to the sides of the double joists with skewable (adjustable) metal anchors.*

F. *Fill the 2 × 4 form for the stair pad with concrete, then screed the top with a straight piece of 2 × 4.*

following the STRINGER TEMPLATE: Starting at one end of the board, position the framing square along the top edge of the board. Align the 11" mark on the square's blade (long part) and the 7" mark on the tongue (short part) with the edge of the board. Trace along the outer edges of the blade and tongue, then use the square to extend the blade marking to the other edge of the board. The tongue mark represents the first riser.

2. Measure 1½" from the bottom mark and draw another line that is parallel to it—this is the cutting line for the bottom of the stringer. (The 1½" is an allowance for the thickness of the treads of the first step.)

3. Continue the step layout, starting at the point where the first riser mark intersects the top edge of the board. Draw lines for the tread of the first step and the riser of the second step. Repeat this process to draw one more step and a top cutting line.

4. Measure 10½" from the top riser and make a mark on the top cutting line. Draw a perpendicular line from the cutting line to the opposite edge of the board—this line represents the top end cut.

5. Cut the stringer and test-fit it against the stair pad and perimeter beam. Make any necessary adjustments. Using the stringer as a pattern, trace the layout onto the two remaining stringer boards, then cut the stringers.

6. Attach the stringers to the perimeter floor beam with metal angles, following the layout shown in the FLOOR FRAMING PLAN on page 434.

7. From scrap pressure-treated 2 × 4 lumber, cut kicker blocks to fit between the bottom ends of the stair stringers. Fasten the blocks to the concrete pad with construction adhesive and masonry screws or nails, then nail through the sides of the stringers into the kickers with 16d galvanized common nails.

Step H: Install the Decking

1. Cut an octagonal starter piece from a cedar 2 × 8: Draw two lines across the board to make a 7¼ × 7¼" square. Make a mark 2⅛" in from each corner, then connect the marks to form an octagon. Cut the starter piece and position it in the center of the floor frame, with each point centered on a double joist. Drill pilot holes and attach the piece with 3" deck screws.

2. Cut the 2 × 6 deck boards for each row one at a time. The end cuts for each board should be 22½°, but you may have to adjust the angles occasionally to make tight joints. Gap the boards, if desired, but make sure the gaps are consistent—use scrap wood or nails as spacers. Drill pilot holes and drive two screws wherever a board meets a framing member. Measure periodically to make sure the boards are parallel to the perimeter beams. Overhang the perimeter beams by ½" with

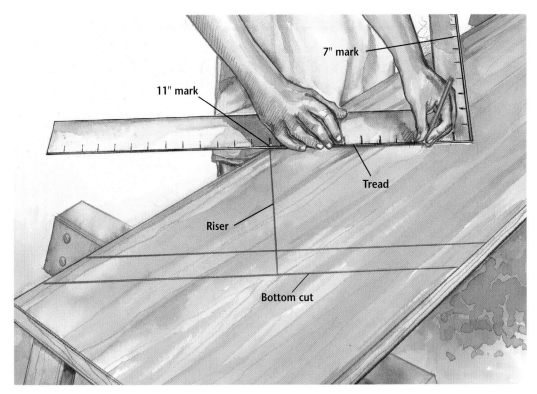

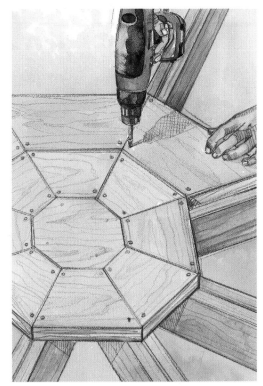

G. *Align the framing square with the top edge of the board. Make the 11" tread mark by tracing along the square's tongue, the riser mark along the blade.*

H. *Install the decking by completing one row at a time.*

439

the outer row of decking.

3. Install the 2 × 6 treads and 1 × 8 riser boards on the stairs following the STAIR DETAIL, on page 433.

Step I: Set the Roof Beams

1. Measure up from the floor deck and mark one of the posts at 101½". Transfer that mark to the remaining posts, using a mason's line and a line level. Mark a level cutting line around all sides of each post, then cut the posts with a reciprocating saw or handsaw.

2. On the top of each post, draw a line down the middle that points toward the center of the structure. Cut each of the four 6 × 8 timber beams in half so you have eight 5-ft.-long beams.

3. Set each beam on top of two neighboring posts so its outside face is flush with the outside corners of the posts. Mark the inside face of the beam where it meets the post centerlines—these marks represent cuts at each end (see the CORNER DETAIL AT ROOF BEAM LINE, on page 434). Also mark the underside of the beam by tracing along the outside faces of the posts—these lines show you where to trim off the beams so they will be flush with the outside post faces. Use a square to extend the marks down around the post sides to help keep your cuts

straight.

4. Starting from the end-cut marks, cut the beam ends at 22½°. Trim off the corners at the underside marks. Mark and cut the remaining beams, test-fitting the angles as you go.

5. Install the beams, securing them to the posts with metal T-anchors. Bend the side flanges of the anchors, as shown in the CORNER DETAIL AT ROOF BEAM LINE, on page 434, and fasten the anchors with the recommended fasteners. Tie the beams together with galvanized metal plates fastened with 16d galvanized box nails.

Step J: Install the Hip Rafters

1. Cut the roof hub from an 8 × 8 post, following the RAFTER HUB DETAIL on page 435. You can have the hub cut for you at a lumberyard or cut it yourself using a table saw or circular saw. Cut the post at 16", then mark an octagon on each end: make a mark 2⅜" in from each corner, then join the marks. The cuts are at 45°. If you use a circular saw, extend the cutting lines down the sides of the post to ensure straight cuts.

2. Draw a line around the perimeter of the hub, 3½" from the bottom end. Center a metal anchor on each hub side, with its bottom flush to the line, and fasten it to the hub using the

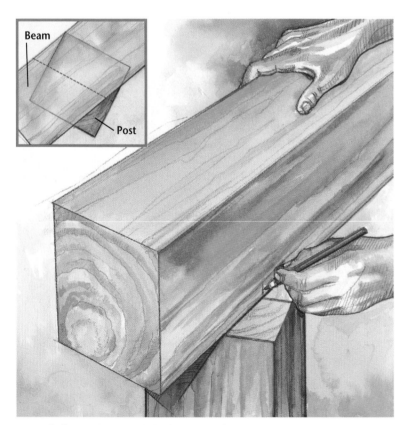

I. *Mark the inside faces of the beams at the post centerlines. Mark the beam undersides along the outside post faces (INSET).*

J. *Attach the rafters to the anchors on the roof hub, driving the nails at a slight angle, if necessary.*

recommended nails.

3. Cut two pattern 2 × 6 hip rafters, following the RAFTER TEMPLATES on page 435. Tack the rafters to opposing sides of the hub and test-fit the rafters on the roof beams. The bottom rafter ends should fall over the post centers. Make any necessary adjustments to the rafter cuts.

4. Use a pattern rafter to mark and cut the six remaining hip rafters. Install the rafters, toenailing the bottom ends to the roof beams with one 16d common nail on each side. Fasten the top ends to the anchors with 1½" galvanized joist hanger nails, then install metal anchors at the bottom rafter ends, using the recommended nails.

Step K: Install Purlins & Intermediate Rafters

1. On each side of each hip rafter, measure up from the cut edge at the lower rafter end and make a mark at 51¾"—these marks represent the lower faces of the purlins (see the ROOF FRAMING PLAN, on page 435, the BUILDING SECTION, on page 432, and the RAFTER TEMPLATES, on page 435).

2. Cut the 2 × 6 purlins, beveling the ends at 22½°. Position them between the rafters so their top edges are flush with the top edges of the rafters. Endnail or toenail the purlins to the

rafters with 16d common nails.

3. Mark the layout for the intermediate rafters onto the tops of the roof beams, following the ROOF FRAMING PLAN, on page 435.

4. Cut a pattern intermediate rafter, following the RAFTER TEMPLATES, on page 435. Test-fit the rafter and make any necessary adjustments. Use the pattern rafter to mark and cut the fifteen remaining rafters.

5. Install the rafters, endnailing their top ends to the purlins and toenailing their bottom ends to the beams with 16d nails. Install metal anchors to secure the bottom rafter ends to the beams.

Step L: Install the Collar Ties

1. Cut two 2 × 6 collar ties to span between the outsides of the roof beams, as shown in the ROOF FRAMING PLAN, on page 435. Clip the top corners of the ties so they don't project above the top edges of the intermediate rafters.

2. Install the ties to the outside faces of neighboring intermediate rafters, as shown in the ROOF FRAMING PLAN—it doesn't matter which rafters you use, as long as the basic configuration matches the plan. Fasten the ties with 10d facenails.

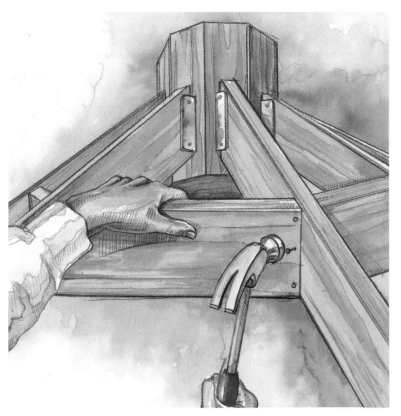

K. *Bevel-cut the ends of the purlins so they meet flush with the rafter faces, and install them between the hip rafters.*

L. *Install the collar ties so that the upper pair rest on top of, and are perpendicular to, the lower pair.*

M. *Miter the ends of the sheathing boards and make sure the tongue-and-groove joints are tight before nailing.*

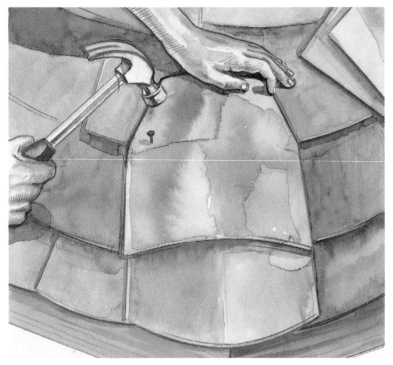

N. *Shingle the roof sides individually, then cover the hip ridges with caps, overlapping the shingles equally on both sides.*

3. Set two uncut 2 × 6 collar ties on top of—and perpendicular to—the installed collar ties so both ends extend beyond the intermediate rafters on opposing sides of the roof (see the ROOF FRAMING PLAN, on page 435). Mark the ends of the ties by tracing along the top rafter edges.

4. Cut the marked ties, then clip the top corners. Fasten the ties to the outside faces of the rafters with 10d nails.

Step M: Add the Fascia & Roof Sheathing

1. Cut the 2 × 4 fascia, mitering the ends at 22½°. Install the fascia with its top edges ¾" above the rafters so it will be flush with the roof sheathing—use 16d galvanized casing nails.

2. Install the 1 × 6 tongue-and-groove roof sheathing, starting at the lower edge of the roof. Angle-cut the ends of the boards at 22½°, cutting them to length so their ends break on the centers of the hip rafters. Fit the tongue-and-groove joints together, and facenail the sheathing to the hip and intermediate rafters with 8d galvanized box nails.

Step N: Install the Roofing

1. Install metal drip edge along the bottom edges of the roof, angle-cutting the ends.

2. Add 15# building paper over the sheathing and drip edge. Overlap the paper at each hip by 6".

3. Install the asphalt shingles on one section of the roof at a time. Trim the shingles flush with the hip ridges.

4. Cover the hip ridges with manufactured cap shingles or caps you cut from standard shingles.

5. Piece in metal flashing around the roof hub, and seal all flashing seams and cover all exposed nail heads with roofing cement.

6. Install the wood sphere on the center of the roof hub, using a large dowel screw.

Step O: Build the Overhead Lattice Screens

1. On the side faces of each post, mark the center of the post width. Then measure over, toward the gazebo center, one-half the thickness of the lattice panels and make a second mark. Use a level to draw a plumb line, starting from the second mark and extending down 17½" from the roof beam (see the ROOF EDGE DETAIL, on page 432). Draw a level line across the post face at the end of the vertical line (at the 17½" mark). Also, snap a chalk line between the vertical lines on the underside of the beams—these will guide the placement of the top inner stops.

2. Cut a cedar 2 × 4 rail to span between each set of posts, so the bottom rail edge is on the level line and the side face is on the plumb line—bevel the ends at 22½°. Fasten the rails to the posts with 3" deck screws.

3. Cut ¾" × ¾" (about 1⅛" × 1⅛" actual dimension) cedar inner stops to span between posts underneath the roof beams. Bevel the ends at 22½° and fasten the stops to the beams with 8d galvanized finish nails so their side faces are flush to the chalk lines.

4. The vertical stops of the overhead screens and the screens below the railings (Step P) are ¾" × ¾", with one edge beveled at 22½°. It will save time to rip all of them at once, using a table saw, if available—you'll need about 100 linear feet.

5. Cut and install the inner vertical stops with their sides flush to the plumb lines drawn on the posts.

6. Cut eight lattice panels at 16 × 39⅝". Set the panels against the inner stops and rails and fasten them with 3d galvanized finish nails.

7. Cut and install the outer rails and stops to complete the screens. Fasten the rails with 3" deck screws driven through the inner rails, and fasten the stops with 8d galvanized finish nails driven into the posts and beams.

Step P: Build the Railings & Lower Lattice

1. Measure up from the deck and mark the side faces of each post at 3" and 36". Draw level lines across the faces at these marks. Draw a plumb line between the level marks by finding the post center and moving inward one-half the thickness of the lattice, as you did in Step O.

2. Cut the 2 × 4 cedar top rails to fit between seven pairs of posts (skipping the two posts flanking the stairs), as shown in the DETAIL AT DECK EDGE, on page 432. Miter the rail ends at 22½° and install them with 3" deck screws so they are centered on the posts and their top faces are on the upper level lines.

3. Cut and install the 2 × 4 inner bottom rails and ¾" × ¾" stops, following the procedure in Step O.

4. Cut the lattice panels at 31 × 39⅝". Fasten the panels against the stops and lower rails with 3d galvanized finish nails.

5. Cut and install the outer bottom rails, securing them with screws, then cut and install the outer horizontal and vertical stops.

O. *Fasten the beveled inner stops (INSET) and rails so their outside faces are set back from the post centers by ½ the thickness of the lattice.*

P. *Set the lattice panels against the inner stops and rails, and fasten them with 3d galvanized finish nails.*

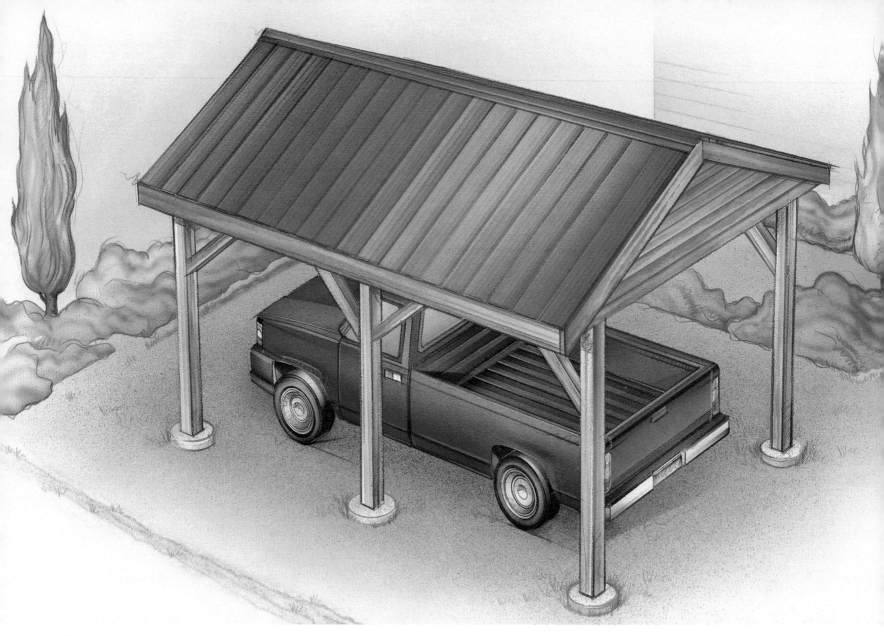

Carport

A carport provides a low-cost alternative to a garage, protecting your vehicle from direct rain, snow, and sunlight. Because it is not an enclosed structure, a carport is not held to the same building restrictions as a garage, making it a viable option in areas with strict zoning regulations.

Our carport provides a 10 × 16-ft. coverage area, large enough to accommodate most full-size vehicles. To help ease the building process, premanufactured trusses are used. When ordering trusses, specify the roof pitch, distance being spanned, and the amount of overhang of the rafter tails. Also, place your order a few weeks in advance of your project start date. Many home

centers and lumber yards carry trusses in standard dimensions and roof pitches, such as a 10-ft. span with a 6-in-12 pitch—the dimensions used in this project.

This project also features metal roofing, an attractive and easy-to-install roofing material that does not require the installation of plywood roof sheathing. Tie trusses together with 2 × 4 purlins, which provide a nailer for the metal roof panels. The panels are fastened with self-tapping metal roofing screws with rubber washers to prevent water leakage.

NOTE: Because of the scale of this project, recruit the help of at least one other person.

Materials

Description	Quantity/Size	Material	Description	Quantity/Size	Material
Foundation			Gable sheathing	2 @ 4 × 8'	¾" CDX plywood
Batterboards	10 @ 8'-0"	2 × 4	Gable fascia	4 @ 8'-0"	1 × 6 cedar
Drainage material	1⅓ cu. ft.	Compactible gravel	Side fascia	4 @ 10'-0"	1 × 8 cedar
Concrete tube forms	6 @ 14"-dia.		Siding	14 @ 8'-0"	cedar siding with 6" reveal
Concrete	field measure	3,000 PSI concrete	**Fasteners**		
Beam framing			1½" deck screws	110 screws	
Posts	6 @ 12'-0"	6 × 6 rough-sawn cedar	2½" deck screws	140 screws	
Side beams	4 @ 16'-0"	2 × 8 pressure-treated	6d galvanized common nails	1 lb.	
End beams	2 @ 12'-0"	2 × 8 pressure-treated	8d galvanized common nails	1 lb.	
Lateral beams	4 @ 10'-0"	2 × 8 pressure-treated	8d joist hanger nails	160 nails	
Diagonal supports	4 @ 8'-0"	4 × 4 cedar	10d galvanized common nails	2½ lbs.	
Roof Framing			⅜ × 4" galvanized lag screws	48 screws with washers	
Gable braces	4 @ 10'-0", 2 @ 8'-0"	2 × 4	⅜ × 5" galvanized lag screws	12 screws with washers	
Trusses	13 @ 10'-0" span	2 × 4 with 6-in-12 pitch	10d ringshank nails	4 lbs.	
Purlins	20 @ 8'-0"	2 × 4	6d galvanized casing nails	¾ lb.	
Metal hurricane ties	22, with nails	Simpson H-1	6d siding nails	1½ lbs.	
Metal hurricane ties	4, with nails	Simpson H-2.5	1" metal roofing screws with rubber washers (as specified by the metal roofing manufacturer)		
Roofing			2½" metal roofing screws with rubber washers (as specified by the metal roofing manufacturer)		
Metal roofing panels	8 @ 4' × 8'	with ridge cap and sealer strip	**Misc.**		
Gable Finishes			Exterior-grade silicone caulk	2 tubes	
Gable-end purlin blocking	3 @ 8'-0"	2 × 2	Stain or sealer	as needed	
Nailers	5 @10'-0"	1 × 6			

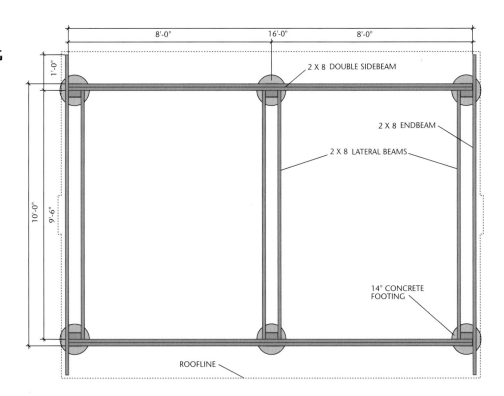

BEAM FRAMING PLAN

8'-0"   16'-0"   8'-0"

1'-0"

2 X 8 DOUBLE SIDEBEAM

2 X 8 ENDBEAM

2 X 8 LATERAL BEAMS

10'-0"

9'-6"

14" CONCRETE FOOTING

ROOFLINE

FRONT ELEVATION

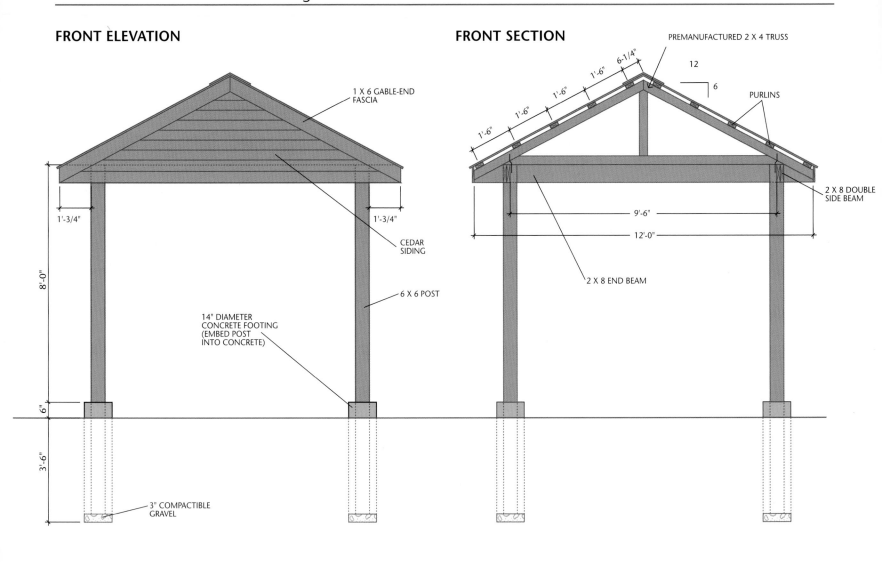

1 X 6 GABLE-END
FASCIA

1'-3/4"

1'-3/4"

CEDAR
SIDING

8'-0"

6 X 6 POST

14" DIAMETER
CONCRETE FOOTING
(EMBED POST
INTO CONCRETE)

6"

3'-6"

3" COMPACTIBLE
GRAVEL

FRONT SECTION

PREMANUFACTURED 2 X 4 TRUSS

6-1/4"

1'-6"

1'-6"

1'-6"

1'-6"

12

6

PURLINS

2 X 8 DOUBLE
SIDE BEAM

9'-6"

12'-0"

2 X 8 END BEAM

DIAGONAL SUPPORT DETAIL

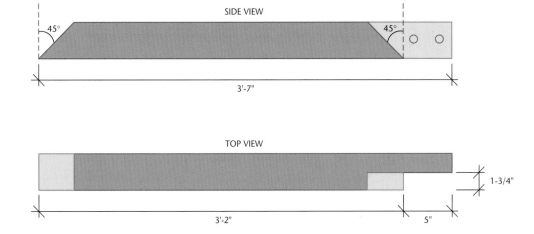

SIDE VIEW

45°

45°

3'-7"

TOP VIEW

1-3/4"

3'-2"

5"

446

SIDE ELEVATION

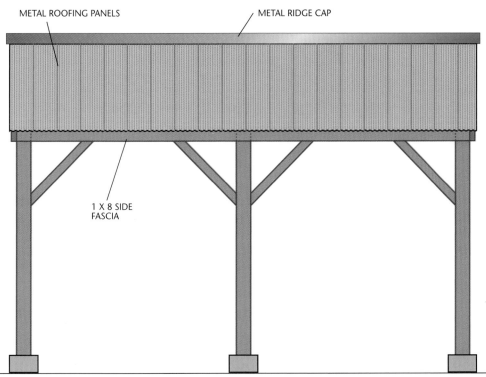

METAL ROOFING PANELS

METAL RIDGE CAP

1 X 8 SIDE FASCIA

GABLE-END DETAIL

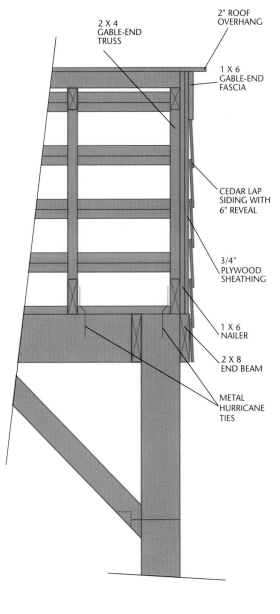

2 X 4 GABLE-END TRUSS

2" ROOF OVERHANG

1 X 6 GABLE-END FASCIA

CEDAR LAP SIDING WITH 6" REVEAL

3/4" PLYWOOD SHEATHING

1 X 6 NAILER

2 X 8 END BEAM

METAL HURRICANE TIES

SIDE SECTION

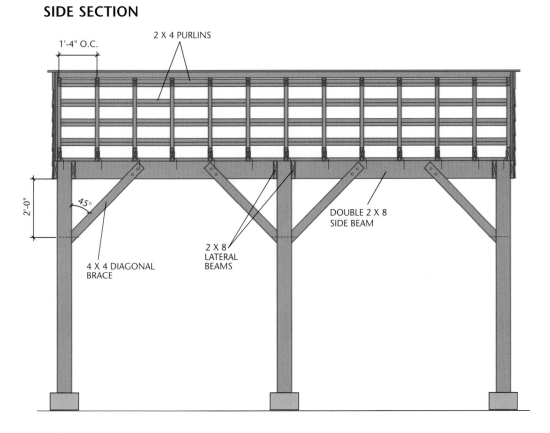

2 X 4 PURLINS

1'-4" O.C.

2'-0"

45°

4 X 4 DIAGONAL BRACE

2 X 8 LATERAL BEAMS

DOUBLE 2 X 8 SIDE BEAM

HOW TO BUILD A CARPORT
Step A: Locate the Footings

1. Lay out the rough location of the carport with stakes and string, an area 10 ft. wide and 16 ft. long. Make sure the surface is relatively flat and even.

2. Build ten 2 × 4 batterboards (pages 215 to 216). Fasten the cross pieces about 2" below the tops of the stakes, using 2½" deck screws.

3. Following the rough layout, establish the exact location of the front walls by positioning a pair of batterboards 12" outside the front rough layout string. Run a level mason's string roughly 3" inside the layout string, then remove all the rough layout stakes and string.

4. Measure along the front mason's string, and mark the centerpoint of the first post at 12", using masking tape. Measure and mark the second post at 114" from the first mark.

5. Set up additional batterboards and stretch two mason's strings perpendicular to the front wall string, so the strings intersect the centerpoints of the front posts. Use the 3-4-5 triangle method to establish right angles for both side wall strings (refer to pages 216 to 217).

6. Measure along both side wall strings and mark the centerpoint of the end posts with masking tape at 186". Set up batterboards and run a mason's string that intersects the centerpoints for the back wall.

7. Check the mason's strings for square by measuring diagonally from corner to corner, adjusting the strings until the measurements are equal.

8. From the centerpoint of the front posts, measure along the side walls 93" and mark the centerpoints of the center posts, using masking tape. Set up batterboards and run a mason's string across the centerpoints.

9. Transfer the six post centerpoints to the ground using a plumb bob, then drive wooden stakes to mark their locations.

Step B: Install the Posts & Pour the Footings

1. Remove the mason's strings, leaving the batterboards in place. Dig 14" footings at least 42" deep, using a power auger or clamshell digger. Make sure the holes are centered on the stakes. NOTE: Some local building codes may require flared footing bases and footings that extend below the frostline.

2. Pour 2" to 3" of compactible gravel into each footing hole. Cut 14"- diameter concrete tube forms to length, so the footings will be 6" above the ground. Insert the forms into the holes, then pack soil around each for support.

3. On each batterboard, measure 3" out from the original location and tack a new nail, then retie the mason's strings to establish the outside-face of each wall.

4. Place a 12-ft. 6 × 6 rough-cut cedar post into the front corner concrete form tube. Align the post with the mason's strings in both directions.

Batterboard

A. *Run mason's strings to determine the exact locations of the centerpoints of the posts.*

B. *Place a 12-ft. post in the footing hole and align with the mason's strings. Plumb the post and brace it on adjacent sides with 2 × 4s staked to the ground.*

5. Attach two 2 × 4 braces to the post on adjacent sides, using 2½" deck screws. Drive a pointed 2 × 2 stake into the ground next to the end of the brace. Check the post on adjacent sides for plumb, using a carpenter's level, making adjustments as necessary. Attach the braces to the stakes with two 2½" deck screws.

6. Install and brace the five remaining posts, then mix concrete and fill the form tubes to anchor the posts. Tamp the concrete with a long stick or rod to eliminate any air pockets. Recheck the posts for plumb, making any necessary adjustments to the braces. Let the concrete cure for 1 week.

Step C: Notch the Posts

1. Measure up from the ground 102" and mark one of the front posts. Transfer the mark onto each side of the post, using a combination square.

2. From the height reference line, run a level mason's line across the faces of each of the five remaining posts and mark. Transfer the line to all sides of the posts with a combination square, then cut off the tops of all the posts at the line, using a reciprocating saw or handsaw.

3. Scribe a 3 × 7¼" notch on the outside face of each post—the dimension of the double 2 × 8 side beams. Rough-cut the notches with a circular saw, then use a reciprocating saw to finish. Make sure to cut all the notches the same.

Step D: Install the Side Beams

NOTE: Refer to the BEAM FRAMING PLAN on page 445.

1. Cut four 2 × 8s at 192", using a circular saw, then clamp the boards together in pairs to make the side beams. Make sure the crowned edges are up and the ends are flush. Nail together using 10d common nails in rows of three, spaced every 16".

2. From one end of each side beam, measure across the top edge and mark the truss locations at 1½" and 15¼". Then, measuring from the 15¼" mark, make a mark every 16"—at 32", 48", 64" and so on, to the end of the side beam. Make a mark 1½" in from the remaining end. Following the plans, draw an "X" next to each mark, designating to which side of the line the trusses go. NOTE: Refer to the SIDE SECTION on page 447.

3. Lift the beams into the notches with the crown up. Clamp into position so the ends of the beams are flush with the edges of the posts. NOTE: Installing boards of this size and length, at this height, requires care. You should have at least one helper.

4. Counterbore two ½"-deep holes using a 1" spade bit, then drill ¼" pilot holes into each beam at the on-center locations. Drive ⅜ × 5" galvanized lag screws with washers into each hole. Seal around the screw heads with silicone caulk.

Step E: Install the End Beams

NOTE: Refer to the BEAM FRAMING PLAN on page 445.

1. Cut two 2 × 8 end beams at 144", using a circular saw, then measure in from each end and mark a reference line at 12".

2. Lift and position the end beams against the ends of the posts, with the top edge flush with the post tops. Match the

C. *Mark 3 × 7¼" notches on the outside face of each beam and cut out with a reciprocating saw.*

D. *Build the double side beams and lift into the notches. Drill counterbored pilot holes at each post, and secure with lag screws.*

E. *Cut the end beams to length, clamp in position, and drill counterbored pilot holes into the post and side beams. Fasten with lag screws.*

reference lines to the outside face of the side beams, and clamp the end beams in place. NOTE: Because of the size and length of the end beams, have the help of at least one other person.

3. Drill a pair of ½"-deep counterbore holes using a 1" spade bit, then drill 3½"-deep, ¼" pilot holes at each location. Position the holes side-by-side, so one bores into the 3" post top created by notching, and the other into the end of the side beams.

4. Fasten the end beams to the posts, using ⅜ × 4" lag screws with washers. Seal around the screw heads with silicone caulk.

Step F: Install the Lateral Beams

NOTE: Refer to the BEAM FRAMING PLAN on page 445.

1. At each pair of posts, measure the span between the interior faces of the side beams. Cut four 2 × 8 lateral beams to size, approximately 114", using a circular saw.

2. Lift each beam into position, between the side beams and against the side of the remaining 3" section of the post tops. Make sure the top edge of the beams are flush with the tops of the posts and clamp in place.

3. Drill a pair of ½"-deep counterbore holes using a 1" spade bit, then drill 3½"-deep, ¼" pilot holes at each location.

4. Fasten the lateral beams with ⅜ × 4" lag screws with washers. Seal the screw heads with silicone caulk.

Step G: Install the Diagonal Supports

1. Cut eight 4 × 4 diagonal supports to size, following the DIAGONAL SUPPORT DETAIL on page 446.

2. At each post, measure down from the side beam and mark at 26". Position the mitered end of the support against the post, aligned with the mark, and the notched-out end against the bottom edge of the inner member of the side beam (half the full double beam). Make sure the support is centered on the post, then clamp it to the side beam.

3. At the notched end, drill a pair of ½"-deep counterbore holes, using a 1" spade bit, then drill ¼" pilot holes into the side beams. Attach the support with ⅜ × 4" lag screws with washers. Seal the screw heads with silicone caulk.

4. Measure up from where the support meets the post and mark 3" on-center. Drill a ½"-deep counterbore hole straight into the support at the mark, using a 1" spade bit, then drill a ¼" pilot hole into the post. Drive a ⅜ × 4" lag screw with washer into each hole and fasten tightly. Seal the screw head with silicone caulk.

Step H: Install the Gable-end Trusses

1. To make the gable-end truss braces, cut 2 × 4s at 36" and 120", using a circular saw. Cut four pieces of each dimension to build four braces. Fasten the 36" pieces at one end of the 120" pieces, using 2½" deck screws.

2. Use two braces at each gable end. Place the 36" end of the brace at the top of the end beam, roughly 36" in from the post. Position the opposite end of the brace at the post, place a scrap

F. Measure and cut the lateral beams to size, and clamp in position. Drill counterbored pilot holes and secure the beams with lag screws.

G. Notch out one end of the diagonal supports and cut the other end at a 45° angle. Fasten the supports in position with ⅜ × 4" lag screws.

H. Align gable trusses with the reference lines on the side beams. Check for plumb, then clamp trusses to 2 × 4 braces. Toenail in place with 10d common nails. INSET: Gable-end hurricane tie.

piece of 2 × 4 between the brace and post, then clamp the brace at both the post and end beam.

3. Place the gable trusses on the ends of the side beams, flush against the braces. Align each truss with the reference marks on the side beams, then measure the overhang of each rafter tail to ensure proper placement.

4. Check to make sure the truss is plumb using a level, and clamp the truss to the braces. Use wood shims at the braces to keep the truss plumb, if necessary. Toenail the truss in place, using 10d galvanized common nails.

5. Drive a 10d nail into the rafter tail of each gable truss and stretch a mason's string between the two ends. Make sure the string is flush across the tails; this string will serve as a guide for installing the common trusses.

Step I: Install the Common Trusses

1. Install three common trusses, following the layout on the top of the side beams. Align the tails of each truss with the mason's line, and make sure they overhang the side beams evenly. Toenail into place with 10d galvanized common nails.

2. On the side of one 96" 2 × 4 starter purlin, measure from one end and mark the 16" on-center truss spacing, following the measurements used for the side beams: mark at 1½" and 15¼", then every 16" for the remaining trusses. Following your plans, mark an "X" on one side, indicating the truss placement.

3. Measure and mark 8" down from the peak on the installed trusses. Align the side of the starter purlin with the reference marks on the trusses, and the gable-end truss reference mark on the purlin with the gable truss. Check to make sure the gable-end truss is plumb, then fasten the purlin in place with 10d galvanized ringshank nails. Align the remaining trusses with the reference marks on the purlin, and fasten in place.

4. Continue installing trusses, working along the purlin and aligning each truss with the reference marks on the side beams and the starter purlin. Check each truss for plumb, then toenail in place with 10d galvanized common nails and fasten to the purlin using 10d galvanized ringshank nails.

5. At the end of the first starter purlin, measure and mark a second 96" 2 × 4 with the same truss spacing, continuing the span to the opposite gable-end truss. Align the new purlin with the reference mark on the gable-end truss and common trusses, make sure the gable-end truss is plumb, and attach the purlin with 10d galvanized ringshank nails.

6. Install the remaining trusses. Align each with the marks on the side beams and starter purlin. Check each for plumb, then toenail in place with 10d galvanized common nails, and fasten to the starter purlin with 10d galvanized ringshank nails.

7. With the trusses installed, secure each using metal hurricane ties. Fasten the hurricane ties to the side beams and 8d galvanized

I. *Align the common trusses with the reference lines on the side beams and the starter purlins. Toenail trusses in place using 10d common nails. INSET: Hurricane tie for common trusses.*

J. *Install 2 × 4 purlins across the rafter chords of the trusses, spaced every 18" on-center. Fasten with 10d ringshank nails.*

common nails and to the rafter tails with 8d joist hanger nails.

Step J: Install the Purlins

1. At each gable end, measure from the leading edge of the starter purlin and mark every 18" along the rafter chords to the tails, following the FRONT SECTION on page 446. Snap a chalk line across the rafter chords between each pair of marks.

2. Align 2 × 4 purlins across the trusses, flush with the ends of the gable-end trusses and aligned with the chalk lines, then fasten with 10d galvanized ringshank nails. (The last purlin should fall 2¼" from the ends of the rafter tails.) Repeat for the other side of the roof, then remove the gable truss braces.

3. Fasten 2 × 2 blocking to the top of each gable-end rafter chord between the purlins, using 10d galvanized common nails.

Step K: Install the Blocking & Gable-end Sheathing

NOTE: Refer to the GABLE-END DETAIL on page 447.

1. Install 1 × 6 blocking to the chords and struts of the gable-end trusses. Measure and cut pieces to length as needed, using a rafter square to mark the angles for the 6-in-12 roof pitch. (Refer to page 314 for rafter square techniques.) Install the blocking over the rafter chords so the top edge is flush with the top of the purlins and blocking. Fasten the blocking to the truss members with 6d common nails.

2. Measure the triangular shape of the gable-end wall, from the top edge of the end beam to the top edge of the blocking. Divide the area into two equal-sized triangular areas, and cut ¾" CDX

plywood to fit. Attach the sheathing with 1½" deck screws.

Step L: Install the Fascia

1. Measure, mark, and cut 1 × 6 fascia boards—two for each gable end—long enough to extend from the peak to several inches past the end of the rafter tails, using a circular saw. Use a rafter square to mark the peak-ends of the boards for a 6-in-12 roof pitch, then cut the angles, using a circular saw. NOTE: Refer to the FRONT ELEVATION on page 446.

2. Fasten the fascia boards to the gable sheathing, so the top edge of the boards are flush with the top of the sheathing. Use 6d galvanized casing nails.

3. Measure the span between the gable-end fascia boards at each end of the carport, then cut 1 × 8s to size for side fascia boards. Cut smaller board lengths to fit, if necessary, making sure seams fall on the ends of rafter tails. Fasten with 6d galvanized casing nails driven into the ends of the rafter tails. Make sure the top edge of the fascia boards do not protrude above the top of the last row of purlins.

4. Trim the ends of the gable-end fascia flush with the side fascia, using a handsaw. Drive three 6d galvanized casing nails through the gable-end fascia, into the ends of the side fascia.

Step M: Install the Metal Roofing

NOTE: Follow the instruction provided by the manufacturer when installing metal roofing.

1. Lay the first roof panel across the purlins and position it so

K. *Attach 1 × 6 blocking to the chords and struts of the gable-end trusses. Make sure the blocking covers the ends of the purlins. Cut triangular pieces of plywood sheathing and fasten to the blocking with 1½" deck screws.*

L. *Cut side fascia boards to span the length between the gable-end fascia boards. Fasten to the ends of the rafter tails with 8d galvanized finish nails.*

the finished edge of the panel extends approximately 1" beyond the gable-end fascia, and 1" past the side fascia.

2. Drive 1" metal roofing screws with rubber washers through the roof panel into the purlins. Space the fasteners according to the manufacturer's directions. NOTE: Do not drive screws into the portion of the panel that will be overlapped by the next panel.

3. Install the subsequent panels, overlapping each preceding panel according to the manufacturer's directions. Work from one gable end to the other. Install the final panel so the finished edge overhangs the gable-end fascia by 1".

Step N: Install the Ridge Cap

1. Measure and mark the location for the pre-formed rubber sealer strip at the on-center location of the starter purlin, 6¼" from the peak of the roof. Mark a reference line along the entire length of the roof.

2. Run a bead of exterior-grade silicone caulk along the reference line, then install the sealer strip. Install sealer strips to both sides of the peak.

3. Apply a caulk bead to the top of the sealer strip, then center the pre-formed metal ridge cap over the peak so it overhangs the finished edges of the gable-end roof panels by 1". At each ridge of the metal roof panels, drive 2½" metal roofing screws with rubber washers through the ridge cap and sealer strip, and into the starter purlins.

Step O: Install the Gable Siding

NOTE: Refer to the FRONT ELEVATION on page 446, and the GABLE-END DETAIL on page 447.

1. At each gable end, measure along the end beam—from fascia board to fascia board—and cut a 2"-wide starter strip (ripped from a piece of siding) to length. Use a framing square or rafter square to mark cutting lines on the ends to match the 6-in-12 roof pitch, then trim with a circular saw. Nail the strip to the end beam, flush with the bottom edge, using 6d siding nails.

2. Measure and mark a cutting line that matches the 6-in-12 roof pitch onto the end of a scrap piece of siding, using a framing square or a rafter square. Cut the siding at the roof pitch line, and use it as a template to mark siding for cutting.

3. Measure, mark, and cut the first piece of siding to length, using the template to mark the ends for cutting. Place the siding over the starter strip, overlapping the bottom edge of the strip by ¼". Fasten with pairs of 6d siding nails, spaced every 12".

4. Cut the next siding board so it overlaps the one below, creating a consistent reveal (amount of exposed siding). Be sure to keep the siding level. Continue to cut and install siding pieces until reaching the peak of the gable.

5. Stain or seal any exposed cedar, such as the gable ends, side fascia, and posts.

M. *Install metal roofing so each subsequent panel overlaps the previous. Fasten to the purlins, using self-tapping screws with rubber washers.*

N. *Attach the sealer strips (INSET) near the roof peak with a bead of caulk, then drive screws at each ridge in the roofing panels to secure the ridge cap.*

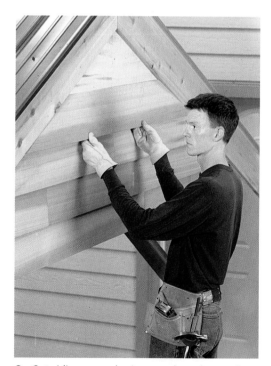

O. *Cut siding so each piece overlaps the previous to create a consistent reveal. Continue to install siding until reaching the gable peak.*

Shed & Outbuilding Ideas

© Saxon Holt

© Saxon Holt

(above) **This rustic shed is ideally suited** to the expansive garden and rural atmosphere of this landscape. The extended shed roof provides cover for a work space with potting bench.

(left) **An elegant, open gazebo** provides a spot for enjoying this large water feature and bulb garden. Gazebos are best placed where they take advantage of key landscape features.

© ColdSnap Photography/John Gregor

(above) **This large outbuilding** blends well with the landscape. Lush vines climb up the side of the structure, and an integrated fenceline ties the shed to the rest of the landscape.

(below) **A studio outbuilding** creates private space for work, study, or hobby. Outbuildings can provide space that is lacking in the home.

© Derek Fell

(right) **This classic lean-to shed** blends mortared stone walls, metal roofing, and a simple wooden door to create a charming back yard original.

© Derek Fell

© Jerry Pavia

Accessories

With your larger projects (such as decks, porches, and sheds) completed, there are many other elements you can add to your outdoor home that will not only make it a more functional and usable space, but also a more enjoyable one.

Building an arbor over a patio or deck can help block out the glaring sun and provide shade for wide-open, treeless yards. Garden ponds and ornamental fountains can be used to establish unique focal points and help create a tranquil setting. Installing a fire pit in the backyard can create a cozy campfire retreat—the perfect way to end a day with family and friends.

When choosing a site, consider the ways you will use the element. A play structure may be better suited farther back in the yard, but within view of an accessible window in the house so you can keep an eye on the kids.

Also research your local building codes—they can be determining factors in where and how you install certain projects. For instance, most codes require that a fire pit be positioned a minimum distance from the house or any other combustible materials, such as a wood fence or deck.

Adding elements such as these increase the overall value of your entire home, and make it a much more comfortable place to live.

Children's Play Structure

Children like to be active, and a play structure provides them with a space all their own, designed specifically with playtime in mind. Play structures provide places for children to have fun, and help them develop physical strength and skills, such as balance and agility.

The play structure shown here has been carefully designed to provide a fun and safe activity area for your children. The ladders leading up to the clubhouse tower are angled to maximize the play areas above and below the structure. Balusters and stringers frame all entrances and exits to enclose the clubhouse, reducing the risk of injuries due to falls. Also, milled cedar timbers are used in the construction to soften sharp corners and prevent splintering.

Though the play structure is installed on a grass surface, it can easily be adapted for a softer, loosefill floor, like sand, pea gravel, or wood chips. Just add the depth of the loosefill flooring material—typically 8" to 12"—to the length of the ladder legs,

and anchor the structure at the solid subbase level. Refer to pages 64 to 65 for information on installing loosefill material. NOTE: Page 492 provides resources for play structure hardware—such as metal gussets—and full kits.

TOOLS & MATERIALS

- Tape measure
- Reciprocating saw or handsaw
- Drill
- 1⁵⁄₁₆" Forsner bit or spade bit
- Round file
- Mallet
- Framing square
- ⅞", 1⅛", 1⅜" spade bits
- Ratchet wrench
- Circular saw
- Bar clamps (various sizes)

- Level
- Combination square
- 6-ft. steel fence post
- 36¼" tubular steel ladder rungs (10)
- 4", 5", 6½", 7", 7½", 11" carriage bolts with washers
- ⁵⁄₁₆ × 1½", ⁵⁄₁₆ × 2½", ⁵⁄₁₆ × 3½", ⅜ × 1½", ⅜ × 4", ⅜ × 5½", galvanized lag screws with washers
- 2", 2½", 3" galvanized deck screws
- Angled metal braces (4)

- 16" 2 × 2 green-treated stakes (6)
- Metal A-frame gusset
- Swing hanger clamps (6)
- #10 × 1½" sheet metal screws
- String
- ¾" galvanized hex bolts with lock washers
- Angle irons with ¾" screws (2)
- 4" mending plates with ¾" screws (2)

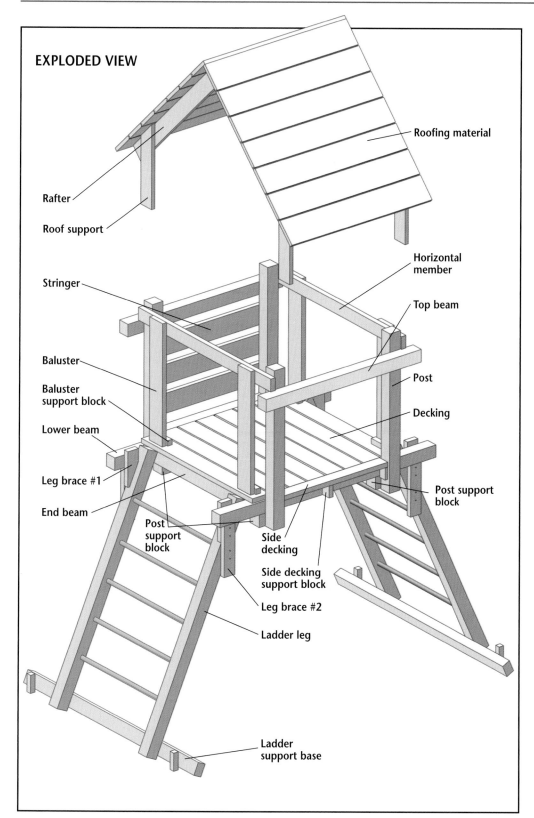

EXPLODED VIEW

Rafter

Roof support

Stringer

Baluster

Baluster support block

Lower beam

Leg brace #1

End beam

Post support block

Roofing material

Horizontal member

Top beam

Post

Decking

Post support block

Side decking

Side decking support block

Leg brace #2

Ladder leg

Ladder support base

Lumber List

Qty.	Size	Part
4	4 × 4" × 70"	Ladder leg
2	3 × 4" × 72"	Ladder support base*
2	4 × 4" × 71"	Lower beam
4	2 × 4" × 12¾"	Leg brace #1
4	2 × 4" × 15¼"	Leg brace #2
8	⅝ × 6" × 47"	Decking
3	4 × 4" × 41"	Deck end beam, mid-beam (not shown)
4	4 × 4" × 44"	Post
4	4 × 4" × 7"	Post support block
2	4 × 4" × 51"	Top beam
2	2 × 4" × 56"	Horizontal member
4	2 × 4" × 18"	Roof support **
2	1 × 4" × 34"	Side decking
4	1 × 4" × 2¼"	Side decking support block
2	2 × 4" × 3½"	Side decking mid-support block
3	⅝ × 6" × 37"	Stringer
4	⅝ × 6" × 34"	Baluster
4	2 × 2" × 7"	Baluster support block
2	4 × 4" × 113"	Double swing beam
2	4 × 4" × 96"	A-frame leg
1	2 × 4" × 41"	A-frame brace
1	3 × 4" × 96"	A-frame support base *
4	2 × 4" × 39"	Rafter **
14	1 × 6" × 66"	Roofing material ***

Use cedar building materials unless otherwise noted

*Landscape timber stock

**Green-treated

***Tongue and grove cedar

FIGURE 1

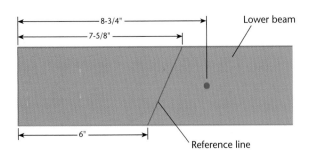

8-3/4"
7-5/8"
Lower beam
6"
Reference line

FIGURE 3

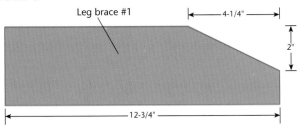

Leg brace #1
4-1/4"
2"
12-3/4"

FIGURE 2

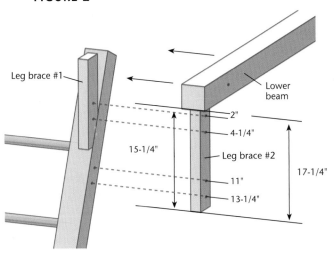

Leg brace #1
Lower beam
2"
4-1/4"
15-1/4"
Leg brace #2
11"
13-1/4"
17-1/4"

FIGURE 4

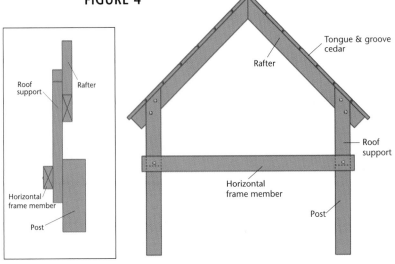

Roof support
Rafter
Tongue & groove cedar
Rafter
Roof support
Horizontal frame member
Post
Horizontal frame member
Post

FIGURE 5

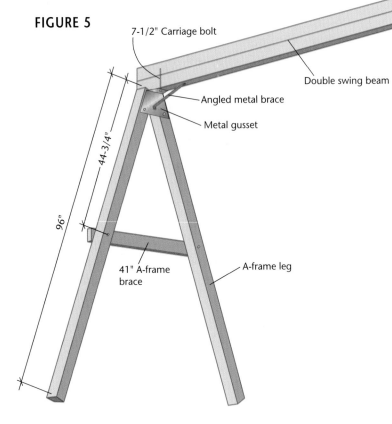

7-1/2" Carriage bolt
Double swing beam
Angled metal brace
Metal gusset
44-3/4"
96"
41" A-frame brace
A-frame leg

FIGURE 6

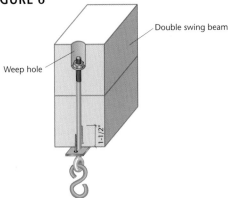

Double swing beam
Weep hole
1-1/2"

HOW TO BUILD A CHILDREN'S PLAY STRUCTURE

Step A: Assemble the Ladders

1. Cut four 4 × 4 ladder legs at 70", using a reciprocating saw. Draw a reference line down the middle of each leg, using a straightedge. Measuring from one end, mark each leg along the reference line at 3¾", 13", 24", 35", 46", and 57".

2. At the 3¾" mark, drill a ⅜" hole through each ladder leg. At the remaining marks, drill 1⅜"-deep holes using a 1⁵⁄₁₆" Forsner bit or spade bit, then round over the edges of each to a ¼" radius, using a round file.

3. Drive five 36¾" tubular steel ladder rungs into the holes of one ladder leg, using a scrap 2 × 4 and a mallet. Check the alignment of the rungs with a framing square to make sure they are straight. If the rungs are difficult to insert, apply petroleum jelly to the inside of the holes. NOTE: Loose rungs can be tightened by inserting aluminum flashing into holes. Cut flashing into ¾ × 2" strips, and install so edges are ⅛" below the edges of the holes.

4. Align the rungs with the holes of the second ladder leg, and fit them in place. Place a scrap 2 × 4 over the leg, and use a mallet to drive the rungs into the holes of the second leg, creating a 41"-wide ladder. Repeat to build the second ladder.

Step B: Build the Clubhouse Leg Assembly

1. Cut two 4 × 4 lower beams to 71". Measure in from each end and mark at 8¾", centered on the beams. Drill ⅝"-deep counterbore holes at each, using a 1⅜" spade bit, then ⅜" holes through the lower beams.

2. On the side of the beams opposite the counterbore holes, measure from each end along the top edge and mark at 7⅞". Measure along the bottom edge and mark at 6". Connect the marks with a straightedge and draw a reference line. (Refer to Figure 1 on page 460.)

3. Place the ladders between the lower beams with the counterbore holes facing out. Align the counterbore holes with the pilot holes at the tops of the ladder legs. Use a ratchet wrench to loosely fasten the structure together, using 7" galvanized carriage bolts with washers.

Step C: Assemble the Leg Braces

NOTE: refer to Figure 2 on page 460 for the leg brace assembly detail.

1. Cut four 2 × 4 leg brace #1s, following Figure 3 on page 460. Also cut four leg brace #2s to 15¼", using a circular saw.

2. Align the ladder legs with the reference lines drawn on the beams, then clamp leg brace #1 in place so the angled edge rests on the ladder leg, and the top is 1¼" above the top face of the lower beam.

3. From the top of leg brace #1, measure down and mark at 2" and 4" on-center. Drill ¼"-deep counterbore holes at each location using a 1⅛" spade bit, then drill ⁵⁄₁₆" pilot holes through the braces. Drive ⁵⁄₁₆ × 2½" galvanized lag screws with washers through

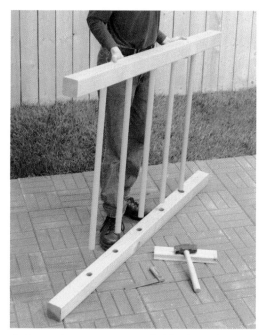

A. *Insert the rungs into one ladder leg, using a mallet and scrap board. Lift the assembly and fit the rungs into the holes of the second leg.*

B. *Position the two ladders between the lower beams, align the pilot holes, and loosely fasten with carriage bolts.*

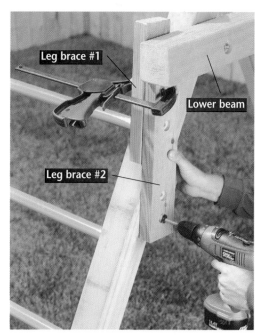

C. *Clamp the leg braces in place, drill counterbored pilot holes, and fasten to the ladder with lag screws with washers.*

brace #1 and into the lower beam, using a ratchet wrench.

4. Clamp leg brace #2 to leg brace #1, so leg brace #2 is flush with leg brace #1, and butted to the bottom face of the beam. From the top of leg brace #2, measure down and mark at 2", 4¼", 11", and 13¼", centered on the brace.

5. Drill ¼"-deep counterbore holes at each mark, using a 1⅛" spade bit, then 5⁄16" pilot holes through the braces. Fasten with 5⁄16 × 2½" galvanized lag screws with washers, using a ratchet wrench.

6. Brace the next corner, then raise and brace the other side of the structure. Fully tighten the carriage bolts joining the lower beams to the ladder legs.

Step D: Install the End Beams & Mid-Beam

1. Cut eight 5⁄4 × 6 decking boards to 47", using a circular saw. Lay one decking board across the lower beams at each end, tight against the tops of the ladders, and aligning one end flush with the edge of one beam. Drill a pair of 5⁄16" pilot holes, and use 2½" galvanized deck screws to fasten only this one end of the decking boards to the lower beams.

2. Cut two 4 × 4 end beams to 41". Clamp the end beams to the underside of the decking boards, between the lower beams and tight against the ladder legs.

3. Drill pairs of ⅝"-deep counterbore holes, using a 1⅜" spade bit, then drill ¼" pilot holes through the lower beams and into the ends of the end beams. Also drill ⅜" clearance holes for lag screw shanks to a 1" depth. Fasten the beams with ⅜ × 1½" galvanized lag screws with washers, using a ratchet wrench, until the unattached ends of the decking boards are flush with the edge of the other lower beam.

4. Drill pairs of 5⁄16" pilot holes through the unattached ends of the decking boards, and fasten to the other lower beam, using 2½" galvanized deck screws.

5. Cut one 4 × 4 mid-beam at 41". Center it between the end beams and clamp to the decking boards. Drill pairs of ½"-deep counterbore holes, using a 1⅜" spade bit, then ¼" pilot holes through the end beams and into the mid-beam. Also drill ⅜" clearance holes, 1" deep, for the lag screw shanks. Fasten with ⅜ × 5½" galvanized lag screws with washers, using a ratchet wrench.

6. Drill 5⁄16" pilot holes and fasten the decking boards to the mid-beam, using 2½" galvanized deck screws.

Step E: Add the Ladder Support Base

1. Cut two 3 × 4 landscape timbers at 72" for ladder support bases, using a reciprocating saw.

2. Check to make sure the clubhouse is level. Center the ladder support bases against the inside faces of the ladder legs. Set each base into the ground, using a mallet.

3. Clamp the support bases to the ladders. Drill a ½"-deep counterbore hole, using a 1⅜" spade bit, then a ¼" pilot hole through each leg and into the base. Also drill ⅜" shank clearance holes 1" deep at each counterbore hole. Fasten with ⅜ × 5½"

D. *Attach decking boards on top of the lower beams, set tightly against each ladder. Fasten on one side only. Position and secure the end beams and mid-beam, then fasten the other ends of the decking boards.*

E. *With the lower structure on level ground and the ladder support bases attached to the bottom of the ladders, drive anchor stakes into the ground at each end of the base, then attach the stakes to the bases with lag screws.*

galvanized lag screws with washers, using a ratchet wrench.

4. To add strength and stability, attach angled metal braces between the ladders and bases, using ⁵⁄₁₆ × 1½" galvanized lag screws. Also drive 16"-long 2 × 2 green-treated stakes into the ground at each end of the bases, and attach to the support bases with ⁵⁄₁₆ × 3½" galvanized lag screws.

Step F: Install the Decking & Posts

1. Evenly space the six remaining decking boards across the lower beams and mid-beam. Drill pairs of ⁵⁄₁₆" pilot holes, then fasten with 2½" galvanized deck screws.

2. Cut four 7"-long 4 × 4 blocks. Measure along one side of each post support block and mark the midpoint.

3. From one end, measure along each lower beam and mark at 16¾" and 54¼". Clamp the blocks to the underside of the lower beams, aligning the midpoint with each mark on the beams.

4. Drill 1¼"-deep counterbore holes, using a 1⅜" spade bit, then drill ¼" pilot holes through the bottom of the blocks, up into the clubhouse. Also drill 1"-deep, ⅜" shank clearance holes. Fasten with ⅜ × 4" lag screws with washers, using a ratchet.

5. Cut four 4 × 4 posts at 44". Center the posts against the lower beams and blocks at the midpoint and flush with the bottom of the blocks. Square the posts to the clubhouse using a combination square, and clamp in place.

6. At each post, drill two ⅝"-deep counterbore holes, using a 1⅜" spade bit, then drill ¼" pilot holes, one through the post and into the lower beams and one into the blocks. Also drill ⅜" shank clearance holes to a 1" depth. Fasten the posts to the lower beams with 7" galvanized carriage bolts with washers, and to the blocks using ⅜ × 5½" galvanized lag screws with washers, using a ratchet wrench.

Step G: Install the Top Beams & Horizontal Members

1. On the front side of the posts, measure down from the top and mark at 6".

2. Cut two 4 × 4 top beams at 51". Position the top beams across two posts, parallel to the lower beams, and with the top edge of the top beams at the reference marks. Make sure the ends evenly overhang the sides of the posts, check for level, and clamp in place.

3. Drill ⅝"-deep counterbore holes, using a 1⅜" spade bit, then drill ¼" pilot holes through the top beams and into the posts. Also drill ⅜" shank clearance holes to a 1" depth. Fasten the top beams to the posts with 7" galvanized carriage bolts with washers, using a ratchet wrench.

4. Cut two 2 × 4 horizontal members at 56". Also cut four 2 × 4 roof supports at 18" and angle one end at a 45° angle.

5. On the ladder sides of the posts, measure down 1½" from the tops and mark. Position the horizontal members across the posts, aligning the top edge with the marks, and sandwiching the roof supports between the members and posts (refer to Figure 4 on page 460). Make sure the members are level, then clamp in

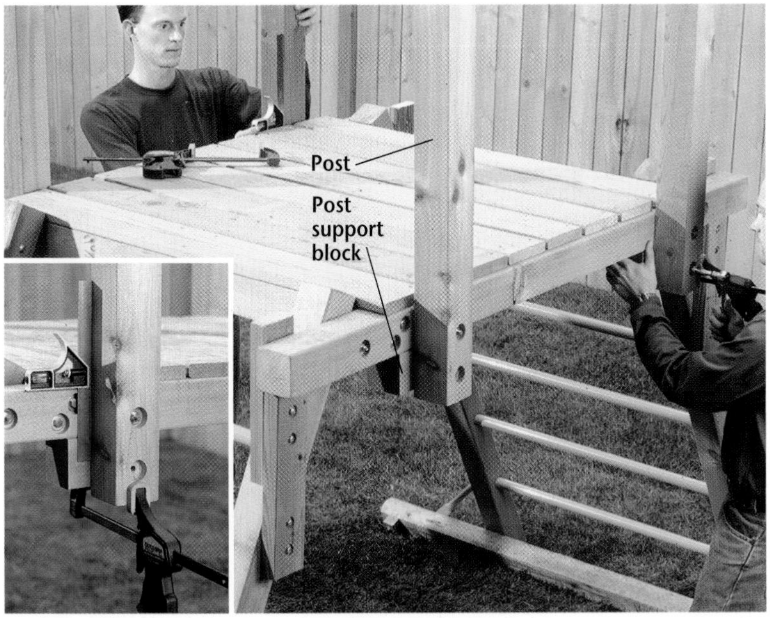

F. *Clamp the posts in place, make sure they are properly aligned and plumb (INSET), then attach to the lower beams and support blocks with lag screws.*

G. *Attach the top beams to the posts with 7" carriage bolts. Also attach the horizontal members and roof supports in place, using 6½" carriage bolts.*

place, so the ends evenly overhang the posts.

6. On the deck side of the posts, drill ½"-deep counterbore holes, using a 1⅜" spade bit, then drill ⅜" pilot holes through posts and roof supports, and into the horizontal members. Also drill ⅜" shank clearance holes to a 1" depth. Fasten using 6½" galvanized carriage bolts with washers, using a ratchet wrench.

Step H: Install the Side Decking

1. Cut two 2¼"-long 2 × 2 side decking support blocks. On the swing side of the clubhouse, place one block against each post so it is flush with the top of the lower beam. Drill two ⁵⁄₁₆" pilot holes, then fasten each with 2" galvanized deck screws.

2. Cut a 1 × 4 side decking boards at 34". Position the board on the blocks, drill a ⁵⁄₁₆" pilot hole at each end, and fasten with 2" galvanized deck screws.

3. Cut a 3½"-long 2 × 4 side decking mid-suport block. Center the block against the lower beam with the top flush against the underside of the side decking board. Drill a 1½"-deep counterbore hole, using a ⅞" spade bit, then drill a ⁵⁄₁₆" pilot hole through the block and into the lower beam. Fasten with a 3" galvanized deck screw.

4. Drill a ⁵⁄₁₆" pilot hole through the top of the side decking board into the block. Fasten with a 2" galvanized deck screw.

5. Repeat the steps to install side decking on the opposite side of the clubhouse.

Step I: Install the Stringers & Balusters

1. Cut three ¾ × 6 stringers at 37". On the side of the clubhouse with the side decking, clamp the stringers to the posts, spaced 2½" apart. Rip a scrap board to use as a spacer.

2. Drill pairs of ⁵⁄₁₆" pilot holes through each stringer, into the posts. Fasten with 2" galvanized deck screws.

3. Cut four ¾ × 6 balusters at 34", and four 7"-long 2 × 2 baluster support blocks. At one end of each baluster, fasten a block to the interior face, flush with the bottom edge. Drill a pair of ⁵⁄₁₆" pilot holes, then fasten with 2" galvanized deck screws.

4. Position the balusters so they do not obstruct the ladder entrances to the clubhouse, with the block ends on the deck and the tops against the horizontal members. Loosely fasten the top ends with 2" galvanized deck screws.

5. Check the balusters for plumb, then drill a ⁵⁄₁₆" pilot hole through the blocks and into the decking. Fasten using 2½" galvanized deck screws, then fully tighten the screws at the top ends.

Step J: Build the Swing A-frame & Beam

NOTE: refer to Figure 5 on page 460 for the A-frame and beam assembly.

1. On the swing side of the clubhouse, install two angled metal braces extending from the lower beam to the posts, using ⁵⁄₁₆ × 1½" galvanized lag screws.

2. Cut two 4 × 4 A-frame legs at 96", and one 2 × 4 A-frame brace at 41".

H. *Position a support block flush with the bottom of the side decking, and attach to the lower beam with a 3" deck screw. Attach the side decking to the block with 2½" deck screws.*

I. *Install stringers between the posts in the clubhouse tower over any opening that does not house any accessories. Fasten to the posts with deck screws.*

3. Lay the legs on a flat surface, and mark on top at 1¾" and 44¾"—this will be the inside face of the A-frame when the legs are installed. At the 1¾" mark, drill ⅜" through holes centered on the legs. At the 44¾" mark, drill ½"-deep counterbore holes, using a 1⅜" spade bit, then drill ⅜" through holes. Also drill ⅜" through holes in each end of the brace, 1¾" in from each end.

4. Attach the metal gusset to the inside faces of the legs so the gusset flange faces up. Align the top screw holes of the gusset with the 1¾" through holes on the ends of the legs. Attach the gusset with 4" galvanized carriage bolts so the washers and nuts are at the inside face. Loosely tighten each nut.

5. Position the brace against the outside face of the legs, aligning the through holes of the brace with the through holes at 44¾" on the legs. Fasten the brace to the legs with 5" galvanized carriage bolts, so the washers and nuts fit in the counterbore hole. Loosely tighten each nut.

6. Adjust the A-frame legs to create a symmetrical triangle, then tighten all the nuts. Drill a ⁷⁄₃₂" pilot hole into each leg at the two remaining screw holes in the gusset, then secure with ⅜ × 1½" galvanized lag screws with washers.

7. Cut two 4 × 4 swing beams at 113". Clamp the beams together, then measure and mark at 5¼", 19¾", 26⅞", 34", 49⅜", 56½", 63⅝", 79", 86⅛", 93¼", and 107¾".

8. Drill 1½"-deep counterbore holes using a 1⅜" spade bit at the

marks for 19¾", 34", 49⅜", 63⅝", 79", and 93¼", then ⅜" holes through the beams at all of the locations. Also drill ¼" weep holes from the bottom edge of each counterbore hole out to the outer face of the beam for water drainage.

9. At the three pilot holes between the counterbore holes, use 7½" galvanized carriage bolts with washers to fasten the beams together.

10. Turn the beam so the bottom faces up. Install swing hanger clamps at the six counterbore pilot holes (refer to Figure 6 on page 460). Align each hanger clamp and fasten to the bottom beam with #10 × 1½" sheet metal screws. Secure the hangers at the top beam with washers and nuts.

Step K: Install the Swing A-frame & Beam

1. On the swing beam side of the clubhouse, run a level string between the two ladders at the bottom of their outside legs. Measure along the string from one end and mark the midpoint with masking tape.

2. Place the double swing beam on the ground, perpendicular to and 3½" out from the midpoint of the string. Check that the beam is square with the string, using a framing square.

3. Drive a fence stake in the ground 1½" away from the far end of the beam. Position the A-frame in front of the stake so it is perpendicular to and centered on the swing beam, using a framing square. Secure the A-frame to the stake with string.

4. With a helper, lift the beam into place, with one end on the

Counterbore hole at inside face of A-frame

Metal gusset

J. After adjusting the A-frame legs to form a symmetrical triangle, fully tighten all the carriage bolts and install ⅜ × 1½" lag screws at the remaining screw holes in the gusset to secure the A-frame.

K. With someone's help, lift the double swing beam into position. Make sure it is level and square, then fasten it to the gusset with a 7½" carriage bolt, and to the clubhouse with an 11" carriage bolt.

gusset and the other end on the top beam of the clubhouse.

5. Check that the swing beam is square and level, then align the hole in the end of the beam with the screw hole on the top of the gusset and fasten, using a 7½" galvanized carriage bolt and washer.

6. At the clubhouse, make sure the beam is centered on and squared to the top beam. Using the pilot hole in the beam as a guide, drill a ⅜" pilot hole through the top beam. Fasten together using an 11" galvanized carriage bolt with washer.

7. Position angled metal braces to connect the swing beam and top beam. Drill ⁷⁄₃₂" pilot holes, then fasten using ⅜ × 1½" galvanized lag screws with washers.

8. Drill a ⁷⁄₃₂" pilot hole into the bottom swing beam at the second screw hole of the gusset, then fasten using a ⅜ × 1½" galvanized lag screw. Attach an angled metal brace to the gusset and beam, using a ¾" hex bolt, lock washer, and nut at the gusset, and drill a ⁷⁄₃₂" pilot hole at the beam location and use a ⅜ × 1½" galvanized lag screw.

9. Connect the beam to the A-frame legs using brace plates. Drill ⁷⁄₃₂" pilot holes, then fasten the plates using ⅜ × 1½" galvanized lag screws.

10. With the beam and A-frame in place, check to make sure the beam is level and the A-frame plumb. Cut and install a 96"-long 3 × 4 landscape timber leg support base, following the same techniques in step E.

Step L: Build the Rafters

1. Cut four 2 × 4 rafters at 39". Mark and cut one end of each at a 45° angle. Butt the angled ends of two rafters together, install an angle iron at the bottom edge of the joint and fasten it, using ¾" screws. Also center a 4" mending plate over the joint and fasten it with ¾" screws.

2. Place the rafter assemblies against the inside face of the roof supports, with the mending plate facing into the structure and so the top edge of the rafters are flush with the top of the roof supports. Clamp in place.

3. Drill pairs of ⁵⁄₁₆" pilot holes and fasten the rafters to the roof supports with 2½" galvanized deck screws.

Step M: Install the Roofing

1. Cut fourteen 1 × 6 tongue and groove cedar boards at 66". Position one board on top of the rafters, flush with the ends, and with the tongue pointing toward the peak. Allow the ends to overhang the outside edges of the rafters by 6" on both sides, then clamp in place. Drills pairs of ⁵⁄₁₆" pilot holes, then fasten with 2" galvanized deck screws.

3. Working toward the peak, position subsequent boards so the groove fits over the tongue of the previous board, and so they overhang the rafters by 6" on each end. Drills pairs of ⁵⁄₁₆" pilot holes, then fasten with 2" galvanized deck screws.

4. If the last board overhangs the peak, position the board and mark the backside at the peak, then rip to size. Repeat for the other side of the roof.

L. *Cut the ends of the rafters at 45° angles, butt the ends together, and secure the joint with an angle iron and a mending plate (INSET). Align the rafter assembly with the roof supports, and secure with deck screws.*

M. *Use tongue and groove cedar to cover the roof, fastening it to the rafters with deck screws. Allow the ends to overhang the rafters by 6".*

VARIATION: PLAY STRUCTURE ACCESSORIES

A play structure is most fun when it provides a range of options. There is a wide variety of play equipment available, from simple favorites, such as swings and slides, to more elaborate equipment, like gliders, horizontal ladders, cargo nets, and rock climbing walls.

Other accessory items are designed to make play areas safer. Handles and railings help to direct appropriate play routes, while shade walls and enclosures provide shaded areas for less active play. Most equipment and accessories are made of plastics or use powder-coat paints to provide non-slip, grippable surfaces.

Many of these items can be purchased at home centers, or ordered directly from the manufacturer. Always follow the manufacturer's installation instructions when installing play structure accessories.

A sturdy slide is a play structure standard, providing a thrilling ride out of the clubhouse.

A shade wall shades the play area and provides a colorful alternative to wooden balusters or rails.

A glider is built to seat two, allowing children to swing together.

A rock climbing wall is a fun addition that creates a greater climbing challenge than a ladder.

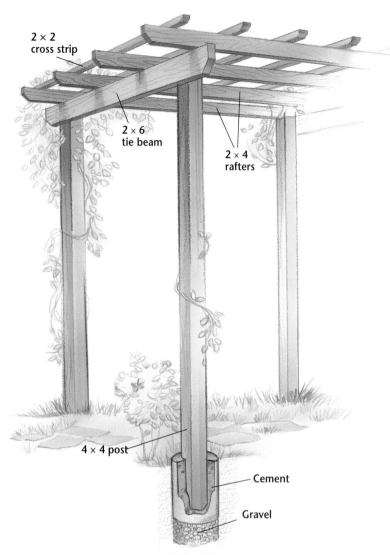

2 × 2
cross strip

2 × 6
tie beam

2 × 4
rafters

4 × 4 post

Cement

Gravel

Arbor

Arbors create a lightly shaded space and add vertical interest to your landscape. For increased shade, you can cover an arbor with meshlike outdoor fabric or climbing vines. You can even transform it into a private retreat by enclosing the sides with lattice.

Our version of a post-and-slat arbor is a 5 × 5-ft., freestanding cedar structure with an extended overhead. You can easily adapt the design to different sizes, but don't space the posts more than 8 ft. apart. If you want to build a larger arbor, add additional posts between the corner posts. Before you begin construction, check your local building code for footing depth requirements and setback restrictions.

If you want to add climbing vines, such as clematis or wisteria, plant one vine beside the base of each post. Attach screw eyes to the outside of the posts, then string wire between the eyes. As the vines grow, train them along the wires.

TOOLS & MATERIALS

- Basic tools (page 18)
- Stakes and string
- Line level
- Posthole digger
- Reciprocating saw
- Paintbrush

- Wood screw clamps
- Concrete mix
- Gravel
- Wood sealer
- 10-ft. 4 × 4 posts (4)
- 6-ft. 2 × 6 tie beams (2)

- Galvanized nails
- 7-ft. 2 × 2 cross strips (7)
- 7-ft. 2 × 4 rafters (4)
- Galvanized deck screws
- 3" lag screws (8)
- Rafter ties (8)

A. *Lay out the location of the arbor posts, then measure the diagonals to check for square.*

B. *Brace the posts into place, then use a level to make sure they are plumb.*

C. *Level and clamp the tie beam against the posts, then secure it with lag screws.*

HOW TO BUILD AN ARBOR

Step A: Dig Holes for the Footings

1. Lay out the location of the posts, 5 ft. apart, using stakes and string. Make sure the layout is square by measuring from corner to corner and adjusting the layout until these diagonal measurements are equal.

2. Dig postholes at the corners to the required depth, using a posthole digger.

3. Fill each hole with 6" of gravel.

Step B: Set the Posts

1. Position the posts in the holes. To brace them in a plumb position, tack support boards to the posts on adjoining faces. Adjust the posts as necessary until they're plumb.

2. Drive a stake into the ground, flush against the base of each 2 × 4. Drive galvanized deck screws through the stakes, into the 2 × 4s.

3. Mix one bag of dry concrete to anchor each post. Immediately check to make sure the posts are plumb, and adjust as necessary until the concrete begins to harden. Be sure to let the concrete dry at least 24 hours before continuing.

Step C: Install the First Tie Beam

1. Measure, mark, and cut all the lumber for the arbor. Cut a 3 × 3" notch off the bottom corner of each tie beam, a 2 × 2" notch off the bottom corner of each 2 × 4 rafter, and a 1 × 1" notch off the bottom corner of each cross strip.

2. Position a tie beam against the outside edge of a pair of posts, 7 ft. above the ground. Position the beam to extend about 1 ft. past the post on each side.

3. Level the beam, then clamp it into place with wood screw clamps. Drill two ⅜" pilot holes through the tie beam and into each post. Attach the tie beam to the posts with 3" lag screws.

Step D: Add the Second Tie Beam

1. Use a line level to mark the opposite pair of posts at the same height as the installed tie beam.

2. Attach the remaining tie beam, repeating the process described in #2 and #3 of Step C.

3. Cut off the posts so they're level with the tops of the tie beams, using a reciprocating saw or handsaw.

Step E: Attach the Rafters

Attach the rafters to the tops of the tie beams, using rafter ties and galvanized nails. Beginning 6" from the ends of the tie beams, space the rafters 2 ft. apart, with the ends extending past each tie beam by 1 ft.

Step F: Install the Cross Strips

1. Position a cross strip across the top of the rafters, beginning 6" from the ends of the rafters. Center the strip so it extends past the outside rafters by about 6". Drill pilot holes through the cross strip and into the rafters. Attach the cross strip with galvanized screws. Add the remaining cross strips, spacing them 1 ft. apart.

2. Finish your arbor by applying wood sealer/protectant.

D. *Attach the other tie beam and trim the tops of the posts flush with the tie beams.*

E. *Attach the rafters to the tie beams with rafter ties and galvanized nails.*

F. *Space the cross strips 1 ft. apart and attach them to the rafters.*

Raised Garden Bed

Raised beds are attractive, functional, and easy to build and maintain. Especially if your yard has poor soil, raised beds are an ideal way to add ornamental or vegetable gardens to your outdoor home. If you build a raised bed properly, fill it with high-quality topsoil and water it frequently, growing healthy plants is practically foolproof. Because these gardens are elevated, they're perfect for children as well as disabled or older family members.

In addition to their functional appeal, raised beds can serve as strong design features. They provide excellent opportunities to repeat materials used in other landscape elements. You can build raised beds from a variety of materials, including brick, cut stone, interlocking block, and landscape timbers.

As you plan your raised bed, think about the types of plants you want to grow and the amount of sunlight they need. Vegetables and most flowers need 6 to 8 hours of full sun during the day. If your yard doesn't have that much sun, plant it with woodland and other shade-loving plants.

Our version of a raised bed is 5 ft. × 3 ft., 18" deep. To build this bed, you simply stack 4 × 4 cedar timbers flush on top of one another in three layers, and secure them with galvanized nails. Then drill holes into the frame to provide drainage, which helps keep the plants healthy. Once the frame is complete, line the bed and frame with landscape fabric to prevent weed growth and keep dirt from clogging the drainage holes. If you're planting shrubs or vegetables in your raised bed, put landscape fabric on the sides only, since these plants typically have deeper root growth than flowers.

TOOLS & MATERIALS

- Basic tools (page 18)
- Reciprocating saw
- Stakes and string
- 8-ft. 4 × 4 timbers (6)
- 6" galvanized nails
- Landscape fabric
- Galvanized roofing nails
- Topsoil
- Plantings
- Mulch
- Wood sealer/protectant

3" layer of mulch

Staggered end joints

½" drainage holes

Landscape fabric

Topsoil

A. Use a shovel to remove the grass inside the outline, then dig a trench for the first row of timbers.

B. Level timbers in the trench, then lay the next layer, staggering the joints. Drill holes and drive nails through them.

HOW TO BUILD A RAISED BED

Step A: Prepare the Site

1. Outline a 5-ft. × 3-ft. area with stakes and string to mark the location of the bed. Use a shovel to remove all of the grass or weeds inside the area.

2. Dig a flat, 2"-deep, 6"-wide trench around the perimeter of the area, just inside the stakes.

Step B: Build & Level the Base

1. Measure and mark one 54" piece and one 30" piece on each 4 × 4. Hold each timber steady on sawhorses while you cut it, using a reciprocating saw.

2. Coat each timber with a wood sealer/protectant. Let the sealer dry completely.

3. Lay the first row of the timbers in the trench. Position a level diagonally across a corner, then add or remove soil to level it. Repeat with remaining corners.

Step C: Complete the Raised Bed

1. Set the second layer of timbers in place, staggering the joints with the joint pattern in the first layer.

2. Drill ³/₁₆" pilot holes near the ends of the timbers, then drive in the galvanized barn nails.

3. Lay the third row of timbers, repeating the pattern of the first row to stagger the joints.

4. Drill pilot holes through the third layer, offsetting them to avoid hitting the underlying nails. Drive the nails through the pilot holes.

5. Drill ½" drainage holes, spaced every 2 ft., horizontally

through the bottom layer of timbers.

6. Line the bed with strips of landscape fabric, overlapping the strips by 6".

7. Drive galvanized roofing nails through the fabric, attaching it to the timbers.

Step D: Fill with Soil & Plants

1. Fill the bed with topsoil to within 4" of the top. Tamp the soil lightly with a shovel.

2. Add plants, loosening their root balls before planting. Apply a 3" layer of mulch, and water the plants.

C. *Place the third layer of landscape timbers over the second, staggering the joints. Secure the timbers in place with nails. Drill 1" drainage holes through the bottom row of the timbers. Line the bed with landscape fabric.*

D. *Fill the bed with topsoil, then plant your garden. Apply a 3" layer of mulch, and water the garden.*

Fire Pit

A fire pit creates a unique space for enjoying fun and safe recreational fires. When determining a location for a fire pit, choose a spot where the ground is relatively flat and even, and at least 25 ft. from your home, garage, shed, or any other fixed, combustible structures in your yard. It is also important that a garden hose or other extinguishing device be accessible at the location.

In this project, two courses of 6" manhole block are used to create a fire pit with a 26" interior diameter, ideal for backyard settings within city limits. Manhole blocks are designed specifically to create rounded tunnels and walls and can be purchased from most concrete block manufacturers.

Three ¾" gaps have been factored into this design to act as air vents, allowing the natural airflow to stoke the fire. This layout makes the circumference of the second course roughly ½" smaller than the first. A slightly thicker layer of surface-bonding cement is added to the top course to make up the difference.

Surface-bonding cement starts out as a white paste and can be tinted to match or complement any color of capstone. The 8 × 16" landscape pavers used here are cut at angles to allow ten pieces to fit around the rim of the fire pit (see illustration on page 473). Pages 52 to 55 contain basic techniques for cutting and building with brick.

There are usually heavy restrictions for pit fires within city limits, regarding pit size, seasonal burning, waste burning, and more. Many municipalities also require that you purchase a recreational burning permit issued by an inspector from the fire department. Check with your local building department for restrictions specific to your area.

When not in use or during winter months, you may want to cover the top of the fire pit to prevent damage that may occur in inclement weather.

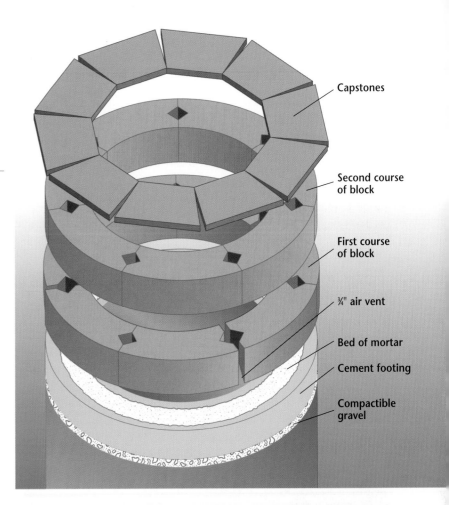

Capstones

Second course
of block

First course
of block

¾" air vent

Bed of mortar

Cement footing

Compactible
gravel

NOTE: It is important to allow your fire pit to cure for at least 30 days before building a fire in it. Heat can cause concrete with a high moisture content to greatly expand and contract, causing the material to severely crack or fragment.

TOOLS & MATERIALS

- Hammer or hand maul
- Tape measure
- Shovel
- Hand tamp
- Wheelbarrow or mixing box
- Mason's trowel
- Spray bottle
- Jointing tool
- Square-end trowel

- Tuck-point trowel
- Circular saw with an abrasive masonry blade
- Eye & ear protection
- Wire brush
- 2 × 2 wooden stakes (2)
- Mason's string
- Spray paint
- Compactible gravel
- 60-lb. concrete (12)

- Sheet plastic
- 6" manhole blocks
- ¾" wood spacers (3)
- Chalk
- Refractory mortar
- Surface-bonding cement
- Mortar tinting agent
- ½" plywood
- 8 × 16" landscape pavers (10)

HOW TO BUILD A FIRE PIT

Step A: Excavate the Site

1. Use a hammer or a hand maul to drive a wooden stake into the centerpoint of the planned fire pit location. Then drive a temporary stake into the ground 10½" from the center stake.

2. Tie a mason's string to the center stake—the string should be just long enough to reach the temporary stake. Hold or tie a can of spray paint to the end of the string. Pull the string taut and spray paint a circle on the ground.

3. Remove the temporary stake and drive it into the ground 22½" from the center stake. Pull the string taut, and spray a second circle on the ground.

4. Strip away the grass between the two circles and dig a trench 10" deep.

5. Fill the base of the trench with 2" of compactible gravel. Tamp the gravel thoroughly.

Step B: Pour the Footing

1. Mix concrete in a wheelbarrow or mixing box and shovel it into the trench until the concrete reaches ground level. Work the concrete with a shovel to remove any air pockets.

2. Screed the surface of the concrete by dragging a short 2 × 4 along the top of the natural form. Add concrete to any low areas and screed the surface again. Finish the concrete with a trowel.

3. When the concrete is hard to the touch, cover it with a sheet of plastic and let it cure for 2 to 3 days. Remove the plastic and let the concrete cure for an additional week.

Step C: Lay the First Course

1. When the concrete has sufficiently cured, lay out the first course of 6" manhole blocks with three ¾" gaps for air vents, using ¾" wood spacers.

2. Mark the internal and external circumference of the first course on the footing with chalk, and remove the blocks. Take

A. *Outline the location of the footing using spray paint and a piece of string. Then dig a circular trench 10" deep.*

B. *After tamping a 2" layer of compactible gravel in the bottom of the trench, fill with concrete and screed it with a scrap of 2 × 4. Float the surface with a trowel.*

note of any low or high spots on the footing, remembering that low spots can be leveled out with extra mortar at the base.

3. Mix a batch of refractory mortar and lightly mist the footing area with water. Throw a bed of mortar on the misted area, covering only the area inside the reference lines.

4. Set a manhole block into the bed of mortar, centering it on the footing and the chalk reference lines. Press the block into the mortar until the joint is approximately ⅜" thick. Place the second block directly against the first block with no spacing between the blocks and press it in place until the tops of the blocks are flush. Use a scrap of 2 × 4 to help you position the tops of the blocks evenly along the first course.

5. Continue laying the blocks, making sure the spaces for the three air vents are correctly positioned with the ¾" wood scraps. Do not allow the wood spacers to become set in the mortar.

6. Continue laying blocks until the first course is set. Remove any excess mortar with a trowel and finish the joints with a jointing tool.

Step D: Lay the Second Course

Dry-lay the second course of blocks over the first, offsetting the layout of the joints between the blocks. NOTE: Because of the air vents in the first course, the second course is slightly smaller in diameter. When laying the second course, line up the internal edges of the blocks, leaving a slight lip along the outer edge.

C. *Mist the footing with water and spread a bed of mortar inside the reference lines. Place the blocks of the first course in position, with three ¾" spacers in the course to create air vents.*

D. *Dry-lay the second course of block ⅜" from the outside edge of the first course. Fill any block hollows with mortar.*

Step E: Apply Surface-bonding Cement

1. Mix a small batch of surface-bonding cement according to the manufacturer's instructions. Add a mortar tinting agent, if desired.

2. Mist the blocks of the fire pit with water. Apply the surface-bonding cement to the exterior of the fire pit walls using a square-end trowel. Make up the difference in diameter between the two courses with a thicker coating of surface-bonding cement on the second course. To even out the cement, angle the trowel slightly and make broad upward strokes. Keep the top of the fire pit clear of surface-bonding cement to ensure the cap will bond to the wall properly.

3. Use a tuck-point trowel to layer the surface-bonding cement inside the edges of the air vents. Do not cover the air vents completely with surface-bonding cement.

4. Use a wet trowel to smooth the surface to create the texture of your choice. Rinse the trowel frequently, keeping it clean and wet.

Step F: Install the Capstones

1. Make a capstone template from ½" plywood, following the illustration (above right). Use the template to mark ten 8 × 16" landscape pavers to the capstone dimensions.

2. Cut the pavers to size using a circular saw with an abrasive masonry blade and a cold chisel. When cutting brick with a

masonry blade, make several shallow passes, and always wear ear and eye protection. Refer to pages 52 to 55 for techniques on building with brick.

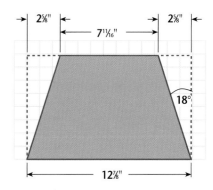

3. Mist the top of the fire pit with water. Mix a batch of mortar and fill in any block hollows, then throw a bed of mortar along the top of the second course.

4. Butter the leading edge of each capstone, and position it on the mortar bed so the front edges overhang the interior diameter of the manhole block by roughly ⅛". Adjust the capstones as you work so the joints are ⅜"-thick and evenly overhang the exterior edge of the pit. Also make sure the entire layer is even and level. Tool the joints as you work.

5. Use a jointing tool to smooth mortar joints within 30 minutes. Cut away any excess mortar pressed from the joints with a trowel. When the mortar is set, but not too hard, brush away excess mortar from the faces of the capstones with a wire brush.

6. Allow the fire pit to cure for 30 days before its first use.

E. *Mist the surface of the walls and apply surface-bonding cement with a square-end trowel. Use more surface-bonding cement on the second course to even out the gap between the courses.*

F. *Lay a bed of mortar on top of the second course and set the cap stones into place, maintaining a uniform overhang.*

Brick Barbecue

The barbecue design shown here is constructed with double walls—an inner wall, made of heat-resistant fire brick set on edge surrounding the cooking area, and an outer wall, made of engineer brick. We chose engineer brick because its stout dimensions mean you'll have fewer bricks to lay. You'll need to adjust the design if you select another brick size. Proper placement of the inner walls is necessary so they can support the grills. A 4" air space between the walls helps insulate the cooking area. The walls are capped with thin pieces of cut stone.

Refractory mortar is recommended for use with fire brick. It is heat resistant and the joints will last a long time without cracking. Ask a local brick yard to recommend a refractory mortar for outdoor use.

The foundation combines a 12"-deep footing supporting a reinforced slab. This structure, known as a floating footing, is designed to shift as a unit when temperature changes cause the ground to shift. Ask a building inspector about local building code specifications.

A note about bricks: The brick sizes recommended here allow you to build the barbecue without splitting a lot of bricks. If the bricks recommended are not easy to find in your area, a local brick yard can help you adjust the project dimensions to accommodate different brick sizes.

TOOLS & MATERIALS

- Tape measure
- Hammer
- Brickset chisel
- Mason's string
- Shovel
- Aviation snips
- Reciprocating saw or hack saw
- Mason's string
- Masonry hoe
- Shovel, wood float
- Chalk line
- Level
- Wheelbarrow
- Mason's trowel
- Jointing tool
- Garden stakes
- 2 × 4 lumber
- 18-gauge galvanized metal mesh

- #4 rebar
- 16-gauge tie wire
- Bolsters
- Fire brick (4½ × 2½ × 9")
- Engineer brick (4 × 3⅓ × 8")
- Type N mortar
- Refractory mortar
- ⅜"-dia. dowel
- Metal ties
- 4" T-plates
- Engineer brick (4 × 2 × 12")
- Brick sealer
- Stainless steel expanded mesh (23¾ × 30")
- Cooking grills (23⅜ × 15½")
- Ash pan

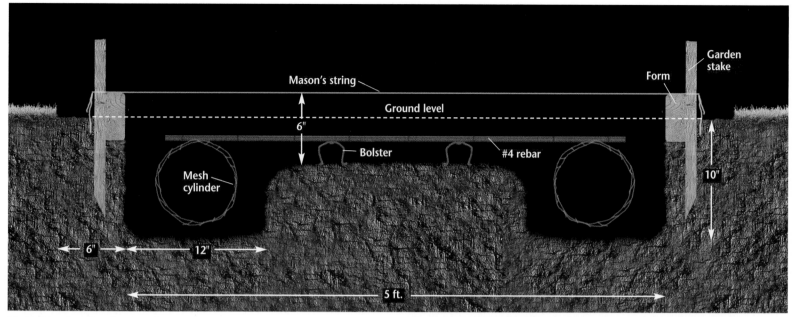

To build a floating footing, lay out a 4 × 5-ft. area. Dig a continuous trench, 12" wide × 10" deep, along the perimeter of the area, leaving a rectangular mound in the center. Remove 4" of soil from the top of the mound, and round over the edges.

HOW TO BUILD A FLOATING FOOTING

1. Lay out a 4 × 5-ft. area with stakes and string. Dig a continuous trench, 12" wide × 10" deep, along the perimeter of the area, leaving a rectangular mound in the center.

2. Remove 4" of soil from the top of the mound, and round over the edges.

3. Set a 2 × 4 wood form (page 42 to 43) around the site so that the top is 1" above the ground along the back, and ½" above the ground along the front to create a slope to help shed water. Use a mason's string and a line level to ensure that the forms are level from side to side.

4. Reinforce the footing with metal mesh and five 52"-long pieces of rebar. Roll the mesh into 6"-dia. cylinders and cut them to fit into the trench, leaving a 4" gap between each. Use bolsters where necessary to suspend the rebar.

5. Coat the forms with vegetable oil, and pour the concrete (pages 44 to 47).

HOW TO BUILD A BRICK BARBECUE
Step A: Dry-lay the First Course

1. After the floating footing has cured for one week, use a chalk line to mark the layout for the inner edge of the fire brick wall. Make a line 4" in from the front edge of the footing, and a centerline perpendicular to the first line. Make a 24 × 32" rectangle that starts at the 4" line and is centered on the centerline.

A. *Dry-lay the outer wall, as shown here, using engineer brick. Space the bricks for ⅜" mortar joints.*

B. *To make a story pole, mark one side of a straight board for eight courses of fire brick, leaving a ⅜" gap for the bottom mortar joint and ⅛" gaps for the remaining joints.*

2. Dry-lay the first course of fire brick around the outside of the rectangle, allowing for ⅛"-thick mortar joints. Start with a full brick at the 4" line to start the right and left walls. Complete the course with a cut brick in the middle of the short wall.

3. Dry-lay the outer wall, as shown here, using 4 × 3⅝ × 8" engineer brick. Space the bricks for ⅜" joints. The rear wall should come within ⅜" of the last fire brick in the left inner wall.

4. Complete the left wall with a cut brick in the middle of the wall. Mark reference lines for this outer wall.

Step B: Make a Story Pole

1. Make a story pole, using a straight 1 × 2 or 2 × 2. On one side of the board, mark eight courses of fire brick, leaving a ⅜" gap for the bottom mortar joint and ⅛" gaps for the remaining joints. The top of the final course should be 36" from the bottom edge. Transfer the top line to the other side of the pole.

2. Lay out eleven courses of engineer brick, spacing them evenly so that the final course is flush with the 36" line. Each horizontal mortar joint will be slightly less than ½"-thick.

Step C: Lay the First Course in Mortar

NOTE: Refer to pages 52 to 55 for Building with Brick techniques.

C. *Lay the first course of the outer wall, using type N mortar. Use oiled ⅜" dowels to create weep holes behind the front bricks of the left and right walls.*

D. *Place metal ties between the corners of the inner and outer walls, at the second, third, fifth, and seventh courses.*

1. Lay a bed of refractory mortar for a ⅜" joint along the reference lines for the inner wall, then lay the first course of fire brick, using ⅛" joints between the bricks.

2. Lay the first course of the outer wall, using type N mortar (page 15). Use oiled ⅜" dowels to create weep holes behind the front bricks of the left and right walls.

3. Alternate laying the inner and outer walls, checking your work with the story pole and a level after every other course.

Step D: Lay the Subsequent Courses

1. Start the second course of the outer wall using a half brick butted against each side of the inner wall, then complete the course. Because there is a half brick in the right outer wall, you need to use two three-quarter bricks in the second course to stagger the joints.

2. Continue adding courses offsetting the joists from row to row, and alternate between laying the inner and outer walls. Place metal ties between the corners of the inner and outer walls, at the second, third, fifth, and seventh courses. Use ties at the front junctions and along the rear walls.

3. Mortar the joint where the left inner wall meets the rear outer wall.

4. Smooth the mortar joints with a jointing tool when the mortar has hardened enough to resist minimal finger pressure. Check the joints in both walls after every few courses. The different mortars may need smoothing at different times.

Step E: Add T-plates

Add T-plates for grill supports above the fifth, sixth, and seventh courses. Use 4"-wide plates with flanges that are no more than ³⁄₃₂" thick. Position the plates along the side firebrick walls, centered at 3", 12", 18", and 27" from the rear fire brick wall.

Step F: Add the Capstones

1. Lay a bed of type N mortar for a ⅜"-thick joint on top of the inner and outer walls for the capstones.

2. Lay the capstone flat across the walls, keeping one end flush with the inner face of the fire brick. Make sure the bricks are level, and tool the joints when they are ready.

3. After a week, seal the capstones and the joints between them with brick sealer. Install the grills.

E. *Add T-plates for grill supports above the fifth, sixth, and seventh courses.*

F. *Install the capstones in a bed of type N mortar with a ⅜"-thick joint.*

Cobblestone Fountain

A cobblestone fountain, typically set flush with a paved garden path or surrounding grass, is attractive when the water isn't running, and delightful when it is. The cobblestone surface could be cut stone or smooth river rock, depending on your taste and what's available.

In one afternoon, with just one wheelbarrow-load of very ordinary materials, a boring corner of a garden can be transformed into a special place.

And anyone can do it—the construction is simple and the materials are inexpensive.

You can use something as simple as a five-gallon bucket for the basin. In fact, any watertight plastic vessel at least 12" in diameter and 15" deep will work. To protect children and animals, you need to cover the opening of the basin with a sturdy grate. This project uses 9-gauge ¾" expanded metal mesh, which is available at some building centers or at any steel yard.

To eliminate weeds and help keep debris out of the basin, cover the excavated area with landscape fabric.

Set the pump on a brick to keep it above the floor of the basin and out of the residue that will collect there. For extra protection, you could put the pump in a clay pot, and then fill the pot with lava rocks that will filter debris.

The illustration at right shows dimensions that worked for the fountain built here, but you can adapt them as necessary to suit your location.

If you want to build a cobblestone fountain in an area not currently served by a GFCI outlet, install one near the proposed fountain location, or call a professional electrician to install one for you.

TOOLS & MATERIALS

- Shovel
- Tape measure
- Level
- Bolt cutters
- Metal file
- Hand tamp
- Plastic bucket or tub

- Sand
- Gravel
- Bricks (2)
- Submersible pump with telescoping delivery pipe
- Landscape fabric

- 9-gauge ¾" expanded metal mesh, 30 × 36"
- 6" paving stones, (approximately 35)
- Plants and decorative stones, as desired

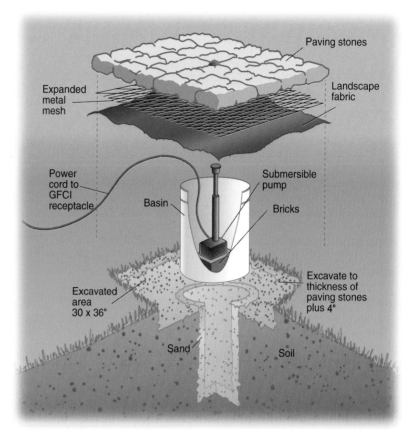

HOW TO BUILD A COBBLESTONE FOUNTAIN

Step A: Dig the Hole & Test-Fit the Basin

1. Begin digging a hole 2" to 3" wider than the diameter of the bucket or tub you selected for the basin of the fountain. Keep the edges of the hole fairly straight, and the bottom fairly level.

2. Measure the height of the basin, add the height of the paving stones you've chosen, and then add 4" to this total. When the hole is approximately as deep as this combined measurement, test-fit the basin and check it with a level. Remove dirt from the hole until the basin is as close as possible to level.

Step B: Dig the Paving Area

1. Cut out the grass or soil in a 30 × 36" rectangle surrounding the hole. To bring the surface of the fountain to ground level, dig this area 2" deeper than the height of the paving stones.

2. Spread sand over the paving area, and then dampen and

A. Dig a hole approximately as deep as the combined height of the basin and the paving stones plus 4".

B. Cut out a 30 × 36" rectangle surrounding the hole, digging 2" deeper than the height of the paving stones.

C. *Add a layer of gravel and then sand, tamping and adding sand until the top of the basin is level with the paving area.*

D. *Place the pump in the bucket, centered on the bricks. Position the electrical cord to run up and out of the hole.*

TIP: WINTER CARE

In the winter, you'll need to drain the fountain and remove the pump for storage. To empty the basin, remove the paving stones and the grate, and then place a small bucket under the spray, positioned to catch the water.

When the water level is as low as possible, remove the pump. Bail out whatever water remains, replace the grate and cover the fountain area with a tarp or sheet of heavy plastic.

tamp the sand. Continue adding and tamping the sand until you've created a level 2" layer over the entire area.

Step C: Position the Basin

1. Add about 3" of gravel to the hole, and then add a 3" layer of sand. Dampen and tamp the sand; then test-fit the basin again. Adjust until the top of the basin is level with the prepared paving area.

2. Fill the edges of the hole with gravel and/or sand to hold the basin firmly in place.

Step D: Install the Pump & the Grate

1. Clean out any sand or dirt, and then put two clean bricks on the bottom of the basin. Center the pump on top of the bricks, then extend the electrical cord up over the edge of the basin and out to the nearest GFCI receptacle.

2. Lay landscape fabric over the paving area. Extend the fabric over the edges of the basin by 5" or 6", and then trim it to shape.

Step E: Fill the Basin & Adjust the Flow Valve

Fill the basin with water. Turn on the pump and adjust the flow valve, following manufacturer's instructions. Adjust and test until the bubbling effect or spray appeals to you. (Keep in mind that the fountain's basic dimensions will be somewhat different when the paving stones are in place.)

Step F: Add the Paving Stones

1. Place the grate over the paving area, making sure the water delivery tube fits cleanly through an opening in the grate. If necessary, use bolt cutters and a metal file to enlarge the opening.

2. Put the paving stones in place, setting them in evenly spaced rows. Be sure to leave an area open around the water delivery pipe so the water has room to bubble up around the stones and then return to the basin.

Step G: Camouflage the Pump's Electrical Cord

Place plants and stones at the edge of the fountain to disguise the electrical cord as it exits the basin and runs toward the nearest GFCI receptacle.

E. Fill the basin with water and adjust the flow valve on the pump to create a pleasing effect.

F. Position the grate, and then set the paving stones in place. Be sure to leave space for water to recirculate between stones.

G. Arrange plants and stones to disguise the electrical cord as it runs to the nearest GFCI receptacle.

VARIATION: STONE OPTIONS

You can pave the fountain area with river stones, overlapping them in a fish-scale pattern.

You can even pave the fountain floor with a collection of colorful pebbles, if you cover the grate with a second layer of landscape fabric to keep the pebbles from falling into the basin.

Wash Tub Fountain

This simple wash tub fountain creatively uses common materials to create a stylish focal point for any yard or garden. Colored glass accent marbles—arranged in a yin/yan pattern here—perfectly complement the metallic sheen of the galvanized wash tub. The gentle spray of water from a submersible pump adds a soothing effect that makes this fountain a spectacular sight.

Installing a wash tub fountain can be completed in a single afternoon. Most of the materials can be purchased at a home building center, while the 9-gauge ¾" expanded aluminum grate can be found at a steel yard. The expanded aluminum grate provides a solid bed for the accent marbles, and also protects children and animals from harm.

The pattern yin/yan symbol provided below can be enlarged on a photocopier and used as a template. Or you can create a design of your own to personalize your fountain.

When determining a location for the fountain, make sure there is a GFCI receptacle nearby, or install a new one in a convenient location. After the wash tub fountain is installed, place plants and stones around the edges of the wash tub to disguise the electrical cord as it exits the basin and runs toward the nearest GFCI receptacle.

During winter months you'll need to drain the fountain and remove the pump for storage (see the TIP on page 482).

NOTE: Many of the building techniques and maintenance for a wash tub fountain are the same as for a cobblestone fountain. Refer to pages 480 to 483 for more information.

TOOLS & MATERIALS

- Drill with ¼" bit
- ½" hole saw
- Caulk gun
- Permanent marker
- Jig saw
- Shovel
- Tape measure
- Hand tamp
- Level

- Grease pencil
- Scissors
- Galvanized wash tub
- ½" watertight electrical box bushing
- Angle irons (4)
- ¼" × ½" hex bolts & nuts (8 of each)
- Silicone caulk
- Sand

- 9-gauge ¾" expanded aluminum grate
- Bricks (2)
- Fountain water pump
- Bell spout
- Clear extension tube (10" to 12")
- Landscape fabric
- Black & white glass accent marbles

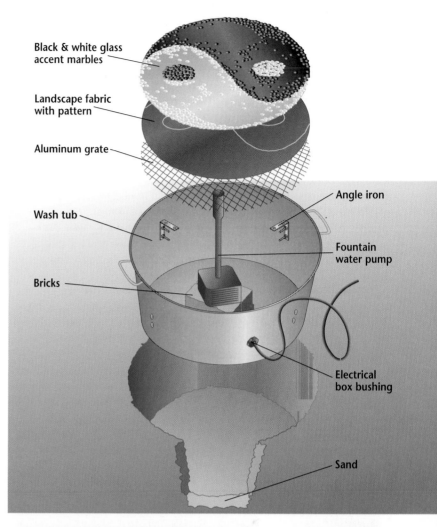

HOW TO BUILD A WASH TUB FOUNTAIN

Step A: Prepare the Wash Tub

1. Mark the location for four angle irons around the perimeter of the wash tub, 2" below the rim. Drill pairs of ¼" holes at each location, matching the hole spacing on the angle irons.

2. Fasten an angle iron on the inside of the wash tub at each location, using ¼ × ½" hex bolts with nuts.

3. Drill an exit hole for the water pump cord, 6" below the rim, using a ½" hole saw. Install a ½" watertight electrical box bushing in the hole, then run a caulk bead around edges of the bushing.

Step B: Install the Grate

1. Place the wash tub upside down on top of the expanded aluminum grate. Trace the outline of the rim on the grate, using a permanent marker.

A. *Drill four pairs of holes in the wash tub and bolt angle irons 2" below the rim, around the perimeter of the tub.*

B. *Cut the expanded metal grate to fit within the tub, then enlarge a hole in the center for the water delivery tube, using a jig saw.*

485

2. Use a jig saw with a metal cutting blade to cut the grate ½" inside the rim outline, so the grate will fit within the tub. NOTE: Line the base of the jig saw with duct tape to prevent the surface from being scratched or damaged.

3. Mark the center of the grate and cut a hole large enough for the water delivery tube of the water pump, using a jig saw.

Step C: Install the Wash Tub

1. Dig a hole that is 3" shallower than the depth of the wash tub and 2" to 3" wider than its diameter.

2. Add a 3" layer of sand to the hole. Dampen and tamp the sand, then position and level the wash tub, adding sand as necessary, until the top of the tub is 6" above ground level.

3. Position the tub so the exit hole for the water pump electrical cord is facing in the direction of the nearest GFCI receptacle. Backfill around the sides of the wash tub with black dirt to hold the tub in place.

Step D: Install the Water Pump

1. Clean out any sand or dirt, and then put two clean bricks on the bottom of the wash tub.

2. Center the pump on top of the bricks, then thread the water pump electrical cord through the hole in the side of the tub and out to the nearest GFCI receptacle. Caulk between the cord and bushing to create a watertight seal.

3. Place the expanded aluminum grate in the wash tub on the angle irons so that the water delivery tube fits cleanly through the center hole in the grate.

4. Add the bell spout to the water delivery tube, following manufacturer's instructions.

5. Fill the wash tub with water. Turn on the pump and adjust the flow valve, following manufacturer's instructions. Test and adjust the spray pattern until you find one that appeals to you.

Step E: Create the Pattern

1. Remove the grate and trace its outline and the hole for the water delivery pipe onto a piece of landscape fabric. Cut the fabric to fit on top of the grate.

2. Draw the yin/yan symbol—or other design of your choice—onto the top of the fabric with grease pencil. (Enlarge the pattern on page 484 to use as a template.)

3. Return the grate to its position in the wash tub and place the landscape fabric over it. Arrange the fabric so the symbol is in the position you prefer.

Step F: Arrange the Stones

1. Arrange black and white glass accent marbles on top of the landscape fabric, following the pattern.

2. Place plants and stones at the edge of the fountain to disguise the electrical cord as it exits the wash tub and runs toward the nearest GFCI receptacle.

C. *Dig the hole for the tub, then add a 3" layer of sand. Position and level the tub in the hole, so the top of the tub is 6" above the ground.*

D. *Set the water pump on bricks in the tub, and put the grate in place. Attach the bell spout according to the manufacturer's instructions.*

E. Cut landscape fabric to fit on top of the grate, then draw a yin/yan pattern on the fabric. Position the fabric in the tub, over the grate.

F. Set black and white glass accent marbles on top of the landscape fabric, following the yin/yan pattern.

VARIATION: PERSONALIZED PATTERN

Decorating a wash tub fountain may be the most satisfying part of the project. Glass accent marbles are available in many colors. Use them to create specific designs or mix them together to add random splashes of color. Use different materials, such as polished stones (LEFT), to add texture and contrast. Decorative grates or copper ornaments (RIGHT) can also be used.

Garden Pond

The simplest way to build a garden pond is to use a prefabricated pond liner. These easy-to-use liners, available at home centers and garden shops, come in a variety of shapes and sizes.

Most pond liners are made from PVC, rubber, or fiberglass. We've chosen a fiberglass pond liner, which is more durable than a PVC liner and less expensive than rubber. If you live in an area with exceptionally cold winters, use a rubber liner instead; fiberglass can crack if it's exposed to severely cold weather for prolonged periods.

To give the pond a more natural appearance, we set coping stones around the perimeter. When adding coping stones, don't place them over the edges of the liner—the weights of the stones can weaken and crack it.

Select the site for your garden pond carefully. A low-lying, level area provides the most natural setting, and requires far less digging than a sloped site. Ponds should not receive too much direct sunshine, however, so choose a location that is shaded for at least half the day. Do not build your pond directly under a tree—you can easily damage the tree's roots during excavation, and bacteria from fallen leaves can contaminate the pond's water. If you're going to stock the pond with fish or delicate plants, let the water sit for at least three days before you add them, to give the chlorine time to evaporate.

TOOLS & MATERIALS

- Basic tools (page 18)
- Rope
- Fiberglass pond liner
- Long 2 × 4
- Sand
- Flagstone coping stones
- Dry mortar mix

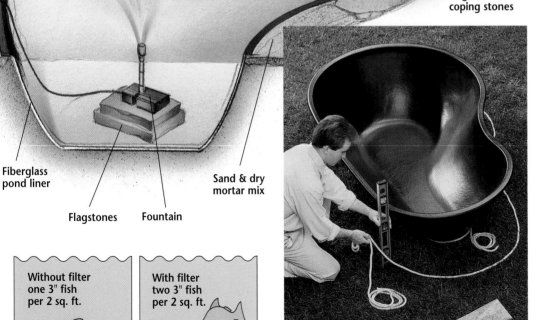

Flagstone coping stones

Fiberglass pond liner

Flagstones   Fountain

Sand & dry mortar mix

Without filter one 3" fish per 2 sq. ft.

With filter two 3" fish per 2 sq. ft.

A. Set the liner in place. Carefully outline both the base and the outside edges of the liner, using rope.

B. Excavate the site for the liner, sloping the sides toward the center. Test-fit the liner, adjusting the hole until the liner fits.

HOW TO INSTALL A GARDEN POND

Step A: Outline the Pond

1. Set the fiberglass liner in place. Outline the base of the liner, using a rope.

2. Hold a level perpendicular against the outside edge, and use it as a guide to outline the perimeter of the liner.

Step B: Excavate the Site

1. Measure the depth of the liner at the center. Excavate the base area to this depth. Dig out the remaining part of the outlined area, sloping the sides toward the flat bottom. Make this area as deep as necessary to hold the edges of the liner slightly above ground level.

2. Test-fit the shell repeatedly, digging and filling areas until the shape of the hole matches the shell.

Step C: Level the Liner

Remove any rocks or sharp objects remaining in the excavated site, then set the liner into the hole. Check the liner for level, and adjust as necessary.

Step D: Fill the Pond & Excavate for the Edging

1. Begin slowly filling the liner. As the water level rises, pack wet sand between the shell and the sides of the hole.

2. Dig a shallow trench around the perimeter of the liner, wide enough to hold the stones.

Step E. Set the Coping Stones

1. Spread a mixture of 20 parts sand to one part dry mortar evenly in the trench. Lightly spray the sand mixture with water.

2. Fit the stones together in the trench, placing them so they

VARIATION: FLEXIBLE LINER

Garden ponds can also be built with soft, PVC or rubber flexible liners that conform to any shape and size. To install, excavate the pond area as desired, add a 2" layer of sand to the floor, then place the liner into the pond bed, folding and tucking it so it conforms to the shape of the hole. Smooth it out as much as possible. Anchor the liner's corners with a few stones and fill the hole with water. Trim the excess around the perimeter of the pond, then install some form of edging, such as flagstone pavers.

don't touch the edges of the liner. Create an overflow point for excess water by setting one of the stones ½" lower than the others.

C. *Remove any rocks from the hole, and set the liner in place. Adjust the liner until the edges are slightly above the ground level.*

D. *Begin filling the liner slowly with water. Pack wet sand into any gaps between the liner and the ground.*

E. *Dig a shallow trench around the liner. Line the trench with a sand and dry mortar mix, and set the stones.*

Accessory Ideas

© Crandall & Crandall

© Angela Hartwell

(above) **This clever "outdoor room"** is created with freestanding framed walls, complete with windows. The structure creates shade and a wind shelter that can be important in food-preparation areas.

(left) **Outdoor kitchens** are convenient spaces for entertaining guests. This small patio includes integrated food-preparation accessories and built-in plumbing.

© Charles Mann

© Saxon Holt

© Saxon Holt

(above) *A large raised garden bed* built with natural stone introduces important visual interest in an otherwise flat yard.

(near right) *A well-planned play structure* has plenty of open space around it, and is placed within clear view of the house, making it easy to keep an eye on the kids.

(far right) *Water features, like this pond,* enhance the beauty of a well-groomed yard. The local stone and vegetation add to the natural appearance of the pond.

491

Conversion Charts

Metric Equivalents

Inches (in.)	1/64	1/32	1/25	1/16	1/8	1/4	3/8	2/5	1/2	5/8	3/4	7/8	1	2	3	4	5	6	7	8	9	10	11	12	36	39.4
Feet (ft.)																								1	3	3 1/12
Yards (yd.)																									1	1 1/12
Millimeters (mm)	0.40	0.79	1	1.59	3.18	6.35	9.53	10	12.7	15.9	19.1	22.2	25.4	50.8	76.2	101.6	127	152	178	203	229	254	279	305	914	1,000
Centimeters (cm)							0.95	1	1.27	1.59	1.91	2.22	2.54	5.08	7.62	10.16	12.7	15.2	17.8	20.3	22.9	25.4	27.9	30.5	91.4	100
Meters (m)																								.30	.91	1.00

Converting Measurements

TO CONVERT:	TO:	MULTIPLY BY:
Inches	Millimeters	25.4
Inches	Centimeters	2.54
Feet	Meters	0.305
Yards	Meters	0.914
Miles	Kilometers	1.609
Square inches	Square centimeters	6.45
Square feet	Square meters	0.093
Square yards	Square meters	0.836
Cubic inches	Cubic centimeters	16.4
Cubic feet	Cubic meters	0.0283
Cubic yards	Cubic meters	0.765
Pints (U.S.)	Liters	0.473 (Imp. 0.568)
Quarts (U.S.)	Liters	0.946 (Imp. 1.136)
Gallons (U.S.)	Liters	3.785 (Imp. 4.546)
Ounces	Grams	28.4
Pounds	Kilograms	0.454
Tons	Metric tons	0.907

TO CONVERT:	TO:	MULTIPLY BY:
Millimeters	Inches	0.039
Centimeters	Inches	0.394
Meters	Feet	3.28
Meters	Yards	1.09
Kilometers	Miles	0.621
Square centimeters	Square inches	0.155
Square meters	Square feet	10.8
Square meters	Square yards	1.2
Cubic centimeters	Cubic inches	0.061
Cubic meters	Cubic feet	35.3
Cubic meters	Cubic yards	1.31
Liters	Pints (U.S.)	2.114 (Imp. 1.76)
Liters	Quarts (U.S.)	1.057 (Imp. 0.88)
Liters	Gallons (U.S.)	0.264 (Imp. 0.22)
Grams	Ounces	0.035
Kilograms	Pounds	2.2
Metric tons	Tons	1.1

Converting Temperatures

Convert degrees Fahrenheit (F) to degrees Celsius (C) by following this simple formula: Subtract 32 from the Fahrenheit temperature reading. Then, mulitply that number by 5/9. For example, 77°F - 32 = 45. 45 × 5/9 = 25°C.

To convert degrees Celsius to degrees Fahrenheit, multiply the Celsius temperature reading by 9/5. Then, add 32. For example, 25°C × 9/5 = 45. 45 + 32 = 77°F.

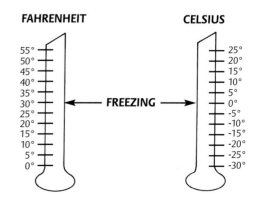

Nails

Nail lengths are identified by numbers from 4 to 60 followed by the letter "d," which stands for "penny."

For general framing and repair work, use common or box nails. Common nails are best suited to framing work where strength is important. Box nails are smaller in diameter than common nails, which makes them easier to drive and less likely to split wood. Use box nails for light work and thin materials.

Most common and box nails have a cement or vinyl coating that improves their holding power.

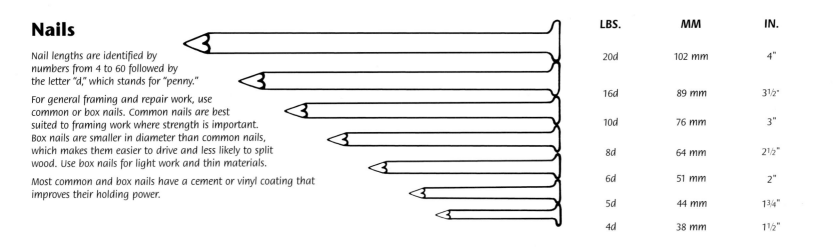

LBS.	MM	IN.
20d	102 mm	4"
16d	89 mm	3 1/2"
10d	76 mm	3"
8d	64 mm	2 1/2"
6d	51 mm	2"
5d	44 mm	1 3/4"
4d	38 mm	1 1/2"

Lumber Dimensions

NOMINAL - U.S.	ACTUAL - U.S.	METRIC
1 × 2	3/4" × 1 1/2"	19 × 38 mm
1 × 3	3/4" × 2 1/2"	19 × 64 mm
1 × 4	3/4" × 3 1/2"	19 × 89 mm
1 × 5	3/4" × 4 1/2"	19 × 114 mm
1 × 6	3/4" × 5 1/2"	19 × 140 mm
1 × 7	3/4" × 6 1/4"	19 × 159 mm
1 × 8	3/4" × 7 1/4"	19 × 184 mm
1 × 10	3/4" × 9 1/4"	19 × 235 mm
1 × 12	3/4" × 11 1/4"	19 × 286 mm
1 1/4 × 4	1" × 3 1/2"	25 × 89 mm
1 1/4 × 6	1" × 5 1/2"	25 × 140 mm
1 1/4 × 8	1" × 7 1/4"	25 × 184 mm
1 1/4 × 10	1" × 9 1/4"	25 × 235 mm
1 1/4 × 12	1" × 11 1/4"	25 × 286 mm
1 1/2 × 4	1 1/4" × 3 1/2"	32 × 89 mm
1 1/2 × 6	1 1/4" × 5 1/2"	32 × 140 mm
1 1/2 × 8	1 1/4" × 7 1/4"	32 × 184 mm
1 1/2 × 10	1 1/4" × 9 1/4"	32 × 235 mm
1 1/2 × 12	1 1/4" × 11 1/4"	32 × 286 mm
2 × 4	1 1/2" × 3 1/2"	38 × 89 mm
2 × 6	1 1/2" × 5 1/2"	38 × 140 mm
2 × 8	1 1/2" × 7 1/4"	38 × 184 mm
2 × 10	1 1/2" × 9 1/4"	38 × 235 mm
2 × 12	1 1/2" × 11 1/4"	38 × 286 mm
3 × 6	2 1/2" × 5 1/2"	64 × 140 mm
4 × 4	3 1/2" × 3 1/2"	89 × 89 mm
4 × 6	3 1/2" × 5 1/2"	89 × 140 mm

Metric Plywood Panels

Metric plywood panels are commonly available in two sizes: 1,200 mm × 2,400 mm and 1,220 mm × 2,400 mm, which is roughly equivalent to a 4 × 8-ft. sheet. Standard and Select sheathing panels come in standard thicknesses, while Sanded grade panels are available in special thicknesses.

STANDARD SHEATHING GRADE		SANDED GRADE	
7.5 mm	(5/16 in.)	6 mm	(4/17 in.)
9.5 mm	(3/8 in.)	8 mm	(5/16 in.)
12.5 mm	(1/2 in.)	11 mm	(7/16 in.)
15.5 mm	(5/8 in.)	14 mm	(9/16 in.)
18.5 mm	(3/4 in.)	17 mm	(2/3 in.)
20.5 mm	(13/16 in.)	19 mm	(3/4 in.)
22.5 mm	(7/8 in.)	21 mm	(13/16 in.)
25.5 mm	(1 in.)	24 mm	(15/16 in.)

Saw Blades

Carbide blade

Panel blade

Planer blade

Masonry blade

Metal-cutting blade

Adhesives

TYPE	CHARACTERISTICS	USES
WHITE GLUE	**Strength:** moderate; rigid bond **Drying time:** several hours **Resistance to heat:** poor **Resistance to moisture:** poor **Hazards:** none **Cleanup/solvent:** soap and water	**Porous surfaces:** Wood (indoors) Paper Cloth
YELLOW GLUE (carpenter's glue)	**Strength:** moderate to good; rigid bond **Drying time:** several hours; faster than white glue **Resistance to heat:** moderate **Resistance to moisture:** moderate **Hazards:** none **Cleanup/solvent:** soap and water	**Porous surfaces:** Wood (indoors) Paper Cloth
TWO-PART EPOXY	**Strength:** excellent; strongest of all adhesives **Drying time:** varies, depending on manufacturer **Resistance to heat:** excellent **Resistance to moisture:** excellent **Hazards:** fumes are toxic and flammable **Cleanup/solvent:** acetone will dissolve some types	**Smooth & porous surfaces:** Wood (indoors & outdoors) Metal Masonry Glass Fiberglass
HOT GLUE	**Strength:** depends on type **Drying time:** less than 60 seconds **Resistance to heat:** fair **Resistance to moisture:** good **Hazards:** hot glue can cause burns **Cleanup/solvent:** heat will loosen bond	**Smooth & porous surfaces:** Glass Plastics Wood
CYANOACRYLATE (instant glue)	**Strength:** excellent, but with little flexibility **Drying time:** a few seconds **Resistance to heat:** excellent **Resistance to moisture:** excellent **Hazards:** can bond skin instantly; toxic, flammable **Cleanup/solvent:** acetone	**Smooth surfaces:** Glass Ceramics Plastics Metal
CONSTRUCTION ADHESIVE	**Strength:** good to excellent; very durable **Drying time:** 24 hours **Resistance to heat:** good **Resistance to moisture:** excellent **Hazards:** may irritate skin and eyes **Cleanup/solvent:** soap and water (while still wet)	**Porous surfaces:** Framing lumber Plywood and paneling Wallboard Foam panels Masonry
WATER-BASE CONTACT CEMENT	**Strength:** good **Drying time:** bonds instantly; dries fully in 30 minutes **Resistance to heat:** excellent **Resistance to moisture:** good **Hazards:** may irritate skin and eyes **Cleanup/solvent:** soap and water (while still wet)	**Porous surfaces:** Plastic laminates Plywood Flooring Cloth
SILICONE SEALANT (caulk)	**Strength:** fair to good; very flexible bond **Drying time:** 24 hours **Resistance to heat:** good **Resistance to moisture:** excellent **Hazards:** may irritate skin and eyes **Cleanup/solvent:** acetone	**Smooth & porous surfaces:** Wood Ceramics Fiberglass Plastics Glass

Abrasive Paper Grits - (Aluminum Oxide)

VERY COARSE	COARSE	MEDIUM	FINE	VERY FINE
12 - 36	40 - 60	80 - 120	150 - 180	220 - 600

Drill Bit Guide

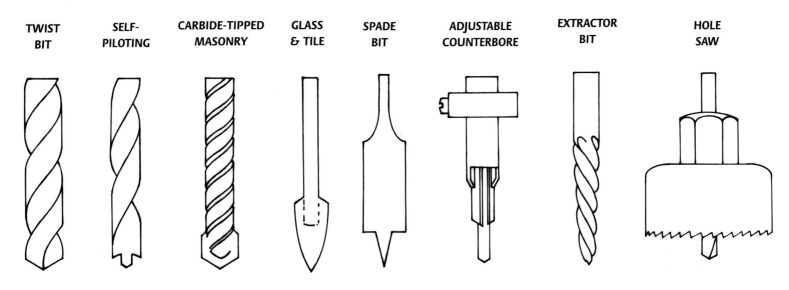

TWIST BIT   SELF-PILOTING   CARBIDE-TIPPED MASONRY   GLASS & TILE   SPADE BIT   ADJUSTABLE COUNTERBORE   EXTRACTOR BIT   HOLE SAW

Counterbore, Shank & Pilot Hole Diameters

SCREW SIZE	COUNTERBORE DIAMETER FOR SCREW HEAD	CLEARANCE HOLE FOR SCREW SHANK	PILOT HOLE DIAMETER	
			HARD WOOD	SOFT WOOD
#1	.146 ($9/64$)	$5/64$	$3/64$	$1/32$
#2	$1/4$	$3/32$	$3/64$	$1/32$
#3	$1/4$	$7/64$	$1/16$	$3/64$
#4	$1/4$	$1/8$	$1/16$	$3/64$
#5	$1/4$	$1/8$	$5/64$	$1/16$
#6	$5/16$	$9/64$	$3/32$	$5/64$
#7	$5/16$	$5/32$	$3/32$	$5/64$
#8	$3/8$	$11/64$	$1/8$	$3/32$
#9	$3/8$	$11/64$	$1/8$	$3/32$
#10	$3/8$	$3/16$	$1/8$	$7/64$
#11	$1/2$	$3/16$	$5/32$	$9/64$
#12	$1/2$	$7/32$	$9/64$	$1/8$

Resources

**American Institute
of Architects**
800.364.9364
www.aiaonline.com

**American Society of
Landscape Architects**
Washington, DC
202.898.2444
www.asla.org

**Asphalt Roofing
Manufacturers Association**
202.207.0917
www.asphaltroofing.com

Black & Decker (U.S.) Inc.
Townson, MD
800.544.6986
www.blackanddecker.com
www.bdk.com

Brick Institute of America
Reston, VA
703.620.0010
www.brickinfo.org

California Redwood Association
888.225.7339
www.calredwood.org

Certified Wood Products Council
503.224.2205
www.certifiedwood.org

**Construction Materials
Recycling Association**
630.548.4510
www.cdrecycling.com

Eon Outdoor Systems Inc.
(Plastic decking products)
877.433.9133
www.eonoutdoor.com

Eull Concrete Products Inc.
(Manhole block)
Albertville, MN
763.497.2136

Masonry Society
303.939.9700
www.masonrysociety.com

**Master Mark Plastics/Rhino Composite
Decking and Railing Systems**
800.535.4838
www.rhino.com

**National Concrete
Masonry Association**
Herndon, VA
703.713.1900
www.ncma.org

Paint Quality Institute
www.paintquality.com

Portland Cement Association
Skokie, IL
847.966.6200
www.portcement.com

Simpson Strong-Tie Co.
800.999.5099
www.strongtie.com

Timbertech
(Composite decking products)
800.307.7780
www.timbertech.com

Photographers

**Jim Baron
The Image Finders**
Cleveland, OH
© Jim Baron/The Image Finders: p. 202

Chandoha Photography
Annandale, NJ
© Walter Chandoha: p.120

ColdSnap Photography
Minneapolis, MN
© John Gregor/ColdSnap Photography:
pp. 370, 455

Crandall & Crandall
Dana Point, California
© Crandall & Crandall: pp. 78, 98,
156, 163, 164, 368, 490

R. Todd Davis Photography
Saint Louis, MO
© R. Todd Davis: p. 99

Derek Fell's Horticultural Picture Library
Pipersville, PA
© Derek Fell: p. 455

Firth Photobank
www.firthphotobank.com
© Bob Firth: pp. 100-101

Angela Hartwell
Minneapolis, MN
© Angela Hartwell: pp. 202, 369, 490

Saxon Holt Photography
www.photobotanic.com
© Saxon Holt: pp. 99, 176, 178, 196,
202, 454, 491

Charles Mann Photography Inc.
Santa Fe, NM
© Charles Mann: pp. 177, 203
© Charles Mann for the
following designers:
Keeyla Meadows; Albany, CA: p. 62
Greg Trutza; Phoenix, AZ: p. 116
Steve Martino; Phoenix, AZ: p. 177 (top)
Glen Ellison/Land Design; Vail, CO: p. 491

Jerry Pavia Photography Inc.
Bonners Ferry, ID
© Jerry Pavia: pp. 79, 98, 176, 180, 456

Andrea Rugg Photography
Minneapolis, MN
© Andrea Rugg: pp. 368, 369

Materials Contributors

Anchor Fence of Minnesota
Richfield, MN
612.866.4961

Buechel Stone Corp.
Chilton, WI
800.236.4473
www.buechelstone.com

CONstruct Architects, Inc.
Minneapolis, MN
612.724.9877
www.constructarchitects.com

Cultured Stone Corp.
Napa, CA
800.255.1727
www.culturedstone.com

DECKBRANDS, Inc.
(Dek-Block Piers)
800.664.2705
www.deckplans.com

Hedberg Aggregates
Plymouth, MN
612.545.4400
www.shadeslanding.com/hedberg/

Interlock Concrete Products Inc.
Jordan, MN
800.780.7212
www.interlock-concrete.com

International Masonry Institute
Minneapolis, MN
800.464.0988
www.imiweb.com

Midwest Fence
St. Paul, MN
651.451.2221
www.midwestfence.com

Minnesota Vinyl & Aluminum
Shakopee, MN
952.403.0805
www.mvas.com

Pittsburgh Corning Corp.
Pittsburgh, PA
800.624.2120
www.pittsburghcorning.com

Pultronex Corporation/E.Z. Deck
(Fiberglass reinforced plastic
decking products)
800.990.3099
www.ezdeck.com

Smith and Hawken
3564 Galleria
Edina, MN 55416
www.smithandhawken.com

The Quikrete Companies
Atlanta, GA
800.282.5828
www.quikrete.com

Warner Manufacturing Company
Minneapolis, MN
800.444.0606
www.warnertool.com

**Wooden Whispers Play Systems
G.L. Huppert Enterprises, Inc.**
(Play structure and hardware kits)
1792 Ruth St.
Maplewood, MN 55109
651.779.8002

Photography Contributors

Anderson Design Services Ltd.
612.473.8387
www.land-design.com: p. 29

Archadeck/US Structures Inc.
800.722.4668
www.archadeck.com: p. 296

California Redwood Association
988.225.7339
www.calredwood.org:
pp. 113, 204, 296, 298

CertainTeed EverNew
800.233.8990
www.certainteed.com:
pp. 124, 127

Lindal Cedar Homes, Inc.
800.426.0536
www.lindal.com: p.296

Master-Halco
562.694.5066
www.mhfence.com: p.128

Western WoodProducts
503.224.3930
522 S.W. 5th Avenue
Portland, OR 97204: p.297

Index

New from
CREATIVE PUBLISHING
INTERNATIONAL

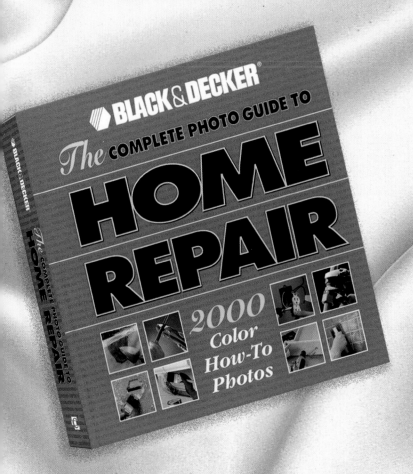

The Complete Photo Guide to Home Repair

The Complete Photo Guide to Home Repair is the most useful, up-to-date home repair manual you can own. It includes more than 300 of the most important home repair projects—from patching cracks in a basement floor to replacing your roof. Each project is illustrated with step-by-step color photography and detailed how-to instructions that leave nothing to chance.

ISBN 0-86573-753-3 $34.95

The Complete Photo Guide to Home Improvement

The Complete Photo Guide to Home Improvement is the most comprehensive and up-to-date remodeling guide ever published. It contains more than 250 of the most important, money-saving projects for improving the quality of life in your home.

In addition to basic construction, this book includes the information you'll need to complete the mechanical aspects—wiring and plumbing—of major projects. It also includes tips and advice on Universal Design—methods for designing or adapting living spaces to meet the needs of people of all ages, sizes, and abilities.

ISBN 0-86573-580-8 $34.95

Also available

Basic Wiring & Electrical Repairs
Advanced Home Wiring
Home Plumbing Projects & Repairs
Advanced Home Plumbing
Carpentry: Remodeling
Remodeling Kitchens
Bathroom Remodeling
Flooring Projects & Techniques
Easy Wood Furniture Projects
Built-In Projects for the Home
Decorating With Paint & Wallcovering
Refinishing & Finishing Wood
Designing Your Outdoor Home
Building Your Outdoor Home
Building Garden Ornaments
Landscape Design & Construction
Building Decks
Great Decks & Furnishings
Advanced Deck Building
Building Porches & Patios
Exterior Home Repairs & Improvements
Outdoor Wood Furnishings
Home Masonry Repairs & Projects
Stonework & Masonry Projects
Finishing Basements & Attics
Complete Guide to Painting & Decorating
Complete Guide to Home Plumbing
Complete Guide to Home Wiring
Complete Guide to Home Storage

ISBN 1-58923-041-8 $16.95

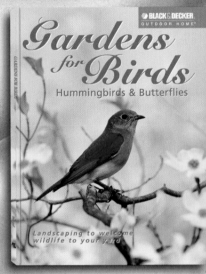

ISBN 1-58923-001-9 $16.95

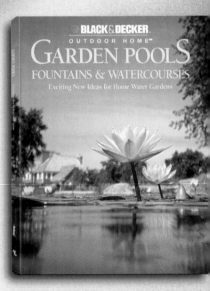

ISBN 0-86573-443-7 $16.95

ISBN 0-86573-466-6 $16.95

CREATIVE PUBLISHING INTERNATIONAL

5900 GREEN OAK DRIVE
MINNETONKA, MN 55343

WWW.HOWTOBOOKSTORE.COM